Reading
Sociology

Third Edition

Reading Sociology

Canadian Perspectives

EDITED BY

Patrizia Albanese
Lorne Tepperman
Emily Alexander

Published in partnership with

THE CANADIAN SOCIOLOGICAL ASSOCIATION
LA SOCIÉTÉ CANADIENNE DE SOCIOLOGIE

OXFORD
UNIVERSITY PRESS

OXFORD
UNIVERSITY PRESS

Oxford University Press is a department of the University of Oxford. It furthers the University's objective of excellence in research, scholarship, and education by publishing worldwide. Oxford is a registered trade mark of Oxford University Press in the UK and in certain other countries.

Published in Canada by
Oxford University Press
8 Sampson Mews, Suite 204,
Don Mills, Ontario M3C 0H5 Canada

www.oupcanada.com

First Edition published in 2007
Second Edition published in 2012

Library and Archives Canada Cataloguing in Publication
Reading sociology : Canadian perspectives / edited by Patrizia Albanese, Lorne Tepperman, and Emily Alexander. — Third edition.

Includes bibliographical references.
ISBN 978-0-19-902004-1 (softcover)

1. Sociology—Canada—Textbooks. 2. Canada—Social conditions—1991- —Textbooks. 3. Sociology—Textbooks. 4. Textbooks. I. Albanese, Patrizia, editor II. Tepperman, Lorne, 1943-, editor III. Alexander, Emily M., editor IV. Canadian Sociological Association, issuing body

HM586.R43 2017 301.0971 C2017-900531-6

Cover image: Hero Images/Getty Images
Cover and interior design: Laurie McGregor

Oxford University Press is committed to our environment. This book is printed on Forest Stewardship Council® certified paper and comes from responsible sources.

FSC www.fsc.org MIX Paper from responsible sources FSC® C014174

Printed and bound in the United States of America
1 2 3 4 — 21 20 19 18

Contents

PART VIII YOUTH AND FAMILIES 156

PART IX EDUCATION 182

Making Connections

Chapter/ Author	HISTORY	THEORY	CLASSIC	MARX	WEBER	DURKHEIM	CONTEMPORARY	BOURDIEU	QUEER	FEMINIST	CULTURE	MEDIA	SOCIAL MOVEMENT	ART	CHILDREN	YOUTH
PART 1 WHAT IS SOCIOLOGY? THEORY AND METHODS																
Chapter 1 Hiller	x	x														
Chapter 2 Kennelly et al.		X						X								X
Chapter 3 Matthews	X	X	X	X	X	X	X				X					
Chapter 4 Powell		X	X	X	X	X	X	X		X	X		X			
Chapter 5 Tepperman & Meridith		X														
Chapter 6 Warren	X	X											X			
PART 2 CULTURE AND CULTURE CHANGE																
Chapter 7 Curtis	X	X					X	X			X					
Chapter 8 Davidson	X										X	X		X	X	
Chapter 9 Klostermann										X	X			X		
Chapter 10 Martin		X					X				X			X		
PART 3 SOCIALIZATION																
Chapter 11 Chen							X								X	
Chapter 12 Dell																
Chapter 13 Doucet								X		X						
Chapter 14 Hillier & Aurini							X	X							X	

Chapter/ Author	ANIMALS	FAMILIES	CARE	LIFECOURSE/AGING	DISABILITIES	MASCULINITY	GENDER	SEXUALITY	WOMEN	RACE/RACISM	MIGRATION	CITIZENSHIP	INDIGENEITY	SOCIAL JUSTICE	INEQUALITY/EQUALITY	EDUCATION
PART 1 WHAT IS SOCIOLOGY? THEORY AND METHODS																
Chapter 1 Hiller																
Chapter 2 Kennelly et al.												X		X	X	X
Chapter 3 Matthews																
Chapter 4 Powell										X		X		X	X	
Chapter 5 Tepperman & Meridith					X											
Chapter 6 Warren																
PART 2 CULTURE AND CULTURE CHANGE																
Chapter 7 Curtis																
Chapter 8 Davidson							X						X			
Chapter 9 Klostermann														X		
Chapter 10 Martin																
PART 3 SOCIALIZATION																
Chapter 11 Chen										X		X	X	X	X	
Chapter 12 Dell	X		X												X	
Chapter 13 Doucet		X	X				X									
Chapter 14 Hillier & Aurini		X													X	X

Chapter/ Author	CLASS	WORK	ECONOMY	CAPITALISM	NEOLIBERALISM	STATE	POLICY	GLOBAL	ENVIRONMENT	RELIGION	HEALTH	MENTAL HEALTH	SPACE	CRIME	DEVIANCE	VIOLENCE
PART 1 WHAT IS SOCIOLOGY? THEORY AND METHODS																
Chapter 1 Hiller																
Chapter 2 Kennelly et al.	X												X			
Chapter 3 Matthews			X	X			X		X		X	X	X			
Chapter 4 Powell	X	X	X	X	X	X		X	X							X
Chapter 5 Tepperman & Meridith											X	X			X	
Chapter 6 Warren																
PART 2 CULTURE AND CULTURE CHANGE																
Chapter 7 Curtis	X							X								
Chapter 8 Davidson						X							X			
Chapter 9 Klostermann	X	X														
Chapter 10 Martin		X														
PART 3 SOCIALIZATION																
Chapter 11 Chen																
Chapter 12 Dell							X		X		X	X				
Chapter 13 Doucet																
Chapter 14 Hillier & Aurini	X						X									

PART 4 DEVIANCE AND CRIME																																																
Chapter 15 Dawson		X								X													X	X	X	X			X	X	X								X						X	X	X	X
Chapter 16 Hahmann		X					X																																								X	
Chapter 17 Nevin												X										X	X																							X	X	
Chapter 18 Pavlich	X	X									X		X										X							X			X													X	X	
Chapter 19 Weissman	X	X							X		X	X	X			X		X			X		X		X	X		X		X	X		X	X	X	X	X	X	X		X		X	X		X		
PART 5 SOCIAL INEQUALITY																																																
Chapter 20 Armstrong										X										X			X								X			X				X					X					
Chapter 21 Evans & Fanelli	X						X						X																	X	X			X	X	X	X	X	X	X								
Chapter 22 Grillo		X	X				X																							X	X					X	X	X										
Chapter 23 McDaniel																		X		X								X			X			X	X	X	X	X	X				X					
PART 6 GENDER AND SEXUALITY																																																
Chapter 24 Green		X						X			X													X																								
Chapter 25 Horgan and Liinamaa	X		X							X													X		X		X				X	X		X														
Chapter 26 Lee		X					X		X	X					X			X	X				X	X	X					X	X		X	X	X	X	X	X	X				X					
Chapter 27 Luxton							X			X													X							X	X			X		X	X	X										

Chapter/Author	HISTORY	THEORY	CLASSIC	MARX	WEBER	DURKHEIM	CONTEMPORARY	BOURDIEU	QUEER	FEMINIST	CULTURE	MEDIA	SOCIAL MOVEMENT	ART	CHILDREN	YOUTH	ANIMALS	FAMILIES	CARE	LIFECOURSE/AGING	DISABILITIES	MASCULINITY	GENDER	SEXUALITY	WOMEN	RACE/RACISM	MIGRATION	CITIZENSHIP	INDIGENEITY	SOCIAL JUSTICE	INEQUALITY/EQUALITY	EDUCATION	CLASS	WORK	ECONOMY	CAPITALISM	NEOLIBERALISM	STATE	POLICY	GLOBAL	ENVIRONMENT	RELIGION	HEALTH	MENTAL HEALTH	SPACE	CRIME	DEVIANCE	VIOLENCE
PART 7 RACE AND ETHNIC RELATIONS																																																
Chapter 28 Denis & Bailey	X	X					X						X													X		X	X	X	X	X				X		X	X		X		X	X				X
Chapter 29 Howe		X					X	X			X		X													X			X									X	X									
Chapter 30 Wilkinson		X					X				X		X													X																						
Chapter 31 Winter	X	X					X				X															X	X	X		X	X						X	X	X	X		X						
PART 8 YOUTH AND FAMILIES																																																
Chapter 32 Antonelli & Mooney				X	X											X																		X	X	X	X				X							
Chapter 33 Molina-Girón																X												X		X	X																	
Chapter 34 Kobayashi & Khan							X		X	X	X				X			X	X	X			X	X	X	X	X				X		X	X			X		X	X			X					
Chapter 35 Mata															X			X										X											X									
Chapter 36 Mathieu										X					X			X	X						X														X									
PART 9 EDUCATION																																																
Chapter 37 Harrison & Albanese															X	X		X	X	X			X		X						X	X		X				X	X	X			X	X				
Chapter 38 Boyo							X				X							X									X					X								X								
Chapter 39 Frideres	X						X				X	X																				X		X	X				X									
Chapter 40 Wotherspoon	X	X					X	X					X		X	X										X			X	X	X	X							X									

PART 10 WORK AND THE ECONOMY																																																
Chapter 41 Boyd					X													X								X					X			X														
Chapter 42 Foster	X			X	X			X																										X	X	X	X				X							
Chapter 43 Livingstone				X			X						X																				X	X	X			X										
Chapter 44 Nichols	X	X					X			X									X				X		X					X	X			X	X	X	X		X									
Chapter 45 Schneider							X									X					X										X	X		X					X									
PART 11 HEALTH AND CARE																																																
Chapter 46 Beaujot, et al.										X					X			X	X				X		X						X	X		X					X									
Chapter 47 Chappell & Penning	X						X												X	X	X										X	X	X						X				X	X				
Chapter 48 McKay							X																															X	X				X					
PART 12 RELIGION																																																
Chapter 49 Brym et al.											X		X																		X		X					X				X						X
Chapter 50 Helmes-Hayes	X												X																	X	X	X											X					
Chapter 51 Kleinknecht											X																															X						
Chapter 52 Reitz	X	X					X			X	X				X	X		X		X			X		X	X	X	X			X			X	X				X			X						X

Chapter/ Author	HISTORY	THEORY	CLASSIC	MARX	WEBER	DURKHEIM	CONTEMPORARY	BOURDIEU	QUEER	FEMINIST	CULTURE	MEDIA	SOCIAL MOVEMENT	ART	CHILDREN	YOUTH	ANIMALS	FAMILIES	CARE	LIFECOURSE/AGING	DISABILITIES	MASCULINITY	GENDER	SEXUALITY	WOMEN	RACE/RACISM	MIGRATION	CITIZENSHIP	INDIGENEITY	SOCIAL JUSTICE	INEQUALITY/EQUALITY	EDUCATION	CLASS	WORK	ECONOMY	CAPITALISM	NEOLIBERALISM	STATE	POLICY	GLOBAL	ENVIRONMENT	RELIGION	HEALTH	MENTAL HEALTH	SPACE	CRIME	DEVIANCE	VIOLENCE
PART 13 Politics																																																
Chapter 53 Béland																																						X	X									
Chapter 54 Clément	X	X					X						X																	X	X							X	X	X								
Chapter 55 Eichler											X		X															X		X	X	X					X	X	X	X	X							
Chapter 56 Nakhaie		X					X				X		X																						X													
PART 14 Social Movements																																																
Chapter 57 Benn-John		X								X			X			X		X					X		X	X			X	X	X			X			X											X
Chapter 58 Warren	X	X									X		X			X						X	X			X		X			X		X		X	X		X	X								X	X
Chapter 59 Wood	X	X					X						X												X	X			X	X	X		X		X	X	X	X		X	X							
PART 15 International Relations and Government																																																
Chapter 60 Follert		X									X																											X										
Chapter 61 Knezevic							X																							X	X			X	X	X	X	X	X									
Chapter 62 Visan		X					X				X	X	X														X													X								
Chapter 63 Winter & Patzelt	X	X									X																X	X		X							X	X	X									
PART 16 Technology and Mass Media																																																
Chapter 64 Lyon	X	X					X				X	X														X	X	X		X	X		X						X							X		X
Chapter 65 Roberge & Crosbie		X					X				X	X																								X												
Chapter 66 Sarbu	X										X	X																		X	X					X	X				X	X						
Chapter 67 Stoddart & Smith												X	X																X	X	X							X	X	X	X							

Introduction

It is a pleasure to present the third edition of *Reading Sociology*, a book prepared under the auspices of the Canadian Sociological Association to showcase current sociological thinking in Canada.

Before you start reading this book, here are a few caveats, to let you know what this book is not. First, despite its general title, this is not a book about all sociology: it is about Canadian sociology. What's more, it is not about all Canadian sociology—only about recent Canadian sociology. And it is not even an exhaustive survey of recent Canadian sociology: it is a small sample of recent Canadian sociology, cobbled together in two main ways. On the one hand, it contains some of the most interesting work presented at the Annual Conference of the Canadian Sociological Association in Ottawa, June 2015. On the other hand, it also contains some of the most interesting recent work of senior sociologists whom we commissioned to write a piece for the book.

Now, you will have noticed the brevity of the 67 pieces in this short book. From that brevity, you will have correctly concluded that this book is not an in-depth examination of any single issue, debate, theoretical perspective, or line of thought. It is more like one of those boxes of chocolates many of us like to receive, with dozens of miniature pleasures presented for our delectation. If you find a particular paper, topic, or author to your liking, we urge you to find out more—to seek more information about that paper, topic, or author in the published literature. Feel free to write the author and express your appreciation; everyone likes hearing praise (and receiving suggestions for improvement). Or send a box of chocolates!

You will have also noticed that this book does not cover all of the many topics that sociologists—including Canadian sociologists—like to study. A book of this size could not completely or even adequately capture all of the topics, themes, and discussions that one finds in Canadian sociology today.

That said, this is an identifiably Canadian book that contains many of the themes that Canadian sociologists currently discuss and, to a large degree, have always discussed. For example, the topics of diversity and equality enjoy central attention in this and any other collection of Canadian work. That includes discussions of gender, ethnic, racial, class, and other forms of diversity and equality (and inequality). Also to be found in this book are themes that are widely discussed in all modern sociological communities: themes around work and employment; stresses in family life; health, welfare, and care issues; and problems associated with crime, to mention a few.

Likely, there will be another edition of this book, four years from now. In that edition, many of the authors and topics will be different, but the Canadian content will still be central. Let us know what you think of this book and what it tells you about recent Canadian sociology.

Acknowledgments

As always, we are grateful to Oxford University Press for producing this handsome volume. Special thanks go to Tanuja Weerasooriya, who served as developmental editor on this project. Since it is always easy for editors to forget details in a large project, Tanuja kept reminding us to prepare this book in a way that we had intended and promised to do. We are also grateful to the anonymous reviewers who read a first draft of this book and offered helpful suggestions for improvement. We want to thank Tara Tovell, who edited the copy for this book and made it smoother and more consistent than it had been, in content and appearance. Most important of all, we are grateful to our authors, who put up with our many demands (especially, our demands for brevity and timeliness) and let us show off their talent in this collected series of miniature gems.

This book is dedicated to the instructors who will adopt this book for their classroom teaching; to the students who will read and study these pieces; and to the academic readers from Canada and abroad who find something interesting to take away from this exhibition of sociological talent.

Patrizia Albanese
Lorne Tepperman
Emily Alexander

Toronto, 2017

Contributors

Patrizia Albanese, Ryerson University
Robert Andersen, Western University
Fabrizio Antonelli, Mount Allison University
Pat Armstrong, York University
Janice Aurini, University of Waterloo
Kerry Bailey, McMaster University
Roderic Beaujot, Western University
Daniel Béland, University of Saskatchewan
Jacqueline Benn-John, OISE—University of Toronto
Monica Boyd, University of Toronto
Toju Maria Boyo, Employment and Social Development Canada
Robert Brym, University of Toronto
Neena L. Chappell, University of Victoria
Xiaobei Chen, Carleton University
Dominique Clément, University of Alberta
Thomas Crosbie, University of Maryland
Bruce Curtis, Carleton University
Tonya K. Davidson, Ryerson University
Myrna Dawson, Guelph University
Colleen Anne Dell, University of Saskatchewan
Jeff Denis, McMaster University
Andrea Doucet, Brock University
Margrit Eichler, OISE—University of Toronto
Bryan Evans, Ryerson University
Carlo Fanelli, Ryerson University
Mike Follert, University of Guelph and University of Toronto Mississauga
Karen Foster, Dalhousie University
J.S. Frideres, University of Calgary
Adam Green, University of Toronto
Carmen Grillo, York University
Tara Hahmann, University of Toronto
Deborah Harrison, University of New Brunswick
Rick Helmes-Hayes, University of Waterloo
Harry H. Hiller, University of Calgary
Cathlene Hillier, University of Waterloo
Mervyn Horgan, University of Guelph
Adam Howe, University of British Columbia
Jacqueline Kennelly, Carleton University
Mushira M. Khan, University of Victoria
Steven Kleinknecht, Brescia University College
Janna Klostermann, Carleton University
Ivanka Knezevic, University of Toronto
Karen M. Kobayashi, University of Victoria
Robyn Lee, Brock University
Saara Liinamaa, University of Guelph
D.W. Livingstone, University of Toronto
Jianye Liu, Lakehead
Meg Luxton, York University
David Lyon, Queen's University
Chris William Martin, Memorial University of Newfoundland
Fernando Mata, University of Ottawa
Sophie Mathieu, l'Université de Montréal
Ralph Matthews, University of British Columbia
Susan McDaniel, University of Lethbridge
Lindsey McKay, Brock University
Nicole Meredith, University of Toronto
Scott Milligan, Western University
L. Alison Molina-Girón, University of Regina
Taylor Mooney, Mount Allison University
Reza Nakhaie, University of Windsor
Andrew D. Nevin, University of Toronto
Leslie Nichols, McMaster University
Anke Patzelt, University of Ottawa
George Pavlich, University of Alberta
Margaret J. Penning, University of Victoria
Christopher Powell, Ryerson University
Zenaida Ravanera, Western University
Jeffrey G. Reitz, University of Toronto
Jonathan Roberge, Université du Québec, Institut national de recherché scientifique
Mihai Sarbu, University of Ottawa
Lynette Schick, Carleton University
Cornelia Schneider, Mount Saint Vincent University

Jillian Smith, Memorial University
Valerie Stam, Carleton University
Mark C.J. Stoddart, Memorial University of Newfoundland
Lorne Tepperman, University of Toronto
Laura Visan, University of New Brunswick
Jean-Philippe Warren, Concordia University
Eric Weissman
Lori Wilkinson, University of Manitoba
Elke Winter, University of Ottawa
Lesley J. Wood, York University
Terry Wotherspoon, University of Saskatchewan

PART I
What Is Sociology? Theory and Methods

In April 2013, in response to a foiled terrorist plot to attack a Via Rail passenger train, the then Canadian prime minister, Stephen Harper, said that this was not the time to "commit sociology." What exactly was he referring to? What should we *not* be doing? What was he implying that we should do? It appears that Harper was asking us to trust our gut, go with our feelings, accept things at face value, and use common sense. He was warning us to *not* ask critical questions, to not look for deeper and more complex explanations using concrete evidence, and to not stop and think deeply and rationally about something that we don't fully understand. Many of the authors in this book have committed their lives to committing sociology. This means that we have chosen a discipline that challenges taken-for-granted, superficial explanations of social phenomena. This also means that we are passionate about and committed to developing and testing theories (explanations) using a range of rigorous social research methods and evidence. Sociologists ask a great many questions: Why do we have poverty, crime and/or homelessness? What does the sexualization of women in the media say about the value that we place on women in our society? How has the evolution of technology changed the way that people interact with and experience others around them?

Sociology is the study of society and social behaviour. It is the job of a sociologist to ask and explore questions like the ones asked above, to challenge the social order and understand the social lives of individuals. Sociology is a broad discipline that focuses primarily on the interrelationship between individuals, social structures, and social institutions. Social structures refer to mechanisms that influence the social arrangement of society, such as race, social class, and gender. Additionally, social institutions are formalized groups within a society that reinforce social structures, such as education, family, and political institutions. Together, social structures and social institutions form the social context in which people live, shaping their attitudes, values, and beliefs.

As noted above, in order to understand the social world, sociologists rely on social theories and methods. A theory is a set of interrelated concepts that can be used to describe, explain, or predict different phenomena. Sociologists use theories as a framework or lens from which to see and understand society. For instance, conflict theory is an example of one lens through which a sociologist approaches the social world. That lens focuses upon power differences at the root of social, political, or material inequalities that exist across individuals and groups in any given society. Feminists, for example, use that critical lens to focus on the impact of gender (sometimes in conjunction with other things like class, race, ethnicity, sexuality, ability, etc.) on access to power and privilege.

The sociologists in this collection all have a particular theoretical lens through which they have approached their area of research. This lens has in turn shaped the kinds of questions they have asked, the methods that they have chosen to use, and the insights that they have shared in their chapters. Throughout this collection, you will see examples of a wide range of research methods or research tools used to test, measure, uncover, and explore the complex phenomena that make up our social world. At first glance, even someone new to sociology will be able to determine whether a chapter's author has taken a quantitative or qualitative approach (or both). Quantitative methods typically look for causal explanations (they identify a series of variables that help explain why things are happening) using mathematical or statistical models and report their results using numbers. Qualitative methods, on the other hand, often ask individuals to share experiences or insights in more rich, personal and descriptive ways—in their own words and in their own ways. Each of the methodological approaches that you will encounter in this and other sociology books aims to provide answers to many of the large (macro) and small (micro) things that make up our often taken-for-granted social worlds. It is this deeper look into the everyday that appears to have made Prime Minister Stephen Harper uncomfortable with what we might find—or worse, what we might do with that knowledge.

Throughout this book you will see examples of individuals committing sociology. In this first section, you will be introduced to some of the more recent discoveries and challenges that have pushed sociology to advance as a discipline. To begin, Harry Hiller describes the difference between micro and macro perspectives in sociology, emphasizing the changing popularity of these perspectives in Canada over time. Then, Chapter 2 explains the struggle that sociologists face when they try to perform research in the community, and how adapting their approach using practical, rather than academic, knowledge can help them achieve their goals. In the next chapter, Ralf Mathews advocates for a sociology that acknowledges the importance of the brain in determining human behaviour, suggesting that we need to link the social and biological together. Moreover, Chapter 4 describes theory as a dimension of knowledge, emphasizing the relationship between theory and practice. In Chapter 5, Lorne Tepperman and Nicole Meredith explore "accident proneness" and the various perspectives that have been used to understand this phenomenon. Lastly, Jean-Philippe Warren emphasizes the importance of recognizing sociology that is written in languages other than English by using the example of Québécois sociology.

1 Macro Sociology: Its Evolution and Relevance to Canada

Harry H. Hiller

What do sociologists do? How do they determine what to study?

Client-Based Research vs. Independent Research

Sociologists practice their craft in many different ways. Some apply their knowledge and research skills in work for government, in the private sector, or as consultants. Sociologists who do this kind of work are sometimes called clinical sociologists because they are practice-oriented in real-life situations with the responsibility to analyze concerns and issues as identified by a client or employer.

In contrast, sociologists who work in academic settings usually engage in independent research in that the topic of research is determined solely by the researcher rather than a client or employer. For example, we may need to know more about changing family patterns, white-collar crime, how high-rise living affects people, or the impact of immigration on a host society. The goal, then, is to engage in research using the discipline's technical tools and theories that moves our knowledge about that phenomenon forward.

The advancement of knowledge normally is a separate objective from that of responding to the research objectives of a client. Michael Burowoy (2005) has argued that **professional sociology** always needs to be supplemented by **public sociology** that brings sociology into dialogue with important public issues beyond the academy.[1] He distinguishes this kind of sociology from **policy sociology**, which is directed to research done in the interests of clients (government, corporations, agencies).

Professional Sociology in the Public Realm

In many cases, topics for research emerge from sociologists' own experiences or observations of what is happening around them, which then serve as a catalyst about what to research. For example, observing discrimination or the wealth–poverty gap can serve as a significant motivating factor in choosing a research topic. Sociologists can also be motivated by social changes occurring around them that affect the way society works. For example, the cellphone, the smartphone, and the Internet have had enormous social consequences that need analysis. A third motivation in research theme selection is the desire to develop new perspectives or interpretations in understanding social life and to contribute to theory-building. Each of these motivations stand at the core of what sociologists do, not only to contribute to their discipline, but also to contribute to the public's understanding of what is happening around them.

Macro Sociology vs. Micro Sociology

Much sociological research is carried on at the **micro** level, meaning that the focus is on individual actors or groups of actors. If the goal is to study prostitution, then the focus of the study is on prostitutes and how they interact with those who control them and their clients. If the goal is to study single parent families, then single parents and their children and how they interact are the focus of study. In contrast to micro sociology, **macro sociology** examines populations and social systems on a large scale, particularly whole societies. Many of the early sociologists, such as Émile Durkheim and Max Weber, were intrigued by how Western society had evolved over time with the advent of capitalism and industrialization, and sought to explain societal/social change and how these new social forms resulted in a different kind of society. Macro sociology, then, examines larger groups of people and attempts to explain their structures and how they change over time. Nation-states and their sub-units (regions) often serve as the unit of analysis.

In Canada, the emergence of sociology as a discipline was intimately tied to macro questions—i.e., what is the nature and structure of Canadian society, how has it changed over time, what factors explain its evolution and unique character, and what are the conflicts and divisions that threaten its existence? No attempt will be made here to identify all of the studies done by early sociologists in Canada, but a few of the most significant studies related to a macro analysis can be identified. C.A. Dawson led a team of researchers looking into how the settlement of the Canadian west was impacting Canadian society (*Group Settlement: Ethnic Communities in Western Canada*, 1936, and *Pioneering in the Prairie Provinces: The Social Side of the Settlement Process*, 1940). Everett Hughes produced an insightful account of how Quebec was changing from its rural agrarian past (*French Canada in Transition*, 1943) and the impact this shift was having on Canada. S.D. Clark noted the role that staples (e.g., fish, fur, lumbering in demand by European metropoles) played in the formation of Canadian society with his book *The Social Development of Canada* (1942). Somewhat later, John Porter wrote an award-winning book called *The Vertical Mosaic* (1965), which examined the patterns of social class divisions in Canadian society. Another classic study by S.M. Lipset attempted to explain the election of the first socialist government in North America in Saskatchewan in 1944 (*Agrarian Socialism: The Cooperative Commonwealth Federation in Saskatchewan*, 1950). Part of what motivated him was the desire to explain not only the factors that made this election possible but what it revealed about how Canada was different from the United States (*Continental Divide: The Values and Institutions of the United States and Canada*, 1989), a fascinating macro question that has often intrigued Canadian sociologists. For a relatively young society only formed in 1867 but that was experiencing the challenges of growth such as in the Canadian West or change such as in Quebec and seeking to establish an identity different from the United States, sociologists responded to the need for Canadians to understand their own society's unique evolution and character.

The Growing Relevance of Macro Sociology in Canada

It was the explosive growth of sociology as a discipline in the 1960s in Canadian universities that gave new impetus to these macro questions. Primarily due to the rapid expansion of universities and student enrolment that led to the increased demand for sociologists to teach courses in the field, newly developed sociology departments required more sociologists than were available in Canada, which meant recruitment from outside the country, and particularly from the United States. Many of these new arrivals knew very little about Canadian society and brought with them models of society and examples of social life that were irrelevant to Canadians. Related to this problem was the fact that there was very little Canadian material (and particularly text material) for them to use in their classes. At around the same time, national identity issues emerged in the 1960s and 1970s as Canadians reacted to their subordinate position in relation to more dominant powers as a former colony of Britain and a branch plant of the United States. The ferment occurring in Quebec, which called into question language and culture, led to the creation of the Royal Commission on Bilingualism and Biculturalism by the federal government in 1963, which ultimately reconstructed Canada as a bilingual society and later established multiculturalism as official policy. The emergence of Quebec nationalism, which gave rise to the election of the separatist Parti Québécois in 1976 in particular, reminded Canadians that the question of societal solidarity could not be taken for granted.[2] In short, the rapid expansion of sociology in Canada in the 1960s and 1970s took place at a time in which many questions were being raised about the nature and future of Canadian society. It was not surprising that a special study called the Symon's Report made recommendations in 1976 that identified the need for Canadians to better understand their own society. Around the same time (1977), the federal government established the Task Force on Canadian Unity to address the crisis caused by French/English duality, regionalism, and the mutual sharing of powers and benefits of Confederation. It was this societal context that prompted sociologists in Canada to address macro issues.

How did Canadian sociologists do this? First, they attempted to develop a larger cohort of Canadian-trained sociologists who were more familiar with Canadian issues. Sociology departments in Canada developed graduate programs to support that goal and not just serve undergraduate students. Second, they began writing textbooks in all sub-disciplinary fields of sociology that would show how sociology was relevant to the analysis of aspects of Canadian society. Third, they engaged in research that was important to the issues Canadians were facing, whether it was background papers to a Royal Commission or Task Force or other topics of national/regional concern. Some of the research themes included continental corporate power and the corporate elite (Clément), ethnic group clustering (Breton) and Canada as an ethnic mosaic (Driedger, Li, Reitz), regionalism (Schwartz) in Atlantic Canada (Brym, House, Matthews) and the West (Conway), social inequality (Curtis), social change in Quebec (Fournier, Guindon), shifting ideological patterns (Marchak), and Aboriginal relations (Frideres, Ponting).[3]

It is possible to refer to this development as the "Canadianization" of sociology—i.e., that sociology had to move through a phase in its development in Canada in which the discipline had to prove its relevance to a society in crisis and change.[4] However, through the 1980s and 1990s, sociology in Canada experienced consolidation in which macro questions no longer served as a dominant catalyst for sociological research. Perhaps Canada itself had grown more confident in its own structures and institutions just as sociology had become more firmly established. The membership of the Canadian Sociological Association (CSA) had grown steadily to around 1,000 members by 2015, and many more were not members of the Association. The number of persons attending the annual meetings of the CSA had grown as well as the number of sessions offered at these meetings. Twenty-five organized research clusters had formed at the national level dealing with everything from gender and sexuality to migration and health studies. Research had become more global in scope, but considerable research by sociologists was also Canadian in orientation and used Canadian data. This pluralization and fragmentation of the discipline did not mean that macro questions of significance to Canada had been lost; it was just that the discipline had become more complex. The need for Canadians to understand their own society, however, was still of importance, particularly because of changes occurring within the society. For example, if at one time Canada was a British-oriented society primarily made up of Caucasians from Europe, this was surely no longer the case. Aboriginal peoples had developed a much higher profile in the national dialogue, and international migration continued to change the composition of Canadian society. Therefore, it should not be surprising that two of the most recent winners of the John Porter Award of the Canadian Sociological Association engaged in research on questions of macro importance: Elke Winter, *Us, Them, and Others: Pluralism and National Identity in Diverse Societies* and Abdolmohammad Kazemipur, *The Muslim Question in Canada: A Story of Segmented Integration*.

Ralph Matthews (2014) recently distinguished between a "sociology of Canada" and a "Canadian sociology." Whereas a "sociology of Canada" referred to all the work that is done in describing and analyzing Canadian society, he argued that a "Canadian sociology" should seek to explain how and why Canadian society is different from other societies.[5] Long ago, Everett Hughes (1959) proposed as the objective of sociology in Canada what he called the "more-so" principle—i.e. what are the features of Canadian life from which we would learn something more about human society than we might learn elsewhere. Both approaches work well for a macro sociology because it is important to gather data and interpret important trends and changes in Canadian society. It is critical for a sense of society that Canadians understand the transformations and consequences of what is happening around them. While some might argue that globalization has made bordered societies meaningless, a macro perspective will continue to be important to Canadians as they address the future.

Notes

1. For a discussion of these distinctions in the Canadian context, see McLaughlin (2005) and the *Canadian Journal of Sociology* 34(3), 2009.
2. For a good discussion of the relation between sociology and collective identity in Quebec, see Fournier (2001).
3. This is only a selected list of sociologists who did work on these topics in the 1970s and early 1980s.
4. No attempt has been made here to list all of the studies dealing with the history and evolution of sociology in Canada. See the work of Robert Brym, Rick Helmes-Hayes, Jeffrey Cormier, Neil McLaughlin, David Nock, and Marlene Shore for discussions on this topic.
5. For a discussion of the debate generated by this distinction, see the *Canadian Review of Sociology* 51(4), 2014.

References

Burawoy, Michael (2005). "For Public Sociology." *American Sociological Review* 70(1): 2–28.

Fournier, Marcel (2001). "Quebec Sociology and Quebec Society: The Construction of a Collective Identity." *Canadian Journal of Sociology* 26(3): 333–47.

Hughes, Everett (1959). "The Dual Mandate of Social Science: Remarks on the Academic Division of Labour." *Canadian Journal of Economics and Political Science* 25(4): 401–10.

Matthews, Ralph (2014). "Committing Canadian Sociology: Developing a Canadian Sociology and a Sociology of Canada." *Canadian Review of Sociology* 51(2): 107–27.

McLaughlin, Neil (2005). "Canada's Impossible Science: Historical and Institutional Origins of the Coming Crisis in Anglo-Canadian Sociology. *Canadian Journal of Sociology* 30(1): 1–40.

2 "*Breaking* with Inside Experience": Dilemmas in Negotiating Practical Knowledge and Scholarly Knowledge in Research with Young People

Jacqueline Kennelly, Valerie Stam, and Lynette Schick

This paper explores both theoretical and pragmatic issues related to doing academic research with young people. Academic researchers working with children and youth must often navigate institutional gatekeepers in order to gain access to their research participants. Such negotiations may be straightforward or fraught, but each takes place within a specific context of academic and community norms and practices that shape the response of each to the other. Drawing on ongoing qualitative and **participatory action research** with three youth-serving organizations in Ottawa, Ontario, we use Pierre Bourdieu's concepts of ***habitus, doxa,* and *field*** to argue that competing, overlapping, and sometimes clashing fields can complicate the research relationship between academics and those in non-academic organizations. We theorize some of these instances using reflective fieldwork "vignettes" that we each wrote about the instances in our research when we felt the worlds of academia and community social services brushing up against each other, not always comfortably.

Attempting to gain enough analytical distance from our own experience, in order to provide an adequate theoretical account of it, is no easy task. The title of the paper reflects this tension, and is drawn from Bourdieu's English introduction to his book *Homo Academicus*:

> In choosing to study the social world in which we are *involved*, we are obliged to confront, in *dramatized* form as it were, a certain number of fundamental epistemological problems, all related to the question of the difference between practical knowledge and scholarly knowledge, and particularly to the special difficulties involved first in *breaking* with inside experience and then in reconstituting the knowledge which has been obtained by means of this break (Bourdieu 1990, 1, emphasis his).

The difficulties of our task here are very much reflected in Bourdieu's words above. We are seeking to analytically separate our *practical* knowledge from our *scholarly* knowledge, understand how the one influences the other, and take into account the manner in which our practical knowledge and academic knowledge do not always sit easily together. As sometime insiders to both the community worlds in which we are researching and the academic worlds in which we are currently positioned, we seek to "break" with that insider experience that informs our actions in both and step back in order to see more clearly where the fault line and fissures lie between these two related but also separate worlds.

Bourdieu uses *field* to specify a particular "social space" that constitutes the symbolic arena within which actors take action and make specific choices (Bourdieu and Wacquant 1992). The field is not necessarily a physical space, though it may be delimited as such in certain situations. It is, rather, the social arena within which certain norms and common sense assumptions are at play—which is the doxa of the field. When actors enter a particular field, their habitus shapes their actions and responses within the field. *Habitus* consists of the embodied beliefs, dispositions, and habits that constitute the subject's capacity to act and make choices within certain situations. If individuals are situated within a field that carries a doxa that is consistent with their own habitus, they will be at ease within that field and be able to conduct themselves in a manner that others within the field recognize as normal; in other words, they will have a "feel for the game" (Bourdieu 2000, 151). However, if individuals' habitus does not match the doxa of the field, then they may be at a loss as to the language or behaviour that is considered acceptable within that field (Bourdieu and Wacquant 1992; Bourdieu 2000; Bourdieu 1977). By theorizing both our practical knowledge and academic knowledge as elements of distinct fields and doxas that shape the research relationship in specific ways, we are seeking to "break with inside experience" (Bourdieu 1990), in the sense of trying to gain some reflective distance from our own embodied knowledges of both social services and academic fields. We do so by looking at three themes: practical knowledge, conflict between academic and social services doxa, and our **presentations of self**.

Theme 1: Practical Knowledge

Here we explore the forms of practical knowledge that we brought to bear in navigating the worlds of academia and the social services sector, drawing on our respective intuitive "feel for the game" that comes from our collective years of experience in both. One shared knowledge that we brought was understanding the importance of building trust with the community organizations with which we sought to work and establishing that our research was relevant and useful to their own aims and goals. Valerie was particularly conscious of the importance of this and drew strategically on her years of experience in community organizations to help "smooth out" the possible tensions that might emerge:

> Valerie: I feel like my previous workplace connections help build trust because there is a history there that people can refer to, and that I can also draw on in my interactions with others. My previous work holds the possibility of helping to smooth out academic-practitioner relationships.

Our social services doxa did not always translate directly across different players within this field. Specifically, there were hierarchies and sub-fields within the social services sector that influenced the manner in which we were read and how we could position ourselves:

> Lynette: I was mindful that most of my work with homeless communities has been adult-oriented, and that my experience with homeless youth has, in contrast, been wildly unsuccessful at times and thus short-lived. For these reasons I wondered—and even worried—about how the youth would read me and my various identity markers.

Cognizant of the norms of the social services sector, we designed a research project that was participatory, involved a lot of stakeholder feedback, and culminated in an advocacy project that drew on participatory action research (PAR) methodology. This research design, drawn from our "feel for the game" within the social services sector, clashed with certain subsets of academic doxa. This was particularly apparent when Carleton's Research Ethics Board questioned the research value of the advocacy project we had proposed, and whether it might be coercive toward the youth involved. This experience highlights our second theme: the tension between the doxa of the social services sector and the doxa of academia.

Theme 2: Conflict between Academic and Social Services Doxa

The doxa of a field is described by Bourdieu as the set of common sense norms that help subjects navigate a specific field. These are typically unspoken and often only noticed by those who are part of that field when the norms have been broken. Because of this, it is sometimes easier for those unfamiliar with the field to discern its doxa. As a tenured professor with more than a decade of enculturation in the field of academia, Jackie was less attuned to the ways in which academic norms might seem foreign or irrational to those in the social services sector. Valerie, on the other hand, had spent the last decade working within the field of community organizations. Valerie was finding the transition to academia challenging, in part because of the shifting norms and practices associated with the respective sectors. In reflecting on a conversation, Valerie notes:

> Valerie: Having Dan[1] introduce me using my former workplace connections, I believe, reassured Jenny that I not only knew the sector, but that I was a respected worker in the social services world. It gave me some credibility.

As a fish who is still slightly out of water in academia, Valerie finds herself trying to translate the value of academic research to the community organizations—and also to herself at times.

In order to bridge the gap between differing doxas in academia and the social services sector, all three of us worked to "translate" between these two worlds, often through the use of different language depending on the context in which we were working. Jackie reflects on her struggles to accurately describe the research we are doing to the community partners:

> Jackie: I am also conscious of the language I use; I typically frame the research project as being about "youth civic engagement" with the community partners, though I actually intensely dislike the language of "civic engagement," co-opted as it has been to be about becoming the well-behaved, self-regulating neoliberal citizen (see Kennelly and Llewellyn 2011 for a critique of the language of "active citizenship" in Canadian curricula).

(Jackie's enculturation to the academic doxa is so thorough that she even cites her own research in her vignette.)

Theme 3: Presentation of Self

The third and final theme discusses our "presentations of self" (Goffman 1959) and how we drew strategically on specific signifiers to mark ourselves as "belonging" to different fields as we worked across diverse settings. Bourdieu marks an interesting relationship between one's habitus and one's appearance, specifically clothing and bodily movements such as "walking, talking, looking, sitting, etc." (Bourdieu 2000, 141). Here, he describes habitus as being that which a subject knows "in a sense, too well, without objectifying distance, and takes it for granted, precisely because he is caught up in it, bound up with it; he inhabits it like a garment [*un habit*], or a familiar habitat" (Bourdieu 2000, 143). To the extent that we are attentive to the differential doxas that exist across differing fields, we are able to adjust our presentations of self to a certain extent, and to attempt to mark ourselves as belonging or "in the know."

> Lynette: My efforts to overtly self-manage began on the morning of that first focus group, even before I got dressed for the day. I needed something to wear that would speak to the audience that reflected the version of me most appropriate for the occasion.

> I opted for something hopefully relatable to the youth: skinny jeans, Blundstones, a leopard print shirt, hoop earrings. Donning my metaphorical power-suit, I hoped the participants would read me as youthful, current, and maybe even stylish.

This vignette demonstrates the efforts we made to be "read" in a certain way. Lynette strove to connect through clothing choices that she hoped the youth would recognize and appreciate, and perhaps even admire. We each made strategic choices designed to bridge the distance between academic and community norms.

Conclusions

Through the use of self-reflective "vignettes," we have sought to explore some of the tensions, contradictions, and confluences between the worlds of academia and the social services sector, when researching across the two. Bourdieu's theoretical concepts, specifically *field*, *habitus*, and *doxa*, provide a useful framework for our analysis. In considering the themes of practical knowledge, conflict between academic and social services doxa, and presentations of self, we have sought to illustrate the manner in which all three of us worked to negotiate our various identities as they manifested in relationship to the research project. With the reflective opportunity offered through writing vignettes, we have done our best to "break" with our own inside experience, by gaining some critical perspective on our habitus, doxa, and field. While always only partial, some awareness of these differences allows us to activate various behaviours, actions, or ways of being depending on the context we are navigating. In a research context, this allows for a certain fluidity when navigating the lines between practice and scholarship. It also enables us to translate more effectively the doxa of social services into academic terms and, conversely, to make the academic doxa more accessible to practitioners or youth. These negotiations are ongoing. As we continuously reflect and "break" with insider experience, we seek to develop a research practice that is ethically responsive to the academic and social services sectors with which we engage.

Note

1. All names used in the paper are pseudonyms.

References

Bourdieu, Pierre. 1977. *Outline of a Theory of Practice*. Translated by Richard Nice. 1st edition. Cambridge, UK; New York: Cambridge University Press.

———. 1990. *Homo Academicus*. Translated by Peter Collier. 1st edition. Stanford, Calif.: Stanford University Press.

———. 2000. *Pascalian Meditations*. Translated by Richard Nice. 1st edition. Stanford, CA: Stanford University Press.

Bourdieu, Pierre, and Loïc J. D. Wacquant. 1992. *An Invitation to Reflexive Sociology*. 1st edition. Chicago: University of Chicago Press.

Goffman, Erving. 1959. *The Presentation of Self in Everyday Life*. 1st edition. New York: Anchor.

Kennelly, Jacqueline, and Kristina R. Llewellyn. 2011. "Educating for active compliance: Discursive constructions in citizenship education." *Citizenship Studies* 15(6–7): 897–914.

3 Reimagining the Sociological Imagination: Including the Brain, Environment, and Culture

Ralph Matthews

Introduction: A New Sociological Imagination

With very few exceptions, for the past century sociology has been written as if the biological individual had little or no presence in the explanation of the social one. This stems largely from a negative response to the work of many prominent early sociologists who used biological determinism (often described as Social Darwinism) to explain social behaviour. Founders of sociology, such as Comte and Spencer, either made biological analogies comparing parts of society to parts of the body, or developed racist and sexist frameworks based on the supposed biological superiority of whites, males, and European societies (Martindale, 1960: 62–7). As social scientists became aware of the horrors of anti-Semitism in Europe and black racism in the United States and elsewhere, sociological writing began to employ a perspective that treated the human at birth as being "a **blank slate**" on which experience was solely responsible for human behaviour and social relationships (Pinker, 2002). Highly regarded sociologists such as Durkheim and Weber developed perspectives that either denied biological influences on human social behaviour or declared them of no relevance to understanding it (Schutt et al., 2015: 1–28). An exception was G.H. Mead (1934: 347*)* who included "mind" in his analysis, but sociologists have focused primarily on his theories of the social self (Franks, 2010: 7; Rose and Abi-Rached, 2013: 160).

Putting Human Biology into Sociological Explanation: The "Social Brain" and Plasticity

A lot has changed in our knowledge of the "social" in the past 50 years. New discoveries in brain science show that social behaviour has a brain-informed dimension. Through inventions such as CAT scans and MRIs, together with experimental research using electrodes embedded in the brain, it is now possible to observe brain functions in connection with social behaviour and to demonstrate clearly that significant brain activity actually precedes human behaviour. We also now know that the brain creates timely succession and defines connections, with both sides of the brain working together to create our perceptions of reality (Taylor, 2009: 9–35; Pinker, 2002: 143). Likewise, developments in genetics and genomics have demonstrated conclusively that small changes in the brain and brain proteins can lead to massive differences in both **cognition** and behaviour, largely independent of the social situation and social constructions of the individuals involved (Pinker, 2002: 45–7). Also, geneticists have identified genes and proteins that are directly associated with cognitive and behavioural activities—particularly those associated with abnormalities. Indeed, so great is the supportive evidence of the role of the brain in social behaviour that the concept of "the **social brain**" is now commonly used in neuroscience as well as in the new sub-discipline of neurosociology (Pickersgill, 2013; Rose and Abi-Rached, 2013: 141–63; Keshavan, 2015: 29–40).

If neuroscience developments require that sociologists now consider the impact of brain processes and genetics on human social behaviour, the discovery of brain "plasticity" has done much to return a significant focus of analysis to social science. There is substantial evidence that individuals' brain structure and its functions are influenced by relatively recent occurrences in both their social and ecological environments (Rose and Abi-Rashid, 2013: 22). Acceptance of this perspective has been particularly influenced by evidence that people with brain damage can improve and restore their brain functioning capacity, often in ways different from their original form (Taylor, 2009: 126-7).

There is also growing evidence that a brain can change as a result of the environmental experience of the individual. The relatively new field of epigenetics is focused on studying this interaction and its implications. Brain plasticity implies that the brain and its experiences are in constant interaction, with experiences changing connections in the brain, and the brain having a similar facility to alter how experiences are understood and interpreted. How we "know" is derived in part from biology and in part from experience. The challenge of sociological social inquiry today is to understand how to incorporate neurological knowledge into sociological explanations. For example, in sociological analyses about "sensing nature" and "nature and time" (Macnaghten and Urry, 1999: 107–71) we should now consider how brain-influenced dimensions of vision, taste, touch, hearing, and smell are complicit in our social definitions of nature and time and their implications for social action.

The title of this paper pays homage to C.W. Mills, whose *The Sociological Imagination* (1959) critiqued prevailing sociological approaches of his day. In their place, he proposed a sociology that linked history and biography, arguing that individual lives cannot be understood except in such broader contexts. Similarly, in this paper I advocate that a "reimagined" **sociological imagination** needs to accept new neuroscience knowledge and incorporate the role of the brain in shaping social behaviour. But, as I argue below, this also requires consideration of both the environment and cultural context in which that interaction takes place.

Putting the Environment into Sociological Explanation

Somewhat surprisingly, as is true of biology, it is only recently that the environment has played a significant role in sociological analysis. Just as early sociologists wished to develop sociology into a field in which humans were treated as purely social beings, they also wished to develop a perspective on the social that was general and not environmentally specific. The comparison was largely with sciences such as physics, in which the aim was the widest generalization and not the local one (Martindale, 1960: 27).

Geography, by definition, focused on the impact of local ecology on social life. Anthropology focused on the socio-cultural processes developed to survive in unique ecological niches. In contrast, sociology frequently was written as if ecology and space didn't matter. To be fair, there were distinct fields of rural and urban sociology, for example. But the focus of each was rarely about the way in which local ecological conditions led to unique societal forms; rather, the focus was on the more general conditions of rural and urban life. The same was true of regional and national sociologies. As I have noted elsewhere, more frequently than not, local "sociologies" were written as comparative analyses of the way that a region or area was alike or different in social processes when compared with major national states such as the USA. There was little analysis of the way in which they were shaped by their unique ecological conditions (cf. Matthews, 2014a; 2014b).

In recent years, this has changed, primarily due to growing awareness of the impact of climate change on all aspects of social life and **culture**. Indeed, sociological literature is now replete with work examining how climate, behaviour, ecology, social organization, and culture are intricately related. Of critical relevance to our analysis here is work that shows clear linkage between the brain, the environment, and social context. The work dealing with understanding of the passage of time is a particularly significant example of this.

While neuroscience provides compelling evidence that the capacity to perceive time is very much related to left brain development (Taylor, 2009: 29–30), TenHouten's (1997) work on Indigenous versus non-Indigenous perceptions of time demonstrates that it is also cultural and learned through environmental experience. He demonstrates that time is understood cyclically by Indigenous persons and linearly by non-Indigenous persons and implies that such differences come from different experiences of living in and experiencing one's ecological surroundings. In short, though time may be brain-defined, time is also socio-culturally derived through experience. TenHouten was the first to label the field that links brain function, environment, and social structure as neurosociology. As he explains, "The case for neurosociology begins with the observation that no social relationship or social interaction can possibly be carried out in the absence of human mental activity" (Ibid 8). That is, the brain and social experience, interacting in an environment, shape our understanding of both ourselves and where we are.

There is another way to examine the relationship between the environment and brain, one that focuses particularly on the ethical issues involved in this relationship. This author and colleagues have been developing a field they call "environmental neuroethics," which, for example, examines whether environmental changes that are deliberately created through resource extraction have neurological implications for brain development and assesses the ethical issues involved (Illes, Davidson, and Matthews, 2014). We also examine how unique approaches to both knowledge and ethics by Indigenous peoples create a unique understanding of neurological development and environmental impacts *on* the brain (Tesluk, Illes, and Matthews, 2016).

Putting Culture into Sociological Explanation

While sociology needs to incorporate knowledge about the interactive influence of brain and environment on social behaviour, up to this point we have primarily presented an understanding of the bio-social character of individuals. We have ignored the primary focus of sociology, the role of society in this process. To offset this and following Mills's directive, we also need to examine the historical and social context in which people live, as these impact both their individual social biographies and their brains. In this, culture plays a key role and may be considered the social imperative, paralleling the biological imperative from the brain as jointly shaping action. Just as brain functions provide an important context for individual action, so does culture provide a similar social context as the "glue" through which society and its organizations have a parallel social influence.

It may be surprising to those who have not previously encountered the neuroscience perspective that the role of culture in social behaviour remains contentious. For example, Pinker regards culture as historically embedded in the brain through experience and as having no external validity as a social process. In his terms, "The best explanation today is thoroughly cultural, but it depends on seeing a culture as a product of human desires rather than a shaper of them" (2002: 66).

In contrast, I argue that culture is the basis on which social organization is formulated and distilled and becomes the template within which social behaviour is channelled. While it may be partly formed in the context of the "social brain," it is primarily an aspect of social organization existing "out there" in the experienced social world. Rose and Abi-Rached capture this aspect of culture as both part of the social brain and also an independent entity, stating, "It is important constantly to remind neuroscientists that neither animal nor human brains exist in individualized isolation.... That they are enabled by a supra-individual, material, symbolic, and cultural matrix" (2013: 233).

On the other hand, culture should not be seen as a static and impenetrable "cake of custom" (Bagehot, 1948). Culture, in the form of institutional patterns guiding behaviour, is to organizations what habits are to individuals. Acting individuals negotiate institutional cultures and the organizational structures behind them in determining appropriate action. Such a formulation owes much to the sociological perspective known as New Institutional Analysis (Nee, 2001; Hall and Taylor, 1996; Young, King, and Schroeder, 2008) which focuses on the actor in cultural matrices related to organizational structures. In C. Wright Mills's terms, culture is the distillation of history and social context as acting individuals experience them. It is, for any individual at any time, the *social a priori* that contextualizes social life in much the same way that the social brain contextualizes individual cognition.

Conclusion: Consilience as the Way Forward

In 1999, E.O. Wilson, a Harvard University–based biologist and essayist, published a book entitled *Consilience: The Unity of Knowledge*. In it, he made a case for the increasing convergence (i.e., consilience) of scientific with non-scientific knowledge from the humanities and social sciences (1999: 136–7). Since Wilson's book appeared, there has been a vast development of our scientific knowledge about how brain activities direct and intersect with individual behaviour. Sociologists cannot continue to largely ignore this evidence of how social life is influenced by prior cognitive direction. On the other hand, we have much yet to learn about how "society gets into our brains," shaping them in ways that were hitherto thought to not be possible. The time for consilience is now.

References

Bagehot, Walter (1948). *Physics and Politics*. New York, NY: Alfred Knopf.

Cabrera, Laura Y., Jordan Tesluk, Michelle Chakraborti, Ralph Matthews, and Judy Illes (2016). Brain matters: From environmental ethics to environmental neuroethics. *Environmental Health*. Under review.

Durkheim, Émile (1951/1997). *Suicide: A Study in Sociology*. New York, NY: Free Press.

Franks, David D. (2010). *Neurosociology: The Nexus between Neuroscience and Social Psychology*. New York, NY: Springer.

Hall, P. and R.C.R. Taylor (1996). "Political Science and the three New Institutionalism," MPIRG Discussion Paper 96/6. Kiln, Germany: Max Planck Institute.

Illes, Judy, Jacqueline Davidson, and Ralph Matthews (2014). Environmental Neuroethics: Changing the environment—changing the brain: Recommendations submitted to the Presidential Commission for the Study of Bioethical Issues. *Journal of Law and the Biosciences* 1(3): 1–6.

Kant, I. 1953. *Critique of Pure Reason*. Translated by N. Kemp Smith. New York, NY: Macmillan.

Keshavan, Matcheri S. (2015). The evolution, structure and functioning of the social brain, pp. 29–40 in Russell K. Schutt, Larry J. Seidman, and Matcheri S. Keshavan (eds), *Social Neuroscience: Brain Mind and Society*. Cambridge, MA: Harvard University Press.

Macnaghten, Phil and John Urry (1999). *Contested Natures*. London, UK: SAGE.

Martindale, Don (1960). *The Nature and Types of Sociological Theory*. Cambridge, MA: Houghton Mifflin.

Matthews, Ralph (2014a). Committing Canadian sociology: Developing a Canadian sociology and a sociology of Canada. *Canadian Review of Sociology* 51(2): 107–27.

Matthews, Ralph (2014b). Committing more sociology: Responses to the commentary on committing Canadian sociology. *Canadian Review of Sociology* 51(4): 409–17.

Mead, George Herbert (1934/1959). *Mind, Self and Society: From the Standpoint of a Social Behaviorist.* Chicago, IL: University of Chicago Press.

Mills, C. Wright (1959). *The Sociological Imagination.* New York, NY: Oxford University Press.

Nee, Victor (2001). Sources of the new institutionalism, pp. 1–16 in M.C. Brinton and V. Nee (eds), *The New Institutionalism in Sociology.* Stanford, CA: Stanford University Press.

Pikersgill, Martyn (2013). The social life of the brain: Neuroscience in society. *Current Sociology* 6(3): 322–140.

Pinker, Steven (2002). *The Blank Slate: The Modern Denial of Nature.* New York, NY: Penguin Group.

Rose, Nikolas and Joelle M. Abi-Rached (2013). *Neuro: The New Brain Sciences and the Management of the Mind.* Princeton, NJ: Princeton University Press.

Russell K. Schutt, Larry J. Seidman, and Matcheri S. Keshavan (eds) (2015). *Social Neuroscience: Brain Mind and Society.* Cambridge, MA: Harvard University Press.

Schutt, Russell K., Larry J. Seidman, and Matcheri S. Keshavan (2015). Changing perspectives in three disciplines, pp. 1–28 in Russell K. Schutt, Larry J. Seidman, and Matcheri S. Keshavan (eds), *Social Neuroscience: Brain Mind and Society.* Cambridge, MA: Harvard University Press.

Taylor, Jill Bolte (2009). *My Stroke of Insight: A Brain Scientist's Personal Journey.* London, UK: Plume Books, Penguin Group.

TenHouten, W. (1997). Neurosociology. *Journal of Social and Evolutionary Systems* 20(1): 7–37.

Tesluk, Jordan, Judy Illes, and Ralph. Matthews (2016). First Nations and environmental neuroethics: Perspectives on brain health in a world of change, in L. Syd, M. Johnson, and Karen S. Rommelfanger (eds), *The Routledge Handbook of Neuroethics.* NY: Routledge Publishers. Under review.

Weber, Max (1947). *The Theory of Social and Economic Organization.* New York, NY: Free Press.

Wilson, Edward O. (1999). *Consilience: The Unity of Knowledge.* New York, NY: Alfred Knopf.

Young, Oran R., Leslie A. King, and Heike Schroeder (2008). *Institutions and Environmental Change.* Cambridge, MA: MIT Press.

4 What Can a Theorist Do?

Christopher Powell

1. Humanity

How should I begin? In hope? In fear? In fury? Or in love?

I sit on the steps of my back porch in the early morning. It's the very heart of white middle-class first-world prosperity. Birds sing in the pre-dawn light. Trees wave softly in a breeze. The grass smells of morning dew. My world feels peaceful. But somewhere, out of sight, a fire is burning. I can't see it, or smell it, but I know it's there, and it's growing. Coming for me, and for everyone I love.

* * *

As a species we have accomplished wonders: walked the moon, cured smallpox, built the Internet. There are 7 billion of us and we have formed a single global society. We are all connected, we are all coming to know each other, and we all share a common fate.

Our economic system, capitalism, depends on constant expansion of production in order to survive. But it can't expand forever. Some combination of diminishing marginal returns on capital investment (Marx 1981; Wallerstein 1974) and ecological limits to growth (Meadows, Randers, and Meadows 2004; Bardi 2011) will, sooner or later, push profits toward zero.

Our political system, the global network of sovereign states, maintains social order through local monopolies of force, each of which competes with the others for regional and global dominance (Wallerstein 2012). This system has created enough military force to annihilate our species many times over (Goodman and Hoff 1990). There is now one firearm for every seven people in the world (Small Arms Survey Project 2007, 39).

Humans experience the world through the medium of culture. Each culture produces a unique form of human experience, a unique reality (Goodman 1978; Davis 2007). Human cultural diversity is diminishing (Crystal 2000). Of the 6,000 languages spoken today, half are not being taught to children, and only 600 are stable and secure (Davis 2007, 6). Genocide and assimilation come too easily. Living with deep difference is hard.

When the global economy stops growing, the many small fires of human conflict could become a holocaust the likes of which our species has never seen. Global fascism, civilizational collapse, human extinction—these are real possibilities.

My stepdaughter's small hand slips into mine as we cross the street.

2. Systems

The crisis we face does not come from our genetically inherent human nature. That nature is flexible, adaptable, protean (Keller 2010; Lock and Farquhar 2007). An alphabet, not a script.

Our crisis does not come from moral choice, from our failure to be moral. Long ago we invented morality (Durkheim 1992), and then forgot we invented it (Berger and Luckmann 1966). Morality is not a compass point toward which we should steer; it is a treaty that we make with each other, and with ourselves, a treaty we continually renegotiate.

Our crisis does not come from any conscious, intentional choice at all. Nobody chose *this* world. We might choose our actions, but we cannot choose the conditions under which we act (Marx 1979), nor can we choose the consequences of our actions. Frequently, we do not even know where our actions will lead (Elias 2000). In the turbulence of history we move blindly, making more history which we do not see coming.

The crisis we are in today is a crisis of **social systems** (Marx 1976; Parsons 1951; Luhmann 1995; Wallerstein 2012). When we act, our actions have consequences, for the physical world and for the people who share that world with us. The interplay of those consequences creates a social world, *both* physical *and* symbolic (Marx and Engels 1976; Mead 1934). This world exceeds our intentions (Elias 1978). From the social world come the forces that motivate us and constrain us, the rewards and the costs of our actions, the objects of all our fears and desires.

We still understand this social world poorly. We have mapped the human genome and we know the origin and structure of the stars, but *we still have no social science*. What we call the social sciences can interpret the world for us in various ways, but they cannot tell us how to solve our problems.

But that is what we desperately need: new solutions for the old problems of how to live together.

3. Theory

I'm going the long way around here. Theorizing. Because I'm trapped, as we all are trapped. "The way out of a trap is to study the trap itself, learn how it is built" (Gunaratana 2002: 98). So I theorize.

But what is theorizing? What is theory?

Imagine three dimensions, present in all knowledge. Like the x, y, and z axes of a Cartesian graph, these dimensions are distinct, they do not reduce to each other, but they are inseparable. Let's call them the practical, the empirical, and the conceptual.

We use knowledge to do things, and doing things generates more knowledge. That's the practical dimension.

We use knowledge to make sense of our sensory experience, and we use our sensory experiences to generate more knowledge. That's the empirical dimension.

Knowledge also has a third dimension, the *conceptual*. A **concept** is any abstraction that gives form to our experiences. Concepts turn the undifferentiated flow of unique sensations into objects, events, relationships, and so on.

When you were born, you had no idea of the distinction between yourself and the rest of the universe (Whitney 2012). Without that distinction, you were the universe, and the universe was you. The discovery of your own particularity was your first concept.

* * *

Concepts organize sensations into phenomena. Think about the difference between Marx and Weber's definition of class, for example (Marx 1975; Weber 1978a). When they each talk about class struggle, they are not referring to the same phenomena. Their theories address different worlds.

A **theory** is any assemblage of concepts that work together in some way. Theories can connect phenomena, but they can also make divisions. Theories can settle questions, or raise new ones. Theories can simplify our understanding of complex things, but they can also complicate and unsettle our established understandings. And so on.

Theorizing, then, is any work along the conceptual dimension. It is working on problems like how to define and use concepts, how to relate different concepts to each other, and so on.

This type of work generates questions that are not strictly empirical or practical. Theoretical questions emerge out of empirical research and social practice, but they have their own quality. They cannot be settled by an appeal to evidence alone, nor by simply trying something out in practice. Sometimes we have to rethink what our concepts should mean and what work they should do.

This is especially true when our existing concepts are part of what has trapped us.

* * *

Here's the thing: social life is itself partly made up of our knowledge of it.

Let me say that again. The social systems on which our lives depend, systems like capitalism, sovereignty, language, and so on, are made up partly of our knowledge of them. Money, the law, the right way to shake hands—to say nothing of sex/gender, race, citizenship, and so on—these things are partly constituted by our knowledge of them and by the ways that we *act* on that knowledge. This is called **reflexivity**.

Reflexivity implies that social life is partly *made of* social theories. So, a change in our theories could change the world. In fact, it happens all the time. We just can't control it—yet.

4. Science

There are two notions we have to get beyond: objectivity and subjectivity, meaning knowledge as a mirror held up to nature, and knowledge as mere ideology.

Sometimes we do advance our knowledge by testing hypotheses against empirical observations (Popper 2002). But some kinds of theories aren't falsified this way. These theories, called **paradigms**, do more than propose hypotheses; they define the objects to be investigated, the general methods of investigation, and the types of findings to be considered valid (Kuhn 1996). And when we change paradigms, we step from one universe of experience to another.

Here's how that works: Our body-minds use concepts to convert experience from an undifferentiated flow of sensation into recognizable objects and events (Merleau-Ponty 2002). We acquire concepts—even basic concepts like time and space—through social interaction (Bourdieu and Wacquant 1992; James 2007; Mead 1962; Durkheim 1995). Our ability to take ordinary, everyday reality for granted depends on innumerable social negotiations (Schutz 1932; Garfinkel 1967). What we experience as real comes to us as a product of social relations (Bloor 1976; Barnes, Bloor, and Henry 1996). Even the most objective science depends on an ultimately subjective decision to value certain ways of knowing over others (Weber 1949, 1978b).

But it's not just all in our heads. The social world is material. When we produce knowledge, we always do so by acting in the world. Even scientists in laboratories *act*, moving things around to see what happens, what would happen if we weren't around (Callon 1988; Latour 2005; Law and Hassard 1999). Every time we produce knowledge we do it by changing something. We act on some stuff, the stuff acts back. We change the world, the world changes us. Reflexivity again.

The upshot is that scientific knowledge is not a mirror held up to nature; nor is it a mere projection of our minds. The production of scientific knowledge about anything—stars, microbes, social systems—is a practical relationship. Sometimes a dance, sometimes a battle, ideas and things mix together and change each other. In the process, new worlds are born.

Since Pasteur did his work there is a lot more penicillin in the world today. The human world changed the non-human world, and vice-versa. Since Lavoisier, there is a lot more carbon dioxide in the atmosphere. Since Bohr, a lot more uranium in silos.

5. Revolution

Today, social theory contributes to social practice in three general ways: by mapping the terrain of struggle (McKay 2005), by critiquing the gap between our ideals and our reality (Adorno 2007), or by cracking open the certainties of our social order to find hidden possibilities of freedom (Foucault 1997). These all have their uses. But none of them can ever make a discovery capable of revolutionizing social practice.

Scientific revolutions tend to give birth to social revolutions by enabling new practical technologies that change the way people relate to each other. Social science has never made this kind of breakthrough—yet. But it will. And when it does, the answers it finds will depend on the questions that it asks.

* * *

How can we produce the goods and services we need while enabling working people to retain ownership of their own labour-power? (Marx 1975, 1976)

How can we live with our political and cultural differences, instead of using violence to suppress or eliminate those differences? (Powell 2011, 2016)

How can we solve the problems of collective action (Olson Jr. 1971) in ways that are egalitarian, inclusive, democratic, but also *effective*?

To build a sustainable and humane world we need answers to these questions. These are not just normative or communicative questions (Parsons 1951; Habermas 1998; Luhmann 1995). These are questions about how to reprogram the *material* dynamics of social systems. To do this, we need new theories, new *kinds* of theories, and whole new paradigms.

And we need them urgently. Because that fire is coming for us all.

* * *

Theorizing, working with concepts, can help change the way turn experience and practice into knowledge. These changes can enable new kinds of experience and practice. Theory fuels our most distinctive human attribute: our unequalled ability to change our circumstances through action.

With the right social theory, we can change our world.

With the right theory we could still save it.

References

Adorno, Theodor. 2007. *Negative Dialectics*. New York: Bloomsbury Academic. Original edition, 1966.

Bardi, Ugo. 2011. *The Limits to Growth Revisited*, *Springer Briefs in Energy/Energy Analysis*. New York: Springer.

Barnes, Barry, David Bloor, and John Henry. 1996. *Scientific Knowledge: A Sociological Analysis*. Chicago: University of Chicago Press.

Berger, Peter, and Thomas Luckmann. 1966. *The Social Construction of Reality: A Treatise in the Sociology of Knowledge*. London: Penguin Books.

Bloor, David. 1976. *Knowledge and Social Imagery*. London: Routledge and Kegan Paul.

Bourdieu, Pierre, and Loïc J. D. Wacquant. 1992. *An Invitation to Reflexive Sociology*. Chicago: University of Chicago Press.

Callon, Michel. 1988. "Some elements of a sociology of translation: domestication of the scallops and the fishermen of St. Brieuc Bay." In *Power, Action, & Belief*, edited by J. Law. London: Routledge.

Crystal, David. 2000. *Language Death*. Cambridge: Cambridge University Press.

Davis, Wade. 2007. *Light at the Edge of the World: A Journey Through the Realm of Vanishing Cultures*: Douglas & Mcintyre.

Durkheim, Emile. 1992. *Professional Ethics and Civic Morals*. London: Routledge.

———. 1995. *The Elementary Forms of Religious Life*. Translated by K. E. Fields. New York: The Free Press.

Elias, Norbert. 1978. *What is Sociology?* Translated by S. Mennell and G. Morrissey. New York: Columbia University Press. Original edition, 1970.

———. 2000. *The Civilizing Process: The History of Manners and State Formation and Civilization*. Translated by E. Jephcott. Revised ed. Oxford: Blackwell.

Foucault, Michel. 1997. "What is Enlightenment?" In *Ethics, Subjectivity, and Truth: Essential Works of Michel Foucault 1954-1984, Volume I*, edited by P. Rabinow. New York: The New Press. Pp. 303–20.

Garfinkel, Harold. 1967. *Studies in Ethnomethodology*. Cambridge: Polity Press.

Goodman, Lisl Marburg, and Lee Ann Hoff. 1990. *Omnicide: The Nuclear Dilemma*. New York: Praeger.

Goodman, Nelson. 1978. *Ways of Worldmaking*. Indianapolis: Hackett Publishing Company.

Gunaratana, Bhante Henepola. 2002. *Mindfulness in Plain English*. Updated and Expanded ed. Somerville, MA: Wisdom Publications.

Habermas, Jürgen. 1998. "Actions, Speech Acts, Linguistically Mediated Interactions, and the Lifeword." In *On the Pragmatics of Communciation*, edited by M. Cooke. Cambridge, MA: MIT Press. Pp. 215–55.

James, William. 2007. *The Principles of Psychology, Volume 1*. New York: Cosimo Books. Original edition, 1890.

Keller, Evelyn Fox. 2010. *The Mirage of a Space Between Nature and Nurture*. Durham, NC: Duke University Press.

Kuhn, Thomas S. 1996. *The Structure of Scientific Revolutions*. Third ed. Chicago: University of Chicago Press. Original edition, 1962.

Latour, Bruno. 2005. *Reassembling the Social Sciences: An Introduction to Actor-Network Theory*. Oxford: Oxford University Press.

Law, John, and John Hassard, eds. 1999. *Actor Network Theory and After*. Oxford: Blackwell.

Lock, Margaret, and Judith Farquhar, eds. 2007. *Beyond the Body Proper: Reading the Anthropology of Material Life*. Durham, NC: Duke University Press.

Luhmann, Niklas. 1995. *Social Systems*. Chicago: University of Chicago Press.

Marx, Karl. 1975. "Estranged Labour." In *Karl Marx Frederick Engels Collected Works*. New York: International Publishers. Pp. 270–82.

———. 1976. *Capital: A Critique of Political Economy, Volume I*. Translated by B. Fowkes. Toronto: Penguin Books Canada Ltd. Original edition, 1867.

———. 1979. "The 18th Brumaire of Louis Bonaparte." In *Karl Marx, Frederick Engels: Collected Works, Volume 11, Marx and Engels: 1851–53*. Moscow: Progress Publishers. Pp. 99–7.

———. 1981. *Capital: A Critique of Political Economy, Volume III*. Translated by D. Fernbach. Edited by E. Mandel. Toronto: Penguin Books Canada Ltd. Original edition, 1894.

Marx, Karl, and Frederick Engels. 1976. "The German Ideology." In *Karl Marx, Frederick Engels: Collected Works, Volume 5, Marx and Engels: 1845–47*. Moscow: Progress Publishers.

McKay, Ian. 2005. *Rebels, Reds, Radicals: Rethinking Canada's Left History*. Toronto: Between the Lines.

Mead, George Herbert. 1934. *Mind, Self, and Society*. Chicago: University of Chicago Press.

———. 1962. *Mind, Self, and Society*. Chicago: University of Chicago Press.

Meadows, Donella, Jorgen Randers, and Dennis Meadows. 2004. *Limits to Growth: The 30-Year Update*. White River Junction, VT: Chelsea Green Publishing.

Merleau-Ponty, Maurice. 2002. *The Phenomenology of Perception*. Translated by C. Smith. London: Routledge Classics. Original edition, 1945.

Olson Jr., Mancur. 1971. *The Logic of Collective Action: Public Goods and the Theory of Groups*. Revised ed. Cambridge, MA: Harvard University Press. Original edition, 1965.

Parsons, Talcott. 1951. *The Social System*. New York: The Free Press.

Popper, Karl. 2002. *The Logic of Scientific Discovery*. London: Routledge Classics. Original edition, 1935.

Powell, Christopher. 2011. *Barbaric Civilization: A Critical Sociology of Genocide*. Montréal: McGill-Queen's University Press.

———. 2016. "Revitalizing the Ethnosphere: Global Society, Ethnodiversity, and the Stakes of Cultural Genocide." *Genocide Studies and Prevention: An International Journal* Vol. 10, No. 1: pp. 44–59.

Schutz, Alfred. 1932. *The Phenomenology of the Social World*. Translated by G. Walsh and F. Lehnert. Edited by J. Wild, *Studies in Phenomenology and Existential Philosophy*. 1967: Northwestern University Press. Original edition, 1932.

Small Arms Survey Project. 2007. *Small Arms Survey 2007: Guns and the City*. Cambridge: Cambridge University Press.

Wallerstein, Immanuel. 1974. "The Rise and Future Demise of the World Capitalist System: Concepts for Comparative

Analysis." *Comparative Studies in Society and History* Vol. 16, No. 4: pp. 387–415.
———. 2012. *World-Systems Analysis: An Introduction.* Durham, NC: Duke University Press.
Weber, Max. 1949. "'Objectivity'" in Social Science and Social Science Policy." In *The Methodology of the Social Sciences*, edited by E. A. Shils and H. A. Finch. Glencoe, IL: The Free Press. Pp. 50–112.
———. 1978a. *Economy and Society*. Vol. 1. Berkeley: University of California Press.
———. 1978b. "Value-judgments in Social Science." In *Weber: Selections in translation*, edited by W. G. Runciman. Cambridge: Cambridge University Press. Pp. 69-98.
Whitney, Shiloh. 2012. "Affects, Images and Childlike Perception: Self-Other Difference in Merleau-Ponty's Sorbonne Lectures." *PhaenEx* Vol. 7, No. 2: pp. 185–211.

5 The Debate about Accident Proneness

Lorne Tepperman and Nicole Meredith

Despite nearly a century of failed efforts to locate a psychological source, the notion of "**accident proneness**" continues to fascinate the public. It's true that some people—and some broader groups of individuals—have more accidents than others. Explaining this trend, however, continues to be a problem.

Some claim that people with a history of injuries are **subconsciously** *trying* to harm themselves (Rawson, 1944). Sigmund Freud, for example, proposed that some people harbour a sense of guilt surrounding their sexual desires. In response, they feel an unconscious need to inflict self-harm as a way of punishing themselves for those "shameful" sexual yearnings (Whitbourne, 2013; Arbous and Kerrich, 1951.) This is part of a larger theory that views all "accidents"—including memory distortions and slips of the lip—as evidence of unconscious motivation. This theory views self-harming behaviour as revealing guilt-driven, neurotic needs for punishment.

There may indeed be a psychopathology or personality trait called "accident proneness" that accounts for an observed **correlation** between, for example, on-the-job injuries and poor health, low productivity, and clumsiness. Two British researchers, Eric Farmer and E.G. Chambers, observed this very correlation in 1926 in their studies of candy-factory, military, and dockyard workers alike. However, the variable of accident proneness is not necessarily needed to explain the trends they observed: for example, workers who are in poor health may be less productive, clumsier, and more susceptible to on-the-job injuries.

A second explanation is that another variable, yet unmeasured—call it X—causes all of these problems, including a high rate of accidents. Imagine that X is bipolar disorder, malnutrition, marital strife, the hatred of a particular job, or harassment by a boss. In fact, many variables may account for a correlation of accidents, ill-health, unproductivity, and apparent clumsiness.

The problem is choosing the right variables to measure, ensuring we measure them well, and then finding out the effects of all these variables. Then, some accidents will be explainable by mental or physical health problems. Some will be explainable by medications people may be taking, or due to normal aging. Others will be explainable by risks associated with a particular location (i.e., dangerous neighbourhoods), lifestyle (i.e., dangerous lifestyles), or type of work (i.e., dangerous lines of work).

Outstanding Questions

To date, researchers have not been able to prove there *is* an accident-prone personality or temperament, nor to agree on its nature. How much of an "accident" is due to the individual's inherent nature, versus her mode of behaviour, the location, and the time or moment, is impossible to say.

In contrast with the personality-focused accident-proneness approach, a public-health approach focuses on external environments: it examines accident rates under different circumstances, effectively holding constant other factors by "washing them out." For example, the risks associated with highways are many. Armed with statistics from hundreds of millions of miles of highway travel, we can safely say that highway X is twice as dangerous or risky as highway Y, in the sense that people are twice as likely to have accidents on highway X. With so many cases, we can ignore other competing explanations. On both highways, some of the victims will have been good drivers, others bad; some will have been inclined to take risks, others not; some will have driven the highway in the winter, others in the summer; some at night, others in daytime; and so on.

We can follow the same process in evaluating daytime versus nighttime driving, winter versus summer driving, driving after drinking versus driving sober, and so on, using millions of miles of driving as our data. There are so many cases, with so many variations, that the unmeasured variables can reasonably be ignored.

All we know today is that an individual who lives, works, and drives in a "dangerous" part of the city—characterized by poverty, a dense population, and limited housing and public services—is more liable to suffer unexpected injuries than a person who lives, works, and drives in a safer part of the city. "Accident liability" describes risk, but risk is never based on a single factor (af Wåhlberg and Dorn, 2009), and certainly not on an unmeasured personality trait.

Now, back to history again. In 1919, Greenwood and Woods gathered information about munitions-factory workers and their injuries for just over a year (Rodgers and Blanchard, 1993; Visser et al., 2007; James and Dickinson, 1950). They found that 20 per cent of workers had suffered 80 per cent of all the injuries. There are two possible conclusions to be drawn from their findings: either these workers were especially clumsy or unlucky, or they were especially unfit for this kind of work. We cannot conclude, however, that these munitions workers were accident-prone without finding out if they also had a high number of accidents in other domains of life. To date, researchers have not done so.

Alternative Explanations

In recent decades, injury, health, and safety researchers have jettisoned the idea of accident proneness (af Wåhlberg and Dorn, op. cit.), chalking it up to a lot of "unsound over-generalization," or even "folklore" (Rogers and Blanchard, op. cit.). Here are alternatives to the theory of accident proneness.

(a) Drugs and Medications

Some industrial injuries may be side effects of medicines prescribed to workers. For example, research has shown that antidepressants and sedatives are related to unexpected injuries. These and other drugs cause apathy, drowsiness, and disorientation and disrupt people's short-term memory, coordination, information-processing skills, and mental abilities as a result. The same is true of recreational alcohol and drug use.

(b) Group Proneness

Today's researchers tend to look at people with a history of injuries as a collective group, who potentially share social and demographic features. They call this group proneness (Lee and Wrench, 1980). If people of certain ethnic or social groups are more likely to injure themselves than members of other groups, cultural factors could be at work—not personal, psychological, or pathological ones. For example, people tend to imitate their friends, even in doing dangerous things.

(c) Risk-Taking Attitudes

Some people crave danger and excitement and pursue these sensations through a range of related activities (see, for example, Volkert et al., 2013;

Junger, West, and Timman, 2001; Maslowsky et al., 2011; Chaumeton et al., 2011). For example, people who gamble are also likely to abuse alcohol, tobacco, and other dangerous substances. In turn, people who abuse alcohol or drugs also tend to drive recklessly, even when they are sober (see, for example, Junger and Dekovic, 2003; Junger, van de Heijden, and Keane, 2001; Junger, Stroebe, and van der Laan, 2001). Researchers call this "cross-domain consistency": people tend to make similar decisions in different situations (Murphy et al., 2011; Martens et al., 2009; Chaumeton et al., 2011).

Men, in our culture, enjoy risk-taking considerably more than women and have correspondingly higher injury rates (Harris, Jenkins, and Glaser 2006; Suchman, 1970; Visser et al., 2007). For example, men are more likely than women to run yellow lights and avoid wearing seatbelts (Junger, West, and Timman, op. cit.), hinting at their greater willingness to take risks and avoid precautions.

(d) Normalized Risk-Taking

Today, almost everyone believes that unexpected injuries are a "normal" part of life. Most children have broken an arm playing; most adults have cut or burned themselves while cooking. But by dismissing these all-too-common injuries as "part of growing up," or common, daily experiences, many of us have become complacent about the harm we do to ourselves.

This is particularly true in certain social environments, such as places designed for recreation, like casinos, clubs, and resorts. Take Las Vegas, the sin capital of North America. Drivers in Las Vegas are 21 per cent more likely to have a collision than the national average (Hansen, 2010).

(e) Lack of Social Integration

Lastly, research shows that the factors that contribute to low suicide rates—marriage and religion—also contribute to lower-than-average accident rates (see Tepperman and Meredith, 2015). As with suicide, the mechanisms by which **social integration** reduces unexpected injury are numerous. For example, both marriage and religion tend to reduce risky behaviour.

Conclusions

Repeat injuries pose a costly health problem for employers and governments who want closure on this problem so they can increase productivity and lower health costs.

To build a safer society, we need to rid ourselves of a careless, risk-taking mentality. We also need to move beyond the thinking that "accident proneness" is a personality defect. "Accidents" are *not* the product of a mysterious personality disorder; they are built into the fabric of our society. Reducing their prevalence therefore requires shifting our deeply entrenched customs and beliefs.

References

af Wåhlberg, Anders, and Lisa Dorn. "Bus driver accident record: The return of accident proneness." *Theoretical Issues in Ergonomics Science* 10.1 (2009): 77–91.

Arbous, Adrian Garth, and J.E. Kerrich. "Accident statistics and the concept of accident-proneness." *Biometrics* 7.4 (1951): 340–432.

Chaumeton, N.R., S.K. Ramowski, and R.J. Nystrom. "Correlates of gambling among eighth-grade boys and girls," *Journal of School Health* 81 (2011): 374–84.

Engel, Ralf. "Social and cultural factors," *Traffic Accident Causation in Europe* (2007). Retrieved from: http://www.trace-project.org/publication/archives/trace-wp5-d5-4.pdf

Farmer, Eric, and Eric Gordon Chambers. "A psychological study of individual differences in accident rates." *Industrial Fatigue Research Board Report. Medical Research Council* 38 (1926).

Greenwood, Major, and Hilda M. Woods. *The Incidence of Industrial Accidents upon Individuals: With Special Reference to Multiple Accidents.* No. 4. HM Stationery Office [Darling and son, Limited, printers], 1919.

Hansen, Kyle B., "Report: Las Vegas drivers more prone to accidents," *Las Vegas Sun*, Sept. 2, 2010, http://www.lasvegassun.com/news/2010/sep/02/report-las-vegas-drivers-more-prone-accidents

Harris, Christine R., Michael Jenkins, and Dale Glaser. "Gender differences in risk assessment: Why do women take fewer risks than men?" *Judgment and Decision Making* 1.1 (2006): 48–63 .

James, Fleming, and John J. Dickinson. "Accident proneness and accident law." *Harvard Law Review* 63.1 (1950): 769–95.

Junger, Marianne, and Maja Dekovic. "'Crime as risk-taking: Co-occurrence of delinquent behavior, health endangering behaviors and problem behaviors." In Chester L. Britt and Michael R. Gottfredson (Eds), *Control Theories of Crime and Delinquency: Advances in criminological theory.* Transaction Publishers, New Brunswick, 2003, pp. 213–48.

Junger, Marianne, Peter van der Heijden, and Carl Keane. "Interrelated harms: Examining the associations between victimization, accidents, and criminal behavior." *Injury Control and Safety Promotion* 8.1 (2001): 13–28.

Junger, Marianne, Robert West, and Reinier Timman. "Crime and risky behavior in traffic: An example of cross-situational consistency." *Journal of Research in Crime and Delinquency* 38.4 (2001): 439–59.

Junger, Marianne, Wolfgang Stroebe, and André M. Laan. "Delinquency, health behaviour and health." *British Journal of Health Psychology* 6.2 (2001): 103–20.

Lee, Gloria, and John Wrench. "'Accident-prone immigrants'": An assumption challenged." *Sociology* 14.4 (1980): 551–66.

Martens, M.P., Rocha, T.L., Cimini, M.D., Diaz-Myers, A., Rivero, E.M., and Wulfert, E.. The co-occurrence of alcohol use and gambling activities in first-year college students. *Journal of American College Health*, 57.6 (2009): 597–602.

Maslowsky, J., D. Keating, C. Monk, and J. Schulenberg. "Planned versus unplanned risks: Evidence for subtypes of risk behavior in adolescence." *International Journal of Behavioral Development*, 35.2 (2011): 152.

Murphy, Sherry L., Jiaquan Xu, and Kenneth D. Kochanek. "Deaths: Final data for 2010." *National Vital Statistics Reports: From the Centers for Disease Control and Prevention, National Center for Health Statistics, National Vital Statistics System* 61.4 (2013): 1–117.

Newbold, Ethel M. "A contribution to the study of the human factor in the causation of accidents." *Industrial Fatigue Research Board Report* 34 (1926).

Rawson, Arnold J. "Accident proneness." *Psychosomatic medicine* 6.1 (1944): 88.

Rodgers, Mark D., and Robert E. Blanchard. 1993. *Accident proneness: A research review.* Federal Aviation Administration, Oklahoma City: Oklahoma Civil Aeromedical Institute.

Suchman, Edward A. "Accidents and social deviance." *Journal of Health and Social Behavior* (1970): 4–15.

Tepperman, Lorne, and Nicole Meredith. 2015. *Waiting to happen: The sociology of unexpected injuries.* Toronto: Oxford University Press.

Visser, E., Y.J. Pijl, R.P. Stolk, J. Neeleman, and J.G. Rosmalen. "Accident proneness, does it exist? A review and meta-analysis." *Accident Analysis & Prevention*, 39.3 (2007): 556–64.

Volkert, J., J.S. Randjbar, S. Moritz, and L. Jelinek, "Risk recognition and sensation in seeking in revictimization and posttraumatic stress disorder." *Behaviour Modification* 37.1 (2013): 39–61.

Whitbourne, Suzanne Krauss. "Clumsy? Put away the Band-Aids and take out the mind-aids." *Psychology Today* (2013). Retrieved from: https://www.psychologytoday.com/blog/fulfillment-any-age/201310/clumsy-put-away-the-band-aids-and-take-out-the-mind-aids

6 French Language Sociology in Quebec

Jean-Philippe Warren

In North America, sociological works published in French are almost totally ignored for the simple reason that the vast majority of scholars don't read French.

I'm of the opinion that the prevalent "**linguistic solitude**" is detrimental to the vitality of mainstream North American sociology, which should seek diversity and not homogeneity in its legitimate quest for objectivity and universalism. Of course, this statement holds true for every linguistic group. In theory, one cannot not see why the incapacity of reading French would be more detrimental than that that of reading Chinese, Spanish, or Urdu.

Yet, two factors contribute to make the ignorance of French-language scholarship particularly regretful for North American sociologists. On the one hand, the French sociological tradition is historically very rich.

Bourdieu and Foucault are today's most quoted sociologists in the world. On the other hand, Quebec, the only North American jurisdiction where a majority of French speakers live, shows a series of traits that make it a relatively "distinct society" on the continent. Studying Quebec may therefore be stimulating for those interested in the issues of immigration, unionism, nationalism, and so forth.

A Different Sociology

In many respects, and notwithstanding numerous exceptions, francophone sociology is different from its anglophone counterpart. I shall restrict myself here to two prominent features: the place of the **public intellectual** and the influence of cultural studies. These differences should not be overblown. Yet, they exist and they play a role in the troubled relationship between anglophone and francophone sociologies.

For a French speaker the idea of a public intellectual is curious and sounds like a pleonasm. Is not an intellectual always public? Has anyone ever heard of a private intellectual? Such labelling points to another concept that doesn't exist in the French language, that of the scholar. There is not a direct equivalent to the term *scholar* in French. Hence, in French, a university professor of sociology is always a public intellectual to some extent, and, at least in words, cannot be a scholar.

Perhaps this partly explains why, in French Quebec, all the great sociologists have been profoundly engaged in social and political debates. From Fernand Dumont (1927–1997) to Jacques Beauchemin (b. 1955), an impressive number of francophone Quebec sociologists have stepped up to present their critical views of society and have been invited to contribute to the crafting of government policies. Their names regularly appear in magazines and dailies (most notably *Le Devoir*, the best newspaper in Canada if you prefer intellectual debates to sports or lifestyle sections), as well as radio and TV shows. For example, Joseph-Yvon Thériault is a guest on the Radio-Canada program *Ouvert le samedi*, and one can hear Yves Gingras talk about science on the radio program *Les Années lumières*. Watched by 1.2 million people (a proportional score would require 53 million viewers in the United States, nine times the audience of the late *Oprah Winfrey Show*), *Tout le monde en parle* sometimes features sociologists (I don't recall Oprah ever inviting a university professor of sociology to her show). Scholars like Gérard Bouchard or Mathieu Bock-Côté have become household names in Quebec.

Nothing of the sort can be said of even the most celebrated North American sociologists in the United States, who are only known by their peers and . . . family.

As a consequence, in French Quebec the best scholarly presses are not university or academic presses. Of course some sociologists published excellent monographs with Les Presses de l'Université de Montréal or Les Presses de l'Université Laval. However, the most prestigious presses are Boréal, Fides, and VLB, which also publish novels and even poetry. The same observation can be made of the publishing system in France. Michel Foucault was published by Gallimard in France and translated by Routledge (among others), and Pierre Bourdieu was published by Les Éditions de Minuit in France and translated by Stanford University Press (again, among others). The publishers are different from one side of the Atlantic to the other, because their audience is not the same.

Considering the wide discussion around the notion of public sociology in the United States, and Michael Burawoy's (2005) passionate plea for engaging multiple publics, it seems that francophone Quebec leads the way in many respects. Here is an example of a discipline firmly rooted in the most pressing issues of our time and forwarding public sociology far beyond the academy. Shouldn't its accomplishments serve as a testimony to what sociology can do to illuminate and refine our critical understating of the world?

The other difference between anglophone and francophone sociologists is the impact cultural studies has had on their practices and approaches. Cultural studies has exercised great influence in American sociology in the past 25 years, and much less in French Quebec.

Such contrast is remarkable considering that the great scholars cited by those involved in cultural studies are French (prominently Foucault, but also Derrida, Deleuze, Lefebvre). Looking at the history of sociology in the last two decades, one could be struck by fact that the dominance of French thinkers in the American sociological milieu has not fostered greater exchange with French-Canadian sociologists beyond the recognition that the works of the French thinkers recycled in North American cultural studies bears little resemblance to those read in France. In other words, Foucault in Chicago or Los Angeles does not sound like Foucault in Paris or, for that matter, Montreal.

The key to this different take on the French intellectual tradition is where anglophone and francophone sociologies come from. In the aftermath of the Second World War, one was dominated by functionalism and the other by structuralism and Marxism. This is not innocuous. Fifty years later, the two traditions still bear the traces of their different origins. For instance, Michel Freitag (1935–2009), who taught at UQAM (Montreal) and has a flock of disciples in CEGEPs and universities, funded a school of thought based on a revisiting of Marxism, structuralism, and Weberism. Freitag published major books on globalization and liberalism that are both philosophically informed and critically engaged. His publications are far removed from the cultural studies stream and can be seen, by those who dwell upon the later field, as belonging to the library of "dead white males," a comment that I have often heard from my English-speaking colleagues. Indeed, Freitag was not interested in the issues of gender and race (at least as they are commonly understood in sociology 101), and built a comprehension of society in which the notions of narrative and storytelling are blatantly absent.

For many American sociologists, Freitag's ideas are not only perplexing, they are ethnocentric and androcentric. And Freitag's assessment of American sociology was no more enthusiastic. He believed that American sociology is divided into two camps. Some scholars are implicitly continuing the functionalist tradition and crunching numbers according to a series of abstract variables with the objective to gauge people's behaviours, while others are centring their analysis on the "self," weaving together a patchwork composed of Husserl, the Frankfurt School, Derrida, and Simmel, in which the idea of "a" society no longer exists and social life has become nothing more than a "phenomenal environment." In this last case, sociologists cease to endeavour to grasp society in its objectifying reality, as a global structuring force.

Freitag's statement is too blunt, but it captures something of the divide between French-speaking and English-speaking sociologists on the continent. When one enters an anglophone bookstore, one finds a social studies but not a sociology section. For a francophone, such a division of scholarly literature in bookstores is revealing.

Hence, by fuelling a conversation with French Quebec sociologists, American sociologists can familiarize themselves with a different approach to the social world. They may not agree with everything they see, but they are sure to learn from this scholarly immersion.

A Different Society

It is easy to claim that all regions of North America are sociologically different. Joel Garreau (1981) stated that there are nine nations in North America, including New England, Dixie, and Mexiamerica. But Quebec is the only state or province that is generally recognized as a distinct region in itself. For that reason alone, a look at what Quebec sociologists are doing is not without benefit.

Interested in social movements? You may inquire about the Front the Libération du Québec (FLQ), a terrorist organization that was responsible for nine deaths from 1963 to 1970, and that perpetrated the only political kidnapping in the United States or Canada. Or you can study the evolution of the Parti Québécois, which is advocating the separation of Quebec from Canada and organized two referendums on the question in 1980 and 1995, the last one which it lost by only 0.58 per cent. You think we should know more about feminism? Quebec was dubbed "the closest thing to a feminist paradise" by French feminist activist Montreynaud. You prefer the study of workers' unions? Quebec unionization level reaches 40 per cent, whereas it is 30 per cent in the rest of Canada and a low 11 per cent in the United States. You were always intrigued by the student movement? In 2012, the "Printemps érable" was the longest and most radical student strike in the history of North America, lasting almost eight months. At one point, there were 300,000 supporters of the student strike marching in the streets of Montreal, which, for the United States, would be the equivalent of 12 million people protesting in Washington.

You believe that the question of rights is worth debating? For better and for worse, Quebec was the stage of very intense discussions around the right for religious groups to demand "reasonable accommodations"—i.e., modification of rules that hamper people's capacity to follow their faith's prescriptions (not work on the Shabbat, wear an Islamic veil in school, etc.). The issue of reasonable accommodations has been hotly debated for roughly 10 years. Co-headed by Gérard Bouchard (a sociologist), a provincial commission was set up (2007–2008) to inquire about the alleged ills caused by the clash between religious expressions and the rule of law. Outside Quebec, many believed that French Quebeckers were racist and xenophobic, and there was more than a kernel of truth to this assertion. However, there was also a fundamental misunderstanding between people who adhere to an Anglo-Saxon interpretation of rights and those who sided with the French Republican model.

I often say that, as a citizen, Quebec sometimes brings me close to despair; as a sociologist, I cannot but find this society extraordinary. Here are a people who seem at the same time more postmodern and more traditional, more politically conscious and more conservative than other populations around it. Quebeckers were the first to recognize same-sex marriage and are the last to open up to religious diversity. They are the most ardent nationalists and among the most likely in Canada to support free trade and economic globalization. How, dare I say, can American sociologists not find Quebec one of the most fascinating playgrounds in North America to launch vast quantitative investigations and conduct fieldwork?

Toynbee's Prophecy

I will have arrived at my goal if this short piece gives American sociologists a taste of what Quebec may bring to the understanding of global issues. Other peoples, populations, or locations may provide fertile grounds for sociological analyses. French Quebec certainly doesn't have the monopoly when it comes to offering stimulating objects of study. Far from it.

It is nonetheless true that Quebec is unique in North America in two respects. The French intellectual tradition it stems from gives it a particular flavour, and the society it is connected to is one of the most intriguing on the continent. Toynbee (1948) once argued that "whatever the future of mankind in North America, I feel pretty confident that these French-speaking Canadians, at any rate, will be there at the end of the story." I don't know if Toynbee's prophecy is right. But French Canadians are part of the story now and American sociologists would be better at what they do if they were to recognize it.

References

Burawoy, Michael. 2005. "For Public Sociology." *American Sociological Review*, vol. 70 (February): 4–28.

Garreau, Joel. *The Nine Nations of North America*. Boston: Houghton Mifflin, 1981.

Toynbee, Arnold Joseph. 1948. *Civilization on Trial*. New York: Oxford University Press.

Questions for Critical Thought

Chapter 1 | Macro Sociology: Its Evolution and Relevance to Canada

1. What motivated professional sociologists to do work in the public realm?
2. Describe both macro and micro sociology. What is the difference between these approaches? How is recognizing the difference between these levels of analysis important?
3. What prompted Canadian sociologists to focus on macro issues? Refer to the social context in Canada during the 1960s and 1970s.
4. How did Canadian sociologists address macro issues? Describe all three methods.
5. What is the difference between "Canadian sociology" and "the sociology of Canada"? Why is this an important distinction?

Chapter 2 | "*Breaking* with inside experience": Dilemmas in Negotiating Practical Knowledge and Scholarly Knowledge in Research with Young People

1. What is the difference between practical knowledge and scholarly knowledge?
2. How can previous work in a community help an academic gain access to that community? Draw on the experiences of Valerie and Lynette.
3. What conflict can arise between academic and social service doxa/norms? How can you bridge a gap between these doxa?
4. How does one's presentation of self influence others' ability to accept them in various fields?
5. What is the value of self-reflection and having an awareness of others' perceptions of you as a sociologist?

Chapter 3 | Reimagining the Sociological Imagination: Including the Brain, Environment, and Culture

1. How has the sociological explanation of human behaviour changed? What factors can influence behaviour?
2. What is brain plasticity? How does the discovery of brain plasticity link the social and biological together?
3. What impact does the environment have on the brain? How does this influence development?
4. What impact does cultural context have on the brain? How does this influence development?
5. Mathews says that sociologists need to stop ignoring the relationship between social life and the brain. Why is bridging the gap between sociology and biology important?

Chapter 4 | What Can a Theorist Do?

1. Powell comments on humanity. He briefly describes capitalism, politics, and culture. Why does he focus on these three structures?
2. What does the crisis of social systems tell us about the social sciences? What is social science missing?
3. What are the three dimensions of knowledge? How does theory contribute to knowledge?
4. Scientists aim to produce new knowledge. What is the impact of new knowledge on existing knowledge?
5. How does social theory contribute to social practice? Describe three ways.

Chapter 5 | The Debate about Accident Proneness

1. Tepperman and Meredith describe the importance of choosing the right variables to measure accident proneness. Why is it important to carefully choose the variables for a study? What can happen if you choose the wrong variables? Draw on the example of accident proneness in your answer.
2. What have psychologists previously hypothesized is the cause of accident proneness?
3. How can sociology be used to determine risk? Use the car accident example that is given by Tepperman and Meredith to describe some of the social determinants of "accident liability."
4. Looking at the alternative explanations that are given by Tepperman and Meredith for accident proneness, can you describe elements of each that are using a micro (individual) and/or macro (structural) perspective? Some explanations may have elements of both.
5. How can understanding the accident proneness literature help build a safer society?

Chapter 6 | French-Language Sociology in Quebec

1. What two factors make the ignorance of French-language scholarship particularly regretful for North American sociologists?
2. In Canada, how do French intellectuals engage with the public? Is their strategy the same or different than that of English intellectuals? Explain.
3. Using the given example of cultural studies, what is the difference between the way that anglophone and francophone sociologists have impacted this area of study?
4. Why is Quebec considered a distinct region in Canada?
5. By using the French language as an example, Warren demonstrates the value of recognizing multilingual sociology. What do you think is the value of recognizing academic contributions that have been written in languages other than English?

PART II
Culture and Culture Change

The common word *culture* has many different meanings, for sociologists and non-sociologists alike. However, for most sociologists, *culture* broadly refers to the knowledge, traditions, values, practices, and beliefs held by members of an organization, community, or society.

Defined this way, we are all familiar with culture and, indeed, with "cultures." In past generations, sociologists tended to think of culture as synonymous with the values and beliefs of an entire society. For example, they might talk about the features of Canadian culture, speculating that certain traditions—for example, playing and watching hockey—were uniquely and generally Canadian. And of course, this hockey tradition is important to many Canadian families, yet it is unimportant to many other equally Canadian families. Hockey is also important to many non-Canadians, as Canadians have learned by watching the fans of international hockey competitions. Another supposedly unique Canadian cultural tradition is "politeness"—for example, saying "sorry" when bumping into someone or even being bumped into. Again, this practice turns out to be neither universal among Canadians nor unique to Canadians.

So, it may be better to think of "culture" as a set of beliefs and practices from which members of a community are encouraged to draw. When we take this approach to culture, it becomes more apparent that there are important regional, ethnic, and other cultural subgroupings within any society. These groupings, called subcultures, are composed of likeminded individuals who share values and norms that may be distinct from the supposed majority beliefs and practices.

Consider post-secondary institutions and their unique colours, homecoming rituals, and values. These institutional subcultures are important to a school's students, faculty, and maybe alumni, but not a part of the dominant culture. And even within universities and colleges, we find departmental subcultures, professional subcultures, and of course, clubs, fraternities, and sororities. In short, there are many subcultures within a given society. Sociologists have even found it useful to name some of these, calling special attention (for example) to ethnic subcultures, organizational subcultures, and deviant subcultures.

In short, everyone has a culture and, in fact, most people have more than one. This is largely because most people belong to multiple groups, communities, and organizations, each with their own subculture. It is also because society is constantly being bombarded with new ideas, values, and practices, and members of society adopt these "innovations" at different rates. So, people routinely disagree over what should be considered part of their own culture or other cultures, and sometimes this translates into disagreements about social policy-making and law enforcement.

Equally, such disagreements lead to cultural change. For example, Canadians did not always support the belief that men and women should be treated equally, though this disagreement was often muted. In the nineteenth century and earlier, Canadians tended to endure, if not always support, the notion of male supremacy. Then, in the 1921 Canadian election, most women finally gained the right to vote (some exceptions included Asian and Indigenous women). Over the course of the twentieth century, feminists fought for equality in all aspects of Canadian life, including equal access to education and jobs. Today, the idea of gender equality is a central feature of Canadian culture, as reflected (among other things) in the Canadian Charter of Rights and Freedoms. Thus, Canadian culture is constantly changing and adapting to accommodate the changing opinions of the masses.

All of the chapters in this section highlight important aspects of culture, showing how cultural beliefs and activities are maintained or changed over time. First, Bruce Curtis draws our attention to the role of music in culture, showing how the meanings we associate with different genres have changed over time. Next, Tonya Davidson discusses monuments as cultural artifacts that evoke emotional responses in their viewers and present significant cultural narratives. Then, Janna Klostermann, in her institutional ethnography of the art world, reveals how dominant or mainstream cultures influence subcultures. Finally, Chris William Martin gives us an up-close view of tattoo culture, using ethnographic accounts of the production of culture to describe how tattoo artists manage impressions to succeed in their business.

7 Can Pierre Bourdieu Give Us the Blues?

Bruce Curtis

This paper comes out of two orders of interest that have been feeding and tussling with each other in my thinking: fandom, and the historical and political sociology of "**musicking**" (Small, 1999). Here I probe some of the analytic resources and impediments offered by the work of Pierre Bourdieu for coming to grips with the politics of music, especially in relation to African-American musical production.

Long a music fan, I was intrigued by the mobilization of blues, gospel, R&B, and hip hop in Barack Obama's 2008 electoral campaign and inaugural celebrations. In another paper (Curtis, 2012), I argued these events were importantly musical, from Obama's rhetorical devices on the campaign trail to the widespread popular use of websites for musical political engagement. One fascinating aspect was the presence at the inauguration—the ritual consecration of state power—of what half a century earlier had been excoriated as offensive subaltern music. I tried to map out the lines of descent through which blues, jazz, and gospel went from bars, brothels, barrelhouses, and churches into the civil rights movement, underpinned black power, and were domesticated in the American commercial mainstream. I pointed to the New Orleans composer Allen Toussaint, the author both of "Yes We Can Can," which was poached for the campaign slogan, and of a large number of cross-over R&B and rock'n'roll hits, to argue that varieties of blues and gospel are embedded in mainstream culture and were mobilized selectively by the Obama campaign.

One aspect of the work has to do with method and evidence: in the nature of the case it is difficult to demonstrate causal links between musical form and content on the one hand and political platform or ideology on the other. It is even more difficult to make a causal connection between the music people heard in an electoral campaign or sang in a social movement and the shaping of their political consciousness. I have been disappointed by most attempts to make such connections. Thomas Turino (2008), for instance, provided a useful typology of varieties of musical performance and participation to study the politics of music in the American civil rights movement and in Nazi Germany. Yet in practice, he rehearsed a well-known account of Nazi musical policy and reproduced the lyrics from a number of songs. He drew on some older literature to discuss the fate of popular choirs and the denigration of jazz, but said little of what made Nazi musical taste substantively totalitarian. For the civil rights movement, Turino only pointed to some musical devices, such as call and response in gospel, that were put in the service of protest songs, cited some song lyrics, and remarked on how moving he finds the music.

Richard J. Evans's (2005) more comprehensive account of Nazi musical politics gives more information about what the Nazis detested and tried to promote, showing that the campaigns against jazz and in favour of Wagner both failed. Yet when it comes to making a case for a specifically Nazi musical aesthetic, he uses the example of Carl Orff's opera *Carmena Barana*: the Nazi Party promoted loud and heroic sounding music and propagandized in favour of the wholesome peasant life; Orff's opera is full of crescendo and peasant themes, so it is what loud and brutish Nazis would like. The relation is of one of homology (similarity with a difference) and for Turino and Evans, the proof is in the hearing.

The problem here is one that Pierre Bourdieu warns against repeatedly, in *Distinction* (1984; cited in 1993:18), of substituting our "intuitive half-understandings" (e.g., it sounds the same to me) for careful analysis of the process of constituting our categories and of the relationships between them—in this case between music and politics. Yet Bourdieu helps to reproduce the problem by focusing on the homologous or parallel relations between class cultural location and the formation of taste. It is not that the logic of political practice is opaque to preferences and strategies, but pointing to homologous relations does not establish the mechanisms and practices that might lead to such relations. We can see that Obama's electoral campaign drew on particular kinds of popular African-American musical resources, and we know that Obama polled in the high 90s among African-American electors. And we can see and hear that the brass band waltzes at G.W. Bush's 2005 inaugural ball had a very different groove and enclosed a very different set of cultural references than did Stevie Wonder's performance at Obama's 2009 inaugural ball. But the possible proofs are based on recognition and intuition: one has to listen and to hear, and hence one's tastes may intervene in the analysis.

Bourdieu argues that for bourgeois society nothing "more clearly affirms one's class, nothing more infallibly classifies, than tastes in music" (1993:18). For the bourgeoisie, he claims, appreciation of the legitimate forms of music expresses a deep and rich interiority, and music is the best exemplar of high bourgeois art, since it serves no ulterior purpose and since its appreciation thus involves a complete negation of the world. According to Bourdieu, musical taste is organized in keeping with the structure of the distribution of cultural and economic capital and thus in keeping with the distance from economic necessity in which groups are located.

Bourdieu (1984; 1993) points to what he claims are regular relations between differential distance from necessity and differential preferences for and attention to form and function. Those with the least amounts of cultural and economic capital prefer music that is simple and stable in its formal properties and whose functional dimensions are most evident. In Bourdieu's account, popular songs are meant to deliver messages or to provide entertainment, and formal variation is frowned upon as an obstacle to such functions. Conversely, those furthest from economic necessity and who have the greatest amounts of cultural capital are indifferent to the functional dimensions of music, but are most interested in its formal properties and formal variations. Music for music's sake has no immediate social function, apart from its certification of distinction. The battle for distinction and for cultural and economic domination leads to the consecration of some musical forms and validates them as exemplars of good music as such, in distinction to vulgar and popular music.

Bourdieu claimed that, in normal times, the space of positions determines the nature of position-takings (where you are is what you'll like). There is a complex attempt continually to embed a structuralizing account in human subjectivity and practice. One consequence is the absence of any autonomous working-class musical culture characterized by formal innovation or internal transformation. Bourdieu's cultural referents in *Distinction* as well as in "The Field of Cultural Production" (1993) are almost exclusively high bourgeois, and there is a consistent neglect of (and probably ignorance about) other cultural products. Bourdieu persists in maintaining a distinction between the legitimate and the popular, with the former institutionalized and the latter conceived in terms of the size of its audience. In a manner that encapsulates a particular understanding of French culture, he assumes that there is a legitimated elite culture that all cultural producers attempt to replicate or to replace with their own cultural products. While he recognizes competing means and standards of legitimation, and while he sees the cultural avant garde as capable of playing a counter-hegemonic role in periods of political crisis, there is little or no consideration of the possibility of autonomous proletarian, working-class, or subaltern cultural production. That the blues can be internally differentiated and characterised by formal variation is not possible, nor does fixing a musical map whose coordinates are high and low culture explain how rough proletarian music might come to consecrate high state power.

Still, Bourdieu affirms repeatedly that the relation between position in social space and taste is not mechanical, but is shaped by a number of forces: Increasing distance from economic necessity leads to increased possibilities of and tastes for the stylization of life in the quest for distinction; entrants into a field of cultural production or consumption will follow either successor or transgressive strategies, depending upon their possession of capital of different kinds and value; and the acquisition of titles of nobility in the academy carries with it the expectation that the titled will not restrict themselves to a narrow technical culture, but will acquire a broad range of dominant cultural attributes (1993: 55–6). One could draw on these and other elements to analyze counter-hegemonic strategies in relation to musicking.

A missing element in the analysis is the ways in which subjectivities may be affected by techniques of self-fashioning. Such techniques have their own histories and trajectories, but it is not only those distant from necessity who may seek to fashion themselves. Foucault (1988) drew our attention to the phenomenon with his account of technologies of the self, and the governmentality literature has also focused on the ways in which neoliberal strategies in a digitized world fashion an "**enterprise self**" (McNay, 2009). Projects of self-fashioning extend well below elite positions, and "musicking" can be both a medium and a means.

Bourdieu's promise for understanding the relation between music and politics lies partly in his recognition that it is characterized by much greater indeterminacy than is the case for other fields. The costs of entry to the field of cultural production are frequently quite low (e.g., the garage band) and so many producers may enter and compete for advantage. At the same time, in a digitized universe, the volume of musical products available to consumers has increased dramatically, and so have the possibilities for a creative engagement in the field of musical production. Genre boundaries become increasingly vague and combinations and re-combinations of past forms are commonplace. That subaltern musical production itself comes to involve a great deal of formal variation, leading to new forms that combine diverse elements, undermines simple divides such as those of high/low taste and musical form/content. To follow Bourdieu now means redrawing the musical map.

A final avenue in using Bourdieu's approach to study music and politics is his insistence that social relations and practices reappear as bodily habitus. He gestures toward a regression theory of listening (Adorno, 1982), but notices that to understand a work of art or music we need to understand the "spirit of the age." Music making is profoundly visceral; it is implicated in ways of being in the body, in movement, in the unfolding of experience in time, in emotion. Encounters with music may command the body; the work I examined above demands that we listen and hear in order to understand. Yet such an injunction may contain a scholastic fallacy: blues and jazz was music to dance to and to work with. If the need to hear in particular ways challenges sociology's capacity to deal with the relations of music and politics, the need to move, play, and dance, to grasp the matter viscerally, does so even more (Keil, 1994; Kenney, 1993; Wald, 2009). Like Walter Benjamin (2006) stoned on hashish, sociologists need to allow themselves to tap their feet.

References

Adorno, T.W. 1982 [1938]. "On the Fetish Character of Music and the Regression of Listening." Pp. 270–299 in *The Essential Frankfurt School Reader*, edited by Andrew Arato and Eike Gebhard. New York: Continuum.

Benjamin, Walter. 2006. "Hashish in Marseilles." Pp. 117–26 in *On Hashish*. Cambridge: Belknap Press.

Bourdieu, Pierre. 1984. *Distinction: A Social Critique of the Judgement of Taste*. Cambridge: Harvard University Press.

———. 1993 [1983]. "The Field of Cultural Production, or: The Economic World Reversed." Pp. 29–73 in *The Field of Cultural Production: Essays on Art and Literature*, edited by Randal Johnson. New York: Columbia University Press.

———. 1994. *Raisons Pratiques: Sur la Théorie de l'action*. Paris: Éditions du Seuil.

Bourdieu, Pierre, and Loïc Wacquant. 1992. *An Invitation to Reflexive Sociology*. Chicago: University of Chicago Press.

Curtis, Bruce. 2012. "Barack Obama's Electoral Blues. An Exploration in the Sociology of Music and Emotion." Ottawa: Carleton University.

Evans, Richard J. 2005. *The Third Reich in Power, 1933–1939*. New York: Penguin Books.

Foucault, Michel. 1988. "Technologies of the Self." Pp. 16–49 in *Technologies of the Self: A Seminar with Michel Foucault*, edited by Luther H. Martin and et al. Amherst: University of Massachusetts Press.

Keil, Charles, and Steven Feld. 1994. *Music Grooves*. Chicago: University of Chicago Press.

Kenney, William Howland. 1993. *Chicago Jazz: A Cultural History, 1904–1930*. Oxford: Oxford University Press.

McNay, Lois. 2009. "Self as Enterprise: Dilemmas of Control and Resistance in Foucault's *The Birth of Biopolitics*." *Theory, Culture and Society* 26: 55–77.

Small, Christopher. 1999. "Musicking—The Meanings of Performing and Listening. A Lecture." *Music Education Research* 1: 1–21.

Turino, Thomas. 2008. *Music as Social Life. The Politics of Participation*. Chicago: University of Chicago Press.

Wald, Elijah. 2009. *How the Beatles Destroyed Rock'n'Roll: An Alternative History of American Popular Music*. Oxford: Oxford University Press.

8 The Social Lives of Statues

Tonya K. Davidson

Introduction

On 22 October 2014, a lone gunman shot and killed Nathan Cirillo, a reservist standing guard at Canada's National War Memorial in Ottawa. Shortly after, Bruce MacKinnon created the cartoon on the next page for the Halifax *Chronicle Herald*. The cartoon was quickly picked up by several national and international news organizations. The cartoon suggests that the 22 bronze soldiers in the National War Memorial are alive and responding to the violent shooting of Cirillo. While the cartoon poignantly captured the national shock and grief that followed the 22 October shooting, MacKinnon's image also speaks to an unspoken but felt understanding of monuments: that they are urban objects that do not sit silently but rather engage with and have effects on their visitors.

In my research on monuments I have adopted the language of the **virtual** to understand the pull that monuments have on us. Following Proust, Rob Shields (2003) understands the virtual as those elements which are "real without being actual" (p. 3). Dreams and haunting are virtualities. So are nostalgias, nationalisms, and other modes of belonging. Virtualities are made visible through actualizations: the material effects of the virtual. In other words, actualizations are indexes to virtualities; they are the tangible evidence of intangible social relations. I understand monuments, especially in the context of the national capital city of Ottawa, as pulsing with virtualities. As the recipients of various emotional investments throughout their lives, monuments produce certain effects: collective experiences of belonging, mourning, or exclusion. Furthermore, monuments generate memories and effects that are neither fixed nor homogeneous.

In this study I focused on the social lives of a series of monuments in Ottawa, including Canada's National War Memorial and a monument to an Indigenous scout that for 70 years was located at the base of a monument to Samuel de Champlain. I took a multi-method ethnographic approach that included archival research, interviews with key participants, and fieldwork that involved observing and participating in various ceremonies that took place at the monuments. Because my research question focused on accessing and analyzing intangible virtualities, I paid particular attention to material artifacts left at the monuments as indexes of these relationships. In the cases presented here, I read these offerings as acts that simultaneously reinforce and challenges narratives of national belonging.

The Scout's Knee

In Ottawa's Major's Hill Park, there is a statue of an Indigenous man. The man's knee is polished from years of being caressed by visitors. From 1924 to 1996,

Republished with permission from The Chronicle Herald

FIGURE 8.1 Cartoon by Bruce MacKinnon

the statue sat on a ledge at the base of a 1915 monument to Samuel de Champlain at Nepean Point, enjoying a panoramic view of the national capital. Together, Champlain and the statue of the scout stood as an iconic celebration of white settler conquest. Sherene Razack (2002) defines a **white settler society** as "one established by Europeans on non-European soil. Its origins lie in the dispossession and near extermination of Indigenous populations by the conquering Europeans" (p. 1). She continues, "a quintessential feature of white settler mythologies is . . . the disavowal of conquest, genocide, slavery, and the exploitation of the labour of peoples of colour" (p. 2). The named, clothed, and celebrated Champlain standing high on a pedestal embodies this white settler mythology.

On a visit to Ottawa in 1996, Assembly of First Nations chief Ovide Mercredi visited the scout monument. Noting the scout's subservient position and historically inaccurate dress, Mercredi covered the scout in blankets and demanded its removal. This protest (and the responses to this protest) can be understood as actualizations of various virtualities—feelings of patriotism, attachments to colonial logic—embodied in the monument.

The protest inspired multiple responses. Some people wanted the monument to stay where it was. They anchored their arguments in nostalgic childhood memories of visiting the scout decades earlier. Ottawa resident Bob O'Connor demonstrated this in a letter to the editor:

> I am 60 years old, and I have pictures of myself and my family, taken when I was about 10 years old. I was kneeling on both knees beside the Indian guide, and he sure didn't look like a lower-class native, and he

FIGURE 8.2 Samuel de Champlain Monument, 1998, Nepean Point Park, Ottawa, Ontario

> still doesn't. To me, this is a magnificent piece of work, and it belongs to the people of Ottawa, and it's part of the history of the area. It should not be removed for any reason (O'Connor 1996, p. A.11).

While expressing childhood memories, I interpret this statement as an expression of imperial nostalgia, a nostalgia for a time when racist representations of Indigenous peoples were accepted and commonplace. Daniel Francis (1992) argues that many common white settler understandings of Indigenous peoples come from children's books and summer camp pedagogies in which Indigenous peoples were and are represented as childlike. This context, combined with the scout's location at eye level for children, make it possible to understand how the scout was a favourite for child visitors. The scout's worn knee represents various public, affective engagements with the logic of colonialism. The knee is a site where imperial nostalgia is expressed; this is not just an allegiance with white settler logic, but affection for this logic.

In 1999, the National Capital Commission relocated the scout monument to Major's Hill Park. Separated from Champlain, the scout continues to produce a fraught representation of an eroticized, nameless Indigenous figure. However, symbolically, the scout's anonymity was challenged in 2013 when the scout was officially given a name by Algonquin elder Annie Smith St Georges. The scout is now Gichi Zibi Omaami Winini Anishinaabe ("Aboriginal Artists in Ottawa" 2013).

A White Poppy Wreath

The National War Memorial in Ottawa was the only federally funded war memorial erected in Canada after World War I (Gardam 1982). While Canada's entry into World War I was as an extension of the British Empire, many historians have understood Canada's participation in the war as a national coming of age (Vance 1997; Hayes et al. 2007; McKay and Swift 2012). If the National War Memorial (NWM) is a site for producing particular meanings of what it means to be Canadian, these meanings often include the message that being Canadian continues to mean allegiance and affection for Canada's imperial past. At the NWM, rituals secure not only the commemorative meanings of the monument, but also particular relationships between race, gender, and the nation. These rituals express and renew virtualities of patriotism born at the monument.

Many of the practices that take place at the NWM can be understood using Hobsbawm's (1983) concept of **invented traditions**, which he defines as "a set of practices, normally governed by overtly or tacitly accepted rules and of a ritual or symbolic nature, which seek to inculcate certain values and norms of behaviour by repetition, which automatically implies continuity with the past" (p. 1). Wreath-laying traditions are political in that they tie

FIGURE 8.3 "Why Do The Indians Always Have To Move?" 2001, Major's Hill Park, Ottawa, Ontario

certain war memories to feelings of national belonging in organized and consistent ways. Visitors are encouraged to remember Canada's white settler colonial origins at the expense of remembering Canada as a nation produced through the violent displacement of Indigenous peoples, and created through the intersection of multiple diasporic mobilities.

At the NWM, imperial nostalgia is expressed through the obligatory and central presence of the governor general or members of the royal family at Remembrance Day and Vimy Ridge Memorial Day services, the singing of "God Save the Queen," and the occasional flying of the Red Ensign (a previous Canadian flag that included the British Union Jack). Imperial nostalgia is also produced through the insistence that only Canadians or members of the Commonwealth be mourned at the NWM. In fact, in the 1950s, the Association of Baltic Canadians made several applications to the committee on the use of Parliament Hill and the National War Memorial to lay a wreath to commemorate the anniversary of 14 June 1941, a day when thousands of Estonians were deported to Russia. The applications were routinely denied because of the committee's policy of restricting the monument's uses to the memories of Canadian and Allied soldiers (Davidson 2012).

During my fieldwork, I noticed after the Remembrance Day service in 2008 that three sides of the base of the monument were covered in official green wreaths. Different groups like the Mothers of Canada, the Royal Canadian Air Forces Prisoners of War Association, the Royal Canadian Mounted Police Veterans Association, and the League of Merchant Mariners Veterans of Canada had all laid wreaths. In this ritual, women are invited to mourn primarily as mothers, reinforcing the dominant gender norm that suggests that women's identities are defined in relation to men. At the back of the monument, there was a single large white poppy wreath. It was made of white and green felt, with a diagonal banner that read "Peace."

Tonya Davidson

FIGURE 8.4 National War Memorial

Tonya Davidson

FIGURE 8.5 White poppy

The white poppy was first designed and produced by the Women's Co-operative Guild in the United Kingdom as a symbol of peace in the 1930s. In the decades immediately following World War I, a pacifist movement threatened to challenge the seemingly uncomplicated celebration of Canadian war victory (Vance 1997, p. 29–30, McKay and Swift 2012, p. 109). In the early 1930s, these same pacifist groups suggested the abolition of Remembrance Day altogether, arguing that the day "perpetuated militarism" (Vance 1997, p. 214). While red poppies had become more and more sacred as memorial objects, white poppies reemerged as a popular memorial object in 2006 ("White Poppy," n.d.). White poppies were interpreted by some veterans and others as deeply troubling and an offensive challenge to war memorial practices in Canada.

In its singularity, the white poppy wreath presents a striking contrast to the green wreaths placed during the official ceremonies. The white poppy wreath challenges the imperial nostalgia generated by many memorial practices. It suggests that the monument can be a site for other forms of remembrance—in particular the remembrance of peace activists and war resisters.

Conclusion

The scout's knee and the white poppy wreath at the NWM are indexes to broader intangible social relations that circulate through the monuments. Both of these objects highlight how monuments enable the production and challenging of normative memorial narratives. The scout's knee is worn from decades of affection for the colonial order that the Champlain and scout monuments represent. However, the protest of the monument worked to disrupt this narrative. Similarly, the rituals at the NWM, the layers of accepted green wreaths and the solemnity we bestow on the NWM produce a very specific narrative about Canada's birth through war.

The white poppy wreath suggests that other forms of remembrance were, and continue to be, possible. Like the social worlds in which they are a part, monuments are dynamic urban objects; they instruct us on what and how to remember, but also produce opportunities to disrupt and expand these memorial narratives.

References

"Aboriginal Artists in Ottawa want traditional fame for 'Scout' statue." (2013, Aug. 23). *CBC News*, website. Accessed 24 August 2014.

Davidson, T. (2012) "Stone Bodies in the City: Unmapping Monuments, Memory and Belonging in Ottawa." PhD dissertation. University of Alberta: Edmonton.

Francis, D. (1992). *The Imaginary Indian: The Image of the Indian in Canadian Culture.* Vancouver: Arsenal Pulp Press.

Gardam, C.J. (1982). *The National War Memorial.* Ottawa: Veteran Affairs Canada.

Hayes, G., A. Iarocci and M. Bechthold (eds). (2007). *Vimy Ridge: A Canadian Reassessment.* Waterloo: Wilfrid Laurier University Press.

Hobsbawm, E. (1983). "Introduction: Inventing Traditions," in E. Hobsbawm and T. Ranger (eds), *The Invention of Tradition.* Cambridge: Cambridge University Press.

McKay, I. and J. Swift. (2012). *Warrior Nation: Rebranding Canada in an Age of Anxiety.* Toronto: Between the Lines.

O'Connor, B. (1996, October 6). "A few words more: Don't remove statue." *The Ottawa Citizen*, p. A11.

Razack, S. (2002). *Race, Space and the Law: Unmapping a White Settler Society.* Toronto: Between the Lines.

Shields, R. (2003). *The Virtual.* New York: Routledge.

Taussig, M. (1999). *Defacement.* Stanford: Stanford University Press.

Vance, J.F. (1997). *Death So Noble: Memory, Meaning, and the First World War.* Vancouver: University of British Columbia Press.

"White Poppy for a Culture of Peace." Peace Pledge Union website. Retrieved on December 18, 2009: http://www.ppu.org.uk/whitepoppy/white-news.html.

9 Starting with a *Squish*: An Institutional Ethnography of Canada's Art World[1]

Janna Klostermann

> It's a serious issue in the visual art world how language—or writing—has now been squished onto it. It's touchy. I'm not the only person who feels that about writing. I have many visual artists-friends who are the same. There is a bitterness about the art world, and a lot of it comes from the writing. There is a serious resentment and bitterness. [Visual artists] are forced to have to justify themselves in writing.

In one of a series of interviews that I conducted, visual artist Beth McCubbin described a bitterness in the art world that comes from the way written/spoken language had been "squished onto it." Her understanding shaped how my research progressed. The phrase "squished onto it" brushed over the practices and relations involved. It blurred the work of other artists and art professionals. It obscured the who's who and what's what of squishing and of bringing about bitterness. It also opened up a line of inquiry, pointed to a field of activity, and hinted at an institutional terrain to be discovered. It served as a critical point of entry from which to begin my study of the art world. Starting with a *squish*, this chapter makes visible my own research process while making visible the work processes of artists and art professionals in Canada's art world.

Visual artist Beth McCubbin described the Canadian art world as a text-heavy environment. She talked about writing various documents as a part of her work: bio statements, artist statements, CVs, and grant applications. Beth talked about her struggles with language and about her struggles to connect up her work to public galleries, grants, and fancy art-speak. As she put it, "You could just be dismissed because of your writing. It has nothing to do with your art." She said she was considering "letting the whole thing go," and she attributed her difficulties in the art world to her lack of formal education and to the way language had been "squished onto it."

Standing before her, I felt the weight of her words. If Beth wasn't an artist, I didn't know who was. I really couldn't understand why she was being edged out by institutional requirements. My friend Beth had committed her life to visual art. She had worked as a self-taught practising artist for 25 years. She was well known by locals in Peterborough, Ontario, for her commitment to the downtown art scene. She was well known for turning ceramic, concrete, porcelain, and recyclables into works of art, and for recruiting volunteers to help her cart sculptures up and down flights of stairs and across city streets. At one point, I visited her to see her crafting a sculpture between her kitchen sink and kitchen table, to which she explained nonchalantly it would only be there a few more weeks (Figure 9.1). Again, I felt the weight of her words. Her sense that she was being excluded institutionally—after 25 years of working as a self-taught visual artist—shaped how my research into Canada's art world progressed.

Courtesy of the artist

FIGURE 9.1 Beth McCubbin, *eternal spirit*, 2014, concrete installation at the Sisters of Mount St Joseph.

Institutional Ethnography

Responding to Beth's concerns, I used **institutional ethnography (IE)** to explore what was bringing about the *squish* in the art world. Developed by Canadian sociologist D.E. Smith (2005), IE is an analytic method and theorized way of looking at social reality. IE starts with particular experiences—like those of visual artists—and then works to discover how those experiences are brought about through particular institutional processes. In IE, experiences are not stand-alone, but are hooked together with other events and circumstances both near and far-flung. In IE, institutional processes are brought about through particular practices and relations across diverse sites of activity. Starting in actual places where people work and do things together, IE keeps people and **texts** in view while investigating coordinated work that is (sometimes) out of view. For institutional ethnographers, texts—like the bio statements and artist statements Beth described—are integral in coordinating people's everyday activity in local settings.

Recent IE studies have focused on work in a variety of institutions including in health (Rankin and Campbell, 2006; Sinding, 2014), education (Darville, 2014; Kerr, 2014; Wright, 2014), social services (Janz, 2014; McCoy, 2014; Nichols, 2014), and international development (Campbell, 2014; Eastwood, 2005). Entering into the field, I wasn't initially sure how the art world—replete with fancy art-speak and a so-called language *squish*—fit in with studies about standardized reports, educational policies, and behavioural tracking charts. I wasn't sure how—or whether or not—visual artists' experiences were connected to other institutional practices and relations. That said, Beth's concerns about the art world coupled well with the approach, and indeed pointed to a text-based institutional territory to be discovered.

Using IE, I didn't take Beth's experience as an object of study in itself. I didn't study how she *felt* about the art world, nor did I attempt to slot artists' experiences into categories or identify set themes. Instead, I used IE to explicate how particular experiences were being coordinated institutionally. To explicate means to open up, map, uncover, tease out, render visible. As a part of the project, I tried to understand visual artists' and public gallery curators' experiences, to understand how language was a part of them, and to understand how they were coordinated institutionally within the larger art world.

To learn more about the art world, I didn't start in the upper echelon, interviewing bigwigs at Canada's National Gallery or at The Canada Council for the Arts. Instead, I started locally, interviewing practising artists about their work, their workplace writing, and their efforts to participate in the art world. I approached the people I interviewed as expert practitioners of their working worlds, telling me what they know about how things are put together. With a view to learning more about the institutional workings of the art world, I tapped "into people's expertise in the conduct of their everyday lives" (Campbell, 2006, p. 92). What I discovered was surprising.

A Conversation in the Art World

It was striking to see how the work of one artist in one studio was connected to the work of others. Irrespective of the medium of art they worked in—or of their personalities, backgrounds, or cities of residence—artists described similar ways of connecting up with or participating in the art world. The artists I interviewed described needing channels to get their work out there, which happened in relation to others (e.g., purchasers, viewers, curators, jury members) and in relation to art institutions (e.g., public galleries, commercial galleries, funding bodies, art schools, academic art institutions). Artists aren't holed away in their studios painting; they are bringing together their art work and words, responding to particular institutional requirements, and working to get out there.

Artists are responsible for using language to show that their work is conceptual and reputable and to hook up with galleries, grants, and the "conversation" in the art world. Some artists participate by rhyming off their credentials or framing their art "in terms of writing about it and speaking about it" and showing they're "a part of larger conversations in the field" (as Toronto artist Mary Porter mentioned) while others joke about art speak or about "so and so [who] studied with so and so and the humphhh and did this and that and the other thing" (as Ottawa artist Marika Jemma joked). Either way, artists acknowledge that they work in an increasingly text-heavy art world in which an expressivist studio practice is hard to maintain.

While I initially felt like I was tracing an endless institutional art terrain, what artists told me shaped my inquiry, leading me to focus on public galleries as a "site of action" (Smith, 1987, p.3). Artists described showing in public galleries as a way of getting out there, a way of making a buck, and a way of being endorsed by the contemporary art community. As Ottawa artist Jinny Yu put it, public galleries are "recognized by [her] peers as being a legitimate exhibition venue." Artists underscored the importance of showing in public galleries and characterized their public

FIGURE 9.2 Jinny Yu, *Ball; Studio Work Number 37; Ball; Column; Stalker; Painting, Painting, Painting*, 2014, various dimension and materials, installed at Ottawa Art Gallery.

gallery work as increasingly discursive. Artists typically use language to get in (e.g., exhibition proposals), there is language involved in the exhibition itself (e.g., artist talks, "writing on the wall"), and there is language to follow as artists' work is typically taken up, written about, or talked about afterwards (e.g., catalogues, reviews, funding reports). Public galleries are a realm where art and language collide.

Given that public galleries are a key place where the language *squish* plays out, I turned to interviewing public gallery curators about *their* (language) work. I was surprised to see how public gallery curators organized their work in fairly conventional ways. As a part of their roles, they were responsible for watching for, promoting, and showing conceptual and reputable art, for engaging the public, and for contributing to the larger conversation in the art world. They were responsible for hooking the work, words, and reputations of artists into the art world. While they, of course, did have professional objectives and did exercise professional authority, much of their work was shaped by and responsive to the institutional priorities of funding bodies. They were responsible for showing their own institutional standing, and for bolstering the standing of the institutions they were a part of. As Rusted (2006) put it, "Their textual practices, along with producing their own legitimacy, produce the legitimacy of the institutions" (p. 121).

Artists and curators alike talked about their work to bring together artwork and words and to hook into the "conversation" in the art world. They talked about speaking to the conversation, edging in, and moving from the periphery to the centre of it. They participated in, took part in shaping, played with, and poked fun at the discursive conventions of the art world. They enacted the art world through their work, not just their material work but also their discursive work to conjoin visual images with conceptual descriptions. As professionals, their language was adapted and shaped through producing talk and meaning for others, and, in turn, giving shape to a particular social world (Goodwin, 2006 as cited by Gutiérrez, 2008, p. 153). That said, I also learned that within this increasingly institutionally and textually coordinated art conversation, some people's experiences were decentred. Some people's experiences were harder to frame, legitimate, or squeeze into (what I earlier called) the text-heavy conversation. In bringing about the conversation, visual artists and public gallery curators alike brought about the *squish.*

Opening with Beth's rendition of an institutional *squish,* this chapter reported on my research into Canada's art world—making visible how the everyday work of artists and curators brings about the institutions they are a part of while, at times, marginalizing particular experiences. While theoretical concepts can be useful in naming particular phenomena, I want to underscore that this research started with and responded to a *squish.* This research would have developed much differently had I approached artists as an object of study or had I started with an abstraction like "performativity" and gone in looking for, detailing, or categorizing examples of it. Instead, IE gave me a theorized way of opening up the art world—starting with particular experiences, following the lead of my participants as they turned my attention to their work in public galleries, and tracing particular institutional connections. Artists' experiences directed my discovery process. This chapter has been an effort to trace my own research process while also introducing the work processes of visual artists and art professionals. This chapter has been an analytical effort to explicate Canada's art world.

Note

1. An earlier version of this paper was presented at the Canadian Sociological Association (Ottawa, ON). I want to acknowledge the support of Dr. Richard Darville and Dr. Graham Smart, who supervised this research.

References

Campbell, M. (2006). Institutional Ethnography and Experience as Data. In Dorothy E. Smith (Ed), *Institutional Ethnography as Practice*, 91–108. Lanhan, NJ: Rowman and Littlefield.

Campbell, M. (2014). Learning Global Governance: OECD's Aid Effectiveness and "Results" Management in a Kyrgyzstani Development Project. In Alison I. Griffith and Dorothy E. Smith (Eds), *Under new public management: Institutional ethnographies of changing front-line work.* Toronto: University of Toronto Press.

Darville, R. (2014). Literacy work and the adult literacy regime. In Alison I. Griffith and Dorothy E. Smith's (Eds), *Under new public management: Institutional ethnographies of changing front-line work.* Toronto: University of Toronto Press.

Eastwood, L. (2005*). The social organization of policy: An institutional ethnography of* UN *forest deliberations.* New York: Routledge.

Gutiérrez, K.D. (2008). Developing a sociocritical literacy in the third space. *Reading Research Quarterly, 43*(2), 148-64.

Janz, S. (2014). For-profit contractors, accreditation, and accountability. In Alison I. Griffith and Dorothy E. Smith (Eds), *Under new public management: Institutional ethnographies of changing front-line work.* Toronto: University of Toronto Press.

Kerr, L. (2014). E-governance and data-driven accountability: OnSIS in Ontario Schools. In Alison I. Griffith and Dorothy E. Smith (Eds), *Under new public management: Institutional ethnographies of changing front-line work.* Toronto: University of Toronto Press.

McCoy, L. (2014). "If our statistics are bad we don't get paid:" Outcome measures in the settlement sector. In Alison I. Griffith and Dorothy E. Smith (Eds), *Under new public management: Institutional ethnographies of changing front-line work.* Toronto: University of Toronto Press.

Nichols, N. (2014). *Youth work: An institutional ethnography of youth homelessness.* Toronto: Toronto University Press.

Rankin, J., and Campbell, M. (2006). *Managing to nurse: Inside Canada's health care reform*. Toronto: University of Toronto Press.

Rusted, B. (2006). Performing visual discourse: Cowboy art and institutional practice. *Text and Performance Quarterly, 26*(2), 115-37.

Sinding, C. (2014). Institutional circuits in cancer care. In Alison I. Griffith and Dorothy E. Smith (Eds), *Under new public management: Institutional ethnographies of changing front-line work*. Toronto: University of Toronto Press.

Smith, D.E. (1987). *The Everyday World as Problematic: A Feminist Sociology*. Boston: Northeastern University Press.

Smith, D.E. (2005). *Institutional ethnography: A sociology for people*. Lanham, MD: AltaMira.

Wright, S. (2014). Knowledge that counts: points systems and the governance of Danish universities. In Alison I. Griffith and Dorothy E. Smith (Eds), *Under new public management: Institutional ethnographies of changing front-line work*. Toronto: University of Toronto Press.

10 The Art and Artist behind Your Tattoo: A Case Study of Two Tattoo Artists

Chris William Martin

Dramaturgical Analysis

Through persistent efforts in overcoming the obstacles to getting access to the tattoo world, I managed to secure a position as an unpaid receptionist at a tattoo shop. This chapter will tell you about my experiences working for a year at the place I will refer to as "The Studio," which is located in a large Canadian city. In addition to being employed at The Studio, I was tattooed there and observed the activities of the shop's artists. In the following I will weave fieldnote narratives into a depiction of the way two tattoo artists, Philippe and Kraken, try to maintain their status in the **interaction order** and provide a nuanced understanding of the **strategic interaction** and **impression management** used in the day-to-day practice of tattooing. Although they did not realize this, these tattoo artists convinced, deceived, and impressed people by committing aspects of strategic interaction pioneered in terms of theory by the Canadian-born Erving Goffman (1959, 1968), reinterpreted by others exploring his work (Scarborough 2012; Manning 2000), and used here to aid in interpreting my own experiences. The occupational and situational demands these two artists face, specifically around performance and precariousness in tattooing, are common for tattoo artists. Although some experiences might not be the same for all artists, it is important to appreciate the rich complexity micro theories of social interaction can have in interpreting the work of tattoo artists generally.

Understanding the Artist's Perspective

What I immediately found fascinating about tattoo artists was Philippe's (pseudonym, the owner of The Studio and a tattoo artist) anxiety and self-doubt. It can be frightening for these artists to execute widely varying designs their clients pursue while juggling the difficulties that accompany the craft of tattooing: the uncertainty of the canvas—in terms of skin type, pain tolerance, and general attitude; factors like the performance of tattoo machines; and rules about pressing harder or deeper depending on the area of the body. Lines can easily be blurred and skin can be chewed up if the machine is applied with too much pressure in areas covered by thin skin such as joints and crevices.

Several times, Philippe paced the studio wondering how he was going to pull off certain pieces, if a client would show up, what he would do if a client decided to make last-minute changes to the design, etc. Managing a business and maintaining clients—in situations of precarious employment—relies heavily on impression management. Roscoe Scarborough (2012: 543) highlights how Goffman's theories of impression management relate to the face work and maintenance of the front-stage (that is, public) persona of musicians and allows us to compare tattoo artists and musicians in a description of a saxophone player "faking" a jazz solo. "Though the sax player does not have the requisite technical proficiency of someone occupying his position as the de-facto leader . . . he otherwise presents himself in a manner that adheres to the contextually appropriate conventions of a jazz nightclub." For an example of a face-saving technique in a situation of audience doubt let us look at my fieldnotes.

> **24 July 2014**
> Philippe makes the stencil in front of me to show how he uses a drawn or printed image with thermal paper to stencil the image to the skin as a guide during the process. The stencil is the phrase "I want to Believe" along with a UFO. I immediately recognize the phrase from the television show The X-Files.
> During the tattoo, the client's wife suggests colour and shading ideas. Philippe is very receptive to her suggestions and shows a demeanor much different from the tattoo artists I have personally experienced in the past. He is kind in allowing so much input from spectators. He seems to be taking her seriously because he knows he needs to be respectful to customers, especially to repeat customers, but not because he values their opinions. Later, he confirms that he was frustrated by her annoying behaviour. Philippe even allows a client, while wincing in pain, to exclaim "what the fuck are you doing right now?" And laughs, saying "sorry."
> After the happy client leaves, Philippe tells me that he was actually having trouble with one of his new rotary machines, specifically the liner. Rubber bands are used to stabilize the needle so it snugly fits in the tube and Philippe was having difficulty with weak bands which cause a machine to run inefficiently and increase the chance of crooked lines and damaged skin by overworking areas.

This shows how maintaining the definition of a situation in the practice of tattooing involves an air of confidence, regard for client opinions, and a professional appearance. In my past experience, tattoo artists usually displayed confidence by acting so stern that you felt timid about asking if everything was okay or suggesting that something might be changed. My new experiences at The Studio prove that the "artification of tattooing" (Kosut 2013) requires that an occupation as guarded as tattooing must rely on methods of defining the situation which emphasize client reassurance and aesthetic justifications for choices of colour and line. Tattoo artists at The Studio define their choices in the context of what the art requires, whether it is white accents to satisfy theories of light or blood lines (grey) to promote realism. Referring again to Scarborough's (2012) dramaturgical insights about the way musicians "deflect, substitute, underscore, or neutralize" themselves to threats against lost status, I believe tattoo artists like Philippe effectively display cultural capital by "underscoring" (Scarborough 2012: 549) their talents and knowledge in contrast to those of a client.

Kraken's Deceptions

The methods tattoo artists employ to appear competent, clean, professional, and likeable are crucial. There is no guarantee of clients. Technical features of the occupation and the popularity of styles quickly change. Artists who are focused on building their career in a field where image can mean getting well paid commit forms of strategic interaction in order to convince clients to commit their skin canvas to them. They commit acts which can best be described in sociological terms as deception (Gibson 2014; Manning 2000; Ytreberg 2009). According to Goffman (1968: X), strategic interaction involves the "calculative, game-like aspects of mutual dealings." In other words, cultural and artistic knowledge become tools tattoo artists wield while making sense of their unorthodox occupation and convincing clients that they are professional and the person best suited for the job.

Before I met Kraken—a man of large stature and presence—I was told repeatedly by Philippe that it would be great for his shop to get involved with an Asian master artist. Kraken had been tattooing for approximately 16 years and had an impressive portfolio of traditional Asian-style tattoos, including tattoo sleeves, shirts, and full back pieces. When I first met him in autumn 2014, he seemed polite, harmless, and lovable despite his strong accent and interesting mannerisms. He boasted about his training with an Asian master tattoo artist and his experiences in different Asian countries.

But over time, things became strained between Kraken and his apprentices in one camp and me and Philippe in the other. After some discussions with Philippe, even I could tell that although Kraken is a gifted artist with lots of experience, not every tattoo he was turning out met the standards he set for himself as a "master artist," especially when he tackled genres outside the realm of Asian traditional. Moreover, he and his apprentices were sometimes sloppy in looking after their workstations. After three months, more problems, and the dismissal of Kraken's apprentice for drinking on the job and acting unprofessional, Kraken did not show up for work. He left over a dozen appointments hanging and several people with half-finished tattoos.

The reality Philippe and I initially saw at The Studio with Kraken may have been due to our personal and emotional investment in the quality of someone else's performance. When "audience" members have a personal stake in bolstering their own prestige by identifying with a "performer," they may have great difficulty seeing through an act to the hidden reality underneath. This is the central reason the elephant in the room went unnoticed for so long. Even for skilled ethnographers this can be a problem. It takes a major disruption of a dramatized performance in order to expose what is amiss. Goffman (1959: 59) notes "the more closely the imposter's performance approximates to the real thing, the more intensely we may be threatened." In fact, Manning (2000: 287) claims that "the theme of deception is at the center of *The Presentation of Self in Everyday Life*, a book that could have easily and perhaps more appropriately been called *The Misrepresentation of Self in Everyday Life*." Deception requires dramaturgical discipline, a consistent storyline, and appropriate behaviour. Goffman thought that to succeed, both trust and deception required the same ingredients.

In Kraken's case, there was no denying his talent as a tattooist and that in some ways he was a friend. It was only on close inspection in hindsight that we all began to see how some of his tattoos did not hold up to the high artistic level he had convincingly claimed. He may never have really cared whether we were his friends or not. The problem of quality consistency in Kraken's tattooing, combined with his abandonment and dishonesty, caused skepticism about almost everything he told us. Sensitivity to the deceptive tool of skilful, consistent reassurance helps in understanding Kraken. He constantly reminded people that "you are getting a quality piece." Moreover, he so craft-fully appealed to the Asian traditional tattooist title of "master artist" that people still call The Studio asking for "Master Kraken."

Conclusion

To understand the nuances, complexities, and occupational stresses involved in permanently altering the body's largest organ for a living, I needed to become fully acquainted with the tattoo world. I was able to do this by carefully infiltrating a tattoo studio where I learned the tools, techniques, and everyday practices of tattoo artists. Some of these artists have become my friends; others have left my life but still have a strong impact on my research. This chapter has highlighted how two tattoo artists produce and define their work in the eyes of clients and their friends. The maximization of client confidence in a tattoo artist is a key aspect of the trade of tattooing, and is essential for attracting business and achieving artistic freedom and liberty from the proprietor of a skin canvas. This can be achieved in many ways, but this chapter has emphasized how tattoo artists can appeal to stocks of cultural and artistic knowledge and the conventions of interaction in order to convince clients that they are legitimate and worth the pain, the money, and the permanent investment of trust.

References

Gibson, David R. (2014) "Enduring Illusions: The Social Organization of Secrecy and Deception," *Sociological Theory*, 32(4), 283–306.

Goffman, Erving (1959) *The Presentation of Self in Everyday Life*. New York: Doubleday.

Goffman, Erving (1968) *Strategic Interaction*. Philadelphia: University of Pennsylvania Press.

Kosut, Mary (2013) "The Artification of Tattoo: Transformations within a Cultural Field," *Cultural Sociology*, published online, 18 July 2013.

Manning, Philip (2000) "Credibility, Agency, and the Interaction Order," *Symbolic Interaction*, 23(3), 283–97.

Scarborough, Roscoe C. (2012) "Managing Challenges on the Front Stage: The Face-Work Strategies of Musicians," *Poetics*, 40(6), 542–64.

Ytreberg, Espen. (2009) "The Question of Calculation: Erving Goffman and the Pervasive Planning of Communication" in Jacobsen (ed.) *The Contemporary Goffman*. London: Routledge.

Questions for Critical Thought

Chapter 7 | Can Pierre Bourdieu Give Us the Blues?

1. What is the relationship between music and politics? Give examples of how this has changed over time.
2. Curtis explains that people from different cultural backgrounds have different musical tastes. What are the differences? Think about current music and give examples to match the different cultural backgrounds.
3. How has the Internet influenced the relationship between people's cultural backgrounds and their musical tastes?
4. What does Pierre Bourdieu say about music? Why is this important?
5. How is music an important part of culture? In what ways does music influence or represent any one of your cultures?

Chapter 8 | The Social Lives of Statues

1. What are virtualities? How does this term help us to understand people's emotional investments in monuments?
2. Think about the scout's knee monument. What cultural changes have occurred around this monument?
3. How does the white poppy wreath challenge the virtualities that are commonly bestowed on war memorials?
4. What methodological approach did Davidson use? Why did she use this approach?
5. What are the material artifacts found at the site of each monument? How do these artifacts show that the statues are virtualities?

Chapter 9 | Starting with a *Squish:* An Institutional Ethnography of Canada's Art World

1. Klostermann used a method called institutional ethnography. What is institutional ethnography? How did this method influence her findings?
2. This article describes the art world as being a text-heavy environment. How is language being *squished* onto art?
3. Can you think of other examples of dominant culture being forced onto a subculture?
4. How does this article describe art culture? How does imposing language onto art change that culture?
5. How does the art world differ from the dominant culture? What are some of the similarities?

Chapter 10 | The Art and the Artist behind Your Tattoo

1. What characteristics and personality traits are required to be a tattoo artist?
2. How do tattoo artists acquire client confidence? Why is this important?
3. How did Kraken deceive clients? How did he deceive Philippe?
4. What is impression management? Thinking about tattoo artists and people in general, give examples of impression management.
5. Think about the researcher and his role as the tattoo-shop receptionist. What kind of impression management would he need to effectively fill the role of receptionist?

PART III
Socialization

Socialization is a lifelong process through which we acquire the norms, values, and behaviours that are believed to be required in order to successfully participate in social life. Historically, the question of what makes us who we are has been framed as part of the nature–nurture debate. Some, for example, have argued that personalities and behaviour are a product of an individual's innate qualities or their biology (nature), whereas others have argued that we are singularly the product of our interactions with those around us (nurture). Today, most sociologists would agree that we cannot understand one without the other. In fact, many sociologists now focus their work on identifying and theorizing the complex and relational (bi- and multidirectional) ways that our identities are shaped. Many point to the importance of recognizing the role of both agency (seeing the individual as a "doer" or creator of social reality) and social structures in shaping our identities. Not surprisingly, then, some sociological work in the area focuses on the ways in which human experiences and expectations about how to be social vary along the lines of gender, age, class, race, etc. Others focus on how some come to resist social norms that are imposed upon them because of their social location.

Despite resistance by some, there is no doubt that social contexts influence a person's identity and sense of self. Culture, language, institutions, and social structures (i.e., class, race, and gender) shape, constrain, and alter who we are or seek to be. For example, individuals of various class backgrounds may be exposed to and may come to internalize very different values, norms, and social expectations.

In Chapter 11, Xiaobei Chen examines the ways in which children's books treat and portray racial differences, suggesting that authors often depict racial minority characters in a way that is either implicitly or explicitly racist. Chen reminds us of the power that books (and stories and storytelling) can have over children's understanding of their own ethnic/racial identity and of the identities and treatment of others around them. Chen underscores the importance of parents, teachers, and authors as primary socializers in perpetuating or countering stereotypical narratives.

We are reminded by authors in this section that patterns of socialization and expectations around how to be social are not stagnant. Instead, norms, values, and behaviours perceived to be "normal" or even innate at one point in time may change profoundly depending on changing social contexts.

When most of us think about socialization, we often think about the interactions that humans have with other humans, and how these interactions come to shape our sense of self. While so many of us value and depend on interactions with our pets (or "companion animals") for fulfillment, few sociologists have spent time researching and theorizing these relationships. Colleen Dell, in Chapter 12, disrupts this trend by challenging us to consider the social value of these important bonds.

Chapter 13 reminds us that socialization is a lifelong process that is dynamic and ever changing. We see two instances of this in Andrea Doucet's work—in both her own academic journey and in the topic of her research. She reflects on returning to one's older work and building on one's earlier scholarly processes and practices, while considering her scholarly work on men mothering, and the changing patterns and expectations around fatherhood and parenting.

Finally, in Chapter 14, Cathlene Hillier and Janice Aurini examine the literacy practices of children during the summer months. One of their findings is that the value placed on reading by children's parents' influences their child's literacy practices. In turn, children from lower-income backgrounds are less likely to read because their parents do not encourage literacy at home, for various reasons.

11 Children's Literature and Racism in Canada[1]

Xiaobei Chen

Introduction

This chapter reports on some preliminary research for a project that explores the promises and illusions of multicultural citizenship in Canada through a critical examination of children's literature. My interests in children's books arose in part from my previous research on international adoptions from China to Canada, through which I quickly found that children's books were seen as an important tool for adoptive parents to ensure that they properly foster their children's cultural identities. While I was impressed by parents' efforts to use these books, when looking at their content, I often found them unsatisfying. Not only did these books include many culturally essentialist and stereotypical representations of Chinese culture and people in their texts and illustrations, but, most troubling of all, they also tended to overstep discussions of racism and the historical and social meanings of being Chinese in North America (Chen, 2015). I became interested in studying how issues of racism, multiculturalism, and social justice are addressed by current children's literature in Canada. The goal is to contribute a critical sociological understanding of how the growing body of children's literature impacts children's understanding of racism, culture, colonial history, cultural identity, and their sense of belonging in the Canadian nation. My research on children's literature, building on existing critical analyses reviewed briefly below, engages with concepts such as **cultural racism** and **multicultural governmentality** (Chen, 2015, forthcoming in 2017). This short chapter discusses two themes that have emerged from my textual analysis of a small sample of children's picture books suggested to me by a staff member at a school in Ottawa, Canada: (1) cultural racism and (2) power and justice.

Critical Scholarship on Children's Literature and Racist Ideology

A relentless theme in critical scholarship on children's literature is the persistent absence of people of colour. Despite some recent growth, the number of children's books on topics of racism, colonialism, and multiculturalism remains low. In the United States, the Cooperative Children's Book Center at the University of Wisconsin reported that out of roughly 5,000 books published in 2014, only 396 (or less than 8 per cent) were about the perspectives and experiences of people of colour (Cooperative Children's Book Centre, 2015). While comparable statistics are not available in Canada (Chen, Xiaobei, personal communication with Library and Archives Canada, 12 June 2015), my initial research suggests that Canadian public libraries and schools frequently make use of American publications, and that Canadian books about people of colour are not likely to be especially numerous.

Where minority characters do appear in children's literature, how they are represented has been at the centre of much critical scholarship. Characters conforming to negative stereotypes and presented as objects of ridicule and denigration were prevalent in children's literature prior to the American civil rights movement (Larrick, 1965; Kyle, 1978; Deane, 1989), but since the 1970s and 1980s, these stark portrayals of racialized minorities have appeared less in children's books (Deane, 1989; van Belle, 2010).

Nonetheless, Varga and Zuk (2013) remind us that some blatant stereotypes, such as the racialized golliwog character, still find their way into children's literature.

More recent scholarship has taken a cue from Larrick's (1965) foundational work, drawing attention to evolving forms of "gentle doses of racism" in children's literature. Whereas critical analysis of the stereotypical portrayal (or absence) of racialized minorities addresses explicit racism, attention has increasingly been given to implicit, nuanced racism (van Belle, 2010, p.14)—or **structural racism**—in children's literature. This concern grew out of scholars' observations that merely having more and nicer characters of colour cannot adequately counteract the tenacious **white norm** in children's literature. Even though people of colour have been increasingly represented in texts, they have appeared as background characters, or from minority cultures subordinate to a dominant white culture (Fondrie, 2001; Yoon et al., 2010; van Belle, 2010; Varga and Zuk, 2013; Ghiso and Campano, 2013).

Another critique has been made by Stuart Ching (2005), who pointedly asks: "Has the focus on racial harmony caused us to overlook the issue of power in children's literature?" (p. 128). Ching (2005) shows that children's books about people of colour often whitewash narratives about race and culture, effectively preventing opportunities to instill a critical understanding about systemic injustice, subordination, and protest. He argues that when children's books substitute justice concerns with racial harmony, they masquerade as advocacy, but actually undermine minority causes because they do not foster critical awareness of the realities lived by people of colour.

Cultural Racism

My research on children's literature builds on these critical analyses and, additionally, brings in concepts such as cultural racism and multicultural governmentality (Chen 2015, forthcoming in 2017). This section discusses the theme of cultural racism in the context of the relative growth of books highlighting different cultural practices, norms, and languages in children's literature since the 1980s.

In many ways, the turn to diversity is a welcome step forward, making available books highlighting different languages, art forms, values, food and eating customs, and traditional apparel. The majority of books I examined, which could be described as cultural diversity books, however, inform children of differences in a way that can easily fall into what Balibar (1991) terms *cultural racism*—when a culture is objectified and believed to be too fundamentally and innately different to have any connection to another culture in the past, present, or future. Some supposedly progressive children's books actually inculcate an essentialist understanding of culture, such as Shirin Yim Bridges's *Ruby's Wish* (2002), which tells the story of a grandmother who persuaded her family to support her education when she was a little girl in China. While the text explains that it was unusual for girls in China to learn to read or write in the grandmother's time, it fails to explain to the reader that the education of girls in the West was also unusual in the early twentieth century. Without adding this perspective, the book imparts the culturally racist message that in opposition to the West, China is where discriminations against girls exists. Moreover, the book's use of present tense (e.g., "If you walk down a certain road in a certain city in China . . .") and its illustrations of characters—even contemporary ones—dressed in clothing rarely seen in everyday life, convey an impression that Chinese culture is unchanging and static.

One book that avoids the problem of cultural racism is James Rumford's *Silent Music: A Story of Baghdad* (2008), about a boy, Ali, who, like many children around the world, loves playing soccer and listening to "parent-rattling" music. What fascinates Ali most is traditional Arabic calligraphy, like the art of Yakut, a thirteenth-century calligrapher. The beauty of calligraphy brings him consolation and peace as he copes with the wartime devastation around him. This story celebrates the uniqueness of the Arabic language and its meaningfulness to Ali, without reducing his life to history or shying away from how his life is shaped as much by his cultural heritage as by contemporary geopolitical events. To sum up, it is important for children's books to have contents that convey some understanding of the spatial and historical specificities of cultural practices, and to avoid reductionist, binary, and hierarchical understandings of cultures.

Power and Justice

In order to teach children about social justice, we need to first teach them about injustices in the past and present that have shaped our society and the lives of people in it. While it is generally accepted that children's books have an important role to play in teaching diversity, tolerance, and respect, it is rare that they equip the reader with a critical awareness of injustices, inequalities, domination, and resistance. Two such books, which I briefly mention here, act as examples of texts that are valuable for broadening children's awareness of cultural diversity, but that fail to include issues of social justice. The prize-winning *Henry and the Kite Dragon,* by Bruce Edward Hall, is a story about conflict between boys from Chinatown and those from Little Italy. Henry loved to fly kites over Chinatown and the park, but Tony and his friends kept throwing rocks at the beautiful kites. As Henry later found out, this was because the kites scared Tony's pigeons. Although the story teaches mutual understanding, respect, and the lesson that people often have more in common than they realize, it does not explain why, at the time, Italian and Chinese immigrants lived in adjacent, poor, and crowded neighbourhoods. Without such information, the story communicates a depoliticized understanding of reality—the boys' conflict becomes mere ethnic strife resolved through individual acts. Likewise, Sylvia Olsen's *Yetsa's Sweater*, a bestseller in British Columbia, represents a missed opportunity to provide a more complete picture of the life of Cowichan people and colonialism in Canada. It tells the story of Yetsa learning to make Cowichan sweaters from her mother and grandmother. The reader learns about all the steps involved, from preparing the sheep fleeces to designing and knitting, and the narrative, as well as the accompanying "Teacher's Guide" (Sononis Press), focus on craft-making and family tradition. The story might have addressed issues of power and justice by discussing colonialism and its devastating effects on Indigenous peoples, or culture as a process of hybridizing and human resilience and creativity in adverse conditions.

Children's literature's current emphasis on themes of fun, excitement, and getting along, as shown in the above examples, reflects the liberal majority's perspective on issues of racism, colonialism, immigration, and inequalities, and masks the realities of life for people of colour. This tendency may do more harm than good. In my view, this focus on happy harmony is also accentuated by the notion of childhood innocence. While children's developmental characteristics do distinguish them from youths and adults in their experiences, perceptions, and approaches, the notion of childhood innocence is far from neutral. Innocence denotes ignorance with regard to money, adult indulgences and pleasures, and difficult topics such as racism and colonialism. This of course denies the reality that children's lives are affected from birth by both material and symbolic inequalities and that they are exposed to racism in various forms from a young age. The expectation for children's books to be tender, joyful, and uplifting is juxtaposed with the need to explore difficult topics and to provide context for their representations of cultures. This, I argue, is another failing of the children's literature used in Canada.

Conclusion

This paper is an initial step in developing a critical understanding of how children's books have challenged or reproduced modes of nationalist, ethnic absolutist, and culturalist discourses that are organized by racial logics of purity, exclusivity, incompatability, and hierarchy. I have discussed two problematic patterns in contemporary children's literature used in Canada: (1) the tendency to portray cultures in an essentialist manner and in an implicit contrast to the West, entrenching a binary, hierarchical understanding that ultimately subordinates other cultures; and (2) the avoidance of exploring power, exclusion, and injustice in children's books, masking realities and closing off opportunities for nurturing a critical awareness in children. Renowned American writer Walter Dean Meyers explained the social and psychological effect of his books featuring inner-city youth on young people: "They have been struck by the recognition of themselves in the story, a validation of their existence as human beings, an acknowledgement of their value by someone who understands who they are" (Meyers, 2014). The challenge still faces us: how to write books that validate children's experiences and acknowledge their value as they confront racism and colonial mentality, as they navigate ambivalent recognition politics that naturalize identity while reducing stigma (Appiah, 1992; Nicholson, 1996; Comaroff, 1997; Brown, 2006), and as they construct identities through discursive practices "within the play of specific modalities of power" (Hall, 1996, p. 4).

Note

1. My sincere thanks to Yu Shen for her unfailing research assistance and to Elizabeth Paradis for her help with editing and comments on an earlier draft.

References

Appiah, A. 1992. *In My Father's House: Africa in the Philosophy of Culture*. New York: Oxford University Press.

Balibar E. 1991. "Is there a 'neo-racism'?" In E. Balibar and I.M. Wallerstein, *Race, Nation, Class: Ambiguous Identities*, (pp.17–28). London: Verso.

Bridges, Shirin Yim. 2002. *Ruby's Wish*. San Francisco: Chronicle Books.

Brown, W. 2006. *Regulating Aversion: Tolerance in the Age of Identity and Empire*. Princeton, N.J: Princeton University Press.

Chen, Xiaobei. 2015. "Not ethnic enough: the cultural identity imperative in international adoptions from China to Canada." *Children and Society* 29(6): 626–36.

Chen, Xiaobei. Forthcoming in 2017. "Governing cultures, making multicultural subjects." In Deborah Brock (Ed.), *Re-Making Normal: Governing the Social in Neoliberal Times*. Vancouver: UBC Press.

Ching, Stuart H.D. 2005. "Multicultural children's literature as an instrument of power." *Language Arts* 3(2): 128.

Comaroff, J. 1997. "The discourse of rights in colonial South Africa: Subjectivity, sovereignty, modernity." In A. Sarat and T.R. Kearns (Eds*), Identities, Politics, and Rights* (pp. 193–238). Ann Arbor: University of Michigan Press.

Cooperative Children's Book Centre. 2015. "Children's books by and about people of color published in the United States." ccbc.education.wisc.edu, accessed 18 May 2015.

Deane, P. 1989. "Black characters in children's fiction series since 1968." *The Journal of Negro Education*, 58(2): 153–62.

Fondrie, Suzanne. 2001. "'Gentle doses of racism': Whiteness and children's literature." *Journal of Children's Literature* 27(2): 9.

Ghiso, María Paula, and Gerald Campano. 2013. "Ideologies of language and identity in U.S. children's literature." *Bookbird: A Journal of International Children's Literature* 51(3): 47–55.

Hall, Bruce Edward. 2004. Henry and the Kite Dragon. New York: Philomel Books.

Hall, S., and P. Du Gay. (1996). *Questions of Cultural Identity*. London; Thousand Oaks, CA: SAGE.

Larrick, Nancy. 1965. "The all-white world of children's books." *Saturday Review*, 11 September 1965: 63–85.

Kyle, D.W. 1978. "Changes in basal reader content: Has anyone been listening?" *The Elementary School Journal*, 78(5), 304–12.

Meyers, Walter Dean. March 15, 2014. "Where are the people of color in children's books?" *The New York Times*, mobile. nytimes.com, accessed 8 May 2015.

Nicholson, L. (1996). "To be or not to be: Charles Taylor and the politics of recognition." *Constellations* 3(1): 1–16.

Olsen, Sylvia. 2013. *Yetsa's Sweater*. Winlow, BC: Sono Nis Press.

Rumford, James. 2008. *Silent Music: A Story of Baghdad*. New York: Roaring Brook Press.

Sono Nis Press. "Teacher's guide (Yetsa's Sweater)." www.sononis.com/tg126.pdf, accessed 10 June 2015.
van Belle, Leah Allison. 2010. "'Gentle doses of racism': Racist discourses in the construction of scientific literacy, mathematical literacy, and print-based literacies in children's basal readers." PhD dissertation, ProQuest, UMI Dissertations Publishing.
Varga, Donna, and Rhoda Zuk. 2013. "Golliwogs and teddy bears: Embodied racism in children's popular culture." *The Journal of Popular Culture* 46(3): 647–71.
Yoon, Bogum, Anne Simpson, and Claudia Haag. 2010. "Assimilation ideology: Critically examining underlying messages in multicultural literature." *Journal of Adolescent & Adult Literacy* 54(2): 109.

12 Sociology and the Human–Animal Bond

Colleen Anne Dell

Animals are a part of our lives. Consider the fact that more than one-half of North American households have a companion animal living in them (McNicholas and Collis, 2006; Perrin, 2009; Stats, Pierfelice, Kim, and Crandell, 1999) and that these animals are commonly viewed as members of our families (Haraway, 2008; Tedeschi, Fitchett, and Molidor, 2005; Vanier Institute, 2009). Add to this the even greater number of people who wear animal skins and fur, eat their flesh, and engage with them as a form of entertainment (e.g., zoo) (Herzog, 2011).

From the outset, sociology has concentrated on the study of human society (Stark, 1994). The vast majority of sociologists have paid no attention to animals (Irvine, 2008; Peggs 2012). Others, such as Mead, declared that because animals have no verbal language they should not be studied by the discipline (1934). It was not until the late 1970s that a fundamental discussion opened in sociology about accounting for animals in society, from livestock to family pets. It was advanced that by incorporating animals in sociology it "could enhance our understanding of work and occupations, criminology, and the sociology of the family, just to name a few areas" (Irvine, 2008:1958).

The aim of this chapter is not to focus on what sociology has traditionally done or not, or even why, but rather to affirm that including animals in our scholarship is advantageous to the discipline. In one of the few books written on animals and sociology, Peggs (2012) identified several areas in which the consideration of animals could progress sociology. These include understanding: selfhood through its presence in animals, contrary to the position of Mead; social inequalities and oppression by way of humans' treatment of animals; crime and human violence and its relationship to animal abuse; space and place through animal segregation (e.g., slaughter houses) and integration (e.g., family home); consumption through animal and animal by-products; media representation of animals to distinguish "us" from "them"; and social organization via grassroots activism. Peggs draws on the original work of Bryant (1979) and others in the emerging sociological subfield known as "animals and society" (American Sociological Association, 2015).

One area overlooked by Peggs (2012) in her detailed work is the increasing role of **animal-assisted interventions** (AAIs) in the lives of humans. AAI is the umbrella term for any intervention that includes or incorporates animals as a part of a therapeutic process (Fine and Beck, 2010). Their growing presence ranges from therapy dogs visiting on over two-thirds of Canadian university campuses during examinations (J. Gillett, C. Dell, and D. Chalmers, 2016) to a television series about therapy dogs assisting war veterans with PTSD (Custom Productions, Inc. and Redtail Media, LLC, 2015). The underpinning of AAIs is the **human–animal bond**: "the dynamic relationship between people and animals such that each influences the psychological and physiological state of the other" (Center for the Human-Animal Bond, 2015).

Recent scholarship in the health sciences field, including by Hodgson and Darling (2011; 2015), explores how health care providers who ask their patients about family pets can establish the context of their living situations more fully. Others have directly examined the beneficial role of companion animals in human health (Arambasic, Kuterovac-Jagodic, and Vidovic, 1999; Dossey, 1997; Walsh, 2009). Research is also emerging on the beneficial role of therapy dogs (Beck and Meyers, 1996; Kovács, Kis, Rozsa, and Rozsa, 2003; Maujean, Pepping, and Kendall, 2015). The natural sciences have likewise recognized the role of animals in human health. For example, a recent study by Havey, Vlasses, Vlasses, Ludwig-Beymer, and Hackbarth (2014) found that "daily visits with a specially trained dog—even for just five minutes—can significantly reduce the need for pain medication in patients recovering from joint replacement surgery" (Anson, 2014). Other studies have identified how interacting with a dog can decrease cortisol and increase oxytocin levels in humans. Studies of dogs have similarly relayed their increased levels, thus contributing to the human-animal bond (MacLean and Hare, 2015; Nagasawa et al., 2015). So what is it sociology can gain by recognizing the human-animal bond? To help answer this question our research team headed to the farmers' market in Saskatoon, Saskatchewan, Canada to explore how the general public views the role of animals in human health from a sociological lens.

On 21 June 2014, a team of five researchers and three St John Ambulance therapy dogs and handlers attended the local farmers' market for a two-hour period. The market is a community of artisans offering "homemade baking, fresh produce, handmade crafts, specialty foods and much more" (Saskatoon Farmers' Market, 2015). St John Ambulance is a not-for-profit that offers charitable, humanitarian care. The goal of its therapy dog program is to offer support and love to the individuals with whom the dogs and handlers visit (St John Ambulance, 2015). With our team located in a busy section of the market, as people passed they were asked if they would like to meet a therapy dog and answer a few questions. We chose a sociological topic of growing social importance in Canada and the province—addictions and mental health (Mental Health Commission of Canada, n.d.; Stockdale Winder, 2014). Individuals were asked: (1) Do you have, or have you had, a pet? Types? Related comments; (2) Thinking about that pet(s), do you think that people in treatment for addictions or mental health could benefit from spending time with dogs, horses, or other animals? Why?; and (3) Any comments about your visit with the therapy dog(s) today? Ethics exemption was granted from the University of Saskatchewan Human Research Ethics Boards given the exploratory focus of the project. This work was also approved by the University of Saskatchewan's Animal Research Ethics Board and adhered to the Canadian Council on Animal Care guidelines for humane animal use.

With a total of 103 participants, the majority were female (86) (male 13, not stated 4), and over the age of 18 (90), followed by children (12 and under) (6), and teens (13–17) (2) (5 unstated). Eighty-four reported to have or to have had a pet. These mostly included dogs, followed by cats, hamsters, rabbits, birds, llamas, and turkeys. Leading participant comments in answer to the first question included reference to the positive role animals have had in their lives, that they cannot currently have a pet because of housing restrictions (e.g., renting), they consider extended family members' pets a part of their lives, and they fondly remember pets no longer in their lives.

Ninety-four of 95 respondents (1 unsure) felt that people in treatment for addictions or mental health could benefit from spending time with dogs, horses, or other animals. The most prominent reasons were that animals provide unconditional love (25); offer non-judgmental support and comfort (20); are calming and help people to de-stress (18); provide companionship, a bond, and are cuddly (13); are positive, happy, and wonderful (9); and are therapeutic and helpful (7).

Additional comments were provided by 25 participants about their visit with the therapy dogs and these centred on acknowledging the important role of companion animals in individuals' personal lives as well as therapy and other dogs in work environments (e.g., military, hospitals, senior facilities).

It is undeniable that the public sample we interacted with viewed and experienced dogs and other animals, whether companion or working, as integral parts of their own and others' lives, with significant attention paid to the influence of the human–animal bond on people's health. Coupled with the multidisciplinary knowledge reviewed above, the importance of this understanding cannot be overlooked. It is valuable for sociology as a discipline to reflect on this alongside the fact that society is being faced with ever more complex social problems, such as addictions and mental health, and is responding in increasingly unique ways, including with AAIs.

To illustrate the important contribution of a sociological perspective, consider **One Health**, which is a multidisciplinary approach to optimizing the health of humans, animals, and the natural world (One Health Initiative, 2015). It is a rapidly evolving concept, focusing on the interface between humans, animals, and their environment (One Health Global Network, 2015). Originally not inclusive of the social sciences, today it is welcoming them (University of Saskatchewan, 2015). Sociologists and others have expanded, for example, the focus on the environment from a primarily ecological perspective to a socially constructed space accounting for social, cultural, political, and economic factors (Chalmers and Dell, 2015). Chalmers and Dell (2015) explain that "people and animals exist in social communities. For example, those faced with ill health, such as mental health or addictions, need to effectively reintegrate within the ecologies of their families and society at-large" (561).

Working in this area expanded my own knowledge in novel ways as a sociologist. For example, even though I have enjoyed living with pets since my early childhood, they were largely "invisible" to me until I was involved in an AAI study. In our community-based project with a horse therapy program for Indigenous girls in solvent-abuse treatment, a cultural ceremony was held to initiate the study. At it, Elder Gladys Wapass-Greyeyes asked the executive director of the treatment centre and me who was missing. Standing in a barn, with all of our community and research partners surrounding us, we neglected to meaningfully incorporate the horse. This experience set the path for our team to move forward holistically in that project, by offering a ceremonial horse dance in each of the four years of the study. This impacted my involvement in future AAI-related work. To illustrate, I co-authored an academic article with one of the therapy dogs I work with. With some training in dog psychology and thus writing from her perspective the best I could, the article attempts to incorporate the influence of her experiences in my understanding of AAIs from a sociological lens (Dell and Anna-Belle, 2015).

In Peggs's (2012) review of scholarship addressing animals in sociology, she claims that the discipline is not reaching its full potential because it is "largely concentrating on what it expects to find rather than opening itself up to the possibilities of what might be out there, and in doing so has often overlooked other animals" (1). There are many questions a sociologist could ask specific to the human–animal bond to inform the sociological discipline as a whole. These include: gender relations: do women take on an unequal role and therefore attachment in caring for the family pet?; family: does socio-economic status impact the ability of families to benefit from companion animals?; children: does the presence of a family pet increase children's interpersonal coping skills? And consider oppression: "We are central to the lives of other animals, most notably in our oppression of them. We take away their selves, take away their space, take away their freedom, and take away their lives; yet still they seem invisible to us" (Pegg, 2012:145).

"As with all scientific fields, sociology is a systematic process of discovery" (Stark, 1994:33). The sociological areas of critical theory, feminist scholarship, and anti-oppressive frameworks, to name a few, have expanded significantly over the past several decades in their processes of discovery and what they consider. But, as Irvine shares, "In light of the tremendous influence of animals on culture and their numerous roles in society, their [continued] omission from sociological study has given us an incomplete picture of the social world" (2008:1966). He goes on to share that "[r]esearch that includes animals [in society] can illuminate general social processes that many sociologists seek to understand" (2008:1966). He illustrates with the example of selfhood being recognized within animals and the broader sociological implications of this understanding for Alzheimer's patients. Quite simply, the human–animal bond should not be challenging for nearly any discipline to account for, given that humans are a part of the animal species, with many physiological, anatomical, and cultural similarities to non-human animals (Haraway, 2008; Herzog, 2011). The absence of attention itself is a question a sociologist could fully undertake and benefit from the process of considering.

References

American Sociological Association. (2015). Section on animals and society. Retrieved 20 July 2015, from: http://www.asanet.org/sectionanimals/about.cfm

Anson, P. (2014). Study: Animal therapy reduces need for pain meds. National Pain Report. Retrieved 31 August 2015, from: http://americannewsreport.com/nationalpainreport/study-animal-therapy-reducesneed-for-pain-meds-8824406.html

Arambasic, G.K., Kuterovac-Jagodic, G., and Vidovic, V. (1999). Pet ownership and children's self-esteem in the context of war. *Anthrozoos* 12(4): 218–23.

Beck, A.M., and Meyers, N.M. (1996). Health enhancement and companion animal ownership. *Annual Review of Public Health* 17: 247–57.

Bryant, C. (1979). The zoological connection: Animal-related human behaviours. *Social Forces* 58(2): 399–421.

Center for the Human-Animal Bond. 2015. https://www.vet.purdue.edu/chab/

Chalmers, D., and Dell, C. (2015) Applying One Health to the study of Animal-assisted interventions. *EcoHealth Journal* 12(4): 560–2.

Custom Productions, Inc. and Redtail Media, LLC (producer). (2015). *Dogs of war.* United States: A&E Network.

Dell, C., and Anna-Belle (St John Ambulance therapy dog). [By Anna-Belle the St John Ambulance Therapy Dog, as interpreted by her handler, Colleen Anne Dell]. 2015. Questioning "fluffy": A dog's eye view of Animal-Assisted Interventions (AAI) in the treatment of different kinds of people using different kinds of drugs for different kinds of reasons. *Substance Use & Misuse.* Early E-Release 17 March 2015.

Dossey, L. (1997). The healing power of pets: A look at animal-assisted therapy. *Alternative Therapies in Health and Medicine* 3(4): 8–16.

Fine, A., and Beck, A. (2010). Understanding our kinship with animals: Input for health care professionals interested in the human/animal bond. In A. Fine (Ed.), *Handbook on animal-assisted therapy: Theoretical foundations and guidelines for practice* (3rd edn, pp. 3–15). San Diego: Academic Press.

Gillett, J., Dell, C., and Chalmers, D. (2016). *Environmental scan: University therapy dog programs.* Author: University of Saskatchewan.

Handlin L., Hydbring-Sandberg E., Nilsson A., Ejdeback M., Jansson A., and Uvnas-Moberg K. (2011). Short-term interaction between dogs and their owners: Effects of oxytocin, cortisol, insulin and heart rate. *Anthrozoos* 24(3): 301–15. doi: 10.2752/175303711×13045914865385

Haraway, D. (2008). *When species meet.* London: University of Minneapolis Press.

Havey, J., Vlasses, F.R., Vlasses, P.H., Ludwig-Beymer, P., and Hackbarth, D. (2014). The effect of animal-assisted therapy on pain medication use after joint replacement *Anthrozoos* 27(3): 361. doi: 10.2752/175303714×13903827487962.

Herzog, H. (2011). *Some we love, some we hate, some we eat. Why it's so hard to think straight about animals.* New York: HarperCollins Publishers.

Hodgson, K., and Darling, M. (2011). Zooeyia: An essential component of "One Health." *The Canadian Veterinary Journal* 52(2): 189–191. Retrieved 20 August 20 2015, from: http://www.ncbi.nlm.nih.gov/pmc/articles/PMC3022463/pdf/cvj_02_189.pdf

Hodgson, K., and Darling, M. (2015). *Pets impact your patients' health* [brochure]. Toronto: Authors.

Irvine, L. (2008). Animals and society. *Sociology Compass* 2(6): 1954–71.

Kovács, Z., Kis, R., Rozsa, S., and Rozsa, L. (2003). Animal-assisted therapy for middle-aged schizophrenic patients living in a social institution. A pilot study. *Clinical Rehabilitation* 18: 483–6.

Maujean, A., Pepping, C., and Kendall, E. (2015). A systematic review of randomized control trials of animal-assisted therapy on psychosocial outcomes. *Anthrozoos* 28(1): 23–36.

MacLean, E., and Hare, B. (2015). Dogs hijack the human bonding pathway. *Science* 348(6232): 280–1.

McNicholas, J., and Collis, G. (2006). Animals as social supports: Insights for understanding animal assisted therapy. In A. Fines (Ed.), *Handbook on animal-assisted therapy: Theoretical foundations and guidelines for practice* (2nd edn, pp. 49–71). Pomona, CA: Academic Press.

Mead, G.H. (1934). *Mind, self, and society.* Ed. by Charles W. Morris. Chicago: University of Chicago Press.

Mental Health Commission of Canada (n.d.). *Making the case for investing in mental health in Canada.* Retrieved 30 August 2015, from: http://www.mentalhealthcommission.ca/English/system/files/private/document/Investing_in_Mental_Health_FINAL_Version_ENG.pdf

Miller, S.C., Kennedy, C., DeVoe, D., Hickey, M., Nelson, T., and Kogan, L. (2009). An examination of changes in oxytocin levels in men and women before and after interaction with a bonded dog. *Anthrozoos* 22(1): 31–42. doi: 10.2752/175303708×390455.

Nagasawa, M., Mitsui, S., En, S., Ohtani, N., Ohta, M., Sakuma, Y., Onaka, T., and Kikusui, T. (2015). Oxytocin-gaze loop and the coevoluation of human-dog bonds. *Science.* 348(6232): 333–6.

Odendaal, J.S. and Meintjes, R.A. (2003). Neurophysiological correlates of affiliative behavior between humans and dogs. *Veterinary Journal* 165: 296–301.

One Health Global Network (2015). Webportal. Retrieved 21 July 2015, from: http://www.onehealthglobal.net/what-is-one-health

One Health Initiative (2015). One Health Initiative. Retrieved 21 July 2015, from: http://www.onehealthinitiative.com

Peggs, K. (2012). *Animals and sociology.* London: Palgrave Macmillan.

Perrin, T. (2009). The business of urban animals survey: The facts and statistics on companion animals in Canada. *The Canadian Veterinary Journal.* 50(1): 48–52. Retrieved from: http://www.ncbi.nlm.nih.gov/pmc/articles/PMC2603652/pdf/cvj-01-48.pdf

Saskatoon Farmers' Market. (2015). About us. Retrieved 21 July 2015, from: http://www.saskatoonfarmersmarket.com

St John Ambulance (2015). Community services: Therapy dog services. Retrieved 20 July 2015, from: http://www.sja.ca/English/community-services/Pages/Community-services-home.aspx

Stark, R. (1994). *Sociology,* Fifth Edition. Belmont,CA: International Thompson Publishing.

Stats, S., Pierfelice, L., Kim, C., and Crandell, R. (1999). A theoretical model for human health and the pet connection. *Journal of the American Veterinary Medical Association* 214(4): 483–7.

Stockdale Winder, F. (2014). *Working together for change. A 10-year mental health and addictions action plan for Saskatchewan.* Regina: Saskatchewan Ministry of Health.

Tedeschi, F., Fitchett, R., and Molidor, L. (2005). The incorporation of animal-assisted interventions in social work education. *Journal of Family Social Work* 9(4): 59–77.

University of Saskatchewan. (2015). Signature areas. Retrieved 19 July 2015, from: http://www.usask.ca/vpresearch/workshop/areas.php

Vanier Institute. (2009). Our family pets. Fascinating families bulletin (pp. 1). Ottawa: The Vanier Institute of the Family. Retrieved 5 February 2015, from: http://www.vifamily.ca/media/node/248/attachments/ff19.pdf

Walsh, F. (2009). Human–animal bonds I: The relational significance of companion animals. *Family Process* 48(4): 462–80.

13 Revisiting the "Do Men Mother?" Question: Temporality, Performativity, Diffractive Readings, and Cat's Cradles

Andrea Doucet

Introduction

One of the wonderful benefits of receiving the John Porter Tradition of Excellence Book Award from the Canadian Sociology Association (CSA) is the opportunity to deliver a public lecture and to engage in a workshop with esteemed colleagues at the CSA annual meetings. I had this privilege in June 2007 when Dorothy Smith and Roberta Hamilton acted as critics of my book *Do Men Mother*? in a workshop on theoretical and methodological issues.[1] There were many questions and comments that stayed with me long after that session. One such question was from Hamilton, who asked me something along the following lines: "What would your arguments have looked like if you had worked with different discourses and concepts? Would this have been a different book?"

This question and my subsequent process of rethinking *how* we approach our research and "objects of investigation" stayed at the back of my mind for several years after the publication of *Do Men Mother?* With each passing year, the book was cited more and more, as scholars continued to build directly on the book's approach and/or findings (e.g., Almqvist and Duvander, 2014; Dowd, 2012; Farstad, 2015; Featherstone, 2009; Fox, 2009; Green and Pelletier, 2015; Marsiglio and Roy, 2012; Podnieks, 2016; Ranson, 2010, 2015; Miller, 2011; O'Brien and Wall, in press; Wahlström Henriksson, 2010). As the book edged toward its 10-year mark, it felt strange for me to continue to receive (mostly) positive feedback on the book while also quietly harbouring an uncomfortable sense that it was outdated, with respect to the fields where it was located, the debates it spoke to, and my own positioning and thinking. After much deliberation, I agreed to write a second edition. I thought: how hard could it be? As most authors do, I thought that I could just leave the book intact and add a new preface and some new concluding thoughts.

Yet, the process of revising, or more properly—*revisiting*—turned out to be more complicated than I had anticipated. How does one revisit an old work? When I first returned to the book and tried to insert myself back into its pages, the image that came to mind was that of returning to a cherished childhood classroom and trying to sit in my old desk again. The fit was no longer a perfect one. I had outgrown much of what I had written. In fact, I had arrived at a point where I could answer Hamilton's provocative question about how different concepts produce different knowledges. Yet, at the same time, I could see that what I had written had meaning and resonance in a particular place and time. I gradually came to the realization that I needed to find a methodological and conceptual framework for that revisiting.

For this, I turned to the small but growing literature on processes of methodological revisiting (Burawoy, 2003; Thomson and McLeod, 2015; Sefton-Green and Rowsell, 2014; Mauthner, 2015). I thus began to think about the varied dimensions of revisiting—including returning to field sites; longitudinal research; possibly revisiting data; rethinking reflexive relationships between researcher and research participant; and a revisiting of theory, concepts, and **epistemic practices** (Buroway, 2003; Bourdieu and Wacqaunt, 1992).

Overall, my approach to revisiting was informed by tenets that have been guiding my work for several years and are part of recent or new theoretical and philosophical "turns" that are, broadly speaking, temporal, relational, affective, new materialist, performative, and ontological. My gradual positioning within these "turns" meant that I shifted from a focus that included not only questions of *what* and *why*, but also *how*. That is, although my research and writing on men and mothering was initially concerned with *what* was occurring in the lives and stories of fathers, I gradually moved to consider *how* we study, make sense of, and participate in the crafting of the narratives that unfold arise in these simultaneously intimate and political corners of social life. I thus turned more and more of my focus toward scrutinizing the theoretical, methodological, epistemological, and ontological underpinnings of these fields as well as the taken-for-granted concepts that guide research, constitute data, and produce findings. These questions of *how*, in turn, led me to work more with Bourdieu and Wacquant's (1992: 41) concept of "epistemic reflexivity" and more specifically, Margaret Somers's (2008: 172) "historical sociology of concept formation," which is the "work of turning social science back on itself to examine often taken-for-granted conceptual tools of research" (Somers, 2008: 172). As Somers writes (2008: 172): "Social scientists in recent years have come increasingly to recognize that the categories and concepts we use to explain the social world can *themselves be fruitfully made the objects of analysis*."

These moves meant that I began to approach what I was doing as a social scientist in a different way so that, broadly speaking, I was working within performative rather than representational approaches (see Bell, 2012; Mauthner, 2012; Thrift, 2008; Winthereik and Verran, 2011). Briefly, four pieces of my frame for revisiting are: temporality; the performativity of concepts; reflexivity and diffractive readings; and cat's cradles.

Temporality

Feminist philosopher Nancy Hartsock, who passed away in 2015, wrote in the introduction to her seminal text *The Feminist Standpoint Revisited and Other Essays* that all of her writing "responded to questions that arose from the social contexts in which I found myself. . . . [T]hey are autobiographical in that they respond to issues I found urgent at different times" (Hartsock, 1998: 1). About a quarter century ago, the "Do men mother?" question found its way into my thinking in ways that were autobiographical, urgent, and temporal. It was autobiographical in that it was seeded from my own biography as a mother parenting with a man who was judged harshly when he tried, in 1991, to join a local moms-and-tots group in England (Doucet, 2006, 2009). It was urgent as I joined a chorus of feminist scholars who argued that women's socio-economic equality with men was dependent on men's participation in shared parenting or mothering (e.g., Ruddick, 1983, 1990, 1995; Young, 1984). Finally, that "Do men mother?" question was temporal in that it was asked in an historical moment when men faced challenges with being socially recognized as primary caregiving fathers.

It is not only that these social worlds wherein men and mothering questions are explored are different, but also that the concepts we use to frame and make sense of these stories are temporal. This attention to temporality means recognizing that, as researchers, the problems that we take up are made possible in given historical conditions of possibility and within our changing epistemic communities. As Somers argues (1998: 772), our research questions and practices are partly "problem driven," so that we work with "temporary analytic frames constructed . . . by the problem the researcher sets out to explain" (Somers, 2011: 14) as well as from "a space of possible ideas [that] has been formed" (Hacking, 2002: 26). To explicate the connection between conditions of possibility and the knowledges we create, I briefly attend to the performativity of concepts.

Performativity of Concepts

Somers attends to what concepts *do*, rather than what concepts *are*; as she puts it, "all social science concepts lack natures or essences; instead they have histories, networks, and narratives" (Somers, 2008: 268; see also Deleuze and Guattari, 1994; Grosz, 2011; Code, 2006). This, in turn, meant that it gradually became to clear to me that the central concepts of *Do Men Mother?*—such as care, embodiment, masculinities, mothering, equality, responsibilities, reflexivity, and maternal lenses—were "words in their sites" (Hacking, 2002: 68). As Somers maintains, concepts do not sit as isolated ones but rather are part of a "conceptual configuration" (Somers, 2008: 267) so that concepts are "not only related to each other in the weak sense of being contiguous; they are also ontologically related" and "fit" together "[l]ike a point and a line in basic geometry" (Somers, 2008: 267). This also leads to a position whereby "successful truth claims are historically contingent rather than confirmations of absolute and unchanging reality" (Somers, 2008: 267).

Revisiting and revising my earlier work meant thinking through the contingency of my questions and the specificity of my epistemic practices and the knowledges I had created. This was perhaps what Roberta Hamilton was pointing to when she asked me about varied conditions of possibility for alternate discourses and concepts. I thus realized that I needed to approach my informing concepts not only as temporal but as contingent, mobile, and lodged in a tightly wound web with other concepts. This leads me to two other parts of my revisiting frame.

From Reflexivity to Diffractive Readings and Analysis

In recognizing temporality, performativity, and contingency of concepts, I began to work with what Karen Barad (2012) calls "diffractive readings" of my own work and that of others. Diffractive readings build on Donna Haraway's concept of diffraction, which is a complicated set of ideas that, at the risk of simplifying, "is about heterogeneous history, not about originals" (1997: 273). Unlike **reflexivity**, where one positions oneself in data collection and analytic processes as separate from the data that is collected, diffraction refers to how we are deeply entangled within the making of that data. Moreover, while reflexivity tends to be enacted as a process that often stops once one has articulated one's location, diffractive readings and analysis rely "on the researcher's ability to make matter intelligible in new ways and to imagine other possible realities presented in the data" (Taguchi, 2012: 267). This entails a process of working with differences, rather than assuming that we can capture or mirror data that is "out there" waiting to be found. As Barad notes,

> Diffraction does not fix what is the object and what is the subject in advance, and so, unlike methods of reading one text or set of ideas against another where one serves as a fixed frame of reference, diffraction involves reading insights through one another in ways that help illuminate differences as they emerge: how different differences get made, what gets excluded, and how those exclusions matter. (2007: 30)

To read and revisit diffractively is to read generously and "to read through, not against; it means reading texts intra-actively though one another, enacting new patterns of engagement" (Barad, 2012: 14; see also Mauthner, 2015). I thus revisited my own work, and that of others who built on it, and I read "through" and in relational "intra-action" (Barad, 2007). This, in turn, led me to think about how knowledge-making practices involve specific kinds of craftings and weavings.

Cat's Cradle

A final fragment of my framework for revisiting earlier work and the process of building with and from others comes from Donna Haraway. Here I borrow her metaphor of a cat's cradle, the well-known two-person string game, as a way of thinking about dialogue, collective intellectual labour, and the making of new worlds through knowledge making. She writes:

> Cat's cradle invites a sense of collective work, of one person not being able to make all the patterns alone. One does not "win" at cat's cradle; the goal is more interesting and more open-ended than that. It is not always possible to repeat interesting patterns, and figuring out what happened to result in intriguing patterns is an embodied analytic skill. . . . Cat's cradle is both local and global, distributed and knotted together. (1997: 268)

Working with this metaphor, returning to one's older work and building on earlier scholarly processes and practices is partly to engage in a dialogic tapestry—with threads from my own past and present work and those of others that I intra-acted with.

Conclusion

This chapter is a brief overview of my processes of revisiting earlier work and the building of a framework that attends to temporality, performativity, and contingency in knowledge-making practices. As I returned to rewrite and revise an earlier set of arguments on men and mothering, I came to the view that I could not write *over* those arguments, but had to write *through* my work and the work of others. Working in the shadows of several new philosophical turns, these processes were also framed by a reconfigured sense of knowledge making as less about representing what was *out there*, and more about reflexively participating in the crafting of scholarly work as "traces and threads," as "twists and turns of the labyrinth" (Ingold, 2007: 2, 61; see also Ingold, 2013), and as a "kind of storytelling" where "stories should never end, but rather lead to further stories" (Tsing, 2015: 287).

Note

1. *Do Men Mother?* was awarded the 2007 John Porter Tradition of Excellence Book Award. Dorothy Smith's (1987) *The Everyday World as Problematic: A Feminist Sociology* received the award in 1990.

References

Almqvist, Anna-Lena and Ann-Zofie Duvander. 2014. "Changes in Gender Equality? Swedish Fathers' Parental Leave, Division of Childcare and Housework." *Journal of Family Studies* 20(1):19–27.

Barad, Karen. 2007. *Meeting the Universe Halfway: Quantum Physics and the Entanglement of Matter and Meaning.* Durham: Duke University Press.

Barad, Karen. 2012. "'Matter Feels, Converses, Suffers, Desires, Yearns and Remembers': Interview with Karen Barad." Pp. 48–70 in *Materialism: Interviews & Cartographies*, edited by R. Dolphijn and I. van der Tuin. Ann Arbor, Michigan: Open Humanities Press.

Bell, Vikki. 2012. "Declining Performativity: Butler, Whitehead and Ecologies of Concern." *Theory, Culture & Society* 29(2):107–23. doi: 10.1177/0263276412438413.

Bourdieu, Pierre and Loic J.D. Wacquant. 1992. *An Invitation to Reflexive Sociology.* Chicago: University of Chicago Press.

Burawoy, Michael. 2003. "Revisits: An Outline of a Theory of Reflexive Ethnography." *American Sociological Review* 68:645–79.

Code, Lorraine. 2006. *Ecological Thinking: The Politics of Epistemic Location.* New York: Oxford University Press.

Deleuze, Gilles and Felix Guattari. 1994. *What Is Philosophy?* Translated by G. Burchell and H. Tomlinson. London: Verso.

Doucet, Andrea. 2006. *Do Men Mother? Fathering, Care, and Domestic Responsibility.* Toronto: University of Toronto Press.

Doucet, Andrea. 2009. "Gender Equality and Gender Differences: Parenting, Habitus, and Embodiment (the 2008 Porter Lecture)." *Canadian Review of Sociology* 46(2):103–21. doi: 10.1111/j.1755-618X.2009.01206.x.

Dowd, Nancy E. 2012. "Fatherhood and Equality: Reconfiguring Masculinities." *Suffolk University Law Review* 45:1047–81.

Farstad, Gunhild R. 2015. "Difference and Equality: Icelandic Parents' Division of Parental Leave within the Context of a Childcare Gap." *Community, Work & Family* 18(3):351–67. doi: http://dx.doi.org/10.1080/13668803.2014.965661.

Featherstone, Brid. 2009. *Contemporary Fathering: Theory, Policy and Practice.* Bristol: Policy Press.

Fox, Bonnie. 2009. *When Couples Become Parents: The Creation of Gender in the Transition to Parenthood.* Toronto: University of Toronto Press.

Green, Fiona and Gary Pelletier. 2015. *Essential Breakthroughs: Men, Mothering, Fathering.* Toronto: Demeter Press.

Grosz, Elizabeth. 2011. *Becoming Undone: Darwinian Reflections on Life, Politics, and Art.* Durham, NC: Duke University Press.

Hacking, Ian. 2002. *Historical Ontology.* Boston: Harvard University Press.

Haraway, Donna. 1997. *Modest_Witness@Second_Millenium. Femaleman_Meets_Oncomouse: Feminism and Technoscience.* New York: Routledge.

Hartsock, Nancy C.M. 1998. *The Feminist Standpoint Revisited and Other Essays.* Boulder, CO: Westview Press.

Ingold, Tim. 2007. *Lines: A Brief History.* Abingdon, UK: Routledge.

Ingold, Tim. 2013. *Making: Anthropology, Archaeology, Art and Architecture.* Abingdon, UK: Routledge.

Marsiglio, William and Kevin Roy. 2012 *Nurturing Dads: Social Initiatives for Contemporary Fatherhood.* New York: Russell Sage Foundation.

Mauthner, Natasha. 2015. "'The Past Was Never Simply There to Begin with and the Future Is Not Simply What Will Unfold': A Posthumanist Performative Approach to Qualitative Longitudinal Research." *International Journal of Social Research Methodology* 18(3):321–36. doi: 10.1080/13645579.2015.1022298.

Mauthner, N.S. 2012. "'Accounting for Our Part of the Entangled Webs We Weave': Ethical and Moral Issues in Digital Data Sharing." Pp. 157–75 in *Ethics in Qualitative Research,* edited by T. Miller, M. Birch, M. Mauthner and J. Jessop. London: SAGE.

Miller, Tina. 2011. *Making Sense of Fatherhood: Gender, Caring and Work.* New York: Cambridge University Press.

O'Brien, Margaret and Karin Wall. In press. *Fathers on Leave Alone: Work–Life Balance and Gender Equality in Comparative Perspective.* New York: Springer.

Podnieks, Elizabeth. 2016. *Pops in Pop Culture: Fatherhood, Masculinity, and the New Man.* London: Palgrave Macmillan.

Ranson, Gillian. 2010. *Against the Grain: Couples, Gender, and the Reframing of Parenting* Toronto: University of Toronto Press.

Ranson, Gillian. 2015. *Fathering, Masculinity and the Embodiment of Care.* London: Palgrave Macmillan.

Ruddick, Sara. 1983. "Maternal Thinking." Pp. 213–30 in *Essays in Feminist Theory,* edited by J. Trebilcot. Totowa, NJ: Rowman & Littlefield.

———. 1990. "Thinking about Fathers." Pp. 222–33 in *Conflicts in Feminism,* edited by M. Hirsch and E. F. Keller. London: Routledge.

———. 1995. *Maternal Thinking: Towards a Politics of Peace.* Boston: Beacon Press.

Sefton-Green, Julian and Jennifer Rowsell, 2014. *Learning and Literacy over Time: Longitudinal Perspectives.* New York/Abingdon, UK: Routledge.

Smith, Dorothy E. 1987. *The Everyday World as Problematic: A Feminist Sociology.* Boston: Northeastern University Press.

Somers, Margaret. 1994. "The Narrative Constitution of Identity: A Relational and Network Approach." *Theory and Society* 23(5): 605–49. doi: 10.1007/BF00992905.

———. 2008. *Genealogies of Citizenship.* New York: Cambridge University Press.

———. 2011. "Reply to the Critics: Book Symposium: Genealogies of Citizenship: Markets, Statelessness, and the Right to Have Rights." *Trajectories* 22(2):25–33.

Taguchi, Hillevi Lenz. 2012. "A Diffractive and Deleuzian Approach to Analysing Interview Data." *Feminist Theory* 13(3): 265–81.

Thomson, Rachel and Julie McLeod. 2015. "New Frontiers in Qualitative Longitudinal Research: An Agenda for Research." *International Journal of Social Research Methodology* 18(3): 243–50. doi: 10.1080/13645579.2015.1017900.

Thrift, N. 2008. *Non-Representational Theory: Space/Politics/Affect.* Abingdon, UK: Routledge.

Tsing, A.L. *The Mushroom at the End of the World: On the Possibility of Life in Capitalist Ruins.* Princeton and Oxford: Princeton University Press

Wahlström Henriksson, Helena. 2010. *New Fathers?: Contemporary American Stories of Masculinity, Domesticity, and Kinship.* Cambridge, MA: Cambridge Scholars Publishing.

Winthereik, B.R. and H. Verran. 2012. "Ethnographic Stories as Generalizations That Intervene." *Science Studies* 25(1): 37–51.

Young, Iris Marion. 1984. "Is Male Gender Identity the Cause of Male Domination?" Pp. 129–46 in *Mothering: Essays in Feminist Theory,* edited by J. Trebilcot. Totowa, NJ: Rowman & Allanheld.

14 The Summer Reading Blues: Children's Accounts of Summer Literacy Practices

Cathlene Hillier and Janice Aurini

Introduction

Research on education inequality draws attention to the loss of academic skills that occurs over summer vacation. Reading is identified as one skill that is particularly vulnerable to "**summer setback**." Children with highly educated and affluent parents often build their skills over the summer months, while others lose several months of literacy learning (Alexander, Entwisle, and Olson, 2007; Borman, Goetz, and Dowling, 2009; Cooper et al., 2000; Davies and Aurini, 2013; Dexter and Stacks, 2014; Downey, von Hippel, and Broh, 2004; Heyns, 1978; National Summer Learning Association, 2014; Pagan and Sénéchal, 2014). To explain these disparities, sociologists routinely turn to the work of Pierre Bourdieu. Bourdieu's (1998) discussion of different forms of "capital" suggests that people or particular groups of people use their economic (e.g., financial resources), human (e.g., skills), social (e.g., networks), and cultural (e.g., knowing how to act in different social situations) capital to their advantage, including facilitating literacy learning (Phillips and Chin, 2004).

This paper examines children's accounts of their summer reading practices. As Chin and Phillips observe, the literature on capital overlooks children's agency and instead tends to examine how parental resources are "passed on" (2004: 187). Following their lead, we show how "**child capital**"—children's human, social, and cultural capital—influences reading practices. As Chin and Phillips (2004) note, children's dispositions and beliefs about learning can influence whether they seek or resist literacy opportunities. We present children's accounts of their summer reading practices, their efficacy (or lack of) in their reading initiatives at home, and their relative ability to motivate others to help them with their literacy growth.

The data for this study comes from face-to-face semi-structured photo-interviews we conducted in 2014 with 35 children, aged five to eight. We gave children a disposable camera and a series of instructions (e.g., Take a picture of what you like to read at home), and followed up with a 30-minute interview after the photos were developed. The students were recruited from two schools in a Southwestern Ontario school board that were offering a summer literacy camp.[1] These schools are in relatively economically depressed neighbourhoods, and 40 per cent of our participants are from households that fall in the bottom income category ($0–$29,999).

Summer Reading at Home

Children's literacy skills diverge during the summer when school is not in session. Research from Canada and the United States finds that many children lose from one to three months of literacy skills (Alexander, Entwisle, and Olson, 2007; Davies and Aurini, 2013; Downey, von Hippel, and Broh, 2004). Our Ontario-based study shows that that summer learning losses accumulate over time, and for some children, they become quite sizeable (Davies, Aurini and Milne, 2016).

Reading is one of the key factors attributed to the disparity in literacy outcomes. During the summer, children from higher **socio-economic status** (**SES**) backgrounds are exposed to more reading opportunities (Allington and McGill-Franzen, 2003) and enjoy a diverse menu of literacy-enhancing activities.[2] Children from lower-SES backgrounds are more likely to be left to entertain themselves. These children engage in fewer activities that support reading and do not have as many reading materials at home (see Chin and Phillips, 2004). Not surprisingly, researchers find sizable differences in summertime literacy rates between children from higher- and lower-SES backgrounds (Davies and Aurini, 2010–2014). These differences have a profound effect on educational achievement gaps. Alexander and his colleagues (2007), for example, attribute two-thirds of the SES gap in grade 9 to summer setback and also find that summer learning from the elementary grades predicts children's high school grades, dropout rates, and post-secondary attendance.

Summer Reading for Children Who Stay "Plugged In"

Chin and Phillips (2004) document how children's own "capital" plays a large role in summer learning and can sometimes shore up disparities at home. Several of our interviewees support this theory. Child capital includes children taking the initiative to read on their own and orchestrate extra-curricular literacy enhancing activities.[3]

Jasmyn (eight years old)—whose father is a high school graduate and mother is midway through college—is very resourceful and finds several ways to engage literacy learning. While her parents are often too busy to read to her, she reads on her own, writes in her diary every day, and is working through a grade 4 curriculum book that her parents brought home. Jasmyn lives within walking distance to a library and told us: "Yeah, because there's like a summer reading club happening there and I go to the library all the time. I read books there and I join the programs there." Since she is not allowed to walk there on her own, Jasmyn often asks her older sister to walk her to the library.

Other children in our study also exhibit Jasmyn's resourcefulness. These children read independently and find ways to access free programs. They tap into their social networks and enlist the help of parents, friends, or extended family members to take them to programs and to read to them. During the summer, ten children said they read every day and six said that they read "sometimes."[4] Two children said that they read with their mom every night before bedtime, eight said that they frequently read with their mother, and seven sometimes read with their mom when she is not busy.

Some children utilize strategies learned at school and at the literacy camp. Amelia, who comes from a single-mother low-income home, uses a card that she received from her remedial reading teacher and goes through the suggested steps when she encounters an unfamiliar word. Similarly, upon encouragement from her teacher, Ava writes short stories on her computer at home. Other children describe enlisting their parents to search for information on the Internet to learn about a topic of interest. Free books and programs at public libraries are popular sources of reading and literacy activities among our participants.

Child capital is evident in these examples as children enact their human (e.g., reading strategies learned at school), cultural (e.g., understanding the importance of reading), and social (e.g., recruiting a family member to take them to a summer program) capital. While parents and siblings play a supportive role, these children are active participants in their literacy learning.

Summer Reading for Children Who "Check Out"

While some children initiate a variety of reading opportunities, many children "check out" of reading during the summer months. We find this to be especially the case when there are few "rules" about reading at home. Several of these children are unable to read on their own; others do not have parents who can read to them on a regular basis because of work or other commitments. Many of these children told us that they do not get to go to the library as often as they wish. Six children told us that they ask their parents "all the time" to go to the library, but their parents are too busy to take them.

Other children do not like to read. Anthony (eight years, low-income family) describes reading as "stupid" and says, "I don't like to read books." Even though he claims to own numerous books, Anthony said that he never reads at home. His mother works full-time, and her common-law husband is unemployed. He says his mother stopped reading to him when he was little and that he is in the bottom level of reading in his class.

While only two children said they "never" read at home during the summer, several children noted that they do not read very often; this is particularly true among our interviewees who describe having little supervision or rules about reading practices. Chloe and Isabelle told us that they only read during the school year when it is assigned for homework. Some children try to read but are frustrated when they come across difficult words. These children lack the child (e.g., resourcefulness) and parent (e.g., parent who can help) capital to solve difficulties related to literacy (e.g., inability to sound out a word, access to the library). As a consequence, they describe giving up, avoiding reading, or turning to other activities (e.g., video games).

Students like Anthony demonstrate the fragility of child capital and its relative power to compensate for summer setback. While Jasmyn's tenacity demonstrates the potential power of child capital for shoring up literacy learning, many children require more adult-led resources and interventions.

Conclusion

Entwisle, Alexander, and Olson (1998) use the metaphor of a "faucet" to describe summer setback. When school is out, instruction and resources are turned off, and some families cannot compensate for this loss. Similar to Chin and Phillips (2004), some children play a large role in supporting literacy learning during summer vacation in ways that compensate for other kinds of disparities at home (e.g., low level of parental education). These interviewees are quite resourceful and engage in a variety of literacy-enhancing activities on their own or with parents' encouragement and help. In the absence of strong parent interventions, however, many children with lower levels of child capital engage in far fewer literacy building activities and are more likely to avoid or resist reading.

While the potential for child capital to shore up some forms of educational disparities is promising, it is hardly a reliable remedy for summer setback. Instead, researchers find that many children, particularly from lower-SES backgrounds, benefit from structured literacy or numeracy interventions over summer vacation. A meta-analysis of the summer setback literature concludes that summer school programs aimed at removing learning deficiencies and accelerating learning have a positive impact on participating students' math and reading skills (Cooper et al., 2000). In the larger study, an evaluation of the literacy camp finds that even a brief two- or three-week program over summer vacation can slow or reduce summer setback and in some cases close achievement gaps between higher- and lower-SES students (e.g., Davies and Aurini, 2010–2014). It is apparent that for children who do not take the initiative to do reading activities on their own, or who are not encouraged by parents to read, interventions like the literacy camp may provide the only vehicle to build or even maintain their literacy skills.

Notes

1. The interviews are a part of a larger mixed-methods project examining summer learning camps in Ontario schools (e.g., Davies and Aurini 2010–2014). The objective of the broader study is to evaluate an intensive summer learning intervention offered by the Ontario Ministry of Education for elementary students. In the

qualitative arm of the project, we interviewed over 200 parents and teachers about their understandings of parent engagement in schooling (2012–2013). The 2014 photo-interviews with children extend our research into home-based learning practices and early literacy skills further. We only draw from the face-to-face interviews for this paper.

2. For example, the quantity of books read (Allington and McGill-Franzen, 2003) and the number of visits to the library (Heyns, 1978) have a positive relationship with literacy growth when school is not in session.
3. It is important to note that many of the children in our sample have parents who do not have nine-to-five employment. Several children in our sample are living in single-parent households or with a relative. These children are often left to manage their own literacy activities.
4. In total, 16 children said that they read on their own but mentioned that if they had trouble with a word then they would ask their mother for help (mother was most often mentioned as the go-to person for reading and homework help).

References

Alexander, K.L., Entwisle, D.R., and Olson, L.S. (2007). Lasting consequences of the summer learning gap. *American Sociological Review, 72*(2), 167–80.

Allington, R.L., and McGill-Franzen, A. (2003). The impact of summer reading setback on the reading achievement gap. *Phi Delta Kappan, 85*(1), 68–75.

Borman, G.D., Goetz, M.E., and Dowling, N.M. (2009). Halting the summer achievement slide: A randomized field trial of the KindergARTen Summer Camp. *Journal of Education for Students Placed at Risk, 14*(2), 133–47.

Bourdieu, P. (1998). The forms of capital. In Halsey, A.H., Lauder, Hugh, Brown, Philip, Wells, Amy Stuart (Eds), *Education: Culture, economy and society* (46–58). Oxford: Oxford University Press.

Chin, T., and Phillips, M. (2004). Social reproduction and child rearing practices: Social class, children's agency, and the summer activity gap. *Sociology of Education, 77*(3), 185–210.

Cooper, H., Charlton, K., Valentine, J.C., Muhlenbruck, L., and Borman, G.D. (2000). Making the most of summer school: A meta-analytic and narrative review. *Monographs of the Society for Research in Child Development, 65*(1), 1–118.

Davies, S., Aurini, J. and Milne, E. (2016). *The Ontario longitudinal study of summer learning.* Final report to the Literacy and Numeracy Secretariat, Ontario Ministry of Education.

Davies, S. and Aurini, J. (2010–2014). Research reports for the summer literacy learning project in Ontario schools (http://www.ontariodirectors.ca/summer_literacy.html).

——. (2013). Summer learning inequality in Ontario. *Canadian Public Policy, 30*(2), 287–307.

Dexter, C.A., and Stacks, A.M. (2014). A preliminary investigation of the relationship between parenting, parent–child shared reading practices, and child development in low-income families. *Journal of Research in Childhood Education, 28*(3), 394–410.

Downey, D.B., von Hippel, P.T., and Broh, B.A. (2004). Are schools the great equalizer? Cognitive inequality during the summer months and the school year. *American Sociological Review, 69*(5), 613–35.

Entwisle, D.R., Alexander, K.L., and Olson, L.S (1998). *Children, schools, and inequality.* Boulder, CO: Westview Press.

Heyns, B. (1978). *Summer learning and the effects of schooling.* New York: Academic Press.

National Summer Learning Association. (2014). *How to make summer reading effective.* http://c.ymcdn.com/sites/www.summerlearning.org/resource/collection/CB94AEC5-9C97-496F-B230-1BECDFC2DF8B/Research_Brief_03_-_Kim.pdf

Pagan, S., and Sénéchal, M. (2014). Involving parents in a summer book reading program to promote reading comprehension, fluency, and vocabulary in grade 3 and grade 5 children. *Canadian Journal of Education, 37*(2), 1–31.

Phillips, M., and Chin, T. (2004). How families, children, and teachers contribute to summer learning and loss. In Borman, G.D., and Boulay, M. (Eds), *Summer learning: Research, policies, and programs* (255–78). Mahwah, N.J.: Lawrence Erlbaum Associates.

Questions for Critical Thought

Chapter 11 | Children's Literature and Racism in Canada

1. How are children's books used as a tool for socialization?
2. What does Chen say are some of the problems with the depiction of culture in children's books? How can these problems be fixed?
3. How does the portrayal of minority characters in children's books negatively influence children's socialization? What problems can arise?
4. What is meant by implicit and explicit racism? What is cultural racism? How can this be avoided in children's books?
5. What solutions to racism does Chen suggest for children's literature? What role does truth and justice play in teaching children to be tolerant?

Chapter 12 | Sociology and the Human-Animal Bond

1. Dell discusses the influence that companion animals have on humans. What is the impact of companion animals of humans? Why is this important?
2. How do companion animals influence human socialization? What are some of the contradictions of the human–animal relationship that exist in our society?
3. What is AAI? Why is it important for sociologists to study AAI?
4. What are some of the benefits of having an animal companion?
5. Near the end of her paper, Dell asks some potential questions that could be answered about the human–animal bond. What are these questions? How would you answer them?

Chapter 13 | Revisiting the "Do Men Mother?" Question: Temporality, Performativity, Diffractive Readings, and Cat's Cradles

1. What caused Doucet to reconsider the literature and approach that she took in writing her book? Why is this important?
2. What were Doucet's personal experiences with men mothering? How do you think this impacted her work? Why are these experiences relevant?
3. Do men mother today? What are the social expectations around mothering in our society? How does your personal upbringing or socialization influence your opinion of mothering and gender roles?
4. What is diffractive reading? Why was this practice important for reframing Doucet's second book?
5. What is meant by the "cat's cradle" metaphor? How is this important when examining a literature or way of thinking? How can you apply this metaphor to your own life and to the things you believe in?

Chapter 14 | The Summer Reading Blues: Children's Accounts of Summer Literacy Practices

1. What is "child capital"? How does this capital influence children's reading practices?
2. How do parents' resources influence their children's literacy practices?
3. Is literacy an important part of socialization? What do children stand to gain from learning positive reading habits? What do they stand to lose from not learning these habits?
4. Hiller and Aurini describe some children as being resourceful. What strategies do these children use to increase their literacy? Give examples of human, cultural, and social capital.
5. What is the most important predictor of positive literacy behaviours during the summer months? How can we increase child literacy outside of school?

PART IV
Deviance and Crime

People in societies create social stability by creating and enforcing rules of behaviour. As we mentioned in the previous section, it is largely through socialization that people learn the rules of society and behaviours that are expected of them. However, individuals sometimes break the rules of society; all of us break them occasionally, and some people break them often.

The sociological study of deviance is the study of norm violation (or rule-breaking). The rules broken by "deviants" can be either formal or informal. Formal rules are often codified in criminal law, so rule-breaking of this kind may include criminal acts such as murder, rape, or assault. Informal rules—etiquette, mores, and folkways, for example—are enforced less consistently and punished less severely. What people consider deviant changes over time, so laws and other norms, and their enforcement, also change over time. Consider, for example, dramatic changes witnessed in the past 50 years in response to premarital sex, pornography, abortion, homosexuality, and recreational drug use.

While all criminal acts are deviant, not all deviant acts are criminal. Generally, most societies agree on what constitute the most vicious and heinous acts of rule-breaking and punish them severely. Consider the act of murder. In every society, people are arrested, convicted, and punished for brutally murdering a neighbour. There is general agreement that such an act is not only deviant; it is criminal and should be punished by imprisonment (or worse). However, there are obvious exceptions to this rule. People who kill enemies in wartime are less likely to be punished; indeed, they may be commended as heroes instead. And in some societies, men who kill or maim their wives or daughters—committing what some call "honour crimes"—may go scot-free if the community forgives them.

Perhaps because of these blurred and shifting boundaries, many instances of deviance are difficult to categorize. Moreover, it is hard to predict how the law will be enforced and the rule-breaker will be punished. Responses to honour killings and passionate acts of revenge, for example, vary significantly from one society to another and from one time period to another. What that means is that the legal systems of different societies are quite different from each other and change over time, even with respect to extremely serious acts of rule-breaking.

Common sense tells us that acts of deviance, especially criminal acts, are harmful to society. However, Émile Durkheim pointed out, early in the history of sociology, that deviant and criminal acts likely serve a social function. Otherwise, he said, it is hard to explain why crime and punishment are universal. Crime may not be functional (or beneficial) to the victim, but it may be functional to society as a whole. For example, rule-breaking forces people to re-examine their social norms. Questioning the status quo, disagreeing with what is considered deviant, and breaking the rules can result in social change and even social progress. Beyond that, punishing crime and deviance gives law-abiding people an opportunity to close ranks—in effect, to celebrate their social cohesion and good behaviour.

With the constant change in social norms and rule-breaking, sociologists have their hands full examining the rule-breaking we observe in society and its social implications. In the chapters that follow, Myrna Dawson gives us a better understanding of the ways courts respond to domestic violence, including "femicide." Next, Tara Hahmann helps us understand the fine line that exists between "normal" superstition and pathological beliefs that support problem (or addictive) gambling. Andrew Nevin calls our attention to the new opportunities for rule-breaking provided by cyberspace, and the possible motivations behind these crimes. Then, George Pavlich explores the theoretical linkages between social inequality and the sociology of law. Finally, Eric Weissman gives us a new insight into the unfamiliar communities of homeless people.

15 Intimacy, Geography, and Justice

Myrna Dawson

Introduction

In 2000, residents of a small, rural province in eastern Canada took to the streets to protest the 10-year sentence imposed in the killing of Kimberly Ann Byrne by her male partner (Department of Justice [DOJ] 2003). There was also criticism of the judge and Crown attorney for allowing the offender, initially charged with second-degree murder, to plead guilty to a reduced charge of manslaughter (*R v Sheppard* 2001). In contrast, many viewed the sentence as substantial: 10 years is longer than the average sentence imposed for manslaughter (i.e., 5 years in 1999–2000) and is the mandatory minimum for second-degree murder, the initial charge laid in this case (DOJ 2003). Regardless of what outcome was "just," this case draws attention to two questions largely ignored in theory and research in sociology of law and punishment. First, is punishment less harsh for offenders who are violent toward an intimate (i.e., is there an "intimacy discount")? Second, does access to justice vary depending on where the crime occurs (i.e., is there justice by geography)?

The effectiveness of social and legal responses to violence has been the subject of debate internationally in recent decades. Stereotypes about intimacy and violence have been challenged, and major transformations have occurred in legislation and public policy. At one time, Canadian law made no mention of intimacy and its meaning in the criminal process. Today, the sentencing principles in the Criminal Code of Canada stipulate that the relationships offenders have with victims may act as an **aggravating factor** in determining punishments (Section 718.2 CCC). This change is positive: those who impose laws must recognize the seriousness of violence before society can effectively respond. The challenge in moving beyond legislation and policy is the dearth of reliable data documenting how jurisdictions are actually responding to violence on the ground (Doob 2011). Knowing what punishments are imposed, for whom, and where, can help us understand whether what are often viewed as "symbolic" state gestures actually impact everyday practices. The research described below begins to address these gaps, focusing on three research questions: (1) Do punishments for violent crime differ across victim–offender relationships? (2) Have there been changes over time in punishments for violent crime by victim–offender relationship? (3) Are punishments consistent across jurisdictions?

Theoretical Framework

Socio-legal and feminist theorists argue that, as intimacy increases, the presence of law will decrease; therefore, law is most likely in crimes involving strangers and least likely in crimes between intimates (Black 1976, 1993; Rapaport 1994). Relationships change over time, however, so law's presence may vary as relationships begin or end (Black, 1976; Mahoney 1991; Rapaport 1994). At the individual level, various complementary theories emphasize the role of dominant stereotypes in criminal case processing. For example, the focal concerns perspective underscores how punishments for crime may be shaped by stereotypes stemming from characteristics of the violence (e.g., intimate/non-intimate) and those involved (e.g., gender) (Steffensmeier et al. 1993, 1998). It has long been argued these stereotypes evolve through the construction of "normal crime" categories used by court actors to classify and place types of crimes along a continuum of severity (Sudnow 1965; Swigert and Farrell 1977).

However, the way in which "normal crimes" are constructed often depends on the composition of cases regularly encountered (Emerson 1983). Stereotypes may be determined by court environments (e.g., court size, caseload, case composition) and broader community characteristics (e.g., population demographics, socio-economic factors, crime rates). While most statutes/policies have province- or state-wide applicability, existing research demonstrates that justice outcomes vary across jurisdictions (Myers and Talarico 1987; Ulmer and Johnson 2004). Early research demonstrated that harsher sanctions were often imposed in rural compared to urban courts (Austin 1981; Hagan 1977; Helms and Jacob 2002; Miethe and Moore 1986). Beyond this limited and somewhat dated research, the association between location and punishment, referred to by some as the "geography of justice" (Harries and Brunn 1978), is not well understood (Ulmer and Johnson 2004).

Prior Research

A review of sociological and criminological literature reveals common stereotypes supporting the assumption that courts treat (and should treat) violence between intimates more leniently than violence between those sharing more distant relationships (Dawson 2006). Despite this, intimacy is seldom examined as a key variable in criminal justice research; typically, its best available proxy—victim–defendant relationship—is more often included as a control variable in examinations of more commonly studied characteristics such as gender or race/ethnicity. Moreover, although intimacy and gender are interconnected in stereotypes about violence, their combined influence on law has also largely been ignored (Dawson 2016). Similarly, Tonry (2007) has argued that few appear concerned by the geographical problem in which similar crimes may be treated differently across jurisdictions (p. 369). However, given changing constructions of intimacy in law in the past several decades, and legislative and policy initiatives targeting violence against women in particular, understanding what groups have been impacted by these changes, where, and why, is integral to ensuring consistency in access to justice.

The Current Study

Data are drawn from an ongoing project that documents homicides in the province of Ontario. Information is collected on victim, accused, and case characteristics with particular emphasis on victim–offender relationship and criminal justice outcomes. Data sources include coroner's records, police, Crown attorney and court files as well as media reports. Quantitative data has been collected for the total population of homicides that occurred from 1974 to 2013—a period of over four decades. It represents one of the few richly detailed datasets that allows researchers to link case characteristics to punishments for violent crime over a significant period of time. Furthermore, using homicide as the unit of analysis to examine responses to crime is more reliable because reporting and recording bias is minimal compared to other types of violence. Qualitative analysis of court documents and media reports are also being used to answer a variety of research questions about the legal and social construction of these crimes. Finally, current data collection is compiling community-level characteristics to allow for multilevel analyses of the effect of **micro-** and **macro-level factors** on punishment outcomes. Below, using data on case characteristics, several core questions are examined, describing highlights from research findings and several avenues being pursued in current and future research.

Research Findings

The Intimacy Discount

Criminal justice responses to violent crime do vary depending on the degree of intimacy between victims and defendants; however, the association depends on the type of relationship and the criminal justice decision-making stage examined (e.g., charge, sentence). Examining cases disposed in Toronto from 1974 to 1996, results demonstrated that, compared to stranger homicides, defendants closest to their victims—intimate partners—were significantly less likely to be charged with first-degree murder, more likely to resolve their cases through guilty pleas, and more likely to receive shorter sentences (Dawson 2004a, 2004b). However, not all intimate partner relationships were treated equally. Subsequent analyses showed that, in cases of intimate femicide, offenders who killed estranged female partners received significantly longer sentences than those who killed current female partners (Dawson 2003). Those who killed other family members also received shorter sentences compared to strangers. However, there were few differences in the treatment of those who killed friends, acquaintances, and strangers.

Does Intimacy Still Matter?

Legal responses to violence in the context of intimacy have varied significantly over time, paralleling legislative and policy changes (Dawson 2012a). Initial analyses of cases disposed in Toronto courts compared two periods: (1) 1974–1983: the period prior to/including the introduction of pro-charging/pro-prosecution policies in cases of domestic violence; and (2) 1984–1996: the period after policy implementation. Results showed that defendants in intimate partner homicides were more likely to plead guilty than other defendants in both periods. Among cases sent to trial, however, these accused were more likely to be found guilty in recent years than those who killed non-intimates compared to outcomes in early years. Moreover, intimate partner homicide cases were less likely to result in murder convictions in the early period, but this changed in more recent years when no difference was documented. Those who killed intimate partners were now equally likely to be convicted of murder, rather than the less-serious offence of manslaughter, suggesting some support for a reduction in the intimacy discount.

More recently, given international attention to femicide, particularly in Latin America and among missing and murdered Aboriginal women in Canada, subsequent analyses examined the treatment of Ontario femicide cases over time. Data from 1974 to 2013 allowed for the examination of sanctions imposed following sentencing amendments in 1996 (Dawson 2015). Results showed that first-degree murder charges and murder convictions were significantly less likely to occur in the early period (1974–1985) compared to the most recent time period (1997–2013). Further, femicide cases disposed in earlier years resulted in significantly shorter sentences than cases disposed in more recent years. It could be argued, however, that increasingly punitive sanctions for femicide are simply a product of increasing punitiveness overall. Thus, a similar analysis was conducted for male victims that also showed a significant, albeit weaker, increase in sentences. Qualitative analyses of sentencing decisions also documented greater judicial emphasis on intimacy as an aggravating factor since sentencing amendments in 1996 (Dawson 2016). However, cases involving women killed in these contexts continue to be treated more leniently than women killed in other contexts (e.g., acquaintances, strangers).

Current and Future Research

While the above research is limited in focus to one jurisdiction and case-level characteristics, these findings contribute to theoretical development in the sociology of law and punishment by enhancing our understanding of the role played by intimacy in determining punishments for violence over a significant period of time. Many questions remain, however, not the least of which is whether the intimacy discount varies by geography and whether stereotypes about intimacy and violence affect these outcomes (Dawson 2006, 2016).

Intimacy and Geography

One explanation offered for perceptions of injustice in the case of Kimberly Ann Byrne, cited above, can be linked to the "normal crimes" framework (Sudnow 1965). It was argued that since intimate partner homicide "is relatively rare in PEI, it is possible that the same offence and sentence would not have received the same attention in some of Canada's cities" (DOJ 2003). Recall that the way in which "normal crimes" are constructed may depend, in part, on the composition of cases regularly encountered and, therefore, one might hypothesize that "more frequency means less severity" (Emerson 1983). Put another way, crimes encountered more often (e.g., family violence) may be seen as "normal crimes" and attract less serious sanctions whereas those that are less frequent (e.g., stranger violence) are less normalized and reacted to with greater severity. Despite the intuitiveness of this argument, research has yet to examine this question, including how intimacy and geography may interact with other social identities (e.g., gender, age, race/ethnicity, sexual orientation) to impact the construction of and response to "normal crimes." Current research using Ontario homicide data is documenting jurisdictional patterns by court and community characteristics to begin to address this gap. Preliminary analysis suggests sanctions in rural courts are more severe than in urban courts (Dawson 2012b), consistent with earlier Canadian research (e.g., Hagan 1977).

Challenging Stereotypes

Little research has examined the empirical validity of criminal stereotypes and their role in criminal justice decision-making beyond those related to race/ethnicity or gender (Auerhahn 2007; Steen et al. 2005). With one exception (Miethe 1987), the many stereotypes related to intimacy remain unexamined; thus, their role in determining how law responds to violence or the way in which gender may affect this relationship remains unknown. A small exploratory study underscores the importance of such research. Contrary to the stereotype that intimate partner homicides are spontaneous "crimes of passion," evidence of premeditation/intent was more frequent in these cases compared to other types of homicides (Dawson 2006). However, despite greater evidence of premeditation/intent and similar case characteristics, intimate partner homicides resulted in shorter sentences overall compared to other homicides. More qualitative data and analyses are required to shed light on these preliminary findings and analyses of sentencing decisions is one move in that direction.

References

Auerhahn, K. (2007). Just another crime? Examining disparity in homicide sentencing. *The Sociological Quarterly* 48: 277–313.

Austin, T. (1981). "The influence of court locations on type of criminal sentence: The rural–urban factor." *Journal of Criminal Justice* 9: 305–16.

Black, D. (1993). *The Social Structure of Right and Wrong*. San Diego: Academic Press.

Black, D. (1976). *The Behavior of Law*. New York: Academic Press.

Dawson, M. (2016). Intimacy, gender and homicide: The validity and utility of common stereotypes in law. Chapter 2 in *Gender, Murder and Responsibility: An International Perspective*, edited by K. Fitz-Gibbons and S. Walklate (Routledge; in press).

Dawson, M. (2015). Punishing femicide: Criminal justice responses to the killing of women over four decades. (*Current Sociology*, in press).

Dawson, M. (2012a). Intimacy, homicide, and punishment: Examining court outcomes over three decades. *Australian and New Zealand Journal of Criminology* 45(3): 400–22.

Dawson, M. (2012b). Justice by geography? Exploring spatial variation in official responses to violence in one Canadian province. Paper presented in the TC Beirne School of Law Seminar Series, University of Queensland, Brisbane.

Dawson, M. (2006). Intimacy, violence and the law: Exploring stereotypes about victim–defendant relationship and violent crime. *Journal of Criminal Law and Criminology* 96(4): 1417–50.

Dawson, M. (2004a). "Rethinking the boundaries of intimacy at the end of the century: The role of victim–defendant relationship in criminal justice decision-making over time." *Law & Society Review* 38(1): 105–38.

Dawson, M. (2004b). *Criminal Justice Outcomes in Intimate Partner and Non-Intimate Partner Homicide Cases.* Ottawa: Department of Justice Canada.

Dawson, M. (2003). "The cost of "lost" intimacy: The effect of relationship state on criminal justice decision-making." *The British Journal of Criminology* 43(4): 689–709.

Department of Justice Canada. (2003). *Report on Sentencing for Manslaughter in Cases Involving Intimate Relationships.* Ottawa: Department of Justice Canada.

Doob A (2011). The unfinished work of the Canadian Sentencing Commission. *Canadian Journal of Criminology and Criminal Justice* (July): 279–97.

Emerson, R.M. (1983). Holistic effects in social control decision-making. *Law and Society Review* 17(3): 425–55.

Hagan, J. and N. O'Donnel (1978). Sexual stereotyping and judicial sentencing. A legal test of the sociological wisdom. *The Canadian Journal of Sociology* 3(3): 309–19.

Hagan, John. (1977). Criminal justice in rural and urban communities: A study of the bureaucratization of justice. *Social Forces* 55(3): 597–612.

Harries, K.D. and S.D. Brunn. (1978). *The Geography of Laws and Justice.* New York/London: Praeger.

Helms, R. and D. Jacobs. (2002). The Political Context of Sentencing: An Analysis of Community and Individual Determinants. *Social Forces* 81(2): 577–604.

Mahoney M.R. (1991–1992) Legal images of battered women: Redefining the issue of separation. *Michigan Law Review* 90(1): 1–94.

Miethe, T.D. (1987) Stereotypical conceptions and criminal processing: The case of the victim–offender relationship. *Justice Quarterly* 4(4): 571–93.

Miethe, T. and C. Moore. (1986). Racial differences in criminal processing: The consequences of model selection on conclusions about differential treatment. *The Sociological Quarterly* 27(2): 217–37.

Myers, M.A. and S. Talarico. (1987). *The Social Contexts of Sentencing.* New York: Springer-Verlag.

Rapaport, E. (1994). The death penalty and the domestic discount. Pp. 224–51 in *The Public Nature of Private Violence,* edited by M.A. Fineman and R. Mykitiuk. New York: Routledge.

Steen, S., R.L. Engen, and R.R. Gainey. (2005). Images of danger and culpability: Racial stereotyping, case processing, and criminal sentencing. *Criminology* 43(2): 435–68.

Steffensmeier, D., J. Ulmer, and J. Kramer. (1998). The interaction of race, gender, and age in criminal sentencing: The punishment cost of being young, black, and male. *Criminology* 36(4): 763–98.

Steffensmeier, D., J.H. Kramer, and C. Streifel. (1993). Gender and imprisonment decisions. *Criminology* 31: 411–46.

Sudnow, D. (1965). Normal crimes: Sociological features of the penal code in a public defender office. *Social Problems* 12: 255–79.

Swigert, V.L. and R.A. Farrell. (1977). Normal homicides and the law. *American Sociological Review* 42(1): 16–32.

Tonry, M. (2007). Looking back to see the future of punishment in America. *Social Research* 74(2): 353–78.

Ulmer, J.T. and B.D. Johnson. (2004). Sentencing in context: A multilevel analysis. *Criminology* 42(1): 137–77.

16 Modern Superstition and Moderate Risk and Problem Slot Machine Gamblers

Tara Hahmann

Introduction

A relationship between gambling-related cognitive distortions, including superstitious beliefs (Toneatto 1999, 2002; Joukhador, Blaszczynski, and MacCallum 2004), and problem gambling has been established in the gambling literature with a psychological focus (Goodie and Fortune 2013; Ladouceur 2004). **Cognitive distortions** are "erroneous assumptions about the degree of control over chance determined outcomes," and they are also referred to as irrational or erroneous beliefs in the gambling literature (Toneatto 1999:1594). Superstitious beliefs that infer causal connections between independent events (Joukhador, Blaszczynski, and MacCallum 2004:171) are a key component of these distortions. Indeed, these distortions are factored into the treatment of problem gambling (Fortune and Goodie 2012) and are well researched (Goodie and Fortune 2013). A key assumption is that these cognitive distortions are fully believed by heavy and problem gamblers (PGs), though the nature of these beliefs requires further exploration reflecting on sociological insight.

Literature Review

Gambling-related cognitive distortions are reported as a key component in the development, maintenance, and treatment of problem gambling (Goodie and Fortune 2013). A psychological focus on cognition infers a powerful relationship between beliefs and decision making. As Toneatto (1999:1594) explained, gamblers make "decisions that can be powerfully influenced by cognitive biases, distortions in reasoning and errors in judgement." That is, PGs believe there is a way to predict, manipulate, or otherwise know the outcome of a future gambling event where such outcomes are unknown and impossible to decipher. Toneatto (1999, 2002) outlined the varied cognitive distortions all related to this central belief of predicting and/or determining a gambling outcome, asserting that PGs possess false beliefs devoid of reality.

The dearth of research originating in psychology makes two important assumptions: (1) cognitive distortions are linked to problem-gambling behaviour (Toneatto 2002; Goodie and Fortune 2013) and (2) PGs believe their beliefs are valid and practices are efficacious (Griffiths and Bingham 2005; Toneatto 2002; Walker 1992). Dwelling on the second point, the idea that gamblers infer a causal connection between events not logically connected is not a new one. In an earlier study by Henslin (1967), he found that a sample of craps players believed that they could influence the outcome of a game. He claimed that "they also moved within the framework of a system of magical belief," maintaining belief [in] and/or practice in the control over objects or events by verbal or non-verbal gestures (words or actions) where there [was] no empirical (natural or logical) connection between the gesture as cause and the object or event as effect (318).

Henslin (1967) reported that his participants felt that they had control over gambling outcomes with intermittent reinforcement supporting this belief. According to Oldman (1974), Henslin's (1967) perspective fails to acknowledge the possibility that the game, for some gamblers, is something qualitatively different from the game as analyzed by scientific discourse. In a similar vein, Reith (2002) warns against non-contextual understanding whereby these beliefs are said to be reflective of an individual disorder of cognition. Relegating these beliefs to an irrational category assumes a false or misunderstanding on the part of gamblers and thus fails to consider that these beliefs are not necessarily fully believed (ibid).

Reith's (2002) point echoes Campbell's (1996), which takes aim at psychological theories that equate certain beliefs to magic while failing to address their nature. Campbell's (1996) theory of modern superstition, with its sociological focus, could be applied to gambling related cognitive distortions. Defining superstition is a complex task according to Campbell (1996), as the precise nature of these beliefs evolves over time, making them culturally and historically grounded. He warns that attempts to define this phenomenon as irrational or erroneous lead to intense philosophical issues with varied and contrasting perspectives. At a basic level, most psychological theories cannot be applied to the study of modern superstition given the assumption of fixed belief in the efficacy of ritual practices (ibid).

Campbell (1996 cited in Gallagher and Lewis 2001:2) goes on to describe modern superstitions as beliefs that are:

> (1) not integrated into the cultural customs and social institutions and consequently

are highly individualistic; (2) unrelated to a system of belief and therefore lack a rationale; (3) usually denied by its practitioners as having any influence over the outcome of events.

To elaborate on point two, when individuals are asked about their practices and beliefs, they are unable to explain why they take the form that they do and typically recognize them as unjustifiable (Campbell 1996:156). The final point speaks to the concept of *half-belief*, a term coined by McKellar (1952:320) meant to denote the act of "intellectually reject(ing) a superstition nevertheless allow(ing) it to influence thinking and actions." Put differently, half-belief manifests the qualities of belief together with the qualities of disbelief (Garwood 1963 cited in Campbell 1996:158).

Superstition, then, serves as a ritual by becoming an instrumental act to affirm faith in **instrumental activism**, a value widely supported in the western world (Parsons 1965). In other words, it is deviant to give up in situations where you have little control; rather, you do something (i.e., assert agency), despite having little faith that the ritual act will lead to the desired end result (Campbell 1996:162). In what follows, Campbell's (1996) definition of modern superstition is assessed against the beliefs of moderate risk and PGs.

Methods

Sample

A total of 43 moderate-risk (35 per cent) or problem (65 per cent) slot machine gamblers were recruited for this study, and screened using the Problem Gambling Severity Index. Several studies have identified irrational beliefs in samples of slot machine gamblers (Walker 1992; Joukhador, Blaszczynski, and MacCallum 2004), prompting the focus here on PGs with this game type preference. The sample composition (Table 16.1) includes a high percentage of those aged 41 years or older (67 per cent), who engaged in slot machine gambling exclusively (86 per cent), and who had never been married (42 per cent). Most had some

TABLE 16.1 Sample Composition*

	N = 43
Variables	
Female	46.5
Age:	
21–30 years	14.0
31–40 years	18.6
41–50 years	34.9
51–60 years	20.9
≥60 years	11.6
Marital Status:	
Never married	41.9
Married	18.6
Separated	4.7
Divorced	20.9
Widowed	2.3
Cohabitating	11.6
Education Level:	
Secondary	25.6
Trade School	9.3
Some College	4.7
College Diploma	27.9
Some University	9.3
University Degree	14.0
Masters/Professional Degree	9.3
Income Range:	
Less than $20,000	23.3
$20,001–$40,000	32.6
$40,001–$60,000	32.6
$60,001–$100,000	11.6
Ethnic Background:	
Aboriginal	2.3
British Isles	18.6
Caribbean	14.0
Eastern/Other European	4.6
Southern European	25.6
Western European	7.0
Latin/Central/South American	2.3
West and East/South East Asian	14.0
South Asian	11.6
Canadian Born:	
Yes	55.8
No	44.2
Problem Gambling Severity Index Score:	
Moderate-Risk Level	34.9
Problem Level	65.1
Slots Exclusively:	
Yes	86.0
No	14.0

*Statistics are reported as means (SD) and percentages.

post-secondary education (75 per cent) and reported a gross annual income lower than $40,000 (56 per cent).

Analysis

Interviews were audio taped, transcribed verbatim, de-identified, and coded for emergent themes using NVivo qualitative data analysis software. Data was coded using open and axial coding techniques. Open coding involved familiarization with the data and the assignment of codes pertaining to emerging concepts or ideas (Glaser and Strauss 1967). Axial coding helped organize data into thematic categories informed by Campbell's (1996) three point criteria.

Findings

1. Individualized Beliefs: Lacking Social Prescription

While the beliefs shared a root similarity, they were highly individualized: this sample of gamblers held diverse beliefs and engaged in diversified actions—with no two participants holding the same set of beliefs or practising the same set of actions. Table 16.2 exemplifies belief type diversity across participants using Toneatto's (2002:193) categorization of cognitions from which the belief types and definitions were drawn.

The beliefs and accompanying actions lacked social prescription. That is, they did not appear to be a form of collective ritual action, thereby sustaining themselves. The bricks-and-mortar casino is a place where these gamblers congregate and may share a common interest, but their superstitious beliefs and actions are not in line with the expectations of others and took place whether others observed or not. In fact, participants were often hesitant to discuss their personal beliefs or superstitious actions with others, even those with whom they shared the activity (Table 16.3). In the end, social expectation remained unrelated to these beliefs and practices which are dissimilar from socially prescribed superstitions found in traditional societies.

TABLE 16.2 Gambling Beliefs: Illustrative Examples

Selected Belief Types and Definitions*	Illustrative Quotation
Magnified Gambling Skill: Overrated ability to win, exaggerated self-confidence despite persistent losing; efforts to acquire special knowledge and develop gambling systems.	I tend to go during less busy times as well, because I think the slots might be looser or programmed to pay out more at a certain time, when there is less people. Um, if possible, if I have time, I'd rather go from Monday to Friday as opposed to a Saturday or Sunday.
Behavioural Superstitions: Certain actions or rituals can increase the probability of winning (e.g., seating preferences at bingo); verbal (e.g., verbal encouragement) and nonverbal (e.g., rubbing hands) behaviour during actual play of a game (e.g., horse race) believed to modify the outcome.	Sometimes, okay, I'll be sitting there, and you know people like press the button. And sometimes it stops like half way, I don't know. Yes, and I will just like go start and I stop it twice; tap it twice. And then, you know, sometimes I win.
Gambler's Fallacy: Losses interpreted as an indication that a win is imminent and often resulting in chasing.	No. You are just thinking I am going to win and I am going to get my money back and the more you lose, the more you put in, thinking you are going to win, right? So (you continue to gamble so that) you could get your money back.

continued

Over-interpretation of Cues: Over-interpreted ambiguous stimuli to guide decisions to gamble or to persist (e.g. bodily sensations, intuitions, omens, unusual events).	Yeah sometimes I do get a feeling, and it really affects my mood, because sometimes I will (sense a win coming). But I think in my head like, "Maybe I should have gone sooner." Or, "Is this the right time? Now should I like hangout at the casino . . ." like I get all these thoughts. "Should I hang out at the casino for a bit? Or should I go to the machine right now?" And I'm like, I don't know, like I feel like there's all these variables that are very, very important. Like, "Should I leave now?" Or, "Should I have left sooner?". . . Sometimes I have a bad feeling, but I still go anyway. Yeah (I still go) because you never know.
Luck as Contagion: Success in other areas of their life generalizes to success at gambling; consequently, frequency of gambling or size of their wagers may increase; may also believe other gamblers bring either good or bad luck.	And I really think sometimes it has to do with who you are with at the casino, you know, like if you go by the luck thing and all that sort of stuff.

Source: *See Toneatto (2002:193) for his complete list of cognitive distortions.

TABLE 16.3 Meeting the Criteria for Modern Superstition

Campbell's (1996) Criteria for Modern Superstition	**Illustrative Quotation**
1. Beliefs Lacking Social Prescription	No (I don't share my beliefs and practices). Because I think people think you're probably stupid to think like that or whatever. But people do (think that way), right. A lot of people think that way, but they won't admit it and they won't say stuff, right. I don't know. They probably, they just feel shy or they just think that you're going to tease them and laugh at them or something like that. He (my friend whom I gamble with) doesn't (know my beliefs). If I said anything, he'll just turn around, he won't even listen to me and probably think that I am losing it or something (laughs).
2. Recognizing Beliefs as Unjustifiable	I don't know if it works (my superstition to select particular machines) or not, but . . . it's something, I guess. In the worst case if it does nothing, at least you've tried!
3. Half-beliefs	No, I don't actually believe (in my superstitions). Few people really believe in their strategies.

2. Recognizing Beliefs as Unjustifiable

Beliefs and practices lacked a concrete rationale, leaving participants unable to give clear reasons for the specific form of their beliefs and actions. Why they partook in certain practices or held certain beliefs was not easily explained, leading to statements including "I do not know," "It is just my superstition." These participants admitted their beliefs lacked a rationale, but they needed to try "something" (Table 16.3). They used phrases such as "maybe," "I think," "I don't know," and "that's crazy" when reflecting on their beliefs and actions recognizing them as unjustifiable.

3. Half-Beliefs

The lack of faith in the efficacy of their actions was clear when they contradicted previous discussions of superstitions by admitting their ineffectiveness. Although participants seemed to allow superstitions to influence their thoughts and actions, they ultimately rejected them on an intellectual level, admitting that they were untenable. These half-beliefs are interesting: the PGs both used and rejected them (Table 16.3). Half-beliefs demonstrate these gamblers' tenuous connection to gambling related beliefs, unconvinced of the instrumentality of their own efforts to procure or determine an outcome.

Discussion

The study challenges the prevailing perspective on gambling-related beliefs given their alignment with Campbell's (1996) criteria for modern superstition. First, these gamblers displayed a number of diverse beliefs and ritual actions detached from covenantal associations. They were more likely to coordinate their behaviour by "pledging themselves to specific reciprocal activity without pledging to one another's well-being" (Robbins and Bromley 1992:5), making these beliefs and actions particularly modern. Second, these actions appeared unrelated to any belief system and, as such, lacked a concrete rationale. For the most part, they could not formulate concrete reasons why their beliefs or actions took a particular form; if they did provide a legitimation, it was characteristically "not integrated into an institutional framework" (Campbell 1996:156). In other words, these gamblers did not attempt to justify their actions by relating them to other beliefs and, for the most part, when asked, could not explain their origin. When further questioned about their beliefs, they readily admitted they were "unjustifiable." Third, they went so far as to deny the efficacy of their actions and the legitimacy of their beliefs.

The combination of these features raises some questions about existing psychological explanations of these gambling-related beliefs. A key misgiving of psychological theory is the implication that people actually believe in their superstition (Campbell 1996). As noted, most modern practitioners of superstition, including the study's PGs, are not prepared to declare that they believe they have control or absolute insight contrary to prevailing claims that they do (Toneatto 2002; Fortune and Goodie 2012). In fact, they distanced themselves from their superstitions in several ways, for example, choosing words to suggest uncertainty or contradicting previous superstitious statements by denying their ability to control the outcome. This calls into question the relationship between beliefs and problem gambling behaviour; these particular half-beliefs seem to drive ritualistic behaviour, not necessarily problematic behaviour.

Campbell's insight into belief and ritual activity with a cultural focus is highly relevant to the moderate risk and PG. This activistic orientation, grounded in the pervasive value of instrumental activism (Parsons 1965), may be more pronounced in this population. That is, a group displaying what is described as deviant behaviour (King 1990) may be more closely tied to this widely shared value. Abt, McGurrin, and Smith (1985) echoed this sentiment in describing gamblers as even more conventional and ritualistic than non-gamblers. The study suggests a cultural link to gambling belief and ritual action, and sheds light on "half-belief." These beliefs are likely non-rational, rather than irrational, and thusly just as "normal" as many other belief types. Further research should unpack the nature of these beliefs, including their cultural underpinnings, in order to ascertain more clearly if and how these half-beliefs and associated actions are tied to problem gambling.

Conclusion

This study suggests new ways of understanding gamblers' beliefs. Although this study offers a cultural explanation for the ritualistic behaviours of this sample of moderate risk and PGs, it does not provide insight into how these half-beliefs and ritual activity may lead to problem gambling. In trying to understand this link, future studies should apply Campbell's (1996) framework to a larger representative sample of individuals experiencing problem gambling.

References

Abt, V., M.C. McGurrin, and J.F. Smith. 1985. "Towards a Synoptic Model of Gambling Behavior." *Journal of Gambling Behavior* 1(2):79–88.

Campbell, C. 1996. "Half-Belief and the Paradox of Ritual Instrumental Activism: A Theory of Modern Superstition." *The British Journal of Sociology* 47(1):151–66.

Fortune, E.E., and A.S. Goodie. 2012. "Cognitive Distortions as a Component and Treatment Focus of Pathological Gambling: a Review." *Psychology of Addictive Behaviors* 26(2):298–310.

Gallagher, T., and J. Lewis. 2001. "Rationalists, Fatalists, and the Modern Superstitious: Test-Taking in Introductory Sociology." *Sociological Inquiry* 71(1):1–12.

Garwood, K. 1963. "Superstition and Half Belief." *New Society* 18:120–1.

Glaser, B.G, and A.L. Strauss. 1967. *The Discovery of Grounded Theory: Strategies for Qualitative Research.* Chicago, IL: Aldine Publishing Company.

Goodie, A.S., and Erica E. Fortune. 2013. "Measuring Cognitive Distortions in Pathological Gambling: Review and Meta-Analyses." *Psychology of Addictive Behaviors* 27(3):730–43.

Griffiths, M., and C. Bingham. 2005. "A Study of Superstitious Beliefs among Bingo Players." *Journal of Gambling Issues* 13. doi:10.4309/jgi.2005.13.7.

Henslin, J.M. 1967. "Craps and Magic." *American Journal of Sociology* 73(3):316–30.

Joukhador, J., A. Blaszczynski, and F. MacCallum. 2004. "Superstitious Beliefs in Gambling Among Problem and Non-Problem Gamblers: Preliminary Data." *Journal of Gambling Studies* 20(2):171–80.

King, K.M. 1990. Neutralizing Marginally Deviant Behavior: Bingo Players and Superstition. *Journal of Gambling Studies* 6(1):43–61.

Ladouceur, R. 2004. "Perceptions among Pathological and Nonpathological Gamblers." *Addictive Behaviors* 29:555–65.

Ladouceur, R., and M. Walker. 1998. "Cognitive Approach to Understanding and Treating Pathological Gambling." Pp. 588–601 in *Comprehensive Clinical Psychology*, edited by A.S. Bellack and M. Hersen. New York: Pergamon.

Ladouceur, R., and M. Walker. 1996. "A Cognitive Perspective on Gambling." Pp. 89–120 in *Trends in Cognitive and Behavioral Therapies*, edited by M. Salkovskis. New York: Wiley.

McKeller, P. 1952. *A Textbook of Human Psychology.* London: Cohen and West.

Oldman, D. 1974. "Chance and Skill: A Study of Roulette." *Sociology* 8:407–26.

Parsons, T. 1965. *Structure and Process in Modern Societies*. New York: The Free Press.

Reith, G. 2002. *The Age of Chance: Gambling in Western Culture.* New York: Routledge.

Robbins, T., and D. Bromley. 1992. "Social Experimentation and the Significance of American New Religions: A Focused Review Essay." Pp. 1–28 in *Research in the Social Scientific Study of Religion*, Vol. 4, edited by M. Lynn, and D. Moberg. Greenwich, Conn.: JAI Press.

Toneatto, T. 2002. "Cognitive Therapy for Problem Gambling." *Cognitive and Behavioral Practice* 9:191–9. doi: 10.1016/S1077-7229(02)80049-9.

Toneatto, T. 1999. "Cognitive Psychopathology of Problem Gambling." *Substance Use & Misuse* 34(11):1593–604. doi: 10.3109/10826089909039417.

Walker, M.B. 1992. "Irrational Thinking Among Slot Machine Players." *Journal of GamblingStudies* 8:245–61.

17 Cyber-Psychopathy: An Expression of Dark E-Personality

Andrew D. Nevin

Introduction

We are living in an increasingly online society, and our substantial time spent immersed in digital environments has influenced our psychosocial development, shaping expressions of the self both on and off the Internet. Some scholars suggest that cyberspace is a distinctive social context that serves as another platform for self-reflection and self-maintenance, which culminates in virtual identities and personalities that can differ from those in the "real" world (Jewkes and Sharp, 2003; Turkle, 1984). Shifts in personality traits when online are not uncommon, as research has documented heightened extraversion and reduced shyness when individuals are using the Internet (Maldonado, Mora, Garcia, and Edipo, 2001; Stritzke, Nguyen, and Durkin, 2004). These ideas represent a theoretical framework of **context-dependent personality**, which suggests that trait expression is, in part, based on situational cues and environmental factors, rather than being completely stable across all social contexts (Allport, 1937; Kenrick, McCreath, Govern, King, and Bordin, 1990; Mischel, 1973, 1977).

Expressions of online personality ("e-personalities") are not universal among all Internet users. On the one hand, there is potential for positive behavioural outcomes such as more honest self-disclosure in anonymous conversations with others online (Joinson, 2001). However, there is also the possibility for expressing e-personalities that are "less restrained, a little bit on the dark side, and decidedly sexier" which can manifest in harmful or malicious behaviours, such as cyberbullying (Aboujaoude, 2011:20). Such "dark" online personalities may emerge because of several conditions that make cyberspace a unique social context: anonymity, lack of non-verbal cues, asynchronicity, and less salient norms, which together appear to incite perceptions that the Internet is like the Wild West—lawless, open, and ready to be explored and conquered (Taylor, 2003). These characteristics contribute to a diminished sense of accountability and less fear of punishment (Demetriou and Silke, 2003; Suler, 2004), weaker moral values and reduced empathy (Todd, 2014; Whittier, 2013), and "psychological distancing," which makes online victims appear as abstractions who do not actually experience harm (Crowell, Narvaez, and Gomberg, 2005; Trope and Liberman, 2010). In this sense, the Internet can facilitate disinhibition and self-compartmentalization, which together may neutralize morality or responsibility within the online context (Suler, 2004). Some Internet users have reported having a "weaker online conscience" and being "detached from reality" when engaging in misbehaviours they would not normally do offline (Selwyn, 2008, pp. 457–8), making their shifts in conduct online appear "similar to real-life Jekylls and Hydes" (Denegri-Knott and Taylor, 2005:94).

For the present study, dark e-personality is conceptualized in terms of expressions of psychopathy on the Internet. Psychopathy describes a personality construct made up of certain traits that emphasize maintaining power and control over others (see Table 17.1). Psychopathic individuals typically prioritize personal gain, show little regard for others, have a reduced capacity to make pro-social moral judgments, and are frequently involved in anti-social behaviours (Cleckley, 1976; Hare, 1991; Levenson, Kiehl, and Fitzpatrick, 1995). While bona fide psychopathy is rare in the general population,

TABLE 17.1 Psychopathic Traits and Characteristics

Glibness/Superficial Charm
Grandiose Sense of Self-Worth
Need for Stimulation
Pathological Lying
Conning/Manipulativeness
Lack of Remorse or Guilt
Shallow Affect
Callousness/Lack of Empathy
Parasitic Lifestyle
Poor Behavioural Controls
Promiscuous Sexual Behaviour
Early Behaviour Problems
Lack of Realistic Goals
Impulsivity
Irresponsibility
Failure to Accept Responsibility
Many Short-Term Relationships
Juvenile Delinquency
Revocation of Conditional Release
Criminal Versatility

Source: Based on Hare, 1991.

it is possible to measure subclinical psychopathy as the presence of such traits independent of a full classification (Babiak and Hare, 2006; Coid and Yang, 2008; Widom, 1977).

Previous research has found that higher levels of dark personality traits (e.g., psychopathy) are associated with engagement in interpersonal online misconduct such as cyberbullying, cyber-aggression, and flaming behaviours (Ciucci, Baroncelli, Franchi, Golmaryami, and Frick, 2014; Fanti, Demetriou, and Hawa, 2012; Pabian, De Backer, and Vandebosch, 2015). Specifically, psychopathic traits are important characteristics of the personality profiles of cyberbullies (Goodboy and Martin, 2015), while higher levels of sadism have been linked to trolling and extreme violence in video games (Buckels, Trapnell, and Paulhus, 2014; Greitemeyer, 2015).

Overall, the purpose of this exploratory study is to investigate whether the Internet facilitates increased expressions of psychopathic e-personality in some Internet users. I empirically test this "**cyber-psychopathy**" concept while exploring the relationship between dark e-personality and online misconduct behaviours.

Methodology

This quantitative study uses a web-based survey to address the primary research questions (Table 17.2). Self-report data were collected from adult Internet users (N=408) who answered both online and offline psychopathic personality inventories in order to allow for controlled score comparisons between the two social contexts. Measures of cyber-psychopathy and offline psychopathy are the independent variables used to predict tendencies to engage in online misconduct behaviours.

Psychopathy is measured with an adapted version of the Levenson Self-Report Psychopathy Scale (LSRP; Levenson et al., 1995), which is made up of 26 items that employ a four-point Likert-type scale for (dis)agreement.[1] For the current analysis, the LSRP is modified for the purpose of controlling for social

TABLE 17.2 Research Questions

RQ1:	Is there a statistically significant difference between online and offline measures of psychopathy? Are cyber-psychopathy scores higher than offline psychopathy scores?
RQ2:	What are the social predictors of being in the subsample that increases in psychopathic expression when on the Internet?
RQ3:	What is the relationship between cyber-psychopathy scores and the likelihood of engaging in online misconduct behaviours?

context; that is, there are two different scales used that apply to either being on the Internet (Cyber-Psychopathy Scale; CPS) or not being on the Internet (Offline Psychopathy Scale; OPS). Both scales rely on context-specifying instructions: the OPS uses the same items as the LSRP while the CPS modifies the items by adding variations of "when online" or "when on the Internet" in order to make congruent online/offline item counterparts (see Blumer and Doering, 2012).

For the present study, online misconduct is conceptualized as *minor or major* transgressions that are commonly deemed as wrong or improper, and cross either *social or legal boundaries.* Ten misconduct behaviours (Table 17.3) are represented by a series of hypothetical vignette scenarios assessed with a follow-up question: "How likely would you be to behave in a similar manner as the protagonist?" The misconduct behaviours are added together as a composite score of overall/average online misconduct tendency (OMT).

TABLE 17.3 Online Misconduct Behaviours

Cyber-stalking
Digital Piracy
Trolling
Flaming
Online Deception
Cyber-Vandalism
Internet Addiction
Reading Others' Emails
Misuse of Digital Information
Online Sexual Pushiness

Findings

A comparison of scores from the CPS and OPS scales demonstrates that there are statistically significant differences between cyber-psychopathy and offline psychopathy, as well as between the genders (RQ1). First of all, there is a differential of 2.2 points in the overall sample in favour of cyber-psychopathy, which represents a 5 per cent average increase in psychopathic expression on the Internet.[2] Males have higher mean scores than females in cyber-psychopathy and offline psychopathy by 5.5 and 3.3 points, respectively. When comparing psychopathy differentials between the genders, males have a differential of 3.4 points which represents a 7 per cent increase in psychopathic expression online, whereas females have only a 3 per cent increase online. Figure 17.1 shows graphical representation of the psychopathy differentials between these social contexts.[3]

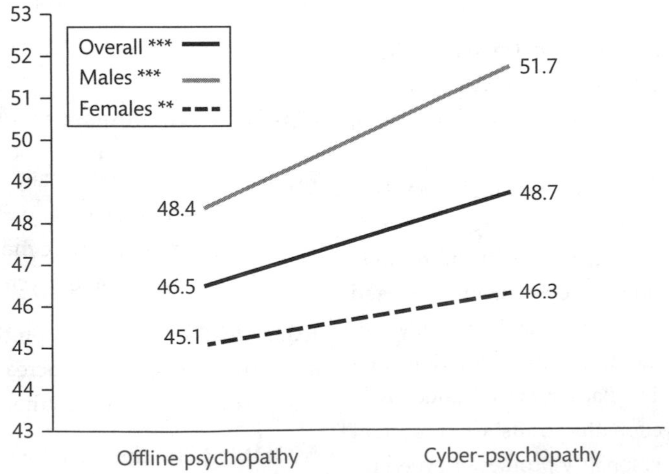

FIGURE 17.1 Psychopathy Scores between Offline and Online Contexts (n=408)

In the overall sample, 20 per cent of participants (n=83) are classified as significantly increasing in their psychopathic expression when on the Internet, with the gender difference being that 31 per cent of males increase online compared to only 12 per cent of females. This classification of "increase online" is determined by individuals having cyber-psychopathy scores that are higher than their offline psychopathy scores by at least one standard deviation of the differential variable (Table 17.4). Among this subgroup the differential between cyber-psychopathy and offline psychopathy is 11 points (24 per cent increase), showing that some individuals are more susceptible to heightened cyber-psychopathy. Logistic regression was then utilized to determine the characteristics of this subgroup who increase in psychopathic expression online compared to those who do not increase online, while controlling for various social predictors (RQ2). This analysis showed that individuals who have substantial increases in psychopathic expression on the Internet can be characterized by the following general profile: being male, being younger in age, and having stronger online skills.[4] Specifically, males are 4.8 times more likely than females to be in this category.

Moreover, do higher levels of cyber-psychopathy predict a greater likelihood of engaging in online misconduct behaviours (RQ3)? Linear regression was used to examine the social predictors of online misconduct tendency through a composite score variable (OMT). There is a positive relationship between cyber-psychopathy scores and one's tendency to engage in online misconduct. Having increases in both cyber-psychopathy and offline psychopathy scores are associated with increases in OMT, with the cyber-psychopathy variable having a larger coefficient. This finding suggests that, when controlling for other variables, psychopathy is generally an important predictor of one's likelihood of participating in online misconduct behaviours. However, when comparing goodness-of-fit (Adjusted R^2) between independent cyber-psychopathy and offline psychopathy models, cyber-psychopathy significantly outperforms offline psychopathy in the ability to predict the variance

TABLE 17.4 Descriptive Statistics for Cyber-Psychopathy and Offline Psychopathy Variables Reported as Means (SD) or Percentages

Full Sample	**Overall (N = 408)**	**Males (n = 180)**	**Females (n = 228)**	***p***
Cyber-Psychopathy Score (CP)	48.7 (10.6)	51.7 (10.7)	46.3 (9.9)	***
Offline Psychopathy Score (OP)	46.5 (10.0)	48.4 (9.9)	45.1 (9.8)	***
Psychopathy Differential (CP-OP)	2.2 (6.7) ***[a]	3.4 (7.2) ***[a]	1.2 (6.1) **[a]	***
Decrease Online (%)	7.6	7.2	7.9	***
No Change Online (%)	72.1	62.2	79.8	
Increase Online (%)	20.3	30.6	12.3	
"Increase Online" Subsample	**Overall (n = 83)**	**Males (n = 55)**	**Females (n = 28)**	***p***
Cyber-Psychopathy Score (CP)	56.4 (10.8)	58.3 (10.1)	52.5 (11.4)	*
Offline Psychopathy Score (OP)	45.4 (9.6)	47.4 (9.1)	41.4 (9.3)	**
Psychopathy Differential (CP-OP)	11.0 (5.3)	10.9 (5.7)	11.1 (4.5)	

Note: The p value column refers to a test of gender difference (independent samples t-test, $\chi2$). The total p value from $\chi2$ test is given for categorical variables

[a] = paired samples t-test between the means of Cyber-Psychopathy and Offline Psychopathy scores

*$p \leq 0.05$, **$p \leq 0.01$, ***$p \leq 0.001$

in OMT. Higher cyber-psychopathy scores specifically predict more hypothetical engagement in the following online misconduct behaviours: digital piracy, trolling, flaming, cyber-vandalism, and online deception.

Discussion

The present analysis shows statistically significant differences between CPS and OPS measures (i.e., cyber-psychopathy scores are, on average, higher than offline psychopathy scores), suggesting that the online context may facilitate shifts in personality expression toward cyber-psychopathy. As such, the results support the hypothesis that expressions of psychopathy are somewhat context-dependent between online and offline environments. Additionally, I have demonstrated evidence supporting the methodological proposition that personality inventories and behavioural outcomes should be measured within the same social context for increased validity.

Furthermore, this study has found substantial gender differences in the expression of cyber-psychopathy, which conforms to similar trends in the psychopathy literature (Forth, Brown, Hart, and Hare, 1996; Salekin, Rogers, and Sewell, 1997). Males have higher mean scores of cyber-psychopathy and also have a much higher likelihood than females to increase in psychopathic expression when online. These findings may be reflective of expressions of **hypermasculinity** on the Internet due to a lack of non-verbal cues and, accordingly, manliness indicators in cyberspace. Previous research has shown that without non-verbal cues, individuals often overcompensate with verbal or physical clarifying reactions (Walther, Loh, and Granka, 2005), and when gender cues are specifically absent, threats to masculinity are typically met with hypermasculine behaviours (Willer, Rogalin, Conlon, and Wojnowicz, 2013). Therefore, masculinity overcompensation on the Internet may be indicative of posturing to demonstrate one's manhood through analogous personality traits that encompass excessive aggressiveness, dominance, and risk-taking (Kimmel, 2004).

Cyber-psychopathy scores are also strong predictors of being more likely to engage in malicious online behaviours, which suggests there is a more complicated process underlying the theoretical relationship between the unique elements of the Internet world (i.e., anonymity, apparent normlessness, and lack of non-verbal cues) and incidences of online misconduct. In this sense, cyberspace characteristics may contribute directly to online misconduct, but may also facilitate the emergence of psychopathy on the Internet by forming an indirect pathway to anti-social behavioural tendencies (see Figure 17.2). For example, being in anonymous digital environments may increase psychological distancing and thus dissociative personality effects, making ordinary

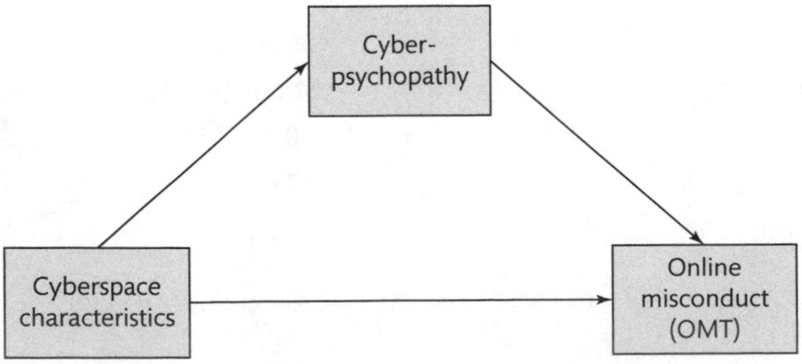

FIGURE 17.2 Cyber-psychopathy Theoretical Model

individuals more likely to express psychopathic traits, which are embodied by both unempathetic moral judgments and impulsive or disinhibited behaviours. Interestingly, previous research has shown that psychopaths generally have reduced eye contact with others (Dadds, El Masry, Wimalaweera, and Guastella, 2008), and the characteristics of cyberspace play right into this, potentially facilitating shifts toward psychopathic expression in online communities that are missing the empathy cues derived from eye contact.

Overall, these findings support a new perspective for offering solutions to address the increasing instances of cyber-crime and cyberbullying. Practical implications from this research should focus on emphasizing the "realness" of cyberspace and online communities should explicitly promote empathy among members to close the psychological distance between them (Barlińska, Szuster, and Winiewski, 2013; Todd, 2014). Additionally, it appears there is a need for online education programs devoted to educating young digital natives about pro-social online behaviours when they are going through crucial stages of identity and moral development. Such education would also be an important contribution for establishing more salient and universal norms in cyberspace, which are largely absent outside of specific online communities.

In conclusion, this study has empirically supported the idea of context-dependent personality expression and has applied this framework to the Internet through the examination of "dark" e-personality (i.e., cyber-psychopathy) and its association with online misconduct.

Notes

1. The scores of the CPS and OPS scales have a range of 26 (minimum) to 104 (maximum). The internal consistency of the scales is very high with Cronbach's $\alpha=0.87$ and $\alpha=0.86$ for CPS and OPS, respectively.
2. The differential is calculated by subtracting the offline psychopathy score from the cyber-psychopathy score (CP-OP).
3. Tests of significance use paired samples *t*-tests between the mean scores of cyber-psychopathy and offline psychopathy for the full sample and each subsample ($*p \leq 0.05$, $**p \leq 0.01$, $***p \leq 0.001$)
4. Digital literacy is measured with the Web-Use Skill Index (Hargittai and Hsieh, 2012). In this study, increasing by one point on this index is associated with a 5 per cent increase in odds of being in the "Increase Online" category.

References

Aboujaoude, E. (2011). *Virtually you: The dangerous powers of the e-personality.* New York: W.W. Norton & Company.

Allport, G.W. (1937). *Personality: A psychological interpretation.* New York: Holt, Rinehart & Winston.

Babiak, P., and Hare, R.D. (2006). *Snakes in suits: When psychopaths go to work.* New York: HarperCollins.

Barlińska, J., Szuster, A., and Winiewski, M. (2013). Cyberbullying among adolescent bystanders: Role of the communication medium, form of violence, and empathy. *Journal of Community & Applied Social Psychology, 23*(1), 37–51.

Blumer, T., and Doering, N. (2012). Are we the same online? The expression of the five factor personality traits on the computer and the Internet. *Cyberpsychology: Journal of Psychosocial Research on Cyberspace, 6*(3).

Buckels, E.E., Trapnell, P.D., and Paulhus, D.L. (2014). Trolls just want to have fun. *Personality and Individual Differences, 67,* 97–102.

Ciucci, E., Baroncelli, A., Franchi, M., Golmaryami, F.N., and Frick, P.J. (2014). The association between callous-unemotional traits and behavioral and academic adjustment in children: Further validation of the Inventory of Callous-Unemotional Traits. *Journal of Psychopathology and Behavioral Assessment, 36*(2), 189–200.

Cleckley, H. (1976). *The mask of sanity.* Augusta, Georgia: C.V. Mosby Publishing Company.

Coid, J., and Yang, M. (2008). The distribution of psychopathy among a household population: Categorical or dimensional? *Social Psychiatry and Psychiatric Epidemiology, 43*(10), 773–81.

Crowell, C.R., Narvaez, D., and Gomberg, A. (2005). Moral psychology and information ethics: Psychological distance and the components of moral behavior in a digital world. In L. Freeman and A.G. Peace (Eds), *Information ethics: Privacy and intellectual property* Hershey, PA: IGI Global.

Dadds, M.R., El Masry, Y., Wimalaweera, S., and Guastella, A.J. (2008). Reduced eye gaze explains "fear blindness" in childhood psychopathic traits. *Journal of the American Academy of Child & Adolescent Psychiatry, 47*(4), 455–63.

Demetriou, C., and Silke, A. (2003). A criminological internet "sting." Experimental evidence of illegal and deviant visits to a website trap. *British Journal of Criminology, 43*(1), 213–22.

Denegri-Knott, J., and Taylor, J. (2005). The labeling game: A conceptual exploration of deviance on the internet. *Social Science Computer Review, 23*(1), 93–107.

Fanti, K.A., Demetriou, A.G., and Hawa, V.V. (2012). A longitudinal study of cyberbullying: Examining risk and protective factors. *European Journal of Developmental Psychology, 9*(2), 168–81.

Forth, A.E., Brown, S.L., Hart, S.D., and Hare, R.D. (1996). The assessment of psychopathy in male and female noncriminals: Reliability and validity. *Personality and Individual Differences, 20*(5), 531–43.

Goodboy, A.K., and Martin, M.M. (2015). The personality profile of a cyberbully: Examining the dark triad. *Computers in Human Behavior, 49*, 1–4.

Greitemeyer, T. (2015). Everyday sadism predicts violent video game preferences. *Personality and Individual Differences, 75*, 19–23.

Hare, R.D. (1991). *The Hare Psychopathy Checklist-Revised.* Toronto: Multi-Health Systems.

Hargittai, E., and Hsieh, Y.P. (2012). Succinct survey measures of web-use skills. *Social Science Computer Review, 30*(1).

Jewkes, Y., and Sharp, K. (2003). Crime, deviance and the disembodied self: Transcending the dangers of corporeality. In Y. Jewkes (Ed.), *Dot.cons: Crime, deviance and identity on the internet.* Cullompton, UK: Willan Publishing.

Joinson, A.N. (2001). Self-disclosure in computer-mediated communication: The role of self-awareness and visual anonymity. *European Journal of Social Psychology, 31*(2), 177–92.

Kenrick, D.T., McCreath, H.E., Govern, J., King, R., and Bordin, J. (1990). Person–environment intersections: Everyday settings and common trait dimensions. *Journal of Personality and Social Psychology, 58*(4), 685.

Kimmel, M. (2004). What about the boys? In H.S. Shapiro and D.E. Purpel (Eds), *Critical social issues in American education: Democracy and meaning in a globalizing world.* Mahwah, NJ: Lawrence Erlbaum Associates.

Levenson, M.R., Kiehl, K.A., and Fitzpatrick, C.M. (1995). Assessing psychopathic attributes in a non-institutionalized population. *Journal of Personality and Social Psychology, 68*(1), 151–8.

Maldonado, J.G., Mora, M., Garcia, S., and Edipo, P. (2001). Personality, sex and communication via internet. *Anuario de Psicologia, 32*(2), 51–62.

Mischel, W. (1973). Toward a cognitive social learning reconceptualization of personality. *Psychological Review, 80*(4), 252–83.

Mischel, W. (1977). The interaction of person and situation. In D. Magnusson and N. Endler (Eds), *Personality at the crossroads: Current issues in interactional psychology.* Hillsdale, New Jersey: Lawrence Erlbaum Associates.

Pabian, S., De Backer, C.J., and Vandebosch, H. (2015). Dark triad personality traits and adolescent cyber-aggression. *Personality and Individual Differences, 75*, 41–6.

Salekin, R.T., Rogers, R., and Sewell, K.W. (1997). Construct validity of psychopathy in a female offender sample: A multitrait–multimethod evaluation. *Journal of Abnormal Psychology, 106*(4), 576–85.

Selwyn, N. (2008). A safe haven for misbehaving? An investigation of online misbehaviour among university students. *Social Science Computer Review, 26*(4), 446–65.

Stritzke, W.G., Nguyen, A., and Durkin, K. (2004). Shyness and computer-mediated communication: A self-presentational theory perspective. *Media Psychology, 6*(1), 1–22.

Suler, J. (2004). The online disinhibition effect. *CyberPsychology & Behavior, 7*(3), 321–6.

Taylor, P.A. (2003). Maestros or misogynists? Gender and social construction of hacking. In Y. Jewkes (Ed.), *Dot.cons: Crime, deviance and identity on the internet.* Cullompton, UK: Willan Publishing.

Todd, P. (2014). *Extreme mean: Trolls, bullies and predators online.* Toronto: Signal, McClelland & Stewart.

Trope, Y., and Liberman, N. (2010). Construal-level theory of psychological distance. *Psychological Review, 117*(2), 440–63.

Turkle, S. (1984). *The second self: Computers and the human spirit.* New York: Simon & Schuster.

Walther, J.B., Loh, T., and Granka, L. (2005). Let me count the ways: The interchange of verbal and nonverbal cues in computer-mediated and face-to-face affinity. *Journal of Language and Social Psychology, 24*(1), 36–65.

Whittier, D.B. (2013). Cyberethics: Envisioning character education in cyberspace. *Peabody Journal of Education, 88*(2), 225–42.

Widom, C.S. (1977). A methodology for studying noninstitutionalized psychopaths. *Journal of Consulting and Clinical Psychology, 45*(4), 674–83.

Willer, R., Rogalin, C.L., Conlon, B., and Wojnowicz, M.T. (2013). Overdoing gender: A test of the masculine overcompensation thesis. *American Journal of Sociology, 118*(4), 980–1022.

18 Critical Sociology and Criminal Accusation

George Pavlich

All societies produce strangers; but each kind of society produces its own kind of strangers, and produces them in its own inimitable way. (Bauman, 1997: 17)

My interest in sociology developed in the 1980s as an unjust apartheid regime in South Africa did its level best to forestall a changing society. I observed firsthand how critical sociology helped to forge new ways of understanding the dangers of a society in which one was socialized and how to conceive of its possible futures. Whether feminist, critical race, post-colonial, social democratic, Marxist, or Nietzsche-inspired, social critics posed direct questions about how power, gender, class, race, and privilege constrained people's lives. They challenged old ways of doing things and tried to imagine what an equal, racially non-segregated and just society might look like. In that ethos, **genres of social critique**—with roots in Kant, orthodox Marxism, praxis-orientated activism, and critical theory—tended to proceed thus: judge particular social contexts against universally assumed or agreed upon criteria in order to secure social progress (see Pavlich, 2000). However, over time, critics also turned their gaze inwards. Some questioned, for instance, how sustainable this approach to critique was in post-colonial societies and whether others might be evoked (see Mbembe, 2014).

Inspired by such questioning, I was eventually pursued a different genre of critique for sociology (Pavlich, 2000, 2013a). My sense was that contemporary socio-cultural conditions had changed such that they could no longer sustain the illusion that universally agreed-upon criteria were possible, or that modern reason could guarantee social progress. In response, I opted for a "dissociative" rather than judgmental critical genre focused on opening, or conceptually separating out, ideas about being with others. To illustrate the stakes of this move, one could point to how this kind of critique reveals forms of governance that erect social limits in support of particular institutions—such as those upheld through a tired language of "crime and punishment" to control historically framed wrongdoing.

Allow me to elaborate. Few sociologists today would deny appealing to some or other type of criticism. Over two centuries ago Kant noted, "Our age is, in an especial degree, the age of criticism, and to criticism everything must submit" (2008: 9). Yet, not all critical genres can be sustained in all social contexts, raising this question: what genres of critique might be mobilized to rethink key issues of our day? One such issue concerns the role of criminal accusation in sustaining massive and costly criminal justice systems. We shall return to this matter below, but responding to the former question, one might say that since current socio-cultural contexts are beset by omniscient uncertainty (Bauman, 1997), it is difficult to agree on which reasoned criteria to adopt, or which social progress to pursue.

Thinkers like Foucault (2000) have also shown how power and ideas shape the limits of any society through subtle and various modes of governance. Since these modes and limits often have dangerous effects, we have to be vigilant of the stories they use to prop themselves. We should recall that social atrocities including the Holocaust happened not by rejecting but precisely by claiming to further reason and progress (Bauman, 1997). Furthermore, colonial claims to "civilized" societies as the most advanced social forms have been revealed as Eurocentric, imperialist, classist, and patriarchal denigrations of others. We might recall too that their violence, bloodshed, and dispossession were justified through claims to reasoned, social progress. Similarly, totalitarian projects, like those envisaged by Stalin and apartheid's architects, engineered divided societies by following various dictates framed through contorted versions of reason, science and social advancement.

Consequently, rather than insisting on a social critique as necessarily operating through founded judgment and social progress, my work has offered an alternative that may be more aligned with our times (Pavlich, 2013a, 2000). Recognizing that social forms are always partially open-ended, indeterminate, and subject to capricious histories, I sought a different—more open, if less comforting—genre of social critique might better respond to emerging relations. This sort of critique would not seek absolute judgments based on universal criteria, offer final solutions, or promise unfettered social progress. Instead, this social critique permanently attempts to expose problematic historical limits, pointing to their dangerous effects and offering tentative social exits from oppressive social forms. Specifically, I called for a "dissociative" genre of critique to chronicle the ideas and practices that enable problematized boundaries or limits (Pavlich, 2009c). The kind of governance that sustains such limits is most effective when it silently, or at least unobtrusively, structures our being with others. Exposing such governance, this critique tries to puncture oppressive meaning horizons. It emphasizes their contingent (rather than necessary) formation, and opens new discussions on future social possibilities (Pavlich, 2013a). As a situated practice, it reflectively shines critical light on shadowy governmental limits, entertains the possibility of not being subject to these, and through that entertains possibilities for social change. The task is an interpretative one born to historical contexts. It names, problematizes, and dissociates governing practices that erect unjust social limits, suggesting possible exits from oppressive ways of being with others.

By way of an example, I relied on a dissociative critique to approach sovereignty and criminal justice at the turn of the nineteenth century in the Cape of Good Hope and in Canada after Confederation (e.g., Pavlich, 2014; 2013b). This genre helped to "dissociate" the familiar view that colonial criminal justice was deployed by imperial rulers. My work considered an alternative possibility: the very imposition of colonial law and order over populations helped to define sovereign control in context. Understood thus, criminal justice—then as now—grows not through the command of sovereigns, but precisely by defining and reinforcing images of what being a colonial sovereign entails. My critique here suggests that our tenacious reliance on idioms of crime and punishment (and criminal justice) have endured precisely because of their political significance for settler-colonial (and subsequent) societies.

This finding allows us to understand why it is so hard to think beyond ways of governing targeted subjects via "crime and punishment." Christie (2013) nicely referred to the rise of a "crime control industry" involved with the production of crime. Amounting to a monopolistic enterprise, this industry defines, processes, and controls crime and criminals. It also remunerates gatekeepers as workers who ensure a steady demand for services—the industry's self-preservation involves unceasing expansion, with moral choices that, by effect, produce mass social exclusion (Reiner, 2007). Entrances to criminal justice are pivotal here; they select and populate criminal justice arenas and determine the latter's expansion. Criminal accusation is a key gatekeeping mechanism that initiates their operations (Pavlich, 2009b).

Over the years, many critical criminologists and sociologists have pointed out many grim consequences of these expansive crime control networks (see Cohen, 1985). Some note the financial drains on both systems and those directly or indirectly affected by mass incarceration (Clear and Frost, 2014; Simon and Sparks, 2013). Others show how punitive, exclusion-based "cultures" of control centred on "crime" undermine democratic institutions (Simon, 2007; Garland, 2002) and create unethical exclusions from society (Reiner, 2007). By targeting specific groups of people for admission, criminal justice entryways generate skewed population profiles that disproportionately select First Nations people (e.g., Comack, 2012), racial minorities (Garland, 2002; Simon and Sparks, 2013), gendered subjects (e.g., Balfour and Comack, 2006), and poor people (Brown, 2009; Wacquant, 2009). Needless to say, generating massive domains of inequitable exclusion has significant effects on society as a whole (Sassen, 2014; Winlow, 2013) and raises questions about the constitutionality of creating such enormous social divisions (Simon, 2014).

Working off that rich critical tapestry, dissociative critique directed my gaze toward governmental practices that initiated and fuelled expanding criminal justice networks. That is, instead of focusing on the criminal justice itself, I turned to an often-overlooked foundation of its governance: the accusatory entryways that select who to process as potential criminals. By naming the limits of social rituals that accuse people, and thereby select them to face courtroom justice, one reveals a starting point for criminalization. With fewer criminal justice entryways and more restrictions on those that govern figurative gates to criminalization, societies could shrink crime control industries and their operations. Limiting the flow and profiles of criminalized subjects, that is, would likely reduce the scale of crime control arenas over the ordering of our societies. Of course, there are many dimensions to this complex matter, including the role of growing forensic and criminal identification technologies—e.g., Bertillon's anthropometry (Ellenbogen, 2012), Galton's composite portraiture (Pavlich, 2009a), eugenics, forensics, and fingerprinting (Cole, 2001; Sengoopta, 2003), criminal imaging (Finn, 2009), and recent biometric techniques (Ajana, 2013). Yet, a dissociative critique helps us to focus attention on governing limits that authorize gatekeepers to select and admit those accused of crimes. In this, the **lore of criminal accusation**, more so than the law of accusation, might be crucial to understanding how "strangers" are created through timeworn notions of crime and punishment (Pavlich, 2007).

Although the previous sketch has covered quite a bit of ground, the ideas are detailed elsewhere (e.g., Pavlich, 2013a; 2006; 2000). However, it highlights a way to approach critical sociology differently; that is, through a dissociated genre of critique that is less concerned with judging or prescribing absolute paths to social progress than naming, opening, and securing governmental patterns that unjustly limit our being with others. By way of illustration, this critique was mobilized to highlight the significance of shrinking accusatory entrances to criminal justice if we are to restrain expanding criminal justice systems and their attendant social exclusions. This may be classed as a problem of history if we consider this wider matter: if unexposed, would accusatory entryways to criminalization produce societies of exclusion where vast swaths of people live out lives in segregated criminal justice systems (as governors or the governed), and where the idea of social inclusion becomes a distant promise of past ages?

If nothing else, the question underscores why we might want to name gatekeeping governance that forges the boundaries of today's criminal justice networks in silence; not only to alter the shape of crime control systems—their size, contours, and population profiles—but also the visions of social order that these arenas secure. Such a critical sociology also points us to this insight: governing historical versions of wrongdoing may be most effective when we try to increase (rather than erode) democratic social attachments. So long as societal forces continue to privilege lexicons of crime and its punishment, the exclusions of governing via criminal justice will continue unabated. However, by naming and seeking exits from certain apparatuses through which subjects enter criminal justice networks as accused criminals, a dissociative social critique might limit the size and profile of criminal justice systems. It promises the possibility of pursuing other, more socially inclusive ways to govern contemporary social limits.

References

Ajana, B. 2013. "Asylum, identity management and biometric control." Journal of Refugee Studies 26(4):576–95.

Balfour, Gillian, and Elizabeth Comack. 2006. Criminalizing women: gender and (in)justice in neo-liberal times. Halifax NS: Fernwood Pub.

Bauman, Zygmunt. 1997. Postmodernity and its discontents. New York: New York University Press. Reprinted with permission from Polity Books.

Brown, Michelle. 2009. The culture of punishment: prison, society, and spectacle. New York: New York University Press.

Christie, Nils. 2013. Crime control as industry. London: Routledge.

Clear, Todd and Natasha Frost, 2014. The punishment imperative: the rise and failure of mass incarceration in America. New York: NYU Press.

Cohen, Stanley. 1985. Visions of social control: crime, punishment, and classification. Cambridge: Polity Press.

Cole, Simon. 2001. Suspect identities: A history of fingerprinting and criminal identification. Cambridge, MA: Harvard University Press.

Comack, Elizabeth. 2012. Racialized policing: Aboriginal people's encounters with the police. Halifax, NS: Fernwood Pub.

Ellenbogen, Josh. 2012. Reasoned and unreasoned images: the photography of Bertillon, Galton, and Marey. University Park: Pennsylvania State University Press.

Finn, Jonathan M. 2009. Capturing the criminal image: from mug shot to surveillance society. Minneapolis: University of Minnesota Press.

Foucault, Michel. 2000. Power. New York: The New Press.

Garland, David. 2002. The culture of control: crime and social order in contemporary society. Chicago: University of Chicago Press.

Kant, Immanuel. 2008. Critique of pure reason. London: Penguin.

Mbembe, A. 2014. What is postcolonial thinking? Retrieved January 30, 2015, from http://www.eurozine.com/pdf/2008-01-09-mbembe-en.pdf

Pavlich, George. 2014. "Criminal justice and Cape law's persons." Social and Legal Studies 23(1):55–72.

———. 2013a. "Dissociative grammar and constitutional critique?" Pp. 31–48 in Karin van Marle and Stewart Motha (eds), Genres of critique: law, aesthetics and liminality. Stellenbosch: Sun Press.

———. 2013b. "Sovereign Force and Crime-focused Law at the Cape Colony." Journal of Historical Sociology 26(3):318–38.

———. 2009a. "The subjects of criminal identification." Punishment and Society 11(2):171–90.

———. 2009b. "Being accused, becoming criminal." Pp. 51–70 in D. Crewe and R. Lippens (eds), Being, justice, and crime: essays in existentialist criminology. London: Routledge-Cavendish.

———. 2009c. G. Pavlich, "Ethics, Universal Principles and Restorative Justice," in G. Johnstone and D. W. Van Ness (eds), Handbook of Restorative Justice (Willan, 2007), pp. 615–30. reprinted in In C. Hoyle (ed, Routledge Major Works Series, Restorative Justice: Critical Concepts in Criminology, Chapter 59, Part 14 (no page numbers).

———. 2007. "The lore of criminal accusation." Criminal Law and Philosophy 1(1):79–97.

———. 2006. "Accusation: landscapes of exclusion." Pp. 85–100 in William Taylor (ed.), The geography of law: landscape, identity and regulation. Oxford: Hart Publishing.

———. 2000. Critique and radical discourses on crime. Aldershot: Ashgate.

Reiner, Robert. 2007. Law and order: an honest citizen's guide to crime and control. Cambridge: Polity.

Sassen, Saskia. 2014. Expulsions: brutality and complexity in the global economy. Cambridge, MA: Belknap Press.

Sengoopta, C. 2003. Imprint of the Raj: how fingerprinting was born in colonial India. London: Macmillan.

Simon, Jonathan. 2014. Mass incarceration on trial: a remarkable court decision and the future of prisons in America. New York: New Press.

———. 2007. Governing through crime: how the war on crime transformed American democracy and created a culture of fear. New York: Oxford University Press.

Simon, Jonathan, and Richard Sparks (eds). 2013. The SAGE handbook of punishment and society. London: SAGE.

Wacquant, Loïc J.D. 2009. Punishing the poor: the neoliberal government of social insecurity. Durham, NC: Duke University Press.

Winlow, Simon. 2013. Rethinking social exclusion: the end of the social? Thousand Oaks, CA: SAGE.

19 Spaces, Places, and States of Mind: A Study of Two Homeless Communities

Eric Weissman, PhD

Historically difficult to define, homelessness is an enduring social problem facing North American cities. For most of the twentieth century, a vagabond sleeping in a park satisfied the public's need to put a face on the problem (Ferguson, 1911; Anderson, 1923; DePastino, 2003). Since the early 1990s, a rise in the numbers of women, families, and able-bodied people living without housing has required new terms reflecting a continuum of precarious housing experiences that transcend the notion of a flawed person. According to the Canadian Observatory on Homelessness (2012),

> Homelessness describes a range of housing and shelter circumstances, with people being without any shelter at one end, and being insecurely housed at the other. That is, homelessness encompasses a range of physical living situations, organized here in a typology that includes . . . Unsheltered . . . Emergency Sheltered . . . Provisionally Accommodated . . . At Risk of Homelessness . . .

This means that some people are literally unsheltered and live on the streets, some people occasionally suffer this way and might use shelters as part of their survival techniques, and many others are very close to losing housing. It is the latter category that is most troubling for us because many people have a false sense of housing security. In Canada, all of these problems are worse for Aboriginal persons, LGBTQ youth, and people with mental health problems. Such diversity confounds attempts at broadly applied housing programming. There are debates about who deserves and who is responsible for social assistance out of homelessness. With such diversity among the homeless, we recognize now that the common root of the problem is a lack of affordable housing.

My research used visually supported ethnographic storytelling based on participant observation in a number of **intentional homeless communities (IHC)** built by homeless people. Intentional communities can be any site that is built around a specific goal or need. The IHC I studied are sometimes called "shantytowns" because they are designed as emergency transitional housing communities for homeless people and are generally very poor places.

In this research, major questions I asked were: what role self-governing IHC could play in official housing policies and if fighting for these communities was a personally empowering experience for homeless activists? The research contributed to political and social theory by asking what freedom and democracy mean when poor people must organize and struggle for the right to self-govern in poverty.

In the United States each month, 146 million people choose between food, shelter, clothes, education, and medical needs. Of these, 52 million are considered to live below the poverty line (NAEH, 2015). It has been argued that between 250,000 and 3 million of these people suffer from temporary, episodic, or chronic homelessness (EHAC, 2011; HUD, 2011). Canada has close to one-tenth the population of the United States, and the homelessness "problem" closely follows this proportional representation (ibid). But as Canada's household debt has grown and the cost of housing has increased, many more

Canadians live in precarious housing even if they don't realize it (Hwang et al., 2006; Hwang, 2010).

Housing First (HF), is part of a rapid-rehousing paradigm, and is the favoured housing model in the United States and Canada. Over 30 years old, HF takes chronically homeless people off the streets and places them directly in conventional accommodations without making any demands on them to solve addictions or work on health issues. Both nations pitch HF in their Ten Year Plans to End Homelessness (Waegemakers-Schiff, 2015). Housing First, with social and medical supports in place, helps people stay housed longer, and helps them to voluntarily address mental health and other personal issues (CMHC, 2014). The cost to taxpayers is far less than that of forcing people to endure street poverty, institutions, and shelters.

For proponents of IHC, HF has limitations, such as limited public support and a very narrow definition of valid housing that excludes alternatives. Some public opposition questions the deserving nature of recipients of HF and wants proof that their communities are safer or that beneficiaries of housing use it wisely. Such resistance hinges on a strong ethic of self-governance and a belief that housing recipients must conform to a dominant vision of "home life." Proponents of HF look at housing as a basic need and as a right, just like health care. They know that self-governance and good health without housing are impossible (Foucault, 1975; Gans, 1991; Fairbanks, 2004).

Residential camping and "tent cities" are not official aspects of the HF paradigm, even though a number of cities in the United States grudgingly recognize them as legitimate survival responses of very poor persons (WRAP, 2010; PHB, 2012; Heben, 2014). Such places seem rough, dangerous, and tragic. Most people equate such places with impoverished slums in the "third world" (Mitchell, 2003; DePastino, 2003; Davis, 2006).

After more than 30 years of HF, and 12 years of it being the official US and Canadian federal model for Ten Year Plans to End Homelessness, only Medicine Hat, Alberta, has ended homelessness. My research argues that this is because it is impossible to end all forms of homelessness in all cities; the concept of "ending" homelessness creates widely held anxiety over this inherent impossibility and demonizes alternate ways of establishing housing such as IHC. Poorer examples of IHC are still looked upon as a kind of homelessness by their critics.

My research on IHC showed that IHC can under certain conditions constitute a valid type of housing. By comparing events in two key shantytowns, Tent City in Toronto and Dignity Village in Portland, Oregon, each beginning in 2000, I showed that one of the keys to such spaces being accepted lay in the history of urban attitudes toward proper use of space in a given urban centre.

Portland, Oregon, is a city with a rich frontier folklore that could imagine campgrounds such as Dignity Village as a common experience, while in Toronto, such phenomena were seen as evidence of failure. Tent City was evicted. Since then, there has not been a strong IHC movement in Canada. Canadian cities have built more shelters, invested in HF and rental supplements, and rigorously enforced laws that prevent people from establishing permanent camps.

By examining the historically recorded tension between popular understandings of deserving and undeserving poor in the United States since 1601, I found that political willingness to accept IHC shifted with economic and social upheavals, such as the Civil War, the Great Depression, and the Great Recession of 2008. Also, Dignity Village activists were able to argue for emergency campgrounds because their state constitution allowed such usage. In short, in Portland, Oregon, in 2000, a group of homeless activists successfully challenged the city in the state Supreme Court for the right to build a "legal" emergency IHC called Dignity Village, and won. Seventeen years later, Dignity Village, the first city-sanctioned emergency campground in the United States remains the controversial legal precedent for activists seeking to build other IHC.

The village's official mission statement suggested a green, sustainable, self-governing democracy, but when I visited there in 2010 and resided there in 2011 for my dissertation research, I found little evidence of these ideals in practice. Instead, I observed infrastructural decay, political apathy, and widespread drug use. To find out what had happened, I asked people at Dignity Village how they understood the community and how they would restore it to its ideal form.

Interviews with villagers and ex-residents revealed that the contract imposed by the city contained conventional rules and codes of conduct especially about drug use that were unrealistic. Also, their location on the outskirts of town made it hard to find work. Furthermore, self-governance was hard to achieve because factions had emerged that interfered with elections and other democratic practices. The freedom to choose a rule-laden, city-approved contract over life on the streets or in shelters was in fact, as Foucault (1991) would have argued, the way the neoliberal "art of government" works through the choices we make about how to be governed, rather than how not to be governed at all. The village became the ideal and evil form of **neoliberal governmentality**, a repository for people who failed at conventional measures of self-conduct and who were deluded enough to think they had won their right to self-govern on a swept-off tarmac next to a composting site (Foucault, 1975, 1991; Dean, 1999).

The village therefore became a physically marginalized community on the outskirts of the city, and people lived there with few if any chances of actually transitioning back into conventional roles. The despair, the drugs, the sloth, and the low morale were the result of a group of terrified and traumatized people forced to live in a **perpetual liminality** understood as a state of protracted limbo. Anthropologists like Van Gennep (1908) and Turner (1967) have shown that all cultures must manage life transitions and transformations because such periods of liminality are threatening to social groups. Generally, though, society facilitates upward transitions from lesser to better roles. Homelessness is a reversal of this "natural tendency." Harper and Baumohl (2004) have argued that the pervasive and attenuated nature of modern homelessness is evidence of a system wide liminality that is reaching drastic proportions. The essential quality, then, that makes housing so central to people, and fuels the anxiety to end homelessness, is that without it, health, employment, family, and home are impossible. Furthermore, even in conventional housing programs, people need assistance with transitions.

What happens when people don't successfully move through expected stages or roles? What happens when people get out of school but can't find work, when people lose their homes, or when the homeless enter transitional housing but never get out of that transition? Since few examples have been established, our knowledge of how the struggle to establish intentional homeless communities helps or hinders people's attempt to transcend liminality was weak. My research has shown how knowledge, like that mobilized in the social activism that began in the social critique of the IHC movement, has temporal and practical attitudes that we can understand using ethnographic methods (Larsen, 2011). In order to do so, one must, as Bruno Latour (2004) suggested, eschew notions of simplicity and confront ambiguity and diversity as the basis for meaningful social critique.

In 2016 the village continues to struggle to evolve. New IHC, moving beyond the lessons learned at Dignity, are growing in number. In particular, Opportunity Village in Eugene, Oregon; Community First Village in Austin, Texas; Quixote Village in Olympia, Washington; and Right to Dream Too in Portland, Oregon, are leading examples of how IHC has moved beyond Dignity Village and can contribute more effectively to the housing needs of major cities. When this research ended in 2014, I noted that despite their popularity, IHC were not considered official parts of 10-year planning and remained outside of official HF language. However, I argued that such spaces would find their way into official planning. Two years later, cities such as San Antonio, Portland, and Sacramento are considering investing millions of dollars to build outdoor shelters and alternative IHC for the many people who need them.

References

Anderson, Nels. 1923. *The Hobo: The Sociology of the Homeless Man*. Chicago: Phoenix Books.

Baumohl, Jim and Hopper Kim. 2004. "Liminality." *Encyclopedia of American Homelessness*. Thousand Oaks, CA: SAGE Publications, pp. 355–6.

Boltanski, Luc. 2011. *On Critique—A Sociology of Emancipation*. Cambridge: Polity.

Bourgois, Phillip and Jeffery Shonberg. 2009. *Righteous Dopefiend*. Berkeley: University of California Press.

Canadian Mental Health Commission (CMHC). 2014. *Final Report, At Home Chez Soi Project—Toronto 2014*. Calgary, AB: Toronto At Home Research Team and Mental Health Commission of Canada.

Canadian Observatory on Homelessness. 2012. "Canadian Definition of Homelessness." http://www.homelesshub.ca/sites/default/files/COHhomelessdefinition.pdf.

Davis, Mike. 2006. *Planet of Slums*, London: Verso.

Dean, Mitchell. 1999. *Governmentality, Power and Rule in Modern Society*. London: SAGE.

DePastino, Todd. 2003. *Citizen Hobo*. Chicago: University of Chicago Press.

Ending Homelessness Advisory Council (EHAC). 2011. "A Home for Hope: A report to the Governor and the Oregon Legislature from the Ending Homelessness Advisory Council November 2011." https://www.oregon.gov/ohcs/pdfs/report-ehac-annual-2011.pdf.

Fairbanks II, Robert P. 2004. "Communal Re-Appropriation of Blighted Spaces: Governmentality and the Politics of Everyday Life in the Kensington Recovery House Movement." PhD dissertation, University of Pennsylvania.

Ferguson, Robert, M. 1911. *The Vagrant: What to Do with Him*. London: J. Nisbett and Co.

Foucault, Michel. 1975. *Discipline and Punish: The Birth of the Prison*. Trans. by A. Sheridan. New York: Random House.

Foucault, Michel. 1991. "Governmentality." Trans. by Rosi Braidotti and revised by Colin Gordon, pp. 87–104 in Graham Burchell, Colin Gordon and Peter Miller (eds), *The Foucault Effect: Studies in Governmentality*. Chicago: University of Chicago Press.

Foucault, Michel. 2007 [1997]. *The Politics of Truth*. Los Angeles: Semiotext(e).

Foucault, Michel. 2007. "What Is Critique?" pp. 41–82 in M. Foucault, *The Politics of Truth*, S. Lotringer (ed.). New York: Semiotext(e).

Gans, Herbert. 1991. *People, Plans and Policies: Essays on Poverty, Racism and Other National Urban Problems*. New York: Columbia University Press.

Gans, Herbert. 1995. *The War against the Poor: The Underclass and Antipoverty Policy*. New York: Basic Books.

Heben, Andrew. 2014. *Tent City Urbanism*. Eugene, Oregon: The Village Collaborative.

Hwang, Stephen, J. Dunn, M. Hayes, J.D. Hulchanski and L. Potvin. 2006. "Housing as a Socio-Economic Determinant of Health: Findings of a National Needs, Gaps and Opportunities Assessment." *Canadian Journal of Public Health* 97(S3) September/October): S11–S15.

Hwang, Stephen 2010. "Canada's Hidden Emergency: The 'Vulnerably Housed.'" *The Globe and Mail*, 22 November 2010.

Larsen, Lars. 2011. "Turning Critique Inside Out: Foucault, Boltanski and Chiapello on the Tactical Displacement of Critique and Power." *Distinktion: Scandinavian Journal of Social Theory* 12(1): 37–55.

Latour, Bruno. 2004. "Why Has Critique Run Out of Steam? From Matters of Fact to Matters of Concern" *Critical Inquiry* 30(2): 225–58.

Mitchell, Don. 2003. *The Right to the City, Social Justice and the Fight for Public Space*. New York: The Guilford Press.

National Alliance on Ending Homelessness (NAEH). 2015. *Snapshot of Homelessness*. Washington. http://www.endhomelessness.org/pages/snapshot_of_homelessness.

Portland Housing Bureau (PHB). 2012. City Contract. Accessed at: http://inpursuitofhappiness.us/philosophers/choices/government-involvement/city-of-portland-draft-dignity-village-contract

State of Oregon. 2011. "A Home for Hope: A 10-year Plan to End Homelessness: Status Report." A report to the Governor and the Oregon Legislature from the Ending Homelessness Advisory Council, 8 November.

Turner, Victor. 1969. *The Ritual Process: Structure and Anti-structure*. Ithaca: Cornell University Press.

Van Gennep, Arnold. 1960 [1908]. *Rites of Passage*. London: Routledge.

Waegemakers-Schiff, J. 2015. *Working With Homeless and Vulnerable People: Basic Skills and Practices*. Chicago, IL: Lyceum Books, Inc.

WRAP. 2010. Strategizing the Right to the City. WRAP Working Paper.

United States Department of Housing and Urban Development (HUD). 2013. The 2007; 2008; 2009; 2010; 2011; 2102; 2013—Annual Homeless Assessment Reports to Congress.

Questions for Critical Thought

Chapter 15 | Intimacy, Geography, and Justice

1. What two questions does Dawson indicate are largely ignored in the sociology of law and punishment literature? What are the three research questions that are asked to fill this gap in the literature?
2. What is the answer to Dawson's question, "Does intimacy still matter"?
3. How has the sentencing of "femicide" cases changed over time? What structural changes may have led to this change in sentencing?
4. What is the "normal crimes" framework? How can this be applied to crimes of intimacy?
5. What are some of the stereotypes surrounding crimes against intimate partners? Conversely, what is the reality?

Chapter 16 | Modern Superstition and Moderate Risk and Problem Slot Machine Gamblers

1. What are superstitions? Why are problem gamblers more likely to believe in superstitions?
2. How does Campbell describe superstitions? List all three aspects.
3. What are "half-beliefs"? How are these tied to ritualistic behaviours?
4. Hahmann's findings indicate that problem gamblers engage in ritualistic behaviours that do not have foundations in beliefs. How does this contradict the psychological theories discussed in the literature review?
5. What is the importance of this study? How do Hahmann's findings help us to further understand problem gambling?

Chapter 17 | Cyber-Psychopathy: An Expression of Dark E-Personality

1. What makes the Internet a distinctive social context? How does this context allow for the development and expression of a dark e-personality?
2. What is psychopathy? What are some traits of psychopathy?
3. What is cyber-psychopathy? Why might higher levels of cyber-psychopathy be associated with greater acceptability and tendencies toward cyberbullying behaviours?
4. Are there gender differences in cyber-psychopathy scores? Why might this be?
5. What solutions does the author suggest for reducing cyber-psychopathy? What additional ways can we address expressions of dark personality on the Internet?

Chapter 18 | Critical Sociology and Criminal Accusation

1. What is critical sociology? What are some genres of critical sociology?
2. What is Pavlich's opinion of social progress? Does everyone agree on progress? What are climates of uncertainty?
3. What is wrong with the "crime control industry"? What does Pavlich suggest will fix this system of crime and punishment?
4. What does Pavlich mean by "dissociative" critical sociology?
5. What insight does Pavlich gain from examining systems of crime and punishment from a different angle? Is this important?

Chapter 19 | Spaces, Places, and States of Mind: A Study of Two Homeless Communities

1. Homelessness is not experienced the same way by everyone. What can be gained from understanding different types of precarious housing situations? How is this a continuum?
2. Weissman uses an ethnographical approach to examine "shanty towns." What insights does he gain from using this approach?
3. Who is most likely to be homeless? What does this tell us about our social structure?
4. What is the Housing First project? Is it effective? Does it have public support? What are the benefits?
5. Compare and contrast Tent City and Dignity Village. What are the positives and the negatives of each? What are the outcomes of these two "shanty towns"?

PART V
Social Inequality

Social inequality is an important area of inquiry in sociological research that often incorporates a number of discrete and intersecting areas, including but not limited to gender and sexuality, social class, and race. Central to this area of study is the idea that there is an unequal distribution of resources and opportunities among individuals and social groups in any given society, and that this unequal distribution is neither random nor necessarily based on ability. The study of social inequality is the study of relationships of power and of economic and political advantage. It involves the study of social status and privilege. Status is bestowed on individuals and groups based on either their ascribed or achieved characteristics. Ascribed characteristics are often involuntary properties that individuals have little control over (often things they are born with or into), such as their physical characteristics, family background, ethnicity, or sexuality. On the other hand, achieved characteristics are earned or chosen and reflect measures of merit, such as educational attainment, marital status, abilities, and skills.

As noted above, many sociologists today note that often it is an individual's ascribed characteristics that carry the most weight in determining their social position rather than their achieved status. Many have come to question the notion that our society is a meritocracy (the hardest working reap the highest rewards). But this was not always the case. Historically, the sociological study of social stratification has included theories that helped to justify existing social inequalities or explain the functional significance of and necessity for social stratification.

In Canada today, many who study social inequality will look to the structural conditions that lead some individuals and groups to succeed at the expense of others. Some also focus on the cultural discourse in formal laws, public policies, and media representations, and reflected in the dominant values of a society that come to normalize or reproduce inequalities.

In Chapter 20, Patricia Armstrong highlights the persistent inequality manifested in the gendered nature of care work. These often taken-for-granted and mundane forms of inequality are exceptionally powerful in normalizing and reinforcing unequal relations in the home and beyond.

In order to combat inequalities within a society, some individuals mobilize through organized resistance to create social movements. Through a range of activities, including protests, members of social moments aim to raise awareness of social injustice and seek social reforms. Two of the chapters in this section show that social movements and social activism can take many forms. In Chapter 21, Bryan Evans and Carlo Fanelli describe the Living Wage Movement, which is protesting economic inequalities through promoting the idea that all workers deserve to be paid a living wage. In Chapter 22, Carmen Grillo describes the role of public sociologists in creating awareness about inequalities and informing social change.

It is important to think carefully about what inequalities exist within our society, who benefits, and what can be done to make a difference. As you will see from the chapters in this section and throughout the book, inequality is pervasive, takes many forms, and can affect individuals and groups in very distinct ways. In Chapter 23, for example, Susan McDaniel gives two Canadian examples of how media representations distort the reality of inequalities that are occurring in the workforce and are experienced by older Canadians. In this chapter, McDaniel shows that public opinion often trumps facts when creating public policies. Unfounded beliefs and their perpetuation inevitably help to maintain and reproduce social inequalities.

20 Working for Care; Caring for Work

Pat Armstrong

This commentary is about my work, about the people with whom I work, and about those who do the work of care.

For us, "the political economy refers to the complex of institutions and relations that constitute not only what are conventionally referred to as the political and economic systems but also the social, physical, ideological and cultural systems" (Armstrong and Armstrong, 2010b:5), or as Marchak (1985:674) put it, it is the "study of power derived from or contingent on a system of property rights, the historical development of power relationships and the cultural and social embodiment of them."

Canadian feminist political economy is unique for many reasons: First, we learn from and with others who take different perspectives, constantly developing our theory and research in response. Second, understanding theory and method as inextricably linked and seeing research as a dialogue between theory and evidence, we do empirical work in various forms. Third, we stress and explore the relationships among all kinds of labour (volunteer, underground, waged, salaried, domestic, private and public sector), deconstructing sectors and categories while developing increasingly complex understanding. Fourth, we do lumping (Stone, 2000) to explore what women have in common, and slicing (Glucksmann, 2000) to understand the multiple and complex lives of particular people in particular places, based on smaller commonalities and fundamental inequities. Fifth, we understand that those who do the work are usually the best source of information on that work, starting from women's standpoints and listening to women's voices (Smith, 1987). Those voices are located within larger contexts and power relations, with the purpose of creating understandings that can lead to structural change. Sixth, we focus on making change in and out of the classroom, which means we have to understand Canada located in a global context and to work with others, such as unions, policy-makers and religious organizations while handling the tensions that arise. Seventh, we work with others to develop and conduct research as well as to turn research into practice. Now called knowledge mobilization, in the sixties we called it praxis.

Our work is focused on Canada, a neglected area when I began. An article on racist segregation in US employment started us thinking about women's segregation in the labour force. Recognizing that numbers matter and seeking to find accessible ways to read evidence, we measured what we called **sex concentration** (proportion of all employed women working in an occupation) and sex-typing (the percentage of the occupation that is female) in the paid workforce. Statistics Canada gave us access to raw data that allowed us to build a historical analysis that met their criteria, something they initially thought could not be done and that could not be done today, given the limited access to such data.

As feminist political economists, it was also important to explore women's work in the home and community, relating this work to what women do for pay. My resulting master's thesis, published as *The Double Ghetto: Canadian Women and Their Segregated Work* (Armstrong and Armstrong, 2010b), led to me serving as an expert witness initially in an *action travail des femmes'* case against Canadian National Railway and later in a dozen others. This landmark Supreme Court decision recognized systemic discrimination against women and that action must be taken to address it.

Canada was a leader in **pay equity**. I learned a great deal working with lawyers, academics, union leaders, and graduate students on figuring out how to explain pay equity and complex Canadian legislation. Stressing that the issue is jobs, not personal characteristics, we demonstrated that gendered labour force segregation is accompanied by wage discrimination that failed to reflect skills, efforts, responsibility, and working conditions in the jobs. Two Ontario Pay Equity Tribunal cases established precedents that are used around the world, leading to huge settlements for women, albeit often years later. Unfortunately, many of those victories are slowly being eroded, as is pay equity itself.

When our daughter broke her leg, we were exposed to the profound gendered and racialized division of labour everywhere in the hospital. We quickly recognized that the hospital represented all aspects of women's work, offering a wonderful site to explore its complexity. We became convinced that health care and health care work are significantly different from other services. We learned why it is not only Canada's best-loved social program but also a defining feature of being Canadian. A research group we formed worked closely with unions, interviewing workers and patients for over a decade. Our books and reports exposed the negative consequences of reforms for work and care, showing that workers faced increasing stress, as women in particular struggled to make up for the care deficit and the increasing routinization of care work.

We took our analysis of the interviews to workers in hospitals where we had not interviewed and asked them what we got right, what we got wrong, and what we had missed, confirming our attempt to capture general patterns. Both the Ontario Government and the Conference Board of Canada were concerned enough about our research to call us to meetings to defend our findings.

Along with others, we produced evidence about the negative impact of privatization on quality and equity. However, the promise of more efficient and effective care, combined with hysterical stories about wait times, meant more and more people were convinced public health care is not sustainable and that privatization is the answer. Privatization is complex, however, and difficult to explain in public meetings. Moreover, much of it is happening by stealth. We deconstructed six forms of cascading privatization: that which trickled down to drown those at the bottom—this included privatization of care work as more care is sent home and less care provided in hospitals and nursing homes; of responsibility—often called responsibilization—for self-care; of care work management with for-profit methods adopted in the public sector; of delivery through contracting out, through handing abandoning services, and through public–private partnerships; of costs through delisting and failing to cover new services; and of decision making, especially with large foreign-owned corporations providing health services. All these forms create more inequities in access and workloads, as well as in quality care.

A group I chaired for more than a dozen years adopted our approach. With Health Canada funding, the mandate of Women and Health Care Reform was to coordinate research across the centres of excellence for women's health, to identify and fill gaps, to influence policy, and to share knowledge with women. Our longevity meant we were able to develop guiding questions and a common theoretical framework, as well as a methodology that drew on multiple disciplines and techniques. We asked: Why is this a women's issue? What are the issues for women, and for which women?

We organized workshops involving care providers, policy-makers, researchers, and people from community organizations. Our first workshop spontaneously resulted in the Charlottetown Declaration on the Right to Care,[1] a policy statement on home care and unpaid care that intrigued other countries and stills provides critical principles to achieve care equity. Our workshops resulted in our popular pieces that were used in classrooms, communities, unions, religious organizations, and governments, and were copied internationally. Our collective experience allowed us to respond quickly to events such as the Romanow Report on the Future of

Health Care and to have gender included in the federal report on wait times. Our books were just one of multiple strategies we used in fulfilling our mandate. Sadly, Health Canada's commitment to women's health has withered away, but our materials are still on the Web.

In a report for the Pan American Health Organization (Armstrong, 2013b), I argued that unpaid health care work is a gender issue because women and girls throughout the world do the overwhelming majority of most demanding and daily unpaid health care; and it's an equity issue because women with the fewest economic resources are the most likely to do the heaviest work, and because those who need care experience inequities in the amount and quality of care they receive as a result. These inequities are too often racialized as well as classed and gendered. Unfortunately, it will be much harder to track this work and who does it in Canada because in 2011 the federal government removed the question from the Census.

It is also harder to track those who do laundry, housekeeping, dietary, and clerical health care work. Informed by the determinants of health literature, we argue in the Gender and Work database and in *Critical to Care* (Armstrong et al., 2008) that these jobs are essential to health services and have a different character when they are done there. We challenged their dismissal as hotel services easily contracted out and argued that privatization removed these workers from the care team, with significant negative consequences for care as well as for the workers.

For us, the conditions of work are the conditions of care. It seems obvious that providing good care is hard to do when you have no time, few resources, little power, and minimum staffing, although the connection is seldom made in policy. Our international survey of workers in long-term residential care was particularly effective in making the case. Personal support workers in Canada were more than six times as likely as those in Nordic countries to say they face violence on a daily basis (Armstrong et al., 2009), yet the residents are similar; it is the conditions that differ. Nordic countries have higher resident-to-staff ratios, and workers have greater autonomy and spend way less time filling out forms saying what they have done.

Our evidence suggests that the differences in violence and absences due to illness or injury result from structures more than from the individual workers' or residents' health. Workers experience a form of **structural violence** (Farmer, 2004: Gultung, 1985), understood as the conditions that prevent people from reaching their potential. Our nursing home research indicates that workers can usually see what needs to be done for residents and usually know how to do it but are too often prevented from doing so, with structures the main the cause. The consequences they feel in their bodies and minds cannot primarily be attributed to their individual practices or the individual residents they care for. This structural violence became obvious in interviews around adult-diaper use. Workers said they could not change the diapers unless the blue line indicated that the diapers were full, denying workers' knowledge and capacity to decide as well as denying resident-focused care, doing violence to both in the process.

This work prompted me to return to skills. Skills have received little attention since the debates over pay equity and, more recently, over emotional labour. Shifting from focusing on deskilling, I argued that we should focus on conditions that prevent people from developing and using the skills they need and from having those skills appropriately valued, and on identifying the ways skills and their evaluation have become gendered and racialized.

Our current projects, "Reimagining Long-Term Residential Care: An International Study of Promising Practices" and "Healthy, Active Aging in Residential Places," involve faculty and students from 12 jurisdictions, 5 union partners, and both a seniors' and an employers' organization. Primarily organized around four themes, the projects involve multiple methods, including analytical mapping and rapid-site switching ethnographies—methods we are developing. Our students/faculty seminar produced

Troubling Care (Armstrong and Braedley, 2013), a book that troubles the categories and identifies troubling aspects of long-term residential care.

These projects are about working for care and caring for work, for project members, for paid and unpaid workers and for the residents and families in order not only to understand the world but also to change it, doing so in a collective, feminist, democratic, and—equally important—fun way. A woman's work is never done.

Note

1. See Women and Health Care Reform website http://www.womenandhealthcarereform.ca.

References

Armstrong, Pat and Susan Braedley, eds (2013) *Troubling Care*. Toronto: Canadian Scholars' Press.

Armstrong, Pat and Hugh Armstrong (2010a) *Wasting Away: The Undermining of Canadian Health Care*. Toronto: Oxford University Press.

Armstrong, Pat and Hugh Armstrong (2010b) *The Double Ghetto: Canadian Women and Their Segregated Work* Toronto: Oxford University Press.

Armstrong, Pat et al. (2008a) *They Deserve Better: The Long-Term Care Experience in Canada and Scandinavia* Ottawa: Canadian Centre for Policy Alternatives.

Armstrong, Pat, Hugh Armstrong and Krista Scott-Dixon (2008b) *Critical to Care: The Invisible Women in Health Services*, Toronto: University of Toronto Press.

Armstrong, Pat (2013a) Puzzling Skills. *Canadian Review of Sociology* 53(3):256–83.

Armstrong, Pat (2013b) *Unpaid Healthcare Work: An Indicator of Equity*. Pan American Health Organization. http://new.paho.org/hq/index.php?option=com_content&view=article&id=2680&Itemid=4017

Armstrong, Pat et al. (2009) *They Deserve Better: The Long-Term Care Experience in Canada and Scandinavia*. Ottawa: Canadian Centre for Policy Alternatives, 2009.

Farmer, Paul (2004) *Pathologies of Power*. Oakland: University of California Press.

Galtung, Johan (1985) Twenty-Five Years of Peace Research. *Journal of Peace Research* 22(2):141–158.

Glucksmann, Miriam (2000) *Cottons and Casuals*. London: British Sociological Association.

Marchak, Patricia. 1985. Canadian Political Economy. *Canadian Review of Sociology and Anthropology* 22(5):673–709.

Smith, Dorothy E. (1987) *The Everyday World as Problematic*. Toronto: University of Toronto Press.

Stone, Deborah (2000) Caring by the Book, pp. 89–111 in M. Harrington Meyer ed., *Care Work: Gender, Labour and the Welfare State*. London: Routledge.

21 The Living Wage Movement in Canada: Resisting the Low-Wage Economy

Bryan Evans and Carlo Fanelli

The idea that workers should be paid a "living wage" (LW) emerged with the rapid expansion of industrial capitalism in late-nineteenth-century Britain, Australia, and New Zealand. The concept was taken up by early trade unions and social theorists like Karl Marx as a principle to guide wage bargaining with employers (Littman, 2014; Jonna and Foster, 2016). This impulse led to minimum wage policies in many jurisdictions. However, minimum wage policies remain vulnerable to political maneuverings and fail to provide adequate compensation for an increasing proportion of workers. As a result, over the past 20 years, a social movement for a LW has emerged. This movement emerged first in the United States and, more recently, in Canada. The demand for a LW is one response to the crisis of quality employment. In what follows we (1) compare and contrast the minimum wage with the LW, (2) explore the strategies and tactics utilized by LW proponents, and (3) briefly discuss the origins of LW movements in British Columbia and Ontario.

Comparing the Living Wage to the Minimum Wage

A living wage is distinct from the minimum wage. A **minimum wage** establishes a government mandated and enforced minimum rate of hourly compensation that applies to all employers. In some jurisdictions the regulation allows for certain occupational variance from the general minimum. In this sense, the minimum wage is set as a "floor" and is not tied to the poverty line or otherwise determined by some measurement of adequacy. This has not always been the case however. In the nineteenth century, as governments contracted with private firms to undertake infrastructure construction, they adopted a minimum wage policy, also known as a fair wage, with the intent to "protect workers from aggressive competition in the bidding process, which always resulted in corners being cut on wages and safety standards" (Hennessy et al., 2013: 11). In the 1920s, minimum wage policy evolved beyond this narrow frame to apply to women and child workers. And by the late 1930s it applied to all workers. Until the mid-1970s and the onset of a global economic crisis, minimum wages both in Canada and the United States more were much closer to the average industrial wage.

For example, in Ontario in 1965 the minimum wage was $1, but this was 42 per cent of the average industrial wage. From 1975 to 1995, there were wide fluctuations in this correspondence, followed by a damaging freeze on the rate between 1995 and 2004. The consequence was that the minimum wage lost 15 per cent of its purchasing power (Hennessy et al., 2013: 12). By 2013, the average minimum wage corresponded to just 46 per cent of average hourly earnings (Statistics Canada, 2014).

One clear problem with the minimum wage history is that the lack of any explicit policy goal, whether to reflect the average industrial wage, to ensure work is paid above the poverty line, or to take wages out of competition. This results in an improvised and politically driven process in wage determination. In contrast, the **living wage** concept is rather distinct from the minimum wage in important ways. The LW "sets a higher test" in that it "reflects what earners in a family need to bring home based on the actual costs of living in a specific community" (Living Wage Canada, n.d). With roughly 1 million Canadians earning the minimum wage, and close to another million earning less than $15 per hour, the LW movement is a call to private and public sector employers to pay wages sufficient enough to provide a modicum of social and financial security (Evans and Fanelli, 2016; Fanelli and Shields, 2016). Unlike the minimum wage, economic need is a central component of the LW. The Canadian Living Wage Framework assumes a family unit composed of two working adults with two dependent children. A basket of goods and services to meet this family's needs is constructed consisting of such items as food, clothing, rent, transportation, child care, non-government-funded health care expenses, adult education, and measures that facilitate a decent life, like the ability to participate in your community or a monthly family night out.

The Living Wage Movement as a Political Strategy

The shift in the balance of political and economic power in favour of business, which began in the 1970s and matured through the 1980s, resulted in a weakening of both trade unions and the political willingness of governments to intervene in markets. This was followed by the erosion of social services spending and a rise in a whole range of precarious and low-paying employment. The notable rise in low-wage work, defined as those earning less than 1.5 times the minimum wage, in part accounts for the dramatic rise in LW movements. Whereas **precarious work** accounted for 13 per cent of all employment in 1989, this rose to more than 20 per cent by 2007. Between 2008 and 2013, part-time jobs grew at twice the rate of full-time work (5.9 per cent versus 3.3 per cent) and accounted for 40 per cent of all job growth. In other words, a glaring 72 per cent of all net new jobs created during this time fall into precarious or low-paid categories (CLC, 2014).

Rapidly increasing income inequality has followed. Between 1980 and 2005, the earnings of the bottom 20 per cent of Canadian workers dropped 21 per cent, while the earnings of the top 20 per cent increased by 16 per cent (Block, 2013: 1). The wealthiest 10 per cent of Canadians own more than 50 per cent of the national wealth, while the richest 86 Canadians alone own more than the bottom 11.4 million. The LW movement is as much a response to deteriorating labour market conditions as it is a reaction to mounting social inequality.

These labour market conditions are not unique to Canada. LW movements, most notably in the United States and the United Kingdom, emerged in response to comparable conditions. The first contemporary LW movement emerged in Baltimore, Maryland, in 1994 where a grassroots community-based campaign led to a local LW policy. By 2002, similar laws had been passed in more than 90 US municipalities. And in the wake of the 2008 economic crisis, many more cities and some states have adopted such policies (Greenberg, 2008: 76). The UK LW movement began in 2001 with the formation of the London Citizens community alliance. This, too, was a broad coalition that lobbied local government and employers to implement LW policies that provided a worker with a sufficient income to live in expensive London. The UK movement achieved its most significant victory in 2015 when the finance minister announced a significant rise in the minimum wage to £7.20 (about $12.50CDN) an hour for all workers over the age of 25 beginning in 2016, and rising by approximately 6 per cent per year to £9.00 ($15.60) an hour by 2020. Canadian LW campaigns resemble their counterparts in their variation and grassroots-oriented outlook. While the specific makeup of LW campaigns varies, they often include segments of organized labour both in the private and public spheres, faith-based groups, charities, non-profits, and public-interest organizations. Women, immigrant, and racialized communities have often been at the forefront of organizing and implementation, since they are disproportionately represented in low-waged work. Tactics can also differ quite widely, including door-to-door canvassing, public hearings, and rallies, as well as direct actions such as squares occupations, sit-ins, and other forms of civil disobedience. To a greater or lesser degree, LW campaigns share the following: (1) an annual calculation of the local LW; (2) advocating for a municipal LW policy to apply to direct employees and the employees of contractors; and (3) lobbying employers to adopt the LW as the minimum rate of pay. As Figure 21.1 illustrates, across Canada there is a growing mismatch between minimum wages and LW. British Columbia and Ontario provide vivid examples of recent efforts to raise the minimum wage to an LW.

The first Canadian LW campaign originated in British Columbia. In 2001, the BC government ripped up the collective agreement with the Hospital Employees' Union (HEU). Eight-thousand workers saw their wages cut by 40 per cent through outsourcing. The union, together with the BC Office of the Canadian Centre for Policy Alternatives, understood through that experience how susceptible the wages of workers, even public sector workers, were to the caprice of governments. Modelled on the London Citizens' LW campaign, the BC CCPA, along with a coalition of unions and community groups, initiated the Living Wage for Families Campaign in 2008, which put forward $15 as a basic LW.

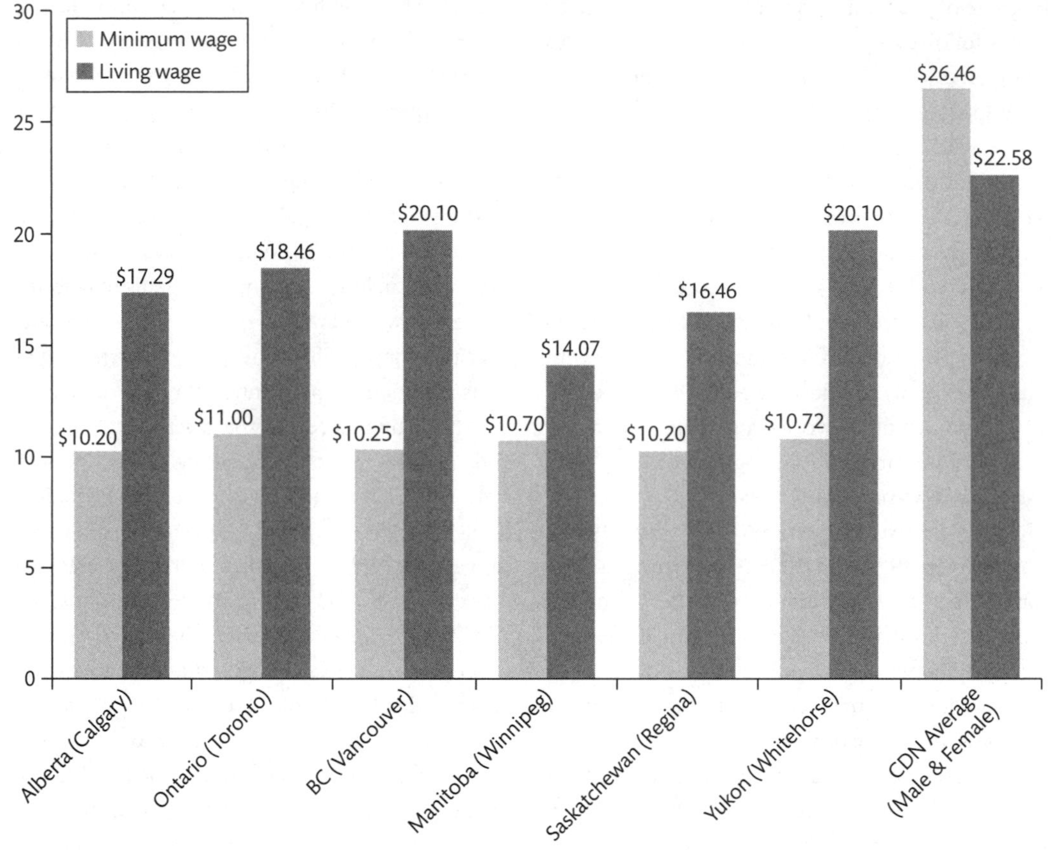

FIGURE 21.1 Minimum Wage vs. Living Wage (Select CDN Cities) Hourly Pay
Source: Living Wage Canada, n.d.

In British Columbia, where two-thirds of minimum wage workers are women and 47 per cent of minimum wage workers are 25 or older, roughly 25 per cent of the total provincial workforce earns less than $15 per hour. In 2011, the city of New Westminster, a municipality within the Greater Vancouver Area, became Canada's first government to adopt an LW policy that requires all firms that are contracted directly or subcontracted by the city to pay a minimum of $19.62 an hour, nearly double the provincial minimum wage. Soon after, the tiny township of Esquimalt set an LW of $17.31, but it has yet to be implemented. Between 2001 and 2011, BC's minimum wage rose from $8 to $9.50; however, this still failed to keep pace with more than a decade of real hourly wage erosion.

In Ontario, activists have made some important strides as well. Between 2004 and 2010, the minimum wage was raised from $6.85 to $10.25. It was frozen, however, for the next three years, which eroded real purchasing power. In 2012, a coalition of more than a dozen advocacy groups and trade unionists came together to form the Campaign to Raise the Minimum Wage to $14. Under mounting pressure from social justice, labour, and community-based organizations, in June 2014 the general minimum wage increased to $11, and in November 2014 it was indexed to inflation. The minimum wage rose to $11.25 in October 2015.

Under pressure from the Campaign to Raise the Minimum Wage, the government of Ontario also established a minimum wage advisory panel set to undertake a formal review of the province's labour and employment standards legislation in a bid to better protect people in low-waged and precarious work.

Conclusion

By challenging the conventional wisdom of neoliberalism, the LW movement has stimulated a broader public debate about low-waged work and social inequality. Beyond the legislative reforms, Canadian LW movements have also been significant in their ability to provide a point of unity between unionized and non-unionized workers. While still in its very early stages, between 40 and 50 LW campaigns have been launched across Canada and are at varying stages of development. If the LW movement continues to grow, it may well be able to exert a greater influence over public policy, ameliorating the conditions of precarious work.

References

Block, Sheila. (2013). *Who Is Working for Minimum Wage in Ontario?* Toronto: Wellesley Institute.

Canadian Labour Congress (CLC). (2014, March 6). *Underemployment Is Canada's Real Labour Market Challenge.* Retrieved from http://canadianlabour.ca/issues-research/underemployment-canadas-real-labour-market-challenge

Evans, B. and C. Fanelli. (2016). "A Survey of the Living Wage Movement in Canada: Prospects and Challenges." *Interface: A Journal For and About Social Movements*, 8(1): 77–96.

Fanelli, C. and J. Shields, eds. (2016). *Precarious Work and the Struggle for Living Wages, Alternate Routes 2016.* Edmonton: Athabasca University Press.

Greenberg, B. et al. (2008). *Social History of the United States: The 1900s.* Vol. 10. Santa Barbara, CA: ABC-Cali.

Hennessy, Trish, Kaylie Tiessen and Armine Yalnizyan. (2013). *Making Every Job a Good Job: A Benchmark for Setting Ontario's Minimum Wage.* Toronto: Canadian Centre for Policy Alternatives.

International Labour Organization (ILO). (2015). *Global Wage Report.* Geneva: International Labour Organization.

Jonna, R.J. and J.B. Foster. (2016). "Marx's Theory of Working-Class Precariousness—and Its Relevance Today". In Fanelli, C. and J. Shields, eds, *Precarious Work and the Struggle for Living Wages, Alternate Routes 2016* (pp. 21–45). Edmonton: Athabasca University Press.

Littman, Deborah. (2014). "The Living Wage: An Idea Whose Time Has Come," *New Zealand Journal of Employment Relations*, 38(2): 70–7.

Living Wage Canada. (n.d.). *Canadian Living Wage Framework: A National Methodology for Calculating the Living Wage in Your Community.* Available online at: http://livingwagecanada.ca/index.php/about-living-wage/about-canadian-living-wage

Statistics Canada. (2014). *The Ups and Downs of Minimum Wage, 1975 to 2013.* Retrieved from http://www.statcan.gc.ca/daily-quotidien/140716/dq140716b-eng.htm

22 Freedom as an Ethical Principle for Sociology

Carmen Grillo

Should sociologists diagnose and treat society's ills? Should they be the vanguard of social change, or should they point out the origins of political ideas and encourage ethical reflection? These questions about sociology's ethical, moral, and political purpose have haunted the discipline since its inception

(See Durkheim, Marx, and Weber, respectively). Over the past 20 or so years, public sociology—a view of sociologists as public intellectuals who have a responsibility to share knowledge with others outside of the university (Burawoy, 2005; Burawoy et al., 2006; Burawoy, Hanemaayer, and Schneider, 2014)—has emerged as a new way of answering those questions. But despite deciding to engage directly with society at large, public sociologists are still confronted with an ethical challenge. Which principles are worthy of sociology's support and which are not? In this chapter, I discuss freedom as one such principle, and explore G.W.F. Hegel's definition of it as a possible foundation for public sociology.

Within public sociology, critical sociology has the task of being sociology's "conscience" (Burawoy, 2005: 11): of considering what is right in society, what is wrong, and how sociology can answer such questions. One way to do critical sociology is to look at current public debates and determine the "social problems" underlying them—an approach called **immanent critique**. According to social theorist Gerard Delanty, sociologists doing immanent critique should identify a social debate, map out the views of different social groups in the debate, determine how those views emerge out of the living situations of those groups, and ultimately find a solution that will resolve the problem (Delanty, 2011: 87–8). For example, in their analysis of a conflict about free speech on a university campus, critical sociologists would identify the groups involved and try to see the issue from each group's point of view. The sociologist would then try to explain the social causes of each group's problems and help formulate policy to solve those problems.

To formulate such policies, however, can be difficult. What is the yardstick by which one can measure "good" or "bad" social policies? Expelling or banning controversial groups on campus is one solution. This might superficially get rid of the tension, but it ultimately does nothing to address the deeper issues. Immanent critique aims to solve problems rather than plaster them over. Still, as the university example illustrates, there needs to be some **ethical principle** to which critical sociology can adhere. Otherwise, the "solutions" might lead to greater social conflict, violence, or oppression (for more on this issue, see Wendy Brown's argument in *States of Injury: Power and Freedom in Late Modernity*).

In modern times, "freedom" has ostensibly become an important guiding principle of social policy. As far as we live in liberal democracies, we learn to applaud freedom and condemn attempts to curtail it. Still, the past few decades have taught us that freedom is not always ethically straightforward; from "free trade" to Gulf Wars, to "freedom of speech," politicians have talked about freedom while trampling people underfoot. If freedom has been used so often to justify violence and injustice, how can it still be the foundation of critical sociology?

Nowhere has this problem been clearer than in the case of neoliberalism. **Neoliberalism** is a set of political ideas, policies, and practices that became popular in the late 1970s, with Ronald Regan and Margaret Thatcher being commonly seen as neoliberalism's official faces. The diversion of funds away from public coffers, the advent of corporate-style government, and an emphasis on individual freedom and choice are some of its hallmarks. It has been called a new ideology (see Harvey, 2005; Žižek, 2009; Hall, 2011), a "truth regime" (see Foucault, 2008; Brown, 2006; Oksala, 2013), and the next phase of capitalism (see Hartmann and Honneth, 2006). In public discourse, its meaning varies, too. To some people, neoliberalism means lower taxes, more responsible governments, and greater choice in consumer goods. To others, it means decreased public services (public transit and health care), increased repression of protest and dissent (like during the G20 protests in Toronto), and widespread destitution and homelessness. In other words, depending on one's point of view, neoliberalism makes people much more, or much less, free. How then, are sociologists to determine whether it is "good" or "bad"? Even though neoliberalism is historically recent, some of the problems it creates around freedom were foreshadowed in the work of the influential German philosopher Georg Wilhelm Friedrich Hegel (1770–1831). Hegel's description of how human freedom works is a good place to start when formulating an ethical position for critical sociology, especially when neoliberalism has made the meaning of freedom ambiguous.

Hegel's analysis of freedom is based on what would later become a classical sociological paradox: on one hand, our minds allow us to constantly reimagine and modify the world around us. We essentially live in social worlds of our own creation. On the other hand, the social worlds into which we are born fundamentally constrain the limits of the possible. Although we all have some degree of choice as to what we do in our lives (Hegel, 1991: 37), that degree is affected by the society in which we live (see Bauman, 1988). For example, when I decide how to get food, I choose between one grocery store and another, between cooking at home and ordering in. I am able to weigh alternatives. Hegel calls this deliberate weighing of preferences "freedom in itself." Nevertheless, the availability of objects to choose from—alternatives for action, acquisition, and reflection—are usually outside of my control. I cannot decide, to continue our example, what the nearest grocery store stocks on its shelves. I am confronted by a social and physical world, an objective reality, from which I am separate, and which is beyond my control (Hegel, 1991: 38).

If our life choices are constrained by what already exists, how can society ever change? How do new social institutions, cultures, and languages come to be? Luckily, people are able to "think beyond" existing social life, and consider the "what if"—to imagine reality as different from how it is ("absolute abstraction" in Hegel's terms, [1991: 37]). Hegel argues that the freest societies provide people ample opportunities to make those "what ifs" real. That is, freedom, in its ideal form, means the capacity not only to choose the life one lives from several options, but to actually change the alternatives on offer; "every relationship of dependence on something other than [one's own will] is thereby eliminated" (Hegel, 1991: 54). In concrete terms, this means that social and political arrangements whose structures are determined by the members themselves, what Hegel calls "institutions of right" (Vernon, 2011: 56)—democratic arrangements—maximize freedom. Although, humans, as social beings, always live in structured groups, we can aspire to social institutions that allow us to consciously and democratically set the terms of our own realities.

Armed with Hegel's definition of freedom, we will see that the neoliberal version of freedom is incomplete; it allows people a great deal of choice but very little opportunity to democratically organize social life. It leaves the individual in a position where she can choose the best of several options but where she has no control over the provision of those options, nor over the terms of choosing. For example, while neoliberal "free" trade policies purportedly offer people cheaper and more diverse consumer goods, those same policies move decision making out of the hands of democratic publics and into the offices of transnational corporations.

We began this chapter with a consideration of sociology's social role, and the problem of formulating ethical principles to guide critical sociology. While the utility of Hegel's definition of freedom is particularly clear in a critique of neoliberalism, it is not limited to this case. Rather, the principle of freedom is a tool that critical sociologists can use in diverse fields of sociology. Whether applied to an analysis of social conflict around gender, around race, or around the distribution of wealth, Hegel's theory tells us that social institutions should be, as much as possible, deliberative and democratic. It tells us that people should have the opportunity to determine their own life circumstances. For immanent critique, it gives sociologists the ability to judge whether the solution to a social problem will alleviate or exacerbate conflict.

References

Antonio, R.J. 1981. "Immanent Critique as the Core of Critical Theory: Its Origins and Development in Hegel, Marx and Contemporary Thought." *The British Journal of Sociology*, Vol. 32, No. 3, pp. 330–45.

Bauman, Z. 1988. *Freedom*. Minneapolis: University of Minnesota Press.

Brown, W. 2006. "American Nightmare: Neoliberalism, Neoconservatism and De-Democratization." *Political Theory*, Vol. 34, No. 6, pp. 690–714.

Brown, W. 2005. *Edgework: Critical Essays in Knowledge and Politics*. Princeton, NJ: Princeton University Press.

Burawoy, M. 2005. "For Public Sociology." *American Sociological Review*, Vol. 70, No. 1, pp. 4–28.

Burawoy, M. et al. 2006. *Public Sociologies Reader*. Lanham, MD: Rowman & Littlefield Publishers.

Burawoy, Michael, Ariane Hanemaayer, and Christopher J Schneider. 2014. *The Public Sociology Debate: Ethics and Engagement*. Vancouver: UBC Press.

Butler, J. 2012. *Subjects of Desire: Hegelian Reflections in Twentieth Century France*. New York: Columbia University Press.

Delanty, G. "Varieties of Critique in Sociological Theory and Their Methodological Implications for Social Research." *Irish Journal of Sociology*, Vol. 19, No. 1, pp. 68–92.

Durkheim, Émile. 1951. *Suicide: A Study in Sociology*. Trans. J.A. Spaulding and G. Simpson, Glencoe, IL: The Free Press, 1951 [1897].

Durkheim, Émile. 1982. "Rules for the Distinction of the Normal from the Pathological." In *The Rules of Sociological Method and Selected Texts on Sociology and its Method*, edited by Steven Lukes, 85–107. New York: The Free Press.

Foucault, M. 2008. *The Birth of Biopolitics: Lectures at the Collège De France 1978–1979*. Trans. G. Burchell. New York: Palgrave Macmillan.

Foucault, M. *The Government of Self and Others: Lectures at the Collège De France 1982–1983*. Trans. G. Burchell. New York: Palgrave Macmillan.

Fraser, N. 2009. "Feminism, Capitalism, and the Cunning of History." *New Left Review*, Vol. 56 pp. 97–117.

Hall, S. 2011. "The Neo-Liberal Revolution." *Cultural Studies*, Vol. 25, No. 6, pp.705–28.

Hartmann, M., and A. Honneth. 2006. "Paradoxes of Capitalism." *Constellations*, Vol. 13, No. 1, pp. 41–58.

Harvey, D. 2005. *A Brief History of Neoliberalism*. Oxford: Oxford University Press.

Hegel, G.W.F. 1991. *Elements of the Philosophy of Right*. Trans. H.B. Nisbet. Cambridge: Cambridge University Press.

Honneth, A. 2010. *The Pathologies of Individual Freedom: Hegel's Social Theory*. Princeton, NJ: Princeton University Press.

Knapp, P. 2009. "Hegel's Universal in Marx, Durkheim and Weber." *Sociological Forum*, Vol. 1, No. 4, pp. 586–609.

Marx, Karl. 1976. "Manifesto of the Communist Party." In *The Marx-Engels Reader*, edited by Robert C. Tucker, 469–500. New York and London: W.W. Norton & Company.

Nichols, L. 2011. *Public Sociology: The Contemporary Debate*. New Brunswick, NJ: Transaction Publishers.

Oksala, Johanna. 2013. "Neoliberalism and Biopolitical Governmentality." In *Foucault, Biopolitics, Governmentality*, edited by Wallenstein S. and J. Nillson, pp. 53–72. Huddinge: Södertörn University Press.

Patten, A. 1999. *Hegel's Idea of Freedom*. Oxford: Oxford University Press.

Read, Jason. 2009. "A Genealogy of Homo-Economicus: Neoliberalism and the Production of Subjectivity." *Foucault Studies*, No. 6, pp. 25–36.

Roberts, J. 2013. "Dialectic and Post-Hegelian Dialectic (Again)." *Journal of Critical Realism* Vol. 12, No. 1, pp. 72–98.

Rose, G. 2009 [1981]. *Hegel Contra Sociology*. London: Verso.

Vernon, Jim. 2011. "Siding with Freedom: Towards a Prescriptive Hegelianism." *Critical Horizons*, Vol. 12, No. 1, pp. 49–69.

Weber, M. 1989. "Science as a Vocation." In *Max Weber's "Science as a Vocation"*, edited by Peter Lasmann P. et al., 1–32. London: Unwin Hyman.

Žižek, S. 2009. *First as Tragedy, Then as Farce*. London: Verso.

23 Inequality, Demographics, and the New World Order

Susan A. McDaniel, FRSC

We live in a world where slogans, propaganda, and politics increasingly triumph over evidence, reason, and goodwill. It may be becoming a 140-character world where illusions prevail. Examples are abundant: unwarranted hope that the various Arab Springs will succeed; that the Internet will set us free; that democracy and capitalism are inextricably linked; that if austerity impositions do not work initially, more austerity might; or that economic models are good estimations of reality. Some illusions are demographic: demography as destiny, demography as predictive, demography as capable of explaining almost everything, population aging as a dominant policy challenge, the list goes on.

What do all of these illusions and slogans have in common? First, they tend to indicate seeing what is wished, not necessarily what is there. Second, they tend to avoid taking note of what may not fit the current belief system or hopeful interpretation. Third, there is a hint of belief triumphing over evidence. Fourth, judgments tend to be made from afar, or in the abstract, without putting them to the test of truth. Fifth, illusions tend to be overly simplistic, gliding over the complexities of real situations. Sixth, there can be a "bandwagon effect" with slogans or simple understandings, which results in what sociologists call **consensual validation**. This occurs when many observers seem to come to the same or similar conclusions, thereby reinforcing each observation as real. Social media has the capacity to amplify consensual validation processes.

In discrepancies between illusions and evidence, there can be light and insights. When a discovery is made that something you believed to be true is actually not true, that tends to get remembered. Myth-busting is something at which sociology is particularly good. In this brief chapter, the findings of two recent research projects, both funded by the Social Sciences and Humanities Research Council of Canada (SSHRC) with the author as principal investigator, are presented in summary, revealing some insights emergent in the space between illusions and evidence.

The first project is a knowledge synthesis project on population aging and the future workforce in Canada (McDaniel, Wong, and Watt, 2015). Aging population, and specifically an aging workforce, is a perplexing policy preoccupation in Canada, as well as in other advanced economies. Demographic panic can take root in the populace when social problems are seen as immutable in the face of the "tsunami" of the baby boomers entering their later years, or shrinking labour force age populations. That is what seems to have transpired in recent decades. The question then becomes, what does the evidence show about policy challenges with an aging population and workforce?

In this project, we first unpacked some issues involved with workforce populations. For example, demographers and policy-makers are often preoccupied with what is referred to as **dependency ratios**, which usually are simple population ratios of those of workforce age to those under age 18 (youth dependency) or over age 65 (old age dependency), or both (total dependency). Everyone can immediately see that these age group ratios are only proxies for actual dependency. Being of working age does not equate with paid labour force participation. Some who are of working age opt for unpaid childrearing; others are unemployed, underemployed, unable to work, or working without pay as interns or as volunteers. At the older end of the life course spectrum, a strong inequality theme comes through, with working-class and disadvantaged people less likely to live as long as better-off people, and more likely to take early retirement due to health issues. The trend toward later retirement is largely, but not exclusively, a white-collar phenomenon. Those who are more skilled not only work longer but are increasingly independent, and in fact, may support younger generations rather than being supported by them (McDaniel, Gazso, and Um, 2013). This is less the case for working-class people, however, therefore widening the gap between what middle-class and working-class parents and grandparents can provide to their younger relatives. Demographic age structure, then, is too simple and too abstract to be a good proxy for workforce realities. And yet, it is typically on the basis of dependency ratio projections that policy concerns are raised about future workforce shortages.

No agreed-upon, universally used, definitions of labour or skills shortages exist. Guy Standing suggests that actually "[the] modern market economy [may have] a 'skills excess,' in that millions of people have bundles of skills that they have not had opportunity to exercise or refine . . . huge numbers have qualifications and diplomas that they do not use and that rust away in their mental lockers" (2011: 122). Canada, in fact, has the highest rate of adult post-secondary education (PSE) attainment in the developed world and spends the highest proportion of its gross national product (GDP) on PSE, according to the Paris-based Organisation for Economic Co-operation and Development (OECD) (2014).

What does the evidence tell us about population aging and possible workforce shortages? SSHRC's knowledge mobilization grant initiative undertakes to answer key policy questions, in this case to shed light on the presumption of future labour shortages due to demographic aging. The McDaniel-led project looked at this through a systematic examination of all published research studies from 2000 to 2013 in Canada, both French and English, that addressed this question in any way. We found no evidence of a national labour shortage at present or into the foreseeable future. In fact, the Canadian labour force is predicted to grow until 2031, but at a slower rate than at present. We did find that there are pockets of shortages in some sectors and regions, but that these have always occurred as national economies never grow evenly. The research also found large under-utilized populations with skills that could be more fully utilized in the workforce—recent immigrants, youth, Aboriginals, disabled persons, and older workers who may be without work. And, we found dramatic increases in reliance on temporary foreign workers, particularly in Alberta.

This research was taken up widely by media as well as by policy-makers. A subsequent study by the Parliamenty Budget Office (2014), using a different methodology, found exactly what we had found earlier. This research led, in part, to changes in various immigration policies in Canada, including changes to the Temporary Foreign Workers program. It also led to McDaniel being named one of the most influential people in Alberta in 2014 (see: http://albertaventure.com/2014/07/susan-mcdaniel-albertas-50-influential-people-2014). Sociological research can have practical outcomes as it dispels illusions with evidence.

The second research project is as interesting as the first in its findings, outcomes, and influence, but it is much more complex. In this multi-year, multi-method project, we sought to find out how those in mid-life in Canada and the United States move through life courses into their later years. We follow the same individuals over time to see what factors contribute to their well-being (physical, mental, and financial) as they age. This approach offers very different insights than the usual one, which looks at those who are in the later years now and projects those patterns for those now in mid-life, most notably the baby boomers. It is this presumption that has led to the illusion that nothing but challenges and problems lie ahead with and for the aging boomers.

What we found in this research is that the challenges ahead are more challenges of inequality than of aging. Working-class people or those who are disadvantaged in mid-life accumulate even more disadvantage as they age; they live less long and tend to retire earlier due largely to health issues, leaving them with fewer resources as they age. And, most importantly, they more often have adult children who are in precarious employment and/or face family or health issues requiring the mid-lifers' support, sometimes for prolonged periods. Entire familial networks are tied together by inequality and **precarity**. These life course outcomes and linked lives were found as well for better-off people in mid-life, but they tend to have less of a disadvantaging effect because of the greater cushion of savings and resources.

One important finding from this research comes from the comparison of Americans and Canadians in mid-life aging in the wake of the Great Recession of 2008. The United States was very much harder hit by this economic downturn, with bank failures, job losses, millions of home foreclosures, and loss of savings and pension funds. The prevailing view, an illusion as it turns out, is that older and younger cohorts were severely affected by the Great Recession, with working-class people hit hardest, but that those in mid-life were not impacted very much. Our research finds, to the contrary, that mid-life people are multiply impacted by economic shocks. Those in mid-life, for example, are called upon by both younger and older relatives to help out in times of strife and difficulty. These demands come at a life course point for the mid-lifers when they are maximizing their retirement resources, which we found were compromised by demands for supports from younger and older relatives and sometimes friends. Americans were significantly more impacted in mid-life by the combination of the economic shock of the Great Recession and the greater reliance on familial or individual support in the United States than in Canada. The political effects of this are now being felt strongly in the US. Canadians "huddled together" in shared multi-generational living situations less often because of the better public risk-insurance nets such as universal health insurance, employment insurance, and in some instances, disability and family care insurance.

A finding from this research dispels another myth or illusion that has shaped much of old-age policy in both Canada and the United States. It is a surprising and important finding. Policy based on previous research as well as common sense, the latter of which can be misleading, has presumed that socio-economic status differentiates those who will be okay and healthy in their later years and those who will suffer. This seems to make sense. That said, we found that in times of economic shocks and widening inequalities, it the degree of precarity—specifically, worry about the gap between expectations about one's older years and realities—that is more important in predicting well-being with aging. In fact, we found that this worry is a larger factor than socio-economic status. This is fascinating since it shows that the key factor is not resources per se, but rather it is contentment, or not, with reaching one's expectations with aging. As more people in times of economic insecurity and widening inequalities find themselves frustrated with realities not coming up to expectations, this could lead to more health and well-being issues in future. It is a fundamentally important new finding.

In conclusion, from two recent research projects, we have seen how sociological research can offer evidence that dispels illusions and mitigates the bandwagon effect of repetition of supposedly known understandings. Policies and public knowledge are better if based on evidence from research than on prevalent beliefs or myths. Underlying these findings is the vital importance of growing inequalities interacting with life courses and demographic change in predicting and responding to both present and future needs. Slogans and politics are no substitute.

References

McDaniel, S.A., A. Gazso, and S. Um. 2013. "Generationing Relations in Challenging Times: Americans and Canadians in Mid-Life in the Great Recession." *Current Sociology* 61(3): 301–21. Accessed 10 September 2014 from http://csi.sagepub.com/content/61/3/301.full.pdf+html

McDaniel, Susan A., Lloyd L. Wong, and Bonnie Watt. 2015. "Aging Workforce and the Future Labour Market in Canada," *Canadian Public Policy—Analyse de politiques* 41(2): 97–108.

OECD (Organisation for Economic Co-operation and Development). 2014. *Education at a Glance 2014: OECD Indicators.* Paris: OECD. Accessed 9 September 2014 from http://www.keepeek.com/Digital-Asset-Management/oecd/education/education-at-a-glance-2014_eag-2014-en#page1

Parliamentary Budget Office. 2014. *Labour Market Assessment 2014.* Ottawa, ON: Office of the Parliamentary Budget Officer (PBO), 25 March. Accessed 15 September 2014 from http://www.pbo-dpb.gc.ca/files/files/Labour_Note_EN.pdf

Standing, Guy. 2011. *The Precariat: The New Dangerous Class.* London: Bloomsbury Academic.

Questions for Critical Thought

Chapter 20 | Working for Care; Caring for Work

1. What is political economy? Why is feminist political economy unique?
2. What inequality sparked Armstrong's interest in studying political economy? How does this interest emerge over time?
3. Who does the majority of unpaid health care? How is this a gender issue? How is this an equity issue?
4. What is structural violence? Give an example of how workers may face structural violence in their workplace.
5. Armstrong says that skills have become gendered and racialized. Give examples of each.

Chapter 21 | The Living Wage Movement in Canada: Resisting the Low-Wage Economy

1. What is a living wage? What is the purpose of this type of policy?
2. What motivated the living wage movement? Describe this movement.
3. What *three* things do many living wage campaigns share?
4. Why is the living wage movement important? What social inequality is being combatted through this movement?
5. Do protests that aim to reduce inequalities work? Think about the living wage movement or Occupy Wall Street. How do these protests reduce inequalities?

Chapter 22 | Freedom as an Ethical Principle for Sociology

1. What is the link between public sociology and critical sociology? Why is this important?
2. What is public sociology? How does it differ from traditional sociology?
3. How does Hegel describe freedom? What are the different kinds of freedom?
4. What two suggestions does Grillo make to public sociologists?

Chapter 23 | Inequality, Demographics, and the New World Order

1. What six things does McDaniel say that most slogans/illusions have in common?
2. Describe project one and the insights that it gives into illusions and evidence. (Hint: the project that examines population aging and the changing Canadian workforce.)
3. Describe project two and the insights that it gives into illusions and evidence. (Hint: the project that examines the life course of middle-aged people as they move into old age.)
4. What demographic patterns emerge in both projects? What inequalities are highlighted?
5. Why is it important to update social policy based on facts and not opinion? What is the benefit of using a sociological approach when updating policy? How (where) can we get the data to make these policy decisions?

PART VI
Gender and Sexuality

Understanding the relationship between gender and sexual orientation is oddly difficult precisely because most people carry assumptions that are gender- or heteronormative. This means that people often assume sexuality and gender are tied together, or that men are naturally attracted to women and women are naturally attracted to men. However, both gender and sexuality are more complicated than that.

Let's start by reviewing the difference between sex and gender. A person's sex is based on physical attributes—for example, reproductive structure and genitalia—that are biologically determined, whereas gender reflects a person's link to the socio-cultural construct that distinguishes between masculine and feminine characteristics. As noted, many people think that gender is determined by sex and that gender is binary, with only two options that are rooted in anatomy—in short, that people must be either male or female. However, researchers have shown that everyone has a unique gender identity that can exist on a spectrum of maleness or femaleness. Essentially, people's gender identity is their innermost concept (or perception) of themselves as male or female. As a result, individuals perceive and express their gender in different ways. In some cases—called "transgender"—a person's gender may not correspond to his or her sex.

Now, consider a third related concept: sexual orientation. Sexual orientation refers to feelings of sexual attraction that people feel toward other people of a specific gender or sex. Some people are attracted to others of the same sex, while others are attracted to people of another (the "opposite") sex. Research shows there are many different sexual orientations, which include heterosexual, gay, lesbian, bisexual, pansexual, and asexual. What's more, people's feelings of sexual attraction fall on a continuum. Although some people are closer to one end of the continuum—meaning that they are mainly or exclusively attracted to women or to men—other people have feelings of attraction that fall closer to the middle. They are sometimes called "bisexual."

Sociologists in recent decades have spent a great deal of time studying the social inequalities that result from differences of sex, gender, and sexual orientation—inequalities that are occasionally related through a process called "intersectionality." The largest fraction of people who study gender and sexuality focus on gender inequalities in the workplace and the home, as well as patterns that emerge from changing sex/gender norms and inequalities. So, for example, researchers have studied changes in gender ideology and socialization; changes in discrimination against women and sexual minorities; gendered violence; and changes in the domestic division of labour.

In the chapters that follow, you will read about how the increasing acceptance of alternative gender roles and sexual partnerships has changed social processes, such as dating, work, and family structures. This critical examination of changing norms helps us to better understand the social implications of wider acceptance of alternative gender roles and sexualities. These chapters also explore the implications of existing gender inequalities. By exploring patterns of violence against women, the historical exclusion of women, and the current marginalization of feminism in sociology, we gain a better understanding of the progress that women have made and the long road that still lies ahead.

In this section, Adam Green gives us an excellent overview of recent research in the sociology of sexuality. Next, the chapter by Mervyn Horgan and Saara Liinamaa, about Annie Marion MacLean, reminds us there have been unjustly forgotten and uncelebrated Canadian women sociologists. Robyn Lee writes about the commodification of that most intimate of family activities: the feeding of babies with breast milk. Finally, Meg Luxton, a celebrated Canadian sociologist of recent vintage, sets out an agenda for an activist, feminist sociology, out to seek social change.

24 Sexual Fields

Adam Green

Recently, scholars of sexuality have sought to make sense of collective sexual life as a particular kind of social life in its own right (Farrer and Dale 2014; Green 2008; 2014; Weinberg and Williams 2014). Drawing from a Bourdieusian field theoretic, these theorists understand sexual social life as comprised of systems of stratification tied to sexual fields whereby individuals vie for sexual partnership and social esteem. This stream of work has sought to move beyond deconstructionist, rational/economic, and traditional social learning accounts in the sociology of sexuality to consider broader questions around the social organization of sexuality (Martin and George 2006). Here, the key insight of a sexual field analysis lies in the recognition that the sexual field is not simply the repository of desire and desirability but, rather, that the sexual field is productive of both in a manner that requires attention to the collective and ecological features of sexual social life.

In this essay, I reflect upon the sexual fields framework, which represents my own effort to extrapolate from Bourdieu's theory of practice to the domain of collective sexual life. Toward this end, first, I provide a historical context in which to locate the emergence of the sexual field. Then, I offer a set of key sensitizing concepts that comprise the sexual fields framework, including sites, sexual field, sexual capital, and structure of desire. I then turn to discuss three ways in which the sexual field is productive of desire and desirability, including via the popularity tournament, socialization, and amplification and intensification processes. Finally, I conclude by noting future directions for sexual fields research.

Late Modernity and the Sexual Field

In the context of macrohistorical shifts related to the development of industrial capitalism and the dominance of an independent wage labour system, coupled with the rise of information and communication technologies, advances in birth control, and women's increasing financial independence, contemporary sexual life has unprecedented independence from traditional institutions of control, such as the church and the family (D'Emilio 1983; Giddens 1992; Halperin 1989). As a consequence, sexual social life has developed as a kind of social order in its own right characterized by sexual fields, each with their own particular institutional and subcultural character. Delayed marriage, high rates of divorce, the precocious milieu of adolescence, and the extension of sexual life into old age contribute to the increasing importance of the sexual field for collective sexual life. It is to the study of sexual social life in this historical period that the sexual fields framework is dedicated.

Key Concepts: Sites, Sexual Field, Sexual Capital, Structure of Desire

In the modern West, just outside the bedroom of the monogamous couple lies a terrain of sexual social life that brings together actors in search of sex, long-term partnership, and social esteem. Be it in local bars, nightclubs, coffee houses, house parties, and gyms, or online in websites designed to meet for a fling or to bring together more serious, relationship-oriented individuals, collective sexual life is bound to physical and virtual sites that facilitate partnership of all kinds. These **sites** are the nodes of the **sexual field**, a stratified domain of interaction comprised of semi-autonomous arenas wherein "actors with potential romantic or sexual interest orient themselves toward one another according to a logic of desirability imminent to their collective relations . . . " (Green 2014:27). Sexual fields are distinguished by their patronage base and by the dominant logic of desirability that underpins the fields' status order.

Sexual capital is that species of capital associated with attractiveness that confers advantage upon those who possess it within a sexual field, including field significance and the ability to obtain an intimate partner of one's choosing. Sexual capital is not simply a characteristic of individuals—e.g., having a fit body or pleasing facial features—but rather, is at once a property of individuals *and* a property of the sexual field. This is so because the personal elements that confer value in a sexual field—including physical, affective, and presentational characteristics—are not strictly personal features but, rather, acquire their value in the context of the specific collective attributions of sexual attractiveness that hold in a given sexual field. Thus, sexual capital is not an essential "thing" that an individual owns, like a personal portfolio that one can take from one field to another (Farrer and Dale 2014), but is field dependent, varying between fields and, sometimes, even within a field. Moreover, to the extent that desired attributes in a partner include characteristics beyond sexual appeal, such as cultural and economic capital, so sexual capital is but one part of a larger, socially constructed portfolio of capitals that is attributed with differential value between communities, social strata, and sexual fields. Indeed, while in some instances economic, cultural, or social capital may simply be "sexy" (Martin 2005)—in which case one has the conversion of non-sexual capitals to sexual capital—in other instances these capitals are desirable in a partner but not themselves sexy, in which case one has a capital portfolio (Green 2014), comprised of a range of capitals, that differentially determines status in a sexual field. As an example, if common wisdom holds true, we can say that men, on the whole, value sexual capital more than other capitals in their prospective female partners, while women, on the whole, value economic and cultural capital more than sexual capital in their prospective male partners. Of course, the extent to which this holds true will vary systematically between sexual fields, the latter that are populated by distinct social strata across time and space, and which place differential value on partner characteristics. Thus among college-aged university students, sexual capital may trump other capitals with respect to an actor's desirability, whereas the same is less likely among the middle-aged divorcee crowd. This example underscores the essential point that partner desirability is socially constructed and field-dependent.

Finally, sexual fields are organized by transpersonal systems of judgment and appreciation, or what I refer to as a **structure of desire**. As an aggregate of individual desires within a given field, structures of desire communicate the sexual status order to players based on a host of local cues, including observable patterns in who is favoured (and who is glossed over), the fronts of patrons, the name and decor of a given site, and the dominant representations of attractiveness that pervade the space, such as those that appear on the cover page of websites designed for dating or long-term partnership. Structures of desire, in turn, form the basis upon which actors locate themselves within the field's sexual status order.

Desire and Desirability as Field Effects

In collective sexual life, to the extent that desire and desirability are not reducible to individual desires, they can be seen as field effects. Fields structure desire and desirability in at least three ways: (1) via the popularity tournament; (2) through socialization processes; and (3) as a consequence of the aggregation and intensification of individual desires.

In the first instance, the popularity tournament, individuals who are regarded as desirable gain desirability as a consequence of their initial popularity and, conversely, those deemed less desirable become even less so. One important element of the popularity tournament is the notion of relative popularity, which is to suggest that actors in a sexual field are engaged in an ongoing process of discernment regarding their own sexual status relative to others. In this context, those attributed with greater popularity become more desirable because they are harder to obtain and because their partnership puts our own desirability in a positive light.

A second way in which desire and desirability emerge as a field effect is through socialization processes. Here, following repeated exposure to a field's structure of desire, novitiates gain appreciation for a given norm of desirability and come to internalize it, thereby reproducing it in their own sexual sensibilities. For instance, the process of sexual socialization has been found to be especially relevant in sadomasochistic subcultures wherein actors quite literally learn to gain new appreciations for pleasure and pain (Hennen 2008). Yet the same processes of assimilation and internalization that occur among practitioners of sadomasochism are likely to occur within sexual fields more generally as actors are newly exposed to particular kinds of bodies, sexual themes, and capital portfolios (Green 2014) and come to appropriate these as matters of cultivated taste.

A third and final way in which desire and desirability arise as a field effect is through a process of aggregation, amplification, and intensification. In this process, otherwise diffusely distributed sexual interests and attitudes in a population are brought together within a given sexual field and, via amplification and intensification, consolidated into a new structure of desire and new institutionalized norms of sexual attractiveness. This process was made especially clear in Levine's (1998) work on the gay clone of the 1970s. Then, individual dispositions related to masculinity were brought together in the gay sexual field of the West Village, New York City, and amplified to produce a hypermasculine sexual lifestyle organized around anonymous rough sex and a hard, muscle-bound, blue-collar aesthetic. In effect, the clone sexual field magnified individually held attitudes about masculinity and transformed them into a new sexual subculture, including new norms around sexual practice and the body. Here, desire and desirability cannot be reduced to any individual actor's disposition but must be seen as the product of collective processes of aggregation, amplification, and intensification.

Future Directions in Sexual Fields Research

Research into sexual fields is still in its infancy. Future research will focus on the sexual field at four levels of analysis, including the intrapsychic, micro, meso, and macro levels.

At the intrapsychic level, individuals come to the sexual field, in part, with preconstituted desires. While the sexual fields framework is primarily designed for analyzing collective rather than individual sexual life, how and to what extent the sexual field acts back on these desires and transforms them is an important question for sexual fields scholarship.

At the micro level, sexual social life occurs over the course of interactions in a nightclub, a coffee house, a gym, a private party, or an Internet chat room. Here, the analyst of the sexual field will want to be attentive to the questions, who is being paid attention by whom?; who initiates conversation and how?; what are the observable patterns in sexual sociality over a given evening, a given weekend, or a given season? Of special significance will be to determine how actors jockey for position and manage the self in light of differential sexual status.

At the meso level, scholars of the sexual field will want to attend to a field's structure of desire, the tiers of desirability that delineate a given sexual status order, the social organization of networks that move in and out of a given sexual site, and the dominant currencies of sexual capital that distinguish one sexual field from another. So too, the analyst of the sexual field will want to consider the relationship of one sexual field to another as these fields come to coincide on a given block, in a given neighbourhood, or within a given community.

Finally, at the macro level, sexual fields are shaped by social, political, and economic processes and structures, including patterns of immigration, gentrification and urban renewal, changing demographic configurations, the rise and fall of sexually transmitted infections, the vicissitudes of local economies, and the state of the law and customs as these pertain to sexual partnership, sexual minorities, and sexual practice, to name only a few.

In total, the study of sexual fields is subject to the full gamut of sociological analysis from the intrapsychic up through the macroscopic levels. Future research into sexual fields will mine each of these levels to generate a more comprehensive portrait of the workings of collective sexual life and sexual stratification.

References

D'Emilio, John. 1983. *Sexual Politics, Sexual Communities: The Making of a Homosexual Minority in the United States, 1940–1970*. Chicago: University of Chicago Press.

Farrer, James and Sonja Dale. 2014. "Sexless in Shanghai: Gendered Mobility Strategies in a Transnational Sexual Field." Pp. 143–70 in Green, Adam Isaiah (ed.), *Sexual Fields: Toward a Sociology of Collective Sexual Life*. Chicago: University of Chicago Press.

Giddens, Anthony. 1992. *The Transformation of Intimacy: Sexuality, Love and Eroticism in Modern Societies*. Stanford, CA: Stanford University Press.

Green, Adam Isaiah. 2008. "Erotic Habitus: Toward a Sociology of Desire." *Theory and Society* 37:597–626.

Green, Adam Isaiah. 2014. "The Sexual Fields Framework." Pp. 25–56 in Green, Adam Isaiah (ed.), *Sexual Fields: Toward a Sociology of Collective Sexual Life*. Chicago: University of Chicago Press.

Halperin, David. 1989. "Is There a History of Sexuality?" *History and Theory* 28:252–74.

Hennen, Peter. 2008. *Fairies, Bears and Leathermen: Men in Community Queering the Masculine*. Chicago: University of Chicago Press.

Levine, Martin P. 1998. Gay Macho: *The Life and Death of the Homosexual Clone*. New York: New York University Press.

Martin, John Levi. 2005. "Is Power Sexy?" *American Journal of Sociology* 111:408–46.

Martin, John Levi and Matt George. 2006. "Theories of Sexual Stratification: Toward an Analytics of the Sexual Field and a Theory of Sexual Capital." *Sociological Theory* 24:107–32.

Weinberg, Martin and Colin Williams. 2014. "Sexual Fields, Erotic Habitus and Embodiment at a Transgender Bar." Pp. 57–70 in Green, Adam Isaiah (ed.), *Sexual Fields: Toward a Sociology of Collective Sexual Life*. Chicago: University of Chicago Press.

25 First but Not a Founder: Annie Marion MacLean and the History and Institutionalization of Canadian Sociology

Mervyn Horgan and Saara Liinamaa

Carl Dawson (1887–1964) was born on Prince Edward Island, studied at Acadia University, and received his PhD from the University of Chicago in 1922. By establishing the nation's first sociology department at McGill, Dawson became widely regarded as the founder of Canadian sociology (Shore 1987), though recently this claim has come under some scrutiny (Helmes-Hayes 2013). Remarkably, like Dawson, Annie Marion MacLean (1869–1934) was also born on PEI and completed undergraduate studies at Acadia University; further, like Dawson, she received her PhD from the University of Chicago. But there is one significant difference: MacLean's PhD predates Dawson's by 22 years. MacLean is the first Canadian to complete a doctorate in sociology, but is not recognized as the "first Canadian sociologist." While institutionalization is central to the emergence and development of an academic discipline—and so Dawson is important—we should not mistake the founding of the first department with actually being the first sociologist. Both *how* and *who* we remember are significant in constituting the discipline's memory. This essay makes trouble with conventional stories of Canadian sociology's origins in the hope that a more complex and multidimensional history can facilitate new kinds of identification with and belonging to the discipline.

Specifically, this chapter builds upon decades of **feminist histories** that have sought to reconstruct women's contributions to sociology and social science more generally (e.g., Bennett 2006; Hill Collins 1990; Eichler 2001; Deegan 1988; 1991, 2014; Delamont 2003; Fitzpatrick 1990; Hoecker-Drysdale 1990; McDonald 1994; Rosenberg 1982). We do this by turning to Annie Marion MacLean, who we treat here as *Canada's first sociologist.* We are not the first, or the only, scholars interested in recovering MacLean's contributions to sociology. We can trace her inclusion in a number of books and articles that challenge the exclusion of women from history of the social sciences (Ainley et al. 2012; Deegan et al. 2009; Fish 1981; Hallet and Jeffers 2008; Lengermann and Niebrugge 2007; Macmillan 1987). Further, she is the subject of a recent book (Deegan 2014) that carefully documents MacLean's impressive accomplishments and unevenly acknowledged contributions. That said, we are stressing a persistent blind spot within both contemporary accounts that refer to her work and contemporary accounts of the history of the discipline in Canada: it seems neither literature foregrounds her status as a *Canadian* sociologist. From this observation, we develop two main arguments. First, we show how MacLean's place as the first Canadian sociologist remains largely unknown, even though her formative research years addressed topics that remain at the core of debates in sociology, both in Canada and elsewhere. Second, we demonstrate how MacLean's academic work can be placed at the fault lines of identity, nationalism, and the disciplinary origins of sociology in Canada. In this respect, we argue for a stronger version of MacLean's contributions to the **history of sociology** in Canada.

Canadian Sociology's "Well-Kept Secret"

Born in St Peter's Bay, PEI, MacLean's family moved to Middleton, Nova Scotia, in 1874. Her father was a Baptist minister in the small town and thereafter, a series of other small towns in the province (Bear River, Falmouth, Waterville, Newport, and Hantsport). After his untimely death at the age of 47 in 1887, MacLean moved to Wolfville (with her mother Christina, sister Mildred, and brother Haddon) where the sisters enrolled in Acadia Ladies Seminary, a high school for girls associated with Acadia University. MacLean then went on to complete her BA (1893) and MA (1894) at Acadia University. At some point in 1893 she moved to the United States, where she received an MA in sociology (1897), and in 1900 she became only the second woman to receive a PhD in sociology (University of Chicago) for her dissertation, "The Acadian Element in the Population of Nova Scotia." Despite her impressive career achievements and publications,[1] MacLean remained "ghettoized for much of her career in the University of Chicago's Extension School" (Lengermann and Niebrugee 1998: 21 n10). Yet, as Deegan argues, she was "among the early sociologists in the world to embark on a professional career" (2014: 3).

The relevance of MacLean's status as Canadian born and educated is generally lost as a significant feature within narratives of her career. For example, MacLean surfaces in a footnote within McDonald's text *The Women Founders of the Social Sciences* (2004; 236 n91), where she is noted for her publication in *American Journal of Sociology* in 1899.[2] MacDonald notes that while she is "Canadian born," she "made her career in the United States." Lengermann and Niebrugee (1998: 232) comment that, although she spent most of her adulthood in the US, she appears to have maintained many life-long ties with Canada. There is a paucity of research on MacLean's early life, with most biographical work beginning post-1894, after her move to the US, until her death in California in 1934. Indeed, it has been left to an American historian of women in social science, Mary Jo Deegan, to rebuild this Nova Scotian-trained social scientist's influence and legacy. Even Deegan's (2014) work only gives a cursory nod to MacLean's early life, focusing almost exclusively on MacLean's professional life in the US rather than her formative experiences in Nova Scotia. Confronted with a lack of information on her early life, Deegan instead speculatively finds parallels between MacLean and PEI's most famous fictional daughter, *Anne of Green Gables*.

While she remains essentially absent from histories of Canadian sociology, and her formative years are only briefly noted in feminist histories, this aspect of her identity and research remains largely unexplored. One exception, however, is a brief exchange within the pages of *Society/Société*, where Campbell (2000) points to MacLean's place as the first Canadian to receive a doctorate in sociology, revising his earlier claim (Campbell 1983: 2) that Walter Alexander Riddell was the first. For Campbell, Riddell's achievement begins the semi-professional phase of the discipline's development in Canada. Of MacLean's achievement, Campbell says it is "not unknown in the Canadian Sociological community but it is a well kept secret" (5). In response to this article, Lazar (2000:15) stresses that her embrace of America as her adopted country and her disparaging views (e.g., MacLean 1905a) of Canada made her easier to exclude. As Lazar comments, she was "from Canada" but not necessary "of Canada" (2000: 16), and so he concurs with Campbell's assessment that she is the first "Canadian-born" rather than straightforwardly "Canadian" sociologist. While MacLean's position on Canada remains to be more fully analyzed, her occasional anti-Canadian commentary or four decades spent in the US do not nullify her place as the first Canadian sociologist. After all, she was born, raised, and educated in Canada. More importantly, her research on Canadian topics is substantial.

Eclecticism and the Origins of Canadian Sociology

MacLean's dissertation on the Acadians in Nova Scotia is almost certainly the first social scientific study of Canada by a professionally trained sociologist. Sadly, no complete copy of this dissertation exists; the copy deposited at the University of Chicago has been missing for decades, though some parts of the dissertation on a francophone minority in Canada were partly serialized by a Quebec-based English-language periodical (MacLean 1901a; 1901b) and elsewhere (1900a). From the outset, MacLean's sociology crossed the two solitudes that have long characterized Canadian history, politics, society, and culture.

A student newspaper article on a talk she gave at her alma mater in 1898 during a return to Nova Scotia to gather data for her doctoral dissertation reported that her presentation, entitled "A People Within Our Borders, or the Acadians of To-day," was a "highly instructive and literary lecture" and went on to note that, on the basis of her success as a student at Acadia University, and the strength of her talk, "great things are prophesied for Miss MacLean in the world of education" (*Acadia Athenaeum* 1898: 24).

MacLean's work on Canada does not end with her doctoral research on the Acadian community. She also published scholarly articles on Canadian factory legislation for women (1899a), a report on the "social value of private schools" for Canadian girls (1900b), an article on Canadian immigrants to the US (1905a), a report on Nova Scotia's response to the threat of tuberculosis (1905b), and a range of magazine articles and anecdotal musings on various elements of Canadian society. In works such as "Significance of Canadian Migration" (1905a) she seems to advocate for Canada's unification with the United States, given what she saw as Canada's position as "weak, fearful of the future, fettered" (823). In addition to her gender, such sentiments also may have contributed to her absence from the history of Canadian sociology, particularly given the general tenor of the **Canadianization debates** that raged at the height of the discipline's institutional growth in the late 1960s and 1970s (Cormier 2004).

More broadly, in addition to her work on Canada, she produced an impressive range of publications that can be broadly categorized as follows (given the quantity of her writings, citations are illustrative rather than exhaustive):

1. Gender as a category of analysis, with particular attention to women's paid work conditions (MacLean 1897; 1899a; 1899b; 1908; 1910)
2. Ethnographic research methods (MacLean 1899b; 1909; see also, Deegan et al. 2009; Hallet and Jeffers 2008)
3. Charity and reform, in Canada, the US and internationally (MacLean 1904)
4. The social and personal impacts of physical disability (MacLean 1914)
5. Reflections on teaching sociology through distance education (MacLean 1923 [1927])
6. Literary and personal works (autobiography, travel writings, human–animal relations, philosophy of life and more).

Taken together, these themes suggest that, by reconsidering her work and history, we can also carve out disparate strands of what Canadian sociology is and has been: attentive to marginalized communities and responsive to diverse features of identity and experience, including gender, work, disability, and ethnicity; conscientious of the relationship between sociological insight and social reform; committed to methodological depth; and dedicated to education. While her work is full of the contradictions and constraints of the time—we are not arguing for an idealized recovery—MacLean's sociology diversifies and complicates the discipline's origins in Canada. By reframing sociology's history with MacLean as Canada's first sociologist, Canadian sociology takes on a longer, deeper, more eclectic—even more contradictory—history than has been previously offered.

Conclusion

Baehr (2002) makes a distinction between sociology's discursive and institutional founders: institutional founders are those who are involved in establishing departments, programs, or journals that consolidate a place for sociology. Carl Dawson, for example, remains significant in this regard. Discursive founders provide concepts, ideas, and theories that mark out a distinctive contribution for the discipline. From our assessment, we would like to put forth MacLean's status as a unique discursive founder whose work prefigures many of the research areas to which Canadian sociologists have turned their attention over the last century. But, as Lengermann and Niebrugee note, the "writing out of the women founders occurred as part of a politics of gender and politics of knowledge within the discipline" (1998: 1); MacLean's case augments our understanding of these processes as it also suggests the politics of nationalism at work at the intersection of gender and disciplinary knowledge production in Canada. While her anti-Canadian sentiments and embrace of America as a nation of "hope" (MacLean 1905a: 823) is somewhat off-putting to any excavation of a *Canadian* history of sociology, we have proposed another interpretation. National identity is an important category of analysis within the puzzle of her history and marginalization. Further, by troubling how we understand the place of Canada in her work and biography, we find new beginnings for Canadian sociologies and sociologies of Canada.

Notes

1. There are too many to list here. See Deegan (2014: 318–23) for a comprehensive list of over 100 of MacLean's academic, popular, and policy publications.
2. In fact, between 1897 and 1926 MacLean published articles in the AJS, two dealing explicitly with Canadian topics.

References

Acadia Athenaeum. 1898. XXIV(6) (June).

Ainley, M.G., G. Rayner-Canham, and M.F. Rayner-Canham. 2012. *Creating Complicated Lives: Women and Science at English-Canadian universities, 1880–1980*. Montreal: McGill-Queen's University Press.

Baehr, Peter. 2002. *Founders, Classics, Canons: Modern Disputes Over the Origins and Appraisal of Sociology's Heritage*. New Brunswick, NJ: Transaction.

Bennett, J.M. 2006. *History Matters: Patriarchy and the Challenge of Feminism*. Philadelphia: University of Pennsylvania Press.

Campbell, Douglas F. 2000. "Annie Marion MacLean: The First Canadian-Born Sociologist" *Society/Sociétè* 24(1):5–6.

Campbell, Douglas F. 1983. *Beginnings: Essays on the History of Canadian Sociology*. Port Credit, ON: Scribblers' Press.

Collins, P.H. 1990. *Black Feminist Thought: Knowledge, Consciousness and the Politics of Empowerment*. Boston: Unwin Hyman.

Cormier, Jeffrey. 2004. *The Canadianization Movement: Emergence, Survival and Success*. Toronto: University of Toronto Press.

Deegan, M.J. 2014. *Annie Marion MacLean and the Chicago Schools of Sociology, 1894–1934*. New Brunswick, NJ: Transaction.

Deegan, M.J. 1988. *Jane Addams and the Men of the Chicago School, 1892–1918*. New Brunswick, NJ: Tranaction.

Deegan, M.J. 1991. *Women in Sociology: A Bio-Bibliographical Sourcebook*. Westport, CT: Greenwood Press.

Deegan, M.J., M.R. Hill, and S.L. Wortmann. 2009. "Annie Marion MacLean, Feminist Pragmatist and Methodologist." *Journal of Contemporary Ethnography* 38(6):655–65.

Delamont, S. 2003. *Feminist Sociology*. London: SAGE.

Eichler, Margrit. 2002. "The Impact of Feminism on Canadian Sociology." *The American Sociologist* 33(1):27.

Eichler, Margrit. 2001. "Women Pioneers in Canadian Sociology: The Effects of a Politics of Gender and a Politics of Knowledge." *Canadian Journal of Sociology/Cahiers canadiens de sociologie* 26(3):375.

Fish, Virginia Kemp. 1981. "Annie Marion MacLean: A Neglected Part of the Chicago School." *Journal of the History of Sociology* 3:43–62.

Fitzpatrick, E. 1990. *Endless Crusade: Women Social Scientists and Progressive Reform*. New York: Oxford University Press.

Hallett, T. and G. Jeffers. 2008. "A Long-Neglected Mother of Contemporary Ethnography: Annie Marion MacLean and the Memory of a Method." *Journal of Contemporary Ethnography* 37(1):3–37.

Hallett, T., G. Jeffers, and E. Bowman. 2009. "There's Something about Annie: Rejoinder to Deegan, Hill, and Wortmann's Comment on MacLean." *Journal of Contemporary Ethnography* 38(6):666–76.

Helmes-Hayes, Rick. 2013. *"The Perfect Sociology, Perfectly Applied": Sociology and the Social Gospel in Canada's English-Language Universities, 1900–1930*. Saskatoon: University of Saskatchewan.

Hill Collins, Patricia. 1990. *Black Feminist Thought: Knowledge, Consciousness, and the Politics of Empowerment*. Boston, MA: Unwin Hyman.

Hiller, Harry H. 1980. "Paradigmatic Shifts, Indigenization, and the Development of Sociology in Canada." *Journal of the History of the Behavioral Sciences* 16(3):263–74.

Hoecker-Drysdale, Susan. 1990. "Women Sociologists in Canada: The Careers of Helen MacGill Hughes, Aileen Dansken Ross, Jean Robertson Burnet," in Ainley, Marianne Gosztonyi, ed., *Despite The Odds: Essays on Canadian Women and Science*. Montreal: Véhicule Press. pp. 152–76.

Lazar, Morty M. 2000. "An Additional Observation on Annie Marion MacLean." *Society/Société* 24(2):15–16.

Lengermann, Patricia M. and Jill Niebrugge. 1998. *The Women Founders: Sociology and Social Theory, 1830–1930: A Text/Reader*. Long Grove, IL: Waveland Press.

MacMillan, Heather Joan. 1987. "Annie Marion MacLean: The Public Career of a Maritime Progressive in the United States 1896–1934." Honours thesis, Acadia University, Wolfville, Nova Scotia.

Magill, D.W., W.M. Michelson, and James Mackenzie Russell, eds. 1999. *Images of Change*. Toronto: Canadian Scholars' Press.

McDonald, L. 1994. *The Women Founders of the Social Sciences*. Montreal and Kingston: McGill-Queen's University Press.

Rosenberg, R. 1982. *Beyond Separate Spheres: Intellectual Roots of Modern Feminism*. New Haven: Yale University Press.

Shore, M.G. 1987. *The Science of Social Redemption: McGill, the Chicago School, and the Origins of Social Research in Canada*. Toronto: University of Toronto Press.

Cited Works by MacLean

MacLean, Annie Marion. 1897. "Factory Legislation for Women in the United States." *American Journal of Sociology* 3:183–205.

MacLean, Annie Marion. 1899a. "Factory Legislation for Women in Canada." *American Journal of Sociology* 5:172–81.

MacLean, Annie Marion. 1899b. "Two Weeks in Department Stores." *American Journal of Sociology* 4:721–41.

MacLean, Annie Marion. 1900a. "Location of the Acadians in Nova Scotia." *Canadian History* 9:241–45.

MacLean, Annie Marion. 1900b. "Schools for Girls in Canada" *Canadian Educational Monthly* XXIII: 300–302.

MacLean, Annie Marion. 1901a. "The Acadian Element in the Population of Nova Scotia." *North American Notes and Queries* 2:264–77.

MacLean, Annie Marion. 1901b. "The Acadian Element in the Population of Nova Scotia." *North American Notes and Queries* 1:247–57.

MacLean, Annie Marion. 1904. "France" in *Methods of Modern Charity*. C. Henderson (ed.), New York: Macmillan. pp. 512–55.

MacLean, Annie Marion. 1905a. "Significance of the Canadian Migration." *American Journal of Sociology* 10(6):814–23.

MacLean, Annie Marion. 1905b. "Nova Scotia's Crusade Against Tuberculosis." *Charities and the Commons* 14:736–38.

Maclean, Annie Marion. 1908. "Life in the Pennsylvania Coal Fields with Particular Reference to Women." *American Journal of Sociology* 14(3):329–51.

MacLean, Annie Marion. 1909. "With Oregon Hop Pickers." *American Journal of Sociology* 15(1):83–95.

MacLean, Annie Marion. 1910. *Wage-Earning Women*. New York: Macmillan.

MacLean, Annie Marion. 1914. *Mary Ann's Malady: Fragmentary Papers Dealing with a Woman and Rheumatism*. New York: Broadway.

MacLean, Annie Marion. 1923 (1927). "Twenty Years of Sociology by Correspondence." *American Journal of Sociology* 28:461–72.

MacLean, Annie Marion. 1926. "Albion Woodbury Small: An Appreciation." *American Journal of Sociology* 32(1):45–48.

MacLean, Annie Marion. 1930. "Conveying Personality at Long Range." *Proceedings of the University Extension Association* 15:130–32.

MacLean, Annie Marion. 1932. "I Become American" *Sociology and Social Research* 16: 427–33.

26 Intimacies and Commodification in Human Milk Exchange: Transforming Families and Kinship

Robyn Lee

Biological relatedness is often taken for granted as the basis for families. Increasingly, however, our understandings of what constitutes a family are being challenged by technological interventions that allow for exchanges of reproductive labour and bodily material outside of the household, involving eggs and sperm, surrogacy, and more recently, human milk.

Sociology has long studied families but is increasingly examining kinship as well. For instance, Jennifer Mason argues for new forms of sociological engagement with kinship, while at the same acknowledging that anthropologists have a longer history in exploring the subject (Mason, 2008).

Queer theory and LGBTQ studies have been driving renewed interest in the concept of kinship, exploring how families are formed outside the confines of heteronormative biological families, and examining how transformations demonstrate the ways in which the "traditional" family has in fact always been socially, culturally, and technologically constructed. The concept of "**families of choice**" (Weston, 1991) has emerged in the context of LGBTQ communities, with friendship and non-procreative sexuality emerging as a foundation for kinship between friends and partners. As well, LGBTQ parenthood is transforming conventional family structures (Berkowitz, 2009; Dempsey, 2010; Stacey, 2004).

Attempts are often made to keep familial relationships separate from the realm of paid employment, with altruism and care associated with private life and contrasted with the realm of economic exchange. But Viviana Zelizer (2007) challenges this view, which she calls the separate spheres or hostile worlds model, instead arguing that economic activity is continually comingled with intimacy.

An example of this comingling can be seen in emerging practices of human milk exchange. As a result of increased attention to the health benefits of breast milk, societal and medical pressure strongly compels mothers to breastfeed. However, many women experience difficulties breastfeeding. This leads some parents to attempt to obtain human milk through alternative means, including wet nursing, cross-nursing, and the use of donated human milk.

Wet nursing and cross-nursing both involve the breastfeeding of a baby by someone other than the baby's biological mother; wet nurses are usually paid employees while cross-nursing is between peers, is usually unpaid, and may be reciprocal.

However, the division between the family and the marketplace is blurred even when breastfeeding is only carried out between mother and child, since a major obstacle to breastfeeding is the difficulty women face in combining it with paid employment (Gatrell, 2007). Breastfeeding bodies challenge the division between public and private, and between personal and professional realms. In the case of breastfeeding, women's bodies are at the centre of conflicts between work and maternity in our society (Hausman, 2004). Breastfeeding is widely regarded as a private act of childrearing, with continuing discomfort being aroused by women breastfeeding in the workplace or in other public spaces (Acker, 2009; Boyer, 2011; Wolf, 2008). Since breastfeeding requires ongoing, embodied interaction with a child, it is extraordinarily difficult to accommodate in the workplace. Breastfeeding impacts women's ability to carry out paid work outside the home, with significant economic costs to women (Rippeyoung and Noonan, 2012).

Treating breastfeeding in terms of its nutritional and medical benefits has fuelled an understanding of human milk as a raw material or product, rather than a fluid produced through the intimate connection between mother and child. Breast pumping has been widely embraced, because it is perceived as disembodied, abstract, and hygienic, and it can potentially be done privately, without intimacy between maternal and child bodies. The focus on breast pumping turns the embodied practice of breastfeeding into a product that can potentially be commodified.

The exchange of human milk through milk banks, cross-nursing, or informal exchanges challenges divisions between the private and the public, the family and the marketplace. The increasing use of breast pumps has made it possible to store, freeze, and transport milk. There has been a dramatic increase in media coverage of human milk exchange, and Internet groups dedicated to the buying, selling, and donation of breast milk have surged in popularity.

In line with trends toward the commercialization of care in other realms of social reproduction, the exchange and sale of expressed breast milk is growing in popularity. The commodification of human milk demonstrates how economics is involved in even the most intimate forms of embodied practice (Boyer, 2011).

Exchanging human milk is controversial because it risks reducing women to objects, commodifying the intimate relationship between mother and child. However, these practices are growing in popularity because dominant understandings of the body, combined with persistent challenges in the division between productive and reproductive labour make it extremely challenging for women to balance paid employment and parenthood.

Women may be motivated to sell their milk in order to offset financial costs of motherhood and compensate for inadequate maternal leaves (Dutton, 2011). Expressing milk and even selling it represent attempts to cope with the difficulties inherent in parenthood. Nevertheless, relying on selling breast milk in order to afford the costs of motherhood risks exacerbating existing inequalities of **stratified reproduction**

(Colen, 1995), under which the ability to reproduce is unequally distributed in society and is stratified along gender, sexual orientation, racial and ethnic, and economic class lines.

The primary focus in debates over milk exchange has been on the health risks posed by these exchanges, with public health authorities viewing the risk of exchanging breast milk as more serious than the risks associated with formula feeding. Public health agencies in Canada, the United States, and France (along with national pediatric associations in those countries) have strongly opposed informal human milk exchange practices, warning parents of the risks posed by transmission of pathogens and chemical residues (Government of Canada, 2014; US Food and Drug Administration, 2010). Parents who attempt to acquire milk from other mothers believe that human milk is very important for children's health and that the benefits outweigh potential harms (Gribble and Hausman, 2012). But beyond the health benefits, some parents describe sharing human milk as forging important social bonds and relationships (Akre, Gribble, and Minchin, 2011; Thorley, 2008) that may be understood as alternative forms of family and kinship. Much attention has been paid to the potential risks of these practices (Gribble, 2013; Keim et al., 2013), but less examination has been given to the bonds created between families who exchange milk and the impact of the income and costs associated with the buying and selling of milk.

Human milk exchange could have a significant impact on LGBTQ families since it allows gay fathers to feed their children human milk. As well, it could eliminate or reduce divisions between birth and non-birth mothers in lesbian-headed families (Zizzo, 2009). It also has the potential to challenge and redefine maternal and gender roles in families generally (Zizzo, 2009).

In the Islamic tradition, breastfeeding an infant you have not given birth to establishes a family connection of "**milk kinship**" (Giladi, 1999). Milk kinship is a family bond established between a woman and an infant she breastfeeds but has not given birth to. It was practised from the beginning of Islam in order to broaden the network of relatives one could rely upon for assistance and co-operation.

Emphasis on the product of human milk and the nutritional benefits it offers has motivated the exchange of human milk beyond mothers and their biological children. There is potential for new forms of intimacies to be created through the exchange of breast milk, including new configurations of historical forms of milk kinship (Parkes, 2007). The donation and sale of milk through the use of online social media may produce new forms of relatedness, with women being motivated to provide milk to others by empathy and a desire to help (Gribble, 2013). Milk exchange can create new forms of intimate relations that go beyond the household, but health risks are a concern and the commodification and commercialization of human milk may exploit women. As human milk exchange practices grow in popularity, it is essential to remain attentive to both the risks and potential benefits of the transformations they produce in families and kinship.

References

Acker, M. (2009). Breast Is Best . . . But Not Everywhere: Ambivalent Sexism and Attitudes Toward Private and Public Breastfeeding. *Sex Roles*, *61*(7–8), 476–90. http://doi.org/10.1007/s11199-009-9655-z

Akre, J., Gribble, K., and Minchin, M. (2011). Milk Sharing: From Private Practice to Public Pursuit. *International Breastfeeding Journal*, *6*(8). Retrieved from http://www.internationalbreastfeedingjournal.com.ezproxy.library.yorku.ca/content/6/1/8

Berkowitz, D. (2009). Theorizing Lesbian and Gay Parenting: Past, Present, and Future Scholarship. *Journal of Family Theory & Review*, *1*(3), 117–32.

Boyer, K. (2011). "The way to break the taboo is to do the taboo thing": Breastfeeding in Public and Citizen-Activism in the UK. *Health & Place*, *17*(2), 430–7.

Colen, S. (1995). "Like a Mother to them": Stratified reproduction and West Indian childcare workers and employers in New York. In F. Ginsburg and R. Rapp (Eds.), *Conceiving the New World Order: The global politics of reproduction* (pp. 78–102). Berkeley, CA: University of California Press.

Dempsey, D. (2010). Conceiving and Negotiating Reproductive Relationships: Lesbians and Gay Men Forming

Families with Children. *Sociology, 44*(6), 1145–62. http://doi.org/10.1177/0038038510381607

Dutton, J. (2011). Liquid Gold: The Booming Market for Human Breast Milk. *Wired Magazine*. Retrieved 10 April 2017 from http://www.wired.com/magazine/2011/05/ff_milk/2/

Franklin, S.B. (2013). *Biological Relatives: IVF, Stem Cells, and the Future of Kinship* (1st edition). Durham, NC: Duke University Press Books.

Gatrell, C.J. (2007). Secrets and Lies: Breastfeeding and Professional Paid Work. *Social Science & Medicine, 65*(2), 393–404. http://doi.org/10.1016/j.socscimed.2007.03.017

Giladi, Avner. (1999). *Infants, Parents and Wet Nurses: Medieval Islamic Views on Breastfeeding and Their Social Implications*. Leiden, The Netherlands: Brill.

Government of Canada, H.C. (2014, May 20). Safety of Donor Human Milk in Canada—Health Canada [guide]. Retrieved 17 June 2015, from http://www.hc-sc.gc.ca/fn-an/nutrition/infant-nourisson/human-milk-don-lait-maternel-eng.php

Gribble, K.D. (2013). Perception and Management of Risk in Internet-Based Peer-To-Peer Milk-Sharing. *Early Child Development and Care*, 1–15. http://doi.org/10.1080/03004430.2013.772994

Gribble, K.D., and Hausman, B.L. (2012). Milk Sharing and Formula Feeding: Infant Feeding Risks in Comparative Perspective? Retrieved 30 August 2013, from http://www.ncbi.nlm.nih.gov/pmc/articles/PMC3395287/

Hausman, B.L. (2004). The Feminist Politics of Breastfeeding. *Australian Feminist Studies, 19*(45), 273. http://doi.org/10.1080/0816464042000278963

Keim, S.A., Hogan, J.S., McNamara, K.A., Gudimetla, V., Dillon, C.E., Kwiek, J.J., & Geraghty, S.R. (2013). Microbial Contamination of Human Milk Purchased via the Internet. *Pediatrics, 132*(5), e1227–35. http://doi.org/10.1542/peds.2013-1687

Mason, J. (2008). Tangible Affinities and the Real Life Fascination of Kinship. *Sociology, 42*(1), 29–45. http://doi.org/10.1177/0038038507084824

Parkes, P. 2007. Milk Kinship in Islam: Substance, Structure, History. *Social Anthropology*, 13, 307–29.

Rippeyoung, P.L.F., and Noonan, M.C. (2012). Is Breastfeeding Truly Cost Free? Income Consequences of Breastfeeding for Women. *American Sociological Review, 77*(2), 244–67. http://doi.org/10.1177/0003122411435477

Stacey, J. (2004). Cruising to Familyland: Gay Hypergamy and Rainbow Kinship. *Current Sociology, 52*(2), 181–97. http://doi.org/10.1177/0011392104041807

Thorley, V. (2008). Sharing Breastmilk: Wet Nursing, Cross-Feeding, and Milk Donations. *Breastfeeding Review, 16*(1), 25+.

US Food and Drug Administration. (2010, November 30). Use of Donor Human Milk. Retrieved 20 September 2011, from http://www.fda.gov/ScienceResearch/SpecialTopics/PediatricTherapeuticsResearch/ucm235203.htm

Weston, K. (1991). *Families We Choose: Lesbians, Gays, Kinship*. Columbia University Press.

Wolf, J.H. (2008). Got Milk? Not in Public! *International Breastfeeding Journal, 3*(1), 11. http://doi.org/10.1186/1746-4358-3-11

Zelizer, V.A. (2007). *The Purchase of Intimacy* (1st edition). Princeton, N.J.: Princeton University Press.

Zizzo, G. (2009). Lesbian Families and the Negotiation of Maternal Identity through the Unconventional Use of Breast Milk. *Gay and Lesbian Issues and Psychology Review, 5*(2), 96–109.

27 Committing Sociology: The Challenges Facing Activist Scholarship[1]

Meg Luxton

In March 2015 at a demonstration opposing House of Commons Bill C-51,[2] a protester carried a sign declaring: "I am not afraid. I do practice Sociology." Her affirmation of the value of sociological practice referred to then prime minister Stephen Harper's 2013 response to an alleged plot against a VIA train,[3] when he said people in Canada should not "commit sociology," but pursue an anti-crime approach, a view he repeated in 2014, arguing that an inquiry into missing and murdered Indigenous women was not needed, because this was not a sociological phenomenon, but simply a series of individual crimes.[4] Her declaration challenged the "climate of fear" and the "death of evidence" that had prompted many scientists to protest the Harper government's policies on research[5] and appears to have silenced others who were afraid to speak out.[6] It also challenged Harper's ideological attempts to render sociological findings illegitimate in the public eye and his efforts to prevent people from being able to identify, and tackle, the structural injustices in Canadian society.[7]

Sociology, like many related social sciences, encompasses a wide range of perspectives, but one of its strongest traditions investigates the links between the personal and the social, or what C. Wright Mills in *The Sociological Imagination* (1959)[8] identified as the links between private troubles and public issues. This approach assumes that many social problems occur because of the social relations involved and can only be solved by changing those social relations, and the related organizations, institutions, and political practices. From this critical perspective, many social scientists strive to understand the world we live in, not just to document the systemic inequalities that shape our lives, but to explain them in order to change them—and that project means that those of us who strive to be both scholars and activists fighting for a more equitable world face serious challenges. There is a long tradition of successful critical scholarship, of academics who have been honoured for their progressive political commitments, and of effective collaborations between academics and other activists. However, here I want to explore some of the difficulties faced by those of us who are scholar activists, engaging in progressive, critical teaching and research, asking how we can strengthen our capacities as scholar activists and build more effective alliances and solidarity movements inside and outside the universities.

The first challenge comes from within academia itself. A long-standing dominant positivist tradition asserts that scholarship must be objective, indifferent to the implications of its findings, and removed from the dominant social concerns of the times. While most people understand that being objective, factual, or accurate is not the same as having no point of view, **positivism** frames critical social science scholarship as biased, ideological, or unscientific. Yet such charges are rarely faced by **neoclassical economists** or business schools, whose theories and orientations confirm the basic premises of liberal democracies and capitalist economies. But scholarship that criticizes the policies and practices of governments is often accused of being political instead of scholarly. A sociology that argues that social inequalities are not inevitable or natural but produced by capitalist economics and that they therefore can be reduced or eliminated threatens the status quo and so risks being charged as "too political." In many cases, the scholars advancing critiques of dominant academic paradigms may well face further discrimination because they are members of the subordinate populations whose situations they investigate (trans, queer, racialized, women, or from working class backgrounds, for example).

Other challenges are posed for academics striving to work with activists outside the universities. Community **activism** and **advocacy** work require a different set of skills, knowledge, and connections than conventional academic work. They usually work on different time frames, with community activism needing information and results more quickly than academic scholarship usually permits. Community activists are often driven by the urgent needs of their community; they need research that promotes actions and offers solutions. Academics are under pressure to produce research that conforms to academic conventions, allowing them to meet the demands of funding agencies, peer reviews, and publishing. This is particularly pressing for contract faculty or pre-tenured faculty hoping for permanent tenured jobs, who may also face discrimination in hiring because of the subjects they teach and research (feminism, anti-racism, Indigenous, trans, or socialist studies, for example).

Universities and their neigbouring communities are often isolated from each other, making alliances more difficult. Differences between academic and community activists may be exacerbated by the power differentials, often class- or race-based, between typically low or unpaid community activists and researchers with research grants in addition to their salaries. Community activists, who usually know very little about the differences between academic ranks or about the demands of academic jobs, may be inclined to assume that academics are readily advancing their careers by doing activist work, which for community activists is sacrifice. They are sometimes suspicious of the sincerity and legitimacy of scholars as political activists. Relative privileges reverberate through such alliances. University professors are often assumed to have expertise, while community activists often have to fight to get their own expertise acknowledged. Sometimes there are debates about who owns the knowledge agenda, whose knowledge is best informed or most accurate, whose knowledge is most legitimate. In some situations, there can be conflicts between our role as activists and as professors. Several Toronto women's studies faculty members, including me, who had been active in feminist organizing in the city, withdrew from that work because we found it too problematic to work with students in both capacities. The cumulative effects of different interests, working conditions, and competing demands create complications that must be negotiated carefully for collaborative efforts to succeed.

A third challenge for activist scholarship stems from the organization of our work, the way it is popularly perceived, and the pressures it imposes on us. Often our commitment to our work is criticized by activist friends (and maybe by ourselves) as revealing career aspirations, as "selling out." Years ago, Angela McRobbie asked a really important question I think every activist academic needs to ask: Why is it, she asked, that women who work in battered women's shelters are seen as doing front-line feminist work, while women who teach hundreds of students every week about feminism are not?[9] To take her point further, why is that most workers who organize in their workplaces and unions are praised for their political activism, but academics actively involved in equity struggles in their workplaces and unions risk being seen as just advancing their own careers?

One reason is clearly because most academics with tenure have good jobs that are well paid, secure, and creative. Those jobs allow us considerable control over what we do, and some of us can advance our careers by our activist politics. That privilege inevitably raises questions about how sincere our activist commitments actually are. Another reason stems from the widespread mystique that surrounds our work. To many outside academia, and even to many of our students, much of what our jobs require is invisible. To many people, our jobs seem to involve only teaching, so the demands seem light. This appearance is compounded by the flexibility of our jobs: we can often choose when and where we do much of our work. The pressures of service, research, and writing, even of preparing courses, grading student papers, and supervising, easily disappear from view. The privileges and flexibility inherent in our work create an impression that many of us "choose" to be unduly busy; that we could be more available if we wanted to be. Finally, research, and especially writing, often require lengthy periods of intense concentration, working alone, and resisting interruptions. Those around us sometimes resent our withdrawals and experience our devotion to work as selfish. As a result, non-academic allies may be skeptical when we withdraw from political engagements because of our workload. How do we convince others that our writing warrants respect? How do we convince ourselves?

Finally, there are two challenges, not unique to academics, that I personally find the most difficult when studying the systemic inequalities that shape our world. The first is how to handle the constant rage I feel about the state of the world. The more I pay attention, the more I learn, the angrier I get. That rage fuels my work and motivates me to keep going, but sometimes it is overwhelming and it is often hard to keep my perspective, my sense of humour, and my delight in life and its pleasures. The second is how to live my life in the current circumstances in ways that prefigure the kind of world I want to live in. I engage in a daily dance of contradictions—where do I shop and what do I buy? How do I treat co-workers who piss me off? How much of my paycheque should I spend on myself, and how much should I give to the local women's shelter and the panhandlers? Which of many issues should I get involved with?

I suggest that while there are obviously no easy answers, the main task for academic activists is to contest and disrupt all such challenges in whatever ways we can. We can start by understanding universities as workplaces and by valuing efforts to make visible their structures, power relations, and inequalities, including the privileges of our economic positions as faculty. Efforts to redress those inequalities are important activist political projects. Which students get admitted, who gets hired and under what terms, what knowledge gets valued for publication, for tenure and promotion, and gets taught—all these either reproduce existing power dynamics or disrupt them. They shape the kind of knowledge produced and legitimated in our society. Equally important are our struggles relating to way the university operates day-to-day. The workplace culture we develop—how meetings are run, how issues like sexual harassment or racism are dealt with, how people from different classes or class backgrounds are treated—all reflect prevailing values and often need to be challenged. Struggles to create more equitable universities raise many questions. How effective are alliances between different campus workers and their unions? Do faculty support other workers such as those who work in food services, cleaning, secretarial work? Does the university recognize trans concerns relating to names, pronouns, bathrooms, and transphobia? Do the new faculty appointments who are the only Indigenous or racialized person in their departments feel safe? Do they face harsher standards in the classroom and in the hiring and tenure and promotion processes? What kind of support do they get? How attentive are we to these dynamics and how diligently do we work to strengthen equity in our universities? And because that work is often really hard, what kinds of support and solidarity do we create for each other as we engage with such issues?

At the same time, as critical social scientists "committing sociology," we need to form alliances beyond the academy, reducing the divides between universities and other communities so we can develop collective understandings of our social conditions and of strategies to resist and change them. How do we move our politics beyond protest and defence? What kind of alternative way of living can we imagine, and how might we try to get there? And how can we, as scholar activists, move away from individualized experiences of anger and guilt and the isolation of the individual academic, to more effectively support each other in our daily lives, in our political practices, and in our struggles to imagine and strive for a better world? It's not easy—but struggles to overcome the systemic inequalities that permeate contemporary society need all our efforts: political engagement with the issues, good scholarship that analyzes those issues, thoughtful demands and political mobilizing that brings together people from as many different constituencies as possible, and a determination to commit sociology despite powerful opposition.

Notes

1. I had the opportunity to present a version of this as a keynote talk at a conference hosted by the Institute of Political Economy, Carleton University, March 2015, and I thank Susan Braedley for organizing it and the audience for their questions and comments. I also thank Susan Braedley, Linda Briskin, Ratiba Hadj-Moussa, Jacinthe Michaud, and Mercedes Steedman, all experienced scholar activists, for their thoughtful comments on an earlier version of this paper.
2. Bill C-51 "An Act to enact the Security of Canada Information Sharing Act and the Secure Air Travel Act, to amend the Criminal Code, the Canadian Security Intelligence Service Act and the Immigration and Refugee Protection Act and to make related and consequential amendments

to other Acts" http://www.parl.gc.ca/HousePublications/Publication.aspx?DocId=6932136

3. Megan Fitzpatrick, "Harper on terrorist arrests: Not a time for 'sociology.'" *CBC News*, 25 April 2013 http://www.cbc.ca/news/politics/harper-on-terror-arrests-not-a-time-for-sociology-1.1413502. Stephen Harper was prime minister and head of a Conservative government from February 2006 to November 2015.
4. Alex Boutillier, "Native teen's slaying a 'crime,' not a 'sociological phenomenon,' Stephen Harper says." *Toronto Star*, 21 August 2014. http://www.thestar.com/news/canada/2014/08/21/native_teens_slaying_a_crime_not_a_sociological_phenomenon_stephen_harper_says.html
5. Terry Pedwell. "Scientists take aim at Harper's cuts with 'death of evidence' protest on Parliament Hill." *The Globe and Mail*, 10 July 2012 http://www.theglobeandmail.com/news/politics/scientists-take-aim-at-harper-cuts-with-death-of-evidence-protest-on-parliament-hill/article4403233
6. Andrea Hill. "Scientists live in a climate of fear; poll suggests researchers can't speak freely." 21 October 2013 http://o.canada.com/news/scientists-live-in-a-climate-of-fear-poll-suggests-federal-researchers-cant-speak-freely
7. Sociologists Brym and Ramos have pointed out that under the Harper government, facts were ignored or suppressed to suit government ideology. http://thechronicleherald.ca/opinion/1126165-harper-adds-sociology-to-list-of-sciences-that-get-short-shrift
8. C. Wright Mills. *The Sociological Imagination* London: Oxford University Press, 1959.
9. Angela McRobbie. "The Politics of Feminist Research: Between Talk, Text and Action." *Feminist Review*, 12 October 1982 http://www.gold.ac.uk/media/politics-feminist-research78.pdf, viewed 22 November 2010.

Questions for Critical Thought

Chapter 24 | Sexual Fields

1. Think about some of the ways in which the sexual social lives of individuals have changed over time. How are some of the sexual social norms different now than in the past?
2. What is sexual capital? Give examples. How does sexual capital vary within fields?
3. What are the three ways in which fields structure desire and desirability?
4. Give examples of sexual social lives at the micro, meso, and macro levels.
5. How do sexual fields vary depending on sexual orientation? Why is this an important distinction?

Chapter 25 | First but Not a Founder: Annie Marion MacLean and the History and Institutionalization of Canadian Sociology

1. Why is recognizing Annie Marion MacLean as the first Canadian sociologist important?
2. What topics did MacLean examine? How did her work contribute to Canadian sociology?
3. What is the influence of gender on MacLean's marginalization in Canadian history?
4. Is MacLean a discursive or institutional founder? Why?

Chapter 26 | Intimacies and Commodification in Human Milk Exchange: Transforming Families and Kinship

1. How has an increased acceptance of LGBTQ sexualities influenced family formation?
2. How has the medicalization of breast milk changed breast feeding?
3. What social pressures accompany a woman's decision to breast feed?
4. How does the human milk exchange influence LGBTQ families?
5. What is the promise of the human milk exchange? What are some of the potential positive and negative effects of the human milk exchange on society?

Chapter 27 | Committing Sociology: The Challenges Facing Activist Scholarship

1. What are some of the limitations of positivism? Why does Luxton think sociology should not have to conform to positivist epistemologies?
2. What subjects does Luxton feel are discriminated against within sociology? Why?
3. What are some of the barriers between academics and the public? Think of ways in which these could be solved.
4. Think about the third struggle of activist scholarship. Is Luxton right? What do you think the answers to these questions might be?
5. What solutions are presented for academic activists? Why is committing sociology so important for creating social change?

PART VII
Race and Ethnic Relations

In our national mythology, Canada is considered a tolerant, multicultural "land of immigrants." But while it may be more tolerant, less racially and ethnically fragmented, and more multicultural than many other countries, Canada is nonetheless a place of intolerance, discrimination, and institutionalized racism. Nowhere is this more obvious than in the treatment of Indigenous peoples, who clearly are not part of the "land of immigrants" mythology.

Every day, the notions of race and ethnicity are implicitly or explicitly imbedded in our conversations and observations—"my black neighbour"; "the arrival and settlement of Syrian refugees." But what exactly do we mean by *race* and *ethnicity*, and what are the implications and social impact of self-identifying or being labelled a member of an ethnic or racialized group? A number of notable Canadian sociologists, including John Porter, have spent a considerable amount of time examining the impact of ethnicity (and others later, of race) on access to power and status in this country.

The term *race* refers to an *ascribed* characteristic that is based on select physical traits, such as skin colour and facial features, that are used to categories people into distinct groups. Although all human beings belong to the same species, the small genetic variations among them have been used to set groups of people apart and to privilege members of one group, most often those deemed "white," at the expense of others. Despite scientific evidence disputing the genetic foundations of racialized differences in behavioural traits (differences in intelligence, criminality, etc.), some individuals, organizations, and states continue to operate under the assumption that some races are superior to others—making race an important social construct worthy of sociological attention.

Ethnicity, on the other hand, refers to a group of people who share a nationality or set of cultural traditions. Ethnic groups often distinguish themselves or are distinguished by others based on their geographic location (country of origin), shared language, religion, or group history. While many people use the terms *race* and *ethnicity* interchangeably, they remain distinct concepts.

Canadian sociology has had a brief but rich history of research and theorizing on race/racialization, ethnicity, prejudice, discrimination, colonialism, nationalism, citizenship, multiculturalism, and identity. In the following chapters, you will learn more about majority and minority relations, which exacerbate inequalities. You will be exposed to case studies and examples of both subtle and more extreme, and at times institutionalized, forms of discrimination and racism. In Chapter 28, Jeff Denis and Kerry Bailey describe the road to reconciliation as they examine some of the ongoing challenges experienced by First Nations individuals and communities in Canada. Adam Howe, in Chapter 29, deepens our understanding in this area by exploring "the rule of difference" in Canadian–Indigenous colonial relations. Racial and ethnic tensions and discrimination are also explored in Chapter 30, where Lori Wilkinson provides examples of overt and covert forms of racism found in the Canadian media. Given these examples, it is not surprising then that in Chapter 31, Elke Winter problematizes and deconstructs our notions of, and the Canadian policy of, multiculturalism.

28 Decolonizing Canada, Reconciling with Indigenous Peoples: How Settler "Allies" Conceive of Their Roles and Goals

Jeff Denis and Kerry Bailey

"Reconciliation is about forging and maintaining respectful relationships. There are no shortcuts."
—Justice Murray Sinclair, Chair, Truth and Reconciliation Commission of Canada

In its 2015 final report, the Truth and Reconciliation Commission (TRC) of Canada—based on six years of national events, statement-gathering, and archival research—described the Indian Residential School system as "cultural genocide" and issued 94 Calls to Action (TRC, 2015:1). While some welcomed the report, others accused it of "half-truths and exaggerations" (Clifton and Rubenstein, 2015), and still others said it did not go far enough (Palmater, 2015; Watts and King, 2015).

Reconciliation requires the engagement of both Indigenous and settler peoples and at least some shared understanding of the kind of society we are working toward. In this light, we interviewed settler-Canadians who participated in TRC events—as statement providers, volunteers, or observers—about how they came to be engaged and how they understood their roles in the process. It soon became clear that participants were there for many reasons, had varying levels of awareness and engagement, and perceived their roles in different and sometimes contradictory ways.

Although most participants identified as **allies**, they attributed diverse meanings to the term, including listening to and learning from Indigenous peoples, educating fellow settlers, speaking out against racism, and lobbying for changes in government policy. While such roles are potentially useful and not mutually exclusive, these same "allies" sometimes conceived of the ultimate goals in divergent ways, ranging from the integration of Indigenous peoples into multicultural Canada to the radical transformation of society (grounded in respect for Indigenous self-determination).

Background and Methods

Self-identified allies sometimes do little to benefit, and might even hinder, the social movements they claim to support (McKenzie, 2014; Park, 2014). In a colonial context, Memmi (1965) argues that settlers can never truly be allies unless they leave the country. However, many Indigenous and non-Indigenous scholars and activists in Canada assert that settlers can make valuable contributions to Indigenous-led movements, at least under certain conditions (Davis, 2010; Gehl, 2012; Regan, 2010; Walia, 2012). Given these debates, we interviewed 24 settlers of various ages and backgrounds who had attended at least one TRC event (in Halifax, Toronto, or Vancouver). While a few were new to such activities, others had been working with Indigenous people for decades.

Each participant was asked to tell the story of how they came to be engaged, but also whether they identify as an ally (and, if so, what being an ally means to them), their vision for the future of Indigenous–settler relations, and the roles that they think Indigenous and settler peoples *should* play in reconciliation and **decolonization**. Below, we summarize salient themes that emerged in our interviews and critically assess the range of roles and goals that engaged settlers see themselves pursuing.

Findings

What Does It Mean to Be an Ally?

Each interviewee was asked if they identify as an "ally," and, if so, what being an ally means to them. More than two-thirds of participants said yes, whereas others were uncomfortable with the label. Some preferred terms such as *supporter*, *friend*, or *advocate*. One participant rejected labels altogether.

For those who did identify as allies, each had a different idea of what being an ally meant, but at least four themes were widely shared. These included "walking together," listening, being educated, and (less frequently) engaging in political activism. Most self-identified allies believed it was their duty to be aware of historical and contemporary issues affecting Indigenous peoples and to support Indigenous causes. But there were major differences in how participants operationalized these concepts. For example, the concept of "support" ranged from building interpersonal friendships to promoting increased funding of social programs to physically standing with Indigenous peoples in defence of their lands and rights.

However, some participants who said they were committed to reconciliation rejected the term *ally*, stating that they were "not on either side" or placing "conditions" on their allyship. For instance, a health care worker in British Columbia said,

> I am not unconditionally an ally.... I think it is healthy for relationships to have conditions.... I am more likely to support First Nations people who are working really hard to ... get out of poverty, [who] want to get into education [and] be a participating member of society....

Such comments confirm what some critics have suggested—that many settlers who participate in reconciliation and solidarity activism have limits and may withdraw their support, especially when their own resources or privileges are challenged.

What Are Participants Trying to Achieve?

When asked about their hopes for the future, participants had diverse and sometimes incompatible ideas, ranging from the inclusion of Indigenous peoples in multicultural Canada to the radical restructuring of society based on recognition of nation-to-nation treaties and Indigenous self-government. The three most common goals were increasing co-operation; building awareness, comfort, and respect; and improving Indigenous peoples' life-chances.

Most interviewees cited relatively vague long-term goals, such as continuing to learn from, understand, communicate, and collaborate with one another. In general, the greater the amount of change required of settlers, the less likely a goal or vision was to be endorsed.

What Does Reconciliation Mean to You?

When participants were asked what *reconciliation* means to them, there was a similar variety of responses. The four most common elements were fostering awareness of how past injustices have affected present circumstances; healing at personal and community levels; story-sharing and mutual learning; and creating more equitable laws, institutions, and socio-economic opportunities and conditions. Echoing the TRC's (2015) final report, many also emphasized that reconciliation is "an ongoing long-term process."

Overall, however, there was a lack of consensus on specific actions that contribute to reconciliation. Many understood it in relatively passive terms such as acknowledgement and awareness. Conveniently, such definitions of reconciliation do not require significant change in settlers' behaviours or policies.

Yet, some participants did recognize that significant change is needed. One said that for reconciliation to occur, settlers must pay their "debt," which "would mean [among other things] change in government policies, the Indian Act, all of the systemic things that mitigate against Aboriginal people." Another stated, "I don't think you can have reconciliation without justice," which, for him, meant eliminating poverty and honouring Indigenous and treaty rights.

A few participants disliked the term *reconciliation*. For example, a recent immigrant did not feel she had "anything to reconcile," but was still seeking "solidarity." Another interviewee noted that reconciliation is contextually specific, so it may look somewhat different depending on the region and peoples involved.

How Do Engaged Settlers Understand Their Role in the Process?

Interviewees were also asked what role, if any, Indigenous and non-Indigenous peoples should play in reconciliation. Altogether, nine roles were identified for settlers. The most frequently suggested roles were learning and sharing knowledge, being open to multiple perspectives, and maintaining awareness of "Indigenous issues." Smaller numbers highlighted speaking out against racism and unjust laws and policies. Yet, most perceived their roles in more passive ways, such as listening, keeping an open mind, and being aware.

Asking non-Indigenous Canadians what role Indigenous peoples should play in reconciliation is potentially problematic. A few interviewees replied that this was a better question for Indigenous people themselves. However, most answered quickly, and nine themes emerged. The most common response was that Indigenous people should "teach" settlers about their experiences and world views and "how to make things right." One interviewee asserted, "[T]hey need to be spending more time engaging non-Aboriginal people and helping to move the educational process along." As critics have noted, the demand to teach settlers places an added burden on Indigenous peoples.

Some self-proclaimed allies also said that reconciliation requires Indigenous people to be open to collaboration, patient, trusting, "not so angry," and willing to heal and take pride in their heritage. While only expressed by a minority of interviewees, such sentiments reproduce paternalistic relations (in which settlers claim to know what's best for Indigenous people).

The Question of Decolonization

Finally, interviewees were asked about the concept of "decolonization" and how, if at all, they see themselves participating. This was a difficult question for many. Among those who did attempt an answer, the meanings attributed to decolonization were more active, suggesting more drastic change than reconciliation—but again, there were large variations.

In terms of roles, the responses were broadly similar to those imagined for reconciliation. For instance, one participant asserted that Indigenous people should "teach non-Aboriginals what colonization really means and what its effects were and how you then could decolonize." For settlers, perceived roles included learning from and collaborating with Indigenous peoples, educating fellow settlers, lobbying Canadian governments, and being aware of one's own biases. One interviewee said,

> To me, decolonization means peeling away the layers of what we call "privilege" and looking at our whole thinking of who we are, where we come from, and what are the assumptions . . . that our culture has made . . . and just facing up to the arrogance. . . .

As this quotation suggests, some participants had more radical ideas for personal and systemic change. However, none expressed support for such extreme measures as removing settlers from Indigenous lands. Indeed, few participants discussed the land at all. The fact that so many self-identified allies are unable to clearly state what decolonization means, and only rarely link it to Indigenous self-determination on Indigenous lands, indicates a profound disconnect between recent Indigenous-led movements (such as Idle No More) and anti-colonial scholarship (e.g., Alfred, 2005; Coulthard, 2014) on the one hand, and the mainstream reconciliation discourse on the other.

Critical Analysis

As critics have stressed, non-Indigenous individuals declaring positive intentions as allies (or supporters) does not mean that racist or colonialist attitudes and behaviours have been eliminated. At least one-third of interviewees expressed paternalism at some point in their interview. For instance, when asked about her vision for the future, an older white female teacher said, "I believe . . . we need to start . . . helping [Aboriginal girls] from the time before they're pregnant and change our education system so [that] those moms would know how to feed their kids and how to read with them."

Several interviewees also expressed colour-blind ideals (Bonilla-Silva, 2010) or laissez-faire racist beliefs (Denis, 2015). One young man of European and Asian descent indirectly blamed Indigenous people for their problems when he said, "What I'd like to see [is] more Native people using the resources that are available to them to succeed," because it is frustrating for him, as a non-Indigenous student, to have to work two jobs to pay his way through university, while Indigenous people allegedly have opportunities for post-secondary funding but do not always take advantage of them (a common misconception). These examples illustrate that having "good intentions" or identifying as an ally does not exempt one from also thinking or acting in ways that could perpetuate racism and colonialism.

Conclusion

Overall, settler-Canadians who have participated in TRC events display tremendous variation in their perceived roles and goals. This diversity creates challenges for reconciliation and decolonization movements in that some would-be allies may be working at cross-purposes or even doing more harm than good. However, as Indigenous scholars (e.g., King, 2013) often note, Indigenous peoples also have diverse political and cultural traditions and visions for the future. To the extent that Indigenous understandings of reconciliation and decolonization also vary by nation and region, the variation we observe among settlers may be necessary. Notwithstanding the utility of general principles for solidarity work (e.g., Gehl, 2012; Walia, 2012), to think that there is any single pathway or role for settlers is perhaps a colonial idea in itself.

At the same time, even settlers who are deeply committed to decolonization and/or reconciliation sometimes make paternalistic or problematic assumptions. Identifying as an ally does not relieve an individual of accountability. That said, what distinguishes many engaged settlers is the high level of critical self-reflection and willingness to learn from mistakes. An older couple recalled once inviting a Haudenosaunee Elder to do a traditional opening for an event they were organizing on Anishinaabe land. After realizing their error, they apologized for it, worked hard to regain trust, and have never repeated the same mistake. Such humility, flexibility, and openness to ongoing learning and dialogue are essential for working in alliance and (re)building respectful relationships with Indigenous peoples.

References

Alfred, Taiaiake. 2005. Wasáse: Indigenous Pathways of Action and Freedom. Toronto: University of Toronto Press.

Bonilla-Silva, Eduardo. 2010. Racism without Racists: Color-Blind Racism and Racial Inequality in Contemporary America, 3rd edition. New York: Rowman & Littlefield.

Clifton, Rodney E., and Hymie Rubenstein. 2015. "Debunking the Half-Truths and Exaggerations in the Truth and Reconciliation Report." National Post, June 4. (http://news.nationalpost.com/full-comment/clifton-rubenstein-debunking-the-half-truths-and-exaggerations-in-the-truth-and-reconciliation-report)

Coulthard, Glen Sean. 2014. Red Skin, White Masks: Rejecting the Colonial Politics of Recognition. Minneapolis: University of Minnesota Press.

Davis, Lynne. (Editor). 2010. Alliances: Re/Envisioning Indigenous–Non-Indigenous Relationships. Toronto: University of Toronto Press.

Denis, Jeffrey S. 2015. "Contact Theory in a Small-Town Settler-Colonial Context: The Reproduction of Laissez-Faire Racism in Indigenous-White Canadian Relations." American Sociological Review 80(1):218–42.

Gehl, Lynn. 2012. "Ally Bill of Responsibilities." (http://www.lynngehl.com/uploads/5/0/0/4/5004954/ally_bill_of_responsibilities_poster.pdf)

King, Hayden. 2013. "We Natives are Deeply Divided: There's Nothing Wrong with that." The Globe and Mail, January 9. (http://www.theglobeandmail.com/globe-debate/we-natives-are-deeply-divided-theres-nothing-wrong-with-that/article7096987)

McKenzie, Mia. 2014. Black Girl Dangerous: On Race, Queerness, Class, and Gender. Self-published.

Memmi, Albert. 1965. The Colonizer and the Colonized. Boston: Beacon Press.

Palmater, Pamela. 2015. "Canada's Residential Schools Weren't Killing Culture, They Were Killing Indians." Rabble, June 9. (http://rabble.ca/blogs/bloggers/pamela-palmater/2015/06/canadas-residential-schools-werent-killing-culture-they-were-)

Park, Suey. 2014. "Anti-Racist Activism and White 'Allies': A Conversation with Dr David Leonard." Rabble, January 6. (http://rabble.ca/news/2014/01/anti-racist-activism-and-white-allies-conversation-dr-david-leonard)

Regan, Paulette. 2010. Unsettling the Settler Within: Indian Residential Schools, Truth Telling, and Reconciliation in Canada. Vancouver: UBC Press.

Truth and Reconciliation Commission (TRC) of Canada. 2015. Honouring the Truth, Reconciling for the Future: Summary of the Final Report of the Truth and Reconciliation Commission. (http://www.trc.ca/websites/trcinstitution/File/2015)

Walia, Harsha. 2012. "Decolonizing Together: Moving beyond a Politics of Solidarity toward a Practice of Decolonization." Briarpatch, January 1.

Watts, Vanessa, and Hayden King. 2015. "TRC Report a Good Start, but Now It's Time for Action." The Globe and Mail, June 5. (http://www.theglobeandmail.com/news/national/trc-report-a-good-start-but-now-its-time-for-action/article24824924)

29 Synthesizing the Canadian Colonial State Field with Contemporary Organizational Network Perspectives

Adam Howe

Introduction

Some recent scholarship on Canadian social movements has focused on the #IdleNoMore movement and related issues of colonialism, Indigenous self-determination, and environmental concerns, among others (e.g. Coates, 2015; Coburn, 2015; Denis, 2015). Understanding this activism requires a better understanding of the social and political conditions within which it occurs. Here I expand upon George Steinmetz's (2008) **theory of colonial state fields**, applying it to the Canadian case to build what I call the Canadian colonial state field (CCSF). I build upon Steinmetz's theory by proposing a synthesis of the CCSF with Mario Small's (2009) theory of **organizationally embedded networks**. This theory views activist networks as existing within particular organizations with their own contexts, rather than as autonomous entities. This represents a useful and potentially more systematic framework for investigating how colonialism affects Indigenous activist social networks and could bolster Indigenous demands for autonomy and self-governance.

The Colonial State Field

According to George Steinmetz,

> Modern colonies can be defined as territories in which (1) political sovereignty has been seized by a foreign political power and (2) the indigenous population is treated by the conquering state as fundamentally inferior. . . . (Steinmetz, 2008, p. 591)

These two requirements are summarized as the "sovereignty" and "rule of difference" criteria. Colonies are governed by the settled colonial state, which must assert independence from both the metropolitan state and the Indigenous society (Ibid, p. 591). Steinmetz wrote about the German case, however, and his ideas need to be applied to the Canadian context. Canada meets Steinmetz's two criteria for modern colonies: (1) the political authority of Indigenous peoples was seized by British and French colonizers (Mihesuah, 2003) and continues to be monopolized by the Canadian state, which is now institutionally autonomous from Britain and France; and (2) Indigenous peoples remain structurally disadvantaged in all areas of social and political life compared to white colonizers (Sunseri, 2011).

Further, early Canadian colonial state autonomy resembled early German colonial autonomy, since in both cases the most important capital was knowledge of the Indigenous society, and only colonial officials could make "coherent policy" (Steinmetz, 2008, p. 592). Additionally, colonial policies in Canada were similar to German colonial policies, as both were "premised . . . on assumptions about the inferiority of the colonized and their incapacity for self-government"—that is, premised on the rule of difference (Ibid, pp. 592–3). Moreover, in both cases colonial governments ensured that the colonized were always understood as different from their own society, and "multiplied distinctions among the colonized in an effort to dilute opposition" against the colonizers (Ibid, p. 593). In Canada, these processes were originally formalized in The Indian Act, 1876, and still characterize Indigenous–state relations today (Neu, 2000). These observations confirm that Steinmetz's theory applies to Canada, and thus the CCSF.

The state is also embedded within the broader colonial field of power, where the dominant form of capital is ethnographic knowledge: one's ability to understand the colonized "Other" (Steinmetz, 2008, p. 594). Hence the rule of difference provides all white European colonizers with substantial "racial" capital compared to their colonized residents (Ibid, p. 591). This capital is a key part of the boundary work done by colonizers to distinguish the colonized society as a separate, subordinate field (Ibid, p. 601). Social struggles within the colonial field of power involve preserving or challenging the "rules" governing the distribution of capital. They may also "attempt to change the very definition of the field's dominant form of capital" (Ibid, p. 591; see also Bourdieu, 1989). In fact, the central aim of colonial policy was to "compel the colonized to adhere to a constant and stable definition of their own culture" (Steinmetz, 2008, p. 593).

Indigenous activists today must also acquire ethnographic capital (i.e., knowledge of colonial politics) to inform their political strategies, making them understandable to the people within the CCSF as a first step; thus, ethnographic capital is one key **network resource** for Indigenous activists. Other key resources are colonial state funds (for Indigenous organizations or autonomous Indigenous groups), access to other key network "nodes" (individuals in a network) who have valuable cultural knowledge/ethnographic capital, and any other resources deemed relevant by Indigenous peoples for political activism. However, Indigenous activist networks are not autonomous, but are embedded within the CCSF and other organizations. Synthesizing Steinmetz with contemporary network theory could help clarify the relationship between Indigenous activism and the Canadian colonial state, and help Indigenous groups to strategically modify future activism.

Organizationally Embedded Networks

Previous research on Indigenous activism has relied on traditional theories of social movements, such as resource mobilization and political opportunity.[1] Few studies deal with social networks, and none do so with any depth. Mario Small (2009) argues that while such analyses are useful, they treat networks as autonomous stand-alone entities, without taking account of the context within which they are established, maintained, and facilitate resource mobilization. In response, Small proposes a theory of organizational embeddedness, which conceives of networks as relations between actors that are dependent on the organizations they exist within. (Small, 2009, p. vi). The ability of networks to mobilize resources depends on the organizations within which they are embedded. The characteristics of these organizations—institutional policies, norms, opportunities to interact, etc.—all contribute to their impact on the social networks within them.

Synthesizing the CCSF with Small's organizational embeddedness is useful for three main reasons. First is the existence of a distribution of ethnographic capital in the CCSF implies inequality, suggesting that some groups benefit more than others. In Canada Indigenous groups are disadvantaged (Sunseri, 2011). Understanding the organizational and network characteristics of Indigenous activism within the CCSF is a useful way of investigating this inequality.

Second, organizational characteristics are commonly influenced by outside factors, mainly the policies of the state (Small, 2009). This is important since colonial policies and institutions—in both the German CSF and modern Canada—are dependent on the practical necessities within the colony (Steinmetz, 2008, p. 597). This means the ability of organizationally embedded Indigenous networks to mobilize valuable network resources is related to colonial state policies, which are strategically designed to disadvantage Indigenous groups.

Finally, the field structure of the CCSF is quite similar to Small's network structures: both entities are made up of social positions related to one another, structured in a hierarchical manner. Moreover, the colonial field contains political institutions similar to Small's broker organizations—those ideally positioned to connect network actors to resources—with similar characteristics and key actors. Steinmetz (2008) argues that competition among elite groups within a colonial bureaucracy can lead to changes in the governance of colonized groups (pp. 590–1). In this way, colonial elite groups (for example, different departments or ministries) resemble broker organizations, while individual bureaucratic elites function like gatekeepers—actors who control access to important resources—within these broker state organizations. This means that these elite groups and individuals affect the social and political lives of colonial field and network actors (Steinmetz, 2008; Small, 2009).

These organizations, and actors within them, also influence the lives of Indigenous peoples through formation, implementation, and interpretation of colonial state policy. Applying Small's (2009) observation that state policies affect organizational networks reveals that colonial policies, which are designed to maintain Steinmetz's two criteria, affect the ability of Indigenous activists to network with colonial gatekeepers, both within and outside the state, and with non-Indigenous people who identify with Indigenous issues. This demonstrates the importance of understanding which broker organizations are central to indigenous activist networks, and the policies affecting their characteristics.

Broker Organizations

Here I enumerate some broker organizations central to facilitating Indigenous activism, both within and outside the colonial state, that are affected by colonial state policies. I also outline how these organizations might alter/constrain the network structure of Indigenous activist networks. Given the network thrust of this chapter, I also focus on identifying network gatekeepers within broker organizations of the state, and investigating access to/ties with these gatekeepers.

Broker organizations would include all national Aboriginal organizations, whose mandates involve mediating relations between the state and Indigenous groups. These include the Assembly of First Nations (Canada's largest Indigenous organization), the Native Women's Association of Canada, and the Congress of Aboriginal People. Also important are band councils—governing units of Canadian Indigenous peoples. Through these organizations, Indigenous activists have great potential for political mobilization given these organizations' knowledge of the CCSF, and the subtle and specific conditions of entry actors are required to understand to gain access to any social field (Bourdieu, 2000 as cited in Steinmetz, 2008, p. 595), which may elude Indigenous groups given Steinmetz's two criteria. All of these organizations are related to Indigenous activist groups, most notably those involved with #IdleNoMore.

Thus, we find a connection between (1) current relations between Canadian Indigenous populations and the federal government (insofar as state policies toward Indigenous peoples are largely determined by this historical relationship), and (2) the ability of Indigenous groups to engage in socio-political activism through organizationally embedded networks (insofar as network organizations are influenced by colonial gatekeepers and partly shaped by colonial state policies). Comparative empirical evidence of discrimination against Indigenous activist networks through colonial organizations could result in meaningful policy changes surrounding Indigenous access to state organizations and funding.

Senior individuals within these organizations might be considered dual network gatekeepers, as they control access to both the state (for Indigenous activists) and Indigenous communities (for the state): they have some control over state access to knowledge of Indigenous social, political, and economic life, while also having much control of activists' access to state funding and network resources. Additional people of interest would include members of the colonial state and activist groups that participate in the field, which "includes all state employees . . . judges, policemen, officers, and soldiers" as well as "[i]ndividuals and groups empowered by the state to carry out official functions" (Steinmetz, 2008, p. 595). However, all of these individuals may not be true gatekeepers, as membership within social fields can be difficult to determine (Bourdieu, 2000 as cited in Steinmetz, 2008, p. 595); hence the need for an exhaustive and accurate network analysis of the CCSF. Scholars should pursue a detailed mapping of Indigenous activist and colonial state networks and organizations and of the network distribution of capital(s) relevant to Indigenous activism within the colonial field of power, as well as the Indigenous field.

Conclusion

I have outlined a synthesis of the CCSF and Small's theory of organizationally embedded networks. Two important commonalities of the theories are (1) the similar characteristics of the field structure on one hand, and of networks on the other, insofar as both are hierarchically structured and affected by state policy; and (2) the existence and importance of gatekeepers in both models, insofar as these individuals/organizations determine who has access/membership to the colonial field, as well as access to valuable network resources. I argue that this framework could facilitate empirical investigations of discriminatory socio-political consequences resulting from the influence of colonial state policies on organizationally embedded Indigenous activist networks.

Note

1. For example, Andrews and Caren (2010); Blomley (1996); Coates (2015); Coburn (2015); Da Silva and Rothman (2011); Davis (2013); Denis (2015); Furniss (2001); Gilchrist (2010); Harding (2006, 2009); Kino-nda-niimi (2014); Wilkes, Corrigall-Brown, and Meyers (2010); Wilkes and Ricard (2007). See also Stoddart and McDonald (2011) pp. 314–15 for a good overview.

References

Andrews, K.T. and Caren, N. (2010). Making the News: Movement Organizations, Media Attention, and the Public Agenda. ASR, *75*(6), 841–66.

Blomley, N. (1996). "Shut the Province Down:" First Nations Blockades in British Columbia, 1984–1995. *BC Studies*, 111, 5–35.

Bourdieu, P. (1989). Social Space and Symbolic Power. *Sociological Theory*, *7*(1), 14–25.

Coates, K. (2015). *#IdleNoMore: And the Remaking of Canada.* University of Regina Press.

Coburn, Elaine. (2015). *More Will Sing Their Way to Freedom.* Halifax, NS: Fernwood Publishing.

Da Silva, P.P. and Rothman, F.D. (2011). Press Representation of Social Movements: Brazilian Resistance to the Candonga Hydroelectric Dam. *Journal of Latin American Studies, 43,* 725–54.

Denis, J.S. (2015). "A Four Directions Model: Understanding the Rise and Resonance of an Indigenous Self-Determination Movement." In Elaine Coburn (Ed.), *More Will Sing their Way to Freedom: Indigenous Resistance* and Resurgence (pp. 208–28). Halifax: Fernwood Press.

Furniss, E. (2001). Aboriginal Justice, the Media, and the Symbolic Management of Aboriginal/Euro-Canadian Relations. *American Indian Culture & Research Journal, 25*(2), 1–36.

Gilchrist, K. (2010). "Newsworthy" Victims? Exploring Differences in Canadian Local Press Coverage of Missing/ Murdered Aboriginal and White Women. *Feminist Media Studies, 10*(4), 373–90.

Harding R. (2006). Historical Representations of Aboriginal People in the Canadian News Media. *Discourses & Society, 17*(2), 205–35.

———. (2009). News Reporting on Aboriginal Child Welfare: Discourses of White Guilt, Reverse Racism, and Failed Policy. *Canadian Social Work Review, 26*(1), 25–41.

Mihesuah, D.A. (2003). *Indigenous American women: Decolonization, empowerment, activism.* U of Nebraska Press.

Neu, D. (2000). Accounting and accountability relations: colonization, genocide and Canada's first nations. *Accounting, Auditing & Accountability Journal, 13*(3), 268–88.

Small, M.L. (2009). *Unanticipated Gains: Origins of Network Inequality in Everyday Life.* Oxford, New York: Oxford Scholarship Online.

Small, M.L., Jacobs, E.M., and Massengill, R.P. (2008). Why Organizational Ties Matter for Neighborhood Effects: Resource Access through Childcare Centers. *Social Forces, 87*(1), 387–414.

Steinmetz, G. (2008). The Colonial State as a Social Field: Ethnographic Capital and Native Policy in the German Overseas Empire before 1914. *American Sociological Review, 73*(4), 589–612.

Stoddart, M.C.J., and MacDonald, L. (2011). "Keep It Wild, Keep It Local": Comparing News Media and the Internet as Sites for Environmental Movement Activism for Jumbo Pass, British Columbia. CJS, *36*(4), 313–35.

Sunseri, L. (Ed.). (2011). *Racism, Colonialism, and Indigeneity in Canada: A Reader.* OUP Press.

Wilkes, R., Corrigall-Brown, C., and Myers, D.J. (2010). Packaging Protest: Media Coverage of Indigenous People's Collective Action. CRS, *47*(4), 327–57.

Wilkes, R., and Ricard, D. (2007). How Does Newspaper Coverage of Collective Action Vary? Protest by Indigenous People in Canada. *The Social Science Journal, 44*, 231–51.

30 How Does Sociology Help Us to Understand and Combat Racism in Canada?

Lori Wilkinson

Have you heard about what happened to Andrew Loku, Jermaine Carby, and Kwasi Skene-Peters? All three were young, black, Greater Toronto Area (GTA) men shot and killed by police in separate incidents during July 2015 (Gillis, 2015). What is ironic is that these deaths were not widely reported outside the GTA and occurred in the same month that #BlacklivesmatterTO was launched. An investigation led by the *Toronto Star* (Gillis, 2015) reveals that "of the 51 fatal shootings involving the Toronto police, at least 18 involved black men, representing 35 per cent of fatal police shootings. Toronto's black population is roughly 9 per cent."

Do you know what Tina Fontaine and Rinelle Harper have in common? Besides being Indigenous, young, and female, both were sexually assaulted and left to die in Manitoba. They are two of the 1,079 murdered and missing Indigenous women in Canada. The number is especially shocking considering it is four times higher in comparison to other women in the country (Amnesty International, 2014). The good news for Ms Harper is that she survived despite being viciously beaten not once but twice by her attackers. Ms Fontaine was not as lucky; she died of her injuries.

In January 2015, *Maclean's* magazine declared Winnipeg as Canada's most racist city (Macdonald, 2015). Like any reputable publication, the article backed its assertion with several prominent and cringe-worthy examples of racism within the city and accompanied the piece with some recent polling results. It shared some data from a 2014 survey sponsored by the Canadian Institute for Identities and Migration (2014) that showed that one-third of Manitoba and Saskatchewan residents (they were combined in the study) believe that racial **stereotypes** (such as that Scottish people are thrifty or that Jewish people are business-minded) have some basis in reality. No other province had such high support for these beliefs in stereotypes. Other research also supports the view that Winnipeg could be one of the most racist cities in Canada. A recent survey conducted by Probe Research (2014) finds that 75 per cent of city residents feel there is a racial divide between Indigenous and non-Indigenous Canadians; it is one of several polls that present a less than harmonious picture of the city.

We have a racism problem in Canada. Whether it involves the shooting of young black men in Toronto, the over 1,000 murdered or missing Indigenous women, or the daily insults faced by **racialized** Canadians that seem to be most prominent in Winnipeg, the fact is that race plays a prominent role in Canadian society. Racism pervades life not just in Winnipeg but across Canada and has real consequences for everyone, not just the persons who are directly victimized by it. **Racism** takes many forms and can be difficult to see and even more difficult to prove, but it influences various aspects of the lives of individuals and the communities they live in, including social cohesion, sense of belonging, happiness, well-being, and even financial security. A good sociologist will ask several questions to learn more about this phenomenon. What is racism and how do we identify it if it is difficult to measure? Who experiences racism and how are they affected by it? Why does the problem persist? How can these problems be alleviated or eliminated? At its core, sociology is about understanding why our seemingly chaotic society is largely functional despite all the problems, competing interests, and calamities that threaten to destroy it. Racism is one of those problems that deeply threaten social harmony and, more drastically, our society's existence. This chapter briefly examines some aspects of racism in Canada, why it persists, and how sociologists understand it.

First, what is racism? At its most basic, racism is "a system of advantage based on race" (Wellman, 1977), referring to "a host of practices, beliefs, social relations and phenomena that work to reproduce a racial hierarchy and social structure that yields superiority and privilege for some, and discrimination and oppression for others" (Cole, 2012). The emphasis is on "system" and not individuals (Tatum, 2015). By focusing on the word *system*, we can come to understand that racism is so much more than the individualized name calling, stereotypes, taunts, and physical violence. Instead, it involves systems within our society that perpetuate faulty beliefs about racial superiority and inferiority that lead to individualized, institutionalized, and systematic forms of oppression.

Racism takes several forms. The one we are most familiar with is individual racism, a form that includes racist attitudes, sentiments, or beliefs directed toward a single individual or group of individuals. This form of racism can be verbal, such as the use of racial slurs or jokes, or may be physical and involve assault and murder. These forms of racism are easy to identify and criticize. They are, however, among the least common. Other forms of racism include subtle racism, institutional racism, systemic racism (Henry and Tator, 2009), and new racism (Satzewich and Liodakis, 2010). These forms are much more difficult to identify, more subtle, more numerous, and more deeply embedded in our society. While it is beyond the scope of this chapter to discuss all these forms of racism, they can be collectively summarized as being real and having detrimental effects on the sense of belonging, acceptance, life chances, and experiences of racialized Canadians.

This leads me to our second question: who experiences racism and what are their experiences? Much sociological research has identified the structural, institutional, and personalized racism directed at racialized persons in our country. From the examples cited at the start of this chapter, we know that Indigenous women have the highest rates of mortality by murder in the country. We also know that black men are greatly overrepresented as victims of police-instigated shootings. From other studies, we know that people with Middle Eastern ethnicities, people who are Muslim, and people with immigrant backgrounds are more likely to be labelled as terrorists than any other group in Canada (Kazemipur, 2014; Welch, 2006). Studies also confirm that white Canadians earn more than racialized groups. Pendakur and Pendakur (2014) find that Indigenous women earn 10 to 20 per cent less than other women, simply for being members of an Indigenous **ethnic group**. For men, the gap is even bigger, between 20 and 50 per cent. Korean-, Iranian-, and Pakistani-origin Canadians have the lowest mean income of all groups (Jedwab and Satzewich, 2015). Data from the 2011 Census reveals that Filipinos (5.2 per cent) and Vietnamese (8.0 per cent) are the ethnic groups least likely to hold management positions. It may be difficult for some readers to comprehend the presence of this kind of labour market inequality in twenty-first-century Canada, but it happens frequently. In July 2015, for example, the Ontario Human Rights Commission launched an investigation of a nursing home in Burlington that advertised for "white only" nursing staff (Carter, 2015).

Racism is not limited to economic issues. Many of Canada's most respected cultural and government institutions have exhibited racism recently. I provide only two examples here. The Bank of Canada apologized to Canadians in 2012 for changing the design of the new Canadian $20 bill from one depicting a female Asian scientist to one showing a woman of "non-descript" (white) background in the final rendering of the new currency (CBC News, 2012). And a branch of the Royal Canadian Legion in Cranbrook, BC, was forced to apologize for a "joke" involving the murder of two "Indians" in their monthly newsletter (Miller, 2012). These are just a small sample of the racism that occurs in Canadian institutions on a daily basis. More serious cases involve the recent shootings of unarmed young black men in Toronto and elsewhere, and the over 1,000 unsolved cases of murdered Indigenous women. Our failure as a society to demand that our police and judiciary services investigate these issues indicates that there is a tacit understanding that this form of injustice is tolerable.

Third, why does racism persist in Canada? That is a tough question. Many people believe that Canada is a place of tolerance and freedom, one that has largely transcended racial and ethnic oppression. It is easy (for some people) to agree with this sentiment. We have a Charter of Rights and Freedoms that prohibits discrimination based on race, ethnicity, colour, nationality, age, religion, physical or mental ability, and sex. It also contains sections regarding minority language preservation and Indigenous peoples. We were the first country to adopt multiculturalism as a policy and as official government legislation.

We have anti-racism workplace legislation and human rights commissions, and all provinces have similar codes and laws in place to ensure that the rights of all peoples are respected.

Yet racism and discrimination still persist. They are embedded in the way we think, speak, and experience our world. A 2014 poll conducted by the Canadian Race Relations Foundation, the Association of Canadian Studies, and Leger Marketing finds that two-thirds of Canadians are worried about racism (Friedman and Jedwab, 2014). Yet conversely, many Canadians are worried about the country having too much diversity. Four in ten Canadians in the same poll report that religious diversity is a liability to Canada (Friedman and Jedwab, 2014). Geography matters. According to a recent survey conducted by the CBC (Lee, 2014), those living in Quebec and the Prairie provinces exhibit greater distrust of ethnic minorities. This finding, backed by other recent opinion polls, is one of the reasons why Winnipeg was singled out by *Maclean's* magazine for its problems with racism.

Finally, our last question is, how can we address these problems? Since racism pervades our way of life, our institutions, the way we think, and the beliefs we all hold, its immediate eradication seems next to impossible. This is where sociology can help. In addition to conducting research that identifies, highlights, and questions the way we organize our society, like the research discussed in this chapter, sociologists have created various theories that attempt to explain why racism persists and what we can do to resolve the racism and discrimination that contribute to social, cultural, and economic inequality in our society. There are many sociological theories that address racism. One popularly used in Canada today is called **critical race theory**. Critical race theorists understand that racism is embedded within the structures of Canadian society and the way institutions operate. They also understand that race intersects with other traits such as sex, class, and education, which together cause further segregation based on race, religion, ethnicity, and creed. The idea is that social justice cannot be attained without questioning, problematizing, and criticizing the way we do things in society with the goal of producing a Canada that is free from marginalization, segregation, or inequality based on race. A sociologist practising the critical race perspective would be working actively to encourage anti-racism as a goal of their studies (Solorzano and Yosso, 2001). Interested readers can read the work of Carl James (2012), Sherene Razack, Malinda Smith, and Sunera Thobani (2010), and Carol Aylward (2003) as examples of the use of critical race theory in Canadian sociology.

In this chapter, we learned that racism is persistent, systemic, and not limited to threats against individuals. We learned that racialized minorities are affected by racism as victims of crime, have lower incomes and advancement opportunities in their jobs, and can be targeted by seemingly respectable government and cultural organizations in the country. We learned that despite the number of laws and policies meant to protect Canadians from racism and discrimination, it still exists. We also learned that sociologists are working hard to uncover these types of discrimination and that new theoretical frameworks such as the critical race perspective help us understand the situation better.

Racism in Canada is a fact. No policy-maker, administrator, educator, or sociologist can argue otherwise. But we are making progress in identifying and eradicating it, and there is some good news to report. Racist attitudes of many Canadians are actually declining. A 2015 survey conducted by the Environics Institute finds that Canadians are less racist than they were in the 1980s. In one measure, it found that 95 per cent of Canadians feel that people born outside Canada are just as likely to be good citizens as those born here. While there is a long way to go to achieve equality, that's something to cheer about.

References

Amnesty International (2014) *Missing and Murdered Indigenous Women and Girls, Understanding the Numbers.* Report by Amnesty International Canada. Accessed online 17 August 2015 at http://www.amnesty.ca/blog/missing-and-murdered-indigenous-women-and-girls-understanding-the-numbers

Aylward, C. (2003) *Canadian Critical Race Theory: Racism and the Law.* Halifax, NS: Fernwood Press.

Canadian Institute for Identities and Migration (2014) "Survey on religion, racism and intergroup relations in Canada shows differences in attitudes among anglophones, francophones and other groups." Accessed online 12 August 2015 at http://www.ciim.ca/en/social-research

Carter, A. (2015) "Company apologizes for white only nurse job ad." CBC News. Accessed online 15 July 2015 at http://www.cbc.ca/news/canada/hamilton/news/company-apologizes-for-white-only-nurse-job-ad-1.3153069

Cole, L.N. (2012) "Racism: A sociological definition." Accessed online 12 August 2015 at http://sociology.about.com/od/R_Index/fl/Racism.htm

CBC News (2012) "Mark Carney apologizes over $100 bill controversy." Accessed online 20 August 2012 at http://www.cbc.ca/news/business/story/2012/08/20/carney-apologu.html

Environics Institute (2015) "Canadian public opinion about immigration and multiculturalism." Accessed online 12 August 2015 at http://www.environicsinstitute.org/institute-projects/current-projects/focus-canada-2015-immigration-and-multiculturalism

Friedman, R. and Jedwab, J. (2014) "Younger Canadians hold more negative views about religious groups." Canadian Race Relations Foundation. Accessed online 12 August 2015 at http://crr.ca/en/component/flexicontent/279-news-a-events/25010-younger-canadians-hold-more-negative-views-about-religious-groups-25010?view=item

Gillis, W. (2015) "How many black men have been killed by Toronto police? We can't know" *Toronto Star,* August 16. Accessed online 17 August 2015 at http://www.thestar.com/news/crime/2015/08/16/how-many-black-men-have-been-killed-by-toronto-police-we-cant-know.html

Henry, F. and Tator, C. (2009) *The Colour of Democracy: Racism in Canadian Society,* 4th Edition. Toronto: Nelson.

James, C.E. (2012) "Students 'at risk': stereotypes and the schooling of Black boys" *Urban Education* 47(2): 464–494.

Jedwab, J. and Satzewish, V. (2015) "Introductory essay: the vertical mosaic 50 years later." Pp. xvii–xxxvii in *The Vertical Mosaic: An Analysis of Social Class and Power in Canada,* 50th Anniversary Edition. John Porter. Toronto: University of Toronto Press.

Kazemipur, A. *The Muslim Question in Canada: A Story of Segmented Assimilation.* Vancouver: UBC Press, 2014.

Lee, D. (2014) "CBC News opinion poll on racism." Accessed online 10 November 2014 at http://www.cbc.ca/news/canada/canadian-attitudes-toward-immigrants-conflicted-poll-says-1.2826022

Macdonald, N. (2015) "Welcome to Winnipeg: Where Canada's racist problem is at its worst." *Maclean's.* Accessed online 22 January 2015 at http://www.macleans.ca/news/canada/welcome-to-winnipeg-where-canadas-racism-problem-is-at-its-worst

Miller, J. (2012) "Legion head says he's appalled by anti-aboriginal joke in B.C. legion newsletter." *Penticton Herald.* Accessed online 16 August 2012 at http://www.winnipegfreepress.com/canada/legion-head-says-hes-appalled-by-anti-aboriginal-joke-in-bc-legion-newsletter-166478076.html

Pendakur, K. and Pendakur, R. (2011) "Aboriginal income disparity in Canada." *Canadian Public Policy* 37(1): 61–83.

Probe Research (2014) *Winnipeg Is a Divided City* CTV News and *Winnipeg Free Press* news release. Accessed 7 October 2014 at http://www.cbc.ca/news/canada/manitoba/deep-racial-division-exists-in-winnipeg-poll-finds-1.2789954

Razak, S., Smith, M., and Thobani, S., eds (2010) *States of Race: Critical Race Feminism for the 21st Century.* Vancouver: Between the Lines.

Satzewich, V. and Liodakis, N. (2010) *Race and Ethnicity in Canada: A Critical Introduction.* Don Mills, ON: Oxford University Press.

Solorzano, D.G., and Yosso, T.J. (2001). "Critical race and LatCrit theory and method: Counter-storytelling." *International Journal of Qualitative Studies in Education* 14(4): 471–95.

Tatum, B. D. (2015) "What is racism anyway? Understanding the basics of racism and prejudice" Pp. 15–23 in *Getting Real about Race: Hoodies, Mascots, Model Minorities and Other Conversations.* Stephanie M. McClure and Cherise A. Harris, eds. Los Angeles: SAGE.

Welch, M. (2006) *The Scapegoats of September 11th: Hate Crimes & States Crimes in the War on Terror.* New Brunswick, NJ: Rutgers University Press.

Wellman, D. (1977) *Portraits of White Racism.* Cambridge, UK: Cambridge University Press.

31 Us, Them, and Others: Canadian Multiculturalism and a Sociology of Pluralist Group Formation

Elke Winter

Introduction[1]

In 1971, Canada was the first country in the world to implement multiculturalism as a policy aiming at the integration of immigrants. It is widely accepted that "no other Western country has gone as far as Canada in adopting multiculturalism not only as a policy towards minorities but also as a basic feature of shared identity" (Bauböck, 2005, p. 93). The Canadian policy stipulates that "ethnic loyalties need not, and usually do not, detract from wider loyalties to community and country" and that "Canadian identity will not be undermined by multiculturalism." Rather, "cultural pluralism is the very essence of Canadian identity. Every ethnic group has the right to preserve and develop its own culture and values within the Canadian context" (House of Commons, 1971).

Over the past 40 years, this approach has attracted much international attention. It has provoked responses both in opposition and in favour of the "Canadian model" of diversity management. While France, for example, has always rejected multiculturalism, several other Western countries such as Australia, the United Kingdom, the Netherlands, and Sweden have adopted similar policies. Within this context, Canadian multiculturalism was more or less successfully imitated, marketed, and exported (Kymlicka, 2004).

At the beginning of the twenty-first century, however, many of these countries have backtracked—at least in political rhetoric—from multiculturalism as a normative framework for both immigrant integration and national identity. While this trend is most noticeable in European countries, a reinforcement of nationalism and citizenship has also been observed in Australia and the United States. Given the alleged "retreat" of multiculturalism internationally (Joppke, 2004), my research examines (a) how the meaning of multiculturalism evolved in the country that initiated it, and (b) how we can apprehend this phenomenon sociologically.

Pluralism as (Sets of) Triangular Social Relations

My theoretical framework holds that ethnocultural diversity is rarely an obstacle to strong national identity and solidarity. Admittedly, some immigrants subscribe to cultural or religious values that are considerably more traditional or patriarchal than the fairly laissez-faire, tolerant, and consumerist way of life that has come to be accepted as the norm by many—but not all—Canadians. Unfortunately, the expression and significance of these values and beliefs are intensified by social differentiation. **Social differentiation** refers to processes where individuals are assigned to socially constructed categories, which are usually conceived as given or "natural." This categorization is then used to assign them to diverse positions and circumstances characterized by unequal resources, opportunities, and life chances (Juteau, 2003). The emergence of modern societies was based upon social differentiation along "national" lines. State-promoted multiculturalism, which assigns symbolic resources to ethnic minorities, serves as a modest remedy to the ongoing process of nationalist marginalization. It promotes the valorization of cultural diversity, as well as equity and integration (Berry, 2013). Thereby, it proposes a two-way street of integration, where both the host society and individuals/groups who hold disturbing values and beliefs are invited to move toward each other through dialogue and, if necessary, nonviolent conflict.

Shared pride about this two-way street of integration may lead to the construction of a multicultural national identity. The latter requires some boundary work (Lamont and Molnár, 2002) toward the outside, where the multicultural "national we" is "bounded" by opposition to (real or imagined) outsiders who do not share or are not invited to share "our" identity. Rather than viewing this process as a binary relation, I argue that the construction of a "multicultural we" is best seen as a specific form of **pluralist group formation**. It describes a dynamic set of triangular relations where the compromise between two, often unequal, categories—"us" and "others"—becomes meaningful only though the presence of outsiders ("them"; cf. Winter, 2011). In the multicultural context, the dominant group acknowledges the particularity of its cultural and social norms. It also values that it shares society with others. These others are integrated within a "multicultural we" not because they are equal in terms of power or similar in terms of culture, but because they are viewed as less different, deviant, or threatening in comparison to a third category. It is the (real or imagined) presence of this third party that forces the national majority to give concessions to minority groups in order to attempt their collaboration and/or cooptation.

Three Phases of Canadian Multiculturalism

In my research, I examine who is included in the Canadian "multicultural we" and how the meaning of multiculturalism as an essential feature of Canadian shared identity has evolved over time. I pay particular attention to socio-ethnic leveraging within processes of national boundary construction. As described above, **socio-ethnic leveraging** implies that minority groups are compared with each other and one is evaluated as more/less different, integrated, or threatening than the other. Using primary and secondary sources, I conduct an analysis of dominant discourses, primarily the mainstream media and speeches by government officials. Not surprisingly, the meaning of Canadian multiculturalism is not immutable over time. My analysis emphasizes three distinct phases.

First, from the early 1960s, through its implementation in 1971, and until the late 1980s, multiculturalism, although promoting equal rights for individuals, is expressed in a language of communities. This is because immigrants, as well as their needs and rights, are framed according to the matrix provided by Québécois nationalists and French Canadians more generally. They are viewed as minority groups of a similar type. Multiculturalism is then conceptualized as a modest remedy to (English-Canadian) nationalist marginalization in cultural and socio-economic terms (Breton, 1984); it is about majority–minority relations, equitable participation, and a shared Canadian identity (Berry, 2013). At least officially, the majority is unmarked: "although there are two official languages, there is no official culture" (House of Commons, 1971). Admittedly, English, French, and other white Canadians remain on top of the socio-ethnic hierarchy (Day, 2000; Mackey, 1999).

Second, in the 1990s, multiculturalism obtains individual and neoliberal connotations (Abu-Laban and Gabriel, 2002). While the focus on improving majority–minority relations remains, the multiculturalism of the 1990s becomes more and more constructed in opposition to allegedly "community-oriented" Québécois nationalism (rather than as an extension of French Canadians' cultural and linguistic accommodation). As such, multiculturalism loses its imputed and potentially society-threatening group-rights connotations. It becomes suitable as pan-Canadian identity (Winter, 2011), but loses its capacity to promote structural (institutional) diversity and the equitable participation of minorities.

Third, in the early 2000s, the neoliberal frame around multiculturalism continues (Kymlicka, 2013). In addition, under a Conservative federal government, "Canadian-Canadian" culture, to use Mackey's (1999) terms, becomes explicitly categorized as the social norm. While white Anglo-Saxons where never really conceived as "just another ethnic group," Canadianness is now even stronger and officially identified with British traditions, values, and institutions such as the monarchy. In fact, former immigration, citizenship, and multiculturalism minister Jason Kenney portrayed integrative pluralism as a "British liberal imperial tradition" (Kenney, 2008–13). The dominant group offers apologies for past injustices, manages (other) ethnic groups' integration and lessens potential hatred and conflict between "them." It is characterized by its allegedly inherent capacity to be the guarantor of peaceful intra- and inter-minority relations. Multiculturalism is no longer about improving majority–minority relations, but rather about managing minority–minority relations.

Pluralism and Socio-Ethnic Leveraging: A Theoretical Account

From the 1960s to the 1980s, Canadian multiculturalism involved socio-ethnic leveraging: comparing immigrants to French Quebeckers and French Canadians more generally turned them cognitively into "ethnic minorities" and hence made them eligible for some kind of culturally sensitive accommodation—i.e., multiculturalism. However, the leveraging did not have a clear direction; it varied between an inclusive and an exclusive logic. According to one logic, immigrant groups seemed the less powerful, less threatening "cousins" of French Canadians and hence more deserving of accommodation. According to the opposing logic, immigrant groups were even multiplying and worsening the centrifugal tendencies inherent in Québécois nationalism and should therefore not be encouraged to pursue multicultural rights. Inclusive and exclusive socio-ethnic leveraging kept each other in check.

What happened in Canada in the 1990s is best described as a conditionally *inclusive* form of socio-ethnic leveraging leading to pluralist group formation/formation of a multicultural national identity. By redefining all French Canadians as Québécois nationalists, and by redefining this nationalism as outdated and ethnically oppressive, in dominant discourses the image of "Quebec" is used as an undesirable contrast conception to a modern, cosmopolitan Canada where individuals of all ethnic and religious backgrounds can trade their talents for membership in the multicultural nation. While French Canadians in Quebec are cast as outsiders, for a certain period of time the members of ethnic minorities who have a "cultural capital" to trade can benefit from this redefinition of Canadian national identity in multicultural terms. However, this pluralist identity formation comes at the expense of redefining multiculturalism in "decommunitarized" (i.e., individualist) neoliberal terms.

The second redefinition that Canadian multiculturalism underwent in the early 2000s cannot be classified as conditionally *inclusive*. Minorities are here unambiguously situated outside the inner core. Their members are pitted against each other. In fact, socio-ethnic leveraging often implies the proclamation that the interests of two minority groups are incompatible, and hence only one of them could be incorporated within the national "we" on a conditional basis. Two types of multicultural subjects are constructed. There are "good" multicultural subjects, namely hard-working individuals with social and cultural capital who are willing to integrate. These individuals' integration efforts, however, are said to be jeopardized by "bad" multicultural subjects, i.e. those who promote inter-group hatred, do not learn English or French, do not adhere to "liberal democratic values," and engage in "abhorrent cultural practices."

The potentially disintegrative nature of "bad" multiculturalism demands that the relations between minority members are to be managed through government intervention on behalf of the dominant group, whose values and institutions alone are viewed to allow for the integration of diversity. This representation of multiculturalism could not be further removed from the original idea that "there is no official culture, nor does any ethnic group take precedence over any other" (House of Commons, 1971). This type of socio-ethnic leveraging is *exclusive*.

Lessons to Be Learned?

What lessons can be learned from the Canadian case at a time where multiculturalism is said to be "in retreat" in almost all Western immigrant receiving countries?

First, the fact that multiculturalism became redefined almost secretly and has not been attacked officially by any of the governing parties underlines the viability of the multicultural ethos in the Canadian context. In a country that strives to distinguish itself from the American melting pot, opinion polls confirm that the notion of multiculturalism remains a core ingredient of national identity (Adams, 2007). It is enshrined in law and in the constitution. As such, Canada remains one of the last strongholds for multiculturalism in the world.

Second, the fact that even in Canada multiculturalism has lost much of its original meaning suggests that the relationship between the national majority and minority groups needs to be re-examined. While the "host society's" rights and traditions should not be taken for granted, they should also not be ignored. As Berry (2013) reminds us, the original policy of Canadian multiculturalism promotes a combination of elements, such as diversity valorization, shared national identity, intercultural dialogue, and equitable participation. These elements should be available to all members of society, regardless of whether they belong to majority or minority populations.

Third, socio-ethnic leveraging as a form of boundary construction can involve both: the national majority's conditional inclusion of some "others" into a more inclusive "we" through contrast with another group ("them"), as well as the manipulation of the alleged characteristics of some minority groups in order to make others guilty by association and, hence, demand their unconditional integration into the dominant national "we" without allowing the latter to become pluralist. My reading of the Canadian case suggests that the presence of a powerful "third party," such as French-Canadian claims-making and/or Québécois nationalism bears some responsibility for the multicultural inclusion of immigrants in the 1990s. Indeed, multiculturalism's reformulation as a "minority affair" in the first decade of the new century runs astonishingly parallel to Quebec's absence from multicultural discourses.

Note

1. This chapter is based upon Winter (2015). The author gladly acknowledges financial support provided by the Social Sciences and Humanities Research Council of Canada.

References

Abu-Laban, Yasmeen, and Gabriel, Christina. (2002). *Selling Diversity: Immigration, Multiculturalism, Employment Equity, and Globalization*. Peterborough, ON: Broadview Press.

Adams, Michael. (2007). *Unlikely Utopia: The Surprising Triumph of Canadian Pluralism*. Toronto: Viking Canada.

Bauböck, Rainer. (2005). If You Say Multiculturalism Is the Wrong Answer, Then What Was the Question? *Canadian Diversity/Diversité canadienne*, 4(1), 90–3.

Berry, John W. (2013). Research on Multiculturalism in Canada. *International Journal of Intercultural Relations*, 37, 663–75.

Breton, Raymond. (1984). The Production and Allocation of Symbolic Resources: An Analysis of the Linguistic and Ethnocultural Fields in Canada. *Canadian Review of Sociology and Anthropology*, 21(2), 123–44.

Day, Richard J.F. (2000). *Multiculturalism and the History of Canadian Diversity*. Toronto: University of Toronto Press.

House of Commons. (1971). *Debates*. Ottawa: Queen's Printer. Retrieved from http://www.canadahistory.com/sections/documents/Primeministers/trudeau/docs-onmulticulturalism.htm.

Joppke, Christian. (2004). The Retreat of Multiculturalism in the Liberal State: Theory and Policy. *British Journal of Sociology*, 55(2), 237–57.

Juteau, Danielle (Ed.). (2003). *Social Differentiation: Patterns and Processes*. Toronto: University of Toronto Press.

Kenney, Jason. (2008–2013). Citizenship and Immigration Canada Newsroom Archives—Speeches. Retrieved from http://www.cic.gc.ca/english/department/media/archives.asp.

Kymlicka, Will. (2004). Marketing Canadian Pluralism in the International Arena. *International Journal*, 59(4), 829–52.

Kymlicka, Will. (2013). Neoliberal Multiculturalism. In Peter A. Hall and Michèle Lamont (Eds), *Social Resilience in the Neo-Liberal Era* (pp. 99–125). Cambridge: Cambridge University Press.

Lamont, Michèle, and Molnár, Virág. (2002). The Study of Boundaries in the Social Sciences. *Annual Review of Sociology* (28), 167–95.

Mackey, Eva. (1999). *The House of Difference. Cultural Politics and National Identity in Canada*. London and New York: Routledge.

Winter, Elke. (2011). *Us, Them and Others: Pluralism and National Identity in Diverse Societies*. Toronto: University of Toronto Press.

Questions for Critical Thought

Chapter 28 | Decolonizing Canada, Reconciling with Indigenous Peoples: How Settler "Allies" Conceive of their Roles and Goals

1. Denis and Bailey use the terms *allies* and *settlers* frequently within this chapter. Who are the allies? Who are the settlers?
2. What four elements were common among participants' answers to the question, "What does *reconciliation* mean to you?"
3. What do non-Indigenous Canadians feel that Indigenous Canadians should do to help with the process of reconciliation?
4. What roles and responsibilities were highlighted during the conversation about decolonization?
5. What are some of the racist or colonialist views shared by participants? How does this hamper reconciliation?

Chapter 29 | Synthesizing the Canadian Colonial State Field with Contemporary Organizational Network Perspectives

1. What two criteria does Steinmetz say make Canada a modern colony?
2. What is the "rule of difference"? How does this perpetuate racism?
3. How does Small's theory of organizational embeddedness add to network theory? Why is this a good theoretical tool to use for understanding activist networks?
4. How do broker organizations influence activism? How do broker organizations fit into the concept of organizational embeddedness?
5. What are two commonalities between the two theories of CCFS and organizational embeddedness?

Chapter 30 | How Does Sociology Help Us to Understand and Combat Racism in Canada?

1. Which city has the reputation of being Canada's most racist? What structural or cultural factors might underlie this reputation?
2. Think about the two examples of racism that are given at the beginning of this chapter. What other examples of racism have you seen in the news?
3. What is racism? What are the forms of racism?
4. Wilkinson gives many examples of racism in Canada. How do these examples contradict the Canadian Charter of Rights and Freedoms?
5. What can be done about racism in Canada? Think about the solutions that Wilkinson gives. What do you think can be done?

Chapter 31 | Us, Them, and Others: Canadian Multiculturalism and a Sociology of Pluralist Group Formation

1. What is the Canadian policy of multiculturalism? How has this changed over time?
2. What is the promise of people sharing a belief in multiculturalism?
3. Does having ethno-cultural diversity affect national identity? Why?
4. What are the three distinct phases of Canadian multiculturalism?
5. What three lessons does Winter say can be learned from examining the case of Canadian multiculturalism?

PART VIII
Youth and Families

This section introduces new sociological research that focuses on youth and families. By exploring these topics, you will gain a better understanding of the social meanings attached to age and learn about key issues that affect people at different ages and stages of life.

In everyday conversation, "youth" refers to a transitional period between childhood and adulthood. During this period, most people begin to take on more responsibility within their families and communities as they become independent and full-fledged members of society. But, although we often refer to people who are 15 to 24 as "youth," there is no specific chronology that sets boundaries to this stage of life. It would probably be fairer to say that "youth" is defined by economic dependency. People may transition out of this youth stage before 15 or after 24, depending on the society they live in and a variety of social factors that include social class and length of formal education. Generally, people who obtain more formal education spend a longer time as youth, which is to say, as economic dependents.

The chapters in this section will expose you to a variety of social patterns and issues that affect youth and families. In sociology, youth research has often included the study of young people's relationships to family, friends, and society at large. It has also looked at how current youth experience the social world, compared to youth of previous generations. In Chapter 32, Fabrizio Antonelli and Taylor Mooney describe the precarious jobs that many youth experience today, whether after school or during the summertime. Specifically, they describe the experience of youth who work in tree-planting camps during the summer. They investigate the economic factors that have pushed youth toward these dangerous and strenuous tree-planting jobs and also examine the unique culture that is being fostered within these camps. (For a longer treatment of this interesting subculture, consider reading the memoir *Six Million Trees*, by Kristel Derkowski.)

In Chapter 33, Alison Molina-Girón describes the changing rates of student participation in public life, and especially their voting patterns/beliefs. In exploring young people's participation in local political actions, she notes important differences in the political engagement of minority and non-minority group members. This chapter explains why youth participation in public life has changed, and points to important consequences for society as whole.

Other chapters in this section examine families and family structures. In the mid-twentieth century, the idealized North American family was made up of a husband, wife, and several children. However, in the twenty-first century we idealize diversity, recognizing that healthy, happy families can take many different forms. Today, we define "family" more in terms of process than structure, as "a group of people who emotionally and economically support each other."

These people, often connected through blood, marriage, or adoption, may even include fictive members as aunts and uncles. This expanded, more diverse definition of family allows for the inclusion of blended (which is a family created through remarriage), single-parent, and same-sex headed families, along with traditional nuclear families and others.

The chapters in this section focus on social patterns that influence the present-day family—for example, the increasingly common practice of delaying marriage and bearing children later in life. In Chapter 34, Karen Kobayashi and Mushira Khan reflect on the changing structure of Canadian families and explore some of the social implications for childhood, parenthood, and even grandparenthood. Fernando Mata, in Chapter 35, describes how families who live together as neighbours influence one another, finding that interactions between neighbours, and especially their exchange of help, shape a new immigrant family's view of civic duty. Finally, Sophie Mathieu explores the issue of child care costs in Quebec, in Chapter 36, noting that as the cost of child care begins to rise again, young parents and two-parent working families are the most affected, resulting in inequalities.

32 "I Knew What I Was Getting Into": A Study of Youth Labour in the Context of a Canadian Tree-Planting Camp

Fabrizio Antonelli and Taylor Mooney

Youth face considerable obstacles in their career development. For many, the daunting task of credentialing involves taking on debt to train for a job market that is shrinking in many sectors (Bernard, 2013). This paper examines how youth navigate early workplaces and presents findings from a study involving young workers in a tree-planting camp in northern Ontario. The conditions of this work—the instability of pay, lodging, equipment costs, to name a few—potentially place young people into vulnerable positions where despite how difficult or unpleasant the work might be, they must take on the work to secure a decent wage and future employment in the industry.

There is clear evidence that students will bring expectations to tree planting that emanate from the dearth of quality employment in home communities. Rather than toil in a "McJob," some young people have taken up the adventure and promise of "fast money" as reason enough to invest the time and money to become a planter (Sweeney, 2009). In essence, although the work could be perceived by youth as lucrative, there is also the potential for workers to see little intrinsic value in tree-planting work. The work itself involves repetitive action, with much of the labour practices being **Taylorized** to the extent that habitual action takes over from more creative and imaginative processes.

The labour is piece-rate work, prompting clear moments of self-motivation that can drive workers to align their interests with that of the company. Similar to Burawoy's (1979) seminal study of Allied's workers, tree planters could be "manufacturing consent" through their efforts to make "fast cash" for the summer. Because planting seasons are short and many of the planters have accrued significant debt over the year (e.g., school tuition, or travel costs), tree planters are not positioned well to resist the actions of their employer. Despite the surface presentation of difficult work associated with planting, this study problematizes the assumptions that **exploitation** and **alienation** necessarily go hand-in-hand, instead exploring how young people are able to gain meaning from their work despite ostensibly exploitive conditions.

In relation to job availability and tempering expectations, the limited availability of "quality work" has placed youth in a position to seek out less traditional benefits from employment. For example, in Besen's (2006) study of baristas, it was uncovered that young people in her study were seeking out the social aspects of work and the "freedom" derived from being out of the home and away from parents. As well, Kidder's (2011) study of bike messengers showed that messengers were able to lessen alienating aspects of their work through the creation of "bike-messenger culture." The aspects of danger within the work, coupled with the challenge of successfully carving out a living as a messenger, helped establish a messenger culture in which challenges on the job enabled workers to find meaning in their work. Much like Burawoy's Allied workers, the games that were played by messengers to maintain a level of interest in the day-to-day operations resulted in workers delivering extra effort and service for an employer that was unwilling to provide a secure income.

As for youth navigating tree-planting work, similarities exist with Besen's baristas and Kidder's messengers. Tree planting presents a "home away from home" where young people can escape the supervision of parents and can enter a world of adventure and promise (Ekers and Farnan, 2010). Much of the "natural allure" associated with tree planting can blur potential moments of exploitation and alienation. The rustic and remote locales of tree-planting camps can provide opportunities for youth to escape the banality of everyday life, enter into Canada's wilderness, and "leave behind their urban bourgeois pretensions and ... approximate the life of the idealized rugged, rural man [*sic*] in order to pursue their 'experience' with nature" (Ekers and Farnan, 2010, p. 100). However, it appears from our study that entering tree-planting work under these romanticized understandings of adventure and escape may cause planters to overlook the potentially exploitative and alienating experiences of the work, and to simply understand these moments as part of the "experience."

The Planter's Experience

Thirteen planters, with varying degrees of experience both in the industry and with the planting company in northern Ontario, were selected for the study. Semi-structured interviews were carried out and respondents were asked a variety of questions related to their decisions to enter the work, what they thought of the work, and experiences in the camp. Findings were coded and classified for themes of workplace control, camp life, planter identity, choice, and reasons for returning.

There appears to be a clear consensus as to why youth choose to take jobs as tree planters. At the front of planters' minds is the potential for a financial windfall for a relatively short time commitment. This arrangement is particularly suitable for students, as they often incur considerable debt in their post-secondary studies while having limited time (primarily summer months) to accumulate funds. As well, choosing to tree plant results largely from the dearth of well-paying, quality work in home communities.

> I needed money for school. And ... I think that I can work hard enough that I can make more than minimum wage tree planting. (Spencer)

Rather than take on low-paying, part-time service work, youth are drawn to the potentially high financial rewards associated with tree-planting's piecework rates.

Although it is clear that financial rewards motivate youth to engage with planting, many participants mentioned non-financial reasons as being important in their decision to return. Matthew notes the remote location of camps as a perk, citing his desire to be away from the city: "That was a big part of it ... getting away." The romanticized wilderness living attached to tree planting spurred many to view the work as an adventure of sorts. Participants noted that the work experience was unique and could not be matched by work found in home communities. In addition to the adventure and change of pace, returning planters noted the closeness to fellow planters as a critical benefit to the work. Lisa reported that she returned to camp for the people and the atmosphere, a finding that was consistent for all participants.

Tree planting, although repetitive in its movements and daily practices, is also unpredictable in terms of the planting conditions related to both environment and company operations. The unpredictable nature of each day is often cited as the most striking observation made by planters when they first enter the work. Many planters take on the job with an idyllic image of clear and flat land, rows furrowed and ready for planting. However, the blocks of land are rarely uniform or square, and are often uneven and covered with trees, brush, and logs.

Despite these difficult environmental conditions, the most challenging part of tree planting is often considered to be the banality of the task. Workers are paid by the piece and are expected to plant, by hand, upwards of 2,000 trees each day in order to make a livable wage.

> [T]he repetitiveness . . . yeah, just basically the repetitive stuff. . . it's going to be a huge mental strain, and it's something that I'm going to have to fight the most when I'm doing it, and I know that I have to be prepared for that. (Brian)

As well, planters must endure and plant in challenging terrain. It can feel pointless to keep going once a planter recognizes that he or she will not likely make a great deal of money in difficult plots. However, the piece needs to be planted in order for the crew to move on, and in some ways, individual success is reliant upon the success of the group. From this understanding, an occupational culture emerges where fellow workers police effort and action in the field, making it undesirable for workers to complain about the task at hand. The expected persistence and determination from workers aligns well with the interests of the employer, yet need not be enforced directly by crew bosses and managers. Rather, this variation on "worker solidarity" fuels the mindset of the planter to complete difficult tasks and overcome the harsh environment as part of the identity and honour of being a tree planter.

Much of the identity tree planters collectively develop is closely tied to the ruggedness of the terrain and the physical demands of the work. It is thematically evident within the interviews that participants found pride not only in their skill and ability to plant effectively, but also in their ability to overcome work-related adversity. For example, a number of participants made reference to the "kind of person" one had to be in order to be successful as a tree planter. Planters are able to derive meaning from their work by understanding it as a skill and as something that few people have the endurance to take on. Participants were more inclined to emphasize the importance of mental endurance over physical endurance, and the mental capacity that makes someone "cut out" for the work also brings a certain cachet to being a planter.

> I'd say that uh, tree planting breaks a person, and then rebuilds the person into a better person, if they get out of it successfully, if they turn into a planter. If they just leave, it won't happen, but if they get bitten by the bug, so to speak, and find something they enjoy about it, it builds character. It does many things to a person. Physically stronger, mentally more balanced, just able to handle more. . . . (Matthew)

In other words, the ability to overcome harsh conditions, physically demanding and repetitive work, and, at times, unfair workplace practices, is what separates a planter from an "ordinary worker" in an "ordinary job."

Participants in this study expressed frustration over a number of issues related to tree planting. However, the disapprovals that were voiced in interviews were followed by statements of tolerance from the participants. This response is part of a greater pattern evident within this research, as participants appeared to internalize and perpetuate their own exploitation. It is possible that participants felt unwilling to criticize their employer because they believed they had finally found work that did not seem to be alienating—a finding that points to the dearth of meaningful employment options currently available to youth. Furthermore, the planters in question may have been operating with an "I knew what I was getting into" mindset, wherein they felt they had been fairly warned by the company about the challenging conditions associated with the work, and therefore felt unjustified in airing grievances. The occupational culture of tree planting perpetuates this mindset. The culture valorizes qualities that align with what the company perceives as essential for a good worker: hard working, deferential, efficient, and accepting of harsh, often exploitive workplace practices.

Conclusion

The norms and values maintained through the tree-planting camp's occupational culture help planters to form their identity and pride, but they also produce workers that will self-regulate to the advantage of the employer. Similar to Burawoy's (1979) findings, by aligning their interests with those of their employer, tree planters may find meaning in their work, but they may also become complicit in their own exploitation. The occupational culture encourages planters to police their co-workers through a valorization of the harsh conditions associated with the work, while condemning those workers who complain about unfair working conditions and who fail or choose not to attain high production rates. However, it should be noted that the creation of planting culture and identity is one of necessity for workers in the planting industry. Failure to insulate oneself from the harsh and exploitive work environment with a culture of identity, reward, and pride would likely result in planters suffering a worse fate. Rather than taking home relatively high financial compensation from a summer's work, youth would be left alienated, lost, and likely less productive.

References

Bernard, A. (2013). *Unemployment dynamic among Canada's youth*. Minister of Industry, Statistics Canada, Catalogue no. 11-626-X — No. 024.

Besen, Y. (2006) "Exploitation of fun?: The lived experience of teenage employment in suburban America." *Journal of Contemporary Ethnography, 35*(3), 319–40.

Burawoy, M. (1979) *Manufacturing consent: Changes in the labor process under monopoly capitalism*. Chicago: University of Chicago Press.

Ekers, M. and Farnan, M. (2010) "Planting the nation: Tree planting art and the endurance of Canadian nationalism." *Space and Cuture, 13*(1), 95–120.

Kidder, J. (2011) "Exploitation and alienation: Using the bike messenger subculture to rethink oppression." Conference Paper, ASA, 2011 Annual Meeting.

Sweeney, B. (2009) "Producing liminal space: Gender, age and class in northern Ontario's tree planting industry." *Gender, Place and Culture, 16*(5), 569–86.

33 How Do Majority and Minority Canadian Youth See Themselves Participating in Public Life?

L. Alison Molina-Girón

The health and stability of Canada's democracy depends on the reflective participation of all its citizens, youth included. Yet, do young Canadians intend to participate in civic and political life? This is the question this paper explores. It is an issue that has garnered increased attention due to reported low levels of youth participation, especially in **electoral politics**, in Canada and elsewhere (Blais and Loewen, 2011; Turcotte, 2015). As a group, young Canadians have the lowest voter turnout rate, affiliation in political parties, and levels of political interest (Bilodeau and Turgeon, 2015; Blais and Loewen, 2011; Gélineau, 2013; Turcotte, 2015). Participation is not only lower among minority youth, but highly unequal: higher-income, better-educated youth are much more likely to participate compared with lower-income, less-educated youth (Bilodeau and Turgeon, 2015; Blais and Loewen, 2011; Turcotte, 2015). Aboriginal, new immigrant, and visible minority youth vote in alarmingly lower numbers compared with majority youth (Bilodeau and Turgeon, 2015; Ladner and McCrossan, 2007; Tossutti, 2007).

Recent research, however, seems to indicate that youth do participate in public life, but have shifted toward more direct, **non-institutionalized** forms of participation, including demonstrating, online activism, consumerism politics, and volunteering (Bennett, 2008; Stolle, Harell, Pedersen, and Dufour, 2013). For example, in 2013, 66 per cent of youth aged 15 to 19 volunteered at much higher rates than any other age cohorts (Turcotte, 2015). Some scholars have warned that such a shift can lead to a "democratic deficit," as it represents "an erosion of the activities and capacities of citizenship" (Boyte, 2004; Macedo et al., 2005, p. 1; Theiss-Morse and Hibbing, 2005). For others, however, direct civic action gives young citizens a voice and a chance to act on issues that are important to them, which can encourage political participation (Bennett, 2008; Dalton, 2008; Kahne, Lee, and Feezel, 2012).

Youth civic engagement research in Canada and elsewhere has primarily focused on electoral political behaviour, such as voting and political knowledge and interest (Griffin, 2005). There is limited research that probes whether young Canadians intend to participate in democratic life and the avenues they may choose for such participation (O'Neill, 2007; Ross and Dooly, 2010). This research is a step in this direction. It investigated the conceptions of good citizenship that majority and minority youth aged 15–18 have, and how they see themselves participating in public life. Three questions guided this inquiry:

1. How do majority and immigrant minority students see themselves as citizens?
2. What actions and behaviours do youth perform or say they will perform in the public sphere as engaged citizens? Are there any similarities and differences in how majority and immigrant minority youth engage or say they will engage in public life?
3. Do they recognize social problems that demand citizen and government attention?

I use Westheimer and Kahne's (2004) citizenship framework to analyze youth's dominant understandings of good citizenship and the ways they see themselves engaging in public life. Findings reveal that immigrant and non-immigrant youth see themselves participating in similar ways, including voting and volunteering in their communities. However, an important difference is that majority youth tend to believe that Canada is a fair, egalitarian country, and while they recognize issues of inequity, they consider them to be minor and somewhat acceptable. In contrast, immigrant minority youth, while appreciating state-granted rights and freedoms, identify poverty, racism, and discrimination as serious problems that undermine Canada's democracy. Further, only youth who recognize social problems regard citizenship action as a mechanism to affect societal change.

Conceptions of Good Citizenship: A Theoretical Framework

Westheimer and Kahne (2004) posit three distinct models of good citizenship: the personally responsible, the participatory, and the justice-oriented citizen. Each one underlies different assumptions of what it means to be a good citizen. The personally responsible citizen fulfills his or her social and civic responsibilities like voting and paying taxes. The law-abiding citizen is a contributing member of society. For example, she or he donates blood and lends a hand in times of crises. Of the three, this is the most minimalist conception of citizenship as it stresses above all else civic responsibility not necessarily for public engagement but for the well-functioning of the state, a conception that may "actually hinder rather than make possible democratic participation and change" (Heater, 1992; Westheimer and Kahne 2004, p. 244).

Both the participatory and the justice-oriented models of good citizenship provide a more demanding vision of citizenship (O'Neill, 2009). Citizens who endorse these conceptions of good citizenship are involved in public affairs. More specifically, they identify problems that demand citizen and government attention and undertake collective, organized efforts to resolve them (Westheimer and Kahne, 2004). The main difference between the two is that for citizens who have a justice-oriented conception, citizen action in the public sphere is directly connected to public governance to affect societal change. Therefore, citizens with a justice-oriented conception of citizenship aim to address existing inequities in order to create a more just and democratic society.

Research Methodology

This exploratory case study focuses on individual and focus group interviews with 25 youth aged 15–18 who at the time of the research were taking the required civics course. Participants were selected from four grade 10 civics classes taught in three urban high schools, data drawn from a larger project (Molina-Girón, 2013). Nine were majority and 16 were immigrant minority students.

Student interviews lasted between 15 and 40 minutes, followed a semi-structured format, were tape-recorded, and then transcribed verbatim. Majority students are those whose parents and they were all born in Canada. In addition, these students identify themselves as white. Minority students included eight 1.5-generation immigrants, or foreign-born students who arrived in Canada at or before age 15, and eight second-generation immigrant students, defined in this research as those who are Canadian born but whose parents were both born outside Canada. The majority of immigrant students in the study come from Asia (including the Middle East) as well as Africa and the Caribbean.

Research Findings

To elicit students' understandings of good citizenship, they were asked questions such as, Who is a good citizen? What do good citizens do? How can young people like you effectively participate in society? To probe whether students had a justice-oriented citizenship stance, they were asked, In Canada, are there any issues of injustice? While I recognize that the sample is too small to represent of all majority and minority youth in Canada and to make generalizations, the research findings provide valuable insights into how these two distinct Canadian youth groups see themselves participating in the democratic process, findings central to the provision of citizenship education programs concerned with the advancement of a more equitable, inclusive society.

Research findings reveal that majority and minority students have similar conceptions of citizenship, and overall they endorse a participatory conception of good citizenship and devise different avenues to participate in public governance. Of 9 majority students, 7 have a participatory conception of good citizenship, compared to 2 students who regard citizenship as acting responsibly. Similarly, out of 16 immigrant students, 9 have a participatory conception, compared to 7 who endorse a personally responsible conception of good citizenship. Youth with a personally responsible conception of citizenship see themselves as contributing members by obeying the law, helping others, and serving the community. They also identified personal traits. Good citizens are "unselfish," "hard workers," and "open-minded." This citizenship conception is well captured by Suzanne. "A good citizen," she affirmed, "knows about the country, how it is run, and is aware of what is going on even if they are not always active."

Students with a participatory conception of citizenship recognize that democracy requires citizens' direct and continuous involvement in matters of public governance. Cemal remarked how "teenagers, don't really get involved." To him, "the civics course is about getting young people involved with the government." Beverly commented on learning "how citizens can affect what the government does [through] direct actions like petitioning and rallies." For these students, politics and public policy is not only what politicians do, but something that directly impacts citizens and their lives. Connor expressed this view: "Every bill that is passed . . . everything that happens in Parliament somehow trickles down and affects us." Being informed, therefore, is seen as critical to a reflective participation. As Omar explained, "When voting or in . . . a referendum, you have to do your research. To me, this is key to be . . . become a full citizen." Students with a participatory conception of good citizenship also recognize that democracy involves working amid competing claims about the common good. Daniel described learning the importance of listening across differences: "I always had my point of view and [did not consider] others." But now I understand the importance of listening to others and to compromise to make decisions that will suit us all." Overall, students with a participatory conception of citizenship have more complex understandings of democracy and see themselves involved in the decision-making process. Jackson's definition of good citizenship captures the participatory conception of citizenship: "Good citizens participate in society. They are informed and talk about important issues. They voice their concerns by sending letters to politicians, going to City Hall. They notice what goes on in society and see what they can do."

While most students understand citizenship in participatory terms, only a few have a justice-oriented citizenship stance—probed by students' identification of issues that challenge Canada's democracy. Of 9 majority students, 7 recognized justice-related issues, but only 4 considered a direct relation between democracy and creating more just societies. Six majority students contended that Canada is a fair, egalitarian country, and that while social issues exist, they are minimal. In contrast, 10 out of 16 minority students named poverty, discrimination, and racism as long-standing societal problems that they often experience. Nine out of 16 immigrant students have a justice-oriented conception of good citizenship. What is different in students who have a justice-oriented conception of citizenship is a stronger sense of citizenry participation being necessary to affect societal change. Edward, for example, explained, "A good citizen is active, trying to make changes and teach other people about the issues concerning the whole country and them." Similarly, Adana said, "I learned . . . not be afraid, to stand up and speak out for what I believe or when I see stuff happening. . . . If you keep quiet, what's the point? Nothing's going to happen."

Discussion

A key finding of this research is that both majority and minority students endorse participatory understandings of citizenship and see themselves participating in the nation's civic and political life in a variety of ways ranging from voting and paying taxes to more substantive actions to affect public decision-making. Overall, the majority of young Canadians see themselves performing public-spirit actions to better their communities.

However, the research findings do raise some concerns. Given space limitations, I will focus on two. First, the number of minority students who endorse a personally responsible conception of citizenship is considerably higher when compared to majority students: 7 out of 16 compared to 2 out of 9, respectively. When a personally responsible citizenship conception dominates, citizenry participation is limited to exercising one's rights and responsibilities. That immigrant students understand citizenship as acting responsible has important consequences to the democratic process. Their voices, interest, and vision of the common good are less likely to be heard. This in turn advances policies and practices likely to benefit already privileged citizens and groups (Boyte, 2004; Theiss-Morse and Hibbing, 2005; Westheimer and Kahne, 2004).

A second cause of concern is with regard to students' understanding of citizenship participation and its role in promoting societal change. While immigrant students are more likely to identify social problems that seriously challenge Canada's democracy, most majority students believe that, for the most part, Canada is an egalitarian country, and that while problems exist, they are minor and acceptable. If interrogating the structures that create and maintain inequity is not part of youth's conception of citizenship, our young citizens may perform public-spirit actions but this engagement may fall short of advancing a more equitable and just society (Theiss-Morse and Hibbing, 2005; Westheimer and Khane, 2004).

References

Bennett, L. (Ed.) (2008). *Civic life online: Learning how digital media can engage youth*. Cambridge, MA: MIT Press.

Bilodeau, A., and Turgeon, L. (2015). *Voter turnout among younger Canadians and visible minority Canadians: Evidence from the provincial diversity project*. Retrieved 15 February 2016, from http://inspirerlademocratie-inspiredemocracy.ca/rsch/yth/vot/index-eng.asp

Blais, A., and Loewen, P. (2011). *Youth electoral engagement in Canada*. Elections Canada. Retrieved from http://www.elections.ca/res/rec/part/youeng/youth_electoral_engagement_e.pdf

Boyte, H.C. (2004). *Everyday politics: Reconnecting citizens and public life*. Philadelphia: University of Pennsylvania Press.

Dalton, R. (2008). Citizenship norms and the expansion of political participation. *Political Studies*, 56, 76–98.

Gélineau, F. (2013). *Who participates? A closer look at the results of the national youth survey*. Retrieved 15 February 2016, from http://inspirerlademocratie-inspiredemocracy.ca/rsch/yth/wpa/wpa-e.pdf

Griffin, C. (2005). Challenging assumptions about youth political participation: Critical insights from Great Britain. In J. Forbrig (Ed.), *Revisiting youth political participation: Challenges for research and democratic processes in Europe* (pp. 145–54). Strasbourg: Council of Europe Publishing.

Heater, D. (1992). Tensions in the citizenship ideal. In E.B. Jones and J. Neville (Eds), *Education for citizenship: Ideas and perspectives for cross-curricular study* (pp. 19–34). London: Kogan Page.

Kahne, J., Lee, N., and Feezell, J. (2012). Digital media literacy education and online civic and political participation. *International Journal of Communication*, 6, 1–24.

Ladner, K., and McCrossan, M. (2007). *The electoral participation of Aboriginal people*. Working paper series on electoral participation and outreach practices: Elections Canada. Retrieved from http://elections.ca/res/rec/part/paper/aboriginal/aboriginal_e.pdf

Macedo, S., Alex-Assensoh, Y., Berry, J.M., Brintnall, M., Campbell, D.E., Fraga, L.R., et al. (2005). *Democracy at risk: How political choices undermine citizen participation, and what we can do about it*. Washington, DC: Brookings Institution.

Molina-Girón, L. A. (2013). Educating active citizens: What roles are students expected to play in public life? In L.E. Bass (Series Ed.) and S.K. Nenga and J.K. Taft (Vol. Ed.), *Sociological studies of children and youth. Vol. 16: Youth engagement: The civic-political lives of children and youth* (pp. 47–72). Bingley, UK: Emerald.

O'Neill, B. (2007). *Indifferent or just different? The political and civic engagement of young people in Canada: Charting the course of youth civic and political participation*. Ottawa: Canadian Policy Research Networks.

O'Neill, B. (2009). Democracy, models of citizenship and civic education. In M. Print and H. Milner (Eds), *Civic education and youth political participation* (pp. 3–21). Rotterdam: Sense Publishers.

Ross, A., and Dooly, M. (2010). Young people's intentions about their political activity. *Citizenship Teaching and Learning* 6(1), 43–60.

Stolle, D., Harell, A., Pedersen, E.F., and Dufour, P. (2013). Maple spring up close: The role of self-interest and socio-economic resources for youth protest. Retrieved 15 May 2016, from https://www.cpsa-acsp.ca/papers-2013/Stolle.pdf

Theiss-Morse, E., and Hibbing, J. (2005). Citizenship and civic engagement. *Annual Review of Political Science* 8, 227–49.

Tossutti, L. (2007). *The electoral participation of ethnocultural communities*. Working paper series on electoral participation and outreach practices: Elections Canada. Retrieved from http://www.elections.ca/res/rec/part/paper/ethnocultural/ethnocultural_e.pdf

Turcotte (2015). Volunteering and charitable giving in Canada. Statistics Canada: Spotlight on Canadians: Results from the General Social Survey (Catalogue number 89-652-X). Retrieved from http://www.statcan.gc.ca/daily-quotidien/150130/dq150130b-eng.htm

Westheimer, J., and Kahne, J. (2004). What kind of citizen? The politics of educating for democracy. *American Educational Research Journal* 41(2), 237–69.

34 Understanding the Changing Nature of Relationships in Aging Canadian Families

Karen M. Kobayashi and Mushira M. Khan

Introduction

Demographic shifts highlight the evolving nature of relationships in aging Canadian families. In particular, the increasing age at first marriage for both men and women in Canada over the past few decades has meant that the transition to parenthood has inevitably been delayed into the thirties for many couples. With the mean age at first birth for women at just under 30 years of age (28.5 years) in 2011 (Statistics Canada, 2013) and average life expectancy at 81 years (81.24 years) (World Health Organization, 2014), Canadians are more likely now to be well into their forties and fifties in experiencing being "caught" between the needs of dependent children, albeit a smaller number, and aging parents (Allen et al., 2000; Milan, 2013). This trend is likely to continue well into the future as the pursuit of career trajectories (i.e., post-secondary education and full-time employment) and of family interests and responsibilities becomes increasingly "normative" for Canadian women.

What are the implications of these changing demographic trends for aging families? This chapter explores the impact of such changes in the broad contexts of social support and diversity, two of the main areas of sociological research on aging families in Canada and the United States, and concludes with a brief discussion on social policy issues.

A. Social Support

Cutbacks to health care and social services over the past decade in Canada have precipitated an increased reliance on the family by governments at all levels for the care of older adults. This issue is particularly salient for aging families—in 2012, most elder care (75 per cent) was provided by those between 45 and 64 years of age (Sinha, 2013). What will be the consequences of changes to public policy and programs then for aging families? This is an important and timely question as Canada faces the challenges of aging in an unusually high proportion of the population early this century.

For the first time in our history, it is estimated that Canadian adults will spend a longer time caring for their aging parents than raising their children (McDaniel, 2005). Given the gendered nature of caregiving in our society, this means that the burden of care will continue to fall on women in mid-life (Dentinger and Clarkberg, 2002; McDaniel, 2005). Although the compression of morbidity to the latter years of old age (80 and above) has resulted in a greater number of disability-free years for older parents, the need for social support from middle-aged children (particularly daughters) remains fairly constant over time. This is because social support comprises three main domains—instrumental, emotional, and informational—and the need for assistance in each of these areas is influenced by the timing of a number of later life-course transitions, namely widowhood, retirement, and the onset of chronic illness. As older parents experience these transitions in later life, their reliance on middle-aged adult children increases either temporarily or long term. The extent to which support is provided by the adult child is dictated both by parents' assistance needs and by the quality of the parent–child relationship. For some mid-life adult children, the competing demands of caregiving for young adult children and older parents can be extremely stressful, leading to negative financial and health outcomes (Gee and Mitchell, 2003).

An older parent's experience of widowhood has consequences for support ranging from temporary assistance with some activities of daily living like bill payments or grocery shopping (instrumental support) to permanent reliance on children for companionship to combat depression (emotional support). Of course, in the latter situation, the long-term need for assistance may require a complete restructuring of children's lives as they try to negotiate caregiving with full-time work and parenting roles and responsibilities. Although multi-generational co-residence may be the best solution, it may cause considerable strain on the relationship between parent and child.

It is less likely that retirement, a transition that older parents are expected to have planned for during their working lives, will have such an onerous effect on middle-aged children's lives. In fact, healthy, financially secure, and retired parents may end up providing financial or instrumental assistance to children in the form of child care and domestic and yard work. Nevertheless, older parents who have a difficult time adjusting financially and emotionally to retirement require the most support and a great deal of attention (temporal, emotional, financial) on the part of middle-aged children who may be required to help them adjust to the truncation of their work trajectory.

Support is transformed into caregiving when a parent becomes ill due to the onset of chronic disease or disability; this transformation is salient because it requires a significant commitment of time and resources mainly from daughters, who often are forced to make life-altering decisions regarding work and family in a very short period of time.

B. Diversity in Aging Families

Studies of satisfaction in marital and parent–child relationships in aging families have tended to examine relationship quality as it is impacted by intergenerational living and/or social support arrangements with children (e.g., Marks, 1995; Mitchell and Gee, 1996; Carr, 2005), only occasionally highlighting the actual relationship between or well-being of members of the dyad. This myopic view of aging families is problematic because it fails to recognize the experiences of separated/divorced, remarried, childless, parentless, ethnocultural minority, gay and lesbian, and long-term or permanent "empty nest" families, groups of emerging importance in the aging Canadian population. We will focus on a few of these groups here.

Remarried

Recent statistics on marriage suggest that remarriage, like divorce, is a mid-life transition, with the average age of remarriage for previously divorced women being 44.8 years and the average age for men, 48.4 years in 2008 (Statistics Canada, 2013). Remarriage in mid-life is also a gendered transition: men are more likely than women to remarry, a pattern that holds well into later life (Ambert, 2005). For women, this could stem from a desire to "enjoy" their new-found independence; conversely, men may find it difficult to make the transition to being "on their own" without the emotional and instrumental support of a partner.

The remarriage of two previously married individuals in mid-life often involves the "blending" of two families, referred to in the literature as a complex stepfamily. The extent to which adult children are involved in the lives of older parents within the complex stepfamily depends largely on the nature of the stepparent-stepchild relationship, the nature of the biological parent–child relationship earlier in life, and perceptions around kinship and kin networks (Pezzin et al., 2014).

LGBT Families

Over the past few decades, family sociologists have begun to question **heteronormative** assumptions around family formation and mate selection (McGuire et al., 2016). Building on the work of Michel Foucault, queer theorists such as Judith Butler and Eve Sedgwick have rejected traditional views around gender and sexuality, arguing instead that gender, like all social identities, is socially constructed. Indeed, LGBT (lesbian, gay, bisexual, and trans) or queer families in mid-life are becoming increasingly diverse as more and more same-sex partners in middle age are making efforts to "blend" existing families or to have children together either via medical technology or through adoption (Epstein, 2003; Miller, 2003). Such emergent family forms may be referred to as "new nuclear" or "new blended," with same-sex dyads forming the nucleus of the family unit.

Recently, the caregiving relationships of aging LGBT individuals have been recognized as important topics in the literature on social support in families. One of the key exploratory studies to emerge in this area focuses on the experiences of mid-life and older gays caring for chronically ill partners (Hash, 2001). Not surprisingly, the findings highlight how homophobic attitudes of informal (family and friends) and formal (health care and human services professionals) resources serve as a major barrier to providing care for chronically ill loved ones. Additionally, unsupportive policies and practices tend to exacerbate the problem of discrimination and/or nonrecognition of same-sex partnerships in the context of caregiving.

Ethnocultural Minority Families

In Canada, multi-generational living, particularly within immigrant and ethnocultural families, is on the rise. In 2011, 21 per cent of recent immigrants aged 45 and older were co-resident grandparents, compared to less than 3 per cent of the Canadian population (Statistics Canada, 2015). Co-residence with older parents within ethnocultural minority families brings about its own set of challenges vis-à-vis cultural values such as **filial piety** and obligation. These challenges are further exacerbated for recently immigrated women who must simultaneously negotiate settlement issues with the provision of care to their older relatives at home (Khan and Kobayashi, forthcoming).

C. Social Policy

This chapter would be incomplete without a discussion of the relationship between aging families and social policy in Canada. Two central issues need to be highlighted in this context: (1) social support in mid-life adult child–parent relationships; and (2) diversity in aging families.

The issue of social support to older parents has been of primary interest to governments in light of reductions to health care spending in this country. At one time, a shared responsibility existed between government and family; now, the provision of social support and caregiving to older adults has become increasingly "informalized" as hospital and community support service budgets have been cut. The onus for this excess burden of care falls squarely on the shoulders of mid-life women—the **sandwich generation**—who are the primary caregivers to older parents and parents-in-law in addition to co-resident adolescent and/or young adult children. As a result of this "caregiving squeeze," middle-aged women have a higher likelihood of transitioning from full-time to part-time employment or of leaving the paid workforce altogether. To date, despite the findings from numerous research studies and reports (e.g., Fast et al., 1997; Keating et al., 1999), neither government nor employer-supported policy has adequately addressed the issue of paid leave for elder care for mid-life women.

Recognition of the diversity in mid-life Canadian families in the policy domain has been limited for the most part to issues of class, gender, and family structure. Governments have focused their efforts on the development of social welfare policy and programs for young to middle-aged single mothers (female-headed lone-parent families) living at or below the low-income cut-off line (LICO), a group characterized by intersecting identity markers of diversity. However, with the continuing emergence of diverse family forms in mid-life, such as LGBT families and childless (by choice or not) couples, it is imperative that governments develop and institute policies that address and attempt to break down systemic barriers (e.g., definitions of "parent" in maternity/paternity leave policy, definitions of "family" for caregiving leave) that have, to date, served to marginalize these groups in Canadian society.

Conclusion

This chapter has provided an overview of some key research areas in the study of aging families in North America. Wherever possible, connections to the Canadian literature have been made. It is important to note that Statistics Canada, through the collection of detailed family data in the census and General Social Surveys (i.e., Cycles 5.0, 10.0, 15.0, 20.0, and 25.0), is a valuable resource for information on changing patterns of family life over time. National data sets can be used to explore topic areas germane to aging families—namely, co-residence, social support, caregiving, work–life balance, and marital transitions.

As contemporary family researchers, we need to expand our definitions of family life course stages and recognize the linkages between lives at individual and structural levels. In addition, in a field that has long been dominated by quantitative research, greater acknowledgement and appreciation are needed of the contributions that qualitative and mixed-method studies have made and are yet to make to the growing body of literature on the family life course. Although this has been an uphill battle for many years, recent published exploratory work by Gee and Mitchell (2003), Mitchell (2009), and Carr (2005) on mid-life families have fuelled our optimism for change. Mid-life family researchers can learn much from family gerontologists such as Bill Randall, Gary Kenyon, Brian DeVries, and Jay Gubrium, who have recognized the value and importance of narrative research in understanding the lived experiences of older adults and their family members.

Finally, research and policy must inform one another in the family domain. Given the increasing diversity of the Canadian population in terms of age, class, ethnicity, immigrant status, sexual orientation, and family structure, it is clear that a broader mandate for family research in this country must be developed. Such an initiative is needed to address some of the critical policy issues for families and the implications for their aging in the coming decades.

References

Allen, K.R., Blieszner, R. and Roberto, K.A. (2000). Families in the middle and later years: A review and critique of research in the 1990s. *Journal of Marriage and the Family*, 62(1), 4–17.

Ambert, A-M. (2005). *Divorce: Facts, Causes, and Consequences*. Ottawa: Vanier Institute of the Family.

Carr, D. (2005). The psychological consequences of mid-life men's social comparisons with their young adult sons. *Journal of Marriage and Family*, *66*(4), 1061–8.

Dentinger, E. and Clarkberg, M. (2002). Informal caregiving and retirement timing among men and women: Gender and caregiving relationships in later mid-life. *Journal of Family Issues*, 23, 857–79.

Epstein, R. (2003). Lesbian families. In Lynn, M. (ed.), *Voices: Essays on Canadian Families*, Second edition (pp. 76–102). Scarborough, ON: Nelson.

Fast, J., Oakes, L., and Williamson, D.L. (1997). *Conceptualizing and Operationalizing the Costs of Informal Elder Care*. NHRDP Project No. 6609-1963-55. Ottawa: National Health Research and Development Program: Health Canada.

Gee, E. and Mitchell, B. (2003). One roof: Exploring multigenerational households in Canada. In Lynn, M. (ed.), *Voices: Essays on Canadian Families*, Second edition (pp. 291–311). Scarborough, ON: Nelson.

Hash, K. (2001). Caregiving and post-caregiving experiences of midlife and older gay men and lesbians. PhD thesis. Virginia Commonwealth University.

Keating, N., Fast, J., Frederick, J., Cranswick, K., and Perrier, C. (1999). *Eldercare in Canada: Context, Content, and Consequences*. Ottawa: Statistics Canada, Housing, Family and Social Statistics Division.

Khan, M.M. and Kobayashi, K.M. (forthcoming). Negotiating sacred values: Dharma, karma and the migrant Hindu woman. In Dossa, P. and Coe, Cati (eds), *Transnational Aging and Kin-Work*. New Brunswick, NJ: Rutgers University Press.

McDaniel, S. (2005). The family lives of the middle-aged and elderly in Canada. In Baker, M. (ed.), *Families: Changing Trends in Canada* (pp. 181–99). Toronto: McGraw-Hill Ryerson.

McGuire, J.K., Kuvalanka, K.A., Catalpa, J.M., Toomey, B.R. (2016). Transfamily theory: How the presence of trans* family members informs gender development in families. *Journal of Family Theory and Review*, *8*(1), 60–73.

Marks, N.F. (1995). Mid-life marital status differences in social support relationships with adult children and psychological well-being. *Journal of Family Issues*, 16, 5–28.

Milan, A. (2013). Fertility: Overview, 2009 to 2011. *Report on the Demographic Situation in Canada*. Ottawa: Statistics Canada. Retrieved 10 April 2017 from http://www.statcan.gc.ca/pub/91-209-x/2013001/article/11784-eng.pdf

Miller, J. (2003). Out family values. In Lynn, M. (ed.), *Voices: Essays on Canadian Families*, Second edition (p. 103–130). Scarborough, ON: Nelson.

Mitchell, B. and Gee, E. (1996). "Boomerang kids" and mid-life parental marital satisfaction. *Family Relations*, *45*, 442–8.

Mitchell, B. (2009). *Family Matters: An Introduction to Family Sociology in Canada*. Toronto: Canadian Scholars' Press Inc.

Pezzin, L.E., Pollak, R.A. and Schone, B.S. (2014). Complex families and late-life outcomes among elderly persons: Disability, institutionalization, and longevity. *Journal of Marriage and Family*, *75*(5), 1084–97.

Sinha, M. (2013). *Portrait of Caregivers, 2012*. Retrieved 28 September 2015 from http://www.statcan.gc.ca/pub/89-652-x/89-652-x2013001-eng.htm

Statistics Canada. (2015). *The Daily: Grandparents Living with Their Grandchildren, 2011*. Retrieved on 14 October 2015 from http://www.statcan.gc.ca/daily-quotidien/150414/dq150414a-eng.pdf

———. (2013). *Fertility: Overview, 2009 to 2011*. Retrieved 1 October 2015 from http://www.statcan.gc.ca/pub/91-209-x/2013001/article/11784-eng.htm

World Health Organization. (2014). *World Health Statistics 2014*. Retrieved 1 October 2015 from http://apps.who.int/iris/bitstream/10665/112738/1/9789240692671_eng.pdf

35 Helping and Receiving Help from Neighbours: A Look at the Canadian and the Foreign-Born[1]

Fernando Mata

Introduction

Neighbourhoods are central arenas for the civic integration of immigrants in Canada (Klein, 2011). One key indicator of this civic integration is the participation in exchange of help with neighbours in the communities of residence (Bourdieu, 1986; Worley, 2005; Cheong, 2006; Van Oorshot, et.al, 2006; Lancee and Donkronkers, 2011). Exchanges of help with neighbours enhance mutual trust, reciprocity, and solidarity between community members (Putnam, 2007; Abbott and Freeth, 2008; Van der Gaag et. al, 2005). Neighbour reciprocity lies at the heart of the **social cohesion** concept developed in Durkheimian classical sociological theory (Kushner and Sterk, 2005). Despite its importance in social policy, however, the phenomenon of exchanging help with neighbours among immigrants has been relatively understudied and lacks strong empirical evidence across countries (Wickes et al., 2013).

Individuals help their neighbours in various ways, such as working at someone's home and providing personal care and assistance such as shopping and so forth. Previous studies have shown that socio-demographic and life-cycle-related factors such as age, gender, marital status, mother tongue, presence of children, and socio-economic status are key drivers of these type of behaviours (Statistics Canada,

2009; Thomas, 2012). In undertaking an analysis of help exchanges with neighbours, it is suspected that the length of residence in the country is a key factor to take into account. As immigrants become more familiar with neighbours over time, they develop stronger bonds with them (Murie and Musterd, 2004; Thomson, 2005; Hooghe, et al., 2009; Vervoot, 2012; Huijts et al., 2014). Attitudinal factors are important to take into account as well. If immigrants perceive the ethnic/racial climate of their neighbourhoods as hostile, then contact and interactions with neighbours may be null or limited (Fischer, 1984; Keller, 1968; Korte, 1988; Stolle et al., 2008).

To what extent do immigrants take part in exchanges of help with their neighbours in Canada? Are patterns similar to those of their Canadian-born counterparts? What socio-demographic and attitudinal drivers are behind these behaviours? To address these research questions, two broad working hypotheses were empirically tested with Canadian data. These hypotheses stated that: (a) the patterns of help exchange behaviour would be different for Canadian and foreign-born groups and, (b) that the impacts of immigrant status and length or residence in the country in defining the patterns of help exchange with neighbours would interact with other socio-demographic and attitudinal correlates of pro-social behaviour. Special attention was paid to four major patterns of help exchanges with neighbours: neither giving nor receiving help (case 1), receiving help only (case 2), giving help only (case 3), and both giving and receiving help (case 4). These patterns were treated as proxies for lower or higher levels of civic integration to the community of residence.

Data and Sample

The data for this analysis is drawn from a pooled sample of the 2010 and 2012 General Social Surveys (GSS) of Canada. The pooled sample contained information on 38,006 individuals aged 15 years and over, who represented a weighted average population of 28.4 million. The composition of the sample was as follows: Canadian-born (82.0 per cent), foreign-born with 20 or more years of residence (10.4 per cent), foreign-born 10–19 years residence (3.9 per cent), foreign-born 5–9 years of residence (1.8 per cent) and foreign-born less than 5 years residence (1.8 per cent). Help exchanges with neighbours were measured by two survey questions: (a) "In the past month, have you done a favour for a neighbour?"; (b) "In the past month, have any of your neighbours done a favour for you?" For each question respondents provided a yes or no answer.

Findings

A first examination of the data suggested that almost half of the adult Canadian population (47.8 per cent) had both given and received help from a neighbour in the last month previous to the GSS surveys (see Figure 35.1). This percentage was higher among Canadian-born compared to the foreign-born (50.2 per cent to 45.3 per cent), a difference found to be statistically significant ($t = 2.04$, $p < .00$). The percentage of individuals who neither gave nor received help (case 1) was higher among the foreign-born compared to the Canadian-born (35.2 per cent to 29.7 per cent, $t = -4.15$, $p < .00$). Approximately one in four immigrants who had resided in Canada less than 5 years or 5–9 years did not report participating in any help exchanges with their neighbours. In terms of unidirectional exchanges (cases 2 and 3), percentages were lower (below 13 per cent), but the difference between Canadian and foreign-born groups was found to be non-statistically significant ($t = +.96$, $p > .24$). For immigrants, bidirectional exchanges of help with neighbours (case 4) did not increase as a function of the length of the years of residence in Canada and hovered around the 50 per cent mark. Immigrants with less than 5 years residence in Canada, older individuals, those who used languages other than English or French at home, and/or who were residents of Quebec and/or British Columbia were the groups most frequently overrepresented in case 1.

Multinomial logistic regressions were carried out to identify the major predictors of help exchanges

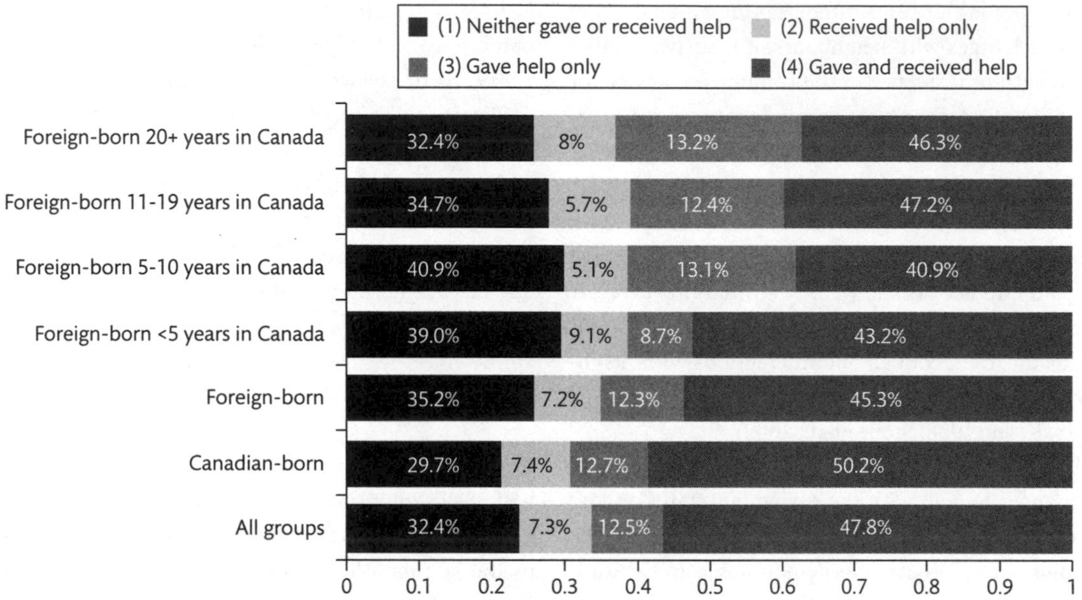

FIGURE 35.1 Neighbourly Help Exchange Types by Immigrant Status Groups
Source: Pooled 2010–2012 GSS Survey

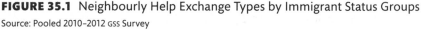

to determine if immigrant status and length of residence remained important predictors after controlling for other major factors of pro-social behaviour. Multinomial regression is a statistical technique aiming at predicting a categorical dependent variable (binary, in this case) by other ones of similar, ordinal, and/or interval nature. The dependent variables used were of the type "0=no, 1=yes" and were assigned to responses to the four patterns of help behaviour using case 4 members (gave and received help) as the reference category. The odds ratios[2] of these multinomial logistic regressions are presented in Table 35.1.

With regard to case 1 (no exchanges), compared to GSS 2010 respondents, GSS 2012 respondents were 1.20 times more likely to report not having participated in any exchanges of help with neighbours. All dummy variables (the binary representations of immigrant status categories) were found to be statistically significant, suggesting that there was a greater propensity of members of these groups to report this behaviour compared to the Canadian-born net from socio-demographic and attitudinal factors (at least 1.15 times greater than the Canadian-born). Older individuals and those residing in the province of Quebec were found among those more likely to not participate in exchanges of help with their neighbours. Greater contact and favourable perceptions of the neighbourhood, being female, and having a child under 14 residing in the household reduced the likelihood of reporting no participation in help exchanges with neighbours. With respect to unidirectional cases 2 and 3, multinomial logistic regressions results complemented those of case 1. For case 2 (received help only), in addition to the cycle effect, those more likely to report this type of behaviour were females, those whose marital status was single, and/or those who resided in all regions excluding the Atlantic region. In case 3 regressions (give help only), these suggested that having positive perceptions of neighbours and having young children at home reduced the likelihood of this behaviour.

TABLE 35.1 Multinomial Logistic Regression Analysis Results: Odds Ratios

	(1) Neither Gives nor Receives Help		(2) Receives Help Only		(3) Gives Help Only	
Predictors	**Odds Ratio**	**sig.**	**Odds Ratio**	**sig.**	**Odds Ratio**	**sig.**
GSS Wave						
2012 wave	1.20	**	1.31	**	1.30	**
Immigrant Groups						
FB: 20+ years residence	1.19	*	1.27	*	1.32	*
FB: 11–19 years residence	1.15	*	0.88	ns	1.23	*
FB: 5–10 years residence	1.18	*	0.75	ns	1.70	*
FB: 5 years or less	1.69	*	1.14	ns	1.30	*
Contact with Neighbours						
Knows a few neighbours	0.44	*	0.37	*	0.23	*
Knows many neighbours	0.28	*	0.21	*	0.09	*
Knows most neighbours	0.30	*	0.17	*	0.10	*
Community perceptions						
Community is a helping one	0.25	*	0.89	ns	0.23	*
Region of Residence						
Quebec	1.20	*	1.27	*	1.19	*
Ontario	1.01	ns	0.82	*	0.85	*
Prairies	0.95	ns	0.75	*	0.76	*
BC	1.08	ns	0.76	*	0.90	ns
Gender						
Female	0.84	*	1.63	*	1.26	*
Age Groups						
35–44	1.34	*	0.68	*	0.83	ns
45–64	1.43	*	0.62	**	0.87	ns
65+	1.46	**	0.79	ns	1.06	ns
Mother Tongue						
French	1.29	ns	0.76	ns	0.89	ns
Other	1.35	ns	0.71	ns	0.88	ns
Presence of Children in Household						
Child under 14 years	0.85	*	0.85	ns	0.64	**
Marital Status						
Single	1.39	*	1.25	*	1.48	*
Other	0.98	ns	1.26	**	0.94	ns
Workforce status						
Student	0.88	ns	1.01	ns	0.87	ns
Retired and Other	1.13	ns	1.18	ns	0.92	ns
Educational Level						
High School Diploma	0.87	ns	0.82	ns	0.87	ns
University/College	0.80	**	0.82	*	0.77	**
Post Secondary	0.72	**	0.92	**	0.79	**

Notes:

Reference categories: Canadian-born, GSS 2010 cycle, males, 15–34 years old, married–common law, no children under 14 in household, full- or part-time work, Atlantic region residence, no high school education, no knowledge of neighbours, neighbours do not help each other.

Symbols: ns=non-statistically significant coefficient, *=significant coefficient at the .05 level, **= significant coefficient at the .01 level.

Discussion

Despite some data shortcomings (e.g., limited counts of recent immigrants, two observation periods, etc.), the GSS 2010–2012 data provides a useful picture of the participation of Canadian and foreign-born populations in help exchanges with their neighbours. **Bidirectional help exchanges** (case 4) were most prevalent, but there were noticeable differences between the Canadian and foreign-born populations. Help exchanges were lower for all immigrants regardless of their length of stay in the country. Unidirectional exchanges of help (receiving or giving help only) occurred more sporadically, representing only a minority of cases. If the community was not perceived as a "helping" one and/or the contact level with neighbours was low, regardless of immigrant status, individuals did not participate in any help exchanges with their neighbours. Multinomial logistic regressions revealed also that, in the presence of other socio-demographic and pro-social drivers, immigrant status and length of residence could not be discarded as potential explanatory factors of help exchange behaviour.

The lower participation of immigrants in help exchanges with their neighbours raises several policy issues. A major one refers to the possible presence of various **cultures of civic engagement** in Canada. For some immigrants, the spectrum of civic engagement (and, for that matter, of citizenship itself) may be more focused on family and kin rather than on surrounding neighbours. Due to their unique experiences with different socialization agents, members of immigrant groups may shape different opinions toward civic duties, rights, and responsibilities of their membership in the community of residence. In a country that is becoming more diverse, understanding these exchange processes is relevant, as neighbours have a tremendous potential to amplify social capital benefits for immigrants and ensure an extended network of social support. Recent immigrants may lack adequate access to extensive social networks and miss opportunities to create strong bonds with their neighbours. To increase social civic engagement, local, provincial, and federal programs should devise initiatives that foster frequent interactions with neighbours, create welcoming images of communities, and build a prejudice-free environment where common goals may be more easily achieved.

Notes

1. Paper presented at the 2015 Canadian Sociological Association Meetings University of Ottawa, Ottawa, Ontario.
2. These odds may be roughly interpreted as the odds ratio of the occurrence of a certain event, controlling for effects of other variables present in the analysis.

References

Abbott, S. and D. Freeth. (2008). "Social capital and health starting to make sense of the role of generalized trust and reciprocity." *Journal of Health Psychology* 13(7): 874–83.

Bourdieu, P. (1986). "The forms of capital." In John Richardson (eds), *Handbook of theory and research for the sociology of education*. New York: Greenwood Press. Pp: 241–58.

Cheong, P. (2006). "Communication context, social cohesion and social capital building among Hispanic immigrants." *Community, Work and Family* 9(3): 367–87.

Fischer, C.S. (1984). *The Urban Experience*. New York: Harcourt, Brace, Jovanovich.

Huijts, T., G. Kraaykamp, and P. Scheepers. (2014). "Ethnic diversity and informal intra- and inter-ethnic contacts with neighbours in The Netherlands: A comparison of Natives and ethnic minorities." *Acta Sociologica* 57(1): 41–57.

Hooghe, M., M. Reeskens, D. Stolle, and A. Trappers. (2009). "Ethnic diversity and generalized trust in Europe: A cross-national multi-level study." *Comparative Political Studies* 42(1): 198–223.

Keller, S. (1968). *The Urban Neighbourhood*. New York, Random House.

Klein, C. (2011). "Social capital or social cohesion: What matters for subjective well-being?" *Social Indicators Research*. Online edition.

Korte, C. (1988). "Increasing help exchange in an urban neighborhood: The effects of a neighborhood directory." *Journal of Applied Social Psychology* 18(3): 228–51.

Kushner, H.I., and C. Sterk. (2005). "The limits of social capital: Durkheim, suicide, and social cohesion." *American Journal of Public Health* 95(7): 1139–43.

Lancee, B., and J. Dronkers. (2011). "Ethnic, religious and economic diversity in Dutch neighbourhoods: Explaining quality of contact with neighbours, trust in the neighbourhood and inter-ethnic trust." *Journal of Ethnic and Migration Studies* 37(4): 597–618.

Marschall, M., and D. Stolle. (2004). "Race and the city: Neighborhood context and the development of generalized trust." *Political Behavior* 26(2): 125–54.

Murie, A., and S. Musterd. (2004). "Social exclusion and opportunity structures in European cities and neighbourhoods." *Urban Studies* 41(8): 1441–59.

Oliver, J.E., and J. Wong. (2003). "Intergroup prejudice in multiethnic settings." *American Journal of Political Science* 47: 567–82.

Putnam, R. (2007). "E pluribus unum: Diversity and com munity in the twenty-first century: The 2006 Johan Skytte prize lecture." *Scandinavian Political Studies*, 30(2): 137–74.

Statistics Canada. (2009). *Caring Canadians, Involved Canadians: Highlights from the 2007 Canada Survey of Giving, Volunteering and Participating*. Catalogue no. 71-542-XPE. Ottawa: Ministry of Industry.

Stolle, D., S. Soroka, and R. Johnston. (2008). "When does diversity erode trust? Neighborhood diversity, interpersonal trust and the mediating effect of social interactions." *Political Studies* 56: 57–75.

Thomas, D. (2012). "Giving and volunteering among Canada's immigrants, Canadian Social Trends." *Canadian Social Trends*, May 17. Catalogue no. 11-008-X

Thomson, I. (2005). "The theory that won't die: From mass society to the decline of social capital." *Sociological Forum* 20(3): 421–48.

Uslaner, E.M., and Conley, R.S. (2003). "Civic engagement and particularized trust—the ties that bind people to their ethnic communities." *American Politics Research* 31(4): 331–60.

Van Oorschot, W., W. Ares, and J. Gelissen. (2006). "Social capital in Europe: Measurement and social and regional distribution of a multifaceted phenomenon." *Acta Sociologica* 49(2): 149–67.

Van der Gaag, M., and Snijders, T. (2005). "The resource generator: Social capital quantification with concrete items." *Social Networks*, 27(1): 1–29.

Vervoot, M. (2012). "Ethnic concentration in the neighbourhood and ethnic minorities' social integration: Weak and strong social ties examined." *Urban Studies* 49(4): 897–915.

Wickes, R., Zahnov, R.,White, G. Mazerolle, L. (2013). "Ethnic diversity and its impact on community social cohesion and neighbourly exchange." *Journal of Urban Affairs* 36(1): 51–78.

Worley, C. (2005). "'It's not about race. It's about Community': New Labour and 'Community Cohesion'." *Critical Social Policy* 25(4): 483–96.

36 The "Quiet" Deconstruction[1]: The Progressive Dismantling of Quebec's Early Childhood Education and Care System

Sophie Mathieu

At the end of the 1990s, and within the difficult circumstances of restructuring social programs with the goal of achieving "zero deficit," the Quebec government, led by the Parti Québécois, decided to develop a new family policy. One of the cornerstones of this policy involved establishing a **universal**,[2] government-subsidized, and low-cost network of child care services for preschool-level children. Between 1997 and 2000, the government opted for a progressive increase in the supply of child care, mainly in non-profit centres known as ***centres de la petite enfance*** (early childhood centres; CPEs). However, these child care centres have been under attack and subjected to a progressive dismantling.

Following the change in government in 2003, from the Parti Québécois (PQ) to the Parti Libéral du Québec (PLQ), the essence of the 1997 policy has been dissolving. Although the discourse on the restoration of fiscal health is nothing new, that for "budgetary rigour" arrived at a timely moment for the Liberals, who had the desire to expand the use of the private sector in the supply of child care services. As a result, Quebec's network of state-funded child care has progressively been dismantled through two processes: (1) an explosion of commercial child care centres, and (2) since 2015, the end of the universality of the program due to the differentiation of costs based on household income.

A Brief History of Quebec's Family Policy

The year 1997 marked a shift in the design of Quebec's family policy. In the turmoil of budget cuts orchestrated by the PQ led by Premier Lucien Bouchard, the government published a White Paper in which it committed to ensure that every child whose parents were working, studying, or undergoing vocational training could benefit from a subsidized low-cost child care space. Having once been centred on the aim of increasing the birth rate from 1988 to 1996 (Mathieu, 2014; Rose, 2010), the new family policy was to be designed to support work and family reconciliation and the development of children in a context of equal opportunities (Gouvernement du Québec, 1997). In tandem with the development of a new Quebec parental insurance plan[3] (McKay, Mathieu, and Doucet, 2016), the central element of this reform rested on the progressive establishment of $5/day child care services for preschool-aged children offered mainly in non-profit centres.

The most striking aspect of the establishment of the reduced-contribution child care network was undoubtedly its universality. The political context of the 1990s was marked by a strong challenging of the suitability of universal services and benefits being offered (Groulx, 2009; Jenson, 2002). The federal government had also opted by the 1980s to move away from universalism in the benefits offered to families. Universal family allowances introduced in 1944 and whose value tripled in 1973 (Battle and Mendelson, 1997) were from 1989 subject to a recovery clause for high-income families, before ceasing to be universal in 1993. The 1997 budget presented by the Quebec government was directed toward the pursuit of restoring fiscal health and the elimination of the budget deficit (Ministère des Finances, 1997). This goal would lead to many cuts in Quebec's public service, and it was also seemingly incompatible with the objective of investment in universal child care. In addition, the 1997 family policy broke with the principle of universalism by putting an end to universal family allowances, which had been available to families in Quebec since 1967. Against all odds, the Quebec government nevertheless opted for a phased introduction of child care services for preschool-age children, with the ultimate objective of creating 200,000 subsidized spaces.

Child Care Services for the Early Childhood Stage under Attack

The development of a network of child care services for preschool-age children was based on two foundations, the first one being a strong bias toward non-profit centres. The 1997 policy was accompanied by a moratorium on the creation of new for-profit daycares. Commercial child care centres already in place were offered three alternatives: to become a CPE following an acquisition of assets made possible by a government program, to remain a for-profit child care centre while offering reduced-contribution spaces, or to remain a for-profit child care centre while offering services at full cost (Lévesque, 2011).[4] Accordingly, between 1998 and 2003, during Quebec's first child care regime, there was a growth in the institutionalization of services, which were mostly made available at low cost, in non-profit facilities (Table 36.1). During this period, the proportion of subsidized spaces in non-profit child care centres[5] went from 70.9 per cent to 84 per cent, due to an increase from 58,367 to 138,694 in the number of spaces in CPEs (in facilities and in family environments). The model in place therefore favoured the development of CPEs (with a growth of 138 per cent), at the expense of commercial child care centres. As a result, only 16 per cent of child care spaces were offered by for-profit centres in 2003 and 99 per cent of the child care spaces were subsidized.

The first foundation of Quebec's network of child care services was attacked when the Liberal under the leadership of Jean Charest came to power in 2003 and chose to make way for a new child care regime. This new regime still supported the institutionalization of child care services, but these were increasingly offered in for-profit centres. While the number of spaces in CPEs (in facilities and family environments) increased by 29 per cent between 2003 and 2014 (from 138,694 to 178,434), that of subsidized private child care

TABLE 36.1 Distribution of Spaces in CPEs, in Subsidized Child Care, and in Non-subsidized Child Care, Quebec, 1998–2014

	Proportion of CPEs among all child care spaces (in facilities and family environment)	Proportion of spaces in for-profit centres among all child care spaces	Proportion of subsidized spaces (in CPEs in facilities and family environment and in subsidized for-profit centres) among all child care spaces	Proportion of non-subsidized spaces among all child care spaces
1998	70.9	29.1	99.7	0.3
1999	74.2	25.8	99.6	0.4
2000	78.2	21.8	99.5	0.5
2001	80.7	19.3	99.5	0.5
2002	82.3	17.7	99.3	0.7
2003	84.0	16.0	99.0	1.0
2004	83.6	16.4	98.9	1.1
2005	83.0	17.0	98.7	1.3
2006	81.7	18.3	98.3	1.7
2007	81.0	19.0	97.8	2.2
2008	80.6	19.4	97.7	2.3
2009	79.6	20.4	96.7	3.3
2010	77.4	22.6	94.9	5.1
2011	74.9	25.1	92.3	7.7
2012	71.9	28.1	88.7	11.3
2013	68.7	31.3	84.8	15.2
2014	66.4	33.6	82.6	17.4

Sources: CSN (2010), FTQ (2015), and Ministère de la famille (2014).

rose by 76 per cent (from 24,740 to 43,549 spaces), while that of nonsubsidized commercial child care centres underwent a meteoric rise of 2779 per cent (from 1,620 to 46,641 spaces). In 2014, more than a third of spaces (33.6 per cent) in institutionalized child care were therefore offered in for-profit centres, while only 82.6 per cent of child care spaces were subsidized.

Although 2003 clearly marked a change in regime for the supply of child care services, the advance in the commercialization of for-profit child care has proved to be at its most dazzling over the past five years, especially with regard to nonsubsidized private child care. For example, between 2005 and 2009, the number of spaces in nonsubsidized private child care increased by 183 per cent, whereas between 2009 and 2014 it jumped by 571 per cent. There thus appears to have been an acceleration in the pace at which the government has been ready to give private enterprise a space in providing child care.

This acceleration has not come about by chance. It has been encouraged by the neoliberal ideology of the party in government since 2003,[6] the PLQ, which promotes parents' use of private child care. The deconstruction of the public, low-cost child care network has come about not only through a dramatic increase in the number of commercial child care centres, but also through rewarding use of this type of child care service with incentives. In Quebec, parents who use nonsubsidized child care are entitled to reimbursement[7] through a tax credit for a portion of the sums they pay. In 2004–2005, the province established the quarterly advance payment, enabling parents to receive help from the government four times a year; this reimbursement would become monthly in 2011. In addition, since 2009 and following the award of the refundable credit for child care expenses, families with a household income of $125,000 or less pay the same price for a space in subsidized child care or in nonsubsidized child care. Together with the growth of the number of spaces in private child care facilities, the award of the refundable tax credit has opened up a significant breach in the essence of the 1997 family policy, which was based on the predominant use of non-profit child care services.

The second attack against the child care network for the early took place in 2015, with the revocation of the universal low flat-rate cost. In spite of the CPEs being considered a success, the Liberals decided to carry out a large-scale consultation in 2003, the *Enquête québécoise sur la qualité des services de garde éducatifs*, to define different scenarios so as "to ensure the sustainability, accessibility and quality of child care services" (Ministère de l'Emploi, de la solidarité et de la famille, 2003: 3). To cope with the pressure exerted on public finances by the costs of early childhood services, the province decided to increase the parental contribution to $7/day in 2004.

Within its permanent reviewing of programs, the Quebec government later announced in 2014 that it would modify the financial aspects of reduced-contribution child care programs by varying the subsidy offered to families in accordance with their income. The government continued to deconstruct an important facet of Quebec's family policy by drawing on arguments related to the financing and sustainability of the network of reduced-contribution spaces. Although the costs paid by parents remain unchanged (at $7.30 per day[8]) under the new funding regime for subsidized spaces, the additional contribution, established on the basis of pre-tax household income, became payable when taxes are filed. In 2015, this contribution remained unchanged for families with a household income of less than $50,000; it was increased to $8 for families earning between $50,001 and $75,000, and it rose to $20[9] for families whose income amounted to $150,000 or more (Table 36.2). This increase in practice affected nearly 64 per cent of all Quebec families (CSF, 2014). The majority of Quebec families therefore received a bill from the government for the difference between the cost paid and the actual cost of a space in child care at the end of the 2015 fiscal

TABLE 36.2 Distribution of Families of Two or More Per Income in Quebec in 2011 and Child Care Costs after the Reform, in 2015

	Percentage of families	Child care cost ($/day/child)
$0 to $50,000	36.5	7.30
$50,001$ to $74,999	28.6	8.00
$75,000$ to $99,999	17.5	8.00–11.41
$100,000 to $119,999	9.8	11.41–14.41
$120,000 to $149,999	3.5	14.41–20.00
$150,000 and over	4.0	20.00

Source: CSF (2014).

year.[10] An important facet of Quebec's family policy had just been silently changed, no doubt due to the ambiguity of the changes to the policy,[11] which allow parents to continue paying $7.30 per day for child care services.

Conclusion

One of the central elements of the 1997 policy, namely the low-cost child care network, has become the victim of a "quiet" dismantling following a change of government from the PQ to the PLQ in 2003. This dismantling cannot be linked to recent discourse on a need for discipline in better managing public finances. The theme of restoring fiscal health is not a new one in Quebec's public discourse. The PQ government installed in 1997 made the commitment in its election platform to eliminate the budget deficit. However, the budget cuts and austerity policies of the late 1990s did not dampen the political will to put a network of universal, low-cost child care in place. More than anything, the dismantling of family policy is the result of a neoliberal ideology that gives the market the responsibility for providing services to citizens (Esping-Andersen, 1990) and that serves as a guideline to the current government. The theme of budgetary rigour and the urgency of restoring fiscal health therefore could not have come at a better time for the Quebec government, which since the beginning of the new millennium has undertaken an increased commercialization of child care.

Notes

1. The expression refers to the "Quiet Revolution," a period of intense changes in the 1960s that led to the creation of the Québécois welfare state.
2. The idea of universalism lacks a widely accepted definition and takes different meanings (Anttonen, Häikiö, and Stefánsson, 2012). In Quebec, up to 2015, universal child care meant that all children were eligible for a government-subsidized space at a low flat-rate cost. Due to the popularity of the program, however, the number of spaces has been insufficient to meet the demand, which has caused some commentators to argue that the program has never been truly universal in access (Anderssen and Mackrael, 2013; Costanzo, 2015).
3. Quebec's new parental leave did not come into force until 2006.
4. Even today, there are two types of for-profit child care centres in Quebec: (1) "subsidized" child care centres that offer spaces at the same cost as those offered by CPEs; and (2) nonsubsidized commercial child care centres, at which parents pay all of the costs related to their child care (around $35 per day) (Ministère de la Famille, 2014). Although parents who make use of subsidized private

child care centres pay the same price as those whose children are enrolled in a CPE, the quality of service is often lower, in part because of the problems they have with retaining staff (CSN, 2010; FTQ, 2015).

5. Non-profit and reduced-contribution child care services can be offered in two types of establishments: (1) CPEs, which accommodate up to 80 children within a facility; and (2) family child care services provided by an educator in his or her private residence, which are under the administration of duly accredited coordination offices.
6. With the exception of a period of 18 months between 2012 and 2014, during which the Parti Québécois was in power.
7. The reimbursement rate depends on net household income.
8. Both the basic and the additional contributions are indexed annually. In 2016, the basic contribution was $7.55 per day.
9. In 2016, the cost was raised to $20.70 per day.
10. However, the 2016–2017 budget provided for, with respect to 2015, a 50 per cent retroactive reduction in the additional contribution for a second child attending subsidized child care.
11. This ambiguity is heightened by the fact that the federal government increased the universal child care benefit in 2015, reducing Quebec families' bills for child care.

References

Anderssen, Erin and Kim Mackrael. 2013. "Better daycare for $7/day: One province's solution for Canada," *Globe and Mail*, October 18.

Anttonen, Anneli, Liisa Häikiö and Kolbeinn Stefánsson. 2012. *Welfare State, Universalism and Diversity*. Cheltenham; Northampton, MA: Edward Elgar.

Battle, Ken and Michael Mendelson. 1997. "Child benefit reform in Canada: An evaluative framework and future directions." Research report for the Government of British Columbia and Human Resources Development Canada. Caledon Institute of Social Policy. Retrieved from: http://www.caledoninst.org/Publications/PDF/255ENG.pdf

Confédération des syndicats nationaux (CSN). 2010. *Des services de garde éducatifs de qualité : un droit pour chaque enfant*, Plateforme sur les services de garde éducatifs à l'enfance.

Conseil du statut de la femme (CSF). 2014. *Avis: Impact d'une modulation de la contribution parentale aux services de garde subventionnés sur la participation des femmes au marché du travail*. Quebec City: Conseil du statut de la femme.

Costanzo, Roslyn. 2015. "Child care subsidy: Why Quebec's $7 per day daycare isn't all it's cracked up to be." *The Huffington Post Canada*, September 29.

Esping-Andersen, Gøsta. 1990. *The Three Worlds of Welfare Capitalism*. Princeton, NJ: Princeton University Press.

Fédération des travailleurs et travailleuses du Québec (FTQ). 2015. *Mémoire sur le projet de loi no°27: Loi sur l'optimisation des services de garde éducatifs à l'enfance subventionnés*. 19 January 2015. Montreal: Fédération des travailleurs et travailleuses du Québec.

Gouvernement du Québec. 1997. *Les enfants au cœur de nos choix. Nouvelles dispositions de la politique familiale*. Sainte-Foy, QC: Publications du Québec.

Groulx, Lionel-Henri. 2009. "La restructuration récente des politiques sociales au Canada et au Québec: Éléments d'analyse." *Labour/Le travail* 63, 9–46.

Jenson, Jane. 2002. "Against the current: Child care and family policy in Québec." In *Child Care Policy at the Crossroads. Gender and Welfare State Restructuring*, edited by Sonya Michel and Rianne Mahon. New York: Routledge, pp. 309–32.

Lévesque, Benoît. 2011. "L'institutionnalisation des services québécois de garde à la petite enfance à partir de l'économie sociale: un processus qui s'échelonne sur plusieurs décennies." *Les cahiers du crises*, juillet.

Mathieu, Sophie. 2014. *Labour markets, family-relevant policies and reproductive behaviours: Québec's fertility regimes between 1960 and 2010*. PhD dissertation,, Department of Sociology, Carleton University.

McKay, Lindsey, Sophie Mathieu, and Andrea Doucet. 2016 (forthcoming). "'Parental-leave rich and parental-leave poor'? Access in/equality in Canadian labour-market-based, temporary leave care policies." *Journal of Industrial Relations*.

Ministère de l'Emploi, de la Solidarité sociale et de la Famille. 2003. *Scénarios de développement et de financement pour assurer la pérennité. l'accessibilité et la qualité des services de garde*, Gouvernement du Québec.

Ministère de la Famille. 2014. *Portrait des garderies non subventionnées du Québec. Enquête auprès des propriétaires de garderies non-subventionnées*, Gouvernement du Québec.

Ministère des Finances. 1997. Budget 1997–1998. Discours sur le budget et renseignements supplémentaires, Gouvernement du Québec.

Rose, Ruth. 2010. "La politique familiale au Québec: La recherche d'un équilibre entre différents objectifs." *Santé, société et solidarité* 2, 31–42.

Questions for Critical Thought

Chapter 32 | "I Knew What I Was Getting Into": A Study of Youth Labour in the Context of a Canadian Tree-Planting Camp

1. What reasons do young people have for working in tree-planting camps? Why are they more likely to accept this type of employment opportunity?
2. Describe the culture created by youth in tree-planting camps? Why is the creation of this culture important?
3. What are some of the physical demands of this job? How are these demands positive? How are they negative?
4. How do the workers police each other's actions? How is this significant?
5. What do Antonelli and Mooney say are some of the positive "employable" traits that young people learn from participating in tree-planting camps?

Chapter 33 | How Minority and Non-Minority Youth Participate in Public Life

1. Are young Canadians voting? How do they participate in public life? Do all categories of youth participate in the same way?
2. Describe Westheimer and Kahne's citizenship framework. What are the three visions of good citizenship?
3. Why are youth drawn to micro-politics over voting? How does this approach make a difference to public life?
4. How do the findings, which explore student's perceptions of citizenship and justice, enhance your understanding of youth participation in public life? How do you feel about the respondents' answers? Do you agree with their perceptions?
5. What two concerns does Molina-Girón say emerge from the findings?

Chapter 34 | Understanding the Changing Nature of Relationships in Aging Canadian Families

1. According to Kobayashi and Khan, how are families changing?
2. What are the three domains of social support? In what way are these areas not getting the support they need?
3. What are some of the positive effects of aging families? How does this impact children, parents, and grandparents?
4. What is the impact of remarrying? How does this change the family dynamic?
5. Describe the two central issues that come up when discussing Canadian social policy and aging families.

Chapter 35 | Helping and Receiving Help from Neighbours: A Look at the Canadian- and the Foreign-Born

1. What benefit can neighbours have on people who have recently immigrated to Canada?
2. To what extent do immigrants take part in exchanges of help with their neighbours in Canada?
3. What does Mata say are the socio-demographic and attitudinal drivers behind helping behaviours?
4. How do experiences with neighbours potentially shape a new immigrant's view of civic duty?
5. Mata gives some suggestions for how immigrant engagement can be increased. How would you increase immigrant engagement? Use your own ideas or build on Mata's suggestions.

Chapter 36 | The Progressive Dismantling of Quebec's Early Childhood Education System: The Progressive Dismantling of Quebec's Early Childhood Education and Care System

1. What progressive family-centric policy was implemented in Quebec? What is happening to the policy now?
2. What was the promise of this policy? How did this policy help combat existing inequalities?
3. How has the child care policy changed in 2015? Why have they divided costs this way? Discuss your opinions and perspectives on the changes.
4. Consider some potential inequalities that could emerge without subsidized daycare. Who would take care of the children? How does poor daycare affect children over the life course?
5. What is a neoliberal ideology? How might the shift to this ideology since 2003 have influenced Quebec's decision to "dismantle" daycare?

PART IX
Education

According to the Organisation for Economic Co-operation and Development (OECD), Canada has one of the most highly educated populations in the world. On the downside, they report that public funding for all levels of education in Canada is considerably lower than the average spending among other OECD countries, resulting in, among other things, Canada being one of the countries with the highest post-secondary tuition. Sociologists working in the area of education have spent considerable time exploring and explaining these trends. The sociology of education examines a wide range of topics, from how social institutions, specific groups, and individuals experience education, to the structure, functioning, processes, and inequalities found within or reinforced by educational institutions. In our increasingly complex societies, studying education has meant tackling issues at various phases throughout the life cycle—well beyond childhood and youth—as we see in the chapters in this section of this book.

Historically, sociological theories of education, and particularly functionalist theories, have focused on the relatively positive and homogeneous aspects of educational systems. They explained that society's institutions, including the educational system, are in place to fulfill specific social needs and functions vital to social survival and equilibrium (promoting a stable social order). Talcott Parsons (1991/1951), for example, argued that education is an important agent of socialization that works to promote our achieved status—the idea that we are judged on merit and hard work. Schools, argue functionalists, are places where students are granted equal opportunity to succeed on a level playing field. Schools are believed to be places that instill the values of achievement and equality of opportunity and perform the function of role allocation—preparing students for their future places in life—by matching inherent talents to the jobs for which students are best suited.

In contrast, conflict theorists argued that society is not in a balanced or ordered state, and is certainly not a meritocracy. They have instead argued that societies are built on struggles for power, wealth, prestige, and control, and those in power also tend to control institutions like schools to promote their interests and goals. Both a formal and hidden curriculum, they argued, aim to reinforce the existing class structure and other social inequalities, despite the fact that some individual teachers were highly committed to equality. Theorists like Pierre Bourdieu (see Bourdieu and Wacquant, 2013) have argued that children of a society's elite acquire most of the valued ideas and resources—cultural capital—long before entering and outside of the formal school system, and thus have an advantage over students of other class and cultural backgrounds. Feminist theorists have pointed to similar inequalities that manifest themselves along gender lines.

Conflict and feminist theorists of education critically assess and deconstruct the idea of education as a great equalizer or as a level playing field. They instead show and explain that in Canada today, as elsewhere, those who come from economically disadvantaged households, who are racialized and/or women (particularly those aiming to study in non-traditional fields, such as engineering), find themselves more likely to struggle in school, compared with those from households with a higher socio-economic status, those who are members of the dominant group, or men (especially in science and math).

As you will see in the chapters that follow, today's sociology of education considers the complexities of education in neoliberal contexts, as affected by political decisions, changes in national economies, and demographic shifts, and as part of broad global trends. For example, in Chapter 37, Deborah Harrison and Patrizia Albanese take a critical perspective when they examine stressors experienced by students affected by the Canadian government's decision to play an active combat role in Afghanistan. They assess the experiences of students with parents in the Canadian Armed Forces and the impact of parental deployments on school engagement, levels of stress, and family responsibilities. In Chapter 38, Toju Maria Boyo describes the impact of highly educated people in Africa migrating to North America, suggesting that Africa is being drained of important intellectual resources. This chapter shows the impact of education on an individual's potential for mobility, but more importantly, the impact of international migrations for the pursuit of education on a national and global level. Also focusing on post-secondary education, in Chapter 39 James Frideres examines educational pathways, specifically for those pursuing a PhD in sociology. Frideres discusses the potential for employment among academics in today's job market, emphasizing some of the changes that have been made to universities and faculty positions. Lastly, in Chapter 40, Terry Wotherspoon advocates for culturally appropriate educational programs for Aboriginal people, one of the groups most profoundly affected by social inequalities in Canadian society. This chapter explores the historical legacy of colonial policies faced by Aboriginal peoples and their limited access to higher education.

References

Bourdieu, Pierre and Loic Wacquant. 2013. "Symbolic Capital and Social Class." *Journal of Classical Sociology* 13(2): 292–302.

Parsons, Talcott. 1991/1951. *The Social System.* London: Routledge & Kegan Paul Ltd.

37 Life at Armyville High School: A Glimpse into How Adolescents Experienced the Afghanistan Missions[1,2]

Deborah Harrison and Patrizia Albanese[3]

Military families resemble other Canadian families: their members care for one another, support each other economically, and raise children. However, military families are also different (Crum-Cianflone et al., 2014; Harrison and Albanese, 2016). While families in general experience a range of stressors, military families experience more than their share.

Adolescents in military families face especially unique stressors whenever they experience a parental deployment. The heightened risk accompanying Canadian Armed Forces (CAF) **deployments** over the last 15 years has also heightened the intensity of military families' deployment-related stressors.

According to recent US research, experiencing a parental deployment is a predictor of depressive symptoms and suicide ideation in military-connected adolescents (De Pedro et al., 2015). In this chapter, we focus on Canadian military-connected students at Armyville High School (AHS),[4] who live on or near a base that vigorously participated in the Afghanistan missions.

Deployments

Seventy per cent of Canadian military families have experienced a deployment at least once, and 17 per cent have experienced more than five deployments (Sudom, 2010). The impact of parental deployments on adolescents is unique for several reasons. First, coping with a deployment interferes with an adolescent's progress toward developing a sense of his or her unique identity (Fitzsimons and Krause-Parello, 2009; Mmari et al., 2009). Second, adolescents are frequently required to become caregivers for siblings and/or undeployed parents, thereby putting their own needs on the back burner (Mmari et al., 2009). **Parentification** has been identified as occurring among these adolescents (Daigle, 2013; West, Mercer, and Altheimer, 1993; Harrison and Albanese, 2012). Third, unlike younger siblings, adolescents are able to empathize with other family members' perspectives on the deployment and anticipate developments during the mission (Mmari et al., 2009). Finally, adolescents are sensitive to, and adept at understanding, the messages that the media communicate (Mmari et al., 2009).

Armyville

In the mid-1950s, almost overnight, Armyville, a tiny town of 250, became a "company town" dominated by CAF personnel. As of 2011, Armyville's population was almost 9,000 (Statistics Canada, 2014). Of these, the base employed 5,000 military members and 1,500 civilians.

Armyville High School (AHS), one of the largest schools in its province, has over 1,270 students, approximately half of them being members of military families. The school and the base enjoy a close relationship: school events are held at the base and military recruiters are frequent school visitors. Many AHS students join the army upon graduation. Recognizing that its staff knew too little about the impact of dangerous deployments on students, the local school board partnered with our research team's endeavour to collect and interpret reliable quantitative and qualitative data during the Afghanistan mission.

Method

The first phase of our **mixed-methods** project was a survey, administered in October 2008, to 1,066 of the 1,270 students attending AHS. Using measures from the National Longitudinal Survey of Children and Youth (NLSCY),[5] we compared the well-being, family functioning, attitudes toward school, and peer relationships of adolescents from CAF families with those of their civilian peers at AHS and their peers in Cycle 7 (2006–7) of the NLSCY.[6] In the second phase, in 2009–10, we conducted two-hour interviews with 61 students: 15 CAF adolescents from each grade (16 from grade 9). We interviewed 35 girls and 26 boys who had 69 parents who were present or recently retired CAF members of various ranks. The interviews covered a range of topics unique to military life, including geographical relocations, deployments, PTSD, family functioning, and participants' perceptions of how their school was supporting them.

Adolescent Deployment Experiences

Since 1994, research has proliferated on the emotional stress suffered by the family members of deployed military members: research on, for example, adolescents (Huebner and Mancini, 2005; Huebner et al., 2007; Mmari et al., 2009; Chandra et al., 2010; Richardson et al., 2011), military couples (Allen et al., 2011), and female spouses (Jensen et al., 1996; Eaton et al., 2008; Dimiceli et al., 2010; Mansfield et al., 2010). According to recent research, adolescents experience significant anxiety about their undeployed parents' well-being (Mmari et al., 2009; Chandra et al., 2011; Richardson et al., 2011). For some of our own interview participants, the parent who remained at home was stressed to the point of being emotionally unavailable to them. For example, when she was living with a father who was unable to provide nurturing to his children, Bridget described her daily life as follows:

> It was pretty much leave for work, come back for dinner, go to bed, leave for work, come back for dinner. That was it. We didn't really talk. It was just "Here's your dinner. I'm going to go watch TV now." . . . That was it. I didn't talk to anybody. I was really, really lonely.

Cindy also worked hard at home when her father went to Afghanistan:

> I was basically the mom. . . . [Mom] worked double shifts from, like, 7 to 3 and then 4 until 12. So she was never home. She had to keep the money going while my dad was away. So it was just me and my brother all the time.

Lorraine said similarly,

> My mom was always at work. So I'd take care of my sister. . . . As soon as my mom would come home, if [my sister] didn't have her homework done or something, she'd get mad at me for it. Saying, "Well, why didn't you help her with it?"

Participants of both genders reported having kept their problems to themselves, in order to minimize the stress to which their mothers were being exposed during the deployment. Marilee, whose father deployed frequently and whose mother was chronically ill, did not tell her parents for four years about the severe bullying she had been subjected to in elementary school.

> I think it's because [of] how independent I had to be once my dad had to constantly go. . . . To be honest, it was kind of just like

> Mom was dealing with all this stuff, so I'll just deal with my stuff alone.

Stewart (father in Afghanistan), whose mother suffered from chronic depression, added:

> Having my dad go away constantly, Mom being depressed . . . It's almost like you're living with yourself. . . . And then you're sitting there like, "What am I going to do?" And you have to come up with your . . . own answers.

Cindy noted,

> I have days where I break down and just want to cry all day. . . . I don't usually talk about my feelings with people because . . . I'm the one who listens to people's problems. So when I cry, it's my way of letting my stress out, instead of talking about it or getting mad.

We found that adolescents' responses to the extra instrumental and emotional burdens that they assume during deployments are complex. On the one hand, the extra burdens exact costs and create stress. On the other, they represent sources of self-esteem and pride. The positive pole is borne out by a recent online survey of 559 US Army adolescents that was conducted by Wong and Gerras (2010). The survey found that adolescents aged 14 to 16 who had a parent currently deployed reported lower stress levels than their peers who did not have a parent deployed. The researchers speculated that these adolescents enjoyed their increased responsibilities (and decreased supervision) around their homes. On the "emotional cost" side of the equation, school personnel recently reported to researchers that, in their experience, long deployments have negative effects on family dynamics. Whereas many families acquire and display resilience in coping with deployments, extended and/or multiple deployments often have the effect of "using up" this reticence and exacerbating the emotional difficulties and costs borne by individual family members (Chandra et al., 2010; Richardson et al., 2011).

According to the adolescents interviewed by Huebner and Mancini (2005), resilience can be created and maintained if sources of extrafamilial support are found. Same-aged friends, especially those from other CAF families, were identified by our participants as the most important sources of extrafamilial support during a deployment, even if a few participants admitted to having derived relatively little comfort from contact with these peers.

Role of Schools

School-based support is also potentially important. Recent research has highlighted the need for educators to recognize the unique circumstances surrounding military students, particularly during a deployment (Mmari et al., 2010; Williams, 2013; De Pedro et al., 2015). The way staff interact with students can either buffer or exacerbate the stress. Our participants had had both good and bad experiences at AHS. Some of them talked about having received excellent support from teachers. In contrast, Brad said that his school had publicized the Afghanistan deployment in such an upbeat fashion that civilian students had not been mobilized, as they might have been, to offer support to their affected peers.

> The school is kind of sugar-coating it . . . saying it's nothing too bad. Like [the civilian students] don't quite understand what's going on there.

Similarly, Zoe believed the school's deployment support had not targeted the students' deep experiences and feelings around their parents' deployments.

> We'll have an assembly. They'll be like "Raise your hand if your father's over there." So 400 kids will stand up: "Yeah,

> my dad's over there." Or "My mom's over there." Or "Raise your hand if your mom or dad have ever been deployed." Almost everyone stands up. We have a situation in our school like so many other schools in military towns; we all have the same problems.... We all had "support the troops" stickers. We all wear red on Friday. But the real stuff that's making these kids sad, it just gets pushed under the table.

Our participants told us much about the isolation that adolescents suffer during deployments, and about the fact that too little support exists for them outside their homes.

In 2011, after our data had been collected and provisionally analyzed, all academic and school board team members, plus other school district staff and a representative from CFB Armyville, participated in a two-day symposium in Armyville, which resulted in 18 recommendations that represented an attempt to improve school-based services to adolescents who are affected by military deployments. Several of these recommendations were implemented.

Conclusion

Fortunately or unfortunately, adolescents are old enough to be very useful at home during a deployment: taking on extra household tasks, co-parenting younger siblings, taking care of the undeployed parent, being discreet and restrained in their communications with both parents, keeping their worries to themselves, and often foregoing extracurricular activities, the companionship of their friends, and other carefree teenage pursuits. As a result, they are proud of their accomplishments, but also struggle with overwork, stress, anxiety, depression, and aloneness.

Although the medium-term future of Canadian military involvement is uncertain, chances are low that the peacekeeping era of the Cold War will soon return to us. Our findings—plus the continual need for children's mental health services in locations such as CFB Petawawa, as documented by the CAF Ombudsman and the media—suggest the existence of a need for school-based mental health support for adolescent offspring of CAF members and veterans. The ideal solution would be a deployment support program, including both staff training and support services, that existed all the time in every military community, and required all school staff to possess at least a minimal level of deployment-related expertise. The advantages of this policy would include the availability of mental health support for CAF adolescents who had been affected by past deployments, and the maintenance of a culture of deployment-related expertise within the school district that did not rapidly have to be reinvented whenever the district was faced with a crisis of the magnitude of Afghanistan. The most effective way to create and maintain a school-based culture of expertise would be through the provision of a form of federal financial support to students from military families of the kind that now exists in England and in the US.

Notes

1. For a more detailed elaboration, see Harrison and Albanese, *Growing Up in Armyville: Canada's Military Families During the Afghanistan Mission*. Wilfrid Laurier University Press, 2016.
2. Funding was provided by the Social Sciences and Humanities Research Council Standard Research Grants Program.
3. The other team members were Karen Robson, Rachel Berman, the late Christine Newburn-Cook, David McTimoney, Mary Mesheau, Lucie Laliberte, Shanyn Small, Margaret Malone, Jennifer Phillips, Riley Veldhuizen, Chris Sanders, Danielle Kwan-Lafond, and Angela Deveau.
4. A pseudonym. All participant names have also been changed.
5. Which excluded children from military families.
6. For discussions of our survey results, see Harrison et al., 2011; and Robson, Albanese, Harrison, and Sanders, 2013.

References

Allen, E.S., Rhoades, G.K., Stanley, S.M., and Markman, H.J. (2011). On the home front: Stress for recently deployed army couples. *Family Process*, 50(2), 235–47.

Chandra, A., Lara-Cinisomo, S., Jaycox, L.H., Tanielian, T., Han, B., Burns, R.M., and Ruder, T. (2011). *Views from the homefront: The experiences of youth and spouses from military families*. Arlington, VA: RAND Corporation and National Military Family Association.

Chandra, A., Martin, L.T., Hawkins, S.A., and Richardson, A. (2010). The impact of parental deployment on child social and emotional functioning: Perspectives of school staff. *Journal of Adolescent Health*, 146(3), 218–23.

Crum-Cianflone, N., Fairbank, J., Marmar, C., and Schlenger, W. 2014. The Millennium Cohort Family Study: A prospective evaluation of the health and well-being of military service members and their families. *International Journal of Methods in Psychiatric Research*, 23(3): 320–30.

Daigle, Pierre (Ombudsman). (2013). *On the home front: Assessing the well-being of Canada's military families in the new millennium*. Special Report to the Minister of National Defence. Ottawa: DND/CF Ombudsman. http://www.ombudsman.forces.gc.ca/assets/OMBUDSMAN_Internet/docs/en/mf-fm-eng.pdf

De Pedro, K.T., Avi Astor, R., Gilreath, T., Benbenishty, R., and Berkowitz, R. 2015. School climate, deployment, and mental health among students in military-connected schools. *Youth & Society*. Published online before print June 30, 2015, doi: 10.1177/0044118X15592296, 1–23.

Dimiceli, E., Steinhardt, M., and Smith, S. (2010). Stressful experiences, coping strategies, and predictors of health-related outcomes among wives of deployed military servicemen. *Armed Forces & Society*, 36(2), 351–73.

Eaton, K., Hoge, C., Messer, S., Whitt, A., Cabrora, O., and McGurk, D. (2008). Prevalence of mental health problems, treatment need, and barriers to care among primary care seeking spouses of military service members involved in Iraq and Afghanistan deployments. *Military Medicine*, 173(11), 1051.

Fitzsimons, V.M., and Krause-Parello, C.A. (2009). Military children: When parents are deployed overseas. *The Journal of School Nursing*, 25(1), 40–7.

Harrison, D., and Albanese, P. (2016). *Growing up in Armyville: Canada's military families during the Afghanistan mission*. Waterloo, ON: Wilfrid Laurier University Press.

Harrison, D., and Albanese, P. (2012). The "parentification" phenomenon as applied to adolescents living through parental military deployments. *Canadian Journal of Family and Youth*, 4(1), 1–27.

Huebner, A.J., Mancini, J.A., Wilcox, R.M., Grass, S.R., and Grass, G.A. (2007). Parental deployment and youth in military families: Exploring uncertainty and ambiguous loss. *Family Relations*, 56, 112–22.

Harrison, D., Robson, K., Albanese, P., Sanders, C., Newburn-Cook, C. (2011). The impact of shared location on the mental health of military and civilian adolescents in a community affected by frequent deployments. *Armed Forces & Society*, 37(3), 550–60.

Huebner, A., and Mancini, J.A. (2005). *Adjustments among adolescents in military families when a parent is deployed*. Lafayette, IN: Purdue University Military Family Research Institute.

Jensen, P.S., Martin, D., and Wantanabe, H. (1996). Children's response to parental separation during Operation Desert Storm. *Journal of the American Academy of Child and Adolescent Psychiatry*, 35(4), 433–41.

Mansfield, A.J., Kaufman, J.S., Marshall, S.W., Gaynes, B.N., and Morrissey, J.P., et al. (2010). Deployment and the use of mental health services among US army wives. *New England Journal of Medicine*, 362(2), 101–9.

Mmari, K., Bradshaw, C., Sudhinaraset, M., and Blum, R. (2010). Exploring the role of social connectedness among military youth: Perceptions from youth, parents, and school personnel. *Child & Youth Care Forum*, 39(5), 351–66.

Mmari, K., Roche, K., Sudhinaraset, M., and Blum, R. (2009). When a parent goes off to war: Exploring the issues faced by adolescents and their families. *Youth & Society*, 40(4), 455–75.

Richardson, A., Chandra, A., Martin, L.T., Setodji, C.M., Hallmark, B.W., Campbell, N.F., Hawkins, S.A., and Grady, P. (2011). *Effects of soldiers' deployment on children's academic performance and behavioral health*. Santa Monica, CA: Rand Corporation.

Robson, K., Albanese, P., Harrison, D., and Sanders, C. (2013). School engagement among youth in Canadian Forces families: A comparative analysis. *Alberta Journal of Educational Research* 59(3), 363–81.

Statistics Canada. (2014). *Census profiles*. Ottawa: Statistics Canada.

Sudom, K. (2010). *Quality of life among military families: Results from the 2008–2009 survey of Canadian Forces spouses*. Ottawa: Department of National Defence Canada.

West, L., Mercer, S.O., and Altheimer, E. (1993). Operation Desert Storm: The response of a social work outreach team. *Social Work in Health Care*, 19, 81–98.

Williams, B. (2013). Supporting middle school students whose parents are deployed: Challenges and strategies for schools. *Clearing House*, 86(4), 128–35.

Wong, L., and Gerras, S. (2010). *The effects of multiple deployments on Army adolescents*. Carlisle, PA: Strategic Studies Institute, US War College.

38 The African Brain Drain and the Social Impact of Family Separation

Toju Maria Boyo

Introduction: The Brain Drain from the African Continent

The number of highly skilled or educated Africans migrating to the West has dramatically increased over the last four decades. According to the International Organization for Migration (IOM), over 300,000 African professionals live outside of the continent, and approximately 20,000 African professionals migrate to Western countries every year (Ite, 2002; Jumare, 1997; Tebeje, n.d.). This sort of movement has been termed **brain drain**—"the situation in which large numbers of educated and very skilled people leave their own country to live and work in another where pay and conditions are better" (*Cambridge Dictionary*, 2013). Today, 40 per cent of some of Africa's brightest minds live outside of the continent (Benedict amd Upkere, 2012). Moreover, "there are more African scientists and engineers working in the United States than there are in Africa" (El-Khawas, 2004: 38). Thus, it is not surprising that Africans have been reported to be "the most educated ethnic group in the United States" (El-Khawas, 2004:38). A similar pattern is reflected in the Canadian and European context (Arthur, 2010). In the span of three years (1999–2002), the University of South Africa lost a staggering total of 100,000 professionals, including doctors, engineers, scientists, academics, and accountants (El-Khawas, 2004). Statistics on the exact figures of migration rates from each African country is highly fragmented.

The literature on the African brain drain is often grounded in the **push–pull theory**, which states that undesirable factors such as unemployment force people to leave a country (push) while desirable factors such as quality education attract others to move to another country (pull). This theory supports a cost-benefit analysis of the countries involved. On one hand, brain drain has cost the continent billions of dollars in lost revenue and expertise and has been cited as a source of cheap labour for Western countries. On the other hand, brain drain has been praised for the amount of cash flow it generates in the continent through remittances. Reasons for the brain drain from Africa include political conflict, corruption, declining access and quality of education, and increased unemployment, which are all rooted in a history of colonization and exploitation. The following section presents a critical appraisal of the current debates on brain drain from the continent.

A Critical Reading of the Literature on the African Brain Drain: Whose Narrative Is It Anyway?

There are a number of issues surrounding the manner in which discussions and debates on the African brain drain is taken up in the literature. While the push–pull theory is the dominant theory used to explain migration, it oversimplifies the process and overlooks some critical aspects. Migration is not unidirectional (Goulbourne, Reynolds, Solomos, and Zontini, 2010). Migrants periodically travel back and forth between their host country and their home country and sometimes return permanently to their home country. The push–pull theory does not explain this aspect of migration; what compels a migrant to move back to their country of origin despite relatively unchanged social and economic conditions at home? This theory assumes that the host country invariably meets all the needs of the migrant. To be sure, the push–pull theory is important for establishing a preliminary understanding of why we migrate. However, we need to build upon this theory in a way that identifies gaps in the literature and points to the diversity and complexity of the migratory experience.

The second point pertains to the displacement of "African voices" in the literature on brain drain. Much of the intellectual debate about brain drain is emerging from outside of the continent. Individuals living in the West overwhelmingly dominate analyses on brain drain. With the exception of scholars such as Adepoju (2008), Tettey (2002), Arthur (2010), Oyowe (1996), Kaba (2007), and a few others, most of the scholars engaging in intellectual discourse about African brain drain are not Africans. This may lead to the appropriation of narratives and a Eurocentric understanding of the phenomenon. A Eurocentric perspective is deeply focused on European culture and history and often assumes European superiority over all other cultures. Such a perspective is likely to be divorced from the lived realities of an African migrant or any African for that matter. It begs the questions, "Who is speaking on behalf of whom?" and "for what purposes?" Furthermore, the predominance of "Western analysts" on the subject of African brain drain grants Western authors significant control over the content and dynamics of the debate and analysis. They determine what is relevant or worthy of focus and what is irrelevant. These distinctions may or may not be compatible with the realities in Africa. As such, prescriptions about how to address the issue of brain drain are limited to finding solutions to what authors deem problematic. This is not to say that Western analysts cannot have the continent's best interest at heart, but we must be mindful of how our social positioning in society informs our work and the lens through which we view the world. Hence, this paper is a call for an increased number of African academics and governments to become more engaged in the process of understanding and finding solutions to brain drain.

Finally, the literature on brain drain is heavily steeped in fragmented quantitative analysis, which only tells part of the story. The discourse on brain drain lacks a qualitative narrative on migrant experiences. The sole preoccupation with statistics does not allow for a deeper understanding of the social and personal implications of migration at the micro level. Moreover, the literature treats the entire process of brain drain like an economic transaction, focusing on what there is to gain or lose in the process. Migrants are reduced to commodities on the global market to be bought by the highest bidder—the highest bidder in this case being the country that is supposedly able to make better use of the commodity. Even the vocabulary we use to describe and analyze the process of brain drain is indicative of a sort of objectification of the migrant. For instance, we speak of emigrants as being "pushed" and "pulled" by certain conditions as though they have no sense of agency. We need to understand more about the decision-making process involved in migration and other important considerations. An **anti-colonial framework** allows for such understandings. At the heart of this framework is the idea of resisting, questioning, and redefining dominant ideologies about the relationship between the colonizer and the colonized (Dei, 2006). This paper utilizes an anti-colonial framework to construct a narrative that highlights some of the lived experiences of many African immigrants in the diaspora. This work contributes to the anti-colonial theory because it points to the transformation and continuity of colonialism to present times. It situates brain drain within a continuum of historical events (slavery and colonization) that have all had the effect of disrupting African family relationships. This work also contributes to the anti-colonial theory by questioning the predominant "cost-benefit" discourse on brain drain by placing the migrant experience and the resulting challenges of family separation at the centre of the discourse. It is important to note that, in many cases, migration leads to successful outcomes in the diaspora. However, the impact it has on family dynamics should not be understated.

Family Separation and Adjustment

Migration can often be a very strenuous experience for both the immigrants and their families. As such, "migration tends to weaken family bonds" (Adepoju 1997: 34). Definitions of the family in the African context deviate from the standard Western notions of what constitutes a family. Citing Locoh (1989), Tiemoko (2004) writes that the African family is characterized by a number of qualities including the "tendency for extended family structures, high separation of gender responsibilities, stronger lineage than conjugal solidarity, integration of reproductive and productive functions, and dominance by elders" (157). This is obviously a broad generalization, as African families are complex and come in multiple forms, but for the purposes of this section we will employ this definition. African households are usually composed of both nuclear and extended family members, whether related by blood or not. The African family functions both as an economic and social unit. As an economic unit, it operates to meet the production and consumption needs of the family and improve the overall quality of life of its members (Adepoju and Mbugua, 1997; Arthur, 2000). Also, "as a social institution, it procreates, socializes and educates the children" (Arthur, 2000: 41). Historically, this conception of the family was challenged with the introduction of transatlantic slavery and colonization. These events both disrupted and reshaped the family unit.

According to Arthur (2000), "to the majority of African immigrants, the journey to America is a family's investment in its future. It is hoped that those who are sponsored to come to the United States will one day assist other relatives as well" (Arthur, 2000: 96). This is because the decision to migrate is often a joint decision that involves the participation of extended family members (Findley, 1997). A study of 304 returning migrants (of varying educational backgrounds) from Ghana and Ivory Coast showed that migration is a family ordeal, in that the decision to migrate is often made as a family, especially among skilled individuals whose family members sponsor the migrant to further their studies abroad (Tiemoko, 2004).

The process of migration is disruptive to kinship relationships as individuals leave family members behind in pursuit of better educational and occupational opportunities abroad. Oftentimes, husbands leave their wives and children behind in the hopes of eventually sponsoring them to reunite abroad. More recently, women are increasingly migrating in search of educational and career opportunities (Adepoju, 2004). This shift in migratory patterns has contributed to the changing roles and expectations of women in the family. As such, traditional gender roles become challenged. Women become more resourceful and have more power to make decisions concerning themselves and their households (Adepoju, 2008).

Expectations from family members can also be a source of tension. Since a number of family members are often involved in facilitating the migratory process, there is usually an expectation that migrants will reciprocate these efforts by regularly remitting money to family members and eventually sponsoring them to join the migrant abroad (Findley, 1997). Other concerns include aging parents and the adjustment of young children to a new environment. Child rearing by individuals other than the biological parents of a child is common in Africa, particularly in West Africa, and the lack of this support system abroad may be disorienting (Coe, 2008). For the most part, African children are known to excel and outperform their peers in Western educational systems (El-Khawas, 2004; Kaba, 2007). However, sometimes the difficulty of adjusting to a new environment can manifest itself through poor academic performance, deviant or delinquent behaviour, and the exhibition of disrespectful behaviour towards their parents.

A study on Senegalese families shows migratory separation can last up to 10 years (Gonzalez-Ferrer, Baizan and Beauchemin, 2012). Distance and time spent apart can take a toll on the quality of family relationships. For those who can afford to return home for a visit, initial feelings of excitement are slowly dissolved by feelings of disorientation and disconnection from the culture and from family and friends as a result of prolonged absences. Most of the literature on transnational families has revolved around migration from Latin American countries to the United States (Mazzucto and Schans, 2011). More attention needs to be devoted to the impact that skilled migration has on shaping the dynamics of African families at home and abroad.

Conclusion and Recommendations

The discourse on the brain drain from the African continent has been limited to a cost-benefit analysis for the countries involved. The anti-colonial framework challenges current debates on brain drain including the push–pull theory, which does not adequately capture some of the lived experiences of African immigrants in the diaspora. These debates are often divorced from a social and historical context. Feelings of isolation, loneliness, and family separation are among some of the challenges faced by immigrants. This study is designed to be a stepping stone for further inquiry on the social impact of brain drain from the African continent. In the future, interviews with focus groups could be conducted with African immigrants in the diaspora, detailing their personal experiences as skilled migrants.

References

Adepoju, A. (2004). Changing configuration of migration in Africa. *Migration Information Source*. Retrieved in September 2012 from http://www.migrationinformation.org/feature/display.cfm?ID=251

Adepoju, A. (Ed). (1997). *Family, Population & Development in Africa*. London: Zed Books.

Adepoju, A. (2008). Perspectives on international migration and national development in Sub-Saharan Africa. In Adepoju, A., Van Naerssen, T., and Zoomers, A. (Eds), *International Migration and National Development in Sub-Saharan Africa: Viewpoints and Policy Initiatives in the Countries of Origin* (pp. 21–48). Leiden, The Netherlands: Koninklijke Brill NV.

Adepoju, A. and Mbugua, W. (1997). The African family: an overview of changing forms. In Aderanti Adepoju (Ed.), *Family, Population & Development in Africa*. London: Zed Books.

Arthur, J.A. (2010). *African Diaspora Identities: Negotiating Culture in Transnational Migration*. Plymouth, United Kingdom: Lexington Books.

Arthur, A.A. (2000). *Invisible Sojourners: African Immigrant Diaspora in the United States*. West Port, CT and London: Praeger Publishers.

Benedict, O., and Ukpere, W. (2012). Brain drain and African development: Any possible gain from the drain? *African Journal of Business Management, 6*(7), 2421–8.

Cambridge Dictionary. (2013). Retrieved 1 June 2013 from http://dictionary.cambridge.org

Coe, C. (2008). The structuring of feelings in Ghanaian transnational families. *City and Society, 2*(2), 222–50.

Dei, G. (2006). Introduction: Mapping the terrain—towards a new politics of resistance. In Dei, G. and Kempf, A. (Eds), *Anti-Colonialism and Education: The Politics of Resistance* (pp. 1–23). Rotterdam and Taipei: Sense Publishers.

El-Khawas, M.A. (2004). Brain drain: Putting Africa between a rock and a hard place. *Mediterranean Quarterly 15*(4), 37–56.

Findley, S.E. (1997) Chapter 7: Migration and family interactions in Africa. In Adepoju, A. (Ed.), *Family, Population & Development in Africa*. London: Zed Books.

González-Ferrer, A., Baizán, P., and Beauchemin, C. (2012). Child–parent separations among Senegalese migrants to Europe: Migration strategies or cultural arrangements? *Migration Between Africa and Europe*, MAFE *Working Paper 17*, pp. 1–31.

Goulbourne, H. Reynolds, T., Solomos, J., and Zontini, E. (2010). Problems of belonging and "return." In Holland, J., and Edwards, R. (Eds), *Transnational Families: Ethnicities, Identities and Social Capital* (pp.120–36). New York: Routledge.

Ite, U.E. (2002). Turning brain drain into brain gain: Personal reflections on using the diaspora option. *African Issues, 30*(1), 76–80.

Jumare, I.M. (1997). The displacement of the Nigerian academic community. *Journal of Asian and African Studies, 32*(1–2), 110–19.

Kaba, A. (2007). The two West Africas—the two historical phases of the West African brain drain. *The Journal of Pan African Studies*, 1(8), 77–92.

Locoh, T. (1995). Familles africaines, population et qualité de la vie. Paris: Dossier du CEPED 31.

Mazzucato, V., and Schans, D. (2011). Transnational families and the well-being of children: Conceptual and methodological challenges. *Journal of Marriage and Family, 73*, 704–12.

Oyowe, A. (1996). Brain drain: Colossal loss of investment for developing countries. *The Courier, 159*, 59–60.

Tebeje, A. (n.d.). Brain drain and capacity-building in Africa. *International Development Research Center (IDRC)*. Retrieved 3 August 2013 from http://www.idrc.ca/EN/Resources/Publications/Pages/ArticleDetails.aspx?PublicationID=704

Tettey, W.J. (2002). Africa's brain drain: Exploring possibilities for its positive utilization through networked communities. *Mots Pluriels, 20*. Retrieved on 3 August 2013 from http://motspluriels.arts.uwa.edu.au/MP2002wjt.html

Tiemoko, R. (2004). Migration, return and socio-economic change in West Africa: The role of family. *Population, Space and Place, 10*, 155–74.

39 The Creative Sociologist: Drivers of Innovative Strategies to Meet the Needs of the New Inorganic Global Economy

J.S. Frideres

Introduction

Let's begin with the meaning of the title Doctor of Philosophy. This term originates from the Latin expression *philosophiae* ("love of wisdom") *doctor*. Dating back to the nineteenth century (Noble, 1994), it has changed very little since the term was first coined. It means that original research has been carried out by the individual and it has been deemed "significant" by his or her peers. It has been a mark of status since its creation and requires the investment of over a decade of post-secondary educational involvement before it is conferred upon an individual. Traditionally, it meant that the education and training would allow the individual to become a university professor. But what about today?

My goal is to show how the new cohort of "retired" professors have shown younger scholars that life outside the academy is alive and well, hence the reference to the "new **inorganic** global economy" in this paper's title. These retired professors are using their skills obtained in the educational process to further contribute to Canadian society and thus confirm that the education and skills obtained in graduate school can easily be put to use outside the academy. New PhD graduates can make the transition from the role of student to one of making a substantive contribution to the social, legal, and economic dimensions of Canadian society, whether inside or outside the academy.

A New Reality: The Twenty-First Century

Politically motivated provincial governments (focusing on **neoliberal** ideology), austerity policies, corporatization, and a singular focus on costs are rapidly undermining traditional post-secondary education and, in the process, the academy's collective ability to fulfil its public mission. As such, post-secondary educational institutions are being forced to make major budget cuts, reducing the number of full-time faculty and at the same time hiring an unprecedented number of **sessionals**. Research in 2012 revealed that in the US, over 25 per cent of the faculty employed in universities were sessional appointments (Curtis, 2014). All of this has reduced the opportunities for new PhDs to find jobs in the academy (Peters, 2014).

Most newly graduated PhDs want to enter the academy; unfortunately, it does not offer many opportunities for such full-time employment. Canadian universities produced about 4,000 new PhDs in 2014 (an increase of 450 per cent since 1970), but less than one-quarter of them find jobs in Canadian universities (Bowness, 2015). According to the Royal Society, just 4 per cent of those who obtain a higher degree in science, for example, gain a permanent academic position, and less than 0.5 per cent end up as professors (Baty, 2012). Just under one-third of Canadians with PhDs were employed as full-time university professors. The trend reveals that this percentage is decreasing each year. The remainder of doctoral graduates must find jobs in industry, business, and government. While this may not be problematic for those doctoral students in the science and engineering faculties, it does raise some questions about the fate of those in the social sciences, arts, and humanities.

In the social sciences, arts, and humanities, many doctoral programs continue to train students for careers in academia. However, today we find that as graduate students emerge from doctoral programs, the long-anticipated university job fails to happen (Mason, 2012). As such, those wanting to pursue an academic career have to consider several alternative pathways. Among the most common options that new PhDs take up are: post-doctoral positions; part-time/contract university teaching, university teaching-stream positions, or community college instructor positions (Maldonado et al., 2013). However, after a few years of fruitless searching for a full-time academic position, many of these individuals move on to "plan B," which is to look elsewhere—e.g., government, **NGO**s, or the private sector—for a sustainable job.

Learning from Your Elders

One day you are teaching, carrying out research, meeting with students, and scheduling a variety of meetings with colleagues and administrators. The next day you find that you have left the academy by retiring and entering a new phase of your life. What happens? And how have your training, your research, and your technical and professional skills prepared you for the next phase of your life? Put another way, what can a sociologist do when he or she leaves the academy?

Some of my retired colleagues have chosen to step aside from their academic pursuits and engage in their personal hobbies or other leisure pursuits. Nevertheless, I see more and more of my retired colleagues use their skills to contribute to the enhancement of Canadian society as well as participate in international programs to support emerging societies. They have joined a league of volunteers (and in many cases have been paid) to support community or regional interests; others have re-entered the workforce, using their skills to add value to a business, and still others have chosen to remain active in the field of sociology through their professional and technical skills. While this suggests that there is "another" life after retirement, it also reminds us that the skills and knowledge obtained during graduate school may provide an alternative avenue for today's graduates as they complete their graduate program and head into the world with their newly minted PhD.

All of this suggests that the skills developed and honed as a sociologist have prepared people for other productive activities that can contribute to the social justice of Canadian society; building an inclusive and accessible society, and bringing about a more knowledgeable and understanding society. Their knowledge and skills also can contribute to the development of other societies as they struggle to deal with issues of security, urbanization, poverty, and political turmoil. In the end, retired sociologists contribute to the enhancement of the quality of life. So, just what are those skills that have been learned, honed, and utilized during graduate school and in the academy that make them so valuable?

Being a Sociologist

Is there something unique about a PhD in sociology that allows individuals to make a contribution outside the academy? Or, are the knowledge and skills obtained in graduate school generic to all doctoral students? My argument is that there are many skills and training that are generic to most disciplines but that sociology is unique in being a discipline that allows its students to make important contributions to society.

One of the most important skills provided to sociology students falls in the area of methodology. Until recently, this focused on the use of statistical procedures to analyze data. Here sociologists were exemplary in their understanding and use of statistics to analyze a variety of data collected by government or the private sector. This skill, combined with a good understanding of theory, continues to provide sociologists with a strategy and technique that distinguishes itself from other disciplines. Sociologists' ability to reduce mass data sets to understandable interpretations has found favour in the world of the academy, business, NGOs, and government. In a related area, research methodology has provided sociologists with the knowledge and understanding of how to go about collecting and interpreting data. Whether the research focuses on research design, the building of questionnaires, or the understanding of what the parameters of an interview are, sociologists have unparalleled knowledge as to how to obtain reliable and valid information that is useful for applied as well as basic purposes. It is true that recently other social sciences and other areas of study—e.g., community health, political science—have come to see the usefulness of these skills, but they still have a lot of catching up to do.

Whether using quantitative or qualitative approaches, an inductive or a deductive perspective, sociology students also have achieved skills that allow them to have the capacity to effectively address complex problems or challenges presented to them. First, by understanding that a research question must be formulated, and then by developing strategies by which the question can be answered. By using a broad knowledge base that understands how the structure of society and the subsequent processes operate (in both domestic and international context), they are able to identify and research the variables that inform it; to appreciate and identify what other knowledge is required to more fully explain it; and to utilize that framework to construct and present a solution to a problem. In other words, inherent in this scheme are the concepts of theory, methodology, statistics, and interpretation.

Sociology students are taught to get beyond the individual level of understanding and develop a deeper understanding of the social. This means they understand what "social" entails and they can focus on the relationship between individual and macro-level factors. Thus sociologists show connections among the elements of its **units of analysis**. It also means that sociologists investigate the form and consequences of these connections. Finally, I should note that sociologists understand the concept of "**contextual embeddedness**" in the collection and interpretation of data (Snow, 1999).

In an articulate, literate way, sociology students are taught to build their writing skills as well as their community-building skills when needed. This requires a good understanding of historical analysis of social structure that embodies the models developed by earlier sociologists, e.g., Marx, Durkheim, Merton, Polanyi. In addition, sociology students learn to be creative and to engage in critical thinking that allows them to adapt to change and to deal with new challenges in a productive way. This perspective also allows sociologists the ability to innovate and to be able to develop new ideas as well as new approaches to problem solving.

The Future: New Directions

Can there really be a purpose for the PhD other than as preparation for the tenure track? For an increasing number of academics and students, the answer is "yes," but in many doctoral programs, outcomes other than permanent academic employment are not viewed positively (Fullick, 2013). Of the new variations of the traditional PhD, professional and work-based doctorates are now receiving some attention. For example, the New Route PhD (most evident in the UK), modelled on the North American doctoral model, includes course-based teaching (including research training), a small thesis, and a shorter time commitment (maximum of four years), but is no less rigorous intellectually. Other PhD programs, such as at Western and Concordia, are offering students training in soft skills, such as communication and teamwork, that will be useful whether they enter the labour market outside the academy or stay within the academy (Yachnin, 2015).

Conclusion

With all the un/under-employment anecdotal stories circulating, why do universities and governments continue to graduate increasing numbers of PhDs while at the same time cutting the institutional support? One reason is that they don't view the PhD as a path exclusively to the professoriate. The logic of the "new inorganic global economy" suggests that increasing the number of people with advanced degrees—"highly qualified personnel"—will lead to more economic development and a more inclusive society. Government doesn't want more professors, but it does want more highly educated people in many areas of the workforce. Unfortunately, governments can't ensure that students enter non-academic areas of the labour market (Fullick, 20130).

Nevertheless, the overall picture shows that many graduate programs are not providing students with the support needed to enter non-academic jobs (Mitchell et al., 2013). It is ironic that while departments and academics acknowledge the role they must play in securing funding and opportunities for PhD students, there is an astonishing culture of non-responsibility when it comes to ensuring that PhD graduates have academic or other jobs when they graduate. Why is this the case?

Two perspectives come to mind. First, evolutionary biology models suggest that equilibrium is based on long periods of relative stability punctuated by periodic bursts of rapid change, adjustment, and adaptation. A second explanation is Kuhn's model of scientific **paradigms**, built on the view of long periods of stability and a continuity of paradigms. These are then interrupted and challenged by phases of rapid change and paradigm shifts, usually driven by external factors (Park, 2005). As such, are we at the point of adaptation and about to undergo a paradigm shift?

Let's end on some good news, and that is that most doctoral graduates who leave the academy eventually find high-paying work. Statistics Canada's *2013 National Graduates Survey* looked at where the class of 2010 ended up three years later. Among doctoral and masters' graduates, employment rates ranged from 90 to 100 per cent (with median salaries ranging from $70,000 to $85,000), demonstrating that jobs are available—whether in or out of the academy.

References

Curtis, J. 2014. *The Employment Status of Instructional Staff Members in Higher Education, Fall, 2011*. Washington, DC: American Association of University Professors.

Baty, P. 2012. "Leader: Too Many Snakes, Too Few Ladders." *Times Higher Education*, June 14. Accessed 6 December 2016, at: www.timeshighereducation.com/comment/leader/leader-too-many-snakes-too-few-ladders/420262

Bowness, S. 2015. "What's Up with Alt-Ac Careers?" *University Affairs*, September 8. Accessed 6 December 2016, at: www.universityaffairs.ca/features/feature-article/whats-up-with-alt-ac-careers

Fullick, M. 2013. "Who Will Hire All the PhDs? Not Canada's Universities." *Globe and Mail*, April 12. Accessed 6 December 2016, at: www.theglobeandmail.com/news/national/education/who-will-hire-all-the-phds-not-canadas-universities/article10976412

Maldonado, V., R. Wiggers, and C. Arnold. 2013. *So You Want to Earn a PhD? The Attraction, Realities, and Outcomes of Pursuing a Doctorate*. Toronto: Higher Education Quality Council of Ontario.

Mason, M. 2012. "The Future of the PhD." *The Chronicle of Higher Education*, May 3. Retrieved from http://chronicle.com/article/The-Future-of-the-PhD/131749

Mitchell, J., V. Walker, R. Annan, T. Corkery, N. Goel, L. Harvey, D. Kent, J. Peters, and S. Vilches. 2013. *The 2013 Canadian Postdoc Survey: Painting a Picture of Canadian*

Postdoctoral Scholars. Canadian Association of Postdoctoral Scholars and Mitacs.

Noble, K.A. 1994. *Changing Doctoral Degrees: An International Perspective*. Buckingham: SRHE and Open University Press.

Park, C. 2005. "New Variant PhD: The Changing Nature of the Doctorate in the UK." *Journal of Higher Education Policy and Management* 27: 189–207.

Peters, W. 2014. "Defending the Academic Job." *CAUT Bulletin* 61: 5.

Snow, D. 1999. "The Value of Sociology." *Sociological Perspectives* 42: 1–22.

Yachnin, P. 2015. "Rethinking the Humanities PhD." *University Affairs*, March 11. Accessed 6 December 2016, at: www.universityaffairs.ca/features/feature-article/rethinking-the-humanities-phd

40 Aboriginal Education in Canada: Opportunities and Barriers

Terry Wotherspoon

Introduction

For several decades, Aboriginal organizations have called for "radical change" in education to address significant inequalities in levels of educational attainment between Aboriginal people and other Canadians (National Indian Brotherhood/Assembly of First Nations, 1972: 3). Their vision for education systems that are culturally appropriate and community controlled, endorsed by the federal government in the early 1970s, has since been echoed in numerous reports and action plans by governments, educational organizations, and other agencies (Assembly of First Nations, 2010; Council of Ministers of Education Canada, 2008). These calls for change have resulted in a vast array of initiatives to change educational orientations and practices, incorporating to some degree Indigenous content and perspectives in educational programming across the country. Despite many successes associated with these initiatives, however, the need to enhance education and improve educational attainment for the Aboriginal population remains one of the most pressing policy issues in Canada. This paper explores why, in the context of a society that has one of the most highly educated populations in the world, many of the objectives to meet educational aspirations for Aboriginal people remain unfulfilled.

Aboriginal People and Schooling in Canada

Canada's formal education system is very complex, reflecting regional and linguistic variations as well as other forms of diversity. Education, under the nation's constitution, is an area of provincial and territorial jurisdiction. In the case of First Nations people living on reserve, by contrast, education and other social services are operated by local bands under federal government jurisdiction. Because the government retains control over funding and other important decisions, First Nations are constrained in their capacity to transform schools effectively. In many cases, levels of funding and resources for band schools are lower than those for their provincial/territorial counterparts (Assembly of First Nations, 2012; Joint Task Force, 2013).

Aboriginal populations are heterogeneous, although they share a distinct heritage as descendants of the original occupants of North America. Various legal, constitutional, and historical arrangements differentiate persons with **Status** as First Nations, Métis, and Inuit from those in **Non-Status groups**. The terms of the Indian Act and treaty provisions, along with land claims and legal settlements, do not apply in the same way to all Indigenous people. **Aboriginal**

rights, which vary across First Nations and status groups, refer to guarantees related to cultural heritage, self-government, and land rights derived from longstanding relations with the land. For those who are eligible for particular types of government services, funding was meant to be derived from revenues produced from lands ceded through the treaties and other agreements with governments.

Aboriginal children and youth represent close to 7 per cent of Canada's school-age population. About four out of five Aboriginal students attend public schools in the provinces and territories in which they live; 17 per cent (representing 60 per cent of First Nations children and youth living on-reserve) attend **band schools** under federal authority; and the remaining 3 to 4 per cent attend private schools (calculated from data at Aboriginal Affairs and Northern Development Canada, 2015, and Statistics Canada, 2013a). Educational outcomes vary within and among Aboriginal status groups.

Table 40.1 illustrates these patterns with reference to an age cohort (25 to 44 years) in which people have typically completed most of their formal education. The ratios represent the proportions of various populations that have university degrees in comparison to those with less than high school (ratios below 1.0 refer to groups with relatively low education while those above 1.0 have higher average education levels). For men, and even more so for women, the ratios are substantially higher among the non-Aboriginal population than for all Aboriginal identity groups. There are also variations within the Aboriginal population. Members of only one Aboriginal population subgroup—Métis women—are more likely to be in the higher-education category, whereas the likelihood of being in the lower education groups is highest among Inuit and First Nations populations, especially those with status as registered or treaty Indians.

TABLE 40.1 Ratio of Population Ages 25 to 44 with University Degree to Those with Less Than High School, by Aboriginal Status and Gender, Canada, 2011

	Female	Male
First Nations	0.41	0.16
Registered or Treaty Status	0.36	0.13
Métis	1.19	0.56
Inuit	0.16	0.08
Aboriginal Total	0.56	0.25
Non-Aboriginal	4.86	2.75
TOTAL	4.30	2.47

Source: Calculated with data compiled from Statistics Canada, 2013b.

Measures to address disparities in educational outcomes and social conditions have drawn mixed public reactions. Greater numbers of Aboriginal people are attaining positions of leadership in important social and economic spheres, presenting strong role models and voices for Aboriginal people. Several high-profile events have also helped foster greater understanding about historical relations among Aboriginal people, European colonizers, and Canadian governments, and have drawn attention to contemporary conditions experienced by many Aboriginal people. A national Truth and Reconciliation Commission, established in 2008, has exposed the role played for over a century by residential schools (mostly operated by religious organizations under the authority of the federal government) in suppressing Indigenous cultures and destroying connections with families and communities for generations of Aboriginal people. Amid these developments, substantial proportions of the population remain wedded to stereotypes that portray the Aboriginal population as one that is largely welfare dependent and unwilling to change their lives (Banting, Soroka and Koning, 2013: 178–9). Aboriginal status is often perceived erroneously by many people as entitlement to special rights, funding, and other resources that are undeserved and not available to other Canadians (Ipsos, 2013). Greater awareness is needed to foster understanding and acknowledgement of conditions that have made it difficult for many Aboriginal people to gain meaningful access to the opportunities and lifestyles associated with life in a relatively affluent society.

Explaining Educational Inequalities

Several interrelated factors in addition to experiences related to residential schooling have contributed to differences in social and educational outcomes for Aboriginal people relative to the general population. These include lack of Aboriginal perspectives in school curricula and practices, limited representation by Aboriginal parents and educators, and differential treatment or racism in schools and other social settings (Joint Task Force, 2013). Action plans and initiatives devoted to eradicate inequalities and enhance education for Aboriginal people have produced some success, but there is a long way to go to achieve targeted objectives (Council of Ministers of Education Canada, 2008). Progress has been slow, due in part to inadequate resources to support implementation, competing demands on teachers' time and energies, and gaps in teachers' knowledge about Aboriginal issues and perspectives (St Denis, 2010; Wotherspoon, 2008, 2014).

Deeper contradictions also influence Aboriginal educational reform. As fundamental social, economic, and technological changes unfold on a global level, different segments of the population experience risks and opportunities in ways that are varied and unequal. Recognition of difference, diversity, and human rights is increasing at the same time that new identities, boundaries, and forms of exclusion are emerging. Sociologist Pierre Bourdieu (1998: 9) emphasizes that persons or groups who command significant resources are more likely to have the capacity to protect themselves against these risks while those not so equipped must struggle to contend with rules and limits set by the powerful. One of the manifestations of these changes occurs in the form of what Henry and Tator (2010) refer to as "democratic racism." This concept describes social conditions in which racism and other forms of discrimination are sustained even when legal and ideological commitments exist to protect democratic practice and principles of equity and socio-economic opportunity.

In the case of Aboriginal educational reform, these contradictions represent a form of "**democratic colonialism**" (Wotherspoon, 2014). Initiatives to reform education are linked with Aboriginal people's desires to achieve their aspirations with respect to recognition of Aboriginal rights and status within broader formal, liberal democratic commitments to equity and opportunity. However, many Aboriginal people continue to encounter racism and other barriers that restrict their chances to succeed in schooling and other social sites.

Schooling represents both part of the experience of colonization and a pathway linked with futures away from colonial legacies. Many early European missionaries and settlers employed education as a tool to devalue Aboriginal people and their knowledge as they occupied their territories or sought to liberate them from what were often considered uncivilized ways of life. Beginning in the late nineteenth century, the Canadian government continued efforts to separate Aboriginal children from their cultural heritage and social ties through residential schooling and other policies focused on assimilation. Although residential school experiences varied across the country, the overall legacy has been devastating to Aboriginal people and their communities, as reflected in the thousands of deaths; high rates of physical, sexual, and psychological abuse; radical breaks in family and cultural connections; and other forms of serious damage in the lives and relationships of many survivors and members of their families and communities (Truth and Reconciliation Commission of Canada, 2015). Governments and other agencies also repeatedly subordinated and regulated the lives of Aboriginal people in many other ways not experienced by other Canadians. Such policies and practices included suppression of food supplies for many communities confronted with serious illness and starvation, failure to respond adequately to outbreaks of communicable diseases in residential schools and First Nations communities, strict regulation of daily reserve life by government agents, and high rates of custody in the context of child welfare and criminal justice agencies (Daschuk, 2013; Truth and Reconciliation Commission, 2015).

By contrast, many recent actions have helped to increase recognition of Aboriginal voices and perspectives while advancing among Canadians in general greater awareness of the significance and nature of Aboriginal issues and experiences. In 2008, the federal government issued a formal apology for its role in establishing residential schools, while the Truth and Reconciliation Commission has drawn attention to the realities encountered by school survivors and their family members. The Idle No More movement has opened conversations about Aboriginal rights and social conditions while highlighting government actions that have endangered these relationships. Several court challenges have also resulted in decisions that uphold or define in more specific terms the nature of Aboriginal rights.

Despite these developments, many Aboriginal people continue to encounter obstacles as they seek to achieve their social and educational aspirations. Negative stereotypes are reinforced through a sense of "otherness" in which Aboriginal people and conditions are differentiated from other Canadians. Aboriginal rights are frequently misinterpreted in accordance with liberal notions that all Canadians should have equal rights. Education gaps are often framed in terms of student "deficits," thereby turning attention away from other systemic factors, including racial discrimination or exclusion that may contribute to unequal outcomes.

More generally, governments have promoted market-oriented policies, including investment in resource extraction industries, as a way to foster economic opportunity for Aboriginal communities. In the process, obligations to consult and work with First Nations on major resource projects that affect Aboriginal lands and communities are often ignored (Wotherspoon and Hansen, 2013). Moreover, many such projects have had little impact on employment prospects for Aboriginal people, and some, more seriously, have endangered water supplies, environmental conditions, and other physical and social conditions in Aboriginal communities. Funding has been diverted from successful early childhood programs and other educational and community development activities in order to support some of these initiatives (Wotherspoon, 2014: 330–1), while schools in many First Nations and other Aboriginal communities frequently lack essential facilities such as safe drinking water, electrical services, or adequate curricular resources (Joint Task Force, 2013; Assembly of First Nations, 2012). In short, numerous interrelated factors have made it difficult to accomplish effective educational and social reform despite widespread commitments to such change.

Future Prospects

Canadians have begun to acknowledge historical relationships that have given rise to differential status and places occupied by Aboriginal people. The recent report of the Truth and Reconciliation Commission (2015: 113) stresses that Canadians must acknowledge the harm of past events and processes that threatened to destroy Aboriginal cultures and communities, and they must simultaneously undertake actions to establish relationships built upon mutual respect and engagement between Aboriginal and non-Aboriginal Canadians. Schooling, which can variously give rise to and impede hopes of a better future, is itself being transformed through these relationships.

References

Aboriginal Affairs and Northern Development Canada. "Federal Funding Levels for First Nations K-12 Education." Ottawa: Aboriginal Affairs and Northern Development Canada, https://www.aadnc-aandc.gc.ca/eng/1349140116208/1349140158945

Assembly of First Nations. 2010. *First Nations Control of First Nations Education: It's Our Vision, It's Our Time.* Ottawa: Assembly of First Nations, July.

Assembly of First Nations. 2012. *A Portrait of First Nations and Education.* Gatineau, QC: AFN Chiefs Assembly on Education.

Banting, Keith, Stuart Soroka, and Edward Koning. 2013. "Multicultural Diversity and Redistribution," in Keith Banting and John Myles, eds. *Inequality and the Fading of Redistributive Politics*. Vancouver: UBC Press, 165–86.

Bourdieu, Pierre. 1998. *Practical Reason: On the Theory of Action*. Stanford, CA: Stanford University Press.

Council of Ministers of Education Canada. 2008. *Learn Canada 2020: Joint Declaration. Provincial and Territorial Ministers of Education*. Toronto: Council of Ministers of Education Canada, April 15.

Daschuk, James. 2013. *Clearing the Plains: Disease, Politics of Starvation, and the Loss of Aboriginal Life*. Regina, SK: University of Regina Press.

Henry, Frances and Carol Tater. 2010. *The Colour of Democracy: Racism in Canadian Society*, 4th edn. Scarborough, ON: Nelson.

Ipsos. 2013. "Fast fallout: Chief Spence and Idle No More movement galvanizes Canadians around money management and accountability," Ipsos News Release, January 15. Accessed 9 March 2015 at: http://www.ipsos-na.com/news-polls/pressrelease.aspx?id=5961

Joint Task Force on Improving Education and Employment Outcomes for First Nations and Métis People. 2013. *Voice, Vision and Leadership: A Please for All. Final Report*. Saskatoon: Federation of Saskatchewan Indian Nations and Government of Canada.

National Indian Brotherhood/Assembly of First Nations. 1972. *Indian Control of Indian Education*. Policy Paper presented to the Minister of Indian Affairs and Northern Development. Ottawa: National Indian Brotherhood/Assembly of First Nations.

Statistics Canada. 2013a. *National Household Survey, Data Tables: Aboriginal Identity, Age Groups*. Ottawa: Statistics Canada, Catalogue no. 99-011-X2011026.

Statistics Canada. 2013b. *National Household Survey, Data Tables: Highest Certificate, Diploma or Degree, Registered or Treaty Indian Status, Aboriginal Identity*. Ottawa: Statistics Canada, Catalogue no. 99-011-X2011037.

St Denis, Verna. 2010. *A Study of Aboriginal Teachers' Professional Knowledge and Experience in Canadian Schools*. Ottawa: Canadian Teachers' Federation and Canadian Council on Learning, March.

Truth and Reconciliation Commission of Canada. 2015. *What We Have Learned: Principles of Truth and Reconciliation*. Ottawa: The Truth and Reconciliation Commission of Canada.

Wotherspoon, Terry. 2008. "Teachers' Work Intensification and Educational Contradictions in Aboriginal Communities," *Canadian Review of Sociology* 45, 4, 389–418.

Wotherspoon, Terry. 2014. "Seeking Reform of Indigenous Education in Canada: Democratic Progress or Democratic Colonialism?" *AlterNative* 10, 4, 323–39.

Wotherspoon, Terry and John Hansen. 2013. "The 'Idle No More' Movement: Paradoxes of First Nations Inclusion in the Canadian Context," *Social Inclusion* 1, 1, 21–36.

Questions for Critical Thought

Chapter 37 | Life at Armyville High School: A Glimpse into How Adolescents Experienced the Afghanistan Missions

1. Imagine what it might be like to have a parent on a dangerous military deployment. How do you think it would affect your daily activities? Your level of school engagement?
2. Describe Armyville. What makes this community unique? How might school experiences in this community be like those in other communities? Do you think the size and location/isolation of a military community affects adolescent experiences in schools? Might youth growing up in military families have difference experiences when bases are located in bigger cities?
3. During a parent's deployment, adolescents typically keep stressful information to themselves in order to avoid placing more stress on their undeployed parent. Give some examples from the chapter of what adolescents kept from their parents. What is the cost of their silence?
4. What role should educators and schools have in mitigating adolescence stress over deployment? How have they handled it in Armyville?
5. What solution do Harrison and Albanese propose for reducing adolescence stress over deployment? Can you think of any other solutions, both in and outside of schools?

Chapter 38 | The African Brain Drain and the Social Impact of Family Separation

1. What might Canada look like if it experienced a "brain drain"? Who would be most affected? In what ways?
2. Boyo explains the African brain drain through a push–pull theory. What does this mean? How does the push-pull affect immigrant and emigrant countries?
3. Who dominates the discussion around "brain drain"? Why is this problematic?
4. What is the effect of migration on families? Comment on family separation and expectations.
5. What is the benefit of examining the lived experiences of African migrants or the anti-colonial approach? How does this help us to better understand the African brain drain?

Chapter 39 | Drivers of Innovative Strategies to Meet the Needs of the New Inorganic Global Economy

1. Consider all the courses you are currently taking. How many of them are taught by "sessional" instructors? How do you think their lives and careers compare to professors with full-time university employment?
2. Have you ever considered pursuing a PhD? If yes, is it so that you can become a professor? Frideres says that only one-third of individuals with a PhD have an academic job. What alternative career options exist for individuals who have a PhD?
3. What can be learned from elders? How do retired academics spend their time? How would you spend your time if you were a retired professor?
4. What skills do sociology students learn? How can these be leveraged on the job market?
5. If the number of jobs in academia is decreasing, why do you think that universities take on so many PhD students?

Chapter 40 | Aboriginal Education in Canada: Opportunities and Barriers

1. What are some of the barriers that hinder the creation of culturally appropriate and community-controlled schools for Aboriginal people?
2. Looking at the entire Aboriginal population, which group of people is most likely to obtain a higher education?
3. What conditions have made it difficult for many Aboriginal people to gain meaningful access to the opportunities and lifestyles associated with life in a relatively affluent society?
4. What is "democratic racism"? How does this impact Aboriginal people?
5. Why is increasing the levels of education among Aboriginal people important? What are some of the barriers that they face?

PART X
Work and the Economy

This section discusses some of the current research that is being done on the sociology of work and the economy. Paid work takes up a large part of many people's lives in Canada. Here and in other countries, we cannot understand the nature and structure of paid work without understanding the organization of the economy.

Here as elsewhere, the "economy" refers to those social institutions that manage the wealth and resources of a country. In Canada, with a capitalist economic system, most "goods" and "services" are privately owned, though they are regulated to various degrees by government legislation. "Goods" are tangible items that meet either essential or non-essential needs, and include food, housing, clothing, iPads, cosmetics, and other consumer items. By contrast, "services" are less tangible but no less important performances by others for our benefit; they may include food preparation, health care, entertainment, and sociology courses.

Under capitalism, people's access to needed goods and services is unequal and, for many, quite uncertain. As noted, the capitalist system is based on private ownership, even including (as Marx pointed out) private ownership of the means of production. This means that wealthy individuals and powerful corporations own businesses that range from coffee shops up to financial institutions. The owners of these businesses control the hiring of workers, with two main consequences. First, the business owners have more wealth than their workers. Second, the workers have less certain employment (and life chances) than the business owners.

This sounds simple and obvious, but it is not always obvious to everyone. Modern capitalism relies on a complex division of labour and social stratification, not to mention what Noam Chomsky called "manufactured consent" by the media and political ruling classes.

As you may remember from Part 5, on inequality, there is a cultural assumption in Canada that if you work hard and get an education, you will be successful, despite the complexity and inequality of our economy. This belief in "meritocracy"—the belief that merit will determine a person's place within the economy—masks a wide range of inequalities that prevent many working-class people from gaining jobs that provide higher pay and more status than that enjoyed by their parents. In Chapter 41, Monica Boyd tackles this issue with particular respect to immigrant offspring.

As Karen Foster reminds us in Chapter 42, the structure and productivity of economically developed countries has only gradually evolved from small agricultural economies to complex knowledge economies. Foster asks us to consider how we came to value "productivity" so highly.

Today, many of the employment opportunities in a developed economy are "knowledge-based," meaning that they require some form of higher education. With the growth of this knowledge-based economy, more people need degrees from post-secondary institutions to be competitive candidates in the job market. And with more highly educated applicants in the job market, employers can be more particular about the people they hire. A job that would have previously required a high school diploma may now require a bachelor's degree; and jobs that previously required a bachelor's degree now require a master's degree. David Livingstone, in Chapter 43, writes about the challenges associated with this credential inflation in the job market, and how this has led to widespread "underemployment." Livingstone shows that today, many people are over-qualified for the jobs they are performing.

In Chapter 44, Leslie Nichols documents how unemployed women struggle to gain employment based on factors that go beyond their "merit." On a very similar note, in Chapter 45, Cornelia Schneider writes about the work experiences of individuals with disabilities.

Among other things, this section focuses on the ways in which the Canadian economy has changed, and how this in turn has changed occupational, education, and social inequalities.

41 Race and the Labour Market Integration of Second-Generation Young Adults

Monica Boyd

Introduction

International migration is a defining characteristic of Canadian life. One in five (22 per cent) is foreign born. In addition, the origins, ethnicities, and phenotypical characteristics of immigrants are diverse; in 2011, six of ten were persons of colour. Finally, because many immigrants are young adults in the family building stages, the **second generation**—Canadian-born children with one or both parents foreign born—is large, standing at 17 per cent or one in six in 2011 (Boyd 2015; Boyd and Alboim 2012; Boyd and Vickers 2016; Statistics Canada 2013).

The 2001 census of Canada was the first since 1971 to include questions on the birthplace of parents, thus separating the Canadian born into those with foreign-born parents (second generation) and those with two Canadian-born parents (**third-plus generation**). Until then, a main concern of sociologists was how well immigrants integrated into the labour market, but these new distinctions have enabled them to ask how well the children of immigrants are doing. Importantly for such research, the 2001 and 2006 censuses document socio-economic differentials between non-white children of immigrants and the third-plus generation (Abada, Hou, and Lu 2014; Abada and Lin 2014; Aydemir and Sweetman 2006; Picot and Hou 2011; Reitz, Zhang, and Hawkins 2011; Skuterud 2010; Wilkinson 2008), with most attention paid to earnings differentials; less frequently studied measures include educational attainments, high school dropout rates, unemployment, and binary indicators of occupations. This chapter extends earlier research by examining recent data on educational, occupational, and earnings outcomes for the **visible minority** second generation in Canada.

Conceptual Models and Data Sources

In North America, the linear "**assimilation**" model envisions that immigrant offspring will fall between the foreign-born and later generations in their economic integration and acculturation. This model was revised in the 1990s, producing three additional models: the "immigrant optimism" model, the "ethnic segmentation" model, and the "reactive segmentation" model (Boyd and Grieco 1998; Kao and Tienda 1995; Portes and Zhou 1993). The optimism model anticipates the socio-economic over-achievement of the second generation compared to parents and the third-plus generation, usually emphasizing educational attainments. In contrast, both segmentation models see second-generation racial and ethnic minorities as continuing to have strong ethnic and racial identities and living their lives either within an ethnic enclave (such as Chinatowns) or rejecting the values of the larger society and experiencing downward mobility with potential for crime-based livelihoods.

The models have two main characteristics in common. First, because they originated in the United States, their terminology emphasizes *assimilation*, generally defined as the decline of ethnic distinctions, in values, norms, cultural practices, and economic outcomes, to the point where great similarity exists between migrant origin populations and a dominant majority (white Anglo-Saxon). In Canada, the term *integration* is used instead, referring to social and economic inclusion in society but with groups free to value and maintain cultural and social patterns associated with their ethnic or national-origin groups (Alba and Foner 2016; Berry 1997); such adherence, however, cannot elicit harm as defined by the norms and laws of Canada—for example, spousal or child violence or refusal to educate children.

Second, no one assimilation perspective fits all groups of immigrant offspring. Some groups seem to fit into one model, such as Chinese offspring in the US who work and live in Chinatowns, or Cubans who are part of "Little Cuba" in Miami. Others, such as Haitian offspring in Miami, seem reflective of segmented assimilation with downward mobility, while still others, such as Dominicans in New York City, have benefited from affirmative action legislation and are upwardly mobile (Portes and Zhou 1993; Kasinitz, Mollenkopf, and Waters 2004). Additionally, different outcome measures can produce different results. Second-generation North Americans often overachieve educationally, supporting the over-optimism model (Boyd 2002, 2008; Boyd and Grieco 1998). Analyses of earnings are less sanguine, however, suggesting that some minorities earn less.

In short, assimilation models represent "**ideal types**"; as elaborated by sociologist Max Weber (1968), each model illuminates characteristics and elements of a particular manifestation of assimilation (or integration), and not all individuals will conform to a specific model. Further, the range of models indicates that groups with different phenotypical characteristics may take different pathways and experience different outcomes.

National censuses do not collect data on many variables and processes identified in segmentation models; these data are better suited for assessing if assimilation or success orientation models hold. Outcome variables of interest are usually educational attainment, occupational location, and earnings. In stratification research, level of education imperfectly captures the impact of social origins to the extent that parental education usually influences the educational attainments of their children. That said, level of education also captures analytical training, often associated with better jobs, higher-status occupations, and higher earnings. Occupations represent bundles of activities performed in the labour force; they are of sociological interest because they indicate the relative locations of workers in an occupational hierarchy, which, in turn, is usually linked to earnings and various other work dimensions, including work autonomy, supervision, and power. In a monetarized economy, earnings are important because they convert into other benefits; for example, earnings permit purchasing goods and services that improve the quality of life, including type and amount of food, shelter, and health care.

This chapter compares the education, occupations, and earnings for minority children of immigrants using the 2011 National Household Survey (NHS), a voluntary survey of a sample of approximately 4.5 million private households. Replicating earlier censuses, the NHS asked, "Is this person XXXX?" thereby producing information on Canada's racial groups, commonly called "visible minorities" (Boyd 2015; Boyd, Goldmann, and White 2000). Although visible minority labels homogenize diverse groups under banner headings (Black, South Asian, etc.) and are socially constructed by federal employment equity legislation, alternative ethnic origin data are problematic because of selective attrition across generations (Duncan and Trejo, 2011). In Canada, persons who self-designate as Arab, West Asian, and Latin American are not considered "white" unless they also respond "white." Persons identifying as Aboriginals (Canada's native peoples) are a separate group under the Employment Equity Act and they are not included here.

The visible minority second generation is young, with two-thirds under the age of 18 and eight in ten under 25 (Table 41.1). In contrast, the white second and third generations are mostly 25 and older. Within the working-age population (25–64), the visible minority second generation is mostly under 40; the white second and third generations are more likely to be 40–64. This means analyses of the overall working population, aged 25–64, conflate

TABLE 41.1 Age Distribution of the Second Generation by Visible Minority Status and of the Third-Plus Generation White Population, Canada 2011

	Second Generation, Visible Minority	Second Generation, White	Third-Plus Generation, White
Total	100	100	100
0–17	64	18	21
18–24	15	8	10
25–39	17	19	19
40–64	4	36	38
65 plus	1	19	12

Sources: Computed by the author especially for this chapter from Statistics Canada 2011 National Household Survey Public Use Microdata File on Individuals.

a young visible minority second generation with a much older white group with greater labour force experience and earnings. Accordingly, this chapter only considers the population aged 25–39. In addition to "white," the second generation is divided into eight visible minority groups, with small groups (Japanese, Korean, etc.) constituting "all other visible minorities." Following earlier studies, these groups are compared to a reference group—in this case, the white third-plus generation, representing six in ten Canadians and consisting primarily of the historically dominant British and French populations.

Education, Occupational Location, and Earnings

Children of immigrants tend to surpass the Canadian third-plus generation in education. Figures 41.1 and 41.2 show the percentages having lower levels of education (no more than a high school diploma) and the percentages having higher educational attainments (bachelor's degrees or higher). Of all second-generation visible minorities, only Latin Americans have higher percentages of low educational attainments when compared to the white third-plus generation (Figure 41.1). Latin Americans also have lower percentages boasting a university education (bachelor's degrees or higher) than the white third-plus generation. On average, the Black second generation is similar to the white reference group in higher educational attainments, with about one in four having received bachelor's degrees or higher. However, most groups, especially those who self-designate as Chinese and South Asians, surpass the white third-plus generation in the percentages having university degrees or post-university degrees (Figure 41.2). These findings of higher-educational attainments for most of the second-generation groups defined by race mirror those of earlier studies (Abada and Tenkorang 2009; Abada, Hou, and Ram 2009; Picot and Hou 2011).

The NHS has organized occupational information on 500 occupational titles. These are collapsed into 30 categories in the Public Use Microdata Files (PUMF) of individuals. Because large arrays make interpreting occupational differences among the second generation cumbersome, two summary measures are used to indicate the occupational locations of the second generation.

One measure is the occupational socio-economic score. This ranks occupational categories according to the educational and earnings characteristics of all incumbents in each category. Following Boyd (2008), socio-economic scores are constructed for the 30 occupational titles; the score indicates what percentages of the overall population hold occupations with lower composite scores for education and earnings. For example, the white third-plus generation has an average score of 56 points, which places them above 56 per cent of the entire labour force who are working in occupations that are ranked lower (Figure 41.3). Here again, second-generation Latin Americans perform poorly, with lower average socio-economic scores than those of the white third-plus generation, indicating that this second-generation group works in occupations characterized by lower educational

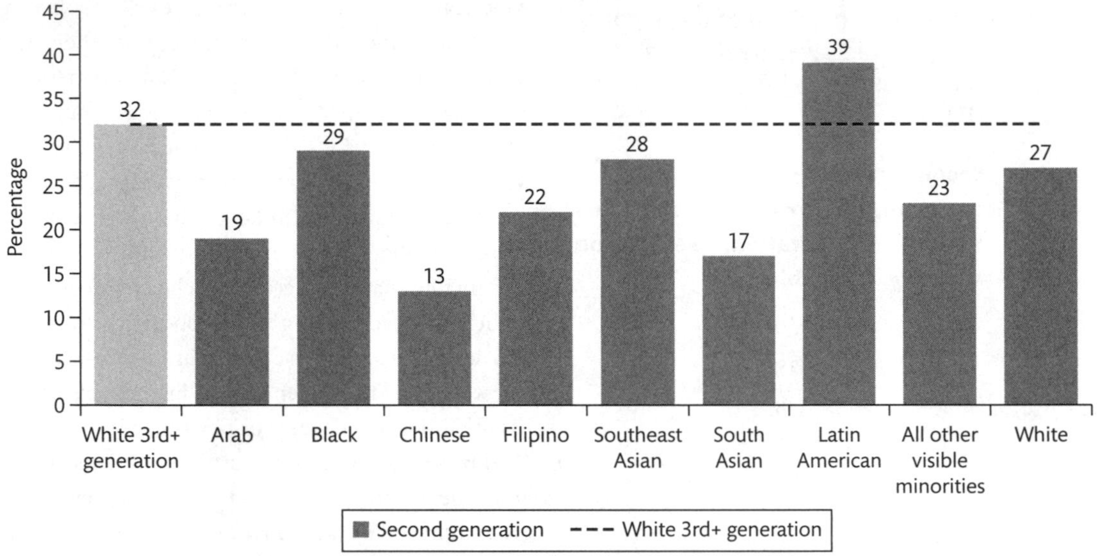

FIGURE 41.1 Percentage with No Post-secondary Degree, by Generation and Visible Minority Status, Age 25–39, Canada 2011

Source: Statistics Canada. 2011 NHS Public Use File of Individuals.

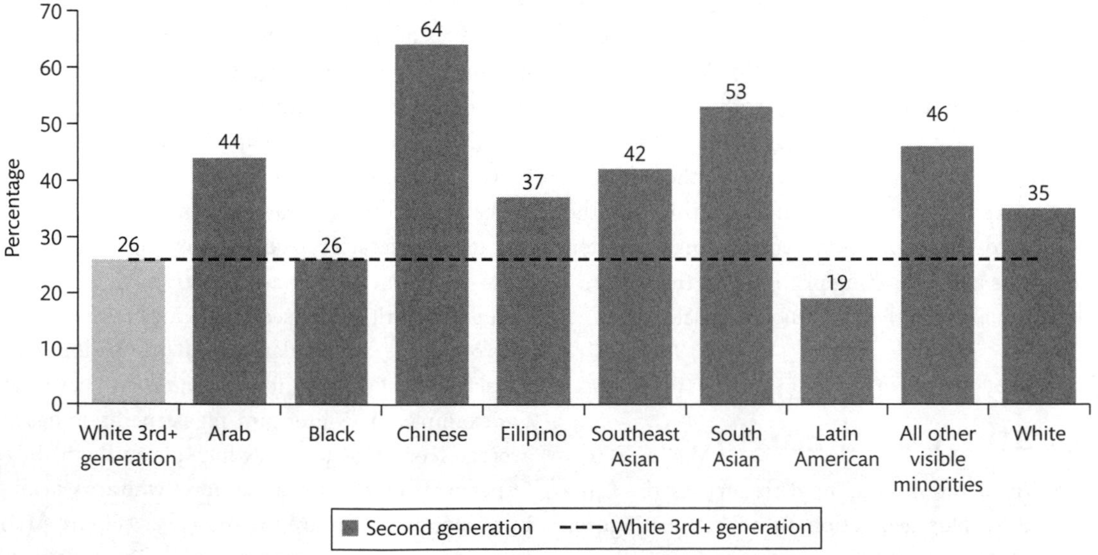

FIGURE 41.2 Percentage with Bachelors' Degrees or Higher, by Generation and Visible Minority Status, Age 25–39, Canada 2011

Source: Statistics Canada. 2011 NHS Public Use File of Individuals.

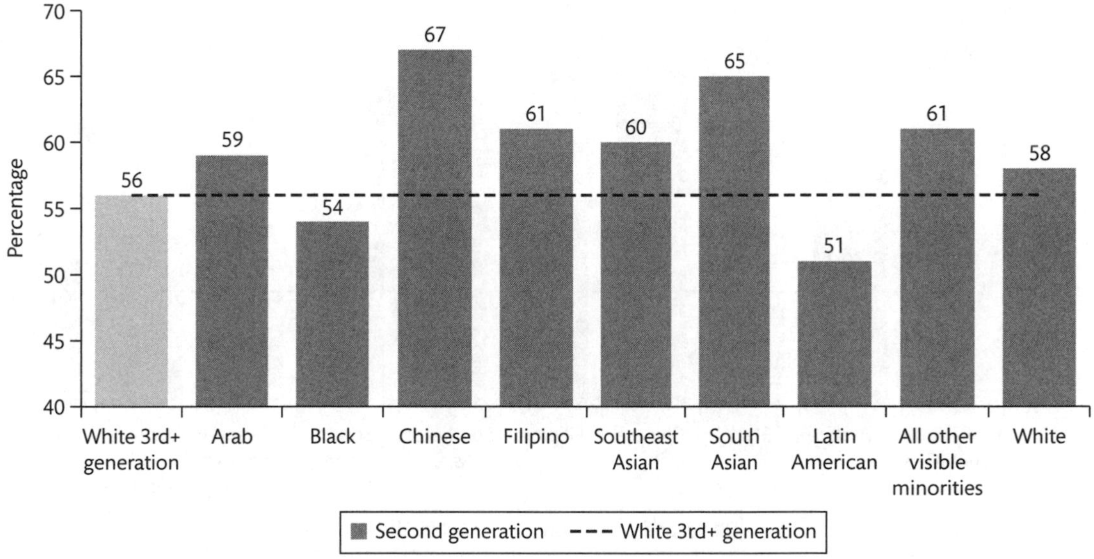

FIGURE 41.3 Average Occupational Socio-economic Scores, by Generation and Visible Minority Status, Ages 25–39, Canada 2011

Source: Statistics Canada. 2011 NHS Public Use File of Individuals, using SES scores calculated by author.

levels and earnings. In contrast, scores for the Black second generation are similar to those for the white third-plus generation. Other visible minority groups have occupational scores suggesting they are in occupations where workers, in general, have higher levels of education and/or earnings than the third-plus generation. The second-generation Chinese and South Asian groups are the most likely to be in highly ranked occupations; average occupational scores place them above nearly two-thirds of the entire work force.

Working in a high-skill occupation is a second measure used to rank groups. The definition is based on the National Occupational Classification developed by Human Resources and Social Development Canada. High-skill occupations are non-management occupations that usually require university education. Second-generation Latin Americans have the lowest percentages in high-skill occupations, while second-generation Blacks approximate the level of the white third-plus generation (Figure 41.4). Other groups have higher percentages than the white third-plus generation; the Chinese, South Asian, and Arab second-generation groups have the highest percentages, at 40, 36, and 31 per cent respectively.

Earnings differentials for second-generation visible minorities compared to the white third-plus generation follow similar patterns: average earnings for most second-generation groups are higher than those for the white third-plus generation (Figure 41.5), with Chinese and South Asians having the highest earnings of all. The Latin American second generation has average earnings below those of the white third-plus generation; second-generation Blacks have the lowest earnings of all groups. This last finding is unexpected; given the similarity between the Black educational and occupational profiles and those of the white third-plus generation, earnings should be similar.

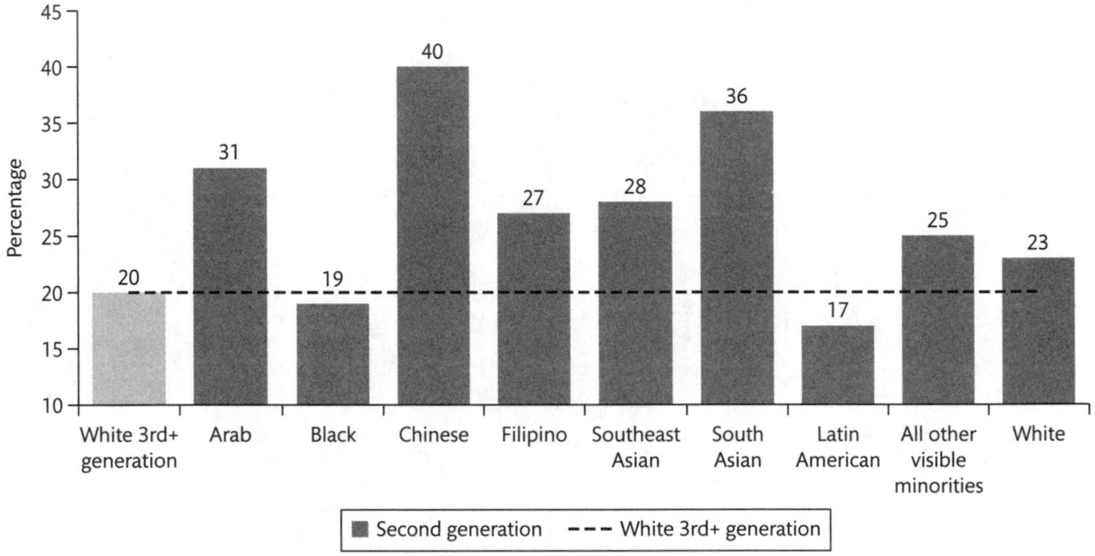

FIGURE 41.4 Percentage in High-Skilled Occupations, by Generation and Visible Minority Status, Age 25–39

Source: Statistics Canada. 2011 NHS Public Use File of Individuals.

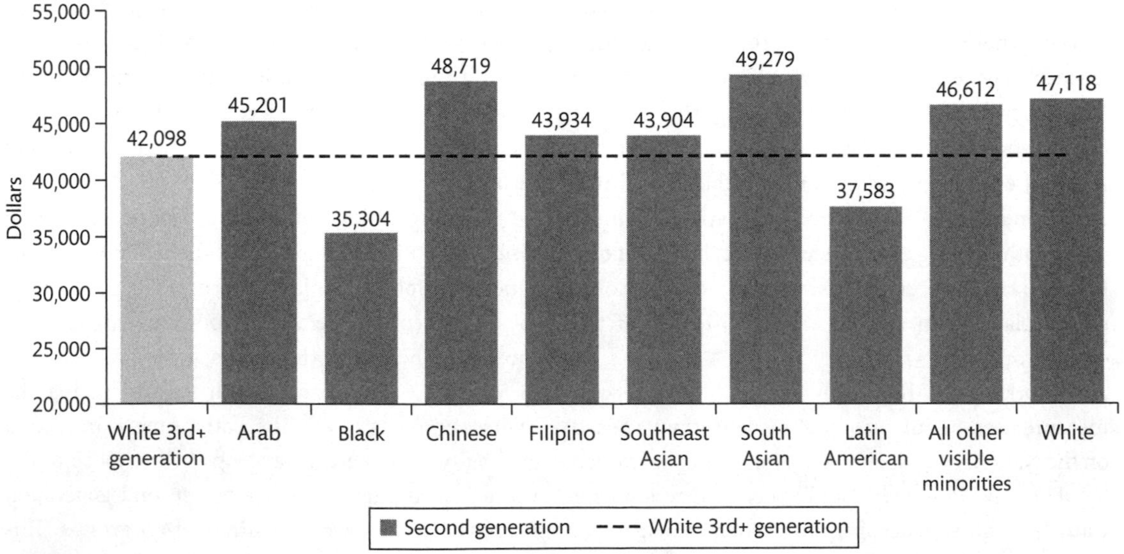

FIGURE 41.5 Average Annual Earning in 2010, by Generation and Visible Minority Status, Age 25–39, Canada 2011

Source: Statistics Canada. 2011 NHS Public Use File of Individuals.

Conclusion

Using the 2011 NHS, this chapter analyzes Canada's second generation in the labour market, focusing on level of education, occupational socio-economic status, per cent in high-skill occupations, and annual earnings. Because educational attainments are highly associated with occupations and earnings, the basic educational profiles tend to be replicated in the occupational and earnings charts. With the exception of the Latin American and Black second generations, most visible minority second generations, on average, have higher occupational status, higher percentages working in high-skill occupations, and higher earnings than the white third-plus generation. The findings are consistent with the immigrant optimism model in that most visible minority second-generation groups have higher levels of education than the white third-plus generation. However, the data also confirm that not all groups have the same labour market experiences; the Latin American and Black second generations either do worse or are similar to the white third-plus population, findings which merit further investigation.

Multivariate research could ask what would be the occupations and earnings of the visible minority second generation if all groups hypothetically had the same educational distributions (see Boyd and Tian 2015). Investigating the roles of other labour market characteristics (full/part-time, sector of employment, ethnic employers, etc.) in shaping the occupations and earnings of second-generation visible minorities would also yield additional insights into their labour market integration.

References

Abada, Teresa, Feng Hou, and Yuqian Lu. 2014. "Choice or Necessity: Do Immigrants and Their Children Choose Self-Employment for the Same Reasons?" *Work, Employment and Society* 28, 1: 78–94.

Abada, Teresa, and Sylvia Lin. 2014. "Labour Market Outcomes of the Children of Immigrants in Ontario," *Canadian Studies in Population* 41, 1-2: 78–96.

Abada, Teresa, Feng Hou, and Bali Ram. 2009. "Ethnic Differences in Educational Attainment among the Children of Canadian Immigrants," *Canadian Journal of Sociology* 34, 1: 1–28.

Abada, Teresa, and Eric Y. Tenkorang. 2009. "Pursuit of University Education among the Children of Immigrants in Canada: The Roles of Parental Human Capital and Social Capital," *Journal of Youth Studies* 12, 2: 185–207.

Alba, Richard, and Nancy Foner. 2016. "Integration's Challenges and Opportunities in the Wealthy West," *Journal of Ethnic and Migration Studies* 42, 1: 3–22.

Aydemir, Abdurrahman, and Arthur Sweetman. 2006. "First- and Second-Generation Immigrant Educational Attainment and Labor Market Outcomes: A Comparison of the United States and Canada," *Research in Labor Economics* 27: 215–70.

Berry, John W. 1997. "Immigration, Acculturation, and Adaptation," *Applied Psychology Review* 46: 5–68.

Boyd, Monica. 2002. "Educational Attainments of Immigrant Offspring: Success or Segmented Assimilation?" *International Migration Review* 36, Winter: 1037–60.

Boyd, Monica. 2008. "Social Origins and the Educational and Occupational Achievements of the 1.5 and Second Generations," *Canadian Review of Sociology* 46, 4 : 339–69.

Boyd, Monica. 2015. "Ethnicity and Race in Canada: Past and Present." Pp. 23–45 in Rogelio Sáenz, David G. Embrick, and Néstor P. Rodríguez (eds) *International Handbook of the Demography of Race and Ethnicity.* Springer: New York.

Boyd, Monica, and Elizabeth Grieco. 1998. "Triumphant Transitions: Socioeconomic Achievements of the Second Generation in Canada," *International Migration Review* 22, 4: 857–76.

Boyd, Monica, Gustave Goldmann, and Pamela White. 2000. "Race in the Canadian Census." Pp. 33–54 in Leo Driedger and Shiva Halli (eds) *Visible Minorities in Canada.* Montreal and Toronto: McGill-Queen's University Press and Carleton University Press.

Boyd, Monica, and Naomi Alboim. 2012. "Managing International Migration: The Canadian Case." Pp. 123–50 in Dan Rodríguez-García (ed) *Managing Immigration and Diversity in Canada: A Transatlantic Dialogue in the New Age of Migration.* Montreal and Kingston: McGill-Queen's University Press, Queen's Policy Studies Series.

Boyd, Monica, and Siyue Tian. 2016. "Educational and Labor Market Attainments of the 1.5- and Second-Generation Children of East Asian Immigrants in Canada." *American Behavioral Scientist* 60, 5–6: 705–29.

Boyd, Monica, and Michael Vickers. 2016. "The Ebb and Flow of Immigration in Canada." Pp. 155–72 in Edward Grabb, Jeffrey G. Reitz, and Monica Hwang (eds) *Social Inequality in Canada: Dimensions of Disadvantage*, 6th revised edition. Toronto: Oxford University Press.

Duncan, Brian, and Stephen J. Trejo. 2011. "Tracking Intergenerational Progress for Immigrant Groups: The Problem of Ethnic Attrition." *American Economic Review: Papers & Proceedings* 101, 3: 603–8.

Kao, Grace, and Marta Tienda. 1995. "Optimism and Achievement: The Educational Performance of Immigrant Youth," *Social Science Quarterly* 76, 1: 1–19.

Kasinitz, Philip, John H. Mollenkopf, and Mary C. Waters (eds). 2004. *Becoming New Yorkers: Ethnographies of the New Second Generation*. New York: Russell Sage.

Picot, Garnett, and Feng Hou. 2011. "Preparing for Success in Canada and the United States: The Determinants of Educational Attainment among the Children of Immigrants." Statistics Canada Analytical Studies Branch Research Paper Series No. 332, March. Available at: www.statcan.gc.ca/pub/11f0019m/11f0019m2011332-eng.pdf

Portes, Alejandro, and Min Zhou. 1993. "The New Second Generation: Segmented Assimilation and Its Variants," *The Annals of the American Academy of Political and Social Science* 530: 74–96.

Reitz, Jeffrey G., Heather Zhang, and Naoko Hawkins. 2011. "Comparisons of the Success of Racial Minority Immigrant Offspring in the United States, Canada and Australia," *Social Science Research* 40, 4: 1051–66.

Skuterud, Mikal. 2010. "The Visible Minority Earnings Gap across Generations of Canadians," *Canadian Journal of Economics* 43, 3: 860–81.

Statistics Canada. 2013. Data table: "National Household Survey: Immigration and Ethnocultural Diversity—Visible Minority (15), Generation Status (4), Age Groups (10) and Sex (3) for the Population in Private Households of Canada, Provinces, Territories, Census Metropolitan Areas and Census Agglomerations, 2011 National Household Survey." Catalogue Number 99-010-X2011029. Available at: http://www5.statcan.gc.ca/olc-cel/olc.action?objId=99-010-X2011029&objType=46&lang=en&limit=0

Weber, Max. 1968. *Economy and Society: An Outline of Interpretive Sociology.* Guenther Roth and Claus Wittich (eds), New York: Bedminster Press.

Wilkinson, Lori. 2008. "Labor Market Transitions of Immigrant-Born, Refugee-Born, and Canadian-Born Youth," *Canadian Journal of Sociology* 45, 2: 151–76.

42 Productivity and Prosperity: A Study in the Sociology of Ideas

Karen Foster

Why Do We Care about Productivity?

In an online essay for the *Sociological Review* in 2015, Nicholas Gane argued that while sociologists have been very good at describing the *consequences* of the global financial crisis of 2008, we have not done nearly enough to explain how it happened. We have also failed to address how it came to be that many "solutions" for the crisis have emerged from the same perspective—what some might call **neoliberalism** or **market fundamentalism** (Somers and Block, 2005; Somers, 2008)—that arguably spurred it in the first place. In Gane's view, the discipline needs to do more "historical and theoretical work" to "address the mechanisms that have made [such solutions] not only possible but also legitimate in the eyes of an electorate" (Gane, 2015). In ignoring this challenge, he wrote, we miss "an opportunity to challenge the hegemony of economic *concepts and ideas* within the public sphere" (Gane, 2015; emphasis added).

I do not wish to comment on whether Gane's claim is true here. But it is interesting to me that concepts and ideas are central to his understanding of sociology's critical function. There is a great and long tradition in sociological thought of reflecting on the power of ideas to constrain and enable action: Weber (1920) wondered how religious beliefs affected people's conduct, especially in work; Marx and Engels (1976) dissected the relationships among ideology, consciousness, and reality; Gramsci exposed how ruling classes used ideas to mystify subordination (Gramsci and Hobsbawm, 2000); Mannheim (1954) asked how everyday "social knowledge" kept the political sphere under control. Many continue to work in this tradition.

A key puzzle that all these works confront is how some ideas come to exercise a disproportionate amount of power over social (including political and economic) life. For the late sociologist Pierre Bourdieu, these are ideas with "the means of making [themselves] true" (Bourdieu, 1998: 95): certain ideas, because they reflect, protect, and legitimate the interests of powerful people and institutions (e.g., senior government officials, owners of the world's largest corporations), have an easier time accessing the gears that make the world turn.

In research conducted from 2012 to 2014, I examined one such idea—the concept of *productivity*—in Canadian political and economic **discourse** (Foster, 2016). I wanted to know why we seem to care about productivity—whether as individuals who desire "productive" lives (and therefore worry about retirement and unemployment even when money is no object) or as nation-states concerned about gross domestic product (GDP)—enough to have our national statistics agency report on it monthly, and to have it peppered so liberally throughout the organizational and government discourse we absorb daily. I was intrigued by the productivity concept's capacity to justify all kinds of political decisions and economic processes that, in my view and in the immediate term, seemed to hurt more people than they helped.

So I conducted a **genealogy** of the concept itself in economic thought, from 1700s **political economy** to present-day statistical economic indicators, connecting this to three case studies of Canadian government apparatuses: the Dominion Bureau of Statistics (DBS, now Statistics Canada); the short-lived National Productivity Council (NPC); and the Atlantic Canada Opportunities Agency (ACOA). In influential economic texts and government archival records, I found the narrative resources for a politically charged history of a contemporary concept whose forms and uses are anything but inevitable.

The Historical Sociology of Concept Formation

I was inspired and helped by Margaret Somers's *historical sociology of concept formation*. This approach "demands that we question and problematize as *historical* objects much of what has long been taken to have been *discovered* in science" (Somers, 1995: 137). Productivity is precisely that kind of object. Somers's concept of the "ideational regime" is especially helpful in this task, as it describes "those public narratives and assumptions that have become widely taken for granted in the political culture," setting "the parameters for what counts as worthwhile argument in social and political debates" (Somers, 2008: 2).

In the historical records of the DBS, the NPC, and the ACOA, I found what I came to understand as a *productivist ideational regime*. I argued that it is comprised of several cultural assumptions: first, that more productivity is good in and of itself; second, that productivity fully or partly determines standards of living and prosperity; and third, that there is a singular "national economy" that circumscribes and contains the social—an assumption that only works *because* we collect statistics at the national level (Mitchell, 1998). Overall, the productivist ideational regime supports and is in turn supported by a persuasive "metanarrative" (Somers, 2008) that connects economic growth to progress, increased average incomes, happiness, and freedom. This is a myth that draws selectively from human history to say that productivity growth has made us happier and richer and is indeed essential for our quality of life.

For one brief moment—precisely the time when the DBS and other national statistical agencies were developing the tools to measure aggregate (i.e., national) economic productivity—this connection between productivity and prosperity was backed up by statistical evidence. Ordinary people's incomes rose in tandem with national productivity. In the 1950s, Stanley Kuznets, one of the first to experiment with a system of "national accounts" measuring all economic activity in a country, came up with a historical series that showed that as the economy grew and productivity rose, the lowest and highest incomes converged. Taking his data as indicative of a fundamental law, he theorized that "income inequality would automatically decrease in advanced phases of capitalist development, regardless of economic policy choices or other differences between countries, until eventually it stabilized at an acceptable level" (Piketty, 2014) His findings were widely embraced, and "the philosophy of [Kuznets's] moment," as Piketty writes, "was summed up in a single sentence: 'Growth is a rising tide that lifts all boats'" (2014: 8). This is **productivism** in a nutshell.

Over this same period, labour unions began to use the newly created productivity statistics in collective bargaining. An approach known as "productivity bargaining" linked workers' wages to aggregate productivity indicators, so that as national productivity grew, workers would be guaranteed a fair share of that growth (Block and Burns, 1986). The idea was that productivity growth depended on workers' efforts and they should therefore share in the economic gains. Strong, export-driven economic growth, weak economies elsewhere, steady business investment and expansion, and an entrenched gender division of labour helped productivity bargaining reify the notion that productivity and prosperity went hand in hand. But in the economic stagnation from the mid-1960s through the 1980s, increasingly neoliberal governments sought to fix the North American "productivity crisis" by decreasing labour costs. The link that labour unions made between productivity and workers' wages was turned back on them: if labour should benefit when productivity grew, they should also suffer when it slowed or stopped (Block and Burns, 1986).

By the time national productivity picked up steam again—from the late 1980s onward—it had effectively been decoupled from wages (Stanford, 2014). And yet productivism—and its idea that productivity meant rising incomes—persisted. I found it throughout my case studies. It was the foundation for many DBS reports from the 1950s, '60s, and '70s, and central to the activities of the NPC. The latter, following the model of similar "productivity councils" established across the world, held a series of labour management seminars bringing together government, business leaders, and union representatives to talk about how all three could work together to improve productivity. Curiously, the productivity–prosperity myth popped up in ACOA's mandate *after* the organization had been in existence for 15 years, long after the statistical link between productivity and wages began to weaken. One of the biggest puzzles that emerged from this research was how it could be possible for so many people and organizations to believe that increased productivity would naturally translate into greater standards of living, even after the empirical evidence began to destabilize the correlation.

More puzzling was the ambiguity and fragility of the productivity concept within and across these organizations. DBS researchers candidly questioned the validity of their data (as did the inventors of aggregate productivity statistics in the US, according to Block and Burns, [1986]). They referred to the national accounts, from which productivity data were drawn, as feats of "fanciful imagination and prejudice" (Marshall, n.d.: 38). Members of the NPC struggled so ungracefully with the concept that it was, at times, humorous to read their meeting minutes. In private meetings, they tried out many different definitions: "productivity means progress," "more for everyone," "more jobs," and it's "an attitude of mind" (NPC, 1962). In public, they coined the definition "work smarter and get on with the job" (Coates, 1964: 39). Their imprecision is even more striking considering they came to see their job as a matter of public relations, imploring Canadians to embrace productivity as a national priority and to do whatever they could (i.e., work harder) to advance it. In ACOA, policy-makers got creative, taking the straight productivist line between productivity and prosperity and replacing the latter with "opportunities." There is no empirical basis for this switch; in my view, based on this research, it was simply a way to explain and justify the increasingly fragile connection between productivity growth and ordinary people's incomes. The idea that productivity growth was necessary for expanding *opportunities* to prosper, rather than prosperity itself, did the trick.

Productivism's persistence suggests that it is one of those ideas with the power to make itself true. Looking at the inner workings of the NPC, the DBS, and the ACOA with Bourdieu's insights in mind, I am led to conclude that it has this power because it *benefits* the powerful—those people and institutions whose incomes continued to grow along with productivity while the "average" income lost ground, the big businesses that can always threaten to move operations in search of higher productivity (i.e., the same output at lower wages). This is not to say that workers who have not benefited as much from productivity gains (Krugman, 2012) do not play some role in keeping productivism afloat; research on the work ethic, from Weber (1920) to Weeks (2011), shows that work and productivity are widely internalized as inherently good—as ends in and of themselves—even if they do not deliver the prosperity they promise.

Alternatives to Productivism

There are always alternative ideas. In asserting that dominant modes of thought channel and control what can be said, we never mean that they completely silence everything else. It is just that alternatives never get the traction they need to influence the "mechanisms" by which society's institutions are "shaped, regulated and organized" (Somers and Block, 2005: 263–4). A key function of the historical sociology of concept formation is to expose the fleeting moments when a choice between alternative futures arose and "all of the forces of [the] world" went one way, taking the rest of the world with them (Bourdieu, 1998). This should not lead us to believe things will never change. Rather, it reminds us that we get chances sometimes.

In this spirit, my work concluded with a look at "anti-productivism" from the 1700s to the present. I found revealing patterns of thought that suggest that as long as there has been a productivism, there has been an alternative to it. And what is especially intriguing is the way in which the productivity concept has factored into these alternative discourses. Those who challenge the pursuit of economic growth for growth's sake often do so by challenging the endless pursuit of productivity gains, by calling into question the assumed link between productivity and prosperity, by asking why increased productivity has failed to give ordinary people more free time, and by proposing that we redraw, in various ways, the connection between "productive" labour and human well-being (Russell, 2004; Latouche, 2010).

But anti-productivism has, in productivism, a formidable opponent. The latter is reinforced by ideas and practices that venerate work—whether we understand these ideas and practices as comprising a "work ethic," a "dogma," or an "ideology" of work (Weeks, 2011). It is sustained by willful blindness toward ecological signs and the common sense that growth cannot go on, unabated, forever (D'Alisa et al., 2014). It is fortified by attachment to consumer society, especially when consumption is understood as something to be earned only by working for income, and when consumer goods and services are designed to be disposable—to serve single purposes and become obsolete. It is difficult to get at these factors—which are ideational, historical, and sociological—without doing sociological research that is historical and focused on ideas.

References

Block, F., and Burns, G.A. (1986). "Productivity as a Social Problem: The Uses and Misuses of Social Indicators." *American Sociological Review, 51*(6), 767–80.

Bourdieu, P. (1998). "Utopia of Endless Exploitation: The Essence of Neoliberalism." *Le Monde Diplomatique.* December 1998. Retrieved 8 December 2016, from: http://mondediplo.com/1998/12/08bourdieu

Bourdieu, P., and Wacquant, L. (1992). *An Invitation to a Reflexive Sociology.* Chicago: University of Chicago Press.

Coates, D. (1964). *The National Productivity Council of Canada.* Ithaca, NY: Cornell University Press.

D'Alisa, G., Demaria, F., and Kallis, G. (2014). *Degrowth: A Vocabulary for a New Era.* New York: Routledge.

DBS Sub-Committee of the Inter-departmental Advisory Committee on Labour Statistics. (1951). *The Measurement and Analysis of Productivity.* Report to the Dominion Bureau of Statistics. Ottawa, September 1951. RG17 Vol. 3131 File no. 66-10.

Foster, K. (2016). *Productivity and Prosperity.* Toronto: University of Toronto Press.

Foucault, M. (2012). *The Archaeology of Knowledge.* New York: Vintage Books.

Gane, N. (2015). "Swimming Upstream: Sociology Beyond Description." *The Sociological Review Online.* Retrieved 26 May 2015, from: http://www.thesociologicalreview.com/information/blog/swimming-upstream-sociology-beyond-description.html

Gramsci, A., and Hobsbawm, E.J. (2000). *The Antonio Gramsci Reader: Selected Writings 1916–1935.* D. Forgacs, Ed. New York: New York University Press.

Krugman, P. (2012). "Where The Productivity Went." *New York Times Blog.* Retrieved 16 September 2015, from: http://krugman.blogs.nytimes.com/2012/04/28/where-the-productivity-went/?_r=0

Latouche, S. (2010). *Farewell to Growth.* Malden, MA: Polity Press.

NPC. (1962). *Minutes of NPC Meeting, January 29th & 30th, 1962.* Ottawa, RG20 Vol. 859, File 40-2.

Mannheim, K. (1954). *Ideology and Utopia.* New York: Harcourt Brace.

Marshall, H. (n.d.). "History—Manuscript, pt. 3." *The National Accounts, Standard Classification Systems, and Research and Development.* RG 31 Vol 1434. Library and Archives Canada.

Marx, K., and Engels, F. (1976). "The German Ideology." *Karl Marx–Frederick Engels Collected Works* (Vol. 5). New York: International Publishers.

Mitchell, T. (1998). "Fixing the Economy." *Cultural Studies, 12*(1), 82–101.

Piketty, T. (2014). *Capital in the 21st Century.* Cambridge, MA: Harvard University Press.

Purvis, T., and Hunt, A. (1993). "Discourse, Ideology, Discourse, Ideology, Discourse, Ideology . . ." *The British Journal of Sociology, 44*(3), 473–99.

Russell, B. (2004). *In Praise of Idleness and Other Essays.* New York: Routledge.

Somers, M.R. (1995). "What's Political or Cultural about Political Culture and the Public Sphere? Toward an Historical Sociology of Concept Formation." *Sociological Theory, 13*(2), 113–44.

Somers, M.R. (2008). *Genealogies of Citizenship: Markets, Statelessness, and the Right to Have Rights.* Cambridge: Cambridge University Press.

Somers, M.R., and Block, F. (2005). "From Poverty to Perversity: Ideas, Markets, and Institutions over 200 Years of Welfare Debate." *American Sociological Review, 70*(2), 260–87.

Stanford, J. (2014). "Canada's Transformation under Neoliberalism." *Canadian Dimension.* Retrieved 8 December 2016, from: https://canadiandimension.com/articles/view/canadas.

Weber, M. (1920). *The Protestant Ethic and the Spirit of Capitalism.* London: Routledge and Sons.

Weeks, K. (2011). *The Problem with Work.* Durham, NC: Duke University Press.

43 Underemployment in Advanced Capitalism: Patterns and Prospects

D.W. Livingstone

Introduction

Underemployment (also known as: "underutilization," "over-education," "over-qualification," or much of the "education–jobs gap") generically refers to the less than optimal use of labour potential. However, agreement on appropriate uses of labour and extent of utilization is problematic in all class-based societies. In advanced capitalist societies, most paid labour is related to the sale of goods and service commodities. From private employers' standpoints, labour utilization is the efficient application of workers' capacities to ensure the greatest number of units is produced and sold in a given time, thereby enabling maximum profits. From hired workers' standpoints, appropriate utilization may involve spending sufficient time and care to ensure high quality and social usefulness of finished units, as well as adequate monetary benefits and recuperation to enable maintenance of continuing good quality of work. Most of the literature on underemployment ignores this difference, but it is implicit in discussions that argue that connections between knowledge and work are mediated by negotiating the powers of those in different social groups (e.g., Grugulis 2003). With greater power comes greater influence over what is deemed to count as valuable labour and the extent to which its use is recognized and rewarded. Workers with little workplace power may be relegated to "getting a little of our own back" by withholding some skill or effort (e.g. Hamper 1991). Effective labour utilization from the employer's perspective may equate to being used up and excreted as waste from workers' standpoints (Yates 2011).

Diverse theoretical perspectives have been used to explain relations between labour capacity and employers' job requirements, including classical economic theory, human capital theory, segmented labour market theories, and credentialism.[1] I use a historical materialist theory positing that interfirm competition, conflicts between employers and employees over working conditions, and technological innovation all provoke incessant shifts in the number of enterprises, employees, and types of jobs available. Through technological innovation and workers' learning on the job, increased efficiency leads either to expanded production or to unemployment, in either case modifying the overall demand for labour. Popular demand for general education and specialized training increases cumulatively as people seek more knowledge, different specific skills, and added credentials in order to live and qualify for jobs in such a changing economy. In advanced capitalist countries, mismatches are inevitable between employers' aggregate demand and requirements for employees on the one hand, and the aggregate supply and qualifications of job seekers on the other. With liberal democratic state regimes that proclaim the right to equal educational opportunity and widespread public access to knowledge through such means as the Internet, the predicted tendency is for the supply of qualified job seekers to exceed the demand for most jobs—a growing reserve army of qualified labour.

This paper identifies basic conceptual dimensions of underemployment, briefly summarizes empirical research on patterns of underemployment, and more briefly discusses current prospects for underemployment and possible alternatives for reducing it.[2]

Basic Dimensions of Underemployment

Three basic dimensions of underemployment can be distinguished: *time, skill*, and *intensity of effort*.

The underemployment of potential labour time is the most evident dimension. The amount of time people are gainfully employed may vary from zero to virtually all their waking hours. Primary time-based aspects are *unemployment* (including those actively looking for employment, discouraged workers, and others such as prisoners and retired people who want paid work but are restricted from the labour market), and *involuntarily reduced employment* in temporary, part-time jobs of those who want more employment.

Skill-based underemployment refers to the surplus capacities, skills, education, or knowledge that workers bring to the job, in comparison with what is needed for the job. There is much dispute over the notions of skills, relevant education, and knowledge. Numerous ways of conceiving dimensions of the gap between employed workers' capabilities and the requirements of their jobs have been suggested (e.g., Kalleberg 2008; McKee-Ryan and Harvey 2011). Three relatively straightforward aspects of the skill gap between workers' capacities and their job requirements are widely recognized:

- *entry credential gap* between the training credentials that job entrants bring and those required by employers;
- *performance gap* between the performance capability of workers and the performance level actually required to do the job;
- *subjective gap* between job holders' personal assessments of their capabilities and their perceived job requirements.

With regard to *intensity of effort*, those who begin a job become more efficient as they gain experience needed to perform it (Pankhurst and Livingstone 2006). The level of production of goods and services in a given time will be closely related to the intensity of effort given by experienced workers. Employers' imperative is to ensure that workers maintain or increase their intensity of effort to continue to produce more goods and services in that time. Workers' overriding objective is to ensure they provide sufficient effort to keep the job without exhausting themselves and losing it. Underemployment of effort by workers is a continual threat to employers' profitability; supplying adequate effort but not becoming over-employed to the extent they threaten their subsistence is a continual challenge for workers.

Consider these three dimensions together. For employers, having an ample supply of qualified workers to employ for varying amounts of time and skill use with high intensity of effort is central to profit maximization. For workers, being fully employed in a job that allows them to use their accomplished skills without exhausting efforts is the optimal condition.

So, underemployment is a highly contradictory phenomenon. Without pretending to resolve the contradiction between standpoints of capital and labour, we will look briefly at empirical patterns and then at prospects/alternatives.

Empirical Patterns

Time-Based Underemployment

In global capitalism today, the vast majority of the labour force is located in developing and underdeveloped countries. As a result of agricultural enclosures and limited urban industrialization, there are now *massively* more adult people in these countries without any meaningful employment or only involuntary part-time jobs than the number of people with full-time paid employment, a burgeoning "relative surplus population" (Neilson and Stubbs 2011). In advanced capitalist countries, official unemployment rates of those actively seeking employment, the long-term unemployed, discouraged workers, and involuntary part-time employed all have been generally increasing to the point that chronic structural unemployment and involuntary underemployment are becoming widely recognized as major social problems (e.g., OECD 2014). In Canada, current estimates put official unemployment at around

7 per cent of the eligible labour force, involuntary part-timers at around 5 per cent, and discouraged workers (including many not actively searching but who want to work) at up to similar magnitudes (OECD 2014; Jackson 2010). So, up to 20 per cent of the potential Canadian labour force could now be underemployed on the basis of time, a very substantial proportion and a growing trend in recent decades.

Skill-Based Underemployment

If the focus is limited to the employed labour force, a primary issue is the extent to which workers are able to use their skills in their jobs. Leaving aside the issue of different conceptions and measures of "skill,"[3] a series of Canadian national surveys in 1998, 2004, and 2010 using self-report measures found that credential over-qualification for job entry increased from 27 per cent to 31 per cent, while under-qualification dropped from 22 per cent to 18 per cent during this period. The same series of surveys found that the over-qualification for performance requirements remained at about 28 per cent through this period, while the proportion under-qualified dropped from 20 per cent to 15 per cent. Thirdly, this series found subjective feelings of over-qualification increasing from 22 per cent to 30 per cent over this period while subjective under-qualification remained at around 5 per cent (Livingstone 2012, 2013). If these three measures are combined, by 2010 a small majority of the employed Canadian labour force reported experiencing one or more of these forms of skill-based underemployment. While few other studies have considered such combined effects, there are now many others that have found similar magnitudes of specific aspects of underemployment (see Livingstone 2016). The basic conclusion is that skill-based underemployment is being experienced by a large and growing portion of the employed labour force in Canada and throughout the advanced capitalist world.

Underemployment of Effort

The weight of evidence suggests that the intensity of effort required of many employees has been increasing in recent decades. Average wages have generally been stagnant over this period while productivity rates have increased significantly (Carchedi 2011). Many workers have taken on heavier workloads without comparable compensation. For example, in the US the proportion of salaried workers entitled to receive overtime pay for their effort dropped by about three-quarters in the 1979–2014 period (Eisenberry 2015). Increasing numbers of workers have been doing more work for less pay. There is widespread evidence of intensification and few signs of increasing underemployment of effort.

In sum, both time-based and skill-based aspects of underemployment are found to be very substantial and growing in recent times, while evidence of underemployment of effort is becoming more and more rare.

Prospects/Alternatives

Time- and skill-based underemployment are now persisting for the potential labour force of advanced capitalist economies through different phases of business cycles. Workers' knowledge and extent of learning activities increasingly exceed the narrow formal requirements of existing jobs. Such underemployment also applies to computer skills in purported "knowledge economies." Higher and sometimes extreme levels of such underemployment occur among youths, recent immigrants, people of colour, and disabled people. Workers have also been found to continually reformulate their knowledge to "micro-modify" their jobs. A growing corpus of workplace learning studies indicate that workers' rich array of learning activities increasingly exceed current actual job requirements and that people generally are already intently engaged in an "educational arms race" for credentials (Livingstone 2009).

Advocates of both human capital theory and a knowledge-based economy persist in asserting educational investment—increasingly funded by students themselves—is the answer to our economic problems. Indeed, from employers' standpoints, a surplus of skills may continue to be both a short-term and long-term benefit. Dominant discourse still insists that more training and more information about available (and generally diminishing) qualified jobs is the basic solution to time- and skill-based underemployment. The fact that oversupply of qualified workers is essential to the reproduction of advanced capitalism is rarely hinted at.

Education provisions can always be improved, as well as more equitable guidance services for transitions between school and paid work. But effective policies for reducing time- and skill-based underemployment are more likely to come from economic reforms—the adoption of job designs and organizational practices that permit workers to more fully use *existing* skills (e.g., Warhurst and Findlay 2012), as well as from public policies that facilitate the redistribution of paid work time, wider recognition of workers' prior learning, incentives for workplace participation, and creation of sustainable green jobs (Livingstone 2009).

Gaining more knowledge to cope with our environment is the most inherently human activity and virtually always valuable. It is only in the narrow sense of qualifications in excess of what employers require for specific jobs that the concept of "over-education" is intelligible as wasted investment. On the other hand, the notion of "over-employment" is rarely heard; it is absurd from an employers' standpoint, which is committed to maximizing the profit-generating efforts of employees. To some employees, this notion *is* intelligible as intensification of work, or exploitation. Wider recognition among employees is a precondition of movement toward alternative forms of production based on economic democracy, sustainable relations with our environment, and decent, fulfilling jobs. The increasingly pervasive condition of underemployment within capitalism also provides more potential time for workers to create such alternative forms of production (e.g., Baiman et al. 2012).

Notes

1. For fuller discussions of theories of mismatches between workers' competencies and labour market needs, see Desjardins and Rubenson (2011); Livingstone (2009); and McKee-Ryan and Harvey (2011).
2. Parts of this paper have been adapted from Livingstone (2016). For fuller development, see Livingstone (2009).
3. Illustrations of the effects of different measures of skill on underemployment measures may be found in Livingstone (2016).

References

Baiman, R., B. Barclay, S. Hollander, H. Kurban, J. Persky, E. Redmond, and M. Rothenberg. (2012). A permanent jobs program for the US: Economic restructuring to meet human needs. *Review of Black Political Economy,* 39(1), 29–41. doi:10.1007/s12114-011-9118-y.

Carchedi, G. (2011). Behind and beyond the crisis. *International Socialism: A Quarterly Review of Socialist Theory* 132. Retrieved 22 May 2015, from: http://isj.org.uk/behind-and-beyond-the-crisis.

Desjardins, R., and K. Rubenson. (2011). An analysis of skill mismatch using direct measures of skills. *OECD Education Working Papers* 63: 01.

Eisenberry, R. (2015). The number of salaried workers guaranteed overtime pay has plummeted since 1979. *Economic Policy Institute.* Retrieved 11 June 2015, from: http://www.epi.org/publication.

Grugulis, I. (2003). Putting skills to work: Learning and employment at the start of the century. *Human Resource Management Journal, 13*(2), 3–12.

Hamper, B. (1991). *Rivethead: Tales from the Assembly Line.* New York: Warner Books.

Jackson, A. (2010). *Work and Labour in Canada: Critical Issues*, 2nd Edition. Toronto: Scholar's Press.

Kalleberg, A. (2008). The mismatched worker: When people don't fit their jobs. *Academy of Management Perspectives, 22*(1), 24–40.

Livingstone, D.W. (Ed.). (2009). *Education and Jobs: Exploring the Gaps.* Toronto: University of Toronto Press.

Livingstone, D.W. (2012). Probing the icebergs of adult learning: Comparative findings and implications of the 1998, 2004 and 2010 Canadian surveys of formal and informal learning practices. *Canadian Journal for the Study of Adult Education 25*(1) (November), 47–71.

Livingstone, D.W. (2013). Skill utilization for sustainable economies: The illusion of an optimal skills mix. Keynote Address to International Conference on "The Optimal Skill Mix for a Modern Economy," Marbach Castle, Lake Constance, Germany, September 12.

Livingstone, D.W. (2016). Skill underutilization. In J. Buchanan, D. Finegold, K. Mayhew, and C. Warhurst (eds). *Oxford Handbook of Skills and Training.* Oxford: Oxford University Press. (Chapter 15).

McKee-Ryan, F., and J. Harvey. (2011). "I have a job, but . . .": A review of underemployment. *Journal of Management, 37*(4), 962–96.

Neilson, D. and T. Stubbs. (2011). Relative surplus population and uneven development in the neoliberal era: Theory and empirical application. *Capital & Class 35*(3), 435–53.

OECD (2014). *Preventing Unemployment and Underemployment from Becoming Structural.* Paris: OECD. Report prepared for the G20 Labour and Employment Ministerial Meeting, Melbourne, Australia, 10–11 September.

Pankhurst, K.V. and D.W. Livingstone. (2006). The labour process: Individual learning, work and productivity. *Studies in Continuing Education 28*(1) (March): 1–16.

Warhurst, C. and P. Findlay. (2012). *More Effective Skills Utilisation: Shifting the Terrain of Skills Policy in Scotland.* Cardiff: School of Social Sciences, Cardiff University. SKOPE Research Paper No. 107, January. Available at: www.skope.ox.ac.uk

Yates, M. (2011). The human-as-waste, the labor theory of value and disposability in contemporary capitalism. *Antipode, 43*(5), 1679–95.

44 Unemployment Experiences of Women in Toronto and Halifax

Leslie Nichols

Introduction

In Canada, workers who become unemployed expect to have access to unemployed worker supports by virtue of an automatic deduction from their wages for **employment insurance (EI)**. Yet, since 1996, when unemployment policy was restructured from **unemployment insurance (UI)** to EI, not all workers have had access to this support. The restructuring led to tougher rules and regulations, particularly regarding the number of previous hours worked needed to receive EI benefits (MacDonald, 2009a, 2009b). This process has not affected everyone to the same degree. Notably, individuals who are more marginalized in society, including women and those with a low socio-economic status, have experienced a greater impact (McGregor, 2004; Nichols, 2014a, 2014b; Silver, Shields, Wilson, and Scholtz, 2005; Silver, Wilson, and Shields, 2004). Women face household demands that make it more complicated for them to remain in the labour market, let alone access it (Shields, Silver, and Wilson, 2006; Silver et al., 2005; Townson and Hayes, 2007).

I conducted a study in 2013 on the lived experiences of unemployed women with a variety of intersecting identities—15 from Toronto and 15 from Halifax—to explore the effects of Canadian unemployed workers' supports. Two main findings from the study are pertinent. First, the **neoliberal policy** paradigm has eroded state infrastructure. This has led to a reduction in supports for unemployed women workers. Second, women who are unemployed face not only inadequate EI support but also a lack of supports in relation to child care, health care, and re-entry into the labour market. As a result, many women who cannot rely on a domestic partner experience poor living conditions.

Changes from UI to EI

UI was introduced in the early 1940s to address large-scale unemployment arising from the Great

Depression. The program was administered by the federal government, which contributed 20 per cent of employer and employee contributions to the program. The aim of the program was to provide assistance to Canadian workers during times of unemployment (Lin, 1998). At the beginning of the program, UI eligibility was based on the number of weeks worked in the year prior to the claim. Depending on the region, the claimant needed to have between 12 and 20 weeks of work, with a minimum of 15 hours per week to qualify (Townson and Hayes, 2007). The benefits given to an individual were based on the total hours of work during the previous year and the total earnings for the year in which the benefits were given (Townson and Hayes, 2007).

In 1996, when UI was replaced by EI, the policy changes included an increase in the work hours required to receive benefits and lower benefit payouts. Under the new system, to receive benefits, a worker needed 180 days of paid labour with a 35-hour week within the last two years. This doubles the number of paid hours that were required to qualify for benefits under UI. (Townson and Hayes, 2007). In 2014, the average EI claimant received $514 per week, compared to $595 in 1995, taking an inflation adjustment into account (Battle, 2009; Government of Canada, 2014). Furthermore, in 2009, only 39 per cent of unemployed workers received EI benefits, whereas in 1990, 83 per cent would have qualified (Mendelson, Battle, and Torjman, 2010).

Women and EI

Current EI policy does not consider the wide variety of reasons that someone can end up unemployed. Thus, women are affected when they temporarily leave the labour market to raise children (Cooke and Gazso, 2009; Townson and Hayes, 2007). EI policy views workers as re-entrants or new entrants to the labour market when they have not been employed for a period of time. This means that they are not credited with any hours they may have worked before the time they were away from the labour market. In addition, EI regulations require workers to have worked 910 hours during the prior 52 weeks (Townson and Hayes, 2007). Thus, having to reach the 910-hour threshold in order to gain supports for re-entering the labour market, many cannot get beyond this hurdle (Bezanson and McMurray, 2000).

Theory and Methods

My 2013 study drew its data from qualitative interviews with 30 diverse women participants (15 from Toronto and 15 from Halifax). This study was designed to explore the ways in which diverse women deal with their unemployment in Canada. These women had a wide range of intersecting identities, including (a) being precariously employed prior to the period of unemployment; (b) being a single parent, a parent of a child, or a parent of multiple children; (c) caring for parents; (d) lacking a partner's income; (e) having a precariously employed or unemployed partner; (f) having a racialized identity or immigrant status; and (f) having various gender, class, and age identities. The key goal of this study was to analyze the effects of EI policy on the lived experiences of that subclass of unemployed women who were caring for children and other dependants.

I explored the interviews through intersectionality theory and methodology and coded the responses through grounded theory, which helped provide "a clearer picture of the way the intersections of identity impact individuals' access to social policies, and, indeed, to full social citizenship" (Nichols, 2013: 234–5; see also Manual, 2007). Intersectionality theory provides a fuller understanding of individuals' lives, particularly in relation to the choices they have available to them and the decisions they make (Manual, 2007). The insight central to intersectionality theory is that an individual does not have a single salient identity; rather, the effects of identities are context dependent.

Discussion

This section overviews some key themes that developed from the interviews with the subject subclass of unemployed women in Toronto and Halifax. These themes allude to the difficulties that unemployed women of the subject subclass experienced in both communities.

Denial of EI Benefits

Three participants from Halifax and four from Toronto were denied EI during either during their current episode of unemployment or during a previous episode. All of these participants applied for EI, but some experienced more complications than others, such as difficulties in finding out that they were not approved. For instance, Sharon, a single mother of one from Halifax, waited a long time to hear whether she was approved. "So I applied on the last day of work, so that was back on June 24th or so. I didn't hear anything whatsoever from the EI department until I called them at the end of August to follow up and find out if—like, what was taking so long. And that's when they told me that I don't qualify." Such poor and disrespectful communication with those who were denied benefits made their situations worse.

After being denied EI benefits, three participants were told that if they could find a temporary job that would give them a few more hours, they would qualify. Sarah, for example, a racialized, married mother of one from Toronto, was in this situation, but even with assistance from an employment counsellor, she was only able to find volunteer work. Still, she did not qualify, because a temporary agency did not properly claim her employment. Kathryn from Halifax, a single mother of one who was pregnant, was told that she could be approved if she acquired more hours through temporary employment. Although she tried, Kathryn was not able to find a single temporary job. EI policy discourse informed these participants that unemployment was their fault and that they had had the *opportunity* to solve their situation. Yet, none were able to do so. Caring for their children simply added more obstacles to meeting the conditions for EI.

Dependent Care Needs While Trying to Find Work

Many scholars, such as Cleveland et al. (1996: 132, 133), have stated that child care costs negatively affect women's participation in the labour market. Others, such as Jenson (2006) and Lefebrve and Merrigan (2008), have argued that a strategically enacted social policy of universal child care can help reduce the marginalization faced by young parents in relation to labour markets. Thus, participation in the labour market is related not only to wages and issues of social reproduction, but also to the direct costs of child care (Cleveland et al., 1996: 133). Indeed, issues regarding child care expenses are clearly related to the kinds of labour markets young parents, particularly mothers, are able to access.

Six participants in Toronto and two in Halifax articulated the implications of child care or dependent care needs for their employment status. Jessica, a single racialized mother of one from Toronto, noted, "It is hard because he is so young. I have to get a babysitter and everything . . . that is also money. Right now I have to put him on subsidy. . . . He is on subsidy waiting list for daycare, which takes up to a year." Danielle in Halifax perceived the same difficulty, particularly due to her very young children. Both Jessica and Danielle referred to the complications of having young children and the trend for women to work through their childbearing years. Belsky (1990) observed that parent involvement during infancy is essential for a child's healthy development. Even with such social programs as maternal or parental leave, which are designed to support the parents' two roles—as workers and child care providers—families still find it difficult to address the competing needs for income and child care (Marshall, 1999: 18). As a rule, this role conflict affects women more than men.

Health Care Costs While Unemployed

Ten participants each in Toronto and Halifax noted that during their period of unemployment, they were able to rely on their partners for support for health care costs outside the realm of public health care. Another three participants—Claire and Kathryn from Halifax and Emily from Toronto—noted that they relied on social assistance for supporting their health care needs. Even so, however, Kathryn stated that in order to be covered for some of her dental care, she had to wait for a couple of cavities to become worse so that she would be covered for an emergency root canal procedure.

Many participants had difficulties meeting health care costs during their period of unemployment. Kathryn disclosed that in spite of her coverage, she still could not meet health care costs. She mentioned that she had just received a phone call from a debt collection agency asking her to "pay some $200 dental bill and I'm like, I can't even give you a payment plan right now." When the agency asked for a payment plan, she told them that she had no money and that she was not sure how she could even attempt to pay them. Ann, a married racialized mother of one from Toronto, addressed a similar concern about her son's dental care, for which social assistance was denied because of the savings requirement to apply for immigration to Canada.

Conclusion

The findings of this research indicate that context-specific identity facts are the reason for the differences in these women's social well-being in terms of personal and structural circumstances. Prominent among these identity categories are precarious employment prior to the period of unemployment, single parenthood, lack of a partner's income, and a precariously employed or unemployed partner. These circumstances greatly influence women's employment experiences, which in turn affect their unemployment experiences. The significance of this study was that it revealed the need both to analyze and to change state policies by exploring individuals' fluid, context-specific identities. As Danielle, one of the study participants, noted, EI "needs to be customized per situation more . . . to actually tailor each situation to the person's needs or their situation."

References

Battle, Ken. "Gender Aspects of Employment Insurance." Presentation to the Commons Standing Committee on the Status of Women, Ottawa, 2009. Accessed on 2 May 2013: http://www.caledonist.org/Publications/PDF/767ENG.pdf

Belsky, Jay. "Parental and Nonparental Child Care and Children's Socioemotional Development: A Decade in Review." *Journal of Marriage and the Family* 52, no. 4 (1990): 885–903.

Bezanson, Kate, and Susan McMurray. "Booming for Whom? People in Ontario Talk about Income, Jobs and Social Programs." (2000). Accessed on 2 May 2013: http://www.caledoninst.org/Publications/Detail/?ID=181

Cleveland, Gordon, Morley Gunderson, and Douglas Hyatt. "Childcare Costs and the Employment Decision of Women: Canadian Evidence." *Canadian Journal of Economics* 29, no. 1 (1996): 132–51.

Cooke, Martin, and Amber Gazso. "Taking a Life Course Perspective on Social Assistance Use in Canada: A Different Approach." *Canadian Journal of Sociology*, 34, no. 2 (2009): 349–72.

Government of Canada. *Service Canada: People Serving People*. Ottawa: Government of Canada, 2014. Accessed on 2 February 2013: http://www.servicecanada.gc.ca/eng/sc/ei/sew/weekly_benefits.shtml

Jenson, Jane. "Against the Current: Child Care and Family Policy in Quebec." In *Rethinking Canada: The Promise of Women's History,* 5th edn, edited by Mona Gleason and Adele Perry, 346–64. Don Mills, ON: Oxford University Press, 2006.

Lefebrve, Pierre, and Phillip Merrigan. "Child-Care Policy and the Labour Supply of Mothers with Young Children: A Natural Experience from Canada." *Journal of Labour Economics*, 26, no. 3 (2008): 519–48.

Lin, Zhengxi. "Employment Insurance in Canada: Policy Changes." *Statistics Canada*, (1998): 41–47. Accessed on 2

May 2013: http://www.statcan.gc.ca/studies-etudes/75-001/archive/e-pdf/3828-eng.pdf

MacDonald, Martha. "Income Security for Women: What about Employment Insurance?" In *Public Policy for Women: The State, Income and Labour Market Issues,* edited by Marjorie Griffin Cohen and Jane Pulkingham, 251–70. Toronto: University of Toronto Press, 2009a.

———. "Women and EI in Canada: The First Decade." In *Women and Public Policy in Canada,* edited by A. Dobrowolsky, 65–86. Don Mills, ON: Oxford University Press, 2009b.

Manuel, Tiffany. "Envisioning the Possibilities for a Good Life: Exploring the Public Policy Implications of Intersectionality Theory." *Journal of Women, Politics and Policy* 28, no. 3 (2007): 173–203.

Marshall, Katherine. "Employment after childbirth." *Perspectives on Labour and Income* 11.3 (1999): 18–25.

McGregor, Gaile. "The Myth(s) of Globalization: Gender Bias in 'EI' Policy as a Case in Point." *Canadian Women's Studies* 23, no. 3/4 (2004): 30–9.

Mendelson, Michael, Ken Battle, and Sherri Torjman. "EI Financing: Reset Required." Caledon Institute of Social Policy, 2010. Accessed on 2 May 2013: http://www.caledoninst.org /Publications/PDF/902ENG.pdf

Nichols, Leslie. "Employment Insurance in Canada: The Gendered Implications." *International Journal of Gender and Women's Studies* 2, no. 2 (2014a): 357–85.

———. "Analyzing Policy Frames for Unemployed Workers' Supports within Canada." *AG: International Journal of Gender Studies* 2, no. 3 (2013): 219–45.

———. "Unemployed Women in Neo-Liberal Canada: An Intersectional Analysis of Social Well-Being" (unpublished doctoral dissertation). Ryerson University, Toronto, ON, 2014b.

Shields, John, Susan Silver, and Sue Wilson. "Assessing Employment Risk: Dimensions in the Measurement of Unemployment." *Socialist Studies: The Journal of the Society for Socialist Studies* 2, no. 2 (2006): 105–12.

Silver, Susan, John Shields, Sue Wilson, and Antonie Scholtz. "The Excluded, the Vulnerable and the Reintegrated in a Neoliberal Era: Qualitative Dimensions of the Unemployment Experience." *Socialist Studies: The Journal of the Society for Socialist Studies* 1, no. 1 (2005): 31–56.

Silver, Susan, Sue Wilson, and John Shields. "Job Restructuring and Worker Displacement: Does Gender Matter?" *Canadian Women's Studies*, 23, no. 3/4 (2004): 7–13.

Townson, Monica, and Kevin Hayes. *Women and the Employment Insurance Program.* Toronto: Canadian Centre for Policy Alternatives, 2007. Accessed on 2 May 2013: http://www.policyalternatives.ca/sites/default/files/uploads/publications/National_Office_Pubs/2007/Women_and_the_EI_Program.pdf

45 Transitioning into Adulthood: Disability, Barriers, and Accessibility

Cornelia Schneider

It is estimated that about 3.8 million Canadians currently live with a disability. These disabilities take many forms, including physical, sensory, or intellectual. While it is true that many Canadians will acquire a disability with age, 4.4 to 6.5 per cent of people with disabilities are under the age of 30 (Statistics Canada, 2013).

Access rates of people with disabilities (PWD) to the labour market and to social participation are well known to be low (49 per cent employment rate for PWD compared to 79 per cent of the general population, dropping as low as to 26 per cent of people with a "very severe" disability; Statistics Canada, 2014). Many people with disabilities continue to be seen as incapable of making their own decisions or participating meaningfully in the broader society. An ableist society and labour market pressures have especially contributed to the exclusion of young people with disabilities from the labour market. However, the growing field of **disability studies** (see e.g., Barnes and Mercer, 2010) has contributed to a shift in thinking, and to the increasing participation of people with disabilities in research (as researchers and participants), as well as in social and political activism. Research and practice are slowly evolving from the **medical model of disability** (the assumption that there is "something wrong" inside the person that needs to be fixed) toward a **social model of disability** (e.g., Oliver, 1998), which analyses the barriers and obstacles in society that are hindering access and participation.

Using the social model of disability, I will introduce a case study based on data from two ethnographic and qualitative research projects of a transition program for youth with disabilities (ACEE—Access to Community, Employment and Education) which supports their transition from high school to adult life. My focus will be the transition of one particular research participant named Daniel, who was a participant in both projects. His transition from student to working adult and father was remarkable, but it also revealed numerous barriers that young people with disabilities face in Nova Scotia.

Methodology

In the first project, I conducted a one-year ethnographic study in the "Dollarstore," a training business for people with disabilities where the ACEE participants completed the work component of the program. I was a trainee myself, beginning my work at the same time as a cohort of young adults who mostly had graduated from high school the previous year. I chose this role because I wanted to be as close to the experience of those young people as possible. While all the research participants knew that I was a researcher, it still meant that I had to learn the same tasks as other apprentices in the store, such as merchandising, customer service, and working the cash register (Schneider, 2010).

In the second project, we investigated if and how participating in this program had impacted the lives of those adults, years after their graduation. We contacted every alumni of the ACEE program (7 cohorts representing 143 young adults with disabilities), and obtained consent from 66 participants to fill out a survey investigating their current life situation. Eleven of the 66 agreed to participate in an interview or a focus group to give a better insight into their transition into adult life (Schneider et al., 2015).

Daniel, a young man with a learning disability, was one of the few participants who participated in all three components of the studies: the ethnographic study in the Dollarstore, the follow-up survey, and an interview. His evolution demonstrates some of the successes and challenges for youth with disabilities who transition toward adult life.

Learning How to Be an Employee

At the beginning of the year, the store orientation that all ACEE participants, including Daniel, received immediately set the tone for their professional training: dress code, organization of the shifts, accepting the supervisors' authority, bathroom breaks, etc. were made explicit to the trainees. This marked a shift from what Daniel (19 years old at the time of the ethnographic study) was used to in school. Unlike the school setting, where he had more freedom, here he had to learn the normative workplace environment. He had to learn to be responsible for himself, and not allow his parents to call in sick for him. He had to learn to negotiate issues with the supervisor, and to come to work on his own. He was expected to display manners, and to be courteous with staff, supervisors, and customers, even in cases where they were not respectful with him.

Daniel had worked as a dishwasher in a restaurant before. Field notes characterize him as "concentrated on the task," "helping," "friendly," and "supportive." In his training at the store, he had to learn to be confident about his skills on cash and in merchandising, as he struggled with reading and writing. In interactions with his co-workers, he "seems to have a lot of maturity, in terms of keeping up conversations, of politeness, of work attitude" (field notes 2009-10-25). He considered himself to be a "team player," in sports as well as at work.

The following shows how he struggled, in the beginning, with having to work a shift on Halloween evening. It also shows that he developed strategies to adapt to a work schedule:

> Daniel is preoccupied by having to work on Halloween evening on closing shift, he says that no one will be in the store on that night, he tries with several people to switch shifts, but does not have success. . . . Daniel asks every new person coming into the storage room if they could not switch with him." (field notes 2008-10-25)

Daniel ended up working on that evening, as his only alternative was to skip the shift at the store. He realized that he was expected to be there, even if he would rather be "trick and treating" on Halloween.

Later that year, Daniel was one of the first in his cohort to move on to paid employment, at a hotel in their parkade. While he had been a team player in the store, he now had to get used to working by himself. An excerpt from an interview shows how he adopted a strategy, suggested by his job coach, to manage feelings of loneliness and boredom:

> D: It gets lonely down there. Haha! Lonely and boring [laughs].
>
> CS: Oh really? Already?
>
> D: Sometimes. It gets boring, it gets boring down there, not . . . because, sometimes, you work, you have stuff to do, but . . . you can't find it, or, like if, you find and you're done in . . . quickly.
>
> CS: Yeah. So what are you doing then?
>
> D: Ah . . . actually, Doris [job coach] has me reading, ah . . . she, she tells me to study up on, because I wanna do concierge, get into concierge, I've been reading, ah . . . little books that she got, like, from upstairs in the . . . lounge and stuff. For . . . little facts around the city, and all of that, and . . . restaurants in the city.
>
> CS: Oh, so that you can tell people . . .
>
> D: Yeah, what to recommend, and stuff, yeah.

Life as a Young Adult

About three years after graduating from the ACEE programme, I meet Daniel again as part of the project on ACEE alumni. He is 23 years old, has a spouse, is father to a toddler, and works three different jobs (no longer in the parkade). It also becomes clear that he has trouble making ends meet. At the time of the interview, Daniel was living with his parents; his spouse and daughter lived separately. When asked why he had moved back with his parents, he replied, "Uh, just I couldn't afford it by myself." He is working three jobs, and is "studying for a test to go for, to become, the guys that do the signs for roadwork," as this occupation would pay better. His ultimate goal is to become financially independent so that he and his spouse and daughter can once again live together as a family. Even though they live apart, he is actively involved in his daughter's life. He says, "[I] take my daughter out to the mall, let her walk around. Yeah. And sometimes after work I go over and visit my daughter, over at her mom's place, yeah."

Daniel also speaks about his busy social life, which is strongly connected to his network of friends dating back to the ACEE program, as well as to organizations such as Independent Living Nova Scotia (Christmas galas and dance parties) and the Special Olympics. Daniel's involvement with sports is impressive. He not only plays lacrosse and hockey, he also travels with a hockey team and "videotaped the games and stuff like that." He also says that he "used to fill up the water bottle and stuff, and I do that, go to practices and stuff."

He shares his plans, "I'm actually trying, I'm thinking about it, I'm trying to get into coaching, like me and my dad might try and coach like lacrosse or something, eventually or something like that, and I want to try and get into helping out coaching hockey, stuff like that."

Discussion and Conclusions

When Daniel started his training, he was faced with learning the norms of a business environment. Like Hochschild's flight attendants (Hochschild, 1983; 1998) who had to manage their emotions in the flight cabin and be able to deal with passengers in a restricted space, trainees were expected to do similar emotion management in the store, in their interaction with customers, supervisors, and co-workers. Daniel learned that once in the store, his immediate needs, desires, and feelings were secondary to the customers'—the customer is king. There were also moments of boredom (Collinson, 1992) and fatigue (Wilton, 2008) that needed to be managed. Emotional labour, in particular, means submitting to norms that are at times difficult to deal with for some people with disabilities. Some face physical or mental conditions that make it hard to be in a very normative and ableist work environment.

Daniel's story illustrates some of the successes and challenges that young people with disabilities are facing when transitioning to adulthood, entering the workplace, and participating in the community. In interviews, Daniel often referred to his family, whose support included helping him to find work. Research has shown that the socio-economic background and the social and cultural capital of the family remain essential for a successful transition (Trainor, 2008; 2010). Daniel has achieved many things that other people with disabilities have not been able to: he has a partner with whom he has a daughter; he holds several jobs; and he has activities outside work that he enjoys doing, mostly related to sports. On the other hand, while working three jobs, he is still not able to support his young family, and, for that reason, is forced to live with his parents. This shows the dearth of affordable housing options for people with disabilities. Often, the only options available to them are either to live with their families or to access group homes. More flexible arrangements are underdeveloped. Related to housing, we need to consider the type of work and salaries that people with disabilities are subjected to (e.g., Holwerda et al., 2012; Howlin, 2003; Shattuck et al., 2012). Even Daniel, who is able to work three jobs simultaneously, is not able to sustain a lifestyle that could afford him independent living with his new family.

Daniel stands out because he is very active outside work, thanks to organizations such as Independent Living Nova Scotia and the Special Olympics. He also participates in athletic activities in the broader community, which is less common for people with disabilities. While many have questioned how inclusive organizations such as Special Olympics are for people with intellectual disabilities (see e.g., Storey, 2008; Counsell and Agran, 2013; MacLean, 2008), Daniel and other alumni from the ACEE program have repeatedly pointed to the importance of those events for their lives.

Recognizing and removing barriers and fostering accessibility and opportunities for participation are essential to recognizing the agency of people with disabilities. We need to empower young adults with disabilities to make decisions about their lives, pay them equitably for the work they do, and offer them meaningful and inclusive ways to engage with the community. Research with people with disabilities offers direction for policy development so that they can live their lives in dignity and to their full potential.

References

Barnes, C., and Mercer, G. (2010). *Exploring disability: A sociological introduction* (2nd edn). Cambridge, UK; Malden, MA: Polity Press.

Collinson, D. (1992). *Managing the shopfloor: Subjectivity, masculinity, and workplace culture.* Berlin; New York: W. de Gruyter.

Counsell, S., and Agran, M. (2013). Understanding the Special Olympics debate from lifeworld and system perspectives: Moving beyond the liberal egalitarian view toward empowered recreational living. *Journal of Disability Policy Studies, 23*(4), 245–56. doi:10.1177/1044207312450751

Hochschild, A.R. (1983). *The managed heart: Commercialization of human feeling.* Berkeley: University of California Press.

Hochschild, A.R. (1998). The sociology of emotion as a way of seeing. In G. Bendelow, and S. J. Williams (Eds), *Emotions in social life. critical themes and contemporary issues* (pp. 3–15). London: Routledge.

Holwerda, A., van der Klink, J.J.L., Groothoff, J.W., and Brouwer, S. (2012). Predictors for work participation with an autism spectrum disorders: A systematic review. *Journal of Occupational Rehabilitation, 22,* 333–52.

Howlin, P. (2003). Longer-term educational and employment outcomes. In M. Prior (Ed.), *Learning and behavior problems in Asperger syndrome* (pp. 269–93). New York: Guilford Press.

MacLean, W.E., Jr. (2008). Special Olympics: The rest of the story. *Research & Practice for Persons with Severe Disabilities, 33*(3), 146–9.

Oliver, M. (1998). Theories in health care and research: Theories of disability in health practice and research. *British Medical Journal, 317*(7170), 1446–9.

Schneider, C. (2010). "Ready for work": Feeling rules, emotion work and emotional labour for people with disabilities, *Interactions, 4.* Retrieved from: http://dc.msvu.ca:8080/xmlui/bitstream/handle/10587/1601/schneider_en.pdf?sequence=1&isAllowed=y

Schneider, C., Chahine, S., Hattie, B. (2015). Trajectoires et transitions de vie de jeunes en situation de handicap. *La nouvelle revue de l'adaptation et de la scolarisation, 68,* 209–25.

Shattuck, P.T., Narendorf, S.C., Cooper, B., Sterzing, P.R., Wagner, M., and Taylor, J.L. (2012). Postsecondary and employment among youth with an autism spectrum disorder. *Pediatrics, 129*(6): 1042–1049. doi: 10.1542/peds.2011-2864

Statistics Canada. (2013). *Disability in Canada: Initial findings from the Canadian survey on disability.* Retrieved from: http://www.statcan.gc.ca/pub/89-654-x/89-654-x2013002-eng.pdf

Statistics Canada (2014). *Study: Persons with disability and employment.* Retrieved from: http://www.statcan.gc.ca/daily-quotidien/141203/dq141203a-eng.pdf

Storey, K. (2008). The more things change, the more they are the same: Continuing concerns with the Special Olympics. *Research & Practice for Persons with Severe Disabilities, 33*(3), 134–42.

Trainor, A.A. (2008). Using social and cultural capital to improve postsecondary outcomes and expand transition models for youth with disabilities. *Journal of Special Education, 42,* 148–62.

Trainor, A.A. (2010). Re-examining the promise of parent participation in special education: An analysis of cultural and social capital. *Anthropology and Education Quarterly, 41,* 245–63.

Wilton, R.D. (2008). Workers with disabilities and the challenges of emotional labour. *Disability & society* 23.4, 361–73.

Questions for Critical Thought

Chapter 41 | Race and the Labour Market Integration of Second-Generation Young Adults

1. What two things does Boyd think suggest that international migration is a defining characteristic for Canada?
2. Boyd describes several models that can explain immigrant offspring's economic potential. How do these models differ?
3. Thinking about Boyd's research, why is examining all minority groups together problematic? How might this impact the results of this study?
4. Which of the second-generation minority groups earn substantially less income? Describe the problem with this.

Chapter 42 | Productivity and Prosperity: A Study in the Sociology of Ideas

1. Foster says that ideas have the ability to constrain or enable action. Using the 2008 financial crisis, how is this statement true? How did ideas constrain action? How did ideas enable action?
2. What is the role of ideas in sociological studies? Think about what sociologists study and what they do with the information they gather.
3. What is productivism? Who does it benefit? Draw on Weber's idea of work ethic.
4. How have ideas of productivism changed? Use the examples from this chapter of various schools of thought that emerged over time.
5. Foster ends this chapter by discussing anti-productivism by comparing it to productivism. What is anti-productivism? What tension exists between the ideas of productivism and anti-productivism?

Chapter 43 | Underemployment in Advanced Capitalism: Patterns and Prospects

1. What is underemployment? What are some other terms that are used to describe this phenomenon?
2. What are the three basic dimensions of underemployment? Briefly explain each of the three.
3. What percentage of the Canadian population is underemployed? Break this down into subgroups. Is this number higher or lower than you expected? Explain.
4. Do educational requirements always align with job requirements? What are the social implications of this relationship?
5. What solutions are suggested to decrease underemployment? What else can be done?

Chapter 44 | Unemployment Experiences of Women in Toronto and Halifax

1. What are UI and EI? How did the shift from UI to EI impact women?
2. Nichols draws on intersectionality theory to understand the experiences of the unemployed women in her study. What is intersectionality theory? Why is this theory appropriate for understanding the experiences of these women?
3. How does child care impact women's employability or employment status? Draw on the experiences of the women in Nichols's study.
4. What health care costs did these women sustain while they were unemployed? How does this tie into the earlier discussion on the denial of EI benefits?
5. List the factors that impact women's employment and unemployment experiences. Drawing from this list and intersectionality theory, what can be done to improve EI?

Chapter 45 | Transitioning into Adulthood: Disability, Barriers, and Accessibility

1. Describe the medical versus social model of disability. Why is the evolution toward the social model important?
2. Schneider collected rich data using multiple methodologies. Why use multiple methodologies?
3. Describe the ACEE program. What skills did Daniel learn through this program? How did this help him acquire employment opportunities?
4. Through ACEE and other programs, Daniel received many opportunities that he might not have had otherwise. What struggles did Daniel face after graduating from ACEE?
5. What is the importance of studying access to employment for individuals with disabilities?

PART XI
Health and Care

Canadians attach a great deal of importance to good health and good health care. There are many reasons for this prioritization. First, good health is a common concern among people around the world; it's hard to enjoy success and prosperity, let alone endure poverty, if you are sick. Second, Canadians consider their health care system to be progressive and egalitarian compared to that of other modern societies (most especially the United States); for Canadians, good health is a measure of societal success and commitment to shared well-being. Third, much research has shown that good health and good health care are generally correlated with a wide range of other safety net commitments, like good access to public education, housing, welfare, and justice.

In health and health care research, sociologists contribute a better understanding of both the social processes that affect health and the impact that illness has on patients and their loved ones. Currently, the sociology of health is one of the most dynamic fields in sociology, and it is constantly changing as it adapts to new illnesses and technologies. The sociological work on this topic often overlaps with the work of epidemiologists and other public health researchers, but sociologists specifically focus on the impact of health and illness on social life, and vice versa. Their areas of study include how families deal with illness, doctor–patient relationships, attitudes toward illness, strategies of health promotion, and health delivery policy.

Here, we see a strong contrast between sociological approaches and the biomedical approach to illness. This latter approach to health reflects the Western medical profession's focus on curing sickness rather than preventing it from occurring. In the biomedical model, the doctor is like a mechanic and the human body is like a machine that occasionally needs repair. However, defining health in strictly somatic terms is inadequate in several ways. There is a growing recognition that the symptoms of biologically identical illnesses vary with differences in personal history, socio-economic condition, and cultural background (Ritsatakis, 2009), leading doctors to understand the importance of "treating the patient rather than simply the disease."

Modern ideas about health have therefore moved away from a solely physiological model toward a more holistic understanding. Here, health is viewed synonymously with well-being—that is, as a state of existence characterized by happiness, prosperity, and the satisfaction of basic human needs. The World Health Organization (WHO), for example, defines health as "a state of complete physical, mental, and social well-being," a definition that has gone unchanged since the organization's formation after World War II (WHO, 1948/2017). Health Canada takes an equally broad stand on the meaning of health, viewing it as a state of social, mental, emotional, and physical well-being that is influenced by a broad range of factors, including biology and genetics, personal health practices and coping skills, social and physical environments, gender, socio-economic factors such as income and education, and cultural practices and norms (Health Canada, 1999).

The chapters in this section reflect these modern sociological ideas about health and health care. In Chapter 46, Rod Beaujot, Jianye Liu, and Zenaida Ravanera show that health care can be as simple as tending to day-to-day strategies of care and illness prevention. These researchers examine the distribution of care-based tasks within families to identify who is mostly responsible for care. As it happens, women or mothers are most often responsible for care; however, these researchers find that men are increasingly taking on more care responsibilities. Thus, these researchers draw our attention to the frontline responders to health care—the family.

This attentiveness to the need for home care becomes especially pressing as the population ages. Accordingly, in Chapter 47 Neena Chappell and Margaret Penning examine health in aging populations. These authors look beyond the physical by using WHO's definition of health, which as we have seen includes the physical, the psychological, and the social. When looking at trends in the health of older adults, this chapter reveals that (a) physically, they are likely to face degenerative diseases; (b) mentally, they have high levels of happiness and life satisfaction despite some instances of depression; and (c) socially, some experience elder abuse or violence. Overall, this chapter presents evidence that helps us to understand trends in the health of older adults that will become increasingly important with the passage of time.

Lastly, Chapter 48 examines the politics that are involved in organ donation. Here, Lindsay McKay describes the public discourse surrounding organ donation while also acknowledging the impact of policy-makers and experts. Mostly, this chapter focuses on the important issue of consent for donation, and how it may be possible to convince the public to give consent more often. Understanding the politics involved in illness and medicine is an important aspect of the sociology of health.

The chapters in this section are meant to provide a better understanding of health research by describing patterns of caregiving and the politics of health care in Canada. They reflect the biopsychosocial view of health and illness. As the name implies, this perspective recognizes that health and disease are products of the interaction of body, mind, and environment, and not just of biology alone. As well, the research in this section reminds us that health is not an all-or-nothing condition. The relative contributions of each factor—mind, body, and social environment—vary from condition to condition and from case to case. The challenge is to find out the role of each factor and to tailor interventions—medical as well as social—accordingly.

References

Health Canada. 1999. Building the Relationship between National Voluntary Organizations Working in Health and Health Care: A Framework for Action. Ottawa: The Joint Working Group on the Voluntary Sector, Health Canada.

Ritsatakis, Anna. 2009. Equity and social determinants of health at a city level. Health Promotion International, 24(Suppl 1): i81-i90.

World Health Organization (WHO). 2017. Constitution of WHO, http://www.who.int/about/mission/en

46 The Converging Gender Trends in Earning and Caring in Canada

Roderic Beaujot, Jianye Liu, and Zenaida Ravanera

Following on *Earning and Caring in Canadian Families* (Beaujot 2000), this article updates the data on the central family activities of earning a living and caring for each other. We consider the gender side of participation in these activities, along with alternate models of the division of earning and caring. This article is based on the idea that there are two components to the gender revolution: **gender relations in the public sphere** and **gender relations in the private sphere** (Goldscheider et al. 2015).

Gender and Earning

The gender changes in earning a living are especially observable in women's increased education and employment (Beaujot et al. 2014: 22). For the population aged 20–64, employment rates and mean work hours, by gender, have moved in a converging direction (Table 46.1). Nonetheless, important differences remain: 78.8 per cent of men and 64.1 per cent of women were employed in 2011; for those working, the mean hours worked were 42.5 for men and 35.2 for women.

Table 46.1 further differentiates employment rates and mean work hours, both by marital status (married/cohabiting versus other) and by parental status (not living with children versus living with children). Men still have the highest employment when they are married or cohabiting, with children at home. However, women's employment rate is no longer suppressed when they are living with children. For married or cohabiting women, the employment rates are the same for those living with and without children at home (66.1 per cent versus 66.3 per cent in 2011). For persons who are not in relationships, both women and men have higher employment rates when they are living with children.

Gender and Time Use in Earning and Caring

The link between gender and caring has not changed as rapidly (Beaujot 2000). However, there has been some change, with men doing more housework and child care than in the past (Doucet 2006; Ranson 2010; Marshall 2006).

Time-use surveys present useful measures to document both earning and caring activities on the basis of the same metric. Table 46.2 divides the time use over a 24-hour day among the following categories: paid work (including commuting to and from work, and education), unpaid work (including housework, household maintenance, child care, elder care, and volunteer work), personal care (including eating and sleeping), and leisure or free time (including active and passive leisure). The table shows hours per day, averaged over a seven-day week, in various activities.

Adding paid work and unpaid work shows that the average total productive activity of men and women has been very similar in each of the survey years. From 1986 to 2010, the work hours have converged as women's paid work hours and men's unpaid work increased. In 1986, women's paid work plus education represented 58.9 per cent of men's time, compared to 74.0 per cent in 2010. For unpaid work, men's time in 1986 represented 46.3 per cent of women's time, compared to 65.9 per cent in 2010. In 2010, for both men and women, the total time in productive activities increases from persons who are not in relationships with no children, to those

TABLE 46.1 Employment Rate and Hours Worked at All Jobs in a Week, by Gender, Marital, and Parental Status, Persons Aged 20–64, Canada, 2006 and 2011

		Male		Female	
		Employment rate	Mean work hours	Employment rate	Mean work hours
		2006			
Mar/Coh	Total	87.0	45.2	64.1	36.2
	No Child	79.2	44.1	65.9	37.6
	Child(ren)	91.5	45.8	62.9	35.3
Other	Total	68.5	41.7	61.8	37.4
	No Child	67.2	41.5	58.7	37.3
	Child(ren)	83.2	44.0	69.5	37.7
Total	Total	81.1	44.2	63.3	36.6
	No Child	72.7	42.7	62.6	37.5
	Child(ren)	91.0	45.7	64.1	35.8
		2011			
Mar/Coh	Total	86.4	43.9	66.2	35.2
	No Child	78.1	42.6	66.3	35.8
	Child(ren)	91.0	44.6	66.1	34.8
Other	Total	61.9	39.1	59.5	35.2
	No Child	60.7	38.9	56.4	34.5
	Child(ren)	77.6	42.0	68.1	37.2
Total	Total	78.8	42.5	64.1	35.2
	No Child	68.7	40.6	61.6	35.2
	Child(ren)	90.4	44.4	66.4	35.2

Source: Beaujot et al. 2013: 231 and authors' calculation based on General Social Survey in 2011.

married/cohabiting without children, to the married/cohabiting parents (Beaujot et al. 2014: 25).

Marshall (2011) also showed a converging trend in gender roles by comparing the division of work across three generations: late baby boomers (born 1957–1966), Generation X (1969–1978), and Generation Y (1981–1990). She found increasing gender similarity in the involvement in paid work and housework from the earlier to the later generation. Compared to older generations, among young adults (aged 20–29) in dual-earner couples, women had increased their hours of paid work and men increased their share of household work. However, even for the younger generations, the presence of children reduced the woman's total paid work time and increased her time in housework. It is among persons working full-time that the average hours of child care are lowest, and most similar for men and women (Ravanera and Hoffman 2012: 33).

Models of the Division of Earning and Caring at the Couple Level

Another way of measuring the variability in earning and caring is at the couple level. By comparing spouses, we can determine whether a given person

TABLE 46.2 Time Use (Average Hours Per Day) of Total Population Aged 15+ and Employed Persons, by Gender, Canada, 1986–2010

	1986		1998		2010	
	M	F	M	F	M	F
			Population 15+			
Total productive activity	7.5	7.4	8.0	8.0	7.9	8.1
Paid work and education	5.6	3.3	5.2	3.5	5.0	3.7
Unpaid work	1.9	4.1	2.8	4.5	2.9	4.4
Personal care	10.8	11.2	10.3	10.6	10.6	11.0
Leisure/free time	5.7	5.3	5.7	5.3	5.5	4.9
Total	24.0	24.0	24.0	24.0	24.0	24.0
			Employed Persons			
Total productive activity	9.0	9.2	9.5	9.7	9.6	9.7
Paid work and education	7.2	6.0	6.9	5.8	6.9	6.1
Unpaid work	1.8	3.2	2.6	3.9	2.6	3.6
Personal care	10.2	10.6	9.8	10.1	10.0	10.4
Leisure/free time	4.8	4.2	4.7	4.2	4.4	3.9
Total	24.0	24.0	24.0	24.0	24.0	24.0

Source: Beaujot et al. 2008: Table 1 and authors' calculation based on General Social Survey in 2010.

does more, the same amount, or less of each of paid and unpaid work (Table 46.3). For the couples where neither is a full-time student and neither is retired, we have combined these patterns into five models of the division of paid and unpaid work.[1]

The most predominant model is the complementary-traditional where the man does more paid work and the woman does more unpaid work; however, it has declined from 43.5 per cent of couples in 1992 to 33.4 per cent in 2010. The women's double burden, where she does more unpaid work and at least as much paid work, has been constant at some 26 to 27 per cent of couples. The shared role model, where they do about the same amount of unpaid work, has increased the most, from 22.6 per cent in 1992 to 28.8 per cent in 2010. Men's double burden, where he does more unpaid work and at least as much paid work, has increased from 5.8 per cent to 8.8 per cent. The complementary-gender-reversed model is the least common, but it has increased from 1.7 per cent to 3.2 per cent of couples between 1992 and 2010.

Other analyses indicate that the models where women do more unpaid work (complementary-traditional or women's double burden) are more common when there are young children present, while the models where men do a more equal share of unpaid work are more likely when women have more education and other resources (Ravanera et al. 2009). Furthermore, average household incomes in 2005 and 2010 are highest in the shared roles model, intermediate in the models involving the double burden, and lowest in the complementary roles model (Beaujot et al. 2014: 11). This is contrary to the proposition of Becker (1981) that gender specialization presents more efficiency in total household production.

TABLE 46.3 Distribution of Couples by Models of Division of Work, Canada, 1992–2010

	Persons in couples			
Models of Division of Work (%)	1992	1998	2005	2010
Complementary-traditional	43.5	39.1	32.9	33.4
Complementary-gender-reversed	1.7	2.7	3.0	3.2
Women's double burden	26.5	26.8	26.8	25.9
Men's double burden	5.8	7.6	10.7	8.8
Shared roles	22.6	23.8	26.5	28.8

Note: Calculated for couples where neither is a full-time student and neither is retired.

Sources: Beaujot et al. 2008: Table 7 and authors' calculation based on General Social Survey in 2010.

Discussion

The trends in earning and caring have moved in the direction of reduced gender inequalities, especially a greater sharing of paid work, and some change toward men's greater participation in unpaid work. However, the differences remain large, and the inequalities are accentuated by the presence of young children.

As a report for the United Nations Economic Commission for Europe proposes: "transforming gender norms is vital to the success of family policies" (United Nations 2013: 11). In particular, the two-income model should be promoted at the expense of the breadwinner model. This necessitates further changes both in the public and private spheres.

In the past, family policy followed the breadwinner model, with an emphasis on men's family wage and associated pension and health benefits, along with widowhood and orphanhood provisions in the case of the premature death of breadwinners. The focus of family policy was on dealing with the loss of a breadwinner and supporting the elderly who were beyond working age.

In the contemporary context, both lone-parent and two-parent families would benefit from promoting a more egalitarian type of family that includes greater common ground between women and men in family activities. Just as policy has promoted the de-gendering of earning, we should discuss the types of social policy that would further modernize the family in the direction of co-providing and co-parenting. Key questions here include parental leave and child care. Parental leave supports the continuing earning roles of parents, and public support for child care reduces the costs for working parents. The Quebec model for parental leave, including greater flexibility and a dedicated leave for fathers, has promoted the greater participation of men in parental leave (Beaujot et al. 2013). The higher Quebec support for child care has also promoted women's earning activities.

Note

1. These models are based on questions regarding time use in the previous week, relating to the respondent and the respondent's spouse. Combining the paid and unpaid work hours for the couple, we first divided each of paid and unpaid work hours of respondent and spouse into three categories: respondent does more (over 60 per cent of the total), respondent does less (under 40 per cent of the total), and they do the same (40–60 per cent of the total).

From the nine models in terms of a given partner doing more, the same or less of each of paid and unpaid work, we derived the five models as specified in the table. The 2010 questionnaire used categories, rather than specific number of hours, for spouse's time use over the week. Based on the respondents of given sexes and presence of children, we established point estimates from these categories.

References

Beaujot, Roderic. 2000. *Earning and Caring in Canadian Families*. Peterborough, ON: Broadview.

Beaujot, Roderic, Ching Du, and Zenaida Ravanera. 2013. "Family Policies in Quebec and the Rest of Canada: Implications for Fertility, Child Care, Women's Paid Work and Child Development Indicators." *Canadian Public Policy* 39(2): 221–39.

Beaujot, Roderic, Jianye Liu, and Zenaida Ravanera. 2014. "Family Diversity and Inequality: The Canadian Case." *Population Change and LifeCourse Cluster Discussion Paper Series* 1(1). Available at: http://ir.lib.uwo.ca/pclc/vol1/iss1/7/

Beaujot, Roderic, Zenaida Ravanera, and Jianye Liu. 2008. *Models of Earning and Caring: Trends, Determinants and Implications*. Report prepared for Human Resources and Skills Development Canada. Available at: http://sociology.uwo.ca/cluster/en/publications/docs/research_briefs/RB-02_final_report.pdf

Becker, Gary. 1981. *A Treatise on the Family*. Cambridge, MA: Harvard University Press.

Doucet, Andrea. 2006. *Do Men Mother? Fathering, Care, and Domestic Responsibilities*. Toronto: University of Toronto Press.

Goldscheider, Frances, Eva Bernhardt, and Trude Lappegard. 2015. "The Gender Revolution: Understanding Changing Family and Demographic Behavior." *Population and Development Review* 41(2): 207-39.

Marshall, Katherine. 2006. "Converging Gender Roles." *Perspectives on Labour and Income* 18(3): 7–19.

Marshall, Katherine, 2011. "Generational Change in Paid and Unpaid Work." *Canadian Social Trends* 92: 13–24.

Ranson, Gillian. 2010. *Against the Grain: Couples, Gender, and the Reframing of Parenting*. Toronto: University of Toronto Press.

Ravanera, Zenaida, Roderic Beaujot, and Jianye Liu. 2009. Models of earning and caring: Determinants of the division of work. *Canadian Review of Sociology* 46(4): 319–37.

Ravanera, Zenaida and John Hoffman. 2012. Canadian Fathers: Demographic and Socio-Economic Profiles from Census and National Surveys. Pp. 26-49 in J. Ball and K. Daly (Eds), *Father Involvement in Canada: Diversity, Renewal, and Transformation*. Vancouver: UBC Press.

United Nations, 2013. *Enabling Choices: Population Priorities for the 21st Century*. Report of the UNECE Regional Conference on ICPD beyond 2014. United Nations, Economic and Social Council, Economic Commission for Europe ECE/AC.27/2013/2.

47 Health Declines in Old Age, or Does it?

Neena L. Chappell and Margaret J. Penning

Everyone knows health declines in old age; the older we become, the worse our health becomes. Consequently, old age and poor health tend to be viewed as synonymous: it is one of the reasons we disparage old age. Gerontology has a long history of recognizing this fact and has a major focus on health, especially from a **biomedical perspective**. Although the field has broadened considerably in recent decades to embrace many disciplinary perspectives, a preoccupation with physical decline, disease, and chronic illness remains evident. This is so despite the fact that long ago the World Health Organization (1948) embraced a multidimensional definition of health that includes physical, psychological, and social dimensions. As sociologists, we were interested in the extent to which the view of old age and aging, particularly within old age, as a process of health-related decline applies when acknowledging the non-biomedical (social, psychological) as well as the more biomedical aspects of health. We did so for a report for the Public Health Agency of Canada (Chappell and Penning 2012). We draw on that report to illustrate the value of a social perspective on health, focusing on Canadian research.

Gerontological Distinctions

Distinguishing between younger and older adults as well as among older adults, typically on the basis of declining health together with related social factors, has a rich history in gerontology. Neugarten (1974; 1975) was the first to distinguish among older age groups, differentiating between young-old (55–74) and old-old (75+) categories based on health status, economic, work, family, and political differences. Since then, authors have added middle-old and oldest-old age categories and have also distinguished between third and fourth age categories (Baltes and Smith 2003). Laslett (1991) described the third age as an era of personal achievement and fulfillment and the fourth as an era of dependence, decrepitude, and death.

Importantly, distinctions between age categories tend to map onto those between pathological, usual, and successful aging. There is a plethora of overlapping nomenclature for the latter—productive aging, robust aging, optimal aging, and aging well—that have at times been used synonymously (Baltes and Smith 2003; Kahana, Kahana, and Kercher 2003; Rowe and Kahn 1998). The long-standing MacArthur model defined successful aging in contrast with usual aging (being at high risk of disease and disabilities) and pathological aging (having diseases and disability) as having three main components: avoidance/low risk of disease and disability, high levels of physical and cognitive functioning, and engagement in social and productive activities (Rowe and Kahn 1987).

Attempts to distinguish good or better aging from aging that entails decline stems in part from efforts to present aging in a positive light (i.e., not everyone who is old is in poor health). Nevertheless, they can be said to convey an **ageism**, implying that those who do not age successfully are undesirable and even responsible, thereby blaming the victim (Dillaway and Byrnes 2009). This is especially problematic insofar as risk, embedded in notions of successful aging, is unequally distributed based on social class, ethnic, and other aspects of social location. While there is neither consensus nor consistency in the terms used to refer to health differences among older adults as they age, there is consistency in the general distinction between younger and older seniors, with the latter typically considered in worse health than the former (von Faber and van der Geest 2010, is an exception).

Health, Age, and Aging

How accurate are these distinctions? When examining physical health in terms of diseases and chronic conditions, it seems clear that older adults are more likely to experience declines than those who are younger. Older adults tend to suffer from chronic conditions (such as arthritis, heart disease, and diabetes) with an overall prevalence rate for one or more conditions at over 80 per cent (Gilmour and Park 2006). Importantly, however, not all chronic conditions are more prevalent among older adults (e.g., asthmas—Gilmour and Park 2006) and there are contradictory findings for some illnesses (such as diabetes, stroke, hypertension—Hogan, Ebly, and Fung 1999). Within old age, physical health declines over time and older elderly adults, regardless of how health is operationalized, tend to have poorer physical health than those who are young-old (Gilmour and Park 2006; Orpana et al. 2010).

When moving away from a biomedical focus on health and illness to a social perspective, the picture is less clear. Functional disability relates to the enactment of social roles, typically measured in terms of the ability to complete activities of daily living (such as mobility, eating, driving, and housework) or several combined. The prevalence of functional disability varies depending on the number and type of disabilities considered. Furthermore, even though the majority of older adults have one or more chronic conditions, most do not experience functional disability. Rather, well over 75 per cent of community-dwelling persons aged 65+ are functionally able. Nevertheless, functional disability increases with age, with about 50 per cent of those aged 75+ living in the community experiencing some functional disability (Statistics Canada 2009).

Perceptions fall into the social psychological realm of sociology. Consistent with declines in physical health, older adults are less likely to self-assess their health positively; over three-quarters do, but this is less than younger adults (Conference Board of Canada 2011; Milan and Vézina 2011). Self-assessments of health also appear to decline within old age; yet most report good to excellent health (Milan and Vézina 2011). Importantly, taking objective differences in health status into account reveals older adults (85+) perceive their health as positively as those younger (Hogan, Ebly, and Fung 1999).

Mental, rather than physical, health falls in the realm of social psychology. It has been defined as "the capacity of each person to feel, think and act in ways that allow them to enjoy life and deal with all the challenges they face. . . . a positive sense of emotional and spiritual well-being that respects the importance of culture, equity, social justice, interconnections and personal dignity" (Standing Senate Committee on Social Affairs, Science, and Technology 2004: 67). It is widely acknowledged that **mental health** is more than the absence of mental illness. A dual continuum model (Keyes, Dhingra, and Simoes 2010; Westerhof and Keyes 2009) views the two as distinct phenomena. In terms of mental health, cross-sectional studies indicate that overall levels of life satisfaction and happiness are relatively high in later life. Over 90 per cent of older Canadians rate their mental health as good to excellent; 89 per cent report being satisfied or very satisfied with their lives (Statistics Canada 2002). How such factors change over the life course is not clear (Blanchflower and Oswald 2008; Latif 2011). The evidence on trends within old age is also contradictory yet suggests little or no decline with age after taking physical health problems or other confounding factors into account (Milan and Vézina 2011).

In terms of mental illness, depression has been characterized as the most common mental disorder in older adults (Canadian Coalition for Seniors' Mental Health 2009); yet it is not a normal accompaniment of aging. Twelve-month prevalence rates for major depression range from 2 to 3 per cent in community samples (Østbye et al 2005; Patten et al. 2006). Whether these low rates can be attributed to under-reporting is unknown. Contradictory evidence exists on whether depression increases or decreases during old age (Cairney et al. 2008; Østbye et al. 2005). In one of the few Canadian longitudinal studies, Wu and colleagues (2012: 22) conclude that any "age-related increase of depression symptoms occurs entirely through medical illness, such as dementia, chronic conditions, and functional limitations. . . . [M]ajor depression decreases from age 65 to age 79. Afterwards, it begins to increase, suggesting that old age has 'two faces' when it comes to major depression."

Turning to more directly social measures of health, most seniors are not socially isolated if defined in terms of lack of contact with others. Lindsay (2008) reports that only 2 per cent of older adults say they have no close friend *and* no close relatives. Whether social isolation increases with age depends on the measure used. The prevalence of "poor social health" appears somewhat higher when assessed in terms of having no friends one feels close to, with 12–14 per cent of those aged 65–74 and 18 per cent of those aged 75 and older saying there were none compared with 5 per cent of those aged 25–54 (Lindsay 2008; Statistics Canada 2006). Conversely, the proportion who report daily contact with family (6–11 per cent) and friends (11–15 per cent) increases with age. The number of seniors reporting that they miss having people around increases with age (Statistics Canada 2008). Importantly, we lack good data on social isolation experienced by those resident in nursing homes. In sum, however, it is not at all clear that old age is a risk factor for high levels of social isolation.

The experience of elder abuse can also be considered an indicator of social health. It can be physical, financial, psychological, and/or emotional and can come from many sources (family, friends, health care workers). It refers to harmful behaviour in the context of a trust relationship (Chappell, McDonald, and Stones 2008) and is an act of commission. The extent of abuse is largely unknown, the major concern being under-reporting. It is, therefore, considered a hidden crime. Prevalence figures are inconsistent. Sev'er (2009) reports that the risk increases after age 85. Statistics Canada (2011) reports decreasing rates of family violence with age among those aged 65+ (<1 per cent in all age groups). Decreasing rates may reflect a declining ability to complain or report violence as chronic illnesses and cognitive impairment increase (Sev'er 2009). Despite concern with elder abuse, the data on abuse within families do not provide confirmation and there is a suggestion that family violence may decrease after institutionalization. However, Canadian data on abuse from family members are dated and data on other sources largely non-existent.

Conclusions

Can we equate old age with poor and declining health? In part, the answer is clearly no. Health is a tremendously broad area, has several domains, and many measures can be employed within those domains. Most older adults across all age categories demonstrate good health, whether assessed using physical, social psychological, or social criteria. Does health decline with age? Here, the answer appears less clear. In Canada, for measures of physical health such as the number of chronic conditions, decline is greater the older we become. There does not appear to be an exact age that represents a threshold or turning point. When it comes to social psychological and social domains, however, the results are mixed. Functional disability and self-assessed health decline with age. Happiness and life satisfaction score high in old age and findings on change over the life course are contradictory. The prevalence of depression is low in old age as are rates of social isolation and elder abuse. Therefore, on social psychological and social measures, older adults fare much better than when examining only physical health. Furthermore, even physical health is subject to social effects. Both Beckett (2000), using US data, and Prus (2007), using Canadian data, note the increased delay of morbidity and disability among higher socio-economic status individuals until a shorter period at the end of life compared to lower SES persons (i.e., the social stratification of the compression of morbidity). House, Lantz, and Herd (2005), using US data, found education related to the onset of limitations while income was related to the progression of a health problem after its onset (looking at morbidity, functioning, and mortality).

Overall, these findings attest to the need to clearly define health and acknowledge the importance of a social perspective on health. Social well-being is a fundamental component of health. Including measures of social health leads to acknowledgement that aging is not a uniform process of health decline. It also counters the prevailing view and suggests that being in the oldest-old or fourth-age categories is not inherently or uniformly pathological or unsuccessful, even when chronic illness and disability are present.

References

Baltes, Paul B., and Jacqui Smith. 2003. "New Frontiers in the Future of Aging: From Successful Aging of the Young Old to the Dilemmas of the Fourth Age." *Gerontology* 49(2): 123–35. doi: 10.1159/000067946

Beckett, Megan. 2000. "Converging Health Inequalities in Later Life–An Artifact of Mortality Selection?" *Journal of Health and Social Behavior* 41(1): 106–19.

Blanchflower, David G., and Andrew J. Oswald. 2008. "Is Well-Being U-Shaped over the Life Cycle?" *Social Science and Medicine* 66(8): 1733–49. doi:10.1016/j.socscimed.2008.01.030

Cairney, John, Laura M. Corna, Scott Veldhuizen, Paul Kurdyak, and David L. Streiner. 2008. "The Social Epidemiology of Affective and Anxiety Disorders in Later Life in Canada." *Canadian Journal of Psychiatry* 53(2): 104–11.

Canadian Coalition for Seniors' Mental Health. 2009. *Depression in Older Adults: A Guide for Seniors and Their Families*. Toronto: 2009 Canadian Coalition for Seniors' Mental Health.

Chappell, Neena L., Lynn McDonald, and Michael Stones. 2008. *Aging in Contemporary Canada*, 2nd Edition. Toronto: Pearson/Prentice Hall.

Chappell, Neena L., and Margaret J. Penning. 2012. *Health Inequalities in Later Life, Differences by Age/Stage*. Report submitted to the Public Health Agency of Canada, 23 March 2012.

Conference Board of Canada. 2011. *Health—Self-Reported Health Status*. Accessed 12 December 2011 at: http://www.conferenceboard.ca/hcp/Details/Health/self-reported-health-status.aspx#_ftn1

Dillaway, Heather E., and Mary Byrnes. 2009. "Reconsidering Successful Aging: A Call for Renewed and Expanded Academic Critiques and Conceptualizations." *Journal of Applied Gerontology* 28(6): 702–22. doi:10.1177/0733464809333882

Gilmour, Heather, and Jungwee Park. 2006. "Dependency, Chronic Conditions and Pain in Seniors." *Health Reports* 16(Suppl): 21–31.

Hogan, David B., Erika M. Ebly, and Tak S. Fung. 1999. "Disease, Disability, and Age in Cognitively Intact Seniors: Results from the Canadian Study of Health and Aging." *Journals of Gerontology A: Biological Sciences and Medical Sciences* 54A(2): M77–82. doi: 10.1093/Gerona/54.2.M77

House, James S., Paula M. Lantz, and Pamela Herd. 2005. "Continuity and Change in the Social Stratification of Aging and Health over the Life Course: Evidence from a Nationally Representative Longitudinal Study from 1986 to 2001/2002 (Americans" Changing Lives Study)." *Journals of Gerontology B: Psychological Sciences and Social Sciences* 60(Special Issue 2): S15–26. doi:10.1093/geronb/60.Special_Issue_2.S15

Kahana, Eva, Boaz Kahana, and Kyle Kercher. 2003. "Emerging Lifestyles and Proactive Options for Successful Ageing." *Ageing International* 28(2): 155–80.

Keyes, Corey L.M., Satvinder S. Dhingra, and Eduardo J. Simoes. 2010. "Change in Level of Positive Mental Health as a Predictor of Future Risk of Mental Illness." *American Journal of Public Health* 100(12): 2366–71. doi:10.2105/AJPH.2010.192245

Laslett, Peter. 1991. *A Fresh Map of Life: The Emergence of the Third Age*. Cambridge, MA: Harvard University Press.

Latif, Ehsan. 2011. "The Impact of Retirement on Psychological Well-Being in Canada." *The Journal of Socio-Economics* 40(4): 373–80. doi:10.1016/j.socec.2010.12.011

Lindsay, Colin. 2008. *Do Older Canadians Have More Friends Now Than in 1990?* General Social Survey Matter of Fact Series No. 4. Ottawa: Statistics Canada Catalogue no. 89-630-X.

Milan, Anne, and Mireille Vézina. 2011. *Senior Women: A Component of Women in Canada: A Gender-Based Statistical Report*. Statistics Canada Catalogue no. 89-503-X.

Neugarten, Bernice L. 1974. "Age Groups in American Society and the Rise of the Young Old." *The Annals of the American Academy of Political and Social Science* 415(1): 187–98. doi:10.1177/000271627441500114

Neugarten, Berbice L. 1975. "The Future and the Young-Old." *The Gerontologist* 15(1 Pt. 2): 4–9.

Orpana, Heather M., Nancy Ross, David Feeny, Bentson McFarland, Julie Bernier, and Mark Kaplan. 2009. "The Natural History of Health-Related Quality of Life: A 10-year Cohort Study." *Health Reports* 20(1):1–8.

Østbye, Truls, Betsy Kristjansson, Gerry Hill, S.C. Newman, Rebecca N. Brouver, and Ian McDowell. 2005. "Prevalence and Predictors of Depression in Elderly Canadians: The Canadian Study of Health and Aging." *Chronic Diseases in Canada* 26(4): 93–9.

Patten, Scott B., Jian L. Wang, Jeanne V.A. Williams, Shawn Currie, Cynthia A. Beck, Colleen J. Maxwell, and Nady el-Guebaly. 2006. "Descriptive Epidemiology of Major Depression in Canada." *Canadian Journal of Psychiatry* 51(2): 84–90.

Prus, Steven G. 2007. "Age, SES, and Health: A Population Level Analysis of Health Inequalities over the Lifecourse." *Sociology of Health & Illness* 29(2): 275-96. doi:10.1111/j.1467-9566.2007.00547.x

Rowe, John W., and Rueben L. Kahn. 1987. "Human Aging: Usual and Successful." *Science* 237(4811): 143–9.

Rowe, John W., and Reuben L. Kahn. 1998. *Successful Aging*. New York: Pantheon Books.

Rowe, John W., and Rueben L. Kahn. 2015. "Successful Aging 2.0: Conceptual Expansions for the 21st Century." *Journals of Gerontology, Series B: Psychological Sciences and Social Sciences* 70(4): 593–96. doi: 10.1093/geronb/gbv025

Sev'er, Aysan. 2009. "More Than Wife Abuse That Has Gone Old: A Conceptual Model for Violence against the Aged in Canada and the US." *Journal of Comparative Family Studies* 40(2): 279–92.

Standing Senate Committee on Social Affairs, Science and Technology. 2004. *Report 1: Mental Health, Mental Illness and Addiction: Overview of Policies and Programs in Canada*. Ottawa: Parliament of Canada.

Statistics Canada. 2011. *Family Violence in Canada: A Statistical Profile*. Statistics Canada, Catalogue no. 85-224-X. Centre for Justice Studies. Ottawa: Minister of Industry.

Statistics Canada. 2009. *Canadian Community Health Survey*. Accessed 12 December 2011 at: http://www.statcan.gc.ca/pub/82-625-x/2010002/article/11271-eng.htm

Statistics Canada. 2008. "Study: Caring for Seniors." *The Daily*, 21 October.

Statistics Canada. 2006. *A Portrait of Seniors in Canada, 2006*. Ottawa: Statistics Canada, Catalogue no. 89-519.

Statistics Canada. 2002. *Canadian Community Health Survey, Mental Health and Well-Being—Cycle 1.2*. Ottawa: Statistics Canada.

von Faber, Margaret, and Sjaak van der Geest. 2010. "Losing and Gaining: About Growing Old 'Successfully' in the Netherlands." In *Contesting Aging and Loss*, edited by Janice E. Graham and Peter H. Stephenson, 27–46. Toronto: University of Toronto Press.

Westerhof, Gerben J., and Corey L.M. Keyes. 2009. "Mental Illness and Mental Health: The Two Continua Model Across the Lifespan." *Journal of Adult Development* 17(2): 110–19. doi:10.1007/s10804-009-9082.y

World Health Organization. 1948. Preamble to the Constitution of the World Health Organization as adopted by the International Health Conference, New York, 19–22 June 1946, and entered into force on 7 April 1948.

Wu, Zheng, Christoph M. Schimmele, and Neena L. Chappell. 2012. "Aging and Late-Life Depression." *Journal of Aging and Health* 24(1): 3–28. doi: 10.1177/0898264311422599

48 Deceased Organ Donation and the Other Site of Politics

Lindsey McKay

Why is there a persistent shortfall of organs available for transplant? Significant public resources and social effort are devoted to persuading people to consent to organ donation at death, and there is evidence that higher consent rates would increase the available supply of organs (McKay, 2015). But is raising consent enough? How important is consent relative to the effort made to increase it? Sociologists have shown that organ supply is not explained solely by consent rates or consent regime (see Healy, 2006a, 2006b; Nowenstein, 2013). Social scientists have also criticized organ donation campaigns for obscuring how organ donation and transplantation is practiced (see, among others, Fox and Swazey, 1992; Joralemon, 1995; Sharp, 2002, 2014).

This chapter uses a science and technology studies (STS) lens to argue that the societal emphasis on consent to organ donation is understandable but overstated; consent is only as significant as the size of the potential donor pool. Even a 100 per cent consent rate will be insufficient to meet demand if not enough patients are eligible to donate organs. While the public is engaged in continuous efforts and debates about improving consent to donation rates, medical experts expand deceased donor eligibility criteria. Separate foci create a disjuncture between public understanding of the organ shortage problem, as caused by inadequate consent rates, and expert efforts to make more organs available by changing donor eligibility criteria. This disjuncture illustrates the division of authority between the social and the scientific that theorist Bruno Latour (1993) calls the modern Constitution.

A key scholar in STS, Latour claims that what defines the contemporary West is a "*productive* paradox": the creation of hybrid issues that entail both nature and culture, social and scientific dimensions, and yet a process of continually parsing out ("purifying") each dimension (Blok and Jensen, 2011: 55). Unlike other times and places, what undergirds our society is the belief in and creation of distinct categories between what is considered nature, science, and technical, and what is social and cultural. Important here is that scientific knowledge is seen as apolitical. Since scientists merely interpret nature, science is not social and does not require democratic oversight (Sismondo, 2010).

This chapter is a small part of a larger study of kidney exchange for transplantation in Ontario from 2000 to 2014 (see McKay, 2015). The argument is demonstrated first by evidence that a consent-focused *discourse of donation* is the basis of public knowledge in public policy reports, media coverage, and legislative bills. Second, caveats in public policy reports reveal the weakness of this discourse. Third, the creation of medical guidelines is analyzed as a concurrent process expanding the potential donor pool absent of public engagement. The conclusion returns to Latour's theory of the modern Constitution as one way to explain public understanding of the organ shortage.

The Discourse of Donation

In 2000, Mike Harris, the premier of Ontario, announced a "Millennium Challenge" to double the annual deceased organ donor rate within five years, from 150 to 300. Harris and a provincial advisory board articulated an already established *discourse of donation* that continues to dominate public knowledge of organ transplantation. In this discourse, the problem of organ shortage is a problem of supply, not demand. Two standard solutions to raise supply are to increase consent to deceased donation, and, to a lesser extent, hospital efficacy.

With an ambitious goal ahead of them, Trillium Gift of Life Network (TGLN), an organ procurement organization, was established with a hefty budget and mandate to generate a supply of organs. Over the next decade, TGLN established a logistics command centre, instilled themselves in intensive care units of key hospitals, and launched major organ donation campaigns. Each campaign emphasized the urgency of donation, describing the plight of patients on the transplant waiting list and often quantifying deaths on the list. The overwhelming message conveyed was that consent is the solution.

Four private member's bills were introduced in the Ontario provincial legislature in 2005 and 2006, each declaring the pace of increasing organ donation by TGLN insufficient. All of the solutions proposed focused on consent, isolating the requirement of explicit consent as a central if not the sole problem. One bill proposed "mandated choice" (requiring Ontarians to declare "yes" or "no" to organ donation when renewing health insurance cards), another proposed switching to a presumed **consent system**.

With a change in government, Ontario's minister of health, George Smitherman, also took up the cause. He declared the need for a new public inquiry—the Citizens' Panel on Increasing Organ Donations—with the rationale that "those with the most important role, the citizens of Ontario who make the vital decision to donate or not donate organs, have never been asked their opinions on this vital issue" (Ontario, 2007: i). Over the winter of 2006–2007, Smitherman's citizens' panel toured the province, probing public appetite for presumed consent. After 45 public meetings and 29 discussion groups, the panel found a lack of support for presumed consent. Consent remained nevertheless central to the recommendations, leading to an electronic registry to record advanced consent in 2012.

Yet, there is another story beyond the focus on consent and hospital efficacy. The year 2000 advisory board report included a caveat:

> Simply put, achieving this goal could be more difficult in Ontario because *Ontario may have fewer potential donors than the most successful jurisdictions*. . . . We know . . . that certain types of injuries involving major head trauma are less common in Ontario than in other jurisdictions, probably because seat belt and motorcycle helmet laws are treated more seriously and we have fewer deaths from gun shots. . . . Trillium Gift of Life Network *must get an accurate assessment of the number of potential donors*. (Ontario, 2000: 22, emphasis added)

The same caveat is repeated in the 2007 citizens' panel report:

> Some other jurisdictions . . . *have more brain dead patients, so can get more donors, but they are not to be emulated.* The message in the numbers is clear. *Donations from the brain dead cannot meet the need.* . . . (Ontario, 2007: 13, emphasis added)

These disclaimers—which went unnoticed—identify that the problem of the organ shortage is not solely one of consent (or hospital efficacy); the problem may lie in the size of the **potential deceased donor pool**.

Another Site of Politics

While the public was focused on consent to donation, experts met to expand the size of the donor pool through new criteria for categorizing trauma patients as potential deceased donors. A federal organization, the Canadian Council for Donation and Transplantation, hosted a process of deliberations, starting in 2005, regarding "whether and how to proceed with organ donation after cardiocirculatory death (DCD [for 'death by cardiocirculatory determination']) in Canada" (Shemie et al., 2006: S1). Rather than remain limited to the pool of patients diagnosed as brain dead (now renamed "neurological determination of death"), experts sought to include patients whose hearts have stopped and who have a prognosis of brain death but do not meet brain death criteria. For TGLN, broadening deceased donor eligibility criteria was "one of its main goals" in its 2005–06 annual report and 2006–07 business plan for increasing the volume of organs (TGLN, 2007: 10). These efforts led to the 2006 publication of national recommendations for DCD in Canada (Shemie et al., 2006: S1).

From an STS perspective, medical guidelines are a social construction (Sismondo, 2010). For Latour, organ transplantation is a "hybrid" process involving scientific and social dimensions. Developing guidelines is thus another site of politics—one set apart from public engagement. In the same way that brain death was established through the release of medical guidelines starting in 1969 (Lock, 2002; McKay, 2001), the new medical guidelines legitimated the first DCD case in 2006. This organ donation relied as much on familial consent as a reconfiguring of who counts as dead, as broader criteria for death came to classify more patients as potential donors. Since this time, even though consent rates have gradually improved (12 per cent from 2008 to 2012) (McKay, 2015), it is expanding the size of the deceased donor pool—with DCD—that generates significant change in improving organ supply (raising deceased donor rates by 25 per cent over four years, from 2006 to 2009) (Hernadez-Alejandro et al., 2011).

That the public was not involved in determining new deceased donor eligibility criteria is not a surprise nor should it offend. Following Latour, the divide between public deliberation and expert decisions reflects the modern Constitution. For organ transplantation, it was 1972 *Gift of Life* legislation that embedded the science–social division of authority: physicians are identified in law as the sole arbiters of what constitutes death based on scientific criteria (McKay, 2015). While altering the consent system requires legislative change, determining eligibility criteria that limit or expand the size of the pool of potential deceased donors is not deemed to be a social exercise.

Conclusion

Beyond public attention to issues of consent, there is another site of politics where experts hold court. If the public is to understand Ontario's annual deceased organ donation rate—currently at 271, still short of the 300 donors per year goal set in the year 2000 (TGLN, 2015)—attention must be broadened beyond the issue of consent (and hospital efficacy). The ambitious year 2000 goal to double the annual deceased organ donor rate in Ontario appeared to only put pressure on consent; however, beyond the public realm, it also generated pressure—and perhaps gave licence—to expand the pool of potential deceased organ donors by declaring more patients dead. Latour's theory of the modern Constitution aids sociological understanding of how organs become available, and why the public is not engaged or seemingly aware of all that is at stake in Ontario's annual deceased organ donor rate reaching set goals.

Based on Latour's theory of the modern Constitution, the disjuncture between public knowledge and expert practice is not an outcome; it is part of the social organization of making organs available for transplant. Latour's theory thus aids sociological understanding of how organs become available, and why the public is not engaged or seemingly aware of all that is at stake in Ontario's annual deceased organ donor rate reaching set goals.

References

Blok, A., and Jensen, T.E. (2011). *Bruno Latour: Hybrid Thoughts in a Hybrid World.* London: Routledge.

Fox, R.C., and Swazey, J.P. (1992). *Spare Parts: Organ Replacement in American Society.* New York: Oxford University Press.

Healy, K. (2006a). Do Presumed-Consent Laws Raise Organ Procurement Rates? *De Paul Law Review, 55*, 1017–43.

Healy, K. (2006b). *Last Best Gifts: Altruism and the Market for Human Blood and Organs.* Chicago: University of Chicago.

Hernadez-Alejandro, R., Wall, W., Jevnikar, A., Luke, P., Sharpe, M., Russell, D., . . . Zaltzman, J. (2011). Organ Donation after Cardiac Death: Donor and Recipient Outcomes after the First Three Years of the Ontario Experience. *Canadian Journal of Anesthesiology, 58*, 599–605.

Joralemon, D. (1995). Organ Wars: The Battle for Body Parts. *Medical Anthropology Quarterly, 9*(3), 335–56. Retrieved from http://www.jstor.org/stable/649344

Latour, B. (1993). *We Have Never Been Modern.* Cambridge, MA: Harvard University Press.

Lock, M. (2002). *Twice Dead: Organ Transplants and the Reinvention of Death.* Berkeley: University of California Press.

McKay, L. (2001). Seeking to Cure by Replacement: The Political Economy of Organ Transplantation. Master's thesis, Carleton University, Ottawa.

McKay, L. (2015). Structured Forgetting and the Social Organization of Kidney Exchange in Ontario. PhD dissertation, Carleton University, Ottawa.

Nowenstein, G. (2013). *The Generosity of the Dead: A Sociology of Organ Procurement in France.* Surrey, UK: Ashgate.

Ontario. (2000). *A Plan for Change and Action: Report of Premier Harris' Advisory Board on Organ and Tissue Donation.* Toronto: Government of Ontario.

Ontario. (2007). *Report of the Citizens' Panel on Increasing Organ Donations.* Toronto: Government of Ontario.

Sharp, L.A. (2002). Denying Culture in the Transplant Arena: Technocratic Medicine's Myth of Democratization. *Cambridge Quarterly of Healthcare Ethics, 11*, 142–50.

Sharp, L. A. (2014). *The Transplant Imaginary: Mechanical Hearts, Animal Parts, and Moral Thinking in Highly Experimental Science.* Berkeley: University of California.

Shemie, S.D., Baker, A.J., Knoll, G., Wall, W., Rocker, G., Howes, D., . . . Dossetor, J. (2006). National Recommendations for Donation after Cardiocirculatory Death in Canada. *Canadian Medical Association Journal, 175*(8 (Suppl)), S1–S24.

Sismondo, S. (2010). *An Introduction to Science and Technology Studies* (2nd edn). Oxford, UK: Wiley-Blackwell.

TGLN. (2007). *Annual Report, 2006-2007.* Toronto: Trillium Gift of Life Network.

TGLN. (2015). *Annual Report, 2014-2015.* Toronto: Trillium Gift of Life Network.

Questions for Critical Thought

Chapter 46 | The Converging Gender Trends in Earning and Caring in Canada

1. The authors of this chapter tell us that men are more likely than women to be employed and work longer hours. Drawing on your sociological knowledge, what social mechanisms may be influencing this trend?
2. Do men or women perform more caring tasks? Is this trend changing in recent years in Canadian society?
3. What is the benefit of collecting time-use data? How does this method give us a more accurate idea of the division of labour between spouses?
4. What is the benefit of promoting a more egalitarian family structure for caring responsibilities?
5. Think about your own family. Growing up, how were caring tasks divided among you, your siblings, and parents? Was one person more responsible for caring tasks? Why?

Chapter 47 | Health Declines in Old Age, or Does it?

1. What are the World Health Organization's dimensions of health? Why are these dimensions important for assessing the health of an aging population?
2. Describe functional disabilities. How are they impacted by health? Are they common or uncommon among older populations?
3. What is mental health? Describe the mental health trends among older people.
4. What is social health? Give examples of social health issues that can occur in older people.
5. Which of the three dimensions of health is understudied for older populations? Why should it be looked at more carefully?

Chapter 48 | Deceased Organ Donation and the Other Site of Politics

1. Describe the existing public discourse surrounding organ donation. How does this discourse encourage or discourage people to become donors?
2. What policies and trends exist in Canada that impact organ donation?
3. How is the creation of medical guidelines for organ donation a site of politics? Who is involved in making these guidelines?
4. Why is understanding the politics and trends surrounding organ donation important? What is the main takeaway from this chapter?
5. How much information do you think that the public should have on organ donation? Should donors have a say in creating medical guidelines? Do you think that transparency is important to potential donors?

PART XII
Religion

Religions are social institutions that are founded on the practice of belief. Religious beliefs guide people on how to lead their lives and manage difficult situations. In the Western world, the three most influential religions are Judaism, Christianity, and Islam. But while these three are the most influential in the West, thousands of religions and religious sects exist throughout the world, and even in the West.

While there are many differences across religions, all religions have at least three things in common. First, they are all built around beliefs: they all have a distinct system of ideas and values that guides its members. Often, a distinctive bible, doctrine, or creed instructs members on how to behave in order to achieve spiritual transcendence. The Muslim Quran, Christian Bible, and Judaic Tanakh are all examples of religious texts that guide faith.

Second, all religions have rituals: repeated physical or verbal gestures that often involve sacred objects. Rituals may occur every day or be reserved for special dates of significance. In Christianity, the specialized use of palms on Palm Sunday is a ritual that is only performed once a year, on the Sunday before Easter. It is meant to symbolize and celebrate Jesus's triumphant entry into Jerusalem, thus honouring Jesus and reminding Christian followers of his sacrifice. Such rituals help the members of a religious group feel a deeper spiritual connection to their faith, while reinforcing significant religious teachings. And, as Durkheim pointed out, they provide an occasion for group affirmation of social cohesion and solidarity.

Third, all religions form communities. Religious communities bring people of a common faith together to share in their beliefs and moral values through teaching, prayer, and ritual activity. These communities are a source of support for believers and help group members to lead a faith-based way of life.

Because of their distinctiveness and the emotional intensity they engender, religions can bring people together or divide them. In Chapter 49, Robert Brym, Robert Anderson, and Scott Milligan compare religious groups on the levels of intolerance they show toward other groups. Their goal is to show that, despite widespread misconceptions, Muslims are no more intolerant than other religious groups, especially when you consider their history and the history of some Christian groups.

Currently, there is an emphasis in Canada on being secular: on promoting public attitudes and activities that are not based on religion. Yet, organized religion has always been important in Canada, and even important in the foundation of Canadian sociology. In Chapter 50, Rick Helmes-Hayes notes that sociology developed in Canadian universities before the 1920s, reflecting the ideas of social gospel and the Protestant church.

In Chapter 51, Steven Kleinknecht describes the culture of Old Order Mennonites. It is a conservative religious sect based on Christianity that encourages followers to lead a minimalist, homogeneous, and isolated life, away from temptation. This is only one example of countless Christian sects that exist today, but it illustrates the fact that religious denominations and sects can have a lot to say about people's "proper" lifestyle.

Chapter 52, by Jeffrey Reitz, provides current evidence of how well Muslim individuals integrate into Canadian culture, in comparison to other religious minority groups. Reitz shows that, despite the notoriety of Muslim terrorists, Muslim minorities in Canada are more successful at integrating into Canadian culture than many other groups.

Despite the historic and current importance of religion in Canadian sociology, we should not forget that sociologists never focus on whether religious beliefs are true. Instead, they study how religious beliefs and institutions are organized, how they cultivate communities, and how social forces and institutions influence their stability. Contrary to what sociology's founders might have expected, religion continues as an important social force today, in Canada and elsewhere.

49 Are Islam and Democracy Compatible?

Robert Brym, Robert Andersen, and Scott Milligan

Democracy Needs Democrats

In 2011, the people of the Middle East and North Africa overthrew dictators in Tunisia, Egypt, Libya, and Yemen. Anti-regime movements erupted in Jordan, Bahrain, Syria, and other countries in the region. It was the "Arab Spring" (Brym et al., 2014). Soon, however, a reaction set in. The Egyptian army ousted the country's elected president, jailed and killed thousands of his supporters, and instituted a military dictatorship. Libya, Syria, Iraq, and Yemen descended into civil war. The rulers of other countries in the region offered minor concessions but combined them with increased repression to stifle dissent.

According to one widely used measure, between 2010 and 2014 civil liberties and political rights deteriorated in nine of the region's 18 countries and remained at the same low level in 7 other countries. The state of civil liberties and political rights improved only in Tunisia and Libya (Brym and Andersen, 2015; Freedom House, 2015). However, it is certain that Libya will soon lose its improved status because of its civil war. In short, the balance sheet suggests that, while much was lost during the Arab Spring—most importantly, of course, many thousands of lives—little was gained overall.

Many commentators argue that the region remains mired in autocracy because it lacks a cultural tradition that promotes democracy. In particular, Islam, the region's dominant religion, supposedly lacks affinity with democratic values. As political scientist Samuel Huntington famously put it in 1993, "Western ideas of individualism, liberalism, constitutionalism, human rights, equality, liberty, the rule of law, democracy, free markets, the separation of church and state, often have little resonance in Islamic . . . cultures" (Huntington, 1993; see also Yuchtman Ya'ar and Alkalay, 2010).

Our analysis of survey data collected in 23 Muslim-majority and Western countries from 1996 to 2007 allows us to reconsider whether Islam is incompatible with democracy (Milligan, Andersen, and Brym, 2014). In brief, we failed to find as high a level of incompatibility as some other analysts claim to have observed.

Islam and Tolerance, Present and Past

Liberal democracy rests on the principles of majority rule and minority rights. Majority rule ensures respect for the will of most of the citizenry. Respect for minority rights prevents the formation of a tyrannical majority and protects the interests of all citizens, even those who are not in the majority. Majority rule is relatively easy to achieve because it requires only free and fair elections. Minority rights are relatively hard to achieve because they require tolerance for people one may dislike or even detest. Classic works of political theory all recognize the importance of tolerance as a pillar of liberal democracy.

The relative lack of tolerance in the Middle East and North Africa is well illustrated by the case of Nouri al-Mailiki. Al-Maliki, a Shi'a, was elected Iraq's prime minister in 2006 by a majority in free and fair elections. However, he systematically stripped Iraq's Arab Sunni minority (about a fifth of the population) of political influence. When Sunni Arabs demonstrated against his government, al-Maliki's security forces fired on them. Civil war ensued. Eventually, some Sunni Arabs in Iraq became so angry with al-Maliki's regime that they resolved to form their own state. They aligned themselves with the Islamic

State (IS), an offshoot of al-Qaeda that is even more extreme than its parent organization. In the summer of 2014, IS raced across eastern and northern Iraq, shooting, raping, torturing, beheading, and crucifying Christians, Muslims, and anyone else who refused to accept their ideology. No trace of humanity, let alone tolerance, could be detected in their actions.

Countries ruled by Muslims have not always been relatively intolerant of minorities. In certain times and places during the Middle Ages, the Jewish minority flourished in countries ruled by Muslims. In Spain, the Jews referred to the early period of Muslim rule (from the eighth century to the eleventh century), as their "Golden Age." In contrast, Christian Europe's Jewish minority suffered many episodes of extreme persecution during the Middle Ages. The Jews were expelled from parts of Germany in 1012; from England in 1290; from France in 1306; from Catholic-controlled Spain in 1492; from Lithuania, Sicily, and Warsaw in 1483; from Portugal in 1496; and from Italy and Bavaria in 1593.

A similar story emerges from a comparison of late-sixteenth-century and early-seventeenth-century India and England. During that period, India's Muslim ruler, Akbar the Great, removed a tax on non-Muslims and sought to integrate Hindus and members of other religious groups into the nobility and the military. His actions increased national unity and prosperity and helped to create an atmosphere of tolerance throughout the country (Sen, 2005). In contrast, at about the same time in England, Roman Catholics were being fined, imprisoned, tortured, and put to death for failing to join the Church of England. A Catholic wanting to hold public office had to give up his religion and swear allegiance to the monarch as the supreme governor of the Church of England. William Shakespeare had to conceal his Catholic upbringing (Holden, 1999).

These few historical facts suggest that, while intolerance of minorities is relatively widespread in the Middle East and North Africa today, there was a time when European Christians were on average less tolerant than Muslims were. It follows that there is no necessary connection between Islam and intolerance.

Despite our historical observations, analysis of the respected World Values Surveys demonstrates that the citizens of Muslim-majority countries are today and on average less tolerant than citizens of Western countries are. We now turn to a subset of these surveys, conducted between 1996 and 2007 on nationally representative samples drawn from 23 Muslim-majority and Western countries.

Tolerance in Muslim-Majority and Western Countries

In the World Values Surveys, respondents were asked the following question: "On this list are various groups of people. Could you please mention any that you would not like to have as neighbours?" If respondents said they would not like to have a neighbour who was a member of a racial minority group, an immigrant, or a person who practised a religion different from their own, they were coded as "intolerant." Otherwise, they were coded as "tolerant."

Listed in order from the most to the least tolerant, the Muslim-majority countries in our study included Morocco, Turkey, Pakistan, Indonesia, Iran, Iraq, Bangladesh, Egypt, and Jordan. (Pakistan, Indonesia, and Bangladesh are not in the Middle East and North Africa.) Western countries, again listed in order from the most to the least tolerant, included Sweden, Canada, Norway, Australia, Switzerland, Brazil, Netherlands, Spain, the United States, Germany, the United Kingdon, Italy, Finland, and France. On average, respondents in Muslim-majority countries had about a 50 per cent chance of being tolerant. The comparable figure for respondents from Western countries was about 85 per cent. Can we attribute this disparity to the different prevalence of Muslims in these two groups of countries?

Not entirely. For one thing, one Western country—France—exhibited a level of tolerance lower than or equal to four of the nine Muslim-majority countries in our sample (Morocco, Turkey, Pakistan, and Indonesia). Two of the four are in the Middle East. This finding suggests that it is possible for Muslim-majority countries to be as tolerant as Western countries are.

For another thing, we found that Muslims in Western countries were generally more tolerant than Christians in Western societies were. We suspect that a self-selection process was at work here. On average, Muslim immigrants in the West may be among the most tolerant residents of their countries of origin. They may immigrate partly because of their relatively liberal values. In addition, their high level of tolerance may reflect the fact that they are "outsiders" who experience the consequences of intolerance more than majority Christians do. That circumstance could increase their sympathy for other minority-group members who experience intolerance, making them more tolerant. Nonetheless, this finding suggests that, in some contexts, having a Muslim religious background does not lead to relative intolerance and having a non-Muslim religious background does not lead to relative tolerance.

Finally, we found that in Muslim-majority countries, practising Christians were as intolerant as practising Muslims were. Although Christians represent a significant minority in only three of the nine Muslim-majority countries in our sample (they comprise about 2 per cent of Jordan's population, 7 per cent of Indonesia's, and 10 per cent of Egypt's), this finding suggests that characteristics of Muslim-majority countries other than the influence of Muslim background might be partly responsible for their relatively high level of intolerance.

The Effects of Socio-Economic Context

That is in fact just what we found: a country's level of economic development and its level of income inequality are significantly associated with its citizens' average level of tolerance, independent of the prevalence of Muslims in the country. Let us consider the meaning of this finding in detail.

Sociologists have established that the greater the degree to which people enjoy job security, the less they fear losing their jobs to "outsiders," including immigrants and minority group members. Sociologists have also established that job security is more common in rich, economically developed countries than in poor, less economically developed countries. Using International Monetary Fund data, we compared the rich G7 countries (Canada, France, Germany, Italy, Japan, the UK, and the US) with the countries of the Middle East and North Africa in 2013. We found that the average purchasing power of each individual's annual income was 3.9 times higher in the G7 countries. Moreover, while the unemployment rate in the G7 countries was 7.6 per cent in 2013, the unemployment rate in the most populous countries of the Middle East and Africa was nearly twice as high (for example, 13.6 per cent in Egypt and 13.4 per cent in Iran; World Bank, 2014). The implication of these facts is that job security, and therefore tolerance of immigrants and members of racial and religious minority groups, is bound to be lower in the countries of the Middle East and North Africa, irrespective of the proportion of Muslims in those countries. Our statistical analysis showed that this is in fact the case.

We also found that people living in countries with high levels of income inequality are more likely than people living in countries with low levels of inequality to be tolerant, irrespective of the proportion of Muslims living in them and how wealthy the countries are. Why is this so? In all countries, people in less privileged positions face more job insecurity than do people in more privileged positions. Moreover, the greater the gap between rich and poor, the more job insecurity less privileged people are likely to experience. We found that this generalization holds regardless of how rich a country is and regardless of the proportion of Muslims who live in it. It follows that in countries with more income inequality, intolerance will be higher, even when economic development and the proportion of Muslims are relatively high.

Significantly, the Muslim-majority countries that we studied tend to be relatively unequal and relatively poor (even though some, mainly small Muslim-majority countries in the Middle East and North Africa are oil-rich). In short, a significant part of the reason that the Muslim-majority countries in our study are relatively intolerant is bound up not with the prevalence of Muslims in them but with their socio-economic conditions. If they were richer and less unequal, they would likely become more tolerant.

However, even after taking level of economic development and degree of income inequality into account, Muslim-majority countries in our sample were significantly less tolerant than Western countries were. We speculate that at least part of the reason for the remaining difference has to do with yet another contextual factor: the historical involvement of Western countries in the Middle East and North Africa.

France and Great Britain colonized much of the Middle East and North Africa from the 1830s to the 1940s. The leaders of these European powers drew the national borders of some Middle Eastern countries in a way that maximized ethno-religious conflict and intolerance. They may have done so because they knew little and cared less about the tribal, ethnic, and religious differences that divided the region. Alternatively, they may have known these things only too well and sought to maximize their influence by applying Julius Caesar's advice to "divide and conquer." Iraq is a case in point. It brought Sunni Kurds, Sunni Arabs, Shi'a Arabs, and several smaller ethnic and religious groups uncomfortably together in one political jurisdiction. In the early 1970s, the United States inflamed matters. Iraq's oil resources were owned mostly by large Western petroleum companies. When Iraq sought to gain control over its oil resources, the US arranged to arm Iraqi Kurds to fight against their own government, thus fanning inter ethnic animosity and intolerance.

In other cases, Western powers stunted the growth of budding democratic movements in the region. For example, in Iran the Constitutional Revolution of 1909 and the democratic movement of the 1950s were undermined by a 1953 coup orchestrated by the CIA and Britain's MI6. The Western powers opposed the democratically elected prime minister of Iran because he wanted his country to gain control over its own oil fields. Subsequently, the United States supported a new authoritarian regime, just as it supported other authoritarian regimes throughout the region and continues to support them today. These examples suggest that, if the people of the Middle East and North Africa have mixed feelings about liberal democracy today, the West must take some responsibility for preventing the flowering of democratic movements.

Conclusion

We do not mean to suggest that the contextual and historical factors we have identified account for all of the difference in tolerance between Muslim-majority and Western countries. Cultural psychologists and sociologists have recently demonstrated that political extremism is associated with certain cultural traits that are more common in Muslim-majority countries than in Western countries (Gelfand et al., 2013). These traits include fatalism (putting one's faith in a higher authority rather than taking responsibility for one's actions), cultural "tightness" (low tolerance for deviance and strong justification for punishing people who commit deviant acts), and opposition to gender equality. More research is needed to determine the degree to which these cultural traits independently account for the difference in tolerance between Muslim-majority and Western countries.

One thing is clear even at this stage, however. Observers who attribute the weakness of democracy in the Middle East and North Africa to the prevalence of Muslims in the region oversimplify a complex situation. They tend to ignore the economic and political context of tolerance and intolerance. Our analysis shows that this context is an important part of the story. With further research, it may turn out to be the most important part.

References

Brym, Robert and Robert Andersen. 2016. "Democracy, women's rights, and public opinion in Tunisia." *International Sociology* 31, 2: 253–67.

Brym, Robert, Melissa Godbout, Andreas Hoffbauer, Gabe Menard, and Tony Huiquan Zhang. 2014. "Social media in the 2011 Egyptian uprising." *British Journal of Sociology* 65, 2: 266–92.

Freedom House. 2015. "Freedom in the World 2015." https://freedomhouse.org/report/freedom-world/freedom-world-2015#.VSRRhZPloRE (retrieved 7 April 2015).

Gelfand, Michele J., LaFree, Gary, Fahey, Susan, and Feinberg, Emily. 2013. "Culture and Extremism." *Journal of Social Issues* 69, 3: 495–517.

Holden, Anthony. 1999. *William Shakespeare: His Life and Work*. London: Little, Brown.

Huntington, Samuel. 1993. "The clash of civilizations?" *Foreign Affairs* 72, 3: 22–49. http://www.foreignaffairs.com/articles/48950/samuel-p-huntington/the-clash-of-civilizations (retrieved 7 April 2015).

Milligan, Scott, Robert Andersen, and Robert Brym. 2014. "Assessing variation in tolerance in 23 Muslim-majority and Western countries." *Canadian Review of Sociology* 51, 3: 239–61.

Sen, Amartya. 2005. *The Argumentative Indian: Essays on Indian History, Culture, and Identity*. New York: Farrar, Straus and Giroux.

World Bank. 2014. "Economy and growth." http://data.worldbank.org/topic/economy-and-growth (retrieved 7 April 2014).

Yuchtman-Ya'ar, Ephraim and Yasmin Alkalay. 2010. "Political attitudes in the Arab world." *Journal of Democracy* 21, 3: 122–34.

50 "Building the New Jerusalem in Canada's Green and Pleasant Land": The Social Gospel and the Roots of English-Language Academic Sociology in Canada, 1889–1921

Rick Helmes-Hayes

Canadian sociology students have some sense of the history of sociology in Europe and the United States because they have learned it in theory courses. However, they know little about the history of Canadian sociology. They are unfamiliar with the contributions of the scholars who built the discipline—Carl Dawson, Everett Hughes, S.D. Clark, John Porter—and they do not know early classic works such as Hughes's *French Canada in Transition* (1943) or Porter's *The Vertical Mosaic* (1965). Their lack of knowledge is understandable, if lamentable, because contemporary Canadian sociology is largely (and rightly) presentist—i.e., concerned with contemporary issues and problems such as inequality, migration, religion, and governmentality and focused on the contributions of insightful current scholars. In this chapter, I offer students a glimpse of the roots of the discipline in Canada—what it looked like back in the late 1800s, well over 100 years ago. They will quickly see some crucial differences between today's sociology and the sociology of a century ago, but they will be surprised to find that there are many similarities as well. Then as now, issues such as the place of religion in society, the stature of science as a model for disciplinary practice, a focus on social problems, and the propriety of **value freedom** were important concerns.

According to standard accounts, university-based (i.e., academic) sociology in English Canada began in the early 1920s when Carl Dawson established an outpost of **Chicago sociology** at McGill University (Hiller, 1982; Wilcox-Magill, 1983; Shore, 1987).[1] Thereafter, the discipline grew slowly. As late as 1960, there were just 60 people teaching sociology across the country. However, beginning in the sixties, the picture changed quickly. Between 1960 and 1975, the university system expanded rapidly and undergraduate enrolments more than tripled. The number of sociologists increased to over 900. Most universities founded sociology departments and initiated graduate programs. Sociologists established their own scholarly journals and set up an independent professional association (Hiller, 1982: 20–5). Today sociology is marginally larger and areas of specialization and styles of research have changed, but in organizational terms the discipline looks similar.

I noted above that, according to the standard version of events, academic sociology got its start in English Canada in the 1920s. However, my current research (reported briefly here[2]) demonstrates that this conventional account is wrong. It overlooks the contribution of an entire generation of scholars who taught "social gospel" sociology in the universities between 1889 and 1921. Long before Dawson was hired at McGill, sociology was well institutionalized in the Canadian post-secondary system. Courses were being taught at 11 English-language Canadian universities and colleges, 28 men had taught sociology for two years or more, and a named appointment in sociology had been made at seven institutions. This indicates that we need to add a new first chapter to the history of Canadian sociology. That is my purpose in this chapter.

The Social Gospel

During the period 1890–1920, the Protestant churches were among Canada's most powerful institutions and religion had a salience in people's day-to-day lives that it now lacks. Indeed, the post-secondary educational system was dominated by religion-based institutions founded by Protestant denominations; McMaster was a Baptist college, Queen's a Presbyterian university, etc. Their primary purpose was to train clergy. Other students were admitted and practical subjects such as economics were taught, but religion was the core of the curriculum and the colleges were regarded as places where young people would be moulded into Christian leaders.

During this period, the dominant theological orientation came to be the *social gospel*, a progressive, applied doctrine oriented to social reform. As a result, the sociology taught in the Protestant denominational colleges reflected this social gospel orientation. Its goal? To "Christianize" Canada—to "build the New Jerusalem in Canada's green and pleasant land" (Calvert, 2009: 4). However, while social gospel sociology was unselfconsciously tied to Christian-inspired "do-gooding" (reformism), it was *not exclusively* religious; it was scientific/secular as well. Not only did it draw on social sciences such as political economy, but also it took inspiration from secular philosophies of social reform such as American **progressivism**. As J.S. Woodsworth, one of the leaders of the social gospel movement in Canada, put it, "We should not only find the poor, but should endeavor to change the conditions that lead to poverty. . . . I firmly believe in *scientific Christianity*—in performing our Christian duty according to the light that modern science has thrown on social conditions" (Library and Archives Canada, Woodsworth Papers, vol. II, file 6: "The Wider Evangel," n.d.; emphasis added).

This scientific and reformist conception of the nature and purpose of sociology fit nicely with a new conception of the role of clergy then spreading in the Protestant churches. In the late nineteenth century, rapid industrialization, massive immigration, and unregulated urbanization had created a set of serious and interrelated nationwide social and economic problems—poverty, crime, alcoholism, prostitution, etc. Increasingly, the Protestant denominations regarded their ministers not just as spiritual guides but also as men of affairs, charged with a responsibility and mandate to understand and remedy these problems.

The social gospel that constituted their social and spiritual guide as they did so departed from traditional Protestant doctrine. Historically, the Protestant churches saw their first purpose as the saving of *individual* souls via evangelization; their mission was to convert people to Christianity. They regarded the social problems of the secular world as the consequence of widespread sin. Once people adopted Christian beliefs and behaviours—stopped sinning—*social regeneration* would take place automatically. Social problems would disappear. Social gospellers disagreed with this logic. They argued that people were products of their environment. Where their life circumstances exposed them to vice, unemployment, poverty, and crime, they would likely fall prey to sin (Valverde, 1991: 132–4). Social regeneration—adequate housing, ample wages, safe working conditions—would have to *precede* individual regeneration.

While many Protestants shared reformist views and adopted the language of the social gospel, it was not a unified movement. There were three camps of social gospellers. *Conservatives* were only minimally influenced by the theology and political-economic ideas of the social gospel. In their view, peoples' morals—sinful behaviour—not institutions, were the problem. Therefore, they concentrated their reform efforts on issues such as temperance and prostitution (Valverde, 1991). *Liberal* social gospellers (the majority) had a more structuralist and progressive understanding of social problems. They objected to the abuses and shortcomings of capitalism—child labour, low wages, etc.—but regarded the economic and political foundations of Canadian society as essentially sound, if in need of improvement by tinkering. They sought to solve the problems of the day by expanding the welfare and regulatory state. Most of those who taught sociology in Canada's Protestant denominational colleges and universities belonged in this liberal camp. On the political left—and in a distinct minority—were full-fledged theological *radical* social gospellers. They had no patience for the hesitancy and half-measures of their liberal and conservative colleagues and argued that only sweeping structural changes—some advocated socialism—could Christianize Canada's economic and political systems (Allen, 1973).

Sociology and the Social Gospel

I mentioned above that social gospel sociology combined religion and science. Sociology, for social gospellers, was both an *intellectual orientation* and a *tool*. As an intellectual orientation, it pinpointed the source of social problems in the structure of the social system rather than the character of individual persons. This made sociology an ideal tool for the churches as they tried to solve social problems via what they referred to as "practical theology" or "applied Christianity." In the late 1800s, they began to introduce sociology into the curricula of their denominational colleges and theological schools because they regarded it as a science that could help them in their fight against social problems. The result? By 1921, sociology was well established across the country. There are three indicators that this was the case: (1) sociology courses were being taught; (2) faculty members had been appointed; and (3) sociology programs had been established.

Establishing Social Gospel Sociology in the Colleges and Universities

Courses Taught

Sociology courses in this period were of two types. First to appear, with one exception, were *courses with some sociological content or component, but not titled sociology*. Calendar descriptions for such courses made explicit mention of "sociological themes," a "sociological orientation," or listed a book written by a sociologist among course readings. Note, for example, the course description of an untitled course taught by J.F. Tufts at Acadia in 1899: "Work in this course will be along sociological lines as represented by the following works or their equivalents: Kidd, *Social Evolution* [1895]; Fairbanks, *Introduction to Sociology* [1896]; Schäffle, *Quintessence of Socialism* [1890]" (*Acadia University Calendar 1899–1900*: 20). By 1908, nine such courses had been offered at seven institutions: Queen's, Mount Allison, McMaster, Acadia, University of New Brunswick, McGill, and the Ontario Agricultural College. The first four mentioned were denominational institutions. The instructors of six of these nine courses were clergymen. In each case, the courses were offered as part of a program in theology, philosophy, or economics/political economy.

The second type of course to appear was a course *titled sociology*. By 1921, courses titled sociology had been taught at 14 universities and church colleges. Most were denominational schools where the social gospel was a significant influence. Most were taught by Protestant clergy. Curiously, only two had an obviously Christian title. The earliest such course offered was Christian Ethics and Sociology, taught at Wesley College, Winnipeg, in 1896 (*Wesley College Calendar 1896–97*: 61). The other was Christian Ethics and Practical Sociology, offered at Victoria University, Toronto, in 1915 (*Victoria University Calendar 1915-16*: 14). Other courses called "sociology" did not betray a religious orientation in their respective titles, but did so clearly in their course descriptions. An example is Sociology 1, taught at Victoria University in 1919 by the Rev J.W. Macmillan. Its description reads: "The social gospel of the New Testament and its application to modern life [and] applied Christianity: relief, criminology, industrial accidents, child welfare, etc." (*Victoria University Calendar 1919–20*: 23). Still other first sociology courses betrayed a likely Christian orientation not via their titles or course descriptions but through their reading lists. The Rev B.C. Borden's course at Mount Allison, taught in 1916, is an example. It had a secular course title and description but the required course readings—i.e., F.G. Peabody's *The Approach to the Social Question* (1909) and Walter Rauschenbusch's *Christianizing the Social Order* (1912)—were social gospel classics (*Mount Allison University Calendar 1916–17*: 52).

Sociology, then, emerged as an autonomous subject only gradually. At first, it appeared as a "topic" in a course devoted to another subject, often philosophy or political economy. Later, it appeared as a separate subject, but only as part of the offerings in another discipline, often theology, philosophy, or political economy. Institutions usually experimented with just one course, which often had a "social problems" focus, before expanding course offerings.

Faculty Appointments Made

At least 28 persons taught sociology for two years or more between 1889–90 and 1921–22 (average equalling seven years). All were male. Over two-thirds were Canadian. The social gospel connection is clear. Most of the men (19 of 28) were appointed at church colleges and two others were Protestant clergy who taught at secular institutions. Indeed, 12 of them were clergymen. However, of the 28, only 9 were appointed to a position that had "sociology" in the job title and only four were hired to teach sociology exclusively. Most were hired to teach other subjects—typically theology or political economy/economics. Indeed, eleven of those that taught sociology had degrees in political economy or economics and six had degrees in theology. Only four had taken graduate training in sociology and only one (Rev R.W. Murchie, Manitoba Agricultural College) had a PhD in sociology.

I remarked above that courses in sociology emerged in a stepwise fashion out of other disciplines. So, too, did those that taught the subject. Typically, those who taught sociology before 1920 did so as a secondary part of their teaching load in another discipline and few had formal training in the discipline.

Programs Established[3]

As of 1921–22, none of Canada's universities or colleges had established an independent department of sociology. However, six institutions—Acadia, Brandon, Victoria, McMaster, Presbyterian College (really the United Theological Colleges, Montreal), and Manitoba Agricultural College—had established a program in sociology. With the exception of Manitoba Agricultural College, which was a secular institution, all were Protestant denominational schools. At each institution, a named appointment in sociology had been made. Indeed, at McMaster and the United Theological Colleges, multiple appointments in sociology were in place. Aside from a standard introductory course, the most common course offering was "social problems" or "applied sociology." Only Brandon and McMaster offered the MA.

Conclusion

Together, the men who taught sociology in Canada's English-language colleges and universities from 1889 to 1921 had two long-term impacts: (1) They laid the institutional and intellectual groundwork for the establishment of the discipline. (2) They advocated a slate of piecemeal changes to Canadian society that would humanize the worst aspects of the nation's capitalist economy and contribute to a more just and egalitarian society. Indeed, through their teaching and other political activities, these men helped establish an intellectual and political environment conducive to the growth of Canada's regulatory and welfare state (Christie and Gauvreau 1996).

Notes

1. The account focuses on English-language sociology. French-language sociology has a very different history (Helmes-Hayes and Warren, 2017).
2. For the full version, see Helmes-Hayes (2016).
3. I define a "program" as three or more courses.

References

Allen, R. 1973. *The Social Passion: Religion and Social Reform in Canada, 1914–1928*. Toronto: University of Toronto Press.

Calvert, L. (2009). "Beyond the Social Gospel." Social Address on the 100th Anniversary of the Stella Mission, Winnipeg, MB. Accessed via http://www.knowles-woodsworth.org/docs/LorneCalvert_BeyondtheSocialGospel.pdf

Campbell, D. 1983. "Social Reform, the Social Gospel and the Rise of Sociology in Canada." Pp. 7–52 in D. Campbell (ed.), *Beginnings: Essays in the History of Canadian Sociology*. Port Credit: Scribblers' Press.

Christie, N. and M. Gauvreau. 1996. *"A Full-Orbed Christianity": The Protestant Churches and Social Welfare in Canada, 1900–1940*. Montreal and Kingston: McGill-Queen's University Press.

Crysdale, S. 1976. "The Sociology of the Social Gospel: Quest for a Modern Ideology." Pp. 423–33 in S. Crysdale (ed.), *Religion in Canadian Society*. Toronto: Macmillan.

Fairbanks, A. 1896. *Introduction to Sociology*. New York: Charles Scribner's Sons.

Helmes-Hayes, R. 2016. "'Building the New Jerusalem in Canada's green and pleasant land': The social gospel and the roots of English-language academic sociology in Canada, 1889–1921." *Canadian Journal of Sociology* 41 (1): 1–52.

Helmes-Hayes, R. and J.-P. Warren. 2017. "The Development of Canadian Sociology." In K. Korgen (ed.), *The Cambridge Handbook of the History of Sociology*. In press.

Hiller, H. 1982. *Society and Change: S.D. Clark and the Development of Canadian Sociology*. Toronto: University of Toronto Press.
Hughes, E. 1943. *French Canada in Transition*. Chicago: University of Chicago Press.
Kidd, B. 1895. *Social Evolution*, 2nd edn. New York: Macmillan.
Peabody, F.G. 1909. *The Approach to the Social Question*. New York: Macmillan.
Porter, J. 1965. *The Vertical Mosaic: An Analysis of Class and Power in Canada*. Toronto: University of Toronto Press.
Rauschenbusch, W. 1912. *Christianizing the Social Order*. New York: Macmillan.
Schäffle, A.E.F. 1890. *Quintessence of Socialism*. London: Swan Sonnenschein.
Shore, M. 1987. *The Science of Social Redemption: McGill, the Chicago School and the Origins of Social Science Research in Canada*. Toronto: University of Toronto Press.
Valverde, M. 1991. *The Age of Light, Soap and Water: Moral Reform in English Canada, 1885–1925*. Toronto: McClelland & Stewart.
Wilcox-Magill, D. 1983. "Paradigms and Social Science in English Canada." Pp. 1–34 in J.P. Grayson, ed. *Introduction to Sociology: An Alternate Approach*. Toronto: Gage.

51 Keeping Up with the Martins: Prescribed Change, Homogeneity, and Cultural Continuity among the Old Order Mennonites

Steven Kleinknecht

Introduction

As many Old Order Mennonites take the surname Martin, in my title I play on the idiom "keeping up with Joneses" (and, more recently, the Kardashians) to make an important point about the operation of social life: we understand ourselves and our place within the world through **social comparison**. If you are an Old Order Mennonite, and your **reference group** is other Old Order Mennonites, then "the Martins" you are attempting to keep up with look similar to you, have limited technology, like you, and believe much the same way you do about living a "simple life"—i.e., a life absent of many of the luxuries of the modern, outside world. Part of a larger study on the preservation of culture among the Old Order Mennonites, this chapter explores how Old Order Mennonite religious leaders, in consultation with their community, attempt to prescribe change so as to dictate the limits of an appropriate Christian lifestyle. In defining what is and is not appropriate for brethren, they reinforce **homogeneity** in such things as possession, belief, and activity. Maintaining sameness creates a level playing field among group members, which in turn reduces the desire to compete with one another and want what other members already do not have.

To make my case, I draw on data collected during my field research with the Old Order Mennonite community. My primary interviews for this project were conducted with 14 current and former Old Order Mennonites. Given that my grandfather taught many of the now older generation of Old Order Mennonites, I was successful in gaining access to participants. Old Order Mennonites are Christians in the Anabaptist tradition who shun most forms of advanced technology such as cars and computers. They abide by a strict interpretation of the Bible, emphasizing a rural-based agrarian lifestyle, a clear gendered division of labour, patriarchal family structure, simple modest dress, separate church-funded schooling, and a devotion to a life based on self-sacrifice, community, and non-resistance. They believe strongly in remaining separate and distinct from the secular world. Nonconformity to the outside world is at the heart of the Old Order Mennonite ideology, so much so that they recognize and appreciate that they are a "separate" and "peculiar" people (Horst, 2000). Since the Old Order Mennonites provide particularly clear and intense instances of people's struggles to deal with change and continuity in the broader community, their society represents an exceptionally strategic sociological site for examining central features of human group life.

In the following pages, I describe how religious leaders in this community attempt to prescribe change by defining the boundaries of the community. Then I examine how attempts to achieve homogeneity contribute to **cultural continuity**. The goal of this chapter is to demonstrate how the dual processes of prescribing change and reinforcing homogeneity work together to preserve a particular way of life.

Religious Leaders, Prescribed Change, and Reinforcing Homogeneity

> When you are baptized you are not just adopting of our theological beliefs, you're saying you will adhere to the lifestyle and be under the direction of the brotherhood. (Old Order Mennonite)

In the Old Order community, the rules of the group, as managed by the clergy, delineate the social boundaries of the group so as to limit change. It is through "**prescribed change**" that the Old Order Mennonites are largely able to limit the types of change that would bring them "closer to the world." Prescribed change captures the idea that the leaders of the group are largely responsible for deciding on and designating the changes to their culture. This is not to say that church leaders are the only members of the community involved in mediating change. All adult members have input into the decision-making process. The right to authority over collective decisions is afforded to church leaders by the community through a religious process that members see as legitimate. Guided by their clergy, change is controlled for the benefit of the group as a whole and can be in the direction of greater or lesser conservatism.

Whenever anything new (e.g., the telephone, farm machinery) is considered for inclusion in Old Order society, these things are contemplated and discussed by the church community, and then the ministry prescribes any changes to their way of life. The rules, and any amendments to them, are meant to help ensure that members of the church continue to live by God's Word, while helping to guarantee the preservation of the Old Order way of life. Church rules touch on everything from hairstyle, dress, and possession to playing sports and the use of outside services. Underlying the issue of communal attempts to prescribe change is the group's emphasis on sustaining homogeneity. I posit that Old Orders are particularly vigilant in their expectations of uniformity not only out of their commitment to the scriptures but also because it is crucial for reducing social comparison and competition, and by extension, the desire or temptation to change.

Being an Old Order Mennonite means devoting oneself to the group and God. When baptized—something that happens when potential members are old enough to make a mature decision—they accept to sacrifice individual indulgences for the good of the group. The essence of this form of group submission is captured by the German word *Gelassenheit*, for which there is no English equivalent, but refers to "an attitude that is ready to yield, abandon, or surrender personal desires before God and the community" (Martin, 2003: 364–365). Martin explains that, "Not only does *Gelassenheit* shape the Old Order understanding of salvation, it shapes everyday life in the community" (2003: 365). Individuality is sacrificed for the good of the group, and such expectations go for all members of the community. The consequence, as it is practised by the Old Orders, is that individual submission to the group establishes uniformity among brethren.

Standards in such things as dress, level of technology, beliefs, and religious practices contribute to uniformity across the group such that homogeneity and the maintenance of it reinforce the boundaries of difference. If innovation is limited to that which is in keeping with their group's ideology, then the playing field is levelled and comparisons are made against a group for which there is not much room for variation. Sameness becomes important to a group emphasizing the community over the individual in that it limits the scope of social comparison. As one Old Order lady puts it: "If everyone else doesn't do these things either, then the temptation doesn't arise as much." An Old Order gentleman echoes these sentiments:

> There are a lot of things in our church that they [i.e., Mennonite clergy] really can't base it on religion. I guess they base it on wanting to be very cautious about things that, especially with the young people, giving into too much peer pressure and stuff like that. By doing that, I guess they have to hold back on some things and not allow them. *If I have it, then the next guy wants it too.* (emphasis added)

Emphasizing not only conformity, but also sameness reduces the feeling of competition among brethren and the temptation to want more.

The following statement by an Old Order gentleman illustrates the impact of homogeneity in maintaining their separation from mainstream society: "We believe in sameness in our community to emphasize community. It is human nature to be drawn to compete. A young person in a 'car-driving society' is more apt to compete. Through our sameness we lessen pride in possession." By focusing the group's attention inward, there is less temptation to want what should not be had or act in ways unbecoming of a true Christian. So, while a key aspect of the Old Order Mennonite community is homogeneity, sameness as it is reinforced through social control has the impact of shoring up the boundaries of the group.

The saying "You cannot miss what you have never had" applies here. Within the community, alternative patterns of identity and activity are limited. The Old Order community serves as the legitimate reference group (Shibutani, 1955) to which members compare themselves. Where comparisons are made to the outside world, these options are constructed as inappropriate alternatives. As one Old Order deacon told me, "There may be some good on the Internet and television, but there is also a lot of evil there. We have a willingness to sacrifice for the good of the next generation." With regard to everything from meeting the appropriate dress code to keeping one's tractor to a maximum of 100 horse power (so as not to be tempted to use it for transportation), the rules and their enforcement help to ensure a level playing field, uniformity, and, as a result, separation from mainstream society.

As some participants made clear to me, uniformity is not without its problems. Part of maintaining uniformity involves restricting contact with the outside world. As one participant described it, this can be problematic:

> Steve: Do you think that there's been less contact over the years, since you were younger, with the Mennonite community and the outside world?
>
> Edna: Yes, because the children, as a rule, don't grow up with others that aren't in their community. To a certain extent it makes for more cohesiveness, perhaps. But there's a danger in that, too. Nothing is ever quite good one way or the other, because there's a danger of children thinking that because this is how we do it, that this is the way it should be, and no other way is okay. But that can work for the other side, too.

Being such an insular community may, on the one hand, reinforce cohesiveness and uniformity among brethren as alternative perspectives are limited, but it can also lead to internal conflict. As another participant indicates, a great deal of emphasis on uniformity can mean that it becomes such a highly elevated value, that it can lead to individuals policing one another with negative consequences:

> If everybody has to be so alike, people start really watching each other. And if they start watching each other, then they start finding failures in others' actions and ways of doing things. Then they start backbiting each other. Then that's where the confusion comes in.

When homogeneity is venerated, it can lead to internal disputes over who is and is not living an appropriate Mennonite lifestyle. Taken to this extreme, brethren begin to lose sight of the religious and social value of *Gelassenheit* and general submission of the individual for the good of the group.

Conclusion

Alongside our fast-paced world, where change often seems unbridled, the Old Order Mennonites have developed strategies to preserve their way of life. There is a saying, "Comparison is the thief of joy."[1] To a great extent, the continuance of Old Order culture relies on such a perspective being reinforced through members' homogeneity in dress, language, possession, and perspective. As the rules dictate the limits of possession and establish a common set of expectations, maintaining uniformity reduces the need to compete with fellow group members. Establishing the Old Order community as the group's sole reference group helps to further bolster an inward focus and lessen the possibility of social comparison to external cultures.

For you and me, our postmodern society sets the context for feelings of relative deprivation (Stouffer et al., 1949): we feel materially and socially worse off compared to those who seemingly have more than we do. As we compare ourselves to others, we feel social pressure to pursue the latest trends and technological advances, thus propelling social change ever forward. In studying the Old Order Mennonites, I came to realize that attempts to control change are made more successful when social comparison is limited. Sustaining cultural continuity requires communal effort and a different standpoint on what is worth working toward.

Note

1. Thank you to Dana Sawchuk for bringing this saying to my attention at the 2015 Canadian Sociological Association meetings, and successfully rounding out my trio of popular sayings in this chapter.

References

Horst, I.R. (2000). A separate people: An insider's view of Old Order Mennonite customs and traditions. Waterloo, ON: Herald Press.

Martin, D. (2003). *Old Order Mennonites of Ontario:* Gelassenheit, *discipleship, brotherhood*. Kitchener, ON: Pandora Press.

Shibutani, T. (1955). Reference groups as perspectives. *American Journal of Sociology, 60:* 562–9.

Stouffer, S.A., Suchman, E.A., DeVinney, L.C., Starr, S.A., and Williams, R.M. (1949). *The American soldier: Adjustment to army life*, Vol. 1. Princeton, NJ: Princeton University Press.

52 The Status of Muslim Minorities during the War on Terror[1]

Jeffrey G. Reitz

Introduction

A backlash against Muslim minority communities has swirled across the Western world since the terrorist attacks on the United States on 11 September 2001, exacerbated by myriad subsequent acts of violence whose perpetrators claim a global Islamic agenda. Recent examples include the January 2015 bombing at the offices of the satirical weekly *Charlie Hebdo* in Paris, and the extensive series of attacks across Paris the following November, killing 130 people. Nor is Canada exempt. Eighteen persons plotting various attacks were arrested in Toronto in 2006. In October 2014, Canadian soldiers were rammed by a car, with one killed; in another episode, a man attacked and killed a soldier guarding a war memorial in Ottawa before turning on Parliament. The responses to these attacks, along with the rhetoric on the "**war on terror**," raise questions about how Muslim minority communities are affected. While an obvious concern is the extent to which local minorities feel a sense of kinship with the attackers, underlying this is a deeper concern, perhaps more worrying, that the attacks reveal an alien character to Muslim culture, one difficult to reconcile with basic Western values of democracy, state religious neutrality, and gender equity, or actually hostile to those values.

Are these concerns well-founded? Are Muslim minorities not integrating into society as effectively as other immigrant groups? Do their growing numbers represent some kind of threat? Evidence from social research refutes such concerns. Muslim communities in Western countries represent a variety of cultural and national backgrounds. Each community reflects these individual backgrounds as much as or more than a common Muslim identity. Moreover, Muslim experience in the community or the workplace differs little from other religious minorities—Hindus, Sikhs, and others. Their main problems centre on employment opportunity, recognition of qualifications, and discrimination—problems of visible minority immigrants generally, not Muslims specifically.

Although research suggests the processes of **integration** of Muslim populations into society are determined by ethnic and racial background, not religion, public opinion says otherwise. Accordingly, public discussion of immigrants has shifted from issues of race and ethnicity to religion. Immigrants to Canada from Pakistan, Iran, and other Muslim countries are now simply considered "Muslim." In France, immigrants once called Arabs or Turks are now just "Muslim." This focus on religion is not just wrong-headed; in many ways, it has been counterproductive, leading to policies attempting to repress religious expression, and erecting, not tearing down, barriers to integration.

Integration of Muslim Minorities

Canadian concern about Muslims as a group emerges in public opinion data. The 2010 Environics Focus Canada survey asked: "Do you think most Muslims coming to our country today want to adopt Canadian customs and way of life or do you think they want to be distinct from the larger Canadian society?" A majority (55 per cent) thought Muslims "want to be distinct." Far fewer (28 per cent) thought Muslims want to adopt Canadian customs (Reitz 2011). And despite widespread support for multiculturalism, Canadians want immigrants to "adopt

Canadian customs" and blend in. Fully 80 per cent agreed "ethnic groups should blend into Canadian society and not form separate communities," with 51 per cent agreeing "strongly." Two-thirds (68 per cent) said, "There are too many immigrants coming into this country who are not adopting Canadian values," with 40 per cent "strongly" agreeing.

Characterizations of Muslims as preferring to be "distinct" are challenged by Muslims themselves, with the vast majority viewing their co-religionists as wanting to integrate. A 2006 Focus Canada survey interviewed both mainstream and Muslim populations; 57 per cent of the former viewed Muslims as wanting to remain "distinct," but only 23 per cent of Muslims agreed. By the same token, 55 per cent of Muslims saw their co-religionists as wanting to adopt Canadian customs, but only 25 per cent of other Canadians agreed (Environics Research Institute 2006). Tellingly, Muslim Canadians are as likely as any other Canadians to express pride in their citizenship; in both cases, three in four were "very proud" to be Canadian, with all but 6 or 7 per cent at least "somewhat proud."

Persuasive evidence of Muslim integration comes from large broad-based social surveys, particularly Statistics Canada's 2002 Ethnic Diversity Survey. Based on over 42,000 interviews with mainstream and minority populations across Canada, it provides such indicators of social integration as intercultural friendships, participation in voluntary activities in the community, social trust, voting, sense of belonging, and feeling Canadian (Reitz, Breton, Dion, and Dion 2009; Reitz, Phan, Banerjee and Thompson 2009). The most detailed information ever collected on Canada's minorities, it shows all growing religious minorities, including Muslims, Sikhs, Buddhists, and Hindus, are slower to integrate socially because they are racial minorities not because of their religious beliefs.

The irrelevance of religion to social integration is revealed in the survey in two ways. First, among visible minorities, those whose religious commitments are strongest—whether Muslim or otherwise and including Christians—do not differ in their social integration in Canada from those whose religion is more peripheral in their lives. Second, when visible minorities are asked about problems such as discrimination, both Muslims and other religious groups describe problems as a result of skin colour or national origin, not religion.

One particularly salient issue is gender equity. Muslims are thought to hold traditional views on the status of women, views seen as extreme and impervious to change. In fact, surveys of Muslims suggest many Muslims, including women, feel Canada should accommodate their traditional beliefs about women's rights and roles. But the reality is that given time in Canada, Muslim minorities adopt Canadian beliefs and practices, including on the status of women.

Muslim assimilation to Canadian values on gender equity is powerfully demonstrated in data on labour force participation (Reitz, Phan, and Banerjee 2015). Recently arrived Muslim women follow traditional family roles; relatively few engage in paid work outside the home. In this, they differ little from recently arrived Hindu or Sikh women. Census data show that low levels of labour force participation of recent immigrant women reflect country of origin, not religion: Pakistani Muslim women, for example, have much lower labour force participation than Middle Eastern or European Muslim women. Evidence also suggests those who are strongly religious do not differ from those who are less so.

Importantly, Muslim women's labour force participation rises dramatically over time. Group differences fade for those with more than 10 years in Canada, completely disappearing for their children born in Canada. The bottom line: assimilation is alive and well for Muslims in Canada, particularly for women.

An interesting source of information on integration is a large-scale employment audit study conducted by Philip Oreopoulos (2011). Nearly 13,000 résumés were sent to employers in response to advertised jobs. Résumés containing English or British names prompted calls for an interview 39 per cent more often than résumés with Chinese, Indian, Pakistani, and Greek names, even when the latter indicated Canadian education and experience. (Callback rates were far lower for those with minority names and education or experience outside Canada.) The extent of discrimination against Pakistanis—who are mainly Muslims—is the same as for the other groups. Obviously, we can't know if employers realized Ali Saeed, Chaudhry Mohammad, or Fatima Sheikh probably were Muslim, or Samir Sharma, Panav Singh, or Priyanka Kaur probably were not (names used in the study). It made no difference to their inclination to pass over such résumés in preference for Greg Johnson, John Martin, or Emily Brown (again names used in the study). This is consistent with other information about the social experience of Muslims in Canada. Their problems are the same as those of other ethnic groups and are not related to religion.

Impact on Muslims of the Focus on Religion

The empirical evidence says one thing, the general public says another, and since 9/11, the religious affiliation of Muslims has come to define them in public opinion. Muslims themselves are very aware of the increased salience of religion in their social identity. Understandably, many are resentful and fearful, seeing it as an invitation for negative attention. Many have been attacked. Yet the dominance of religion in public discourse has not substantially altered the pattern of social, economic, and political integration of Muslim communities in Western societies. There is little overall impact on national identity, or on friendship patterns, and so on. Most people, including Muslims, operate on a day-to-day basis with friends and co-workers they know and like, not with hostile people. Bad things happen, but at the same time, there are positive signs. Sometimes even a struggle against stigma/exclusion can bring people into a society and its social and political dynamic. Some Muslims, for example, have engaged with the project of countering anti-Muslim viewpoints; this brings them into closer relations with the political process, producing greater integration in society, not less.

A public discourse of exclusion does not necessarily lead to exclusion; we see this in comparison across settings. In France, the debate over religion in the public sphere as applied to Muslim immigrants is intense, bans on the headscarf for Muslim women have been extended to schools, and the right-wing National Front has made notable political gains based on anti-immigrant and anti-Muslim policies. In Quebec, politics are more muted; the proposed Quebec Charter of Values, which would have imposed French-style bans on headscarves for public employees, failed with the defeat of the Parti Québécois government. Meanwhile, in the rest of Canada, despite debates of Sharia law or headscarf bans, public discourse indicates little interest in policy restrictions.

Yet across these differing settings, we find little difference in Muslim experiences of discrimination, the establishment of social relations with members of other communities, or trust in and identification with the larger society (Reitz, Simon, and Laxer 2014)—with a striking exception. In France, the headscarf policy has backfired. Instead of facilitating integration by making all women alike, many highly motivated and Westernized women simply withdraw from the labour market and other arenas where headscarves are banned.

As noted above, in Canada, gender differences in labour force participation fade and are virtually eliminated for the Canadian-born generation. In France, however, while Muslim women assimilate into the labour market, this is limited; even the French-born Muslim women participate less than others. Whereas the odds of a Canadian-born Muslim woman being in the labour force are identical to the mainstream population, the odds of a French-born Muslim woman being in the labour force are 13 per cent lower than mainstream. In interviews,

Muslim women point to the restricted employment opportunities for hijab-wearing women. Canada, of course, has no headscarf ban.

The evidence is clear: the Muslim community, regardless of national origins, integrates as well into Canadian society as any other visible minority group. Policies restricting religious expression would not be conducive to integration, as the French headscarf ban suggests. Kazemipur (2014) argues we must "shift our attention from the theological to the social" (p. 180). Put otherwise, the prevailing focus on religion diverts attention from those areas of life that actually determine social integration: getting a job, sending children to school, playing a role in community decision making. We should remove existing barriers, not build new ones.

Note

1. Adapted from "The Status of Muslim Minorities Following the Paris Attacks," pp. 21-7 in *After the Paris Attacks: Responses in Canada, Europe and Around the Globe,* edited by Edward M. Iacobucci and Stephen J. Toope, Toronto: University of Toronto Press, 2015.

References

Environics Research Institute, 2006. *Focus Canada Report 2006-4.* Toronto: Environics Research Institute.

Kazemipur, A., 2014. *The Muslim Question in Canada.* Vancouver: UBC Press.

Oreopoulos, P., 2011. "Why Do Skilled Immigrants Struggle in the Labor Market? A Field Experiment with Thirteen Thousand Résumés." *American Economic Journal: Economic Policy,* 3,4: 148–71.

Reitz, J.G., 2011. "Pro-immigration Canada: Social and Economic Roots of Popular Views." Montreal: IRPP, Study No. 20.

Reitz, J.G., R. Banerjee, M. Phan, and J. Thompson, 2009. "Race, Religion, and the Social Integration of New Immigrant Minorities in Canada," *International Migration Review,* 43,4: 695–726.

Reitz, J.G., R. Breton, K.K. Dion, and K.L. Dion, 2009. *Multiculturalism and Social Cohesion: Potentials and Challenges of Diversity.* New York: Springer.

Reitz, J.G., M. Phan, and R. Banerjee, 2015. "Gender Equity in Canada's Newly Growing Religious Minorities," *Ethnic and Racial Studies* 38,5: 681–99.

Reitz, J.G., P. Simon, and E. Laxer, 2014. "Muslims' Social Inclusion and Exclusion in France, Québec and Canada: Does National Context Matter?" Presented at XVIII ISA World Congress of Sociology, Yokohama, July 15. https://isaconf.confex.com/isaconf/wc2014/webprogram/Paper35459.html

Questions for Critical Thought

Chapter 49 | Are Islam and Democracy Compatible?

1. What is the main question being asked in this study? How is it motivated by religion?
2. In this chapter, a historical comparison is made between Muslim and Christian majority countries. Which of these two religious groups is historically less tolerant toward minority groups? Give examples.
3. This chapter compares countries that are either a Christian or Muslim majority to see which countries have the highest levels of intolerance. Currently, which group has a higher level of intolerance? Can this be linked to religion?
4. What is the relationship between a country's level of socio-economic development and level of intolerance?
5. What cultural traits are associated with political extremism? Why is this important to understand?

Chapter 50 | "Building the New Jerusalem in Canada's Green and Pleasant Land": The Social Gospel and the Roots of English-Language Academic Sociology in Canada, 1889–1921

1. What is the social gospel? What religious group was the most involved in its teachings?
2. Sociology is said to have come to Canada in the 1920s; however, Helmes-Hayes argues that it arrived much sooner in the form of the social gospel. How can social gospel be linked to sociology?
3. How is sociology both a tool and an intellectual orientation for social gospellers?
4. Who taught the social gospel? Where did they come from? What were they previously educated in?
5. Why is it important to recognize the social gospel as the beginning of sociology in Canada?

Chapter 51 | Keeping Up with the Martins: Prescribed Change, Homogeneity, and Cultural Continuity among the Old Order Mennonites

1. What does it mean to "keep up with the Martins"? Briefly describe the culture of Old Order Mennonites.
2. Who manages the Old Order community? By what process does prescribed change occur?
3. Why is maintaining homogeneity important to the Old Order Mennonites? From what does this practice protect them?
4. What are some of the potential drawbacks of homogeneity?
5. Kleinknecht finds that the Old Order Mennonites' practice of homogeneity makes them less likely to desire change. Imagine applying this practice to all of Canadian culture. Could homogeneity be achieved?

Chapter 52 | The Status of Muslim Minorities during the War on Terror

1. Public opinion and social research on Muslim integration into North American society are different. How are they different? What factors are at play in understanding these differences?
2. How is public opinion harmful to Muslim minority groups? Comment on the media's discourse about "the war on terror."
3. Why is it problematic to group all people from Pakistan, Iran, Turkey, and other Muslim-majority countries together under a common label?
4. What factors prevent racial and religious minority groups from integrating into North American culture?
5. Describe the trends of integration for Muslim women. What can be learned from their level of integration?

PART XIII
Politics

During the 2015 Canadian federal election campaign, many citizens intently followed political debates because, after nearly 10 years of government by Stephen Harper and the Conservative Party, they were ready for a change. As the major political parties and their leaders put forward their positions on television, citizens followed suit, actively discussing the contending viewpoints at dinner tables, bars, and other public places. As a result, on Election Day 2015, more Canadians turned out to cast their vote than had done so in the previous two decades. This momentous election ended with Justin Trudeau and the Liberal Party winning a majority government and the Conservative Party and New Democratic Party losing their leaders.

Events like these are of great interest to political sociologists, because they are about the processes by which public decision making takes place in Canadian society. While candidates campaigned and debated, private citizens argued over politics, supporters rallied for political parties, and voters made their way to the polls, these sociologists looked for answers to pressing questions about the link between political life and changes in the culture, the economy, and society.

Political sociology generally focuses on the connections between state, society, and citizenry in hopes of understanding the influence of power on politics. This research goes beyond elections, examining the interaction between political actors and the day-to-day business of politicians and the impact that policy has on the public.

Where politics is concerned, sociologists do more than teach and research within the university. The first chapter in this section, Chapter 53, will introduce you to the idea of public sociology and the view that sociologists should take a more active role in public life. Here, Daniel Béland focuses on the benefit of having a sociologist (a) teach the public about the sociological imagination and (b) act as a mediator in political debates. This chapter thus shows the benefit of a sociological education for voters and citizens more generally.

Chapter 54 describes the meaning of human rights and Canada's rights culture. In this chapter, Dominique Clément explains that Canada's liberal culture emphasizes the importance of respecting people's civil and political rights. This liberal approach to human rights can be found in Canada's culture, policy-making, and political dialogue, illustrating the complex interrelation of social forces in politics.

However, in order to fully understand political research, we must also recognize the role that power plays in shaping the social order. Typically, political actors gain their position of authority because of their social standing. Ultimately, power is gained by having access to resources that others do not have access to—in this case, money, influence, pedigree, or a skill. But Canadians have different amounts of access to such standing, and hence to such authority. Social stratification based on gender, race, and class creates unequal opportunities for the acquisition of power in Canadian society. Not surprisingly, many people in positions of power and authority choose to maintain the status quo, which works in their own favour.

For example, as you will see in Chapter 55, former prime minister Stephen Harper made many changes to Canadian policy that diminished public access to information. Margrit Eichler describes how Harper's decision to cut back on both access to scientific findings and census data collection hindered the production of public knowledge. No wonder, then, that one of Justin Trudeau's first acts as the new prime minister of Canada was to reinstate the long-form census and declare his respect for scientific research and transparent policy-making. These decisions had both a practical impact on society and a symbolic impact, by declaring that new power-holders would rule in a different way.

In a democratic society like Canada, voting can make a difference to how the polity works. Accordingly, political sociologists study the factors that influence people's voting patterns, and in Chapter 56 Reza Nakhaie compares pre- and post-Second World War generations to describe how people respond electorally to political and economic stress.

53 Why Sociologists Should Care about Public Policy[1]

Daniel Béland

Introduction

Why should sociologists care about **public policy**? Too often public policy is understood as an overly technical and even technocratic field of inquiry that is distinct from, and even less valuable than, an inquiry into broad theoretical issues or empirical shifts. I seek to debunk this widely shared myth that good sociology and public policy should remain separated. Sociologists are in a good position to provide policy advice on a range of issues, without rejecting the critical perspective they might embrace. In fact, critical voices are much needed in contemporary policy debates, in context of which sociologists can make a difference. In this short chapter, I explain why sociologists should care more about public policy than most of them typically do, despite the excellent policy work members of the discipline have done over the years. To make a strong case for a sociological perspective on public policy that is not merely technocratic or partisan, I discuss general reasons why all sociologists should take policy research and engagement very seriously.

Taking Public Policy Seriously

There are six general reasons why sociologists should really care about public policy. First, from a historical standpoint, key founders of our discipline had clear policy objectives, and they played a central role in the policy debates of their time. For example, Émile Durkheim (2002) wrote extensively about education reform under France's Third Republic. More recently, sociologists all around the world have weighted in key policy discussions on issues ranging from gender equality to environmental policy. In the context of these discussions, sociologists do not have to simply take the position of narrow-focused experts who provide technical advice to policy-makers. However, when necessary, they must take a public stance to put forward concrete, detailed policy proposals, through op-eds, policy briefs, and government testimonies. From this angle, **policy sociology** is not entirely distinct from what Michael Burawoy (2005) calls public sociology. This is true because, as opposed to what Burawoy (2005: 9) suggests, the interface between sociology and public policy is not necessarily about putting "sociologists in the service of a goal defined by a client." Taking a stance in policy debates and putting forward actual proposals is not the same thing as serving the state or another client.

Second, the expansion of state power over the last century means that, today, public policy is literally everywhere. From this perspective, it is impossible to study social processes without taking into account the changing role of the state and, more importantly, the reconfigurations of the relationship between the state and other social institutions. The state is involved in all aspects of our lives, and public policy is an essential component of the "big picture" sociologists seek to understand. For this reason, in Canada as elsewhere around the world, sociological research and intervention are related to crucial policy issues, in one way or another. From immigration and gender inequality to health status and labour relations, social issues are also policy issues. In this context, because of the nature of their research objects and the broad scope of their discipline, sociologists are in an excellent position to shed unique light on contemporary policy problems. Yet, in Canada at least, economists and political scientists are more widely represented in public debates about core policy issues than sociologists. The same remark applies to the growing number of policy schools in Canada, whose faculty are primarily populated by economists and political scientists. This is a pity because, more than economics and at least as much as political science, sociology lends itself to interdisciplinary collaboration. While maintaining their disciplinary identity, to contribute to both policy research and advice, sociologists can reach out to people from other disciplines and from outside academia. Political scientists and, more recently, economists have borrowed extensively from sociologists in the context of their work, something that is excellent news for the discipline. For instance, the recent work of Akerlof and Kranton (2010) shows that economists can engage with sociological thinking in order to move their policy research agenda forward. Economics and sociology are perhaps the two broadest social science disciplines and, thus far, the former has proved far more influential within policy circles than the latter. In fact, from a historical standpoint, as Robert Nisbet (1966) suggested, sociology emerged partly as an alternative (or at least a corrective to) the individualistic world view associated with modern economics. Considering that policy is central to most of the issues sociologists study, it would not be hard for them to make their research even more policy relevant in order to challenge the domination of economics in a host of policy areas.

Third, interdisciplinary policy research is both relevant and legitimate, as long as we understand that disciplinary traditions are here to stay, and that the perspectives they offer must complement one another, with the objective of making citizens and policy-makers more aware of the challenges and opportunities they face. As a consequence of their participation in broad policy discussions and networks, sociologists can become more relevant without necessarily losing their identity as scholars. Yet, sociologists need to contribute to policy debates in a way that could be understood by people outside academia, which is the only way to become relevant outside the Ivory Tower. Being able to write a concise op-ed and take part in what is known as knowledge translation are essential conditions for sociologists to start mattering more in the policy realm, which is not about them becoming mere advocates but about improving the quality of both policy deliberation and decisions. For example, when sociologist Julie Kaye (2015) wrote an op-ed criticizing the Harper government's legislation on the sex trade (Bill C-36), she discussed legislation enacted in New Zealand before explaining why she considered Bill C-36 to be a flawed policy. Instead of attacking the Harper government from an ideological standpoint or simply becoming the voice of a particular group, she offered a rigorous analysis of the new policy in light of available sociological evidence. This is one of the best ways in which sociologists can matter in the policy arena.

Fourth, there is a growing consensus within and beyond sociology as a discipline that globalization has not strongly weakened the potential role of nation-states in society and policy development. Yet, the contemporary debate on globalization stresses the need to take into account the role of transnational actors and processes in policy-making. Sociology is in a privileged position to shape the contemporary debates on the intersection of national and transnational policy actors and processes. For instance, it is possible to explore how international organizations might impact national policy decisions, and how such decisions can shape processes of transnational policy diffusion. Much of the recent political science literature on international organizations and public policy focuses primarily on how formal political actors and institutions shape the impact of international organizations on domestic policy (Orenstein, 2008). In such a context, there is much room available for sociologists to stress the role of non-state, civil society actors in the construction and diffusion of transnational policy influence around the globe. Simultaneously, in the context of globalization, sociologists could play a more central role in the process of international lesson drawing (Rose, 1991), according to which countries and jurisdictions can learn from one another, sometimes through rigorous comparative research. An outstanding example of this approach is the work of Dan Zuberi (2006), who compares the fate of hotel workers in Vancouver and Seattle to assess the impact of cross-national differences in social policy in the lives of low-income people in Canada and the United States. Grounded in more than 75 interviews on both sides of the border and a clever comparative research design, his book *Differences That Matter* is relevant for both scholars and people outside academia who want to understand how policies affect people and how to make such policies more effective (Zuberi, 2006).

Fifth, with the growing interest in public sociology (Burawoy, 2005), it is becoming easier to move the relationship between sociology and public policy beyond the technocratic model that dominated the post-war era. However, while recognizing that our policy positions are related to power relations, sociologists do not necessarily have to embrace a partisan approach. The unique perspective of sociology as a discipline should inform policy debates alongside other disciplinary perspectives, regardless of the partisan orientations of scholars involved in such debates. The last thing we need is to have sociologists act as servants of a political party, which often tend to care less about good policy and more about getting their people elected and re-elected. This is not to say that sociologists should not take a stance in political debates over key policy issues. Sociologists who want to make a difference in these debates, however, should not do so simply to support a partisan agenda.

Sixth, studying policy issues from a sociological perspective is fulfilling the promise of what C. Wright Mills called the sociological imagination (1959). For him, sociological imagination is about understanding the relationship between apparently private troubles like losing one's job and public issues like unemployment—a collective problem. Because the social construction of public problems is a major aspect of both policy and sociological debates, sociology unavoidably deals with policy issues. In this context, the role of sociologists in the realm of public policy is not only to formulate solutions to potential economic, environmental, and social problems but to help identify, measure, and frame such problems. Because sociologists have long contributed to problem definition through their analyses, they are in an excellent position to feed policy debates, when the time comes to assess the nature and scope of the issues of the day that may necessitate public action. What Mills called sociological imagination is at the heart of the construction of problems in a number of policy areas, a situation that empowers sociologists to get involved in them and to make a difference by drawing directly on their knowledge and research findings.

Conclusion

As the above discussion suggests, by understanding the history of our discipline, the enduringly central role of the state in contemporary societies, and the potentially important contribution of the sociological perspective on major policy debates, we should no longer think of public policy as a purely technical and, therefore, inferior topic. In the end, through the analysis of policy issues related to the big picture, our discipline can achieve a crucial element of the sociological imagination. In order to do this, sociologists have to write more op-eds and policy reports. They also need to publish more regularly in policy journals and play a much greater role within policy schools, which should become more interdisciplinary, instead of simply featuring scholars from economics and political science. These schools would surely gain from greater exposure to top-notch sociological, policy-relevant scholarship.

Note

1. This chapter is a significantly revised and extended version of Béland, 2009. The author thanks Patrizia Albanese, Lorne Tepperman, and Neil McLaughlin for their feedback on previous drafts of this chapter. He also acknowledges support from the Canada Research Chairs Program.

References

Akerlof, George A. and Rachel E. Kranton. 2010. *Identity Economics: How Our Identities Shape Our Work, Wages, and Well-Being*. Princeton, NJ: Princeton University Press.

Béland, Daniel. 2009. "Sociology and Public Policy," *Footnotes*, 37(4): 7.

Burawoy, Michael. 2005. "For Public Sociology," *American Sociological Review*, 70(1): 4–28.

Durkheim, Émile. 2002. *Moral Education*. Mineola, NY: Dover Publications

Kaye, Julie. 2015. "Canada's Flawed Sex Trade Law," *New York Times*, January 20. http://www.nytimes.com/2015/01/21/opinion/canadas-flawed-sex-trade-law.html?_r=0

Mills, C. Wright. 1959. *The Sociological Imagination*. New York: Oxford University Press.

Nisbet, Robert. 1966. *The Sociological Tradition*. New York: Basic Books.

Orenstein, Mitchell A. 2008. *Privatizing pensions: The transnational campaign for social security reform*. Princeton, NJ: Princeton University Press.

Rose, Richard. 1991. "What Is Lesson Drawing?" *Journal of Public Policy*, 11(1): 3–30.

Zuberi, Dan. 2006. *Differences that Matter: Social Policy and the Working Poor in the United States and Canada*. Ithaca: Cornell University Press.

54 The Sociology of Human Rights

Dominique Clément

One of the most difficult lessons to teach about **human rights** is that people have not always framed their grievances using the language of rights. In the past, Canadians were more likely to reference socialism, industrial democracy, Christian values, or British justice when they felt wronged and sought restitution. At a meeting of the Victoria School Board in 1922, for instance, Trustee Bertha P. Andrews condemned the systemic segregation of Asians in schools as "a violation of the fundamental principles of British justice and even a greater violation of the basic principles of our Christian religion" (Stanley 2011). When people did speak about rights, it was often in reference to speech, association, assembly, press, religion, voting, due process, and equal treatment. Today, rights talk has gone far beyond political and civil freedoms to include everything from the environment to Internet access.

A sociological approach to human rights understands that rights derive from society and the state rather than an abstract principle. There is a distinction between human rights laws, which are codified rules, and talking about human rights as aspirations or competing moral claims. In this way, human rights are a sociological as well as a legal fact. Human rights should be understood as they are practised in social life (Griffin 2008). Our understanding of human rights must go beyond abstract universalism and recognize that each society has its own rights culture that is socially constructed. Claims to universality confuse the way human rights are realized as a distinct social practice.

When lawyers and judges debate human rights, they often appeal to abstract principles. The legal approach posits that human rights derive from an abstract pre-social individual who has rights by virtue of his or her humanity. In theory, there would be no limit to how we define human rights. In the sociological tradition, however, "any discussion of human rights should be firmly linked to the capacity of the state and society at large to guarantee the enjoyment of those rights" (Madsen and Verschraegen 2013). Human rights are a particular type of social practice. Sociology can help us understand how and why human rights have emerged as a powerful social force; how rights are realized in practice; how society resolves competing rights claims; and what were the social conditions that made rights significant in a particular historical moment. In order to have social meaning, human rights must become embedded in routine practices of societal institutions such as schools, hospitals, families, courts, and government (Madsen and Verschraegen 2013). In other words, a sociological approach helps us understand the societal preconditions for the emergence and practice of human rights.

Sociology's founders scorned the idea of human rights. Émile Durkheim, Karl Marx, and Max Weber believed that rights were nothing more than a philosophical abstraction. They rejected the notion of universal values that were independent of society. Over time, though, sociologists have come to recognize the increasing influence of human rights. They have sought to understand those societal preconditions that facilitated the popularization of human rights.[1] Societal preconditions might include, for example, democracy and capitalism, which facilitated the emergence of human rights. A modern industrial economy combined with a powerful state produces social disruptions arising from mass education, geographic mobility, and segmented family units. Disruptions to social networks, as well as an emphasis on individual autonomy, facilitated the popularization of human rights as a way of framing grievances. The proliferation of rights talk also coincided with the growing repressive capacity of the state, as well as the emergence of expansive state bureaucracies. In this way, rights serve a particular function: to protect autonomy in a liberal society where the individual is paramount.[2]

Rights have, throughout history, been a rallying cry for those committed to equality and inclusivity rather than exclusion and privilege. Conflict is at the very heart of human rights. It is a language that the weak appropriate to challenge the powerful. It is effective because human rights principles such as equal treatment or freedom are embraced by the weak and powerful alike. At the same time, the practice of human rights differs among communities. A **rights culture** is the way a community interprets and applies rights in practice (Clément 2016). Canada's rights culture is most apparent in those rights that are codified in law. But human rights are not simply law. In fact, the law is simply a reflection of existing social practices. To have social meaning, human rights must be part of people's daily lives and integral to societal institutions. A rights culture is constitutive of those rights that are deeply embedded in the practices of social and political life. To say that Canadians have a rights culture is to assert that rights are a product of community, and that they evolve as part of that community over time. Rights are not above politics, nor do they exist in the abstract outside our community. There may indeed be universal principles that should apply to every human being, but each society interprets and applies human rights in its own way. Perhaps the only genuinely universal human right, as **Hannah Arendt** once suggested, was the right to have rights. In other words, the only universal human right is to belong to a community that recognizes and protects rights (Arendt 2004). A stateless person has no human rights.

It is misleading, therefore, to suggest that human rights are based on universal truths or moral absolutes. In fact, human rights have an instrumental or political function (Goodhart 2013). The state might enforce rights through law, but new rights claims emerge from people and movements outside the state who frame their grievances and their vision for social change using the language of rights. Human rights have a social life in that they emerge from shared understandings of what rights should be. As a result, every society has its own rights culture. Human rights have universal appeal as abstract principles, but they are not premised on a shared universal understanding. Rather, institutions, social practice, historical context, and resistance shape rights cultures. One of the most salient examples of how history has shaped Canadians' rights culture is the commitment to the principle of self-determination for Aboriginal peoples and French Canadians (Clément 2016). State policy relating to Aboriginal peoples may be flawed, but there is growing consensus around their collective rights. Moreover, the federal government has acknowledged the collective rights of French Canadians to protect their language and culture. It has even gone so far as to legislate a formula to break the country apart.

There are other notable aspects of Canadians' rights culture (Clément 2016). Capital punishment is illegal. Women have the right to an abortion. There is a history of tolerance toward religious minorities. Sexual minorities enjoy more freedom in Canada than many other countries. The constitution guarantees freedoms of speech, assembly, association, press, and religion as well as due process and equal treatment (with notable limits). The **Charter of Rights and Freedoms** is unique in the world in that it recognizes multiculturalism, minority language education, the equality of men and women, and Aboriginal peoples' rights as human rights.

The most important lesson that history teaches about Canada's rights culture is that it is liberal and individualistic. This focus on individual rights often acts as a type of filter in public debates around the legitimacy of new rights claims. Canadians have traditionally given greater prominence to civil and political rights above economic, social, or cultural rights. For example, people have a right to request legal aid, but receiving legal aid is not guaranteed. Canadians have a right to access health care or education, but many people cannot afford to attend university or pay for expensive medicines. Citizens have the right to vote and to participate in the social, economic, and cultural life of the nation without discrimination. But there is no human right to material equality. Poverty, in other words, is not recognized in law as a human rights violation. Another feature of Canada's rights culture is that, during periods of emergency, the state has often temporarily suspended rights.

Perhaps the most notable feature of Canada's rights culture is the failure to fully embrace economic and social rights. This does not necessarily reflect a failure of rights discourse. Human rights has, throughout history, become so closely aligned with individual autonomy and law that it is hard to imagine rights as a transformative discourse (Stammers 2009). And yet rights discourse has become the dominant vernacular for framing grievances precisely because it is malleable. If framing grievances as human rights violations has failed to produce material equality, the fault lies with our society's lack of commitment to genuine equality as opposed to rights discourse. In this way, liberalism and capitalism have profoundly shaped Canada's rights culture. It is a rights culture largely premised on treating everyone the same and providing equal opportunity, which has allowed systemic inequalities in wealth to flourish. Nonetheless, new rights claims emerge every year. It is not uncommon to hear Canadians today speak of the environment, housing, assisted suicide, natural resources, or communication as human rights. As society changes, so too will Canada's rights culture.

Notes

1. Bryan S. Turner's (1993) pioneering essay on sociology and human rights helps explain why sociologists have been hesitant to engage with the study of human rights in the past. More recent studies on the sociology of human rights include: Armaline, Glasberg, and Pyrkayastha (2015); Hynes, Lamb, Short, and Waites (2010, 2011); Sjoberg, Gill, and Williams (2001); and Sznaider (2006).
2. For a more detailed discussion on the sociological tradition, as well as societal preconditions that facilitated the popularization of rights discourse, see Madsen and Verschraegen (2013).

References

Arendt, Hannah. 2004. *The Origins of Totalitarianism*. New York: Schoken Books.

Armaline, William T., Davita Silfen Glasberg, and Bandana Pyrkayastha. 2015. *The Human Rights Enterprise*. Cambridge: Polity Press.

Clément, Dominique. 2016. *Human Rights in Canada: A History*. Kitchener-Waterloo, ON: Wilfrid Laurier University Press.

Goodhart, Michael. 2013. "Human Rights and the Politics of Contention." Pp. 31–44 in *Human Rights at the Crossroads*, edited by Mark Goodale. New York: Oxford University Press.

Griffin, James. 2008. *On Human Rights*. New York: Oxford University Press.

Hynes, Patricia, Michele Lamb, Damien Short, and Matthew Waites. 2010. "Sociology and Human Rights: Confrontations, Evasions and New Engagements." *The International Journal of Human Rights* 14: 811–32.

———. 2011. *Sociology and Human Rights*. Toronto: Routledge.

Madsen, Mikael Rask and Gert Verschraegen. 2013. "Making Human Rights Intelligible: An Introduction to a Sociology of Human Rights." Pp. 1–24 in *Making Human Rights Intelligible*, edited by Mikael Rask Madsen and Gert Verschraegen. Portland, OR: Hart Publishing.

Sjoberg, Gideon, Elizabeth A. Gill, and Norma Williams. 2001. "A Sociology of Human Rights." *Social Problems* 48: 11–47.

Stammers, Neil. 2009. *Human Rights and Social Movements*. London: Pluto Press.

Stanley, Timothy J. 2011. *Contesting White Supremacy: School Segregation, Anti-Racism, and the Making of Chinese Canadians*. Vancouver: UBC Press.

Sznaider, Daniel Levy and Natan. 2006. "Sovereignty Transformed: A Sociology of Human Rights." *The British Journal of Sociology* 57: 657–77.

Turner, Bryan S. 1993. "Outline of a Theory of Human Rights." *Sociology* 27: 489–512.

55 Making Us Ignorant: Canadian Science Policy under a Neo-conservative Regime

Margrit Eichler

Introduction

When Stephen Harper became prime minister in 2006, Canada took a sharp turn to the right. With the election of a Liberal government in 2015, some (but not all) of the Harper government's **neo-conservative** policies, including those affecting science, have been reversed. Neo-conservatism, as practised in Canada, included turning from peace keeping to actively supporting wars; stressing a supposedly ever-present threat of terrorism that requires drastic counter-measures, including mass surveillance of citizens; and an unmitigated support for extractive industries, at the expense of environmental protection.

It also included a deliberate weakening of democratic institutions, particularly the House of Commons, through the use of omnibus bills that prevented discussion, the prorogation of Parliament, and other means. It included a disdain for human rights and an obsession with crime and punishment. One lesser-known aspect of this approach is the suppression of certain types of scientific knowledge.

Any government needs information in order to govern. Part of the information needed is collected and analyzed by natural and social scientists in its employ. However, the Harper government systematically and deliberately blinded itself—and of course its citizens—by shutting down, defunding, or otherwise destroying world-class scientific organizations that used to provide information on the state of the nation, the environment, and social justice.

In reaction to these assaults on public knowledge, scientists took to the streets in demonstrations—a step that was unprecedented in Canadian history.

Various civil society groups including Evidence for Democracy[1] and Our Right to Know[2] were formed with the specific intent of combatting these changes. Voices-Voix continues to document the suppression of dissent and the erosion of democracy through detailed and well-researched case studies.[3]

In the following, I shall provide a brief summary of some of the ways in which **public science** was decimated, note which of the policies were changed by the new government, and then look at the electoral system in order to explain the gap between the government's policy and public opinion. The majority of citizens did not agree with Harper's "war on science."

Attacks on Public Science by Harper's Neo-conservative Government

The Harper government was *not* uniformly against science. For instance, it provided infrastructure enhancement to Canadian universities and colleges, and supported the Council of Canadian Academies, the Canada Foundation for Innovation, and more.[4] However, science was perceived as the handmaiden of industry, rather than as in the public interest. This was explicitly expressed on the website of the National Research Council, which offered a "concierge service" for enterprises (but does not any longer).[5] While Canada's overall science budget decreased by 7 per cent since the Conservatives came into power,[6] Canada still spent a substantial $10.3 billion on science and technology.[7] The Liberals increased spending on various aspects of science in their first budget.[8]

Harper's attacks were largely targeted toward the census, human rights, and environmental research.[9]

a) The Census

The Harper government abolished the mandatory long-form census against the concerted advice of organizations from all parts of the political spectrum. Cities from coast to coast to coast objected, as did chambers of commerce, professional organizations, health professionals, churches, academics, two former chief statisticians of Statistics Canada, and two former clerks of the Privy Council. More than 400 organizations are on record as having objected,[10] and there were probably many more.

The consequences were as dire as predicted: The voluntary survey that replaced the mandatory survey was about $22 million more expensive,[11] and the data are vastly inferior because the response rate dropped from the previous 93.5 per cent to 68.6 per cent. The responses in 1,813 subdivisions were so low that they had to be dropped from the data. Twenty-one per cent of millionaires did not participate in the survey, and some Aboriginal communities are entirely missing. The very rich and the poor and marginalized, including Aboriginals, people with disabilities, recent immigrants, and people with low levels of education or with difficulties expressing themselves in one of the official languages are the ones who tend not to participate in voluntary surveys. Most importantly, the data are so poor that the voluntary household survey, which replaced the census, cannot be used to correct sampling errors in other surveys, thus negatively affecting all other national surveys. Experts have declared it to be of no scientific value, concluded that it undermines Canadian science, and demanded that it should be withdrawn.[12] On Day 2 after having taken power, the Liberal government reinstated the census.

b) Human Rights

Organizations that research human rights were one of the targets for defunding, closure, and harassment. These included organizations conducting research for Aboriginals, women, refugees, general human rights organizations, and others. Some of the organizations that have been simply shut down include the Sisters in Spirit, a database on missing and murdered Aboriginal women,[13] and the Rights and Democracy Agency, which was created by the Progressive Conservative government of Brian Mulroney in 1988 to encourage democracy and monitor human rights around the world.[14] Many others were likewise abolished. A partial list can be found on the timeline of Our Right to Know.[15]

These organizations cannot simply be restarted. It is easy to destroy research organizations, and very difficult and time-consuming to build them. Some of the research capacity is forever lost to Canada, but hopefully alternatives will be created over time. With respect to Aboriginal issues, the Liberal government committed itself to implementing all of the recommendations of the Truth and Reconciliation Commission,[16] which includes some research aspects.

c) Environmental Research

Environmental research carried on by government scientists was severely circumscribed. In 2007, Environment Canada adopted a new media relations policy that required senior researchers to obtain permission from the government before speaking with the media, and questions were vetted beforehand.[17] The result was that reporting on climate change dropped by 80 per cent within one year. This policy was lifted by the Liberals, and the mandate letter for the minister of science contains an explicit request to ensure "that scientists are able to speak freely about their work."[18]

Contacts between scientists were also monitored. In one famous example, media people shadowed Canadian scientists at a Polar Year Conference hosted by Canada in Montreal. If they received a question from the media, scientists were instructed to ask them for their business card and tell them that they would get back to them with a time for an interview.[19] There was also direct intervention in publishing. Scientists required approval before being permitted to submit articles for publication.[20] They had to submit requests for going to conferences a year or earlier in advance—usually before conferences were even advertised, thus making it very difficult to attend scientific conferences. Permission to attend was sometimes denied even if they had received funding for it.[21] The Liberal government lifted the muzzle off the scientists when they reinstated the census.

When the government changed the Environmental Protection Act in one of its omnibus bills, almost 3,000 environmental reviews were summarily dropped.[22]

On 9 January 2012, the then minister of natural resources, Joe Oliver, sent an open letter criticizing "environmental and other radical groups" who "threaten to hijack our regulatory system to achieve their radical ideological agenda."[23] Further verbal attacks on environmental groups followed, including the statement by the Counterterrorism Unit in Alberta that environmentalism is a terrorist threat.

This was followed by the Canada Revenue Agency's (CRA) auditing of the major environmental groups, after a complaint by Ethical Oil, a group with very close ties to the Conservative Party and government.[24] At a time when its overall staff was cut, the CRA received a total of $13.4 million to audit charities. Charities critical of the government were audited. While auditing of charities is a normal and regular function of the CRA, these audits were political in nature. The Liberal government committed itself to stopping politically motivated audits, but as this is being written,[25] procedures to clarify what constitutes permitted and non-permitted political activities on the part of charities have not been introduced. Nor were the audits that started under the Harper government stopped.

Many organizations were shut down. Perhaps most troublesome is the fact that many environmental and other libraries were shut down; books dumped, burned, or sent to landfills; and archives destroyed. It has been called "libricide" and a "knowledge massacre,"[26] and has been compared to Rome destroying the Royal Library of Alexandria in Egypt.[27] These acts cannot be reversed. The knowledge contained in some of the libraries and archives is irretrievably lost.

To sum up, in spite of investments in research that directly benefitted industry or was seen as having the potential to do so, there was a systematic and targeted attack on basic research in general, and in particular on the census, and on research that documents social injustice or environmental problems.

The public outcry against the dismantling of public science was considerable, but it was ignored by the government. This must be understood within the context of the Canadian electoral system, which allows a government elected by a minority of Canadians to form a majority government, which is then able to ignore opinions that do not fit within its ideological framework.

The Canadian Electoral System

Canada is one of the few democracies that has a "first-past-the-post" electoral system. This means that the person with the most votes wins. That system works well in a two-party system, but it leads to great problems in a country with more than two parties, because parties with a relatively small portion of the popular vote may form majority governments. That is the reason why the majority of democracies have a representative electoral system, in which the number of seats in a house corresponds to the percentage of the popular vote.

Table 55.1 shows how the "first-past-the-post" system worked in Canada in 2006, 2008, 2011, and 2015.

In 2008, the Conservatives won 37.7 per cent of the popular vote, which resulted in their electing 40.3 per cent of the members of the House of Commons. In 2011, with less of a 2 per cent increase in the popular vote, 53.8 per cent of elected MPs were Conservatives. In other words, the majority of Canadians, 60.5 per cent, did *not* vote for the Conservatives, who nevertheless gained an absolute majority. This is due to vote splitting. The situation reversed in the 2015 election, in which the Liberals won an absolute majority with only 39.5 per cent of the popular vote. While the Conservatives lost only 7.7 per cent of the

TABLE 55.1 "First-Past-the-Post" System in Canada

	Conservatives	Liberals	NDP	BQ	Greens	Other
2006 pop. vote	36.3%	30.2%	17.5%	10.5%	–	5.5%
2006 number elected	124	103	29	51	–	1
2006 % elected	40.3%	33.4%	9.4%	16.6%	–	0.3%
2008 pop. vote	37.7%	26.3%	18.2%	10.0%	–	7.8%
2008 number elected	143	77	37	49	–	2
2008 % elected	46.4%	25.0%	12.0%	15.9%	–	0.6%
2011 pop. vote	39.6%	18.9%	30.6%	6.1%	3.9%	1.0%
2011 number elected	166	34	103	4	1	0
2011 % elected	53.8%	11.0%	33.4%	1.3%	0.3%	0
2015 pop. vote	31.9%	39.5%	19.7	4.7%	3.4%	0.8
2015 number elected	99	184	44	3	1	0
2015 % elected	29.3%	54.4%	13.0%	10.0%	0.3%	0

Source: Computed from Parliament of Canada, Electoral Results by Party. Retrieved 19 July 2016 from: http://www.lop.parl.gc.ca/parlinfo/Compilations/ElectionsAndRidings/ResultsParty.aspx

popular vote, their percentage of elected members dropped by 24.5 per cent. Conversely, the Liberals increased their popular vote by 20.6 per cent, but their elected members increased to 54.4 per cent. In both elections, the current electoral system distorts the results of the popular vote. Prime Minister Trudeau made the commitment that the 2015 election would be the last election run under such a problematic system, but as this is being written, it is not yet clear which system, if any, will replace the current one.[28]

Conclusion

The damage that has been done to Canadian public science is serious. Some of it is irreversible. The current Liberal government has ceased the attacks and has started to repair some of the damage. However, unless Canada moves to a representative electoral system, we remain vulnerable to being manipulated by a party that has been elected by a minority of Canadians. Both public science and the electoral system require deep reforms.

Notes

1. https://evidencefordemocracy.ca
2. http://ourrighttoknow.ca
3. See http://voices-voix.ca
4. See the official website of Industry Canada: http://www.ic.gc.ca/eic/site/icgc.nsf/eng/h_07056.html
5. http://www.nrc-cnrc.gc.ca/eng/irap/concierge
6. http://kennedystewart.ndp.ca/latest-statistics-canada-data-confirms-conservative-war-on-science
7. http://www.statcan.gc.ca/daily-quotidien/140528/dq140528g-eng.htm
8. Kondro, Wayne. Canadian scientists smile as Liberals deliver a déjà vu budget. *Science*, 22 March 2016. http://www.sciencemag.org/news/2016/03/canadian-scientists-smile-liberals-deliver-d-j-vu-budget
9. International development has also been a target, but much of the refocusing in this area has been achieved by reorganizing international development goals and rules, rather than focusing on research.
10. http://datalibre.ca/census-watch
11. http://o.canada.com/news/national/statistics-canada-clients-see-gaps-in-latest-survey-analysis?utm_source=dlvr.it&utm_medium=twitter
12. http://neighbourhoodchange.ca/documents/2014/11/2011-nhs.pdf
13. https://docs.google.com/file/d/0B93A7NnBlooMT1lCUVRMbnVwYlU/edit
14. http://www.cbc.ca/news/politics/troubled-rights-and-democracy-agency-to-be-closed-1.1185276
15. http://ourrighttoknow.ca/domestic-events
16. Truth and Reconciliation Commission Canada, http://www.trc.ca/websites/trcinstitution/File/2015/Honouring_the_Truth_Reconciling_for_the_Future_July_23_2015.pdf
17. https://docs.google.com/file/d/0B93A7NnBlooMRjRTMzF0aXJmRlU/edit
18. http://pm.gc.ca/eng/minister-science-mandate-letter
19. http://www.canada.com/technology/Critics+instructions+Environment+Canada+scientists+Montreal+conference/6500175/story.html
20. http://elizabethmaymp.ca/news/publications/island-tides/2013/02/28/tightening-the-grip-muzzling-of-scientists-ramps-up
21. https://unmuzzledscience.wordpress.com/2013/02/26/50-shades-of-muzzle-part-3-conference-approval-denied
22. http://o.canada.com/news/harper-government-kills-3000-environmental-reviews-on-pipelines-and-other-projects
23. http://www.nrcan.gc.ca/media-room/news-release/2012/1/1909
24. http://www.huffingtonpost.ca/2014/04/08/ethjical-oil-greenpeace-elections-canada_n_5111843.html
25. July 2016.
26. http://www.huffingtonpost.ca/capt-trevor-greene/science-cuts-canada_b_4534729.html
27. http://ourrighttoknow.ca/erasing-history
28. Excellent information on different electoral systems can be found on the Fair Vote Canada website: http://www.fairvote.ca.

56 Liberty Aspiration and Political Behaviours

Reza Nakhaie

Introduction

Recently, there has been a significant decline in voting behaviours, and yet there has been a surge of **elite-challenging behaviours** in many of the developed and developing countries. One way to explain these latter forms of direct participation of the citizens is to frame them in Inglehart's theory. He has argued that an increase in economic development tends to increase the proportion of **post-materialist** segments of society who are less involved in elite-directed behaviours (e.g., voting) and more in elite-challenging political behaviours (e.g., protests). Moreover, for Inglehart (1997), the post-materialist deep-rooted changes in mass world views prevail more among those who grew up during the economic prosperity after the Second World War, which in turn helped to shape their political life. Therefore, the effects of post-materialist cultural values on elite-challenging behaviours would be stronger among the post–Second World War and younger generations when compared to pre-war and older generations.

Inglehart's Theory

According to Inglehart, as countries modernize, their cultural values will change, too. Using Maslow's (1970) hierarchy of needs, Inglehart argued that individuals born in less industrialized societies are more concerned with satisfying basic, immediate physiological safety and survival needs (e.g., food, shelter, and other physical comforts). He identified them as "materialists." In contrast, those growing up in post-industrial, affluent, and economically secure societies tend to emphasize Maslow's higher non-materialist values. He referred to them as "post-materialists" (see Inglehart, 1971, 1977, 1997). The latter group, relatively secure with material needs, tends to place more emphasis on symbolic or expressive needs (e.g., self-expression, citizen involvement and concern with freedom and democracy, equality of opportunity, gender and racial equalities). Inglehart's theory predicted that economic development helps with objective wealth and educational expansion as a means of independent economic and intellectual resources for social and political action, which in turn enhances people's aspirations and willingness to invest in campaigning for freedom. Once individuals experience economic security, they will enjoy more "free" time to be informed on political issues, to be politically active, and to demand democratic freedom and civil liberties. Consistent with his emphasis on the importance of cultural values, Inglehart insists that post-materialist individuals will be more involved in elite-challenging "unconventional" political activities (see Inglehart, 1990:3 11–18, ch. 10 and Inglehart, 1997: 307–15). This would be our first hypothesis.

Inglehart's general theory also suggests that as the younger, more educated, post-materialist cohorts replace the older, less educated, and more materialist, the rate of elite-challenging behaviours would increase. He argued that older people who grew up in industrial societies before the Second World War were more concerned with satisfying basic, immediate, physiological safety and survival needs when compared to the relatively younger cohort of individuals whose formative years were shaped during the favourable affluent and economically secure post-war environment. The latter tends to emphasize Maslow's higher non-materialist values. Accordingly, our second working hypothesis is that the effect of post-materialist values on elite-challenging behaviours should be stronger among recent generations (who are also younger) than among older generations.

Inglehart (1971) identified the source of this "silent revolution" toward more post-materialist cultural values and elite-challenging behaviours in the socialization of the younger cohorts whose formative years resulted in different value orientations than their older cohort. As the older generation "died off," the proportional size of the new generation increased. However, the development of such value orientation is expected to be class-based. He argued that the higher-social-class families help with higher educational attainment of their children when compared to the lower social classes. In turn, higher education means higher-social-class position, more economic security, and more free time to achieve self-actualization goals. Teachers are also expected to play a key role in indoctrination of post-materialist values, and since higher social classes are more educated, they tend to be more indoctrinated into these values (1997: 152–3). The importance of education for elite-challenging behaviour is understandable since political participation requires "cognitive mobilization" or types of skills that enable their possessor to manipulate political abstractions allowing coordination of activities remote in time and space (1977: 295). Accordingly, our third working hypothesis is related to increasing effect of generations. Since cultural values are formed through socialization during adolescence, when the most deep-rooted values are formed, post-materialist values should have increasing effects on elite-challenging behaviours among each succeeding generation.

Methodology

Data

The data source for our purpose is the World Value Survey (1981–2014). Since many countries were surveyed more than one time, we will use only the latest study in each of the 88 countries that have been surveyed. The total sample size for the present study includes 102,586 respondents. Given the large sample size, we will rely on standard errors and significance tests in multivariate analysis based on a 5 per cent random sample of all cases. However, given that the average sample size per country is 1,165 cases, we will use the total sample size when we predict elite-challenging behaviours by GDP per capita.

Measurement

In this study, we focused on **liberty aspiration** as the "libertarian aspects of post-materialism" (Welzel and Inglehart, 2005). Accordingly, we summed the scores on three liberty items where each respondent assigned "first," "second," and "no priority" to goals of giving people more say in governmental decisions, seeing that people have more say about how things are done at their jobs, and protecting freedom of speech. If no liberty item on first- or second-priority ranking is mentioned, respondents are assigned a score of 0; if one liberty item on second rank is mentioned, they are assigned 1; if two liberty items on second or one on first rank is mentioned, they are assigned 2; if one liberty item on first and one on second rank are mentioned, they are assigned 3; if one liberty item on first and two on second rank are mentioned, they are assigned 4; and if two liberty items on first and one on second rank are mentioned, they are assigned a score of 5. This index has six categories ranging from 0 to 5.

We used year of birth and created three generations: pre–Second World War, Second World War to 1970, and post-1970 generations. Economic prosperity is measured by per capita gross national income (GNI). Accordingly, countries are grouped into four categories: low income (GNI of less than $4,035), middle income ($4,036–$12,475), and high income (more than $12,476). We also included ex-Soviet countries as a separate category independent of their GNI. We will also use the real gross domestic product (real GDP) per capita in 1980 as a correlate of liberty aspiration and elite-challenging behaviours.

Finally, we will use control variables that may effect liberty aspiration and elite-challenging behaviours. These variables include education, professional occupations, income scale, gender, marital status, and year of birth.

Analysis

Table 56.1 shows the correlation coefficients between predictors with liberty aspiration and elite-challenging behaviours. With the exception of the relationship between gender and liberty aspiration, and between year of birth and marital status, with elite-challenging behaviours, all correlations are significant.[1] Among predictors of liberty aspiration, GDP per capita has the strongest relationship. Among predictors of elite-challenging behaviours, liberty aspiration, followed by GDP per capita and university education, have the strongest relationships.

Figure 56.1 gets to the heart of our hypotheses. We expected that (a) liberty aspiration would affect elite-challenging behaviours more in economically prosperous societies than in the less prosperous societies; (b) it would be stronger among the younger generations than among older generations; and (c) its effect would successively increase from one generation to the next. The results in Figure 56.1 are consistent with the first and second hypotheses. Although the findings are also generally consistent with the third hypothesis, the match is not perfect. We notice that the effects of liberty aspiration are stronger for each generation in high-income countries than middle- or low-income countries. Ex-Soviet countries stand somewhere between the middle- and low-income countries. Moreover, the effects of liberty aspiration on elite-challenging behaviours are stronger in post–Second World War generations than in earlier ones for all countries with the exception of the ex-Soviet countries.

Conclusion and Discussion

This study is generally supportive of Inglehart's theory. We showed that liberty aspiration (a) has a significant relationship with elite-challenging behaviours with and without controls; (b) has a stronger relationship with elite-challenging behaviours in more economically prosperous than less prosperous societies; and (c) has a somewhat stronger relationship with elite-challenging behaviours among the post–Second World War generations than among those born before the war. However, the differences between the two succeeding post-war generations were not substantial and were at times contrary to

TABLE 56.1 Correlation of Liberty Aspiration and Elite-Challenging Behaviours with Predictors

	Liberty Aspiration	Significance	Elite-Challenging	Significance
Liberty Aspiration			.184	***
GDP per capita 1980	.157	***	.136	***
Scale of incomes	.055	***	.086	***
Year of birth	.027	*	−.017	
Elementary education	−.045	***	−.090	***
Secondary education	.040	**	.038	*
University education	.059	***	.108	***
Married	−.052	***	−.006	
Male	.010		.077	***
Professional	.064	***	.083	***

Notes: < .05, ** < .01, *** < .001 Significance tests are based on 5 per cent of the sample.

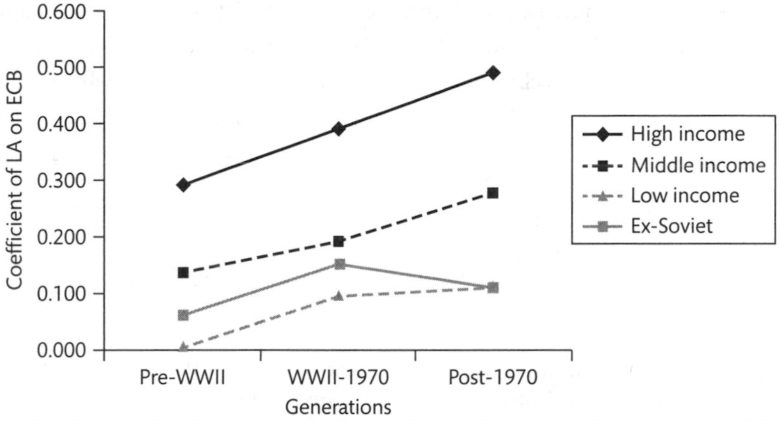

FIGURE 56.1 Liberty Aspiration and Elite-Challenging Behaviours

the expectation. This evidence seems to support Inglehart's (1997) theory that accounts for long-term intergenerational shift and short-term period effects. The fact that the effect of liberty aspiration on elite-challenging behaviours did not change much after the 1970s suggests that the post-1970 economic slowdown and even downturn resulted in a lower economic prosperity for the citizens of most countries and a consequent decreasing effect of post-materialism on elite-challenging behaviours. Economic fluctuations tend to alter the relationship between liberty aspiration and elite-challenging behaviours. This is because people do not act in a vacuum: they respond to prosperity or economic recession or crisis. Recession tends to increase the proportion of the population with materialist values.

However, one should be cautious in overgeneralizing Inglehart's theory. Although economic recession may increase the proportion of the materialist population, it can also increase economic grievances. For example, despite relatively lower economic development in Greece and particularly in Tunisia or Egypt in the recent past, as compared to Canada or the United States, mass protests were significantly higher and more violent in the former than in the latter. With respect to the latter, rule of law and open political opportunity structure resulted in a more peaceful type of elite-challenging behaviours such as the Occupy movement in both countries and the student protests in Quebec. However, lack of rule of law and an open political structure resulted in massive and violent uprisings in Tunisia and Egypt, with the consequent change of regimes. Greece stood somewhere in between these two poles. Its relatively open political opportunity structure, on the one hand, resulted in massive and at times violent elite-challenging protests, but on the other hand, it did not result in regime change.

Nevertheless, we concur with Inglehart that by understanding the cultural shifts in various societies, we can accurately predict future political trajectories of these societies. Our study suggests that some economic and cultural trajectories probably have synergy with certain other political trajectories. Accordingly, it is reasonable to predict that economic development and the subsequent rise of the middle class in countries such as Turkey, Tunisia, Egypt, Syria, Kuwait, Bahrain, and Saudi Arabia will build pressure for more democratic rights, and in countries such as Canada, England, United States, France, Greece, and Italy, the pressure will help prevent the decline of these rights. However, this process is a double-edged sword. If governments do not solve the economic problems of the nation, they risk losing the support of most of the people who are interested in Maslow's lower-order (economic) needs. On the other hand, if they solve these problems and help with the development of a successful middle class, the materialist segment of the population will decline and the post-materialist segment will increase and more likely be involved in elite-challenging types of behaviours, thus potentially destabilizing the country.

Note

1. When the total sample is used, all correlations except for marital status are statistically significant.

References

Inglehart, R. 1971. "The Silent Revolution in Europe: Intergenerational Change in Post-industrial Societies," *American Political Science Review* 65: 991–1017.

Inglehart, R. 1977. *The Silent Revolution: Changing Values and Political Styles among Western Publics.* Princeton, NJ: Princeton University Press.

Inglehart, R. 1990. *Culture Shift in Advanced Industrial Society.* Princeton, NJ: Princeton University Press.

Inglehart, R. 1997. *Modernization and Postmodernization.* Princeton, NJ: Princeton University Press.

Maslow, A. 1970. *Motivation and Personality.* New York: Harper and Row.

United Nations. 2013. *Statistical Annex.* Development Policy and Analysis Division (DPAD), United Nations.

Welzel, C. and Inglehart, R. 2005. "Democratization as the Growth of Freedom: The Human Development Perspective." *Japanese Journal of Political Science* 6(3): 313–43.

World Bank. 2010. *Human Development Report.* United Nations.

Questions for Critical Thought

Chapter 53 | Why Sociologists Should Care about Public Policy

1. What historical roots does sociology have in public policy? Why should we acknowledge these roots?
2. How does sociology intersect with public policy?
3. What role can sociologists play in making policy issues more accessible to the public?
4. How can sociologists help with globalization and the intersection of global policies?
5. How can sociologists be part of the public policy discussion without advocating for a specific partisan agenda? Why is this important?
6. How can sociologists bring the "sociological imagination" to the public through policy debates?

Chapter 54 | The Sociology of Human Rights

1. What are "human rights"? Describe Canada's rights culture.
2. How did sociology's founders feel about human rights? How has sociology's view changed?
3. Clément states that human rights are not based on a universal truth. What are the two functions of human rights? Describe them.
4. Clément says, "The most important lesson that history teaches about Canada's rights culture is that it is liberal, individualistic and ranks civil and political rights above economic, social or cultural rights." Give some examples, either within or outside this chapter, that support this statement.
5. This chapter ends with a statement of caution. What role can sociologists play in shaping Canada's rights culture? Why is this important?

Chapter 55 | Making Us Ignorant: Canadian Science Policy under a Neo-conservative Regime

1. How did Canada's Conservative Party weaken public institutions that produce knowledge?
2. How did scientists react to this "assault" on public knowledge?
3. How did the Harper government attack (a) the census, (b) human rights, and (c) environmental research?
4. Why is funding public knowledge or science important? What is the impact of no longer allowing the production of public knowledge?
5. How does the Canadian electoral system work? What impact can you have by voting?

Chapter 56 | Liberty Aspiration and Political Behaviours

1. According to Inglehart, who would be elite-challenging? Who would be elite-directed? Why?
2. What is the "silent revolution"? Why are the elite-challenging generation important for this revolution to occur?
3. List the three hypotheses tested in this study. What is the outcome of each?
4. How do the findings of this study support or contradict Inglehart's theory?
5. What caution does Nakhaie offer when using Inglehart's theory?

PART XIV
Social Movements

Protesting is not glamorous. You could be standing outside with the sun or rain beating down on you for hours or even days. During the Birmingham civil rights protest of 1962, civil rights supporters accompanying Martin Luther King, Jr., were assaulted by fire hoses and police dogs. So why, then, would anyone take part in a protest or social movement? Why do people risk their comfort, employment, and even their lives?

To answer these questions, we have to first define our terms, so we understand specifically what we are talking about. Social movements are purposeful, organized groups that take action to solve problems. They range from small groups of people who organize in a community to demand a new stop sign, to large, globally recognized initiatives such as the environmental movement. But whatever their size, all social movement groups start by identifying a problem and deciding to take action.

That said, social movements vary in ways other than size. Some are reformative, aiming to change a specific aspect of the existing social structure. Examples include the above-mentioned US civil rights movement, the Indigenous-led Idle No More, and the Arab Spring. Or consider another example, provided by Jean-Philippe Warren in this section, in his chapter on the collective action taken by Quebec taxi drivers in the 1960s. Other social movements focus on changing people's beliefs or behaviours. Many of these movements are religiously motivated; however, some of them are based on secular self-improvement and alternative living. The clean-living movement and the Association for Inner Growth are two examples of such secular lifestyle movements. Finally, some social movements form to prevent or resist change. The Quebec student movement, discussed here in the chapter by Lesley Wood, is an example of a reformative movement aimed at resisting the increase of post-secondary tuition in Quebec.

Social movements use many different strategies and tactics to reach their target audience, which is typically the government, the public, or the media. Tactics can include protests, sit-ins, hunger strikes, marches, boycotts, demonstrations, and petitions, among other things. When movements choose to mobilize, they carefully select tactics that they imagine will be the most effective in reaching their goal, and often they use more than one tactic at a time. For example, the Quebec student movement used a combination of marches, rallies, and a strike to convey their message to the provincial government.

Typically, social movements form when a group of people share the same feelings of discontent. Movement members may endure long days of protesting or striking because they firmly believe the cause they are fighting for is worth the effort. Many theories attempt to explain why people engage in social movements and of course, members of a given movement often have a variety of motives. They are inclined to take action for different reasons. That said, movement members tend to have one thing in common: namely, a deep desire to bring about change.

Reading the chapters in this section will challenge you to think more critically about ways to effectively create social change. In Chapter 57, Jacqueline Benn-John shows the importance of considering black perspectives in activism by focusing on what can be learned from their unique lived experiences. Jean-Philippe Warren, in Chapter 58, explains why Quebec taxi drivers took violent action in the 1960s, concentrating on what can be learned from the conditions that elicited violent protest. Finally, in Chapter 59, Lesley Wood compares the strategies taken by the Quebec Student Movement and by Idle No More to show that there is no recipe for social movement success. Each movement requires its own carefully considered strategy, suited to its particular historical situation.

57 Critical Intervention: Black Women (Re)defining Feminist Resistance, Activism, and Empowerment in Feminist Organizing within Ontario

Jacqueline Benn-John

In its broadest sense, **feminism** constitutes both an ideology and a global political movement that confronts sexism (Collins 1996). However, Wane (2002) argues that feminism is "based on the experiences of White, middle-class, heterosexual women whose lived experiences are analyzed without interrogation of race or colour" (38). Similarly, the Combahee River Collective (1983) notes that although racialized women have been involved in the feminist movement since the 1960s, a combination of "reactionary forces . . . as well as elitism and racism within the movement, have served to obscure Black women's participation" (273). Rediscovering black women's experiences and contributions to feminist organizing is not simply an issue of historical inaccuracy; according to Patricia Hill Collins (2000), "maintaining the invisibility of Black women and our ideas has been critical in maintaining social inequalities" (3) overall for racialized women.

With this reality in mind, this paper examines the experiences and contributions of black women working in rape crisis centres in Ontario, Canada. In this context, I ask, *What does feminist scholarship bring to our understanding of black women workers' perspectives on feminist organizing/practices within rape crisis centres; and what does the hegemonic feminist scholarship exclude?* This work will attempt to offer an intentional analysis of existing feminism in this context, and, where possible, to identify the constructed invisibility of black feminist action, practice, and thought in feminist organizing.

I wish to make clear that this research is a work in progress. Foundational components on context, relevant theoretical frameworks, and the existing literature are described in this paper. I build my arguments on integrative theoretical foundations of anti-colonialism, integrative anti-racism, and African-Canadian feminist discourses. **Anti-colonialism** is defined as "the political struggle and active resistance of colonized peoples against the ideology and practice of colonialism. It emphasizes decolonization and affirming Indigenous knowledge" (Pon, Gosine, and Phillips 2011, 400). **Integrative anti-racism** refers to the intersection of race with other forms of difference, such as sexual orientation, ability, class, and gender identity (Dei 2007). **African-Canadian feminism** creates an inclusive brand of feminism that reflects both race and gender (Wane 2002).

I have carefully selected an integrative approach to this topic for three reasons: first, single-axis theories do not effectively address the experiences of marginalized groups; as many of you know, one size does not fit all. Further, a black woman is never just black or African or woman. Instead, all of her identities come into play, impacting her experience of day-to-day social interactions, privilege, and marginalization. Last, I wish to affirm Indigenous ways of knowing, as employed by black women in social justice work. These frameworks challenge the institutional structures established by and maintained through colonialism, with a necessary privileging of the expertise of black women.

Marginalization of Black Women's Experience

Both historically and today, women of African ancestry have had diverse community and labour experiences in Canada. Their contributions to Canadian workplaces, fields of study, social movements, and community work have been valuable—and often very different than the contributions of black men or white women. Black women bring knowledge that men or white women do not. This might include contributions that reflect the lived experiences, community culture, and needs of racialized communities; the experiences and prevalence of violence against women of colour (different from those of white women); notions of class difference; and lived experiences of anticipating and resisting everyday racism. Despite their contributions, there is a dearth of black women's voices and thought in women's services and feminist organizing.

Black women face erasure because of the colour of their skin. Colonial and patriarchal domination have had the effect of omitting us from history books, curriculums, and narratives—and even feminist scholarly work. Although feminist women's organizations have made efforts to explicitly operate from social justice and anti-oppression frameworks, they have a long history of reproducing inequities, including racist inequities that exist elsewhere in society (see Combahee River Collective 1983; Lorde 1984, "The Transformation of Silence into Language and Action"; Collins 2000; Wane 2002; James 2007; Gulbrandsen and Walsh 2012). This reproduction of inequity occurs via the normalizing and privileging of whiteness within women's organizations and via the universalizing of the issues these organizations aim to address as uniform and representative of the concerns of all women. These phenomena—*privilege* and *universalizing*—are reproductions of and by the racialized hegemony rooted in Canada's colonial past. Within this hegemony, notions of white superiority are supported in both structural and material practices within Canadian society. Further, within this hegemony, the perspectives and voices of racialized people are marginalized —or made invisible. This paper seeks to identify these patterns in rape crisis centres in Ontario, and to present alternative models for identifying and resisting these patterns.

Focus and Locating Self

There are 41 **rape crisis centres** in Ontario delivering counselling, information, and support services to survivors of sexual violence. For over 20 years, I have been active in social justice work and I have volunteered and worked in four rape crisis centres in Ontario. I also represented centres across Ontario as president of the Ontario Coalition of Rape Crisis Centres for three years, and as an executive member for eight years. The inspiration for this paper is my own experience as a black woman with embodied experiences of subjectivity and agency in different contexts in Canada. Specifically, I am motivated by the feeling that feminist studies and feminist organizations have failed to acknowledge the intersectional experience of womanhood and blackness within (and upon) rape crisis centre work within Canada and the United States.

Diversity in Ontario's Rape Crisis Centres

Although there are some academic and "herstorical" texts on rape crisis centres, women's organizations, worker experiences, and feminist organizing in Canada and the United States, neither the academic nor activist literature present African diasporic and other racialized women as *visible research participants*, paid workers, volunteers, and service users within women's anti-violence services within Canada and the United States. This absence has both political economic and theoretical causes.

A number of feminist studies and essays discuss the underfunding of feminist women's services and the implications of this on organizational autonomy, staffing, activism, and social change (internally and externally). For example, in "Implications of the Shrinking Space for Feminist Anti-Violence Advocacy" (Bonisteel and Green 2005), the authors consider women's organizations' struggles to assert political autonomy and a feminist approach in a growing corporatized climate and service delivery model. Maier's 2011 study "Rape Crisis Centers and Programs: 'Doing Amazing, Wonderful Things on Peanuts'" discusses the implications of underfunding at women's organizations for staff, including diversely positioned staff. In the Canadian context, a shortage of financial resources at rape crisis centres has resulted in few permanent full-time positions being available within these agencies. Consequently, black and other racialized women are underrepresented as centre staff, volunteers, and board members. When present, they are overrepresented in precarious employment within centres: for example, in front-line contract staff positions with "less access to decision-making spaces" (Timothy 2007, 379).

At the theoretical level, some feminist researchers ground their research in integrative discursive frameworks such as anti-racism and anti-colonialism, while many feminist studies and best practice guides on how to integrate a feminist anti-racist, anti-oppression approach within women's organizations in Canada exist; however, an anti-oppression framework (that is, framework or intentional practice that aims to address *all oppressions* and discriminatory practices) can incidentally diminish the problematizing of *racist/anti-racist* practice specifically.

The implications of these physical and theoretical erasures for service delivery—including supportive service delivery to diverse women, are illustrated in Llana James's "Censure and Silence." Her interviews with young black women revealed that Ontario's rape crisis centres were not prepared to meet the needs of African women who have experienced sexual violence. In this important study, James asserts that "rape crisis centres' lack of capacity to meet the needs of African Diasporic women is a result of the rape crisis movement's failure to identify and implement a model of solidarity and feminism that is inclusive of racialized women in general, and women of the African Diasporic in specific" (236).

A More Inclusive Feminism

Aligning with bell hooks's thoughts, I believe that the invisibility of black presence in most feminist scholarship compels us, as black female readers, to interrogate the subject further—and with a black feminist lens. Much feminist action can be improved by an anti-oppression and anti-racist lens.

For example, Canadians were incensed by Toronto police officer Constable Michael Sanguinetti's suggestion that women could prevent sexual violence by avoiding "dressing like sluts." The resulting SlutWalk[1] protest unfolded, yet the strategies for resisting Sanguinetti's and other common comments that related women's sexuality to sexual violence reflected analyses and solutions proffered by white women only. A vocal group of black women raised race-conscious concerns about the issue of sexual violence, women's experiences of being targeted for *racialized and sexualized violence*, and the SlutWalk march: "We do not have the privilege or the space to call ourselves 'slut' without validating the already historically entrenched ideology and recurring messages about what and who the Black woman is," a coalition of black women activists wrote, "We don't have the privilege to play on destructive representations burned in our collective minds, on our bodies and souls for generations" (*Wikipedia* 2012). This commentary reflected the missing "herstory" on issues of sexual violence and diverse women in the SlutWalk movement, as well as the important knowledge and lived experiences that black women brought to this issue.

Black women in Canada continue to engage in feminist activism and to resist oppression in innovative ways. They also bring significant and different knowledge to feminist issues. For example, black women's activism integrates resistance from everyday acts of oppression. Moreover, black women's experiences and strategies in activism provide an additional, richer, and concurrent women's "herstory" to the current hegemonic story. As an example, feminist organizing against patriarchal violence has commonly included public displays of resistance, such as women-only Take Back the Night[2] marches and the more recent SlutWalk. Yet, like Aboriginal culture, African ancestral heritage privileges the collective, in contrast to neoliberal discourses that promote an ethos of individualism (Ringrose and Walkerdine 2008, 227). For our communities, women's-only events present limitations, such as decreased capacity to engage men, boys, families, elders, and other integral community members. Further, the engagement of "women only" in ending violence against women has been misinterpreted by the public at large as exclusionary, negative, or punitive. This has led to the perpetuating of myths for example, that addressing violence against women is a woman's issue only.

Comparably, women of colour and Indigenous communities have brought collaborative approaches to engage male allies in addressing violence against women. Many racialized communities believe men must be part of these actions and solutions, as they are overwhelmingly the perpetrators of violence against women. Positive and current examples of this work include the Ontario Federation of Indian Friendship Centres (OFIFC) and the White Ribbon Campaign's "I Am a Kind Man/Kizhaay Anishinaabe Niin" campaign. This campaign, led by the OFIFC and its members, aims to offer Aboriginal "men and youth a safe place to begin to understand their roles and responsibilities to end violence against Aboriginal young girls and women . . . and encourages opportunities for them to reconnect to their traditional roles within families and communities" (OFIFC 2015).

Clearly, it is critical to recognize varied experiences and knowledge and to add arguments that are diverse, embodied, and constructive in new ways. Embodied experience has the ability to identify differences and histories, dismantle structural inequalities, and offer new resistance strategies. I concur with George Yancy (2008) in his assertion that "through resistance, the Black body affirms itself through a set of values historically denied it" (113).

Conclusion

Increasing understandings about black women's feminist organizing can lead to real possibilities for the recognition of both black women's marginalization and their strengths. It can also lead to better collaboration across social justice movements (e.g., feminist, anti-colonial and anti-racist), and to further recognition of the experiences of black women. In addition, allies and academics can consider ways to employ their power to create more space for black women. This will support black women to engage in resistance that gives voice to black women's experiences and multifaceted modes of expressing resistance. Even though we have been relegated to the margins of histories and scholarship, as stated by bell hooks, black women refuse to be "socialized out of existence" (quoted in King 1988, 45).

Notes

1. SlutWalk protest marches began on 3 April 2011, in Toronto and became a movement of rallies across the world in response.
2. Take Back the Night (also known as Reclaim the Night) is an internationally held march and rally intended as a protest and direct action against rape and other forms of sexual violence. The first TBTN was held in Belgium in 1976.

References

Bonisteel, M. and L. Green. (2005). Implications of the Shrinking Space for Feminist Anti-Violence Advocacy. Paper presented at the 2005 Canadian Social Welfare Policy Conference, Forging Social Futures, Fredericton, New Brunswick.

Collins, P.H. (2000). The Politics of Black Feminist Thought. In P. Collins (Ed.), *Black Feminist Thought: Knowledge, Consciousness and the Politics of Empowerment* (pp. 1–19). New York: Routledge.

Collins, P. (1996). What's in a Name? Womanism, Black Feminism, and Beyond. *The Black Scholar*, 26(1), 9–17.

Combahee River Collective. (1983). In B. Smith (Ed.), *Home Girls: A Black Feminist Anthology* (pp. 272–82). New York: Kitchen Table–Women of Color Press.

Dei, G.J.S. (2007). Integrative Anti-racism. Keynote speech at the symposium "Multiculturalism with(out) Guarantees: The Integrative Anti-Racism Alternative," University of British Columbia, Vancouver. Retrieved from http://ccie.educ.ubc.ca/PDFs/georgedei-keynote.pdf.

Gulbrandsen, C. and C. Walsh. (2012). It Starts with Me: Women Mediate Power within Feminist Activism. *Journal of Women and Social Work*, 27(3), 275–88.

James, L. (2007). Censure and Silence. In N. Massaquoi and N.N. Wane (Eds), *Theorizing Empowerment: Canadian Perspectives on Black Feminist Thought* (pp. 228–44). Toronto: Inanna Publications and Education.

King, D. (1988) "Multiple Jeopardy, Multiple Consciousness: The Context of a Black Feminist Ideology." *Signs*, 14(1), 42–72.

Lorde, A. (1984). *Sister Outsider: Essays and Speeches* Toronto: Crossing Press.

Maier, S.L. (2011). Rape Crisis Centers and Programs: "Doing amazing, wonderful things on peanuts." *Women & Criminal Justice*, 21(2), 141–69.

Ontario Federation of Indian Friendship Centres (OFIFC) and the White Ribbon Campaign. (2015). *I Am a Kind Man/ Kizhaay Anishinaabe Niin*. Retrieved 20 September 2015 from: http://www.iamakindman.ca/IAKM/about-us-kizhaay-anishinaabe-niin.html

Pon, G., K. Gosine, and D. Phillips. (2011). Immediate Response: Addressing Anti-Native and Anti-Black Racism in Child Welfare. *International Journal of Child, Youth and Family Studies* 3 & 4, 385–409.

Ringrose, J., and V. Walkerdine. (2008). Regulating the Abject, *Feminist Media Studies*, 8(3), 227–46.

Timothy, R. (2007). "Third World Women," "Women of Colour," "Minority Women": An African/Black Feminist Analysis of Our Identities. In N. Massaquoi and N.N. Wane (Eds), *Theorizing Empowerment: Canadian Perspectives on Black Feminist Thought* (pp. 155–76). Toronto: Inanna Publications and Education.

Wane, N. (2002). Carving out Critical Space: African Canadian Women and the Academy. In N.N. Wane et al. (Eds), *Back to the Drawing Board: African Canadian Feminisms* (pp. 175–196). Toronto: Sumach Press.

Wikipedia. (2012). SlutWalk. Retrieved 16 December 2012 from: http://en.wikipedia.org/wiki/SlutWalk

Yancy, G. (2008). *Black Bodies, White Gazes: The Continuing Significance of Race*, Lanham, MD: Rowman & Littlefield.

58 Factors Leading to Political Violence: Taxi Driving in Montreal

Jean-Philippe Warren

One of the most turbulent sectors of the Quebec economy is the taxi industry. It was the object of a considerable number of public inquiries in the last century, and is again under review in relation to technological changes and security issues today. But the most troubled page of its history was certainly the 1960s.

From 1963 to 1970, the taxi industry was the theatre of a series of violent actions that profoundly shook the province of Quebec. As bombs exploded in Montreal and social turmoil increased, the nationalist movement joined force with the taxi drivers to denounce the oppression of the working class and the alienation of the Quebec nation. To give only one example, taxi drivers Jacques Lanctôt and Marc Carbonneau chose to go underground in 1969 and perpetrated the kidnapping of the British diplomat

James Cross in 1970, igniting the infamous October Crisis, which led to the intervention of the Canadian army and the temporary suspension of habeas corpus.

Why were Quebec taxi drivers among the most likely to engage in violent actions in the 1960s? What factors explain their propensity, at the time, to engage in civil disobedience and non-peaceful protests? Can these factors help us understand contemporary struggles and specific repertoires of contention? Is there a mix of personal experiences and social contexts that is more conducive than others to social upheaval and brutal undertakings?

I shall attempt here to identify some factors that have historically contributed to the legitimization of the use of force by taxi drivers. My research has led me to the conclusion that these factors are sevenfold: the discovery of social inequality; the issue of gender; the difficulty of organizing **collective action** on firm grounds; the lack of political channels to voice popular demands; the strategic alliances with other extremist groups; a revolutionary ideology that suggested the adoption of an urban guerilla strategy; and, finally, a general climate of **political effervescence**.

The Discovery of Social Inequality

While poor, taxi drivers were continuously in contact with the most privileged classes of Canadian society. Working behind the wheel to pay for his university studies, Jacques Lanctôt became one of the most vocal leaders of the radical organization Mouvement de libération du taxi (MLT, 1969–1970) and ended up editing the periodical of the movement, *Le Journal du taxi*. It is during his shifts driving around Montreal, from the east-end to the west-end neighbourhoods, that he realized the profound fractures plaguing his society. "The taxi opened my eyes! It made me discover my city, those who rule it and those who own ($$$) my country, Quebec. I had never seen Westmount, Outremont, Ville Mont-Royal, Côte St-Luc, Hamstead. . . . Now, I know where the real enemies of the Quebecers live, those who have millions in their pockets, a rack full of plants, shops, firms" (*Le Journal du taxi*, 1 June 1969). Picking up clients in tuxedos or evening dresses at the door of five-star hotels and high-end restaurants in downtown Montreal and driving them back to their luxurious mansions, Lanctôt started to realize how mediocre his paycheque and how shameful his dwelling was, on the third floor of a shabby apartment block in Hochelaga-Maisonneuve. He was becoming aware of the necessity for people like him to stand together against the bourgeoisie who controlled the nation's economy and politics.

Gender

The Montreal taxi industry was characterized by an overrepresentation of male drivers (less than 1 per cent were women). Not unlike the construction business, the ethos of the taxi driver was based in values of virility associated with "real men." The definition of manhood in a male dominated sector clearly attributed positive qualities to aggressive action. For instance, the Teamsters (which included many taxi associations in the US and Canada) were one of the most bellicose American unions, not above engaging in intimidation to promote their movement's interests. Another violent strike of the period was the one organized by the former truck drivers of a private contractor, named Lapalme, who had delivered the mail in Montreal for Canada Post. The tone of the debate around the Lapalme strike can be measured by the sentiments of the then prime minister, Pierre Elliott Trudeau, who openly said, "Qu'ils mangent donc d'la merde!" ("Let them eat shit!").

Difficulty to Organize Collective Action

Further, the isolation of taxi drivers and the lack of a solid organizational basis for action made the grouping of progressive forces difficult. The participation of all taxi drivers in a general strike was nearly impossible: some taxi drivers owned their car; others rented it; others were simple employees; many were driving a taxi on top of other, more well-paying jobs; there existed deep linguistic and ethnic divides between allophones, anglophones, and francophones; and nobody could exercise control over every taxi stand in a city as big as Montreal. Therefore it was hopeless to think one could identify and neutralize the scabs who would happily take the place of the striking cab drivers. Having every reason to show solidarity in theory, the drivers were in reality alone behind the wheel and in direct competition with their colleagues. Hence, the violence of an organization such as the MLT was also a consequence of its weakness. Not being able to count on ordinary methods of striking, it had to resort to more spectacular tactics.

Lack of Political Channels

Taxi drivers were also under the impression that no official group really represented their interests and that they had no other choice to make themselves heard but to use violent means. Most doubted that there would ever be a political solution to the crisis of the taxi industry. All politicians were said to be corrupt. Elections only served to legitimize the domination of an economic elite. Painstaking endeavours to lobby political authorities yielded meagre results. Tellingly, in the pages of the *Journal du taxi* the exchanges in the National Assembly were reproduced in a section entitled "Bla . . . bla . . . bla . . . ." The impression that the taxi drivers had to rely on their own means (which was precisely the future title of the 1971 manifesto of the CSN/CNTU, "Let Us Rely on Our Own Means") made the mediation through the democratic process fruitless, if not harmful. Therefore, as long as authorities were projecting the image of a distant and insensitive power, the taxi drivers tended to support revolutionary and spontaneous actions. "Misters the Members of Parliament," warned an activist, "put it in your brain that you are supposed to represent the interests of the majority of the population and not those of the big shots. So move yourself! . . . If you don't, there's gonna be trouble" (*Le Journal du taxi*, 1 May 1969).

Strategic Alliances with Other Extremist Groups

In the 1960s, the two most important social movements in Quebec were, on the one hand, the leftist groups and, on the other hand, the nationalist movement. Immediately, the frustrations experienced by Montreal taxi drivers were associated with the plight of francophones and ordinary workers. The taxi industry, therefore, lay at the crossroads of national and social conflicts. This cocktail was explosive, and the struggle around the Murray Hill Company serves as proof. Murray Hill had obtained a monopoly on the transportation to and from the airport. It was the property of the WASP Charles Hershorn, who lived in a lavish house in Westmount. Worse, the airport monopoly had been granted by the federal government, which meant that Quebec taxi drivers were forbidden to operate in that federal territory and could not participate in what constituted the most lucrative market of the Montreal region. In the 1970 FLQ manifesto, the authors denounced a Canadian regime that "maintains the brave taxi drivers in a state of semi-slavery by shamelessly protecting the exclusive monopoly of the disgusting Murray Hill and of its murderer and owner, Charles Hershorn." Murray Hill embodied everything that was going wrong in Quebec from a socialist and nationalist perspective: leftists of all origins and nationalists of all classes could come together in a firm opposition to the taxi company. On the night of 7 October 1969, activists marched on the Murray Hill garage and burned it down. During that night of terror, one person was killed, seven people were wounded, and the property damage amounted to more than $300,000.

A Revolutionary Ideology

The peculiar ideologies of the 1960s also played a role in an increasingly frequent use of violence. Activists belonging to a wide variety of social movements believed in the necessity of perpetrating violent actions to hasten the liberation of Quebec and the emancipation of the working class. Some students were convinced that the tactic called "shock and offend," which the Students for a Democratic Society was known for, should be implemented in Quebec. As for the urban guerilla tactics promoted by the MLT, the organization was directly reproducing the foco theory developed by Che Guevara. This theory stated that the relentless harassing of power would foster in the masses a will for rebellion and create the perfect conditions for an uprising. First step: brief, repeated, and disturbing attacks. Second step: a very well-orchestrated escalation of violence. Third step: the seizure of power. Translating the watch-word of Che ("Create Two, Three, Many Vietnams"), some militants of the Quebec taxi industry were arguing that they had to create two, three, five, ten Murray Hills. The sitting social order was too strong to be overtaken by an open and frontal assault, and, therefore, the way forward was an intangible insurrection, an invisible yet continuous aggression. To adopt guerilla warfare and fight in the shadows seemed a promising option for those who believed that Canada in general, and Quebec in particular, were under the yoke of a police state that boasted all the characteristics of a fascist regime.

A General Climate of Political Effervescence

Finally, the climate of social turmoil that characterized the Quiet Revolution (1960–1970) reinforced in the hearts of radical activists the hope that the use of violent methods was an efficient way to advance their cause. These years of profound agitation stirred the conviction that a revolution was underway, which awaited only the contribution of young, selfless citizens to fully materialize. A popular song that played on French Quebec radio claimed, "It's the beginning of a new era. The world's clock is set back to zero." Long ago, Alexis de Tocqueville argued that people are more prompt to revolt when their conditions improve, not when these conditions worsen, and the 1960s seem to prove him right. Lifted by the rising expectations of the "glorious thirty" (1945–1975), while still being frustrated by some periodic resistance, impatient Quebec militants were turning to aggressive action. In such a spiral of violence, the riots organized by the MLT were not seen, by the most steadfast activists, as regretful exceptions, but as models to follow. The riots showed the means to shake down once and for all the power structure that had hitherto favoured opulent and anglophone classes.

Conclusion: A Fertile Ground for Political Violence

Although the seven factors mentioned above can always be applied to other groups and contexts,[1] they should not be taken as an irrefutable frame of analysis. Not only can other variables play a role according to a different historical context, but the significance of each factor can fluctuate to a great extent, especially when studying small militant groups that drive a good part of their energy from the engagement of their leaders. Yet I believe that the history of the taxi industry in Montreal constitutes a good basis to define the social, political, economic, and subjective conditions that have made it possible in the past, and continue to make it more likely today, for some social movements to resort to violence. Though it is an episode of the Canadian left now largely forgotten, the story of the Montreal taxi drivers in the 1960s is rich in lessons for scholars, here and abroad.

Note

1. Meshack M. Khosa, "Routes, ranks and rebels: Feuding in the taxi revolution." *Journal of Southern African Studies*, 1992, Vol. 18 Issue 1, pp. 232–52; Graham Russell Gao Hodges, *Taxi! A Social History of the New York City Cabdriver*. Baltimore: Johns Hopkins University Press, 2007.

References

Mills, Sean, *The Empire Within: Postcolonial Thought and Political Activism in Sixties.* Montreal: McGill-Queen's University Press, 2010.

Warren, Jean-Philippe, *Une douce anarchie. Les années 1968 au Québec.* Montreal: Boréal, 2008.

Warren, Jean-Philippe, "Quelques facteurs sociologiques de la violence dans les années 1968: le Mouvement de libération du taxi." In Ivan Carel, Robert Comeau and Jean-Philippe Warren (eds), *Violences politiques. Europe et Amérique, 1960–1979.* Montreal: Lux, 2013, pp. 117–37.

59 Fighting Back and Building Another World: Contention in the Twenty-First Century

Lesley J. Wood[1]

How are social movements in Canada fighting back and building another world? This paper will survey the range and issues of protest in Toronto and Montreal from 1995 to 2005, and will zoom in more closely to examine two more recent, high-profile mobilizations: the Quebec student movement and Idle No More. The Quebec student movement made headlines in 2011 and 2012, when it fought the government's plan to dramatically increase student tuition fees. University, college, and CEGEP students held general assemblies, went on strike, blockaded their campuses, organized community "casserole" marches, lobbied, and built alliances. The movement succeeded at stopping the rise in fees, at least for the short term. Idle No More, an Indigenous-led wave of protest, was sparked by federal government budget bills that removed environmental protection from waterways and limited community control of land. Although those protests failed to stop the bills, they have evolved into broad networks arguing for a different kind of political challenge.

In 2017, social movements in Canada demanding social spending and defending environmental protection face challenges. They are constrained by the dominant neoliberal ideology that refuses government intervention in the economy, favouring "market solutions" of trade and investment as a panacea. As a result, movements to redress exclusion, inequality, and environmental protection fail to make headway. Partly in response, movements are engaging in a dual strategy. On the one hand, they are using the traditional repertoire of marches and rallies to make demands on state/provincial authorities. On the other, they are building new sets of relations and institutions that call the state, capitalism, and colonialism into question.

Since the early nineteenth century, social movements in the Global North have taken a consistent form. Charles Tilly analyzed the changes to popular politics in Great Britain from 1760 to 1834 and found that the rise of the national Parliament corresponded with the rise of the modern social movement. Instead of protesting locally, in particular ways and for particular issues, ordinary people began to form associations that would organize campaigns that make claims on outside authorities, within which they would march, rally, petition, and send delegations in ways that would display their worthiness, unity, numbers, and commitment to political authorities, observers, and opponents. This model succeeded in ending British support for slavery, extending suffrage, and implementing various rights—and as

European control and capitalism gained influence, so did the model (Tilly and Wood 2012).

The effectiveness of this form of action varies, but it is most successful when authorities are relatively "open" and concerned about maintaining the consent of the population, and movements are thus able to threaten disruption or the withdrawal of legitimacy and consent. The approach has changed policy, established new social programs, led to the legalization of gay marriage, ended wars, and limited the use of nuclear power, as well as limited abortion, supported racist policies, and stopped immigration. But social movements do not emerge or succeed everywhere, all of the time. Authoritarian contexts may not tolerate social movements; decentralized or **low-capacity regimes** may make them irrelevant. If social movements do not or cannot exist, contention and the struggles against inequality take other forms—including underground action, lobbying, guerilla movements, and advertising campaigns.

The vast majority of Canadian protests in the twenty-first century resemble those in nineteenth-century Britain. If we look at protests in Montreal and Toronto between 1995 and 2005, we can see the period of 1995–2000 as one of intense struggle against the cuts to social spending demanded by neoliberal restructuring. The frequency of protest events in a given year within this period ranges from 40 (Montreal 1997) to 112 (Toronto 1997). The most frequent tactics in these events were marches and rallies, with walkouts and blockades appearing more often in Montreal than in Toronto. Most of the protests in both cities targeted the provincial governments.[2] After 1999, protesters began to shift their demands to the national and international level—with evidence of the global justice movement and its struggles against corporate control and free trade. While the repertoire didn't change significantly during the period, we do see some experimentation with street parties after 1998. After the attacks of 11 September 2001, the number of protests declined but their size increased, with mass marches against wars in Afghanistan and Iraq, and Israel's policies toward the Palestinians.

Despite such variation, struggles against the state and against international institutions during this decade achieved little success. Without receptive authorities, the goals became unclear and some movements appear to have shifted their emphasis. Beyond protests that make demands, movements were constructing alternative institutions, networks, and cultures. We can see this in both the Quebec student movement of 2011–12 and the Idle No More mobilization of 2012–13.[3]

Quebec Student Movement, 2011–12

The Quebec movement has ebbed and flowed over the years, with student unions providing an "infrastructure of dissent" that is far more cohesive than in the rest of the country, creating a history of "student strikes" with rallies, marches, and general assemblies (Lafrance and Sears 2012). Their success is visible in the fact that Quebec's university tuition fees are the lowest of any province in the country. But this is not due simply to marching and rallying in a routine fashion. Instead, it is due to the widespread disruptive threat that the movement poses. In the fall of 2011, the ruling Liberal Party threatened to raise tuition fees by 75 per cent. On 10 November 2011, 200,000 students began an initial two-day strike, with more than 20,000 students marching on Premier Jean Charest's Montreal office. The movement held frequent popular assemblies where members of the different student unions were able to discuss strategy and tactics. Nonetheless, the government refused to budge. By February, activists held daily night marches and rallies, and the strike involved 200,000 students shutting down the colleges, CEGEPs, and universities, as well as blockades of bridges and provincial institutions. The police used stun grenades, pepper spray, and tear gas, and carried out mass arrests. This and new bylaws against the protest broadened the mobilization, with tens of thousands of Quebeckers marching in May 2012 against police commands, making it "the single biggest act of civil disobedience in Canadian history" (Common Dreams Staff, 2012). Eventually, the pressure became too much, Parliament dissolved, and an election was called. The Parti Québécois (PQ) defeated the ruling Liberals, partly on the promise of a tuition freeze. After classes returned, amid widespread euphoria, some sections of the movement demobilized. Others worked on alliance building and others extended their demands—by moving their attention beyond the state and capitalism—arguing for free education, and an end to **austerity budgets** and capitalism. Within a year, the PQ began to argue that some tuition increases were necessary.

Idle No More, 2012–13

Four women launched Idle No More in the fall of 2012 to challenge federal omnibus budget bills that would erode Indigenous interests and remove environmental protections from land and water. Indigenous communities are some of the poorest in the country, with colonial exploitation and displacement excluding Indigenous people from opportunities for sovereignty. Idle No More initially centred on opposing the bills, but after they passed and the movement continued to grow, demands for respect and assertions of sovereignty became more central. Building on existing networks and using social media, the mobilization spread quickly. The first national day of action corresponded with the United Nations Human Rights Day on 10 December 2012 and included 13 protest actions across the country. The following day, Chief Theresa Spence of Attiwapiskat began a hunger strike, demanding more respect for Indigenous communities. This became a story in the mainstream media and messages spread through Facebook and Twitter. On 17 December, in Regina Saskatchewan, Idle No More activists held a round dance in the Cornwall Centre shopping mall. The video of the event went viral, and four days later, there were 79 actions (including 23 round dances) across the country and around the world.[4] By 5 January 2013, the Idle No More Facebook group had more than 45,000 members, and the number continued to increase after January, when Prime Minister Harper agreed to meet with Chief Spence.

Despite its failure to stop the omnibus bills, the movement grew. Protests and teach-ins increased into the spring of 2013 and shifted into the movements for a public inquiry around murdered and missing Indigenous women, for Indigenous sovereignty, and against oil and gas pipelines and fracking. As this occurred, some argued for a different understanding of political engagement. Michi Saagiig Nishnaabeg writer, activist, and educator Leanne Betasamosake Simpson (2011) argued, "When resistance is defined solely as large-scale political mobilization, we miss much of what has kept our languages, cultures, and systems of governance alive. . . . At this point, to me, it seems rather futile to be engaged in scholarly and political processes, trying to shift these relationships when there is no evidence there exists the political will to do so on the part of the Canadian state" (16–18). As the manifesto of Idle No More reads, "We contend that: there are many examples of other countries moving towards sustainability, and we must demand sustainable development as well. We believe in healthy, just, equitable and sustainable communities and have a vision and plan of how to build them" (Kind-nda-niimi Collective 2014).

How Do We Understand the Strategy?

In their emphasis on the need for disruption of the state and capitalism, and on the need for resurgence and the building of equitable and sustainable communities, both the Quebec student movement and especially Indigenous-led movements for **decolonization** suggest a form of contentious politics that is distinct from the social movement. This is in part due to the way that **neoliberal globalization** has transformed the relationship between the state and capitalism.

Charles Tilly and Lesley Wood (2012) suggested that neoliberal globalization limits the future of claims-making social movements. They argue that increased income inequality and the decline of state capacity to intervene in the economy, as well as increasingly dense global connections, makes states less concerned about the well-being of their own populations. Professional social movement organizations that have the resources to challenge international institutions and corporations may continue to make headway. But especially at the national level, activists fighting for a more equal and just society must innovate. As these examples suggest, some combine traditional social movement work with transnational networking and the building of alternative systems, culture, and infrastructure—what Chris Dixon calls "the infrastructure of a liberatory society in ways that undermine, with the goal of contesting, and ultimately replace ruling relations and institutions" (Dixon 2014, 138).

How do we change the world? The answer, it seems, is changing.

Notes

1. I am writing this as a settler on Mississauga Anishinaabe territory. It has been a home and hunting grounds to many peoples, including the Haudenosaunee, Wendat, and always the Mississauga of the New Credit.
2. Event catalogues of protest constructed from the *Montreal Gazette* and the *Toronto Star* using Lexis-Nexis. Search terms: protest, protesters, demonstrated, and rallied.
3. My relationship to both movements is as a supporter and occasional participant.
4. This event catalogue data is based on map data compiled by Tim Groves, and cleaned and supplemented by the author. It catalogues 200 events during the first two months of Idle No More (November–December 2012), identified through social media, Internet sources, alternative media, and mainstream media.

References

Common Dreams Staff. 2012. "Biggest Act of Civil Disobedience in Canadian History." *Common Dreams*, May 23. Available at: http://www.commondreams.org/news/2012/05/23/biggest-act-civil-disobedience-canadian-history

Dixon, Chris. 2014. *Another Politics: Talking across Today's Transformative Movements.* Oakland: University of California Press.

Kind-nda-niimi Collective. 2014. *The Winter We Danced: Voices from the Past, the Future and the Idle No More Movement.* Winnipeg, MB: Arbeiter Ring Publishing.

Lafrance, Xavier, and Alan Sears. 2012. "Red Square, Everywhere: With Quebec Student Strikers, Against Repression." *The Bullet*, e-bulletin no. 640, May 24. Available at: http://www.socialistproject.ca/bullet/640.php

Simpson, Leanne. 2011. *Dancing on Our Turtle's Back: Stories of Nishnaabeg Re-creation, Resurgence and a New Emergence.* Winnipeg: Arbeiter Ring Publishing.

Tilly, Charles. 1995. *Popular Contention in Great Britain.* Boston: Harvard University Press.

Tilly, Charles and Lesley J. Wood. 2012, *Social Movements 1768–2012.* Boulder, CO: Paradigm.

Questions for Critical Thought

Chapter 57 | Critical Intervention: Black Women (Re)defining Feminist Resistance, Activism, and Empowerment in Feminist Organizing within Ontario

1. In what way is the term *feminism* connected to race in North American society? Is this depiction true or false? How?
2. Why is Benn-John focused specifically on black women's voices? Explain.
3. Why does Benn-John use an integrative approach? Provide two reasons.
4. Why do black women have to be innovative in their activism? How are their experiences left out or silenced in mainstream campaigns?
5. What can be learned from specifically focusing on black women's organizing? Why is this research important?

Chapter 58 | Factors Leading to Political Violence: Taxi Driving in Montreal

1. This chapter draws on the example of violent protests performed by Quebec taxi drivers in the 1960s. What are non-peaceful protests and episodes of civil disobedience? Give examples.
2. What social differences existed between the taxi drivers and their customers? How did this influence the taxi drivers?
3. What seven factors led the taxi drivers to legitimize the use of force? Briefly describe each.
4. Why did activists feel that violence was the most effective way to liberate Quebec? What three steps did they believe they needed to take?
5. How can this case study help us to better understand contemporary struggles?

Chapter 59 | Fighting Back and Building Another World: Contention in the Twenty-First Century

1. What challenges did social movements face in 2015? How can they adapt to overcome these challenges?
2. Briefly describe the Quebec student movement. What tactics did the supporters of this movement use? What is the outcome of this movement?
3. Briefly describe the Idle No More movement. What tactics did its supporters use? What was the outcome of this movement?
4. How are both the Quebec student movement and Idle No More engaged in contentious politics? Explain.
5. Wood summarizes her chapter in the last line by saying, "How do we change the world? The answer, it seems, is changing." Using what you have learned from this chapter, explain the meaning of this statement. Do you think Wood is right?

PART XV
International Relations and Government

We are said, as humans, to be living in a period of rapid globalization. The term *globalization* has many definitions, but in general, it refers to a process of international integration that has come about as a result of a growing interchange of world views, products, ideas, and other aspects of culture. While globalization is not new—ask Christopher Columbus!—the rapid expansion of new and sophisticated information technology has certainly made the instant exchange of ideas the norm. We don't need to physically cross borders to gain access to products or views from around the world. Rapidly expanding information technology has also made the study of things happening around the globe and in international relations relatively easy and very common, as we will see in the chapters in this section.

Sociological research on international relations typically attempts to explain the interaction of actors in international politics. These actors can be politicians, governments, or private/non-government/inter-government institutions or individuals. Sociologists examine the interactions of different actors and social structures to understand outcomes that have national and international implications by shaping policy, conflict, war, terrorism, trade, economics, the environment, and social "development."

International sociology is important for a number of reasons. To start, it helps us to connect individual biography with global histories. By carefully examining international relations and past interactions, we can see how specific historical events have come to shape individuals' behaviours and attitudes. For example, the terrorist attacks that were orchestrated by the Islamic terrorist group Al-Qaeda in the United States on 11 September 2001 had international consequences. These attacks helped to promote a public discourse of fear and hate, and of insecurity and increased surveillance, that affect us to this day and will likely do so for many years to come.

In this section, you will encounter a number of examples of internationally focused social research. Chapter 60, by Mike Follert, for example, discusses the common language of diplomacy that is used between political leaders so that they can effectively communicate with each other by both maintaining goodwill and conveying their potentially controversial views. Being skilled at diplomacy is important not only for political leaders but also for average citizens.

Internationally focused social research can illuminate the origin of, and point to possible solutions to, global social problems, such as colonization and the inequality between countries, as well as systems of stratification, racism, and sexism. Today, technology, and the Internet in particular, have opened up opportunities for people to become more aware of and more socially engaged or active in social struggles that are taking place in nearly all parts of the globe.

Internationally oriented sociology can help, and indeed has helped, Canadian consumers become aware of how their desire for cheap clothing and other goods contribute to maintaining systems of inequality through, among other things, the use of sweatshops for production. This research has informed many about how our everyday consumption patterns and choices directly affect people's quality of life and the environment thousands of kilometres away.

This section will introduce you to current sociological research that focuses on international relations, politics, and governance. As noted above, in Chapter 60, Follert explores the dynamics of diplomacy, commenting on the way that political leaders interact. Ivanka Knezevic, in Chapter 61, describes labour conditions in Croatia, Slovenia, and Serbia in the years since their civil war in the 1990s. This chapter illustrates international policy differences while comparing how these three countries acquire support by primarily leaning on the European Union. In Chapter 62, Laura Visan explores the 2014 Romanian presidential election, focusing on the transnational participation and campaigns of Romanian diasporas. Lastly, Chapter 63 compares the citizenship regulations of Canada and Germany to demonstrate the impact of a government's political party on policy-making. Each of the chapters in this section provides key insights into the importance of doing and of studying international sociology.

60 The Ambivalence of Diplomacy

Mike Follert

At a private retreat during the G20 Brisbane summit in 2014, the Canadian prime minister made international headlines with his departure from customary Canadian politeness. Upon meeting Vladimir Putin, who extended his arm to greet the prime minister, Stephen Harper told the Russian president, "I guess I'll shake your hand but I have only one thing to say to you: You need to get out of Ukraine" (Canadian Press 2014). It was a brusque rebuff that some of Canada's allies revelled in. However, there was more transpiring in this exchange than a verbal rebuke. As the prime minister voiced his reluctance to engage in the formality of the handshake, any civility initially assumed in the act vanished. The handshake's mere customary character was exposed for both parties to see. In such a breach of custom, denuded of its symbolic meaning, the handshake collapses into a mere sequence of anatomical motions. For the sociologist, these moments of ritual exchange are most instructive when they break down; but as Erving Goffman (1956) reminds us, "these antique tributes cannot be neglected with impunity" (p. 479). This friction in the face of an initial "goodwill" gesture among state leaders brings to light the core problem of diplomacy: it is an art that relies upon civility even amidst antagonism.

At the end of the eighteenth century, the philosopher Immanuel Kant (1963) saw the relations between the nations of the world as shaped by an "unsocial sociability" (*ungesellige Geselligkeit*). Nature, in its innate wisdom, had dispersed humanity across the globe and subsequently, by cunning, brought these far-flung peoples back into contact with one another. Nations have since become at once sociable and unsociable, Kant suggested, as if driven into constant tension, but also, through their rivalry, have progressed toward civilization. Diplomacy as a kind of social relation seeks to mitigate this unsociable element within international relations by acknowledging entrenched cultural differences, even when navigating their symbolic dimensions poses challenges. Goffman (1956) recalls the nineteenth-century diplomatic meetings between Britain and China, for example, where "the Kot'ow [i.e., bow] demanded of visiting ambassadors by the Chinese Emperor was felt by some British ambassadors to be incompatible with their self-respect" (p. 492). In recent years President Obama himself was frequently excoriated by those on the right for bowing to foreign leaders during state visits—an act that conveyed "docility." But the customary character of the handshake as an interpersonal ritual has assumed a fairly normative character at international gatherings. Through it, distinctions or disagreements are suspended as parties convey some minimum degree of mutual respect. Even the inwardly begrudged handshake may be salvaged, if one can outwardly lose oneself sufficiently in its ritual form. Like the language of diplomats, it evinces what Richard Sennett (2012) calls the "subjunctive mood." In contrast to the assertiveness associated with hawkish forms of political speech, the subjunctive mediates with conditional statements and qualifications—"perhaps" and "I would have thought" (p. 23). It is a disposition that also enables the reciprocal communication of respect or deference. "Acts of deference," Goffman (1956) tells us, "typically contain a kind of promise, expressing in truncated form the actor's avowal and pledge to treat the recipient in a particular way in the oncoming activity" (pp. 479–80). Deference becomes all the more important when potential antagonists talk. We may take as an example of diplomacy's artfulness the words of Russian foreign minister Sergei Lavrov, regarding his relationship with former US secretary of state John Kerry: "We talk about bad things nicely" (Akkoc and Oliphant 2015). This way of speaking Lavrov points to is suggestive of a type of language game that, through its "guarded understatement[,] enables diplomatists and ministers to say sharp things to each other without becoming provocative or impolite" (Nicolson 1952: 219). Diplomacy as a form of interaction, we may then say, entails a kind of duality or **ambivalence**.

In the foreign service, state representatives are constantly either overtly or covertly conveying political messages. In her study of the social worlds of the US foreign service, Arlie Hochschild (1969) revealed the mix of political and social messaging that gets routed through the unofficial channels of ambassadors' spouses, as hosts or guests at social gatherings. Turning down an invitation to a gathering, leaving a party early, or snubbing a foreign official may carry potent meanings, even if these slights are indirect or unintentional. Alternatively, the pleasantry of a handshake may very well be interpreted as too cordial by some when it comes from the leader of a rival state. This is perhaps why diplomacy is an art best left to those diplomats acting away from the public eye.

At stake alongside these social niceties, of course, are the more serious affairs of states. Negotiations between state officials, some would argue, require a more rational, **ideal speech situation** (Habermas 1985). The parties involved in this dialogic scenario, as Jürgen Habermas defined it, must be considered equals despite any existing real-world power imbalances. They must take as their goal mutual understanding, rather than mere influence. They should assume a conciliatory tone, even as parties may be far from consensus. But there is something at work in diplomacy beyond what Habermas's rational-purposive situation allows—a disposition or outward performance even. We might recall here an expression that came out of the Reagan–Gorbachev arms reduction negotiations in the ebbing years of the Cold War. Reagan at this time spoke openly of his fondness for the Russian saying "*doveryai, no proveryai*"—"trust, but verify." There is an obvious tension in this maxim, and perhaps even a self-contradiction. For "trust, but verify" betrays the conceit that trust can *ever* be anything but a leap of faith. As Seligman (1997) notes, trust necessarily assumes a relation of uncertainty toward the intentions of another actor—toward an agent whose actions are not entirely predictable (p. 63). One can only ever trust in spite of (or *because* of) one's imperfect knowledge of the other. *Doveryai, no proveryai* expresses this tension: one may trust or have faith in the good intentions of the other, but one must nonetheless confirm or verify the truth of the other's claims. It is a curious turn of phrase since trust, in its explicit logic, does not brook part measures: one either trusts or one does not. That is to say, if one does not fully trust, then one has suspicions and is therefore in a state of *doubt*. We might just as well say "doubt, then verify." But perhaps what is most important here is the *outward* appearance of trust, just as the diplomat relies upon making convincing or trustworthy self-presentations. It is akin to Pascal's maxim on faith, notably paraphrased by Louis Althusser (1971): "Kneel down, move your lips in prayer, and you'll believe" (p. 168). In this instance, the maxim might proceed: "trust, or act in a sincere manner, and you will create a reciprocal basis for trust." There is something outside the realm of rational negotiation here. For trust connotes a feeling, or an imagined familiarity. Indeed, if such an expression—*doveryai, no proveryai*—is an effective, if contradictory, convention borne of unsocial sociability, then its effectiveness is perhaps demonstrated best in the success of those US–Russian arms negotiations in the 1980s.

If there is a basis for such feelings of familiarity in diplomacy, however, it is only partly found in the formal rites of shaking hands or bowing heads. Just as the wives of ambassadors in the 1960s would, according to Hochschild (1969), *relax* formalities on more sociable occasions (e.g., hosting a dinner), so too does the shrewd diplomat or minister. We may look back to Canadian history for a telling example. For the better part of the last half-century, Canada's role on the world stage has been that of a "moderate mediatory middle power" (Holmes 1982: 69)—a negotiator. One may recall especially Lester B. Pearson during the Suez Crisis and the introduction of UN peacekeeping missions as pivotal in carving out this legacy. It was Pearson's diplomatic **sociability**, his "extraordinary capacity for getting on with [people]" (Anderson 2015: 74), as one biographer puts it, that was so germane to his success in brokering peace in the Suez: "The outwardly modest Canadian's delightful charm and self-mocking humour," Anderson notes, "made him excellent company in a very communal profession" (p. 82). Outside the ritual formality of the obligatory handshake is the other side of diplomacy: the ability to relax formalities and appear to let one's guard down in a kind of unburdened sociability. The casual conversation, for example, allows for a different kind of reciprocal exchange, stripped of the instrumentality of a negotiation and shorn of status differences or ulterior motives. In such conversation, parties interact as if they are equals, even as this may be a momentary "departure from reality" (Simmel 1949: 257). This is the purview of those middle-power peace-brokers who cannot be overly officious if they are to establish the familiarity and trust necessary to talk about serious things. It is noteworthy that at the 1954 Indochina Conference, Pearson showed no compunction about chatting informally with the then foreign minster of China, Zhou Enlai—a Cold War–era diplomatic leap forward at a time when the US secretary of state, Foster Dulles, chose instead to exit the room when Zhou extended his arm. Curiously, some six decades later in 2015, it appeared to be more the American, John Kerry, than any Canadian minister who could talk amicably with former Communist foes.

If Reagan's canny "trust, but verify" maxim illustrates the ambivalence of Kant's unsocial sociability in international affairs, then Harper's handshake rebuff appears rather as a kind of pure *unsociability* by comparison—a relation that while frank, in one sense, also negates the possibility of a diplomatic rapport. Taking this concept of diplomacy seriously means realizing the limit points of normal, rational-purposive debate, at least in the world of international affairs where interlocutors lack a shared lifeworld. The diplomat must assume the possibility of confronting different world views, and even differing epistemologies. One famous diplomatic historian remarked of the American mind in the 1940s that it "will not apprehend Russia until it is prepared philosophically to accept the validity of contradiction" (Holmes 1970: vii). Putin, according to one spokesman, responded to Harper's demand that the Russians leave Ukraine by saying "that's impossible because we are not there" (Canadian Press 2014). In this, we confront an apparent contradiction that to North American ears may sound preposterous, but from another perspective, perfectly tenable. Perhaps to Putin's mind Russia was not there because there (i.e., Crimea) was not Ukraine. Whether a logical contradiction or a dispute over semantics, the two countries find themselves at an impasse. Diplomacy, however, maintains alongside antagonism or contradiction the possibility of a kind of charm or seduction: from incommensurable positions, even a disapproving remark may magically lose its sting and bring about something more productive. Indeed, for all the fawning over the charms of Justin Trudeau by the international press just after he became prime minister of Canada, there was surely serious work being done alongside to re-craft Canada's image as a conciliatory actor in international affairs. It is a tone or a mood perhaps most notably reflected in the role Canadian officials played in advancing the Paris Agreement on climate change in December 2015.

In the spirit of Georg Simmel, then, we can view diplomacy as a distinct social form. It bears a duality or ambivalence in a manner similar to Simmel's other major examples: the proximity and distance found in the stranger, the knowing and not-knowing of flirtation, the individuality mixed with imitation in fashion, or the connection and disconnection entailed in conflict. Diplomacy, by contrast, finds its distinctive character in its combination of the conciliatory and the more severe, or in the alternation between formality and informality, without allowing the one to fully overtake the other.

References

Akkoc, Raziye and Roland Oliphant. 2015. "Russia kills US-backed Syrian rebels in second day of air strikes as Iran prepares for ground offensive." *Telegraph.co.uk*, October 2. Retrieved 30 October 2015 from: http://www.telegraph.co.uk/news/worldnews/europe/russia/11903702/Russias-Vladimir-Putin-launches-strikes-in-Syria-on-Isil-to-US-anger-live-updates.html.

Althusser, Louis. 1971. *Lenin and Philosophy and Other Essays*. New York: New Left Review.

Anderson, Antony. 2015. *The Diplomat: Lester Pearson and the Suez Crisis*. Fredericton, NB: Goose Lane Editions.

Canadian Press. 2014. "Stephen Harper at G20 tells Vladimir Putin to 'get out of Ukraine.'"

Cbc.ca, November 15. Retrieved 30 October 2015 from: (http://www.cbc.ca/news/world/stephen-harper-at-g20-tells-vladimir-putin-to-get-out-of-ukraine-1.2836382).

Goffman, Erving. 1956. "The Nature of Deference and Demeanor." *American Anthropologist*, 58(3): 473–502.

Habermas, Jürgen. 1985. *The Theory of Communicative Action. Volume I: Reason and the Rationalization of Society*, trans. H. McCarthy. Boston: Beacon Press.

Hochschild, Arlie. 1969. "The Role of the Ambassador's Wife: An Exploratory Study." *Journal of Marriage and Family*, 31(1): 73–87.

Holmes, John W. 1970. *The Better Part of Valour: Essays on Canadian Diplomacy*. Toronto: McClelland & Stewart Ltd.

———. 1982. *The Shaping of Peace: Canada and the Search for World Order 1943–1957, vol. 2*. Toronto: University of Toronto Press.

Kant, Immanuel. 1963 [1784]. "Idea for a Universal History from a Cosmopolitan Point of View." In *On History*, translated by L. White Beck. Indianapolis: Bobbs-Merrill.

Nicolson, Harold. 1952. *Diplomacy*. London: Oxford University Press.

Seligman, Adam B. 1997. *The Problem of Trust*. Princeton, NJ: Princeton University Press.

Sennett, Richard. 2012. *Together: The Rituals, Pleasures, and Politics of Cooperation*. New Haven, CT: Yale University Press.

Simmel, Georg. 1949. "The Sociology of Sociability." *American Journal of Sociology*, 55(3): 254–61.

61 Policy Networks, Policy Transfers, and Recommodification: Actors and Mechanisms of Labour Policy Formation in Post-Yugoslav Countries

Ivanka Knezevic

This paper sketches an analytical framework for an explanation of labour policy formation in Slovenia, Croatia, and Serbia during the last 25 years. Until 1990, all three countries were part of socialist Yugoslavia and shared the same legal regulation of labour and social policies associated with it. Like other **post-socialist countries**, they have changed their laws and policies to accommodate a capitalist economic system, based on private ownership of enterprises and much-reduced government regulation of the economy. One of these changes is the reduced regulation of the labour market, which makes the hiring and firing of workers by corporations easier, but—from employees' perspective—makes both employment and income more insecure.

The position of these countries' economies in the international (and global) economic system is influenced by their membership in the European Union (EU), which provides favourable conditions for investment and trade among its members. Slovenia joined the EU in 2007, Croatia in 2013, and Serbia is now a "candidate country": it must fulfill a number of mostly economic conditions in order to become an EU member.

The framework proposed here focuses on three interrelated factors that influence labour policy formation in these countries: social policy networks, the transfer of international policy preferences, and the resulting social policy consensus. Social policy networks tie the other two factors together. On the one hand, they transmit policy preferences from international agencies to the governments and civil services of the three countries. On the other, they are central in negotiating and maintaining a labour policy consensus—a shared understanding of the role the labour force should play in a country's economy. This consensus guides laws and policies, as well as negotiations between governments, civil society organizations, corporations, and unions. Since these three countries started developing capitalism, the main overall characteristic of their labour policy consensus has been an increasing recommodification of labour. National differences in the composition of policy networks, the exact timing and process of policy transfer, and the content of the adopted consensus help explain why the regulation of labour in these countries now differs.

For the purposes of this paper, we have conducted a qualitative content analysis of labour-related policy documents issued by the EU and its governing bodies (see, for instance, European Union 2000, 2009, 2010; European Commission 2013; Europska komisija 2013). These documents influence legislation and policies not only of member countries (see Baloković 2008; Čujko 2008; Čatipović 2013) but also of candidate countries (such as Serbia), which must prove that their legal environment is compatible with that of the EU. Policy transfer from international financial institutions—the World Bank and the International Monetary Fund (IMF)—is significant in nearly all post-socialist countries whose transformation from socialism to capitalism produced prolonged economic crises and necessitated large international loans.

Context: Post-socialist Countries on the Global Periphery

One early commentator wrote that Eastern Europe had gone from subjugation by a Soviet-led international regime to subjugation by a Western-led regime of global domination (Janos 2002). Most consider that post-socialist countries belong to the global semi-periphery, characterized by considerable industrial and post-industrial development, though dependent on core countries as markets for their products. We would argue that most post-socialist countries that joined the EU since 2007 should be considered peripheral. Privatization of their industrial facilities has led to the closure of many of them and to the sale of the remainder to foreign investors in a situation of a "race to the bottom" (Brecher and Costello 1994), which includes the rapid recommodification of labour. As a result, both Croatia and Serbia are in positions of marked underdevelopment and dependence on foreign investors and international organizations, including the EU. Only Slovenia could be considered a semi-peripheral country: its labour activation rate is at the level of the EU-15 and growing; its unemployment rate is higher than in the old EU members, but has been decreasing steadily (Cantillon and Vandenbroucke 2014); and knowledge-based services form a substantial part of its economy.

Networks in Labour Policy Formation

We propose the concept of "**policy network**" to replace the widely used "epistemic community" (e.g., Galbreath and McEvoy 2013), which carries the ideological connotation of common interests, absence of inequality, and absence of conflict.

We expect policy decisions (including the degree of commodification of labour) to be influenced by power relations among interest-based social groups: governments, corporations, and workers' organizations. Their interests are represented and negotiated in social networks and institutions. Policy networks consist of people whose professional status enables them to influence concrete decisions on public policy, redistribution of state resources, and legislation. Communication and resources are exchanged among network members, whose relationships may be unequal or hierarchical. The degree of their influence on other network members may differ, because they represent organizations with different degrees of power: governments, civil service, universities, international institutions (including the EU), and governmental and non-governmental organizations (NGOs). A policy network includes both institutional and informal relationships among its members. Its defining characteristic is an engagement in policy formation: innovation, standard setting, diffusion, and implementation (Haas 1992; Adler and Haas 1992).

Social policy legislation in Serbia over the last five years (Vuković 2012; Vuković and Babović 2013), for example, has been formulated by experts from a range of fields who are affiliated with the academy, research institutions outside the academy (e.g., the Centre for Liberal-Democratic Studies, financed by and co-operating closely with the World Bank), and NGOs, together with experts from the relevant ministries. A similar composition of policy-formation networks has also been documented in Croatia and Slovenia (Jurčević 2005; Baloković 2008; Čujko 2008).

Three Sections of Policy Networks and Their Roles in Policy Transfer

Each national policy network is differentiated: it consists of a number of smaller sections. Vuković (2012) has identified three: (1) experts and politicians from a relevant ministry; (2) experts and managers affiliated with international organizations; and (3) "domestic" experts affiliated with NGOs, research institutions, and the academy.

The network of government experts is quite stable, because European civil services (including post-socialist ones) do not encourage the change of experts' professional fields during their careers. Experts may move between service-delivery departments (e.g., employment centres), and the policy-making and monitoring areas of a ministry (e.g., ministry of labour and social services).

International governmental and non-governmental organizations (INGOs) have been the key agents of professional socialization of local policy experts—both governmental and academic—during the last 20 years. The customary reference to these organizations as "international development partners" reflects their importance. The actual members of policy networks representing these organizations' interests are international and local consultants, who exert their influence through the management of research and policy-writing projects, and the organization of conferences and seminars. Rarely, as it has happened in Croatia, consultants leave the INGOs and take positions in the civil service or local research institutions.

The influence of international organizations has two dimensions. On the one hand, they finance social policy reforms and their delivery mechanisms, and provide logistical support for them. On the other, their role in education of local experts helps create a policy consensus (Deacon 2007; Vuković 2012).

Croatia and Serbia have taken significant loans from the World Bank, whose "poverty reduction strategies" are conditions of these loans and have made the Bank the most influential international organization in their labour policy formation. The EU does not interfere with these strategies, which are imposed on a number of its members (Yarashevich 2013).

In Slovenia, policy reforms have taken place largely under the influence of the EU experts and with financing from EU funds. Labour policy changes have followed the pattern typical of the "new members" of the EU. Deregulatory/commodifying employment policy reforms are required in order to qualify for membership. Once a country has joined, most EU intervention in labour policy is directed at administrative "capacity building" (Bejaković, Vukšić, and Vratić 2012; Cierco 2013). This is a process of transmission of Western experiences in planning and monitoring of service delivery, subcontracting, decentralization of funding and services, and interdepartmental co-operation. EU consultants present it as entirely unproblematic, despite important differences among societies these organizations should serve, as well as much lower state capacity—a state's ability to organize its service (e.g., education, training, and employment insurance) and enforce its laws (e.g., corporate taxation and worker safety)—in comparison with the developed EU countries. Bickerton, Counliffe, and Gourevitch (2007) write that this formal, technical approach to social services indicates a deliberate effort to depoliticize public policy reforms and stifle public polemic about it. This makes a policy consensus easier to build and maintain.

The third section of policy networks—local academic experts—have also been socialized under the influence of "international developmental partners," even during the international economic sanctions against Serbia from 1992 to 1995, when local professional and academic communities were otherwise isolated (Vuković 2012). Most of these experts are associated with local branches of INGOs propagating "global values" (Boli and Thomas 1999), rather than with advocacy organizations of social policy users—trade unions, associations of the disabled, or women's organizations (Vuković 2012; Čatipović 2013).

In 2000, a party advocating EU membership came to power in Serbia. Following this change, co-operation of academic experts with government bodies has intensified. They have prepared social policy strategies, protocols, and legislation in co-operation with ministries and service provider departments.

Policy Consensus and Policy Outcomes: Recommodification

The concept of "**recommodification**" refers to changes in labour conditions that increase workers' dependence on an uncontrolled labour market for survival (see Visser 2006; Bailey 2009; Krings 2009). Complete commodification of labour exists if workers are fully dependent on market relations (i.e., on wages they receive in exchange for work) for their existence. Humans, however, need a range of non-market institutions—from the unpaid domestic work of their family members to public transportation—to live. State institutions surrounding a capitalist economy therefore always include mechanisms for the decommodification of labour (decreasing its dependence on an uncontrolled labour market). Publicly funded education, health care, and employment insurance are among them. Over the past several decades, the scope and availability of extra-market means of survival have been restricted worldwide under the influence of corporate interests, cash-strapped states, and neoliberal ideology.

The EU labour policies are meant to facilitate labour market transitions and flexible employment careers (Morel, Parlier, and Palme 2012): the relatively easy movement of workers from unemployment to employment, and from one employer to another. So far, however, such policies have facilitated labour market entry into low-skilled work, rather than promoted the training and upskilling of the workforce. Workers, whose previous qualified jobs have been lost to international competition or restructuring, are forced to accept low-skilled work or remain unemployed. They have no opportunities to upgrade their skills and join the knowledge economy, which is the declared long-term goal of the EU policies.

Research on the Croatian labour market supports this conclusion. The EU-sponsored employment policies do not actually improve the lot of the unemployed: those who participated in the EU-sponsored training programs did not find employment any sooner or remain employed any longer than those who did not participate. Both groups found work predominantly in low-skilled, unstable positions (Matković, Babić, and Vuga 2013).

The 2009 Croatian labour law is a good example of the EU-sponsored recommodification policies. The most significant change from the earlier regulation was the weakening of the employment contract by lifting barriers to part-time and limited-term contracts, as well as simplifying layoff and firing procedures. Qualifying conditions, duration, and amounts of unemployment benefits all changed between 2004 and 2008. Unemployment insurance restrictions are now among the strictest in the EU (Baloković 2008). These changes have led some analysts to predict that Slovenia will lose much of its industry to cheaper Croatian labour.

In the domain of employment services (training and employment support), the trend is toward privatization and marketization. The provision of services by private companies is now a part of employment policy in all three post-Yugoslav countries. Marketization is a step further than privatization. This does not involve merely subcontracting or including private service providers among the range of options for provision of social services, but deregulating these services so that the market mechanism of supply and demand determines the availability and cost of services.

Since the interests of workers themselves are not represented by any of the three sections in the policy networks in Slovenia, Croatia, and Serbia, it should not be surprising that the internationally sponsored recommodification policies turn the usual criteria of quality of work on their heads. In the dominant policy consensus, job stability becomes an indicator of the "insufficient dynamism of the labour market," and shuttling between standard and non-standard employment is not understood as a hardship for workers (Šošić 2005).

References

Adler, E. and P.H. Haas. 1992. "Conclusion: Epistemic Communities, World Order and the Creation of a Reflective Research Program." *International Organization* 46:1, 367–80.

Bailey, David J. 2009. *The Political Economy of European Social Democracy: A Critical Realist Approach*. London and New York: Routledge.

Baloković, Snježana. 2008. "Programi pomoći Republici Hrvatskoj u sustavu socijalne sigurnosti: CARDS—regionalni program pomoći." *Revija za socijalnu politiku* 15:2, 225–42.

Bejaković, Predrag, Goran Vukšić, and Vjekoslav Bratić. 2012. "Komparativna analiza zaposlenosti i naknada za zaposlene u javnom sektoru u Hrvatskoj i u Evropskoj uniji." *Društvena istraživanja* 21:1, 101–19.

Bickerton, Christopher, Philip Counliffe, and Alexander Gourevitch (eds). 2007. *Politics without Sovereignty: A Critique of Contemporary International Relations*. London: University College Press.

Boli, John and George M. Thomas (eds). 1999. *Constructing World Culture: International Nongovernmental Organizations since 1875*. Stanford: Stanford University Press.

Brecher, Jeremy and Tim Costello. 1994. *The Race to the Bottom: Global Village or Global Pillage*. Boston: South End Press.

Cantillon, Bea and Frank VandenBroucke (eds). 2014. *Reconciling Work and Poverty Reduction: How Successful Are European Welfare States?* Oxford and New York: Oxford University Press.

Čatipović, Iva. 2013. "Izmjene i dopune Zakona o radu i Zakona o rodiljnim i roditeljskim potporama." *Revija za socijalnu politiku* 20:3, 293–302.

Cierco, Teresa. 2013. "Public administration reform in Macedonia." *Communist and Post-Communist Studies* 46.4: 481–91.

Čujko, Adela. 2008. "Nadzor nad primjenom Europske socijalne povelje u Hrvatskoj: Zaključci Europskog odbora za socijalna prave." *Revija za socijalnu politiku* 15:2, 243–56.

Deacon, Bob. 2007. *Global Social Policy and Governance*. Thousand Oaks, CA: SAGE.

European Commission. 2013. *Monitoring Report on Croatia's Accession Preparations*, Brussels.

European Union, European Parliament. 2000. *Charter of Fundamental Rights of the European Union*, Nice. Accessed 24 January 2014: http://www.europarl.europa.eu/charter/pdf/text_en.pdf

European Union, European Parliament, European Council. 2009. *Directive 20090/38/EC on the establishment of a European Works Council or a procedure in Community-scale undertakings and Community-scale groups of undertakings for the purposes of informing and consulting employees.* Accessed 25 January 2014: http://eur-lex.europa.eu/LexUriServ/LexUriServ.do?uri=OJ:L:2009:122:0028:0044:en:pdf

European Union. 2010. *Consolidated Treaties. Charter of Fundamental Rights*, Brussels. Accessed 15 January 2014: http://europa.eu/pol/pdf/qc3209190enc_002.pdf

Europska komisija. 2013. "Prema socijalnom ulaganju za rast i koheziju—uključujući i provedbu Europskog socijalnog fonda za razdoblje 2014-2020." *Revija za socijalnu politiku* 20:2, 167–90.

Galbreath, David J. and Joanne McEvoy. 2013. "How Epistemic Communities Drive International Regimes: The Case of Minority Rights in Europe." *Journal of European Integration* 35:2, 169–86.

Haas, P.H. 1992. "Introduction: Epistemic communities and international policy coordination." *International Organization* 43:3, 1–35.

Janos, Andrew C. 2002. "From Eastern Empire to Western Hegemony: East Central Europe under Two International Regimes." *East European Politics and Societies*, 15:2, 230–59.

Jurčević, Živko. 2005. "Socijalna skrb u Hrvatskoj od 2000. Do 2004. Analiza pokazatelja stanja i razvoja." *Revija za socijalnu politiku* 12:3–4, 345–75.

Krings, Torben. 2009. "A Race to the Bottom? Trade Unions, EU Enlargement and the Free Movement of Labour." *European Journal of Industrial Relations* 15, 49–69.

Lučev, Josip and Zdenko Babić. 2013. "Tipovi kapitalizma, ekspanzija neoliberalizma i socijalni učinci u baltičkim zemljama, Sloveniji I Hrvatskoj: komparativni pristup." *Revija za socijalnu politiku* 20:1, 1–20.

Matković, Teo, Zdenko Babić and Annamaria Vuga. 2013. "Evaluacija mjera aktivne politike zapošljavanja 2009. i 2010. Godine u Republici Hrvatskoj." *Revija za socijalnu politiku* 19:3, 303–36.

Morel, Nathalie, Bruno Parlier and Joakim Palme (eds). 2012. *Towards a Social Investment Welfare State? Ideas, Policies and Challenges*. Bristol: Polity Press.

Nee, Victor. 2005. "New Institutionalism in Economics and Sociology." In Neil J. Smelser and Richard Swedberg (eds) *The Handbook of Economic Sociology*. Princeton and Oxford: Princeton University Press.

Šošić, Vedran. 2005. "Siromaštvo i politike na tržištu rada u Hrvatskoj." *Financijska teorija i praksa* 29:1, 75–94.

Visser, Jelle. 2006. "More Holes in the Bucket: Twenty Years of European Integration and Organized Labor." *Comparative Labor Law and Policy Journal* 26, 477–521.

Vuković, Danilo. 2012. "Interesi, mreze i institucije: sociološko-pravna analiza novog socijalnog zakonodavstva u Srbiji." *Sociologija* LV:1, 25–46.

Vuković, Danilo and Marija Babović. 2013. "Social Interests, Policy Networks, and Legislative Outcomes: The Role of Policy Networks in Shaping Welfare and Employment Policies in Serbia." *East European Politics and Societies* 28:5, 5–24.

Yarashevich, Viachaslau. 2013. "External Debt of Post-Communist Countries." *Communist and Post-Communist Studies* 46, 203–216.

62 Political Engagement through Civic Transnationalism: Romanian Diasporas and the 2014 Presidential Elections

Laura Visan

This chapter explores the role of social media in facilitating transnational **political participation** and shows that **social networking sites (SNS)** have the potential to produce a space for political debate, to facilitate interpersonal communication, and to educate the public regarding its political options, but that they are not democratic "by nature." In other words, it is the *users* of social media that win **elections**, change political regimes, or endorse a civic cause, and not the media per se. The chapter analyzes the role of Romanian diasporas from Western Europe and North America in determining the result of the Romanian presidential elections from November 2014 through contributions on social media.

SNS and Political Participation

Political participation consists of "contacting a political representative; petitioning or demonstrating for a certain cause; voting in local or national elections; participating in local neighbourhood meetings that address political matters; becoming an active member of a political party or protest organization" (Fennema and Tillie 2008).

The role of SNS in mobilizing political participation has been amply debated. Skeptical researchers consider that political participation via the Internet is too often reduced to "clicktivism," which does not count as a form of participation but is rather seen as a passive form of acknowledgement; arguably, the same argumentation may be applied to "liking" politicians' pages. On the optimistic side, it is argued that if political motivation exists, materialized in posted comments, tweets, blog entries, or other kinds of user-generated content, we may speak of political participation (Hosch-Dayican 2014, 342).

In spite of all their incontestable caveats—the use of personal data for sending targeted advertising messages and the impossibility to opt out from them, the reliance on unpaid labour, a double-standard approach to privacy (Fuchs 2014), and the risks associated with "dataveillance" and the commodification of personal data (Lyon 2009, 2014)—the major SNS have been suggested to facilitate a "networked citizen-centered perspective providing opportunities to connect the private sphere of autonomous political identity to a multitude of chosen political spaces" (Papacharissi 2010). This is due to the versatility of SNS, in comparison to more traditional media, which has led to a blurring of boundaries between "mainstream news media increasingly reliant upon political blogs and citizens-user content" (Loader and Mercea 2011, 762).

SNS also have the potential to create social networks that may be mobilized for political action (Boulianne 2009, 525). The ties produced by such networks facilitate the circulation of information (Gil de Zúñiga, Jung, and Valenzuela 2012), and may increase the visibility of a certain candidate's messages (Boulianne 2015, 525). Core political beliefs and values are unlikely to change as a result of attending online debates or accessing online media material; users, though, tend to be more open in their opinions toward different candidates (Hoff 2010, 178–97).

Digital media, including SNS, provide the public with more opportunities to become informed about politics, and this is particularly useful when it comes to small-scale political initiatives that are not usually presented in mainstream media. The Internet and social media may produce a new model of active citizenship, in counter-response to the "growing disinterest in conventional forms of political participation" (Papacharissi 2009, 35). At the same time, the "always on" features of new technologies allow the political message to reach a much wider audience, in a few seconds (Gibson and Ward 2012, 66). More information usually translates into more "opportunities for action" (Bimber 2012, 123), and in a similar fashion, more content produced by young users on social media usually results in a more consistent participation in politics (Östman 2012). Moreover, a preference for online media has been shown to be a predictor of stronger political engagement, particularly in the case of young users (Bachmann, Kaufhold, Seth et al 2010, 42). However, the correlation between digital media and "offline" political participation needs to be further investigated: it is unpredictable, so generalizations are difficult to make (Bimber 2012). Even Barack Obama's Internet and social media campaign for the 2008 US presidential elections, considered a turning point in the use of new media for political activities, should be approached with a more balanced perspective. Thanks to social media, it was easier to fundraise and to coordinate the teams of volunteers involved in Obama's campaign, but there is "little evidence that... [social media] were successful in changing people's levels of participation... [i.e.], people's likelihood of voting or participating in the campaign" (Boulianne 2015, 534).

Romania 2014: Klaus Iohannis and Victor Ponta—Two Presidential Candidates on Facebook

After a first electoral round with 12 candidates on 2 November 2014, only two candidates remained in the political race for the second round, on 16 November: Victor Ponta from the left-wing party PSD (Social-Democratic Party), and Klaus Iohannis from the centre-right coalition ACL (Liberal-Christian Alliance). Ponta graduated from the University of Bucharest law school in 1995. In 2012 he became the prime minister of Romania, following the resignation of the former right-wing cabinet. In the same year, the scientific journal *Nature* revealed that approximately 80 pages of Ponta's doctoral thesis were plagiarized. The prime minister denied the accusations and refused to resign, in spite of the numerous requests from politicians and civil society. (In July 2016, after evaluating Ponta's doctoral thesis, a national council composed of prominent university professors and researchers ruled that the thesis was plagiarized, and the former prime minister had his PhD revoked).

Klaus Iohannis, a former high school physics teacher and school inspector, was elected the mayor of the Transylvanian city Sibiu in 2000, with the support of the German Forum in Romania. Praised for his efforts to modernize Sibiu by branding it as a tourist attraction and an attractive hub for foreign investors, Iohannis succeeded in obtaining the award of 2007 European Cultural Capital for Sibiu. Iohannis was re-elected as a mayor in 2004, 2008, and 2012, each time with more than 70 per cent of the ballots. In 2013, Iohannis joined the National Liberal Party, becoming its vice-president, and in June 2014, its president. For the first time in its post-1989 history, Romania had a candidate from an ethnic minority—Saxons—a member of the German-speaking Lutheran Church in Transylvania.

Both candidates relied heavily on social media in their campaigns. Ponta's social media campaign was built mostly on personal attacks against Iohannis. His campaign slogan, "Proud to be Romanian—the President who Unites," capitalized on nationalism and portrayed his opponent as a foreigner whose allegiances were not that of the ordinary Romanian—a jab at Iohannis's ethnic background. For his part, Iohannis adopted a moderate tone and chose to ignore all the attacks coming from Ponta's team, emphasizing instead his administrative and managerial skills as well as his ample network of contacts among foreign politicians. The slogan of his campaign was "Romania of Good Things Done," an allusion to the German origins of the candidate, important because, for most Romanians, "German-ness" has a positive connotation of thoroughness and conscientiousness.

"Just a Bunch of Provocateurs": Facebook Discourse between the Two Election Rounds

On 2 November 2004, Victor Ponta won the first round of the presidential election with 40.01 per cent of the ballots, while Klaus Iohannis ranked second with 30.54 per cent. The first round of the election triggered a powerful wave of dissatisfaction among the members of the Romanian diaspora worldwide, who lined up for hours in front of Romanian consulates but did not get a chance to vote. Alternative media outlets and social media channels showcased copious stories of Romanians from Boston, New York, Munich, Brussels, Strassbourg, Paris, and London who complained about the problems in the organization of the election.

The Facebook page of Klaus Iohannis swiftly echoed the wave of public dissatisfaction. Countless photos showed lineups of hundreds or even thousands of Romanian migrants waiting to vote in Munich, Kishinev, Brussels, Stockholm, Paris, London, Bologna, Vienna, Berlin, Valencia, and Dublin. The comments posted on Iohannis's Facebook page showed a spiralling frustration against Victor Ponta and his government, due to the poor organization of the voting process outside Romania. In this context, individuals without political allegiances acted as "political 'produsers,'" responding to the hostile context created by the Romanian government (Dahlgren 2013, 68).

Conversely, Victor Ponta posted only two brief comments on his Facebook page regarding the situation abroad. His statement contained a less than subtle attempt at self-promotion: "I worked and studied abroad, too." During the 14 days that separated the two rounds of the election, Ponta's staff posted countless pictures of him in the company of prominent political, religious, and artistic figures, from Angela Merkel to the Netanyahu family, and from Pope Francis to Arnold Schwarzenegger. No comments were posted, but the photos aimed to convey the image of a political leader with ample external exposure. Furthermore, the minister of external affairs declared that the incidents at the polling stations abroad were largely due to the intervention of some provocateurs—people who came on purpose just to stand in line, to make the queue look thicker (Neagu, 2014).

The malfunctions in the organization of the election at the polling districts outside Romania continued in the second round, too. However, Klaus Iohannis succeeded in winning the election with 54.51 per cent of the votes. Not only did Iohannis succeed in closing the gap that separated him from Victor Ponta in the first round of the election; he received an extra 10 per cent of votes in the second round.

"We were Defeated by Facebook"

Shortly after the score of the elections was officially announced, the vice-president of PSD, who coordinated Ponta's electoral campaign, blamed social media for the defeat. His anger was most likely misdirected, because social media was just one of the factors that contributed to Iohannis's success. His Facebook page delivered text and comments, but most importantly, it encouraged the *grassroots* initiatives, as its creator declared. Though it aimed to acquire over one million likes and a reach of over 5 million people, Iohannis's Facebook page exceeded all expectations by attracting more fans than the Facebook pages of Angela Merkel or Francois Hollande (Vasile 2014).

Social media provided an alternative to the pro-Ponta discourse of most national-coverage television news broadcasts, which dismissed the irregularities at the polls abroad. At the same time, Facebook mediated between the Romanians living abroad and their families and friends from Romania. The former shared via social media their experiences from election day, when they lined up for seven–eight hours or more in front of Romanian consulates, in inclement weather, after travelling several hundreds of kilometres. This was a more powerful incentive to vote pro-Iohannis (or, better said, anti-Ponta) than any electoral message.

However, as Loader and Mercea (2011) aptly note, we should "dispel the deterministic idea that social media are themselves inherently democratic and that politics is dead" (760). It was not Facebook that won the presidential elections in Romania. Without the hours of lining up in front of Romanian consulates, and without the meetings organized in Romania in support of the co-nationals from abroad, it is unlikely that even the craftiest Facebook campaign could have reversed the results of the first round.

At the same time, social media do not carry the promise of long-term political engagement by migrants, and it would be beneficial if further research granted more attention to online forms of participation among diasporas. The fact that Romanians came together for a specific, time-limited cause, and not for a long-term project, was (involuntarily) confirmed by the remark of a person who was extremely committed to posting content and photos on social media between the two rounds of the election. After the victory of Iohannis was announced, her comment was: "Good thing it's over. Now I can finally go back to my stuff."

References

Bachmann I., K. Kaufhold, L. Seth, et al. (2010). News platform preference: advancing the effects of age and media consumption on political participation. *International Journal of Internet Science* 5(1): 34–47.

Bimber, B. (2012). Digital media and citizenship. In H.A. Semetko, and M. Scammell (Eds), *The SAGE handbook of political communication* (pp. 115–27). London: SAGE.

Boulianne, S. (2015). Social media use and participation: a meta-analysis of current research. *Information, Communication & Society* 18(5): 524–38. Available at: http://dx.doi.org/10.1080/1369118X.2015.1008542

Boulianne, S. (2009). Does Internet use affect engagement? A meta-analysis of research. *Political Communication* 26(2): 193–211.

Dahlgren, P. (2013). *The Political Web: Media Participation and Alternative Democracy.* Houndmills, Basingstoke, Hampshire; New York: Palgrave Macmillan.

Fennema, M. and J. Tillie. (2008). Social capital in multicultural societies. In D. Castiglione, J.W. Van Deth, and G. Wolleb (Eds), *The Handbook of Social Capital* (pp. 349–70). Oxford: Oxford University Press.

Fuchs, C. (2014). Social media and the public aphere. *Triple-C* 12(1): 57–101. Available at: http://www.triple-c.at/index.php/tripleC/article/viewFile/552/529

Gibson, R.K., and S. Ward (2012). Political Organizations and Campaigning Online. In H.A. Semetko and M. Scammell (Eds), *The SAGE Handbook of Political Communication* (pp. 62–74). London: SAGE.

Gil de Zúñiga, H., N. Jung, and S. Valenzuela. (2012). Social media use for news and individuals' social capital, civic engagement and political participation. *Journal of Computer-Mediated Communication* 17(3): 319–36.

Hoff, J. (2010). Election campaigns on the Internet: how are voters affected? *International Journal of E-Politics* 1(1): 22–40.

Hosch-Dayican, B. (2014). Online political activities as emerging forms of political participation: How do they fit in the conceptual map? *Acta Politica* 49, 342–6. doi:10.1057/ap.2014.7

Loader, B. and Mercea, D. (2011). Networking democracy? Social media innovations and participatory politics. *Information, Communication & Society* 14(6), 757–69; doi: 10.1080/1369118X.2011.592648

Lyon, D. (2009). Surveillance, power, and everyday life. In Chrisanthi Avgerou, Robin Mansell, Danny Quah, and Roger Silverstone (Eds), *The Oxford Handbook of Information and Communication Technologies* (pp. 449–68). Oxford: Oxford University Press.

Lyon, D. (2014). Surveillance, Snowden, and big data: capacities, consequences, critique, *Big Data & Society* July–December, 1–13.

Neagu, A. (2014). Titus Corlăţean: "There were supporters of some candidates who complicated the process of voting in diaspora." *Hotnews*, 3 November.

Östman, J. (2012). Information, expression, participation: how involvement in user-generated content relates to democratic engagement among young people, *New Media & Society* 14(6), 1004–21.

Papacharlssi, Z. (2010). *A Private Sphere: Democracy in a Digital Age.* Cambridge: Polity.

Papacharissi, Z. (2009). The citizen is the message: alternative modes of civic engagement. In Z. Papacharissi (Ed.), *Journalism and Citizenship: New Agendas in Communication* (pp. 29–43). New York: Routledge.

Vasile, A. (2014). Vlad Tăuşance, unul dintre oamenii care l-au ajutat pe Klaus Iohannis să devină primul politician european care a atins 1 milion de LIKE-uri pe Facebook. 19 November. Available at: http://andreeavasile.ro/2014/11/19/vlad-tausance-omul-datorita-caruia-klaus-johannis-a-devenit-primul-politician-european-care-a-atins-1-milion-de-like-uri-pe-facebook

63 Liberalizing versus Tightening Citizenship Rules in Germany and Canada: A Question of Party Platforms and Politics?

Elke Winter and Anke Patzelt

Introduction

Recently, both Germany and Canada have been undergoing major changes in their citizenship legislation. While Canada has rendered citizenship more difficult to get and easier to lose, Germany has made life-long dual citizenship accessible for those born on German soil to legal foreign residents. While this seems to be a far cry from legislation in Canada, where dual citizenship even for naturalized citizens has been unreservedly tolerated since 1977, it seems fair to argue that the two countries are currently on opposite paths regarding the development of their citizenship laws: Germany is liberalizing its citizenship rules, while Canada is doing the opposite. Our current research examines this trend in some depth. In this paper, we briefly contrast the two country's recent developments in citizenship policy and law. We then debate the extent to which their governments' stance on citizenship policy is related to party platforms and politics.

Germany: On the Move toward More Liberal Citizenship Regulations?

Germany is a classic example of an "ethnic nation" having a long-standing tradition of blood-based citizenship (***jus sanguinis***), and applying fairly strict citizenship regulations (Brubaker, 1992). In fact, until the beginning of the 2000s, Germany had an "exclusionary model" of citizenship, in which naturalization was extremely difficult to achieve[1] and children born on German soil by non-German parents were not granted territory-based citizenship (***jus soli***).

Only at the end of the 1990s did Germany slowly start to shift its perspective and move toward more liberal practices. With the Social Democrats (SPD) and the Green Party (Bündnis 90/Die Grünen) gaining power in the federal elections in 1998, a new citizenship act was decided upon and came into effect on 1 January 2000. The principle of territory-based citizenship was introduced for the first time ever. Thus, children who were born on German soil but of non-German parents were now automatically granted access to German citizenship if at least one of their parents either had been living in Germany as a legal resident for eight years, held permanent residency for at least three years, or had obtained residence entitlement. In addition, these children could also take up the citizenship of their parents. However, holding dual citizenship was only allowed for a limited amount of time, and by the age of 23, they had to decide on one citizenship only. This regulation came to be known as the *Optionspflicht* (the duty to choose) and was one of the most debated elements of the new legislation.

Recently, after a 14-year "experiment," the *Optionspflicht* was abolished, because it was feared that many of the young dual national Germans might decide against German citizenship. The new law was implemented on 13 November 2014 under the coalition government of the Christian Democrats (CDU/CSU) and the SPD. Hence, most of the children born on German soil to non-German parents, who obtained German citizenship upon birth since 2000,[2] are no longer required to choose between keeping their German citizenship or the one of their parents if they can prove that they grew up in Germany. This can be achieved if they have (a) been living in Germany for eight years, (b) visited a school in Germany for six years, or (c) graduated from a school or obtained professional training in Germany. For everybody else, the *Optionspflicht*—the need to choose one nationality only—remains intact.[3]

Canada: A Restrictive Turn in Citizenship Rules

Canada is usually identified as a "civic nation" promoting fairly liberal citizenship legislation that allows for the acquisition of citizenship by birth on national territory and unrestricted dual citizenship (since 1977). Given its multicultural policy since 1971, some scholars have alternatively suggested that Canada represents a "pluralistic-civic nation," which encourages the maintenance and public expression of ethnic group identities in addition to a shared national identity (Castles 1995).

However, between 2006 and 2015, the Canadian Conservative government adopted a more restrictive stance toward citizenship. On 19 June 2014, a new citizenship act received royal assent. Arguably, the Strengthening Canadian Citizenship Act made citizenship harder to get and easier to lose. The most disputed provisions relate to citizenship loss: the minister of citizenship and immigration has received considerable new authority that formerly belonged to the governor in council. The minister's office can now revoke citizenship (mostly for the offence of fraud), or grant it under non-routine circumstances (e.g., honorary citizenship). Specifically, the minister's office can revoke the citizenship of dual citizens who engage in actions contrary to the national interests of Canada (e.g., high treason, terrorism, espionage), and of those charged outside of Canada with an offence that, if committed in Canada, would be considered a serious criminal offence. This last provision is currently being repealed by the Liberal Party of Canada, which came to power in October 2015. While the Liberals softened the tone, as well as some of the stipulations introduced by the Conservatives, many of the tightened provisions regarding the uptake of citizenship have either remained identical or were only slightly altered.[4] For example, residency requirements now require four out of six (rather than three out of five) years of legal residency, as well as proof of physical presence in the country (rather than mere legal residence as was the case before 2014). Furthermore, citizenship candidates are now required to pass a language test before they are admitted to take the citizenship knowledge test in English or French (no translation allowed), which remains more difficult than it was before changes were introduced in 2009. Moreover, adult permanent residents are now required to file Canadian income tax returns as part of their application packages.

Contrasting Germany and Canada: Party Ideologies at Work?

Against the backdrop of the developments in Canada, it seems fair to say that Germany is on a progressive route toward opening up its citizenship regime. The steps may be small, but the direction is forward. In Canada, by contrast, there has been the feeling that previous citizenship provisions were taken advantage of, that the integrity of the system was compromised (e.g. by individuals cheating on the citizenship test), and that more meaning needed to be added to the citizenship acquisition process. As such, in recent years, Canada has been retracting previous provisions and is thereby restricting access to its citizenship. While, arguably, this trend was more pronounced under the Conservatives than under the Liberals, the overall direction is backward or, at the very least, characterized by stagnation. How can we account for this trend?

Joppke (2003) explains that irrespective of how a state defines itself, citizenship usually shows aspects of both ethnic and civic dimensions. Both dimensions are constantly negotiated and are highly dependent on the sitting government and its party's ideology. As such, Joppke (2003) claims that processes of "de-ethnicization"—facilitated access to citizenship through **naturalization**, *jus soli*, and toleration of dual citizenship (2003: 436, 441)—are often undertaken under left-leaning parties (437), whereas processes of "re-ethnicization"—emphasizing ascribed ethnic attributes for defining inclusion and exclusion—are commonly undertaken by right-leaning political parties (446).

How do these party ideologies play into citizenship politics in the German and Canadian case? In Germany, Angela Merkel (CDU) chairs a coalition government together with the more left-leaning SPD. Forming this coalition required that the CDU/CSU made certain concessions in order to be able to govern (Landeszentrale für politische Bildung Baden-Württemberg, 2013). One of the most significant concessions made was in regard to the abolition of the *Optionspflicht*. For the SPD, who had advocated dual citizenship since the late 1990s and taken up the abrogation of the *Optionspflicht* as a central point in their 2013 election platform, it was an absolute necessity to insist on the inclusion of this legislative change in the coalition treaty. Thus, the coalition negotiations were characterized by intense discussions about this issue (*Zeit Online*, 2013; *Taz*, 2013a; *Süddeutsche*, 2013; *Taz*, 2013b), and only after several rounds was a compromise (which now assures infinitive dual citizenship for the majority of those born and raised on German soil) ultimately found (Bundesregierung Deutschland 2013). Whereas for the SPD it was a necessity to fight for their election promise of abolishing the *Optionspflicht*, even the CDU/CSU benefit from the deal they have struck. On the one hand, having accepted dual citizenship for the majority of individuals with a so-called migration background will potentially allow them to recruit votes from this constituency in the upcoming years. On the other hand, this compromise that was "forced" upon them by the SPD also makes it possible to defend the move against more conservative critics from within the party. Thus, Joppke's claim that party ideologies matter for citizenship rules is certainly valid here. This is also true when analyzing the recent changes in Canada.

During their years in power, Stephen Harper's Conservatives pursued a policy of re-ethnicization, or "re-nationalization," as Winter and Sauvageau (2015) put it. Specifically, emphasis was placed on establishing a national identity based on "Canadian history and values" defined along traditional lines with reference to Britain and the monarchy. While the introduced measures did not reduce the overall naturalization rate—which remains one of the highest in the world—citizenship acquisition was made more cumbersome (Winter, 2014a) and potentially more selective along ethnic lines, as visible minorities are particularly affected by a declining citizenship test pass rate (Griffith, 2015). While this trend started under the Conservatives, it was not fully reversed under the Liberals (Griffith 2016). Hence, in this case, the impact of distinct party platforms on citizenship policy cannot easily be identified.

However, Conservatives and Liberals did strike very different *tones* regarding citizenship issues, which do run along party ideologies. One of the most important debates concerns the banning of face coverings at citizenship ceremonies—a 2011 policy by the Conservatives that was unequivocally interpreted as targeting niqab- and burqa-wearing Muslim women. When in 2015 the Supreme Court ruled twice that the ban of the niqab at citizenship ceremonies was unlawful, the Conservative government appealed this ruling both times. The Liberals, by contrast, built their 2015 election campaign on ethnic inclusiveness and stopped the appeal immediately after coming to power.

To conclude, contrary to the German case, where the conservative-leaning CDU/CSU benefited to some extent from citizenship liberalizations requested by the SPD, in Canada, the Liberal Party seems to condone many of the measures introduced by the Conservatives (e.g., physical presence required during residence period, standardized language tests for citizenship candidates, higher citizenship fees, more power to the minister concerning citizenship revocations and attributions). As such, they benefit from Conservative policies by not having to offend their more liberal-leaning constituencies while additionally harvesting praise from these constituencies for eliminating some of the Conservative policies that are very harsh in their consequences (e.g., citizenship revocation for dual nationals, face-veil banning at citizenship ceremonies), but symbolic in that only very few people would suffer their consequences. Recent citizenship policy development in Germany and Canada seems to follow opposing trends not because fundamentally different parties are in power or fundamentally different policy concerns are at stake. Rather, governments in both countries aim to safeguard the meaning of citizenship and the loyalty it commands. They do so according to different party platforms, policy imperatives, strategic considerations, politics, and very different historic starting points and conditions.[5]

Notes

1. Obtaining citizenship for individuals of non-German background was a long and complicated process, which could only be achieved through naturalization after at least fifteen years of residence in Germany (Storz and Wilmes 2007).
2. §4 section 3 of the citizenship act states that children of non-German parents who are born in Germany obtain German citizenship if one of their parents has lived in Germany for eight years and holds a permanent residency or as a citizen of Switzerland or a relative of the same has a residence permit on the basis of the agreement of free movement (from 21 July 1999 between the European Community and its member states on the one hand and the Swiss Confederation on the other hand) (Staatsbürgerschaftsgesetz 2000, §4 section 3(1)).
3. There is, however, a hardship provision for individuals who can prove to have a similar connection to Germany than those who were born and raised on German soil, but who, for diverse reasons, do not fulfill the criteria mentioned above (Deutscher Bundestag 2014, §29 section 1).
4. While Bill C-6 "An Act to amend the Citizenship Act and to make consequential amendments to another Act" (Parliament of Canada 2016, Bill C-6), is still under review, it will likely have been passed by the time this chapter is published.
5. See Winter (2014b) for a historical approach to Germany's and Canada's citizenship policies.

References

Brubaker, Rogers. 1992. *Citizenship and Nationhood in France and Germany.* Cambridge, MA: Harvard University Press.

Bundesregierung Deutschland. 2013. "Deutschlands Zukunft gestalten. Koalitionsvertrag zwischen CDU, CSU und SPD." Berlin. Accessed on 23 March 2015. http://www.bundesregierung.de/Content/DE/StatischeSeiten/Breg/koalitionsvertrag-inhaltsverzeichnis.html.

Castles, Stephen. 1995. "How Nation-States Respond to Immigration and Ethnic Diversity." *New Community,* 21(3), 293–308.

Deutscher Bundestag. 2014. "Gesetzentwurf der Bundesregierung. *Entwurf eines Zweiten Gesetzes zur Änderung des Staatsangehörigkeitsgesetzes.* Drucksache 18/1312 (05.05.2014)." Accessed on 23 March 2015. http://dip21.bundestag.de/dip21/btd/18/013/1801312.pdf.

Griffith, Andrew. 2015. "Canadian Citizenship: 'Harder to Get and Easier to Lose.'" Paper presented at the *Canadian Bar Association, National Immigration Law Conference*, 8 May. Accessed on 25 May 2015. https://multiculturalmeanderings.files.wordpress.com/2015/05/citizenship-cba-8-may-2015-final.pdf.

Griffith, Andrew. 2016. *Various Commentary on Citizenship Act Changes.* Accessed 5 March 2016. https://multiculturalmeanderings.wordpress.com/tag/andrew-griffith.

Joppke, Christian. 2003. "Citizenship between De- and Re-ethnicization." *European Journal of Sociology,* 44(3), 429–58.

Landeszentrale für politische Bildung Baden-Württemberg. "Bundestagswahl am 22. September 2013." Accessed on March 23, 2015. http://www.bundestagswahl-bw.d.

Parliament of Canada. 2016. "Bill C-6." Accessed on 8 January 2016. http://www.parl.gc.ca/HousePublications/Publication.aspx?Language=E&Mode=1&DocId=8380792.

Staatsbürgerschaftsgesetz. 2000. Accessed on March 27, 2015. http://www.gesetze-im-internet.de/bundesrecht/rustag/gesamt.pdf.

Storz, Henning, and Bernhard Wilmes. 2007. "Die Reform des Staatsangehörigkeitsrechts und das neue Einbürgerungsrecht." Bundeszentrale für politische Bildung. Accessed on 8 June 2015. http://www.bpb.de/gesellschaft/migration/dossier-migration/56483/einbuergerung.

Süddeutsche. 2013. "Doppelpass entzweit Union und SPD," November, 7. Accessed on 21 March 2015. http://www.sueddeutsche.de/politik/verhandlungen-zur-staatsbuergerschaft-doppelpass-entzweit-union-und-spd-1.1812917.

Taz. 2013a. "Keine Kompromisse," November 7. Accessed on 21 March 2015. http://www.taz.de/!5055457.

Taz. 2013b. "Gröhe könnte sich da was vorstellen," November 24. Accessed on 21 March 2015. http://www.taz.de/Streitthema-doppelte-Staatsbuergerschaft/!5054256.

Winter, Elke. 2014a. "Becoming Canadian—Making Sense of Recent Changes to Citizenship Rules." IRPP *Study (Montreal Institute for Research on Public Policy)* (44), 1–28. Accessed on March 21, 2015. http://www.irpp.org/en/research/diversity-immigration-and-integration/becoming-canadian.

Winter, Elke. 2014b. "Traditions of Nationhood or Political Conjuncture? Debating Citizenship in Canada and Germany," *Comparative Migration Studies*, 2(1), 295–321.

Winter, Elke, and Marie-Michèle Sauvageau. 2015. "Vers une compréhension nationaliste de la naturalisation au Canada? Analyse des changements récents en matière d'octroi de la citoyenneté dans le contexte canadien," *Canadian Journal of Law and Society/La Revue canadienne Droit et Société*, 30(1), 73–90.

Zeit Online. 2013. "Streit über doppelte Staatsbürgerschaft wird Chefsache," November 7. Accessed on 21 March 2015. http://www.zeit.de/politik/deutschland/2013-11/doppelte-staatsbuergerschaft-koalitionsverhandlungen-union-spd.

Questions for Critical Thought

Chapter 60 | The Ambivalence of Diplomacy

1. What was the significance of Harper and Putin shaking hands? What aspect of this gesture was interesting to sociologists?
2. Is diplomacy an art? How can this be seen through gestures and language?
3. What does the casual conversation offer that diplomacy does not? Why is balancing the two types of communication important for politicians?
4. Referring to Simmel's theory, how is diplomacy a distinct social form?
5. How should sociologists understand the role of diplomacy in political domains? How does this knowledge enhance our understanding of politics?

Chapter 61 | Policy Networks, Policy Transfers, and Recommodification: Actors and Mechanisms of Labour Policy Formation in Post-Yugoslav Countries

1. What three interrelated factors influence labour policy formation in Croatia, Slovenia, and Serbia? How?
2. What is a policy network? Why is this the best framework to use when examining Croatia, Slovenia, and Serbia?
3. Describe the three sections of policy networks using examples from Croatia, Slovenia, or Serbia.
4. What are the labour conditions like in Croatia, Slovenia, and Serbia?
5. From learning about the labour policy and labour conditions within Croatia, Slovenia, and Serbia, what do you think the social stratification is like in these countries? How do you think power is divided?

Chapter 62 | Political Engagement through Civic Transnationalism: Romanian Diasporas and the 2014 Presidential Elections

1. How can social networking sites facilitate political participation?
2. What activities count as political participation? How can these behaviours be performed in-person and online?
3. Compare the campaigning strategies of Klaus Iohannis and Victor Ponta. How were they similar and different? What demographic did they each appeal to?
4. Who won the first round of the election? How did the Romanian diasporas react?
5. Who won the election? What role did social media play in this candidate's success?
6. Will social media play a large role in future political action? What does Visan think? What do you think?

Chapter 63 | Liberalizing versus Tightening Citizenship Rules in Germany and Canada: A Question of Party Platforms and Politics?

1. How have Germany's citizenship regulations changed over time?
2. How have Canada's citizenship regulations changed over time?
3. Look at both Canada's and Germany's current citizenship regulations. Which is more exclusionary? Is this surprising? Why?
4. Why do the authors focus on citizenship? What does this reveal about the social climate in each of these countries?
5. What are the ongoing implications of Stephen Harper's conservative government on citizenship and racial/ethnic relations in Canada?

PART XVI
Technology and Mass Media

The world is constantly changing, and nothing shows that more clearly than the evolution of technology in the last 20 years. As computers emerged, evolved, and became commonplace in North American homes, people became more connected both locally and around the world. Today's technology lets people access and transmit information effortlessly, through the Internet. In this section, you will learn more about the relationship between technology and society: the harms as well as the benefits that new technology can bring.

To begin, *technology* is the application of science for a practical purpose, or to solve a problem that arises in daily life. The flowering of science has hastened the evolution of technologies from primitive stone tools to modern smartphones. In this section, we focus on communication technologies such as computers, cellphones, and tablets—technologies used in everyday life. Understanding the way that communication technologies affect people and their behaviour is of central interest to sociologists.

One of the main ways in which technology affects people is by spreading information. Typically, information is spread by media: that is, by print or digital means of communication. Media take a variety of forms: newspapers, magazines, radio, television, and most recently the Internet. The information conveyed through media shapes people's attitudes, consumption patterns, and sense of what is important. In this sense, the media set the agenda for public discussion of social issues. As media become more accessible, they create new forms of social interaction and new ways for individuals to relate to one another. In the past, for example, people might cut interesting articles out of the newspaper; today, they are more likely to send someone a link to the article, or "share" it.

There would be no modern media without modern technology. With the invention of the printing press, it became possible to efficiently reproduce and disseminate written material. With the invention of the computer and Internet, it became possible to efficiently reproduce and disseminate forms of material for which we scarcely have names yet: they include blogs, tweets, and e-zines. Technology has expanded our ability to communicate easily with distant friends and family, while also allowing us to expand our social circles online through social networking or dating sites. Rather than catching up with friends over the phone, you might be more inclined to send them a text. And rather than raising your hand to ask teachers a question in class, you might prefer to send them an email. Essentially, technology has enhanced our ability to communicate.

So advances in communication technology have brought many positive changes, but they have also brought new associated uncertainties and hazards. In this section, the authors analyze specific elements of information and communication technologies to critically evaluate their potential impact. First, in Chapter 64, David Lyon describes how the collection of "big data" can leave people vulnerable to unwanted surveillance, personal intrusion, and online inequalities. Moreover, Jonathan Roberge and Thomas Crosbie, examining the social character of algorithms in Chapter 65, suggest that biases in these algorithms potentially limit people's access to information. In Chapter 66, Mihai Sarbu describes the important influence of the evolving ideas and technology on nature.

Finally, Mark Stoddart and Jillian Smith, in Chapter 67, explore the news coverage of climate deterioration. These authors find that news reports do not focus on climate justice: the reports blame climate deterioration on the countries that are deteriorating, not the countries that cause deterioration. In short, they blame the victim.

64 The Missing "V" of Big Data: Surveillance and Vulnerability

David Lyon

Recently I had to go to the hospital emergency department, where I showed my Ontario health card and the triage nurse duly entered my details. But when I went to register as a patient, warning bells went off. My story didn't match the record. Apologetically, a nurse cut off my new ID band and gave me another. "Wrong David Lyon," she said. Two minutes later, red-faced now, she was back with her scissors. "Sorry, your band reads 'David Lynn,' but this new one's finally correct."

For the period during which I was wearing the wrong bracelet, I was vulnerable to confused or risky decisions about my health just because of a mistake with my electronic record. What if I'd been given drugs to which I'm allergic or the wrong treatment for my condition? This has been a problem area for the digital world for a long time, but today the situation is further complicated by the fact that our digital makeup includes much that was never entered by us or someone in touch with us, but rather was inferred from many sources, direct and indirect—from us or from others. How does this work?

Facebook's social graph appeared in 2007, using its then three-quarter billion Facebook users to plot a graph, and concluding that our "degrees of separation" are closer to four than the six suggested controversially in the 1960s by Stanley Milgram.[1] Facebook's social graph uses sophisticated graph theory to analyze relationships: who's connected with whom in what ways and what does this mean for our chances and choices? The US National Security Agency (NSA) jumped on this bandwagon in 2010.

Documents obtained from the NSA by Edward Snowden and released in 2013 show that the spy agency used information garnered from phone call and email logs to make graphs of Americans' social connections. They identify users' associates, locations at particular times, and who they may be travelling with, along with other information. They wish to "discover and track" connections between people in the US and overseas intelligence targets by using "large-scale graph analysis on very large sets of communications metadata. . . ."[2]

Phone and email data are combined with other information from public, commercial, and other sources, including "[F]acebook profiles, passenger manifests, voter registration rolls and GPS location information as well as property records and unspecified tax data" to be analyzed in innovative ways. These are "big data" practices, often described in "Vs" such as "volume, velocity, and variety."

Big data practices, says the NSA, are "revolutionizing" data collection and analysis, making possible more "complete and predictive" understanding of behaviour than is available from the content of phone calls and emails. **Metadata** can reveal religious and political affiliations, as well as information about medical conditions and, of course, networks of relationships.

This information, often handled by the NSA's "Mainway" program, seeks so-called entity types of phone numbers, email and IP addresses, and also 164 "relationship types" and "community of interest" profiles showing information such as with whom people travel, who they employ, or what forum they contribute to. These may be combined with social media data, billing records, and bank codes.

The mapping of social connections using sophisticated algorithms and statistical analysis is a key component of big data. Adopted by corporations, government departments, and public health and educational organizations, it addresses questions of efficiency and productivity and pinpoints likely target groups of all kinds—whether voters, consumers, patients, criminals, or high achievers.

How Big Data Makes Some Groups More Vulnerable Than Others

In the US, several studies have shown conclusively that large-scale use of metadata does not produce the results once claimed for them—successfully predicting terrorist attacks, for instance. But other kinds of results may occur. Those results may produce "vulnerability," the missing V of big data. This is hardly surprising given the history of big data.

It was the software-and-statistics amplification of disadvantage that helped make the concept of "**social sorting**"[3] so compelling as a means of showing the effects of surveillance from the 1990s onward. Consumer surveillance had grown as geodemographic marketing methods took off from the later 1980s. This clustered consumers into postal codes (zip codes in the US) on the logic that "birds of a feather flock together"—spawning categories from "rural hardscrabble" or "bohemian mix" to "money and brains."

The computer-enhanced logic of surveillance—to classify populations so that different groups can be treated differently—means advertising can be more precisely targeted. But it also has negative effects for some, not just in the consumer sphere but in an array of contexts. As Oscar Gandy demonstrates so effectively in his work on such "sorting machines," "rational discrimination" can also too easily produce "cumulative disadvantage" for some.[4]

The New Transparency Project in Canada[5] shows clearly that while **surveillance** occurs largely behind a veil of legal and commercial secrecy, it peels back the onion of privacy for those who are studied. We become more visible to organizations that are less visible to us.

Richards and King[6] include this kind of analysis in what they call "big data paradoxes." The "identity paradox" is that while ordinary users of devices say they wish to maintain control over their identity—how they are seen by others—big data defines identity for us in ways that go far beyond what is on a health card, for instance. We depend on how we are identified to corporations or government for the products we see, the information presented to us, and the choices we make. Our profiles affect everything—from pizza toppings to Google data mining to crossing borders. Another paradox, "power," follows. Big data promises to "revolutionize" our lives, but the means of doing so are in the hands of powerful institutions.

A key reason why big data practices must be checked for their contribution to vulnerability is that similar methods are used for different purposes. Big data is all about trends, shifting social graphs, and prediction. The point is to be better prepared to anticipate risk and face the future, to know what's coming so that those who have to make decisions will be ready. But prediction comes in different packages.

What kinds of prediction are enabled by big data practices?[7] Consequential predictions try to show the likely outcomes of actions so that the least risky option can be chosen. Preferential predictions, familiar through online marketing, try to influence consumer decisions and increase sales. But *pre-emptive* predictions have a different purpose: to diminish someone's range of future options. These have less to do with the persons themselves and more with the state or corporation creating no-fly lists or choosing to hire employees on the basis of data profiles.

Big data contributes to vulnerability, for example, by expanding categories of suspicion that end up denying basic rights, such as the presumption of innocence. The supposed "duty to prevent" harms, especially to so-called national security, has led to the denial of human rights to some innocent people. If sophisticated data analysis suggests that someone might be a "threat," then they will be subject to suspicion, whether warranted or not in a traditional sense. As Kerr and Earle say, such challenges cannot be met by tweaking data protection regimes. Basic issues of **due process** and **privacy** are at stake.[7]

It was Gary T. Marx who—in the 1980s—first used the expression "categories of suspicion" in his groundbreaking analysis of the "new surveillance."[8] He noted a negative trend in policing that was enhanced by the use of new technologies. Today, that trend has ballooned into a central feature of surveillance, which in many fields is obsessed with categorical suspicion—profiling people by reference to those with whom they are associated.

And this is not only a matter of police surveillance. It occurs in many fields, all of which now take their lead, effectively, from marketing, Facebook style.

Surveillance and Vulnerability

As noted earlier, the fact that profiles and categories may be constructed from consumer data means that very varied criteria may be at work in assembling a given data double or online persona or profile. Disadvantages across a range of social sectors and life areas may be brought together, making vulnerabilities both intersect and reinforce each other. Different dimensions of inequality may thus be analyzed in relation to each other, creating a complex matrix of vulnerability.

The main vulnerability relates to discrimination, which of course can be negative as well as positive. In 2015, the Truth and Reconciliation Commission report was released in Canada, claiming that "cultural genocide" occurred in Canada and that many kinds of surveillance contributed to the discrimination, neglect, and destruction of Aboriginal groups in this country.

Scott Thompson's work shows clearly the role of surveillance, for example, by the Liquor Control Board of Ontario (LCBO), in sorting between white and Aboriginal groups, protecting and privileging the one and denying and labelling the other.[9] Stereotypes about addiction were fostered through the extensive bureaucratic surveillance engaged in by the LCBO.

Today, discrimination and the vulnerabilities associated with social sorting are amplified by big data practices. Under Canada's Anti-terrorism Act (C-51, 2015) Canadians may be placed on no-fly lists, for example, when the minister of public safety *suspects* that they might commit an act threatening transportation security. Such suspicions are fuelled by big data inferences and produce significant reduction of liberty.

All this means that classic social questions of justice and rights are raised. As big data is increasingly used to predict futures and guide policy decisions, so in its surveillant dimensions it will continue to inform pre-emptive prediction and thereby create fresh forms of vulnerability. The negative effects of such surveillance are mutually reinforcing, thus heightening the risks of certain groups being denied rights more than others.

The story of my health card, which began this paper, sounds like a personal problem, experienced by just me. But many others are misidentifed by health, educational, law enforcement, and other agencies. These are not just individual experiences. Big data practices magnify this problem enormously for individuals and population clusters. As C. Wright Mills[10] would have insisted, these are social and public issues on a huge scale. They are consequences of the increasing digitization of society, particularly the consequences of new forms of surveillance.

This means, in turn, that we have to consider political activities, to engage in research not only on resisting worst case scenarios or minimizing potential harms, but also on how to seek real alternatives through imagining things differently.[11] As questions of rights are raised, we will need to be clear about what rights are, how they are based in human dignity, and what Julie Cohen calls the "structural conditions for human flourishing."[12]

Few question the "volume, velocity, or variety" of big data, but by focusing on these we may easily neglect the missing V of big data—vulnerability. New surveillance practices reveal some of the key conundrums of modernity, in which the liquidity[13] of surveillance is both a challenge to critical analysis—it's a public issue not just a personal trouble—and a reminder that things can be different.

Notes

1. Mike Isaac. 2011. "Facebook study: It's a small(er) world after all." *Wired*. 22 November. At http://www.wired.com/2011/11/facebook-social-graph-study
2. James Risen and Laura Poitras. 2013. "NSA gathers data on social connections of US citizens." *New York Times*, 28 September. At http://www.nytimes.com/2013/09/29/us/nsa-examines-social-networks-of-us-citizens.html. See also, David Lyon. 2015. *Surveillance after Snowden*. Cambridge and New York: Polity.
3. David Lyon, ed. 2003. *Surveillance as Social Sorting: Privacy, Risk and Digital Discrimination*. London and New York: Routledge.
4. Oscar Gandy. 2011. *Coming to Terms with Chance: Engaging Rational Discrimination and Cumulative Disadvantage*. London: Ashgate.
5. Colin Bennett, Kevin Haggerty, David Lyon, and Valerie Steeves, eds. 2014. *Transparent Lives: Surveillance in Canada*. Edmonton, AB: Athabasca University Press.
6. Richards and King. 2013. "Three paradoxes of big data." *Stanford Law Review* 41: 41–46.
7. Ian Kerr and Jessica Earle. 2013. "Prediction, preemption, presumption." *Stanford Law Review* online, 3 September. At http://www.stanfordlawreview.org/online/privacy-and-big-data/prediction-preemption-presumption
8. Gary T. Marx. 1988. *Undercover: Police Surveillance in America*. Berkeley: University of California Press.
9. Gary Genosko and Scott Thompson. 2009. *Punched Drunk: Alcohol, Surveillance and the LCBO 1927–1975*. Toronto: Fernwood.
10. C. Wright Mills. 1959. *The Sociological Imagination*. New York: Oxford University Press.
11. Ruth Levitas. 2014. *Utopia as Method*. London: Palgrave Macmillan.
12. Julie Cohen. 2012. *Configuring the Networked Self*. New Haven, CT: Yale University Press.
13. See Zygmunt Bauman and David Lyon. 2013. *Liquid Surveillance*. Cambridge: Polity Press.

65 Algorithmic Sociology: An Emerging Field

Jonathan Roberge and Thomas Crosbie

Algorithms, the step-by-step procedures for calculations entrenched in software codes, are pervasive features of contemporary life. In the first part of this chapter, we outline the key features of the new sociology of algorithms. In the second part, we introduce an important site for research, namely the cultural, political, and economic dimensions of visualization algorithms. Our focus is on a phenomenon we refer to as "**deep sight**": rich, multi-tiered visual data streams that situate actors in dynamic, meaning-laden environments. We believe that algorithmic visuality will change representation and the interpretation of culture more broadly. We also believe many social scientists will be forced to grapple with the subtle effects of algorithms, and we hope our research on deep sight will help guide the way to a truly algorithmic sociology.

Part 1: Toward a New Sociology of Algorithms

The earliest theories of cyberspace and digital culture often embraced techno-utopianism, a sort of wide-eyed optimism that had much in common with the ideas of the founder of sociology, August Comte (Turner, 2006; Featherstone and Burrows, 1995). However, this enthusiasm soon gave way to pessimistic accounts, many by commenters who followed Karl Marx in warning against the alienating effects of modern technology (Shepard, 1977).

Today, scholars struggle to balance the good and the bad in more or less equal measure. If new technology is neither the salvation of an imperfect society nor its damnation, nevertheless we cannot ignore technology's transformative effect on the social world. And indeed, a very complex reality is quite literally taking form through the exponential growth of the Internet of things (Giusto et al, 2010) and wearable computing (Amyx, 2014). A society of individuals adorned with computing technology that accounts for our health, tracks our movements, connects with global networks, talks to satellites, and provides us with information on command is no longer science fiction but everyday life.

One starting point for a sociology of algorithms is the question of data. Even if we try to keep our use of technology to a minimum, we still produce massive amounts of public- and private-sector data, eagerly but imperfectly gathered by interested parties. The quantification of social life relies on data, but data are never "raw" (Gitelman, 2013). Rather, data must be sorted and organized in order to be used. Algorithms are in this sense mathematical solutions to create order in complex ensembles, "to identify patterns and to provide links between seemingly dissociated or heterogeneous elements" (Willson, 2014: 4). From a computer science perspective, then, algorithms are generally viewed as both objective and rational (Cormen et al., 2009: 4). As such, they are emblems of the process whereby the messiness of reality is translated into tractable computational processes. This appearance of objectivity and rationality is deceptive, of course, since human error and coding biases inevitably seep in.

Because algorithms select, order, and sort the data used in computing tasks, today's technology is algorithmic all the way down. Algorithms create both **path dependence** (Pierson, 2000), meaning that they establish patterns that are ever harder to break, and Matthew effects (Merton, 1968), meaning that these patterns tend to allow for advantages and disadvantages in network placement to keep compounding over and over. This insight has inspired scholars in the fields of science and technology studies (STS) and the social science of finance to develop their own sociologies of algorithms (e.g. Beer, 2009; MacKenzie, 2014). Scholars recognized the vast power of algorithms to shape our access to information, privileging some network nodes while silencing and suppressing others.

Since so much computing is unseen by human eyes, epistemological problems (problems of knowing) may become ontological ones (problems of being). In other words, we are confronted not with technical questions of computing but rather with social questions of legitimacy and representation. Neyland (2015: 131) poses this dilemma in a set of questions: "Who and what is included or excluded, on what terms and to what ends?" When we rely on algorithms to make sense of the world, we thereby change our access to the world. Accordingly, often lacking from the science-focused approaches to the sociology of algorithms is the social dimension, including the intersection of algorithms with culture, politics, and economics. In our case study of algorithmic visuality, we provide a model for tackling how one class of algorithms shape social life across these three dimensions.

Part 2: Deep Sight and Everyday Life

Much of our visual culture was shaped in the age of monitors rendering data in text blocks on a two-dimensional surface. Today, however, we have entered a new regime of algorithmic visuality, in which our access to increasingly automated, mobile, and accurate images is supplemented by artificial intelligence and machine learning capacities. Currently, prominent actors in the technology sector, including Google, Facebook, and Amazon, are shifting their corporate strategy to focus on bringing algorithmic visuality into mainstream consumer culture (Featherstone, 2009). Technologies such as augmented eyewear and drones mounted with and guided by 360-degree high-definition cameras are now being placed in dialogue with one another, creating rich, multi-tiered data streams—"deep sight" that situates actors in dynamic, meaning-laden environments. The outcome is enormously powerful data, crucially linking street-level, virtual, and aerial perspectives.

We view algorithmic visuality as a key site for research in the new sociology of algorithms; at present, it is an understudied sociological phenomenon, with industry understanding far outstripping social scientific inquiry, and with almost no research to date on its cultural, economic, and political consequences. There are of course exceptions, including Parmeggiani's (2009) use of cutting-edge visualization technologies to allow Italian villagers to consider the transformation of their home, and Hoelzl and Marie's (2014) study of Oslo by way of Google Street View. Mostly, however, the sociology of algorithmic visuality is yet to be written.

From a *cultural* point of view, new media technologies are rooted in the complex processes involved in creating, maintaining, and potentially losing cultural support. Indeed, while objects, like the Glass and Rift virtual reality headsets, and practices, like the drone delivery of parcels by Amazon's Prime Air or Google's Wing, may come in time to be viewed as legitimate, they may instead languish, never accepted as elements of the social realm. Nothing is predetermined by the technology. Everyday experience is thus key to the appropriation process. And so, as immersive environments and wearable computing are on the rise, so too affect and embodiment become ever more significant (Featherstone and Burrows, 1995). For deep-sight technologies, meaning is projected onto the world by adding emotional, normative, and aesthetic depth to context and interaction, contributing to a new "everyday aesthetic" (Murray, 2008).

While culture is an important element in the story of algorithmic visuality, the *economic component* is equally significant. The term *gafanomics* captures the key dynamics at play: fusion and acquisition; venture capital; and research and patents (Fabernovel, 2014). More specifically, it refers to the intense competition between Google, Amazon, Facebook, and Apple in the adoption of technological standards. As each endeavours to achieve full integration and interoperability of devices on their own proprietary platforms, they create a "co-operative struggle" with broad ramifications (Crandall, 2010). For example, Google will soon have a fleet of small satellites able to generate one terabyte of imagery per day, enough to boost the accuracy of all of Google Maps, including their "ground truth" and "Google Cars" projects. And yet, full integration and dominance is a long way away. Competitors such as Facebook, Nokia, Sony, and others are all at work on different "live" or "deep" representations of the physical world (Miller, 2014).

Scholars have argued that *power and politics* are "inscribed in the very materiality" of new technologies (Winner, 1980). In the case of deep sight, a concern is the potential for surveillance. Surveillance scholarship has long drawn on the metaphor of CCTV video recordings, but it increasingly recognizes the performativity of data processing and learning algorithms (Andrejevic, 2006). The key difference is that the latter can now shape data automatically and recursively. Image analytics and real-time information mining supplemented by and cross-referenced with multiple data streams facilitate the gathering, detecting, predicting, and targeting capacities of powerful actors with an interest in exerting influence over the lives of ordinary people.

Concluding Thoughts

Algorithms shape our lives in countless ways. For computer scientists, this impact is often viewed as a simple matter of whether a code fixes a problem as efficiently as possible. Sociologists have a more complex view. Science-oriented scholars have noted that algorithms have largely unrecognized effects on how we access data about the social world. They conclude that algorithms are not neutral processes but are rather co-constitutive of the outcome. A new community of scholars is emerging, however, with a more refined conception of the social character of algorithms, teasing out cultural, political, and economic sites where algorithms contribute to the shaping of the social world.

We explore the case of algorithmic visuality, those visualization technologies such as Google Glass, Amazon Prime Air, and Oculus Rift that create immersive, real-time, and multi-dimensional data streams. Here and in many other areas of social life, algorithms create dramatically new configurations of meaning, power, and access to resources. Integrating all of these lessons and more into our practice of social science is the challenge that confronts us today as we work toward a truly algorithmic sociology.

References

Amyx, Scott. (2014). "Wearing Your Intelligence: How to Apply Artificial Intelligence in Wearables and IoT." *Wired*, 4 December. Accessed from: http://www.wired.com/2014/12/wearing-your-intelligence.

Andrejevic, Mark. (2006). "The Discipline of Watching: Detection, Risk, and Lateral Surveillance." *Critical Studies in Media Communication*, 23: 391–407.

Beer, David. (2009). "Power Through the Algorithm? Participatory Web Cultures and the Technological Unconscious." *New Media and Society*, 11: 985–1002.

Cormen, Thomas H., Leiserson, Charles E., Rivest, Ronald L., and Stein, Clifford. (2009). *Introduction to Algorithms*, Third Edition. Cambridge, MA: MIT Press and McGraw-Hill.

Crandall, Jordan. (2010) The Geospatialization of Calculative Operations: Tracking, Sensing and Megacities." *Theory, Culture & Society*, 27(6): 68–90.

Fabernovel. (2014). "GAFAnomics." October. Accessed from: http://www.slideshare.net/faber Novel/gafanomics

Featherstone, Mike and Burrows, Roger (eds). (1995). *Cyberspace/Cyberbodies/Cyberpunk: Cultures of Technological Embodiment*. London: SAGE.

Featherstone, Mike and Yoshimi, Shunya (eds.). (2009). *Ubiquitous Media*. London: SAGE.

Gitelman, Lisa. (2013). *Raw Data Is an Oxymoron*. Cambridge, MA: MIT Press.

Giusto, Daniel, Iera, Antonio, Morabito, Giacomo and Atzori, Luigi (eds). (2010). *The Internet of Things: 20th Tyrrhenian Workshop on Digital Communications*. New York: Springer.

Hoelzl, Ingrid and Marine, Rémi. (2014). "Google Street View: Navigating the Operative Image." *Visual Studies*, 29(3): 261–71.

Johnson, Cathryn, Dowd, Timothy J., and Ridgeway, Cecilia L. (2006). "Legitimacy as a Social Process." *American Review of Sociology*, 32(1): 53–78.

Lash, Scott. (2007). "Power after Hegemony: Cultural Studies in Mutation?" *Theory, Culture & Society*, 24(3): 55–78.

Liker, Jeffrey K., Haddad, Carol J., and Karlin, Jennifer. (1999). "Perspectives on Technology and Work Organization." *Annual Review of Sociology*, 25: 575–96.

MacKenzie, Donald (2014). "A Sociology of Algorithms: High-Frequency Trading and the Shaping of Markets," working paper.

Merton, Robert M. (1968). "The Matthew Effect in Science." *Science*, 159: 56–63.

Miller, Greg. (2014). "The Huge, Unseen Operation Behind the Accuracy of Google Maps." *Wired*, 8 December. Accessed from: http://www.wired.com/2014/12/google-maps-ground-truth/?mbid=social_fb.

Murray, Susan. (2008). "Digital Images, Photo-Sharing and Our Shifting Notions of Everyday Aesthetics." *Journal of Visual Culture*, 7(2): 147–63.

Neyland. Daniel. (2015). "On Organizing Algorithms." *Theory, Culture & Society*, 32(1): 119–32.

Parmeggiani, Paolo. (2007). "'Alas there are only sixteen of us left': Social Disintegration, Identity Transformation, and Visual Changes in a Rural Italian Village." In *Framing Globalization: Visual Perspectives*, P. Faccioli and J.A. Gibbons (eds). Newcastle, UK: Cambridge Scholars Publishing.

Pierson, Paul. (2000). "Increasing Returns, Path Dependence, and the Study of Politics." *The American Political Science Review*, 94(2): 251–67.

Shepard, Jon M. (1977). "Technology, Alienation and Job Satisfaction." *Annual Review of Sociology*, 3: 1–21.

Turner, Fred. (2006). "How Digital Technology Found Utopian Ideology: Lessons from the First Hackers' Conference." In *Critical Cyber-Culture*, David Silver and Adrienne Massanari (eds). New York: New York University Press.

Willson, Michele A. (2014)."The Politics of Social Filtering." *Convergence: The International Journal of Research into New Media Technologies*, 2(2): 218–32.

Winner, Langdon. (1980). "Do Artefacts Have Politics?" *Daedalus*, 109: 121–36.

66 (Re)defining Climate Change as a Cultural Phenomenon[1]

Mihai Sarbu

"It is hard to imagine," argued Mircea Eliade a while ago, "how the human spirit could function without the conviction that there is something irreducibly *real* in the world; and it is impossible to imagine how the conscience could appear without conferring a *signification* to the impulses and experiences of humans" (1976, p. 7).[2] The essential claim of this paper is that our *cultural* heritage is a burden that hinders our efforts of dealing with **climate change**. I examine critically the assumption, common in the Western culture, that we need to "hold on tight," individually and collectively, to what we consider as being *ultimate truths*; this assumption is linked to religious ideas about a transcendent realm accessible only through reason and contemplation, which evolved into ideas separating the body from the mind and the humans from the biosphere, and were materialized in hierarchical social structures. I will also argue in favour of finding alternative ways of thinking that could be helpful in dealing with the challenges that lie ahead.

The Typical Evolution of an "Ultimate Truth"[3]

The questionable "certainties" that are taken, time and again, to constitute *ultimate truths* are, as I will argue below, historically and socially constructed. Without the pretence of providing a thorough account on this matter, I think the steps described below can be taken as being generally valid for what I termed "the typical evolution of an ultimate truth." It is likely that after confronting the difficulties of a given life situation, whether social, economic, conceptual, or a combination thereof, a human community should develop an *emerging awareness* (Hacking, 2010, p. 73) of an eventual solution. The more difficult the challenge, the worthier of praise will be those who can formulate a solution to it, and the greater the danger that their solution will end up being mythologized as an *ultimate truth*.

This danger is always present, because, once adopted and implemented, the solution becomes **path-dependent** (Homer-Dixon, 2008, pp. 26–7), and will increasingly crystallize the energies of the community. Social structures will evolve around this solution and will develop with it symbiotic relationships. If and when it ends up being considered an ultimate truth, the solution becomes one of the unquestionable foundations of that particular culture, and those who have the power to define its meanings will become its ruling elites.

A foundation has to be *fixed*—it becomes dogma, and the fact that the original solution only solved a problem which, although important, was limited in space and time, is conveniently ignored. As the world around changes, the (old) solution and those who represent it become a hindrance for further development. Confronted with the progressive inadequacy of their conceptions, the ruling elites are unlikely to reconsider them, since this would also put in question their role. Although they may agree to some minor adjustments, they are much more likely to dig in their heels and fight change.

As things continue to evolve, the old "solution," now most likely an empty shell, has to be maintained by force[4] and fear; at the same time, a new emerging awareness is likely to indicate the possibility of a new solution. Things may not change immediately, but once the new solution gathers critical mass the cycle leading to another paradigm shift will start again and—if history can be a guide—such turning points can be associated with very serious suffering.

Religion and the "God-given" order of the medieval world have defined the "ultimate truth" of Western societies for many centuries. Due to space limitations I cannot elaborate on the important changes that took place since then; however, I argue that the tendency to mythologize our social arrangements has manifested itself repeatedly and sometimes very conspicuously.[5] I further argue that neoliberalism represents the "ultimate truth" of Western societies today. Neoliberalism is promoted aggressively in spite of its failures: an increasing inability of fulfilling its promise of material prosperity, increasing social inequalities, and the widespread destruction of nature.

There is a slightly different angle that may contribute to improving this analysis. It relates to the "new/old" cycle described above but it is somewhat different; the element to be considered is the *degree of familiarity* of a certain idea or situation. One can only imagine how shocking the idea of a heliocentric universe was when it first appeared. However, with the passage of time, it became normalized, and today it is not even worth mentioning. This is just the way things *are*, because a heliocentric universe is a part of our *life-world*.

The term *life-world* (*Lebenswelt*) has been made famous by Edmund Husserl, although it has been used by others before him (Føllesdal, 2010, p. 27). In Husserl's words, "The life-world is the natural world—in the attitude of the natural pursuit of life we are living functioning subjects involved in the circle of other functioning subjects" (as cited in Føllesdal, 2010, p. 39). In other words, life in the life-world entails just "functioning"—that is, living unreflectively, immersed in everyday routines and surrounded by other people who do the same.

An essential aspect "of any life-world is its *pre-reflective*, taken for granted nature. People exist for the most part in their life-world like fish in water" (Inglis, 2005, p. 12, emphasis added). To materialize this degree of familiarity (or lack thereof) one can think of an idea or situation that is (perceived as) totally foreign and then compare it with another that is (perceived as) an integral part of one's environment. Both extremes are historically and socially constructed and some relevant examples are given below.

Climate and Social Hierarchies

Lucian Boia (2005) provides several accounts on how climate was conceptualized by different ancient civilizations. There are significant commonalities between these accounts, regardless of the geographical locations of their authors. One commonality is the fact that humans are seen as powerless in the face of the forces of nature. But more interestingly, each civilization perceives its own climate as ideal and conducive to great virtues, while seeing the climate of other civilizations as bad—the farther away, the worse (Boia, 2005, pp. 15–40). According to the geographer Strabo,

> The Britons were distinguished by their barbarity, but the Irish were even worse, being both herbivorous and cannibalistic (the two extremes of alimentary otherness brought together). They considered it both a duty and a pleasure to eat their dead kin. An unbridled sexual promiscuity completes the picture: all women were fair game to the men, including their own mothers and sisters. There was nothing to be done—it was all the climate's fault. (Boia, 2005, p. 26)

It is clear that in this case both normality and otherness were socially constructed, and climate was used to rank civilizations from good (one's own) to bad (those of other people). Fast forward 1,500 years and we could see again the pattern of such discourses: the Native people from the territories newly discovered by the Europeans were described in similar terms. In that period "Western Europeans were growing rapidly richer, and were becoming lords of all the world" (Russell, 2005, p. 495). However, this was achieved at the expense of countless Indigenous people from Africa, Asia, Australia, Oceania, and the Americas. A notable exception is Japan; a decisive factor for the different outcome of the interaction between Japanese and Europeans was probably the fact that in the seventeenth-century Japan was unified under the military rule of the Tokugawa shogunate. After 1640, the Japanese treated the Europeans as savagely as the Europeans treated Indigenous people elsewhere.[6]

Hundreds of years have passed, but dominating other humans by force or the threat of using it, in the name of a perceived superiority carefully cultivated by social elites all around the world, still remains a central paradigm of our civilization. This paradigm has worked in the past; however, what we need now is not force but *restraint*. At the time of writing, our consumption of resources amounts to more than 1.6 planets: what Earth can regenerate in a year is consumed in less than seven and a half months.[7] This is a deeply unsustainable path.[8] Dominating and exploiting other people, while risky and ethically repugnant, is a modus operandi of our civilization. Trying to dominate nature is much more dangerous.

Conclusion

The Western culture is impregnated with ideas of separation of body and mind, separation of humans from the rest of the biosphere, superiority of humans over the rest of nature, and superiority of Westerners over all other people. These conceptions constitute a heavy cultural baggage, which burdens us in our fight against climate change. Moreover, the mindset of seeing ourselves special, and our habit of holding on tight to our "ultimate truths" may contribute to the inertia that characterizes our inadequate response to the crisis of climate change.

It is important to be aware of this heavy cultural heritage, because in order to fight climate change we will have to change many of our own preconceived ideas and well-established habits. We need to culturally redefine the preciousness and irreplaceability of the web of life, of which we are only an infinitesimal part, as being of utmost importance for all humans; this task is exceedingly difficult due to the mundane and, at least in the Western culture, repulsive status that is most of the time assigned to biological processes (Inglis, 2005, p. 106). An equally difficult and important cultural task is to redefine many of our current practices, such as the dumping of CO^2 in the atmosphere, the dumping of plastic and effluents in the oceans, overfishing, soil degradation, the over-exploitation of water and minerals, and the widespread destruction of species and ecosystems, as what they are: crimes[9] against the biosphere.

Last but not least, we need to act soon. We need to experiment,[10] to imagine and enact new ways of living and appreciating life within the confines of the biosphere. Such efforts need to mobilize a very large number of individuals, and therefore social learning[11] becomes very important.

Notes

1. Winner of the 2015 Best Doctoral Student Paper Award presented by the Environmental Sociology Research Cluster of the Canadian Sociological Association
2. The English translation of Eliade's work was not available to me at the time of writing. The French passage reads as follows: "Il est difficile d'imaginer comment l'esprit humain pourrait fonctionner sans la conviction qu'il y a quelque chose d'irréductiblement réel dans le monde; et il est impossible d'imaginer comment la conscience pourrait apparaître sans conférer une signification aux impulsions et aux expériences de l'homme" (1976, p. 7).
3. This is how I interpret the expression "something irreducibly real"; if other things can be reduced to it, then their

reality, and therefore truthfulness, become somewhat questionable.

4. According to Berger and Luckmann, "Deviance from the institutionally 'programmed' courses of action becomes likely once the institutions have become realities divorced from their original relevance in the concrete social processes from which they arose" (1967, p. 62).
5. Communism and fascism are two examples.
6. See Jansen, Eyre, Spencer, Scalapino, and Kitagawa, 1969, p. 902.
7. Global Footprint Network, 2015.
8. Climate change may therefore be the symptom of a more serious problem. Fossil fuels provide only the means to power our unsustainable civilization. I have argued elsewhere about the irresponsibility of exceeding the carrying capacity of the planet (Sarbu, 2010).
9. In ancient Greece, those who killed their relatives were supposedly haunted by the Erinyes, deities of vengeance, who were not only terrifying but also unforgiving: "Though just, they are merciless and take no account of mitigating circumstances" (Haley, 1969, p. 681). On a more realistic note, the justice system may be one of the ways to enforce environment rights when other initiatives fail; several cases are in front of the courts in the US (Wood, 2014). Also, a recent judgment ordered the government of the Netherlands to reduce greenhouse gas emissions by at least 25 per cent by 2020 (Holligan, 2015).
10. Hubbard and Paquet (2015, p. 32) provide guidelines which could be applied to such experimentation (which they term *prototyping*).
11. Paquet (2014) argues convincingly that our social learning skills are underdeveloped, due to lack of critical thinking and the widespread rigidity of organizational structures.

References

Berger, P.L., and Luckmann, T. (1967). The social construction of reality: A treatise in the sociology of knowledge. New York: Anchor.

Boia, L. (2005). The weather in the imagination. London, UK: Reaktion.

Eliade, M. (1976). Histoire des croyances et des idées religieuses. [A history of beliefs and religious ideas]. Paris: Payot.

Føllesdal, D. (2010). The Lebenswelt in Husserl. In D. Hyder and H.-J. Rheinberger (Eds), Science and the life-world: Essays on Husserl's 'Crisis of European Sciences' (pp. 27–45). Stanford, CA: Stanford University Press.

Global Footprint Network (n.d.). World footprint: Do we fit on the planet? Retrieved 15 July 2015 from http://www.footprintnetwork.org/en/index.php/GFN/page/world_footprint

Hacking, I. (2010). Husserl on the origins of geometry. In D. Hyder and H.-J. Rheinberger (Eds), Science and the life-world: Essays on Husserl's "Crisis of European Sciences" (pp. 64–82). Stanford, CA: Stanford University Press.

Haley, W. (Editor in chief). (1969). Erinyes. In The encyclopaedia Britannica (Vol. 8, pp. 680–1). Chicago: Encyclopaedia Britannica.

Holligan, A. (2015, June 24). Netherlands ordered to cut greenhouse gas emissions. BBC News. Retrieved 15 July 2015 from http://www.bbc.com/news/world-europe-33253772

Homer-Dixon, T. (2008). The upside of down: Catastrophe, creativity, and the renewal of civilization. Washington, DC: Island Press.

Hubbard, R., and Paquet, G. (2015). Irregular governance: A plea for bold organizational experimentation. Ottawa: Invenire.

Inglis, D. (2005). Culture and everyday life. New York: Routledge.

Jansen, M.B., Eyre, J.D., Spencer, R.F., Scalapino, R.A., and Kitagawa, J.M. (1969). Japan. In The encyclopaedia Britannica (Vol. 12, pp. 876–945). Chicago: Encyclopaedia Britannica.

Paquet, G. (2014). Unusual suspects: Essays on social learning disabilities. Ottawa: Invenire.

Russell, B. (2005). The rise of science. In History of Western philosophy (pp. 484–96). New York: Routledge Classics.

Sarbu, M.B. (2010, October 2). Taking risks as species [Letter to the editor]. The Ottawa Citizen, p. B5.

Wood, M.C. (2014). Nature's trust: Environmental law for a new ecological age. New York: Cambridge University Press.

67 The Endangered Arctic, the Arctic as Resource Frontier: Canadian News Media Narratives of Climate Change and the North[1]

Mark C.J. Stoddart and Jillian Smith

Human-caused **climate change** has become the most visible environmental issue of the early twenty-first century. Climate change is caused by increased emissions of greenhouse gasses, such as CO^2 and methane, as a result of increased burning of fossil fuels such as coal and oil since the Industrial Revolution. The social-environmental impacts of climate change include sea level rise, melting of glaciers and polar ice caps, increased drought, transformations to ecosystems and wildlife habitat, and situations where unpredictable and extreme weather are becoming the new normal. The mainstream scientific consensus, which is communicated by the United Nations' Intergovernmental Panel on Climate Change (IPCC), is that human-caused climate change is happening, it will have significant negative social and environmental impacts, and societies need to enact policy responses to limit our greenhouse gas emissions.

The mass media are a key space for conflict over social understandings of climate change, as well as debate about how societies should respond (Crow and Boykoff, 2014). Mass media coverage focuses on climate change as a global issue, to which we all contribute through transportation, natural resource extraction, and energy consumption. However, there are significant disparities between the countries that are most responsible for historic and ongoing carbon emissions, and those that are most vulnerable to climate change–related disasters, including droughts, sea level rise, and increasingly severe storms. Attention to these disparities between climate change responsibility and vulnerability is called the **climate justice** perspective (Roberts and Parks, 2007).

Climate justice is important for drawing attention to power imbalances between countries, which helps us understand why international climate change policy negotiations are often so difficult. Placing too much emphasis on international power imbalances can distract us from seeing differences in climate change responsibility and vulnerability within countries. In northern countries like Canada, the Arctic is already seeing negative impacts for communities that are far removed from major sites of greenhouse gas emissions (Cunsolo Willox et al., 2013; Trainor et al., 2009). While Arctic communities are faced with living with the impacts of rapid social-environmental change, much of the Canadian carbon footprint comes from the Alberta oil industry, as well as from industrial production and energy consumption in southern Canada (Murphy and Murphy, 2012).

Drawing on articles from the *Globe and Mail* and the *National Post*, which are key national news outlets, we answer two questions. First, how does the Canadian Arctic enter into national news media coverage of climate change debate? Second, do these media provide space for a climate justice perspective on the unequal distributions of climate change harms and responsibilities between the Arctic and southern Canada?

Climate Change and the Media

Research on mass media helps us better understand the social dimensions of climate change. Brulle et al.

(2012) examine links between public opinion about climate change and extreme weather events, media coverage, scientific communication, messages from political elites, and communication from environmental movements. While weather has a weak effect on public opinion, the strongest effects come from the messages of politicians and environmental organizations, and indirectly through mass media as they give space to politicians and social movements to communicate to audiences. News coverage allows groups with a stake in climate policy to argue with each other in publicly visible media space. As key news sources appear repeatedly in news coverage, media audiences learn whose voices and perspectives deserve the most attention in debates over climate change and proposed policy solutions to this issue (Boykoff, 2011).

A recent overview of research on mass media and climate change concludes that climate justice has received limited attention in the media (Olausson and Berglez, 2014). As Dreher and Voyer argue, a "key challenge for climate justice . . . is to ensure a hearing for those people and countries that face the impacts of global warming in their daily lives" (Dreher and Voyer, 2015, p. 59). Examining **media discourse** about climate change, or the recurring themes presented by the media to audiences, tells us a great deal about the connections between climate change and climate justice, and how this is conveyed to media audiences.

Climate Justice

The concept of climate justice highlights that there are social inequalities related to climate change responsibility; vulnerability to the risks of climate change; and the economic and political ability to respond through "mitigation," or reducing carbon emissions, and "adaptation," or making adjustments to live with changing environments (Roberts and Parks, 2007). International climate policy is negotiated within a world system marked by legacies of colonialism and divides between affluent countries and developing countries (Roberts and Parks, 2007). It is generally the affluent countries that are most responsible for historical and present carbon emissions, while it is often developing countries that are most vulnerable to climate impacts like sea level rise, coastal erosion, or drought. Furthermore, the affluent countries of the Global North generally have greater economic, technological, and political abilities to carry out climate change mitigation and adaptation. This is described as a global "risk-responsibility divide," which is often used to claim that poorer countries should bear less of the burden of climate change mitigation, and that it is up to the affluent Global North to take a lead in addressing the issue (Billett, 2009).

While climate justice has often been conceptualized through a national lens, Trainor et al. (2009) note that climate justice also involves unequal responsibilities and vulnerabilities within countries. They focus on the increased vulnerability of Arctic communities to climate change, compared with those living in southern Canada and elsewhere. Though climate change has global environmental impacts, there are localized extreme effects on Inuit communities, for whom "sustainability involves continuing subsistence harvest . . . and cultural and physical health is synonymous with environmental and ecosystem health" (Trainor et al. 2009, p. 154). They argue that the misdistribution of climate change harms should be viewed as "aspects of internal colonialization—the colonization and exploitation of those living in the hinterlands of developed countries" (p. 146).

Ashlee Cunsolo Willox and her co-authors also provide a close examination of impacts of climate change in the Nunatsiavut region of Labrador. Their work finds that "the land was at the heart of what it meant to be Inuit and was deeply connected to individual and community identity, and mental well-being" (Cunsolo Willox et al. 2013, p. 261). Climate change impacts are being felt in everyday life as "access to land and land-based activities were disrupted due to changes in sea ice, snow, and seasonal temperature, as well as wildlife migration patterns due to warming temperatures" (p. 262).

In the next section, we describe our methodology before describing the dominant themes that Canadian news media use to talk about climate change and the Arctic.

Methodology

This analysis is part of a larger project on climate change coverage in the *Globe and Mail* and the *National Post*. Using the Factiva online database, we conducted keyword searches for "climate change" or "global warming" between 1997 (when the Kyoto Protocol was negotiated) and 2010 for the *Globe and Mail*, and from 27 October 1998 (its first date of publication) through 2010 for the *National Post*. We also searched "IPCC" and its full name (Intergovernmental Panel on Climate Change). The number of articles containing one or more of the keywords was 15,021. This data set was cleaned by manually scanning and removing duplicate articles or articles that mentioned the keywords without providing substantive information, resulting in a set of 8,960 articles. Based on available resources, we produced a 20 per cent random sample of 1,792 articles. The results presented here are based on a textual analysis of a sub-sample of 46 articles published from 2006 through 2010 that focus specifically on climate change in the Arctic.

Results

Two of the key media discourses that characterize coverage of climate change and the Arctic assert that global climate change is transforming the Arctic, and that melting sea ice offers new economic opportunities in the Arctic. Most of the news source organizations included in news coverage are from government, universities and research centres, and civil society (such as the Inuit Circumpolar Conference, the World Wildlife Fund, and the David Suzuki Foundation). With a few exceptions, most of these news sources are based outside the Arctic. This is consistent with observations that the "idea of North" has often been created by southerners (Cameron, 2015), a pattern that extends to media coverage of climate change.

In the media discourse, there is tension between the idea of the Arctic as under threat due to rapid sea ice melting and a competing idea that a warming Arctic will lead to new economic opportunities. Examples of the Arctic's environmental transformation include the observation of record high temperatures and an increase in migration of new species (such as insects, birds, or trees not usually seen in the region). These transformations are subsequently altering the Arctic landscape.

The idea of a "new North" has become increasingly visible in Canadian politics in recent years. This emphasizes that rapid environmental change in the Arctic will create a new natural resource frontier (Cameron, 2015; Stuhl, 2013). In line with this idea, media discourse emphasizes that climate change will open up new shipping routes in the Arctic. Opportunities for oil and gas extraction in the north, which John Urry (2013) calls "tough oil" because of its higher costs and risks to extract, also become possible as melting polar ice caps open up access to the Arctic. Other researchers suggest that adopting an oil-oriented perspective on climate change and the Arctic intensifies international conflict over who has sovereignty in the Arctic (Shadian, 2014). News media discourse is consistent with this claim. Media discourse asserts that the potential for developing resources from regions once considered remote and inaccessible is intensifying sovereignty debates among circumpolar countries, leading the Arctic to become an increasingly militarized zone. The militarization of the North is deemed necessary by nations such as Canada, the United States, and Russia in order to claim, maintain, or bolster their northern sovereignty and protect their "national interests" (Axworthy, 2008, p. A15).

Media discourse of rapid environmental change and new economic opportunities produced by climatic change in the Arctic fit a national model of climate justice that divides countries into those that will benefit from rapidly changing environments and those that will bear the risks and costs (Roberts and Parks, 2007). From a nation-state lens, media discourse defines Canada as a potential "winner" and "Arctic superpower" in relation to climate change impacts on the Arctic (Boswell, 2009, p. A4). However, the idea that Canada will prosper from climate change assumes that all Canadians will benefit. This assumption masks the disproportionate distribution of risks and benefits within the country and downplays climate-related harms that are already occurring in northern Canada (Cunsolo Willox et al., 2013; Trainor et al., 2009).

Conclusion

News media discourse produces a binary framework for understanding the impacts of climate change on the Arctic. On one hand, claims about the Arctic as nature under threat are consistent with IPCC assessment reports that stress that circumpolar environments and communities are seeing climate change impacts earlier and more dramatically than other parts of the world (IPCC, 2014). On the other hand, there are claims that climate change will offer new economic opportunities in the Arctic as sea ice melts and this region is transformed. As such, media discourse reinforces long-standing cultural views of the North as both an expansive, untameable wilderness and a natural resource frontier (Jorgensen, 2013).

Media discourse on climate change and the Arctic often puts forward the idea that Canada may be a climate change "winner" by benefiting from access to new pools of natural resources. By making the Canadian nation the focus, this media discourse downplays regional differences in climate change responsibility, risks, and impacts. From a climate justice standpoint, we see how media discourse fails to convey that the positive and negative impacts of climate change on the Arctic are unequally distributed and pose risks for many northern communities and people, while presenting opportunities and benefits that will largely go to economic and political interests located far outside the region.

Note

1. Acknowledgments: The authors would like to acknowledge the research assistance of Noelani Dubeta, Michelle Hay, and Emily Maynard. Jeffrey Broadbent, Philip Leifeld, Ashlee Cunsolo Willox, and Jessica Shadian provided valuable input throughout the development of this project. Funding for this research was provided by the Social Sciences and Humanities Research Council of Canada (SSHRC Grant Number 430-2011-0093). This paper builds on the research methods and data collection instruments developed by the program on Comparing Climate Change Policy Networks (COMPON; http://compon.org/) funded by the US National Science Foundation (NSF Grant Number BCS-0827006, Human and Social Dynamics, "Collaborative Research: Social Networks as Agents of Change in Climate Change Policy Making" October 2007 to September 2014) led by Jeffrey Broadbent, Department of Sociology, University of Minnesota.

References

Axworthy, L. (2008, August 22). A new Arctic circle; There's too much at stake to go it alone in the North. *The Globe and Mail*, p. A15.

Billett, S. (2009). Dividing climate change: global warming in the Indian mass media. *Climatic Change, 99*(1–2), 1–16.

Boswell, R. (2009, June 29). Minister touts arctic strength. *National Post*, p. A4.

Boykoff, M.T. (2011). *Who Speaks for the Climate? Making Sense of Media Reporting on Climate Change*. Cambridge: Cambridge University Press.

Brulle, R.J., Carmichael, J., and Jenkins, J.C. (2012). Shifting public opinion on climate change: an empirical assessment of factors influencing concern over climate change in the US, 2002–2010. *Climatic Change, 114*(2), 169–88.

Cameron, E. (2015). *Far Off Metal River: Inuit Lands, Settler Stories, and the Making of the Contemporary Arctic.* Vancouver: UBC Press.

Crow, D.A., and Boykoff, M.T. (2014). Introduction. In D.A. Crow and M.T. Boykoff (Eds), *Culture, Politics and Climate Change* (pp. 1–20). London: Routledge.

Cunsolo Willox, A, Harper, S.L., Ford, J.D., Edge, V.L., Landman, K., Houle, K., . . . Wolfrey, C. (2013). Climate change and mental health: an exploratory case study from Rigolet, Nunatsiavut, Canada. *Climatic Change, 121*, 255–70.

Dreher, T., and Voyer, M. (2015). Climate refugees or migrants? Contesting media frames on climate justice in the Pacific. *Environmental Communication, 9*(1), 58–76.

IPCC. (2014). *Climate Change 2014: Synthesis Report: Contribution of Working Groups I, II and III to the Fifth Assessment Report of the Intergovernmental Panel on Climate Change.* Geneva, Switzerland: IPCC.

Jorgensen, F.A. (2013). The networked North: thinking about the past, present, and future of environmental histories of the North. In D. Jorgensen and S. Sorlin (Eds), *Northscapes: History, Technology, and the Making of Northern Environments* (pp. 268–79). Vancouver: UBC Press.

Murphy, R., and Murphy, M. (2012). The tragedy of the atmospheric commons: discounting future costs and risks in pursuit of immediate fossil-fuel benefits. *Canadian Review of Sociology, 49*(3), 247–70.

Olausson, U., and Berglez, P. (2014). Media and climate change: four long-standing research challenges revisited. *Environmental Communication, 8*(2), 249–65.

Roberts, J.T., and Parks, B.C. (2007). *A Climate of Injustice: Global Inequality, North-South Politics, and Climate Policy.* Cambridge: MIT Press.

Shadian, J.M. (2014). *The Politics of Arctic Sovereignty: Oil, Ice and Inuit Governance.* London: Routledge.

Stuhl, A. (2013). The politics of the "New North": putting history and geography at stake in Arctic futures. *The Polar Journal, 3*(1), 94–119.

Trainor, S.F., Godduhn, A., Duffy, L.K., Chapin, F.S., Natcher, D.C., Kofinas, G., and Huntington, H.P. (2009). Environmental injustice in the Canadian Far North: persistent organic pollutants and Arctic climate impacts. Concepts of environmental justice in Canada. In J. Agyeman, R. Haluza-DeLay, P. Cole, and P. O'Reiley (Eds), *Speaking for Ourselves: Environmental Justice in Canada* (pp. 144–62). Vancouver: UBC Press.

Urry, J. (2013). *Societies beyond Oil: Oil Dregs and Social Futures.* London: Zed Books.

Questions for Critical Thought

Chapter 64 | The Missing "V" of Big Data: Surveillance and Vulnerability

1. What is "big data"? What types of information are being collected about individuals through computer algorithms?
2. What is the missing "V" of big data? Why should this "V" be included?
3. Who is made the most vulnerable through social sorting software? Why?
4. Lyon asks, "What kinds of prediction are enabled by big data practices?" What does he conclude?
5. How is Lyon's story about his health card more than just a private trouble? Describe how this experience is reflective of a public issue.

Chapter 65 | Algorithmic Sociology: An Emerging Field

1. The sociological study of algorithms is relatively new. Briefly describe the emerging sociology of algorithms.
2. What do Roberge and Crosbie mean by their asssertion, "When we rely on algorithms to make sense of the world, we thereby change our access to the world"?
3. How do algorithms impact culture, the economy, power, and politics? Explain.
4. Roberge and Crosbie suggest that algorithms are not neutral and have a social character. Using what you have learned about algorithms from this chapter, what do you think could give algorithms a more equal/neutral social character? Do you think this is possible?
5. Why is the sociological study of algorithms important? Should consumers of technology be aware of how algorithms limit their access to information?

Chapter 66 | (Re)defining Climate Change as a Cultural Phenomenon

1. What are ultimate truths? How are they historically and socially constructed?
2. Define *life-world*. Using the characteristics outlined by Sarbu, describe the characteristics of your life-world.
3. What similarities can be drawn between ancient civilization's accounts of nature? How is this different from the way that nature is discussed today?
4. How has the evolution of humanity and technology impacted nature?
5. How can we fight climate change? How is technology central to the changes we must make to fight climate change?

Chapter 67 | The Endangered Arctic, the Arctic as Resource Frontier: Canadian News Media Narratives of Climate Change and the North

1. How is climate change portrayed in the media? How is this different from what climate justice activists and scholars are focused on?
2. Describe climate justice. Using this idea, who should be responsible for reducing climate change?
3. How does the Canadian Arctic enter into national news media enactments of climate change debate?
4. When describing both climate change harms and responsibilities between Arctic and southern Canada, does the media provide a space for climate justice discourse?
5. Should the media be held accountable for not conveying climate justice? What do you think can be done to increase people's awareness of climate justice?

Glossary

Aboriginal rights Rights based on recognition of the unique social orders and patterns of land use maintained by Indigenous people prior to contact, in Canada recognized and affirmed under section 35 of the Constitution Act, 1982.

Accident proneness A theory that aims to explain the tendency of certain individuals to experience more accidents than average; attributes a high rate of accidents to the individual's personality.

Activism A practice of deliberate and engaged efforts to change something, often by mobilizing groups of people to work together.

Advocacy Public support for a particular cause or value.

African-Canadian feminism A feminist approach that gives attention to the disadvantages of both race and gender.

Ageism Discrimination on the basis of a person's age that has often involved a tendency to regard older persons as unwell/debilitated, unworthy of attention, or unsuitable for employment.

Aggravating factor A circumstance of a crime that may increase the culpability of an offender at sentencing (e.g., prior criminal record, severity of crime).

Algorithms A process or set of rules to be followed in calculations or other problem-solving operations, especially by a computer but more generally in any systemic or organizational framework.

Alienation A Marxian concept referring to the separation of a worker from the work they perform, from their fellow workers, and from themselves.

Ally Someone who supports a social movement or a cause that primarily benefits another group. In the context of Indigenous-settler relations, it might involve activities such as non-Indigenous people (settlers) listening to, learning from, and building relationships with Indigenous peoples

Ambivalence Social indifference or disconnection. Simmel's most popular example is the stranger, who is at once someone socially in close proximity (i.e., not just wandering by), yet symbolically remote as an outsider to the group—at once both near and far.

Animal-assisted intervention A type of therapeutic intervention that includes or incorporates the use of animals in health, education and human service.

Anti-colonial framework A school of thought that resists, questions, and redefines dominant ideologies about the relationship between the colonizer and the colonized.

Anti-colonialism The practices of political struggle and resistance by colonial peoples against the actions and beliefs of colonizers.

Assimilation (immigrant assimilation) Actions that lead to a decline of ethnic cultural and behavioral distinctions, with the result of greater similarity between people of different origins.

Austerity budgets Budgeting principles that involve cutting education, health, and social assistance spending with the justification that it will lead to economic growth. Adopted by many countries in the Global North after the economic crisis of 2008. See also, *neoliberalism*.

Band schools Schools located on reserves operated by First Nations, under federal government jurisdiction, in accordance with the terms of the Indian Act.

Bidirectional help exchanges Exchanges of help between neighbours that are reciprocated.

Biomedical perspective A conceptual model of illness that excludes social or psychological factors and focuses instead only on biologic factors when attempting to understand or explain a person's illness or disorder.

Blank slate A perspective that argues that social experience and not biological capacities shape our understandings of social life.

Brain drain The situation in which large numbers of educated and very skilled people leave their own country to live and work in another where pay and conditions are better.

Canadianization debates Refers to a moment of cultural nationalism in the discipline of sociology in Canada. The growth of sociology departments in Canada during the late 1960s and early 1970s inspired keen debates around how and why Canadian sociology should distinguish itself from its American counterpart.

Centres de la petite enfance (CPE) Government-subsidized and low-cost childcare services in Quebec that provide educational child care to preschool children, in both centres and private homes.

Charter of Rights and Freedoms An amendment to the constitution in 1982. It lists a series of rights that are protected by law. It only applies to governments.

Chicago sociology The dominant approach to sociology in the United States, 1890–1935. Focused on urban social processes (immigration, race, and ethnic relations). Contributed to the development of qualitative and quantitative research techniques (ethnography, case studies, social surveys, mapping). The early home of human ecology theory.

Child capital The native aptitudes and abilities of children that can be built on to overcome a lack of resources (e.g., money, human capital, social capital) in their lives.

Climate change Human-caused, or anthropogenic, climate change is a major global environmental issue is the result of increasing concentration of greenhouse gases in our atmosphere (such carbon dioxide and methane). Climate change has social causes, as it has been driven by rapid increases in extracting and burning fossil fuels (coal, oil, and gas) for energy and transportation since the industrial revolution.

Climate justice A theoretical perspective on climate change, as well as a distinct branch of the environmental movement concerned with addressing climate change. Climate justice draws our attention to the inequalities in which countries and social groups are most responsible for producing climate change through high carbon footprints, and which countries and social groups are most vulnerable to its impacts.

Cognition The socially conditioned mental process of acquiring knowledge and understanding through thought, experience, and the senses.

Cognitive distortions Erroneous assumptions about the degree of control over chance-determined outcomes.

Collective action Action taken together by a group of people whose goal is to improve their status and achieve a common goal, following a plan or ideological agenda.

Concept Any abstraction that works to organize our experience. Concepts turn the undifferentiated flow of unique sensations into objects, events, relationships, and so on.

Consensual validation This occurs when many observers seem to come to the same or similar conclusions, thereby reinforcing each observation as real.

Consent system (organ donation consent system) An agreement to allow one's organs to be used (after death) by others; in some cases, the agreement is stated or explicit, and in other cases, it is presumed.

Context-dependent personality A theoretical framework that proposes that one's personality can vary across social contexts and that traits are often expressed based on the characteristics of a given situation and other environmental factors.

Contextual embeddedness An understanding of surrounding social institutions and how they interact to complement or conflict with each other.

Correlation A link between two variables, such that a change in one is accompanied by a change in the other.

Critical race theory A theoretical perspective that sees racism as deeply embedded within the institutions of Canadian society and complicated by the often overlapping issues of sexism, ageism, ableism, heterosexism, and other forms of inequality.

Cultural continuity The preservation over time of core elements of a group's culture.

Cultural racism A form of racism that operates around an essentialist notion of culture, which sees cultures as fundamentally different in ways that one could learn to tolerate but never mix.

Culture The formal and informal patterns that are developed in any society or organization that provide guidelines for human behaviour.

Cultures of civic engagement Different social and cultural patterns defining how people are to engage with one another, and with their community at large.

Cyber-psychopathy An expression of psychopathic traits specifically with reference to cyberspace. Cyber-psychopathy is a concept that applies the characteristics of psychopathy to one's behaviours, values, and mindset on the Internet.

Decolonization Refers to the dismantling of foreign political, economic, and military control over another nation and its territory. This may include returning stolen land (and other resources) to Indigenous peoples and respecting their political autonomy.

Deep sight Rich, multi-tiered visual data streams that situate actors in dynamic, meaning-laden environments.

Democratic colonialism The existence of conditions that contribute to negative and unequal treatment of Aboriginal people despite legal recognition of equal rights and democratic participation for all.

Dependency ratios Usually simple population ratios of those of work force age, to those under age 18 (youth dependency) or over age 65 (old age dependency), or both (total dependency).

Deployment Refers to the assignment of people, especially military personnel, to serve in various locations away from home for reasons that include aid-to-the-civil-power operations (e.g., floods), peacekeeping, and combat.

Disability studies Examines and critiques disability as a social and cultural as well as physical, environment that limits or excludes people with disabilities. It advocates for improving inclusion, accessibility, and participation.

Discourse A set of spoken, written, or non-verbal "statements" that, in combination with other discourses, organizes our thinking and social life.

Due process Fair treatment through the normal judicial system, especially as a citizen's entitlement.

Elections The formal and organized process of periodically choosing members of a political body (e.g., elections to Parliament).

Electoral politics Refers to the conventional channels to elect public representatives, such as fair elections, a competitive party system, and running and holding public office.

Elite-challenging behaviour Non-traditional political activities that challenge people in dominant positions—for example, by signing petitions, joining boycotts, attending lawful/peaceful demonstrations, joining unofficial strikes, and occupying buildings or factories.

Employment Insurance (EI) The current system to support unemployed workers in Canada., Currently, unemployed workers in Canada to qualify must have 180 days of paid labour within a 35-hour work week in the past two years.

Enterprise self In neoliberal societies, the existence and creation of social selves that are distinctive but controlled by economic and ideological processes, limiting both autonomy and resistance.

Epistemic practices Knowledge-making practices; processes of knowing distinct pieces of knowledge with the recognition that the these objects can be viewed, understood, and analyzed differently depending on the research contexts, theoretical approach, and purpose of the study.

Ethical principle A rule for deciding between what is immoral or moral.

Ethnic group Refers to a group of individuals who share a common language, history, territory, and sometimes (but not always) language and religion. Ethnic group members recognize one another as members of the same group, and society recognizes them as an individual group.

Exploitation Domination of the working class by the bourgeoisie, using economic and political power to extort surplus value from the labour of wage workers

Families of choice Chosen, rather than fixed, relationships and ties of intimacy, care, and support. LGBTQ families are often seen as the clearest example of this phenomenon.

Feminism An ideology and political movement that confronts sexism by advocating women's rights on the grounds of women's political, social, and economic equality to men.

Feminist histories Feminist histories recognize gender as a central category within historical analysis and research, and identify historical patterns, experiences, and relations of gender and sexuality-based discrimination and inequality.

Filial piety Care, respect, and obedience toward a parent or one's elders or ancestors.

Gender relations in the private sphere The gendered domestic division of (unpaid) labour.

Gender relations in the public sphere The gendered division of paid labour.

Genealogy According to Foucault, a method of doing historical sociological research that traces the lineage of a contemporary idea or event to identify the sequence of conditions that brought it about.

Genres of social critique Different styles of thinking and practice that analyze, challenge, appraise, and open up to new ideas about being with others.

Habitus, doxa, and field Concepts developed by social theorist Pierre Bourdieu to account for the reproduction of inequality in society. The "field" is the social space in which people interact; the "doxa" of the field are the common sense norms associated with that social space; and the "habitus" is the embodied set of dispositions carried by individuals within the social space.

Half-belief Intellectually rejecting a superstition nevertheless allowing it to influence thinking and actions.

Hannah Arendt A German-born Jewish political philosopher who published several important books in the aftermath of the Second World War. Arendt's work is especially noteworthy for her insights on totalitarianism and democracy.

Heteronormative A biased point of view, which suggests that heterosexuality is the "normal" or preferred sexual orientation.

History of sociology An account of the establishment of sociology as an academic discipline, investigating the development of theories and methods, researching key figures and their research contributions, and examining the social, political, and cultural contexts that have shaped how society and social questions are asked and studied during given periods.

Homogeneity The quality of having the same or similar cultural attributes.

Human–animal bond The reciprocal relationship between people and animals, such that each influences the psychology and well-being of the other.

Human rights Those rights that people have by virtue of their humanity. They are a particular type of social practice that has an instrumental and political function.

Hypermasculinity The exaggerated expression of qualities that make up the stereotypical "real" man in contemporary culture, such as excessive aggression, dominance, and recklessness.

Ideal speech situation According to Jürgen Habermas, a dialogic scenario that presupposes a set of criteria necessary for achieving consensus in public discourse. Those involved must be freely and sincerely engaging in dialogue, without disproportionate influence by one party over the other, and the shared goal should be mutual understanding.

Ideal type A conceptual tool which accentuates the characteristics and elements of an aspect of social life.

Immanent critique A method for analyzing conflicting social, moral, or political perspectives according to their origins within a concrete historical and social context.

Impression management The conscious or unconscious efforts social actors make to control and influence the definition of self in the presence of others. This process can be undertaken in face-to-face interaction or can involve other avenues of social interaction

Inorganic Not arising from natural growth, lacking structure.

Institutional ethnography (IE) A way of looking at social reality founded by Dorothy E. Smith, IE helps researchers uncover how people's disparate experiences are coordinated and controlled institutionally, and are not the result of individual choices.

Instrumental activism A widely supported value in the Western world that is enacted by doing something, asserting agency, even if the actor has little faith that the action will produce the desired outcome.

Integration (immigrant integration) The acts and processes that incorporate individuals and/or groups into society—especially referring to the inclusion of migrants in the major institutions of a society (e.g., in education, the economy, and the polity)

Integrative anti-racism The intersection of race with other forms of difference, such as sexual orientation, ability, class, and gender identity.

Intentional homeless communities (IHC) Communities built by homeless advocates to house people permanently or temporarily but usually without government support.

Interaction order According to Erving Goffman, the unspoken rules and conventions that govern social encounters and interactions. The interaction order forms the basis for how individuals can go about their daily affairs while sharing a sense for how things should or ought to proceed.

Invented traditions Ritual or symbolic practices governed by social rules which, through repetition, seek to inculcate values and norms that imply continuity with the past.

***Jus sanguinis* (the right of blood)** A citizenship system that is based on descent. Parents can pass on their citizenship to their children irrespectively of the place the children are born in.

***Jus soli* (the right of soil)** A citizenship system that is based on one's place of birth. Anyone who is born in the territory of a country adhering to this principle has the right to obtain this country's citizenship.

Liberal democracy Rests on the principles of majority rule (respect for the will of most citizens) and minority rights (protection of the interests of all citizens, even those who are not in the majority).

Liberty aspiration Libertarian aspects of post-materialism in that individuals give priority to having input in governmental decisions, more say about how things are done at their jobs, and want to protect freedom of speech.

Linguistic solitude The segregation of intellectual or academic thought within language groups, limiting sharing and co-operation across language groups.

Living wage A wage that reflects the hourly rate at which a household can meet its basic household needs, once government transfers have been added to the family's income and deductions have been subtracted. A living wage sets a higher standard than the minimum wage and is based on the actual costs of living in a specific community.

Lore of criminal accusation Refers to the ideas, rituals, everyday practices and kinds of truth telling required by given societies in order for variously defined accusers to accuse another of committing a criminal offence.

Low-capacity regimes Governing systems in a particular jurisdiction that are unable to effectively respond to the demands of their population.

Macro-level factors Those that relate to or define social life on the larger scale such as communities and societies.

Macro sociology An approach to sociology that emphasizes the analysis of entire societies and populations, as well as the major institutions that make up these societies.

Market fundamentalism The belief that "the free market," with little to no government intervention, is the most efficient and fair way to distribute resources (e.g., income, health care) throughout society.

Media discourse These are the recurring themes used by the mass media and news sources to help audiences make sense of social issues and public debates.

Medical model of disability Views disability as inherent in the individual person, and as a condition that needs to be treated, but does not take into account the social, cultural, or environmental circumstances that might disable an individual.

Mental health The capacity of people to feel, think, and act in ways that allow them to enjoy life and deal with all the challenges they face. A positive sense of emotional and spiritual well-being that respects the importance of culture, equity, social justice, interconnections, and personal dignity.

Metadata Often misleadingly reduced to "data about data," metadata in a surveillance context means sensitive contextual data such as individual locations, preferences, commitments, and orientations.

Micro An approach to sociology that emphasizes the analysis of face-to-face, interpersonal processes of interaction and influence

Micro-level factors Those factors that relate to or define face-to-face social and situational interactions.

Milk kinship A family bond established between a woman and an infant she breastfeeds but has not given birth to. It was practised from the beginning of Islam in order to broaden the network of relatives one could rely upon for assistance and cooperation.

Minimum wage A government mandated and enforced minimum rate of hourly compensation that applies to all employers.

Mixed-methods research Makes use of more than one type of investigative perspective; often involves combining in-depth, contextualized, and natural insights of qualitative research, with the efficient but often less rich, predictive power of quantitative research.

Multicultural governmentality Following Michel Foucault, this views multiculturalism as a particular mode of governmentality, encompassing ideas and logic that shape the mental, emotional, social, and political conduct of racialized Others and the major group.

Musicking The creation and performance of music, highlighting the fact that music is a process, not a product.

Naturalization The process by which an individual asks the state for permission to become a citizen of a country. Often naturalization is bound to certain criteria set out by the country, e.g., having permanent residency status.

Neoclassical economics An economic approach that assumes that, as individuals, people make rational choices reflecting their self-interests to maximize utility and firms make choices based on maximizing profits. As a result, prices, outputs, and incomes are determined by supply and demand.

Neoliberal globalization A form of transnational integration that prioritizes free trade and privatization of economic transactions, over state regulation and intervention.

Neoliberal governmentality A term coined by Foucault (1991) that refers to how citizens in the West have developed a governing mentality that expects people to conduct their lives well and expects little from government.

Neoliberal(ism), neoliberal policy A political and economic perspective that holds that governments should limit their interventions in economic life to protecting free trade, free markets, and private property. It holds that personal liberty is maximized by limiting government involvement in the operation of free markets.

Neo-conservative regime A type of government informed or directed by neoliberal thinking that calls for limited government regulation and the dominance of private interests in a free market economy.

Network resource Anything—including money, information, knowledge, and social influence—that circulates in a social network and affects the outcomes of social action.

NGO Any non-governmental, non-profit, voluntary citizens' group that is organized on a local, national, or international level.

Non-institutional participation Refers to citizen public participation through more indirect, looser, and less hierarchical forms of political participation, such as participation in marches, signing of petitions, and boycotting/buycotting products.

One Health A global initiative to encourage collaboration among health providers to attain optimal health for people, animals, and the environment.

Organizationally embedded networks Social networks lodged within larger organizations that may serve to support, protest, or disrupt organizational goals.

Paradigm A theoretical approach or set of ideas that defines the questions of interest and preferred methods of research for an entire field of study.

Parentification The process of role reversal whereby a child is obliged to act as parent to his or her parent. In some cases, the child is used to fill the void in the alienated parent's emotional life.

Participatory action research An approach to research that makes central the concerns of those who are involved in the research, rather than being solely driven by the researcher. Typically has a social justice, activist, or advocacy orientation.

Path dependence The tendency of many social, economic, and political processes to enhance their own dynamics, leading to a gradual weakening and eventual elimination of competing processes.

Pay equity Stresses that gendered labour force segregation is accompanied by wage discrimination that fails to reflect the skills, efforts, responsibility, and working conditions in jobs.

Perpetual liminality A condition in modern society that makes transitioning from earlier to later roles very difficult.

Pluralist group formation Involves a dynamic set of triangular relations wherin the compromise between two, often unequal, categories—"us" and "others"—becomes meaningful only though the presence of outsiders.

Policy network A network of people whose professional status enables them to discuss and make decisions about public policy. A member's importance in the network usually depends on the power of the organization (such as a government, a corporation, or a trade union) that he or she represents.

Policy sociology According to Michael Burawoy, the work of "sociologists in the service of a goal defined by a client." More broadly, it is the intervention of sociologists in ongoing public policy debates.

Political economy An academic discipline that studies the mutually influential relations between political and economic processes.

Political effervescence (or collective effervescence) A state of group excitement in which people communicate similar thoughts and participate in similar (or joint) activities.

Political participation Any activity that involves people in the political sphere, whether by voting, attending a rally, sending a letter to a representative, donating money to a party, or committing an act of terrorism.

Positivism A philosophy that assumes that the only accurate source of knowledge is the information received by observation and measurement and interpreted by reason and logic.

Post-materialist A term used by Inglehart to refer to people born after the Second World War. Since their needs for food, drink, shelter, sex, security, order, and stability are satisfied by living in developed affluent countries, they tend instead to seek intellectual and aesthetic satisfaction, equality of opportunity, and citizen involvement

Post-socialist countries Formerly socialist countries that transformed to capitalist economic system, privatizing public enterprises and deregulating the market. Most are in a peripheral position in the world economy and are dependent on developed countries and corporations for investment and development.

Potential deceased donor pool The population of patients dying in hospital who meet eligibility criteria (such as the absence of infectious disease) to donate organs at death. Potential donors become actual donors with consent to donation.

Precarious work Non-standard employment that is poorly paid, temporary, part-time, insecure, unprotected, and/or cannot support a household.

Precarity A precarious existence, lacking in predictability, job security, and material or psychological welfare. The social class defined by this condition has been termed the precariat.

Prescribed change The process by which the designated leaders of a group decide on, implement, and enforce the changes to be made to their culture.

Presentations of self A concept developed by sociologist Erving Goffmann to refer to the way in which individuals represent themselves to the world, through speech, dress, ways of moving, and so on. Uses the analogy of a theatre, where individuals are acting on a stage for a particular audience, and adjust their behaviour accordingly.

Privacy The right to be free from observation or disturbance by other people, organizations, or government.

Productivism The ideology that economic growth is both necessary and sufficient to ensure people's prosperous well-being.

Progressivism The philosophy underlying a variety of liberal and social democratic social reform movements focused on empowering the state to remedy social problems (poverty, slums, poor working conditions) that are created by the operation of an unregulated capitalist economy.

Professional sociology Work that is done by highly trained, full-time sociologists, often for the consumption of other highly trained, full-time sociologists.

Public intellectual A person who carries out critical study, thought, and reflection about the reality of society and, to stimulate public discussion, proposes solutions for the problems of that society in the public sphere, gaining public visibility and authority.

Public policy Refers to the actions, programs, and regulations of the state. In Canada, each level of government (municipal, provincial, and federal) operates numerous public policies to address a large number of economic, social, and environmental issues.

Public science Scientific research commissioned and paid for by public funds, intended to inform public policy-making about pressure social and environmental issues.

Public sociology Sociological research intended to inform public opinion and public policy-making on important social issues of the day.

Push-pull theory A theory that supports the idea that migration is induced either by undesirable factors that forces people to leave their country (e.g., unemployment and political instability) or by desirable factors that attract people to move to another country (e.g., employment and security).

Racialized/racialization A term meant to capture all forms that racial and ethnic discrimination, both obvious and non-obvious. Less obvious forms of racialized discrimination would include the differential treatment of individuals who speak English or French with an accent, or are perceived to be in minority religious groups.

Racism A system of social judgment that prioritizes members of one race or ethnicity above others. (See also *racialized/racialization.*) It can take the form of name calling, physical assault, vandalism, theft or destruction of personal property, or murder.

Rape crisis centres In Ontario, centres delivering counselling, information, and support services to survivors of sexual violence. Centres have also been at the forefront of the anti-rape movement in Canada.

Recommodification Increasing dependence of workers on the labour market (i.e., their ability to sell their own work in exchange for wage) to survive. Workers' survival normally relies not only on the labour market, but also on non-market institutions, such as public education or health care. In recent decades, such non-market institutions have become less available.

Reconciliation A process of re-establishing friendship, trust, and respect after a conflict between ethnic or racial groups—for example, between Indigenous and non-Indigenous Canadians.

Reference group Any group that individuals use as a standard for evaluating themselves and their own behaviour.

Reflexivity A research practice requiring researchers to acknowledge their role in producing and analyzing research data at all stages of the research process. Secondarily, any feedback loop in which the parts of a social system (ideas, actions, even people) both shape the workings of that system and are shaped by it.

Rights culture A rights culture is the way a society interprets and applies rights in practice. A rights culture is most apparent in those rights that are codified in law, but it also includes rights that are embedded in the practices of social and political life.

Sandwich generation A population of mid-life adults who provide care to aging parents as well as their own children simultaneously.

Second generation Refers to persons who themselves are born in the destination country but who have at least one parent, and often two parents, who are foreign-born.

Sessional An individual who is hired by a university for a limited time or to teach a limited number of courses.

Sex concentration The proportion of all employed women working in an occupation and sex-typing—the percentage of the occupation that is female in the paid workforce.

Sexual capital The species of capital associated with attractiveness that confers advantage upon those who possess it within a sexual field, including field significance and the ability to obtain an intimate partner of one's choosing.

Sexual field A domain of social interaction in which actors with potential romantic or sexual interest in one another orient themselves according to a culturally defined logic of desirability.

Sites Those physical and virtual locations to which sexual fields are attached.

Social networking sites (SNS) Online platforms that allow users to create a public profile and connect with other users of the same platform.

Sociability According to Georg Simmel, a range of interactional forms that are enjoyed merely for their own sake. Social games, casual conversation, or flirtation number among Simmel's main examples.

Social brain According to recent thinking, a brain and mind that operate in reciprocal relations with society (i.e., human organization and social behaviour).

Social cohesion The attachment that exists between members of a group, community, or society that results from social interaction and shared beliefs.

Social comparison The process people go through in order to understand themselves and their place within the world in relation to other people.

Social differentiation Processes that assign individuals to socially constructed categories, which are usually conceived as given or "natural." This categorization is then used to justify unequal resources, opportunities, and life chances.

Social integration The principles by which individuals or actors are related to one another in a society.

Social model of disability Views disability as created in the interaction between an individual and its environment. Main focus is the analysis of disabling barriers in society and the environment. The social model strives for social change in order to change the living conditions of people with disabilities.

Social sorting Increasingly automated systems for assigning risk to individuals and groups, or assigning the "worth" of customers to corporations. Social processes that "triage" or "filter" individuals and groups into different categories so that they can be treated differently.

Social system A dynamic network of interdependent human actions that generates effects independently of the conscious intentions of the people involved in it. Social systems both constrain and enable different actions at different times and places and for different actors.

Socio-economic status (SES) A term used to describe the class or social standing of a person or groups of people. SES is commonly determined by considering one or more of the following: income, level of education, and/or occupation.

Sociological imagination According to C. Wright Mills, sociology's unique perspective that views individual biographies (e.g., choices and problems) in terms of socio-historical contexts.

Socio-ethnic leveraging Implies that minority groups are compared with each other and that one is evaluated as more/less different, integrated, threatening than the other.

Status and Non-Status groups "Status" is a legal definition that applies to First Nations persons who are registered under the terms of the Indian Act, while "Non-Status" typically refers to those who identify as Indian but are not registered; Non-Status Indians are also typically differentiated from Métis and Inuit.

Stereotype Any process that assumes people who are ethnically, linguistically, religiously, or culturally similar are identical in important respects. Stereotypes are generally negative (such as equating particular groups of people with extremist ideologies), though some can be positive (like the belief that some ethnic groups are more academically inclined than others).

Strategic interaction According to Erving Goffman, "strategic interaction" describes the game-like aspects of self-interested interaction between social actors. It describes how actors may deceive or purposely mislead others in order to influence interaction much like the way opponents play against each other in a game or match.

Stratified reproduction Refers to the fact that certain categories of people in a society are encouraged or coerced to reproduce and parent, while others are not. As a result, the ability to reproduce is unequally distributed in society and is stratified along gender, sexual orientation, racial and ethnic, and economic class lines.

Structural racism The unequal relationship between a white majority and racialized minority groups, creating material and symbolic inequality between the groups and exclusionary processes that collectively reproduce inequality in social institutions.

Structural violence The conditions in the social structure that prevent people from reaching their potential.

Structure of desire Transpersonal systems of judgment and appreciation within a given field that communicate the sexual status order to field participants.

Subconscious The part of the mind of which one is not fully aware but which influences one's actions and feelings; typically explored in psychological or psychoanalytical analyses.

Summer setback Refers to the loss of literacy or numeracy skills that students may experience during the summer break.

Surveillance Any social processes that gather and analyze personal data for purposes of political or corporate gain and influence.

Taylorized (Taylorism) A managerial method that involves a strong managerial presence and reduces work processes to simple steps. In theory, this process allows workers an opportunity for greater economic rewards through greater outputs; in practice, it produces a sense of meaninglessness and alienation.

Text Any document, communication, or information set that can be mined for sociological information.

Theory An assemblage of concepts that work together in some way. Theories can connect or divide phenomena, settle or raise questions, and simplify or complicate our understanding.

Theory of colonial state fields A theory that focuses on the dynamics or "rules of the game" of colonization—how the colonial field is different from the home state (metropole), how colonized people are positioned with respect to the colonizers, and the kinds of capital that are important for effective colonization.

Third-plus generation This group consists of persons who are born in the destination country and whose parents are all born in that country. In Canada, the third-plus generation are those persons born in Canada who also have two Canadian-born parents.

Underemployment Generically refers to the less than optimal use of labour potential.

Unemployment insurance (UI) This was the system of support for unemployed workers in Canada until 1996. It was based on number of weeks worked, with a required minimum of 15 hours per week. The required number of weeks depends on the unemployment level in the unemployed workers' region, ranging from 12 to 20 weeks.

Units of analysis The major entity that you analyze in a study, e.g., individuals, groups, artifacts, geographical units, social interactions.

Universal program/universalism Refers to a benefit or a service that is offered to all citizens, irrespective of income, age or employment status. Universal programs, such as health care in Canada, treat people equally, regardless of their needs. In Quebec, childcare has been described as universal in reference to the low flat-rate cost.

Value freedom (or value neutrality) The notion that it is both possible and beneficial not to make moral judgments about social phenomena. Closely related to the idea of objectivity—i.e., the notion that it is possible and beneficial to remain unbiased in the gathering and reporting of data.

Virtual Those elements that are real (i.e., exist) without being actual (i.e., material), which, like statues, symbolize and express important emotions or ideas.

Visible minority A term first used in the early 1980s in Canada to denote groups distinctive by virtue of their race, colour, or "visibility." Visible minorities are defined as persons who self-identify as Chinese; South Asian (e.g., East Indian, Pakistani, Sri Lankan, etc.); Black; Filipino; Latin American; Southeast Asian (e.g., Vietnamese, Cambodian, Malaysian, Laotian, etc.); Arab; West Asian (e.g., Iranian, Afghan, etc.); Korean; Japanese; and Other (to be specified by the respondent.

War on terror After the 11 September 2001 attacks on the United States, US President George W. Bush used this term to refer to American global military, political, legal, and conceptual struggles against organizations designated as terrorist and the regimes accused of supporting them.

White norm The concept of white norm refers to the ideological belief in the superior position of Western economy, religion, philosophy, and polity, and the social phenomenon of holding these as the universal standard to the disadvantage of non-Western Others.

White settler society A society established by (white) Europeans on non-European soil (i.e., populated by non-white people).

Youth civic engagement A field primarily concerned with research, practice and the development of programs that promote young people's active participation in civic and political life.